SOCIOCULTURAL ANTHROPOLOGY

A Problem-Based Approach

THIRD CANADIAN EDITION

Richard H. Robbins
State University of New York at Plattsburgh

Maggie Cummings
University of Toronto

Karen McGarry
McMaster University

NELSON

NELSON

Sociocultural Anthropology: A Problem-Based Approach, Third Canadian Edition

by Richard H. Robbins, Maggie Cummings, and Karen McGarry

VP, Product and Partnership Solutions:
Anne Williams

Managing Editor Content Development and Acquisitions Editor:
Mark Grzeskowiak

Senior Marketing Manager:
Amanda Henry

Content Development Manager:
Katherine Goodes

Photo and Permissions Researcher:
MRM Associates

Production Project Manager:
Jennifer Hare

Production Service:
Cenveo Publisher Services

Copy Editor:
Kate Revington

Proofreader:
Pushpa

Indexer:
BIM Creatives, LLC

Design Director:
Ken Phipps

Managing Designer:
Franca Amore

Interior Design:
Cathy Mayer

Cover Design:
Cathy Mayer

Cover Image:
© Max Johnston

Compositor:
Cenveo Publisher Services

Library and Archives Canada Cataloguing in Publication Data

Robbins, Richard H. (Richard Howard), 1940-
[Cultural anthropology]
    Sociocultural anthropology : a problem-based approach / Richard H. Robbins, State University of New York at Plattsburgh, Maggie Cummings, University of Toronto, Karen McGarry, McMaster University. — Third Canadian edition.

Previous editions published under title: Cultural anthropology.
Includes bibliographical references and index.
ISBN 978-0-17-657016-3 (paperback)

    1. Ethnology—Textbooks.
I. Cummings, Maggie, 1974-, author
II. McGarry, Karen Ann, 1972-, author III. Title: Cultural anthropology

GN316.R62 2016   306
C2015-906184-9

ISBN-13: 978-0-17-657016-3
ISBN-10: 0-17-657016-0

A Note About the Book's Cover:

The publisher of *Sociocultural Anthropology: A Problem-Based Approach*, Third Canadian Edition, hopes that the inquiry-based approach of this book guides students as they develop an inquisitiveness and openness to cultural diversity. The cover image is an untitled work from 1993 by Max Johnston, an artist whose work is primarily abstract art and who lives in Toronto.

SOCIOCULTURAL ANTHROPOLOGY

A Problem-Based Approach

THIRD CANADIAN EDITION

PUTTING THE WORLD IN PERSPECTIVE

Although all humans that we know about are capable of producing accurate sketches of localities and regions with which they are familiar, *cartography* (the craft of mapmaking as we know it today) had its beginnings in 16th-century Europe, and its subsequent development is related to the expansion of Europeans to all parts of the globe. From the beginning, there have been two problems with maps: the technical one of how to depict on a two-dimensional, flat surface a three-dimensional spherical object, and the cultural one of whose world view maps reflect. In fact, the two issues are inseparable, for the particular projection one uses inevitably makes a statement about how one views one's own people and their place in the world. Indeed, maps often shape our perceptions of reality as much as they reflect them.

In cartography, a *projection* refers to the system of intersecting lines (of longitude and latitude) by which part or all of the globe is represented on a flat surface. There are more than a hundred different projections in use today, ranging from polar perspectives to interrupted "butterflies" to rectangles to heart shapes. Each projection causes distortion in size, shape, or distance in some way or another. A map that correctly shows the shape of a landmass will of necessity misrepresent the size. A map that is accurate along the equator will be deceptive at the poles.

Perhaps no projection has had more influence on the way we see the world than that of Gerhardus Mercator, who devised his map in 1569 as a navigational aid for mariners. So well suited was Mercator's map for this purpose that it continues to be used for navigational charts today. At the same time, the Mercator projection became a standard for depicting landmasses, something for which it was

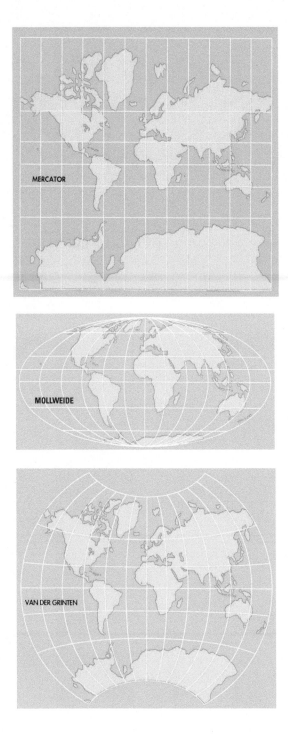

MERCATOR

MOLLWEIDE

VAN DER GRINTEN

never intended. Although an accurate navigational tool, the Mercator projection greatly exaggerates the size of landmasses in higher latitudes, giving about two-thirds of the map's surface to the northern hemisphere. Thus, the lands occupied by Europeans and European descendants appear far larger than those of other people. For example, North America (19 million square kilometres) appears almost twice the size of Africa (30 million square kilometres), while Europe is shown as equal in size to South America, which actually has nearly twice the landmass of Europe.

A map developed in 1805 by Karl B. Mollweide was one of the earlier *equal-area projections* of the world. Equal-area projections portray landmasses in correct relative size, but as a result, they distort the shapes of continents more than other projections. They most often compress and warp lands in the higher latitudes and vertically stretch landmasses close to the equator. Other equal-area projections include the Lambert Cylindrical Equal-Area Projection (1772), the Hammer Equal-Area Projection (1892), and the Eckert Equal-Area Projection (1906).

The Van der Grinten Projection (1904) was a compromise aimed at minimizing both the distortions of size in the Mercator and the distortions of shape in equal-area maps such as the Mollweide. Although an improvement, the Van der Grinten still emphasizes the lands of the northern hemisphere at the expense of the southern. For example, it shows Canada and the former Soviet Union at more than twice their actual size.

The Robinson Projection, which was adopted by the National Geographic Society in 1988 to replace the Van der Grinten, is one of the best compromises to date between the distortions of size and those of shape. Although an improvement over the Van der Grinten, the Robinson Projection still depicts lands in the northern latitudes as proportionally larger than those of the southern, that is, the Third World. And like European maps before it, the Robinson Projection places Europe at the centre with the Atlantic Ocean and the Americas to the left, thus emphasizing the cultural connection between Europe and North America, while neglecting the geographic closeness of northwestern North America to northeastern Asia.

Each of the four maps on the following pages conveys quite a different cultural message. Included among them are the Peters Projection, an equal-area map that has been adopted as the official map of UNESCO (the United Nations Educational, Scientific, and Cultural Organization), and a Japanese map that shows us how the world looks from the other side.

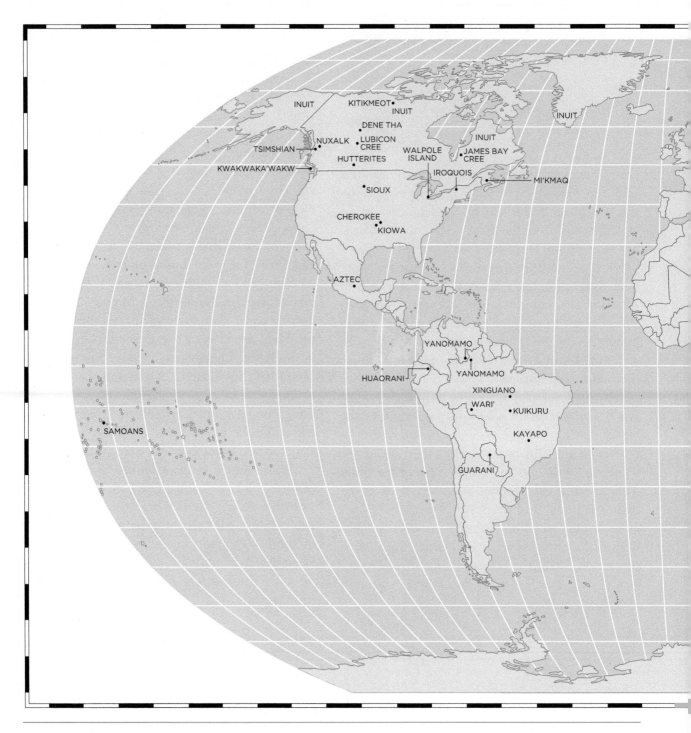

THE ROBINSON PROJECTION

This projection is used today by the National Geographic Society and Rand McNally. Although it distorts the relative size of landmasses, it does so much less than most other projections. Still, it places Europe at the centre of the map. This textbook uses the Robinson.

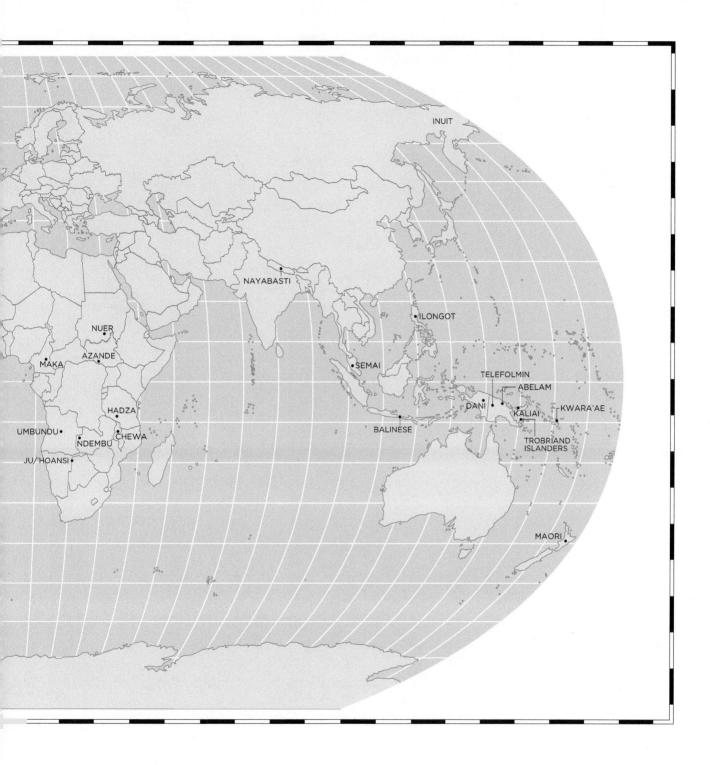

INUIT

NAYABASTI

NUER

MAKA

AZANDE

ILONGOT

SEMAI

HADZA

UMBUNDU

NDEMBU   CHEWA

JU/'HOANSI

TELEFOLMIN

ABELAM

DANI   KALIAI   KWARA'AE

BALINESE

TROBRIAND
ISLANDERS

MAORI

THE PETERS PROJECTION

This projection is based on the Peters. It distorts the continents (countries near the equator are vertically elongated by a ratio of 2 to 1), but it does show all the continents according to their correct relative sizes. Europe is still at the centre but is not shown as larger than the Third World.

JAPANESE MAP

Not all maps place Europe at the centre of the world. This map, besides reflecting the importance the Japanese attach to themselves in the world, has the virtue of showing the geographic proximity of North America to Asia—a fact easily overlooked when maps place Europe at their centre.

RUSSIA

UNITED
STATES

CANADA

GREENLAND

UNITED STATES

MEXICO

THE
BAHAMAS

CUBA

HAITI
DOMINICAN REPUBLIC

JAMAICA

BELIZE
GUATEMALA
EL SALVADOR
HONDURAS

NICARAGUA

COSTA RICA
PANAMA

COLOMBIA

VENEZUELA

FRENCH GUIANA

GUYANA
SURINAM

ECUADOR

PERU

BRAZIL

BOLIVIA

PARAGUAY

CHILE

NEW
ZEALAND

ARGENTINA

URUGUAY

ANTARCTICA

BRIEF CONTENTS

PUTTING THE WORLD IN PERSPECTIVE   IV
PREFACE   XIX
ABOUT THE AUTHORS   XXIX

CHAPTER 1
CULTURE AND MEANING   2

CHAPTER 2
DOING FIELDWORK IN SOCIOCULTURAL ANTHROPOLOGY   36

CHAPTER 3
THE MEANING OF PROGRESS AND DEVELOPMENT   58

CHAPTER 4
CONSTRUCTING REALITIES   92

CHAPTER 5
CONSTRUCTING FAMILIES AND SOCIAL RELATIONSHIPS   128

CHAPTER 6
CONSTRUCTING IDENTITIES   160

CHAPTER 7
SOCIAL HIERARCHIES   186

CHAPTER 8
GLOBALIZATION, NEOLIBERALISM, AND THE NATION-STATE   220

CHAPTER 9
RESOLVING CONFLICT   254

GLOSSARY   281
BIBLIOGRAPHY   287
INDEX   305

CONTENTS

PUTTING THE WORLD IN
PERSPECTIVE   IV
PREFACE   XIX
ABOUT THE AUTHORS   XXIX

CHAPTER 1

CULTURE AND MEANING   2

PROBLEM 1: How can people begin to
understand beliefs and behaviours that are
different from their own?   3

INTRODUCTION   3
  The World Behind Everyday
  Appearances   3
  A Multi-faceted Discipline   4

QUESTION 1.1: Why Do Human Beings
Differ in Their Beliefs and Behaviours?   9

QUESTION 1.2: Is It Possible to See the
World Through the Eyes of Others?   12
  How Do People Explain the
  Beliefs and Behaviours of Others?   12
  The Ethnocentric Fallacy and the
  Relativist Fallacy   13
  Virginity Testing in Turkey and
  Cannibalism Among the Wari'   14
  Objectivity and Morality   16

QUESTION 1.3: How Can the Meanings
That Others Find in Experience Be
Interpreted and Described?   18
  Deciphering the Balinese
  Cockfight   19

QUESTION 1.4: What Can Learning About
Other Peoples Tell Anthropologists
About Their Own Societies?   22
  A Balinese Anthropologist Studies
  Canadian Hockey   22

  An Anthropologist Looks at a
  "Happy Meal"   24
QUESTION 1.5: How Can an
Anthropological Perspective Be Used
Outside Academia?   26
  What Can You Do with a B.A. in
  Anthropology?   26
  Applied Anthropology   27
  Indigenous Issues   27
  Legal Anthropology   29
  Political Ecology   30
  Medical Anthropology   30
  Corporate Ethnography   32
CONCLUSIONS   34
CRITICAL THINKING QUESTIONS   35

CHAPTER 2

DOING FIELDWORK IN SOCIOCULTURAL ANTHROPOLOGY   36

PROBLEM 2: How do sociocultural
anthropologists learn about culture?   37

INTRODUCTION   37

QUESTION 2.1: How Did Ethnographic
Fieldwork Develop During the Formative
Years of Anthropology?   39
  Anthropology from an Armchair   39
  Ethnographic Fieldwork   41

QUESTION 2.2: How Has Fieldwork
Changed over the Past Century?   43
  Changing Notions of Fieldwork   43

QUESTION 2.3: What Are Some of the
Challenges of Conducting Fieldwork?   47
  The Embarrassed Anthropologist   47
  Confronting Witchcraft in Mexico   48

QUESTION 2.4: What Are the Responsibilities of Anthropologists Toward the People They Work With? What Does It Mean to "Act Ethically" as an Anthropologist?   50

QUESTION 2.5: How Do Anthropologists Represent the People They Study and Work With? Why Is Representation an Important Issue Within Anthropology?   51

     Representation and Culture   51

CONCLUSIONS   55

CRITICAL THINKING QUESTIONS   56

CHAPTER 3

THE MEANING OF PROGRESS AND DEVELOPMENT   58

PROBLEM 3: How do we explain the transformation of human societies over the past 10,000 years from small-scale, nomadic bands of foragers to large-scale, urban-industrial states?   59

INTRODUCTION   59

     What Do We Mean When We Talk About Progress?   59

QUESTION 3.1: How and Why Did Foraging Societies Switch to Sedentary Agriculture?   60

     Does the Idea of Progress Help Us Understand the Shift from Foraging to Sedentary Agriculture?   62

     Evolutionary Explanations for Culture Change: Lewis Henry Morgan and Leslie White   63

     What Are the Shortcomings of These Theories of Progress?   65

     Life Among Foragers: The Hadza and Ju/'hoansi   65

     The Transition to Agriculture   68

     Industrial Agriculture: Producing Potato Calories   70

QUESTION 3.2: How Can We Explain the Vast Inequality Between the Rich and the Poor?   71

     The British in India   74

     Cotton, Slavery, and the Trail of Tears   75

     Progress for Whom?   78

QUESTION 3.3: How Do Inequality, Economic Development, and Cultural Diversity Relate to One Another?   78

     The Case of Brazil   80

     Do Progress and Development Inevitably Lead to Inequality?   81

QUESTION 3.4: Have Progress and Development Improved Human Health?   82

     Illness and Inequality   82

     The Meaning of Illness   83

QUESTION 3.5: How Can We Apply a Critical Anthropological Understanding of Progress and Development Outside the Academy?   86

     Anthropologists in Development   86

CONCLUSIONS   90

CRITICAL THINKING QUESTIONS   91

CHAPTER 4

CONSTRUCTING REALITIES   92

PROBLEM 4: Why do people believe different things, and why are they so certain that their view of the world is correct and that other views are wrong?   93

INTRODUCTION   93

     The Central Question   93

QUESTION 4.1: How Does the Use of Metaphor Affect the Meanings People Assign to Experience?   95

     Borrowing Meaning with Metaphors   95

     Kwakwaka'wakw Metaphors of Hunger   98

The Metaphors of Contemporary Witchcraft and Magic 100

QUESTION 4.2: How Does Symbolic Action Reinforce a Particular View of the World? 101

The Kwakwaka'wakw Hamatsa Dance 102
A Ritual of Contemporary Witchcraft and Magic 103
Zombies Are "Good to Think With" 104

QUESTION 4.3: How Does the Way We Live Affect Our Beliefs and Rituals? 106

Sapphire Mining in Northern Madagascar 110
Modern Witchcraft in Cameroon 112

QUESTION 4.4: What Happened to Local Worldviews When They Were Confronted by the Religions of the European Colonizers? 113

The Dene Tha and Christianity 113
Christianity in the Solomon Islands 114
Rastafari in Jamaica 115

QUESTION 4.5: How Can People Reorder Their View of the World if It Becomes Unsatisfactory? 117

Wovoka and the Ghost Dance 118
Haitian Vodou 119
Western Secularism 122

CONCLUSIONS 124

CRITICAL THINKING QUESTIONS 126

CHAPTER 5

CONSTRUCTING FAMILIES AND SOCIAL RELATIONSHIPS 128

PROBLEM 5: What do we need to know before we can understand the dynamics of family life in other societies? 129

INTRODUCTION 129

Family Relations in North American Popular Culture 129

QUESTION 5.1: What Is the Composition of the Typical Family Group? 131

The Family Composition of Ju/'hoansi 133
The Family Composition of Trobriand Islanders 134
The Family Composition of Rural Chinese 137

QUESTION 5.2: How Are Families Formed, and How Is the Ideal Family Type Maintained? 139

The Family Cycle of Ju/'hoansi 140
The Family Cycle of Trobriand Islanders 141
The Family Cycle of Rural Chinese 144

QUESTION 5.3: What Are the Roles of Sexuality, Love, and Wealth? 145

Sex, Love, and Wealth Among Ju/'hoansi 145
Sex, Love, and Wealth Among Trobriand Islanders 146
Sex, Love, and Wealth Among Rural Chinese 146

QUESTION 5.4: What Threatens to Disrupt the Family Unit? 147

Threats to a Ju/'hoansi Family 147
Threats to a Trobriand Island Family 148
Threats to a Rural Chinese Family 149

QUESTION 5.5: How Has the Anthropological Study of Families Changed? 151

Challenges to Theory in Anthropology 151

QUESTION 5.6: How Can Understanding Patterns of Family Relations Be Relevant Outside Academia? 154

AIDS Prevention in Namibia 155

CONCLUSIONS 158

CRITICAL THINKING QUESTIONS 158

CHAPTER 6

CONSTRUCTING IDENTITIES 160

PROBLEM 6: How do people determine who they are, and how do they communicate who they *think* they are to others? 161

INTRODUCTION 161

QUESTION 6.1: How Is Identity, and One's Sense of Self, Learned? 162
- Learning Identities 162
- Learning to Belong 163

QUESTION 6.2: How Does the Concept of Personhood Vary from Society to Society? 167
- The Importance of Self 167
- The Egocentric Self and the Sociocentric Self 168
- Personhood in Japan 170

QUESTION 6.3: How Do Societies Distinguish Individuals from One Another? 171

QUESTION 6.4: How Do Societies Mark Changes in Identity? 173
- The Transition to Adulthood 173

QUESTION 6.5: How Do Individuals Communicate Their Identities to One Another? 174
- Rituals of Gift Giving and Hospitality 175
- Gifts and Commodities 177
- Gift Giving and the Christian Celebration of Christmas in North America 178

QUESTION 6.6: How Do People Form Identities Through Collective Struggles? 180
- The Meaning of "Indigenous" 180
- Social Movements 181
- Palestinian Refugees 182
- Conflict Within Collective Identity: Telefolmin and Land in Papua New Guinea 182

CONCLUSIONS 185
CRITICAL THINKING QUESTIONS 185

CHAPTER 7

SOCIAL HIERARCHIES 186

PROBLEM 7: Why are modern societies characterized by social, political, and economic inequalities? How are certain gender, class, racial, and other identities privileged or marginalized in various social contexts? 187

INTRODUCTION 187
- The Rationale for Social Inequality 187

QUESTION 7.1: How Do Societies Use Class and Caste to Rank People in Social Hierarchies? 189
- Class as a Form of Social Hierarchy 189
- Caste as a Form of Social Stratification 190

QUESTION 7.2: How Do People Come to Accept Social Hierarchies as Natural? 192
- Race as a Form of Social Stratification 192
- Constructing the Ideology of Racism 192
- Class, Race, and the Social Construction of "Intelligence" 196

QUESTION 7.3: How Is Gender a Form of Social Hierarchy? 200
- Constructing Male and Female 200
- Constructing Stratification by Gender 201
- Gender Stratification and the Privileging of Hegemonic Masculinities 202
- Gender Stratification and the Feminization of Poverty 204
- Body Image and Gender Hierarchies 204
- Language, Gender, and Racial Hierarchies 206

QUESTION 7.4: How Are Different Forms of Social Hierarchy Interwoven with Each Other?   207

Race, Class, and Social Hierarchies in Brazil   207

Constructing a New Racism   208

Pakistani Immigrant Women and the Construction of the "Sanitized Body"   209

QUESTION 7.5: Can a Non-stratified Community Exist Within a Large Society?   210

The Hutterites and the Colony of Heaven   210

QUESTION 7.6: How Can Anthropology Be Applied to Alleviate the Effects of Inequality?   212

Anthropology and Human Rights   212

Anthropology and Medical Rights: The Work of Paul Farmer   214

Health as a Human Right   216

CONCLUSIONS   219

CRITICAL THINKING QUESTIONS   219

CHAPTER 8

GLOBALIZATION, NEOLIBERALISM, AND THE NATION-STATE   220

PROBLEM 8: What are the economic and cultural effects of globalization, and what is the relationship between globalization, the nation-state, and neoliberalism?   221

INTRODUCTION   221

QUESTION 8.1: What Is Neoliberalism, and What Role Does It Play in Capitalist Economic Globalization?   223

"The Great Transformation"   223

The Emergence of Neoliberalism   225

QUESTION 8.2: What Role Do Nation-States Play in Market Economies?   226

The Nation-State and the Cost of a Snickers Bar   228

What Is the Role of the Nation-State in an Increasingly Neoliberalized Global Economy?   230

Globalization, Free Trade, and the Canadian Garment Industry   233

QUESTION 8.3: What Is the Relationship Between the Nation-State and Identity Under Globalization?   234

Education and the Nation-State   237

The First Nations' Challenge to the Canadian State   237

Global Challenges to the State   240

QUESTION 8.4: How Do Engagements with Global Capitalism Affect Local Cultural Identities and Livelihoods?   241

Nuxalk Identity in an Age of Globalization   241

Figure Skating, Globalization, and Canadian Identity   243

Intersections of Nationalism and Economic and Cultural Globalization in Vanuatu   244

Globalization and Cultural Diversity   247

Finding Hope in the Face of Cultural Devastation   248

CONCLUSIONS   251

CRITICAL THINKING QUESTIONS   252

CHAPTER 9

RESOLVING CONFLICT   254

PROBLEM 9: How do societies give meaning to and justify various forms of conflict resolution, both peaceful and violent?   255

INTRODUCTION   255

Justifying Violence and Imagining Peace   255

QUESTION 9.1: How Do Societies Create a Bias in Favour of Collective Violence?   257

Horses, Rank, and Warfare
Among the Kiowa   257

Good Hosts Among the
Yanomamö   258

Constructing Religious
Justifications for Violence   259

QUESTION 9.2: How Do Societies Create
a Bias in Favour of Peaceful Conflict
Resolution?   261

Characteristics of Peaceful
Societies   261

QUESTION 9.3: What Are the Economic,
Political, and Social Differences
Between Peaceful and Violent
Societies?   263

The Need to Protect Resources   264

Creating the Conditions for
Violence   265

Sexism and Violent Conflict   266

QUESTION 9.4: What Is the Relationship
Between Violence and the
Nation-State?   267

Violence and the Nation-State   267

Violence, the Nation-State, and
Peace in East Timor   269

QUESTION 9.5: How Is It Possible to
Justify the Creation of Weapons of Mass
Destruction?   272

The Language of Nuclear
Destruction   273

QUESTION 9.6: How Do Anthropologists
Do Fieldwork in the Midst of Violent
Conflict?   274

The Endangered Anthropologist   274

Is There a Place for Anthropology–
Military Collaborations?   275

Making Sense of Combat: Canadian
Soldiers in Kandahar   277

CONCLUSIONS   **280**

CRITICAL THINKING QUESTIONS   **280**

GLOSSARY   281

BIBLIOGRAPHY   287

INDEX   305

PREFACE

A NOTE TO STUDENTS: HOW TO READ THIS TEXTBOOK

"How can you begin to think like an anthropologist?" Each of the chapters in this book addresses a series of questions and problems that are of concern to contemporary anthropologists. This text provides you with the necessary anthropological concepts and tools to begin to think "anthropologically" about these problems. For most of you, thinking anthropologically will involve re-evaluating and critiquing many core ideas and values you have probably been taught as being "true," "right," or "natural." Through cross-cultural examples and case studies, you will learn to appreciate the diversity of beliefs, traditions, and experiences of different cultures. This appreciation, in turn, will challenge you to think differently about aspects of your own culture, upbringing, and beliefs.

Each of the nine chapters in this text includes a problem, chapter questions, exercises, and critical thinking questions. Think of these as a "toolkit" to guide you through the text. Each chapter begins with a specific "problem." While reading a chapter, you should keep the relevant problem in mind so that, once you are finished reading, you will understand how the various cultural examples in the text can help you critically address the central problem or issue of the chapter. Each chapter also opens with a brief epigraph and an opening image related to the respective problem. Together, they are meant to evoke, visually and in literary terms, the issue at hand. Keep them in mind as you read through the chapter.

In addition, in each chapter you will find questions that will help you think anthropologically and more specifically about the problem. To make the broad issues in the chapter manageable, we break down the problem into a series of related questions. Exercises interspersed throughout each chapter are derived from the chapter content; they aim to focus your attention on a meaningful critique of contemporary social practices and to allow you to apply the new knowledge and skills you are learning to particular social concerns. You should therefore do the exercises after you have read the chapter's corresponding section. Finally, the critical thinking questions, located at the end of each chapter, ask you to reflect on broad issues discussed in the chapter. These questions should be considered only once you have read the entire chapter thoroughly. They also make excellent study questions.

You will find key terms in *bold* font throughout this text. These are foundational concepts and ideas in anthropology, and it is important to understand how these key ideas are defined within the discipline. For instance, most people use the term "gender" in everyday language. However, "gender" has a unique meaning in anthropology. To help you remember these bolded key terms, we have provided a running glossary throughout the chapter, an end-of-chapter list of the key terms with pertinent page numbers, and a full glossary at the end of the book.

FOR INSTRUCTORS

This text introduces students to the key concepts and methods utilized by sociocultural anthropology. One of our goals in writing this text is to encourage students to read, think, and write critically. Indeed, we believe that one of the main objectives of first-year sociocultural anthropology courses is to teach students to think differently about the world around them. The text facilitates this by encouraging students to analyze and critique many basic assumptions that they have brought with them to the course. For example, many of us are taught to think about our sense of identity, which encompasses gender, class, race, ethnicity, nationality, and family, as natural, biological, or fixed—as something we are born with. In this text, however, we place particular emphasis on the culturally constructed nature of our world: on the idea that many identities, as well as beliefs and practices, that we view as natural are both learned and the consequences of cultural differences.

We thus adopt a "problem-based approach" to the study of anthropology. Richard Robbins wrote the original edition of *Cultural Anthropology: A Problem-Based Approach* in the hope that such an approach would foster a classroom culture that, regardless of class size and instructional technique, would actively involve students in the learning process, promote critical thinking, and impress on students that they, along with the other people and cultures of the world, are cultural animals worthy of study.

Each chapter is organized around an intellectual "problem" and then subdivided into a series of questions that address the problem from an anthropological perspective. Most sections of each chapter contain short exercises that encourage students to apply the knowledge and skills they have learned to foster a sense of reflexivity about their own behaviours and beliefs. Each chapter ends with a discussion of the ways in which a problem-based approach and anthropological perspective can be put to use outside academia. Ultimately, we hope that after reading this text, students will appreciate that culture, as the way that human beings make their lives meaningful, is fluid, dynamic, contradictory, and subject to critique. Moreover, we hope that students who read this book will understand why and how anthropology *matters* for anyone who wants to understand, and perhaps make a difference in, the contemporary world.

The material in this text is organized by problems and questions rather than by topics. Each of the nine chapters focuses on a specific problem of anthropological as well as general concern:

- How can people begin to understand beliefs and behaviours that are different from their own?
- How do sociocultural anthropologists learn about culture?
- How do we explain the transformation of human societies over the past 10,000 years from small-scale, nomadic bands of hunters and gatherers to large-scale, urban-industrial states?
- Why do people believe different things, and why are they so certain that their view of the world is correct and that others are wrong?
- What do we need to know before we can understand the dynamics of family life in other societies?
- How do people determine who they are, and how do they communicate who they *think* they are to others?
- Why are modern societies characterized by social, political, and economic inequalities? How are certain gender, class, racial, and other identities privileged or marginalized in various social contexts?
- What are the economic and cultural effects of globalization, and what is the relationship between globalization, the nation-state, and national identity?
- How do societies give meaning to and justify various forms of conflict resolution, both peaceful and violent?

These problems have no definitive solutions, yet they drive much intellectual inquiry. Each problem/chapter is broken down into a series of specific questions, each of which can be "answered" by focusing on the ethnographic and theoretical contributions of anthropologists. Such questions include the following:

- Is it possible to see the world through the eyes of others?
- How do people come to accept social hierarchies as natural?
- What are the characteristics of peaceful societies?

TOPIC AND QUESTION CORRESPONDENCE

Topic	Corresponding Chapter or Question
Aboriginal and Indigenous Peoples	Question 3.2; Question 3.3; Question 3.4; Question 3.5; Question 4.1; Question 4.2; Question 4.3; Question 4.4 ; Question 4.5; Question 6.1; Question 6.6; Question 8.3; Question 8.4; Question 9.1; Question 9.2; Question 9.3
Applied Anthropology	Question 1.5; Question 3.5; Question 5.6; Question 7.6; Question 9.6; Chapter 9 (Conclusions)
Caste	Question 7.1
Colonialism	Question 3.2; Question 3.3; Question 3.4; Question 4.4; Question 4.5; Question 6.2; Question 6.6; Question 8.2; Question 8.3; Question 8.4; Question 8.5; Question 9.3; Question 9.4
Conflict	Chapter 9
Corporations	Question 8.1; Question 8.2
Cultural Relativism	Question 1.2
Culture Change	Chapter 3
Culture Concept	Chapter 1
Ecology	Question 1.5; Question 3.3; Question 3.5; Question 8.2; Question 8.3
Economic Anthropology	Chapter 3; Chapter 7; Chapter 8
Education	Question 6.1; Question 8.3
Ethnocentrism	Question 1.2
Family Organization	Chapter 5
Feminist Anthropology	Question 4.5; Question 5.1; Question 6.4; Question 9.3
Fieldwork	Chapter 2
Food Production	Question 2.3; Question 3.1; Question 8.2
Foragers	Question 3.1; Question 9.2
Gender	Chapter 7; Question 6.1; Question 7.3; Question 9.3
Gift Giving	Question 5.3; Question 6.5
Globalization	Chapter 8; Question 3.2; Question 3.3
Human Rights	Question 1.2; Question 7.6
Identity	Chapter 6
Industrialization	Question 3.2; Question 3.3
Inequality	Chapter 7; Question 7.1; Question 7.2; Question 7.3; Question 7.4; Question 7.5; Question 7.6
International Development	Question 3.3; Question 3.5; Question 5.6; Question 6.6
Kinship	Chapter 5
Language and Culture	Question 1.3; Question 4.1; Question 6.3; Question 7.3; Question 9.5
Law and Anthropology	Question 1.5
Marriage	Chapter 5

(Continued)

Topic	Corresponding Chapter or Question
Medical Anthropology	Question 1.5; Question 3.4; Question 5.6; Question 7.6
Nation-State	Chapter 8; Question 9.4
Neoliberalism	Chapter 8
Peasants	Question 2.5; Question 3.1; Question 3.3; Chapter 5
Political Ecology	Question 1.5
Political Organization and Control	Chapter 7; Question 7.5; Question 9.2; Question 9.3; Question 9.4
Race and Racism	Question 7.2; Question 7.4
Religion/World View	Chapter 4; Question 1.1; Question 1.2; Question 6.5; Question 9.1
Ritual	Question 1.3; Question 1.4; Question 4.2; Question 4.3; Question 6.4 ; Question 6.5; Question 6.6
Sexual Stratification	Question 5.1; Question 5.2; Question 5.3; Question 9.3
Sexuality	Question 5.3; Question 5.5; Question 5.6; Question 7.3
Social Stratification	Chapter 7
Status and Rank	Chapter 7; Question 3.1; Question 3.2; Question 3.3; Question 9.1
Subsistence Techniques	Question 3.1; Question 3.2
Symbolism	Question 1.1; Question 1.3; Question 1.4; Question 4.1; Question 4.2; Question 4.3; Question 6.4; Question 6.5
Systems of Exchange	Question 6.5
Tourism	Question 2.5; Question 8.4

Although the problems and questions included in the text are not exhaustive, those that we have selected are central to the concerns of the discipline and include the topics and issues typically covered in an introductory sociocultural anthropology class. We have chosen problems and questions that we hope will capture students' imaginations and whet their appetite for further study in the discipline. The Topic and Question Correspondence chart, which links topics to questions considered in the text, can be used in guiding discussion and in course planning.

A key pedagogical feature of this text is the inclusion of exercises that give students the opportunity to apply what they have read, to think about the implications of the material for their own lives, and to think about various problems "like an anthropologist." These exercises are interspersed throughout the text and can be used in various ways by students and instructors. They might serve as discussion questions in lectures, tutorials, or online discussion posts, or they could be used as the basis for group work. They could also be treated as informal writing assignments, with students preparing brief reading responses based on the exercises, which would then be used as a starting point for classroom discussion. However they are used, the exercises are designed to give first-year students a chance to engage in intellectual debate and to highlight the real-world implications of what they have learned.

In addition to the exercises, each chapter concludes with several critical thinking questions.

The questions, together with updated end-of-chapter glossaries of key terms, encourage students to review what they have learned in two different ways. The lists (whose terms appear in bold throughout the chapter) allow students to review each chapter's material quickly: names, terms, and theories. The critical thinking questions provide students with the opportunity to rethink the material in a way that underscores what they have learned through the problem-based approach.

This third edition of *Sociocultural Anthropology: A Problem-Based Approach* includes maps, which are interspersed throughout the chapters. The inclusion of the different projections that open this book exemplifies one of the key pedagogical goals of an introductory anthropology class: to show how one's entire world is shaped by one's cultural perspective. In addition to these maps, each of the chapters includes two or three smaller maps, each of which corresponds with one of the ethnographic examples in the text. These are intended to help orient students toward the material, especially for places that, in our teaching experience, students tend to be less familiar with (the Trobriand Islands, for example).

Another key feature that contributes to learning stems from Richard Robbins's conviction—evident in the earlier editions and maintained here, and which we share—that students learning about the cultures of others cannot fully appreciate them without first understanding something of their own cultural perspective. In order to appreciate that other people construct their worlds, they must appreciate that they themselves do so as well. Accordingly, we have included numerous comparisons of world cultures with North American cultures, both in the text and through the exercises.

NEW IN THIS EDITION

In this Third Canadian Edition of *Sociocultural Anthropology: A Problem-Based Approach*, we retain the spirit of Richard Robbins's account of what anthropology is all about. We continue to build on Sherrie Larkin's efforts in the first Canadian edition to provide interesting and important examples of the research that Canadian anthropologists are doing, both in Canada and beyond. Larkin's strong focus on Canadian anthropological work with First Nations, Inuit, and Métis peoples remains important as well. In order to give students a sense of both the history of the discipline and its ongoing dynamism and potential, we have added new ethnographic examples from around the world, both classic and contemporary. In response to instructor feedback, and based on our own experiences in the classroom, we have made several additions and enhancements throughout the text. These include a change in the title of the text. Although the first and second Canadian editions were titled *Cultural Anthropology: A Problem-Based Approach*, we have replaced the term "cultural anthropology" with "sociocultural anthropology." We feel that this change better reflects the combined influences of British and American anthropology on Canadian anthropological traditions. In addition, we have made the following chapter-specific changes.

Chapter 1

- We have moved and lengthened our discussion of fieldwork from Chapter 1 to form a new chapter on fieldwork (Chapter 2).
- The discussion of anthropology's four subfields (archaeology, biological/physical anthropology, linguistics, and sociocultural anthropology) is expanded.
- This edition expands significantly upon the second edition's discussion of applied anthropology, with examples drawn from research within legal anthropology, the corporate sector, work among Indigenous groups, and health-related research.

Chapter 2

- This chapter is new to this edition. Much of the material on fieldwork from the last edition has been moved here and expanded upon.

- There is an exploration of how anthropological methods and fieldwork have changed over the past century.
- A new section discusses ethical obligations and concerns within anthropology.
- Issues of representation are expanded from Chapter 1 in the previous edition.

Chapter 3

- The concept of progress is problematized and discussed in greater depth.
- There is a stronger focus upon and discussion of the concept of colonialism.

Chapter 4

- The chapter includes a new section on Western secularism and atheism, with a discussion of the *Charlie Hebdo* incident in France.
- The concept of world view is defined and elaborated upon with the use of religious/spiritual examples as well as a new example using Robbie Floyd-Davis's work on hospital birth as a rite of passage.
- There are updated examples and a discussion of shamanism and witchcraft.

Chapter 5

- The discussion of reproductive technologies and kinship is expanded.
- An updated introduction notes some of the significant features of kinship using contemporary examples that will be well-known to Canadian students.
- Additional attention is paid throughout the chapter to North American kinship and patterns of family relations. Students are constantly encouraged to critically question their own understandings of what makes a family.

Chapter 6

- This new chapter provides a more nuanced discussion of the significance of thinking about identity as learned rather than natural, with the addition of new references about popular understandings of the role of genetics in identity.
- There is further discussion and clarification of the concepts of egocentric and sociocentric notions of personhood.

Chapter 7

- A revised introduction emphasizes the significance of taking a critical approach to social hierarchies, which are often taken for granted as natural.
- Discussion of caste is revised, and there is a stronger critique of the idea of class hierarchy as a meritocracy.
- Statistics on poverty in Canada are updated.
- There is an extended discussion of how different forms of social hierarchies (e.g., race and class) can overlap with each other.
- A new section explores forms of "new racism" with a case study of new immigrants in Canada.

Chapter 8

- The commoditization of sugar and its role in the development of economic globalization is discussed.
- Updated examples of various commodities (e.g. Snickers bar) are included.
- A new section, "Globalization and Cultural Diversity," is now part of the chapter.

Chapter 9

- The chapter clarifies the concepts of peace and violence, and puts a greater focus on different forms of conflict resolution.
- There is a discussion of the potential and role of anthropology in establishing peace and minimizing conflict within different societies.

Finally, in addition to the pedagogical features (updated exercises, critical thinking questions, and maps) and the new material discussed above, there are more photographs in this edition than in the last; they have, however, been added in such a way that they complement a key strength of the earlier editions: the inclusion of many in-depth case studies that encourage close reading. This text should appeal to visual learners, active learners, and those who learn through reading. These learning styles come together in the opening pages for each chapter, each of which includes a visual element (such as a photo) that is explicitly connected, in its caption, to a text element (the epigraph), which, in turn, exemplifies the issues for active learning articulated in the chapter problem.

ACKNOWLEDGMENTS

We remain indebted to Richard Robbins and Sherrie Larkin for their work on earlier editions of this text. In the first Canadian edition, published in 2007, Sherrie Larkin did an excellent job of adapting Robbins's text for a Canadian readership. Much of this third edition is an extension and elaboration of their earlier efforts.

We also thank Maya Castle, Mark Grzeskowiak, Linda Sparks, Jennifer Hare, and Katherine Goodes at Nelson Education for their encouragement, patience, and support throughout the writing of this third edition. Thanks also go to Kate Revington, the copy editor. Maggie would like to thank Karen, once again, for being an imaginative, inspiring, and patient co-editor and a wonderful colleague. And Karen thanks Maggie for her patience, organization, and creativity during the planning, writing, and editing of this text.

We would also like to thank the reviewers, past and present, for their valuable feedback:

Anna K. Boshnakova, Sheridan College
Sean Connaughton, Kwantlen Polytechnic University
Ellen Facey, University of Northern British Columbia

Edward J. Hedican, University of Guelph
Chris Holdsworth, University of Calgary
Teresa Holmes, York University
Branka Maleševi, University of Windsor
Sam Migliore, Kwantlen Polytechnic University
Bruce Miller, University of British Columbia
Brian Pegg, Kwantlen Polytechnic University
Blair Rutherford, Carleton University
Patricia Kelly Spurles, Mount Allison University
Mark Tate, Memorial University
Charisma Thomson, University of Regina
Marilyn Walker, Mount Allison University
Barbara Wilkes, University of Calgary
Saulesh Yessenova, University of Calgary

We would be very grateful to receive questions, comments, and suggestions for improvement from instructors and students. Our e-mail addresses are mcummings@utsc.utoronto.ca and mcgarry@mcmcaster.ca.

Maggie Cummings and Karen McGarry

ANCILLARIES

Instructor Resources

The **Nelson Education Teaching Advantage (NETA)** program delivers research-based instructor resources that promote student engagement and higher-order thinking to enable the success of Canadian students and educators. Visit Nelson Education's **Inspired Instruction** website at http://www.nelson.com/inspired/ to find out more about NETA.

The following instructor resources have been created for Sociocultural Anthropology, Third Canadian Edition. Access these ultimate tools for customizing lectures and presentations at www.nelson.com/instructor.

NETA Test Bank

This resource was updated and revised by Karl Schmid, York University. It includes over 235 multiple-choice questions written according to NETA guidelines for effective construction and development of higher-order questions. Included, as well, are over 120 true/false, over 40 short answer, and approximately 15-20 essay-type questions.

cognero ®
Full-Circle Assessment®

The NETA Test Bank is available in a new, Cloud-based platform. **Testing Powered by Cognero®** is a secure online testing system that allows instructors to author, edit, and manage test-bank content from anywhere Internet access is available. No special installations or downloads are needed, and the desktop-inspired interface, with its drop-down menus and familiar, intuitive tools, allows instructors to create and manage tests with ease. Multiple test versions can be created in an instant, and content can be imported or exported into other systems. Tests can be delivered from a learning management system, the classroom, or wherever an instructor chooses. Testing Powered by Cognero for *Sociocultural Anthropology*, Third Canadian Edition, can also be accessed through www.nelson.com/instructor.

NETA PowerPoint

Microsoft® PowerPoint® lecture slides for every chapter have been created by Terry Webb, Western University. There is an average of 30-35 slides per chapter, many featuring key figures, tables, and photographs from *Sociocultural Anthropology*, Third Canadian Edition. NETA principles of clear design and engaging content with instructor notes have been incorporated throughout, making it simple for instructors to customize the deck for their courses.

Image Library

This resource consists of digital copies of figures, short tables, and photographs used in the book. Instructors may use these jpegs to customize the NETA PowerPoint slides or create their own PowerPoint presentations.

NETA Enriched Instructor Guide

This resource was updated and revised by Terry Webb, Western University. It is organized according to the textbook chapters and addresses key educational concerns, such as typical stumbling blocks student face and how to address them. Other features include responses to the text's Critical Thinking Questions.

The National Geographic Learning Reader Series

This groundbreaking series is brought to you through an exclusive partnership with the National Geographic Society, an organization with a unique tradition of exploration, scientific research, discovery, conservation, and nonpareil publishing. Readers of interest to students of anthropology include *Archaeology*, *Biological Anthropology*, and *Cultural Anthropology*. The readers bring learning to life by featuring compelling images, media, and text from National Geographic Learning. Each article has an introduction to provide context as well as focus questions that suggest ideas to think about while reading the selection. Rich photography and compelling images are used throughout to further enhance understanding of the selections. The chapter culminating section includes discussion questions to stimulate both in-class discussion and out-of-class work. Additional resources are available via a media-rich ebook that contains videos as well as the capability to highlight, take notes, search, and bookmark. For more information, visit www.cengage.com/community/natgeo, or contact your Nelson Education learning solutions consultant.

CourseReader

CourseReader is an easy-to-use and afford-able option to create your own online collection of readings for your course. Simply go online to search or browse Cengage Learning's collection of thousands of text documents and media clips. In just a matter of minutes you can preview, select, and create your customized collection from across many disciplines. To view a demo of CourseReader, visit www.cengage.com/coursereader. To learn more about money-saving bundles, please contact your local Nelson learning solutions consultant.

Student Ancillaries

Free Student Companion Site

The more you study, the better the results. Make the most of your study time by accessing the tools available on the free Student Companion Site at http://www.nelson.com/student:

- glossary
- matching quizzes
- crossword puzzles
- flashcards

ABOUT THE AUTHORS

RICHARD H. ROBBINS Richard H. Robbins is a distinguished teaching professor of anthropology at the State University of New York at Plattsburgh. His teaching interests include courses on global problems, utopian societies, comparative religion, and activist anthropology. He has conducted research among Indigenous peoples of Canada and fishing communities in northeastern New Brunswick. His books include *Global Problems and the Culture of Capitalism,* Fourth Edition; *Darwin and the Bible: The Cultural Confrontation* (with Mark Cohen); and *Globalization and the Environment* (with Gary Kroll). Professor Robbins is the recipient of the 2005 American Anthropological Association Award for Excellence in Undergraduate Teaching.

MAGGIE CUMMINGS Maggie Cummings is an assistant professor, teaching stream, in the department of anthropology at the University of Toronto, Scarborough (UTSC). For more than a decade, she has done fieldwork on gender, modernity, and social change in Vanuatu. More recently, her research interests have expanded to include the ethnography of social media and the institutional ethnography of the contemporary university. Since beginning her teaching career in 2006, she has designed and taught more than a dozen undergraduate anthropology courses, including "Introduction to Anthropology," "Fieldwork in Sociocultural Anthropology," "Genders and Sexualities," and "Culture through Film and Media." She has also been involved in several fieldwork-based student learning initiatives at UTSC, including an interdisciplinary project on citizenship, belonging, and urban life in East Scarborough.

KAREN MCGARRY Karen McGarry is an assistant professor of anthropology at McMaster University in Hamilton, Ontario. Her research focuses upon two areas: the anthropology of sport and educational anthropology. Karen's fieldwork on sport involves ethnographic studies of elite, high-performance sports like figure skating, with an emphasis upon the production, distribution, and reception of particular representations of athletes' bodies in the mass media. Broadly speaking, she is interested in the intersections among gender, race, class, ethnicity, and Canadian nationalism. In the field of educational anthropology, her interests lie within the realm of multicultural education and educulturalism. At McMaster, she teaches introductory anthropology courses ("Sex, Food, and Death" and "Race, Religion, and Conflict"), as well as anthropological theory, and a fourth-year undergraduate course, "The Anthropology of Zombies and the Undead."

PROBLEM-BASED PEDAGOGICAL FRAMEWORK

One doesn't need to change one's instructional approach to adopt a problem-based book. If you'd like your students to question, inquire, think critically, and analyze material, the problem-based pedagogical framework of this text can support that intention.

A Thorough, Robust Map Program

Expanding students' geographical awareness can be achieved through a comprehensive map program. Global ethnographic examples within the chapters are grounded by maps in the prefatory and in-text material. The maps give students a visual sense of both the global diversity of human culture, and of the geographical breadth of anthropology as a discipline. Each chapter includes two or three smaller maps that correspond with one of ethnographic examples in the text. These are intended to help to orient students toward the material, especially for places with which, in the authors' teaching experiences, students tend to be less familiar.

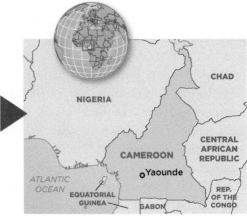

Problems

At the centre of the problem-based approach is the problem that frames each chapter. The material in this text is organized by problems rather than by topics to encourage students to make connections between pressing issues, anthropological lenses, and anthropologists' work. Each of the nine chapters of the book focuses on a specific problem of anthropological, as well as general, concern. Although these problems may have no definitive solutions, they drive much intellectual inquiry.

Problem 3

How do we explain the transformation of human societies over the past 10,000 years from small-scale, nomadic bands of foragers to large-scale, urban-industrial states?

Questions

Each problem/chapter is broken down into a series of specific questions, each of which can be "answered" by focusing on the ethnographic and theoretical contributions of anthropologists.

QUESTIONS

3.1 How and why did foraging societies switch to sedentary agriculture?

3.2 How can we explain the vast inequality between the rich and the poor?

3.3 How do economic development, inequality, and cultural diversity relate to one another?

3.4 Have progress and development improved human health?

3.5 How can we apply a critical anthropological understanding of progress and development outside the academy?

Exercises

A key pedagogical feature of this text is the inclusion of exercises that give students the opportunity to apply what they have read, to think about the implications of the material for their own lives, and to try to think about various problems "like an anthropologist." These can be assigned for homework, worked through in class, or posted to your learning management system. Students can complete them in groups or individually.

EXERCISE 3.1

It is easy to look back at 19th-century anthropological theories, such as Morgan's theory of unilineal evolution, and critique them as being unduly influenced by norms and concerns of the time. It is more difficult to think about how more historically recent theories for thinking about human difference and social change are also culturally and historically situated. What kinds of contemporary issues might shape our theories for understanding humanity, progress, and development today? What kinds of scientific theories from other disciplines might we see imported into sociocultural anthropology?

CRITICAL THINKING QUESTIONS

1. In Chapter 1, we discussed the methodological concept of cultural relativism. How might you apply the idea of cultural relativism to the twin concepts of progress and development?
2. Western environmental activists often point to indigenous cultures and modes of livelihood as examples of a more environmentally friendly way to live. What are the possible advantages and disadvantages of this approach, both from the perspective of the environmentalists and from that of the indigenous groups to whom they refer?
3. Given what you have learned about how population, urbanization, agriculture, and technology relate to one another, what predictions might you make about future modes of livelihood and food production?

Critical Thinking Questions

To extend the inquiry-based philosophy of the text, the authors have provided critical thinking questions at the end of each chapter. The questions encourage students to review what they have learned by giving students the opportunity to rethink the material in a way that underscores what they have learned through the problem-based approach. These questions can be assigned for homework or used for in-class discussion.

Running Glossary

This edition continues to have a running glossary in which key terms are highlighted and defined on the page where they first appear. The glossary (whose terms appear in bold throughout the chapter) allows students to review quickly the chapter's material: names, terms, and theories.

sedentary
A mode of livelihood characterized by permanent or semi-permanent settlements.

progress
The idea that human history is the story of a steady advance from a life dependent on the whims of nature to a life of control and domination over natural forces.

CULTURE AND MEANING

© Yvette Cardozo/Alamy

As noted in the epigraph by Rupert Ross on the next page, it is nearly impossible to accurately interpret people's acts when we do not understand the meanings they attribute to those acts. This photo of an Inuit woman, dressed in traditional regalia, demonstrates the potential pitfalls of misinterpretation. What do you see when you look at the photo? Is this everyday dress, or is this for a special occasion? What is the significance of her finery? Unless you are well versed in Inuit culture and history, it is likely that your interpretation says more about your own cultural context than that of the Inuit. Understanding human beliefs and behaviours requires a similar attention to meaning in context.

Acts are never merely acts. They are also signals of attitude. Those signals, however, are often culture specific. When acts are seen, but their signal-content misinterpreted, it is impossible to avoid forming inaccurate interpretations of others. Until we understand what particular acts mean to the other, we will continually ascribe motivations and states of mind that are well off the mark.

Rupert Ross, Dancing with a Ghost

Problem 1

How can people begin to understand beliefs and behaviours that are different from their own?

INTRODUCTION

The World Behind Everyday Appearances

In **sociocultural anthropology** we strive to look beyond the world of everyday experiences to discover the patterns and meanings that lie behind that world. Take, for example, the typical classroom chair with attached desk.

In our taken-for-granted, everyday world, this piece of furniture is a utilitarian object: something to sit on, or to write on, or even to put our feet on. But for the sociocultural anthropologist, as the epigraph to this chapter suggests, acts are never merely acts, nor are objects, even classroom chairs, merely objects; both are signals whose meaning is culturally specific. The classroom chair tells some interesting tales and poses some interesting questions. For example, why do we have chairs at all? Many societies don't; instead, people sit or squat on the ground or the floor or sit on stools or benches. Historically, the chair likely first appeared in Europe or the Near East, but it wasn't common even in Europe until the 18th century. Another question: Why does the classroom chair take the form it does? One feature of the chair that anthropologists might explore as they try to decipher the meaning of the classroom chair with writing surface is the erect position into which it forces the body, compelling it, in effect, to "pay attention." We might take a clue from the French philosopher Michel Foucault, who refers to the shaping of the human body as a

sociocultural anthropology
A comparative approach to the study of societies and cultures that focuses on differences and similarities in the ways that societies are structured and cultural meanings are created.

"political anatomy." By this, he means that people's bodies are controlled by others to operate with the necessary speed and efficiency. Political anatomy produces, he says, "docile bodies."

An anthropologist might suggest that the classroom chair with desk is part of the political anatomy of educational settings—part of the system of relations that gives meaning to the classroom. In other words, this piece of furniture forms the body into a shape that prepares it (or forces it) to attend to a teacher and not to others in the same room. Moreover, it is appropriate to its unique setting in the classroom, as are other objects of furniture. Imagine, for example, replacing classroom chairs with bar stools, whose main purpose is to promote bodily mobility and conversation with others.

Once alert to the idea that the classroom chair might serve as an instrument of control, we might notice other ways in which classroom design serves as a mode of discipline. The distribution of people in space, with each person in a particular "spot" in neat, ordered rows, serves to discipline people to "pay attention" to the classroom centre and not to others around them. We might also notice the distinctive ordering of time and the use of clocks, bells, and whistles to control the movement and activities of people in school settings. We can even take our analysis a step further and examine the discipline of the school setting sequentially, from

Sociocultural anthropologists find patterns of meaning even in objects as simple as a classroom chair.

© Stacey Newman/Shutterstock

kindergarten through high school. Contrast, for example, the wide-open space of the kindergarten classroom, with its open, movable chairs and tables and teacher's desk set off to the side, with the enclosed, partitioned space of a second- or third-grade classroom, with its neatly arranged desks facing the centred desk of the teacher. This is the evolution of classroom discipline.

Students, of course, do not always obey the subtle commands that direct their bodies to do certain things at certain times. One only has to examine the strange bodily contortions of students as they resist the form into which the classroom chair tries to force them. We also try, occasionally, to resist the isolation imposed by the arrangement of classroom furniture or the timetables set by clocks, bells, and whistles.

The ways in which specific societies order behaviour through the arrangement of space and time is but one small area examined by sociocultural anthropology, but it serves as an example of how, from an anthropological perspective, we cannot take anything about even our own beliefs and behaviour for granted, let alone the behaviour and beliefs of those whose backgrounds and histories differ from our own.

This book is about how sociocultural anthropology can help us see beyond our taken-for-granted world. We will be examining how sociocultural anthropology helps us understand others and, in the process, better understand ourselves. We will also be examining how knowledge of others and ourselves is relevant to careers in social and economic development, public policy and planning, education, medicine, and conflict resolution.

A Multi-faceted Discipline

The term "anthropology" comes from two Greek words: *anthropos*, meaning "human beings," and *logia*, meaning "the study of" or "the knowledge of." This study of, or knowledge of, human beings includes everything that humans do currently or have done

Most anthropologists specialize in one or more of anthropology's four sub-fields. Clockwise, these include biological anthropology, linguistic anthropology, sociocultural anthropology, and archeology.

in the past. It also includes collecting evidence of how and when we became human and comparing humans to other organisms in the world. If asked to describe a typical anthropologist, you might envision an intrepid explorer, like Indiana Jones, searching for priceless artifacts or painstakingly excavating ancient fossils. But it would be more realistic to imagine a sociocultural anthropologist equipped with a notebook and a voice recorder rather than a shovel or a trowel. The kind of knowledge about human beings that interests sociocultural anthropologists is acquired by spending time with people, talking to them, observing what they do, and trying to understand their lives—as anthropologist Bronislaw Malinowski aptly put it—"from the native's point of view" (see section 1.2).

In North America, anthropology is divided into four different approaches to the study of humans. Although these four subdisciplines address some of the same questions about what it means to be human, they focus on different aspects of the anthropological question (hence, the differences among the tools—notebooks versus shovels—used by different kinds of anthropologists). The subdisciplines are biological anthropology, archaeology, linguistic anthropology, and sociocultural anthropology (known as "cultural anthropology" in the United States and "social anthropology" in Britain; in Canada the discipline is influenced by both these traditions). To understand what makes sociocultural anthropology unique among the subdisciplines (and among the social sciences in general), it is important first to understand the points of convergence and divergence among these subdisciplines.

Biological anthropology, the oldest of the four subdisciplines, focuses on the study of the evolution, function, and health of the human body and our closest primate ancestors across time and space. There are many areas of specialization within the field of biological anthropology, three of which are discussed here. Some biological anthropologists, for instance, specialize in *paleoanthropology*, which is the study of the fossilized remains of the earliest humans, and endeavour to understand the history of human biological evolution. Paleoanthropologists excavate ancient sites of early human activity or habitation, and they study fossil remains in laboratories.

Through close examinations of fossil records in Africa, Europe, and parts of Asia, paleoanthropologists study mostly extinct, transitional species between apes and humans called "hominids." Hominids are bipedal primates that first evolved in Africa ("bipedal" refers to the ability to walk on two feet for extended periods). They subsequently spread throughout the rest of the world. Although the history of hominid evolution is changing rapidly as new fossils are discovered, it is currently believed that hominids evolved over 4 million years ago.

By studying and comparing the anatomy of hominid feet and leg joints, as well as preserved footprints, paleoanthropologists can reconstruct such things as the height, gait, and locomotion patterns of ancient hominids. At the site of Laetoli in Tanzania, for instance, famed paleoanthropologist Mary Leakey discovered evidence of bipedalism from hominid footprints preserved in volcanic ash that date to approximately 3.7 million years ago. Other paleoanthropologists study the cranial anatomy of hominids. Tooth structure and tooth wear can help us reconstruct hominid diets. Reconstructions of the physical structure of hominids can also provide evidence for migrations and ancient interactions of hominids. Based upon his excavation and study of Neanderthal sites, Canadian anthropologist Eugene Morin argues that Neanderthals and humans interacted with each other between 30,000 and 40,000 years ago. This interaction may have included, in some cases, interbreeding.

Other biological anthropologists specialize in *primatology*, or the study of our closest nonhuman relatives. One of the most famous primatologists is Jane Goodall. In 1960, she went to Gombe Stream National Park in Tanzania, where she would begin a lifetime study of the behavioural patterns of wild chimpanzees. Given that humans and chimpanzees are closely related genetically, many primatologists believe that the study of apes can help glean information about the behaviour of early hominids that lived between 4 and 5 million years ago. Today, Goodall continues her research. She has worked tirelessly to help establish safe chimpanzee sanctuaries, and she speaks out against the destruction of their ecosystems.

The newest branch of biological anthropology is *forensic anthropology*, which is the study of human remains for identification and cause of death. Forensic anthropologists can often determine the age, sex, health status, height, and cause of death by examining human skeletal material and its surrounding context. Many forensic anthropologists assist with human rights cases, excavating human bones found buried in mass graves. By excavating remains found in war-torn areas of the world, such as the former Yugoslavia, Rwanda, and Darfur, forensic experts can document cases of mass genocide. This information, in turn, can

biological anthropology
A subdiscipline of anthropology that focuses upon the study of the evolution, function, and health of the human body and our closest primate ancestors across time and space.

be used in international human rights tribunals to establish the guilt or innocence of various parties. In addition, by identifying missing individuals, forensic anthropologists are able to provide many families with a sense of closure through confirmation of the death of a loved one. Other forensic experts work on active criminal investigations in tandem with the police in an effort to identify human remains that may be associated with a criminal case.

Archaeology is the branch of anthropology that studies human history and its artifacts. Archaeologists typically look at the material remains of human groups in order to learn how people lived. Tools, pottery shards, and other artifacts offer clues about the social and cultural lives of societies that existed thousands of years ago. Archaeologists excavate archaeological sites (areas that display evidence of past human activity).

Although archaeologists are often romanticized as treasure hunters within our pop culture, they do not keep any artifacts they find. All artifacts discovered are carefully mapped and recorded at a site to preserve their provenience, or specific location in space. For example, it is important to note where an artifact is found inside a house. Is it in the kitchen, a storage room, a bathroom, or a midden, or refuse area? By mapping out the horizontal location of artifacts, archaeologists can make inferences about the functions of different spaces on a site. Some areas, for instance, might be used for cooking, others for making weapons, and other areas for weaving or producing textiles. When recording provenience, archaeologists also record vertical provenience, or how far below the surface that an artifact is discovered. Often, different layers of soil (called "strata") are connected to different dates of occupation. So, it is important to map both vertical and horizontal provenience to understand spatial functions as well as time periods.

Once an archaeological site is excavated, the artifacts discovered are taken to labs where they are washed and further analyzed. Decorations on pottery, for instance, can help date the pot (and, by extension, the site), and they may also reveal other information about past lifestyles. Occasionally, residue may even be discovered inside an artifact such as a pot. Archaeologist Pat McGovern, for instance, conducts chemical analyses on the residue of ceramic pots. In the process, he has discovered (and re-created) some of the world's oldest alcoholic beverages. In Iran, he found the world's oldest barley beer dating to approximately 3400 BCE, as well as the oldest wine made from grapes, from 5400 BCE. Brewing ancient beverages for modern consumers may sound exciting, but more than that, the ingredients in such beverages can tell us a lot about ancient life. For instance, we can learn about trade routes and migrations of people by examining the ingredients in beer. If a particular ingredient is not locally available, archaeologists can trace its source to other cultural areas and try to understand past human interactions, such as trade, on a wider scale.

Linguistic anthropology involves examining the relationship between language and culture. *Linguistic anthropologists* explore how people use language, both in a physical sense with regard to how communication is structured, and in a historical sense with regard to how different languages have developed and spread throughout history. Linguistic anthropologists are interested in studying all languages across time and space, although most focus on language use within a particular

archaeology
The branch of anthropology that studies human history and its artifacts. Archaeologists typically look at the material remains of human groups in order to learn how people lived.

linguistic anthropology
A study of the relationship between language and culture. Linguistic anthropologists explore how people use language, both in a physical sense with regard to how communication is structured, and in a historical sense with regard to how different languages have developed and spread throughout history.

cultural framework. *Sociolinguists*, for instance, are interested in how various aspects of culture shape how we use language. They may analyze the structure and vocabulary used within speech, the study of accents, and even the study of topics of conversation. Language is informed by a society's views on gender, class, race, and other factors such as the context of speaking. Think, for example, about how you may speak differently (in terms of vocabulary choice, intonation, and conversation topics) when you have a conversation with your grandmother versus your best friend.

An early and famous sociolinguistic study was conducted by American linguist William Labov who studied the speech of sales associates working in department stores in Manhattan. Interested in the connection between social class and speech, Labov (1966) studied speech differences among sales associates at three department stores: S. Klein, which offered low-priced merchandise; Macy's, which appeals typically to middle-class consumers; and Saks, a high-end, expensive retailer. Labov noted that sales associates in each store talked differently, with associates from Saks putting greater emphasis on preconsonantal r's, found in such words as "beer" or "floor." A strong emphasis on the pronunciation of "r" is considered to be a subtle and unconscious form of prestige, and it is an emphasis mainly used in upper-class speech in Manhattan.

Historical linguists study the origins of languages and changes in language over time. For example, Canadian anthropologist John Colarusso received international media attention in 2014 when he deciphered writings on an ancient Greek vase referred to as the "New York Goose Play Vase" in New York's Metropolitan Museum of Art. An expert on the ancient Circassian language, Colarusso translated the meanings of ancient scribbles and graffiti on pottery that dates to over 3000 years ago.

The above examples from the fields of biological anthropology, archaeology, and linguistic anthropology highlight the diversity of interests within anthropology.

Given that anthropologists study all aspects of humanity across time and space, it is not uncommon to find an anthropologist studying ancient Egyptian hieroglyphics, observing homeless people in Toronto, or excavating archaeological sites in Peru.

Although all anthropologists specialize in the study of particular peoples, places, and issues, they also tend to work collaboratively, when necessary, to understand various societies. An archaeologist excavating an ancient site in Turkey, for instance, will most certainly call in biological, or physical, anthropologists when and if skeletal material is uncovered. Similarly, a historical linguist, like John Colarusso, will work with archaeologists or art historians to help decipher writings on ancient pottery. But what, then, is sociocultural anthropology, the primary focus of this text? How do the research interests and methods of sociocultural anthropologists differ from those of other anthropologists?

What Makes Sociocultural Anthropology Unique? *Sociocultural anthropologists* look at how societies are structured and how cultural meanings are created. Although these anthropologists are interested in differences among peoples throughout the world, they also look for similarities in how people construct their own versions of what it means to be human. Sociocultural anthropologists, then, explore both the universal and the particular, moving back and forth between these two levels of inquiry and analysis in their work. They do fieldwork and ethnography among the societies and cultures they study (see Chapter 2), gathering data by talking to people and by participating in and observing their day-to-day lives.

This focus on social structures and cultural meanings, in all their forms, is what makes sociocultural anthropology unique among the subdisciplines. Many people, including some anthropologists, wonder whether sociocultural anthropology should be characterized as a science or as one of the humanities. At its best, sociocultural anthropology incorporates aspects of both: the methodological and analytical rigour of the sciences, and the interpretive insights and nuances of the humanities. Eminent anthropologist Eric Wolf (1964, 88) perhaps put it best when he described anthropology as "the most scientific of the humanities, [and] the most humanistic of the sciences." This combination of versatility and breadth is precisely what makes anthropology such an interesting and dynamic discipline.

Moreover, the unique perspective on humanity provided by sociocultural anthropology is well suited to thinking about the complexity of the contemporary world and the human condition. This book is organized around nine general problems that arise from the human condition—problems such as how to understand people with different beliefs and behaviours; why ways of life change; how people justify violence; and whether solving problems of social inequality is possible. These problems concern everyone, not just sociocultural anthropologists, but definitive solutions are not possible. So the goal, instead, is to achieve a greater understanding of why those problems exist and what might be done to address them. Sociocultural anthropologists can ask specific questions about them, applying their unique disciplinary perspective and methodologies. We will be focusing on these nine general problems in this text. At various points you will be asked to supply your own answers to questions and, perhaps, to discuss your answers with others.

Understanding others requires you to recognize that your behaviours and beliefs, as well as those of people in other societies, are socially patterned and constructed. For that reason, you will find in this text many comparisons between North American life and life in other societies. Whether or not you pursue a career in anthropology or a career that explicitly requires anthropological expertise, learning to approach and understand human beliefs and behaviour from an anthropological perspective is a valuable skill in the contemporary world.

QUESTIONS

1.1 Why do human beings differ in their beliefs and behaviours?

1.2 Is it possible to see the world through the eyes of others?

1.3 How can the meanings that others find in experience be interpreted and described?

1.4 What can learning about other peoples tell anthropologists about their own societies?

1.5 How can an anthropological perspective be used outside academia?

QUESTION 1.1: WHY DO HUMAN BEINGS DIFFER IN THEIR BELIEFS AND BEHAVIOURS?

From an anthropological perspective, members of a society view the world in a similar way because they share the same **culture**; people differ in how they view the world because their cultures differ. What do anthropologists mean by "culture"? A good place to start to understand the concept is with the fact that members of all human societies experience specific life events such as birth, death, and the quest for food, water, and shelter. All societies have what are for them appropriate rules for courtship, ideas about child rearing, procedures for exchanging goods, methods of food production, techniques for building shelters, and so on. But from one society to the next, the meanings people assign these events differ. We learn these meanings from, and teach these meanings to, other members of our culture.

culture
The system of meanings about the nature of experience that are shared by a people and passed on from one generation to another, including the meanings that people give to things, events, activities, and people.

CULTURE AND MEANING

Our working definition of culture, therefore, is as follows: "culture is the system of meanings about the nature of experience that is shared by a people and passed from one generation to another." This definition encompasses the meanings that people give to things, events, activities, and people. Anthropologists have debated—and often disagreed about—the substance of culture and the best ways to study it. Our working definition of culture highlights those aspects of this complicated and contentious term upon which most anthropologists *can* agree: culture is about meaning; cultural meanings must be learned; and, once learned, meanings are shared by members of a particular culture. Culture enables human beings to make sense of their life experiences and to understand those experiences as meaningful in particular ways. Human beings share certain basic experiences: hunger and death, for example. Why, though, do people from different backgrounds understand these experiences in different ways? Thinking about culture begins to suggest an answer to this question.

Attitudes toward death provide one example. For some people, death marks the passage of a person from one world to another. For others, death is an ending, the final event in a life span. Still others view death as part of a never-ending cycle of birth, death, and rebirth. The Kwakwaka'wakw of British Columbia, for example, believe that when a person dies, the soul leaves the body and enters the body of a salmon. When a salmon is caught and eaten, a soul is released and is free to enter the body of another person.

Some societies fear the dead; others revere them. In rural China until recently, each household contained a shrine to the family ancestors. Before any major family decision, the head of the household addressed the shrine to ask the ancestors' advice, thus making the dead part of the world of the living. In southern Italy, by contrast, funeral customs were designed to *discourage* the dead from returning. Relatives placed useful objects such as matches and small change near the body to placate the soul of the deceased and to ensure that it did not return to disturb the living.

A Chinese bride makes an offering to an ancestral shrine.

In some societies, death is accepted as natural and inevitable; in others, death is always attributed to the malevolent act of some person, often involving sorcery. In these societies, every death elicits suspicion and a demand for vengeance. Still other societies require great demonstrations of grief and mourning for the deceased. Thus, the Dani of New Guinea require a close female relative of a recently deceased person to sacrifice part of a finger. When the Wari' of western Brazil still lived independent of Western civilization, they disposed of the bodies of their dead by eating the roasted flesh, certain internal organs, and sometimes the ground bones. They ate the dead not because they needed the meat or because they liked the taste of human flesh, but rather out of a respect and compassion for the dead person and the dead person's family (we will explore this example in section 1.2). In southern Europe, widows were required to shave their heads; at one time in India, widows were cremated alive at their husbands' funerals, a practice known as *sati*. In most North American societies, survivors of the deceased are expected to restrain their grief almost as if it were a contagious disease. To many North Americans, the sight of southern Italian women pulling their hair and being restrained from flinging themselves into an open grave is as bewildering as their own restraint of grief would be to southern Italians.

Food provides another telling example of how a culture takes the "raw materials" of human life and makes them meaningful. All humans need to eat; however, no society accepts all items in their edible universe as "good to eat." Only a relatively few items are so designated. Insects such as grubs, beetles, and ants are acceptable fare in some societies, while people in others are horrified by the thought of eating insects. North Americans generally do not define insects as food (although U.S. federal regulations do allow a certain percentage of insect matter to be included in processed food). Most North Americans like and are encouraged to drink milk, yet some people in China consider milk undrinkable. Conversely, the Chinese raise dogs for meat—something that would horrify most North Americans. North American children who have raised pet guinea pigs would have a hard time accepting the Peruvian practice of raising guinea pigs for food.

Of all the 2 million or so species of living organisms that inhabit Earth, only humans dwell largely in worlds that they themselves have created by giving meanings to things. This creation is what anthropologists mean by the term "culture." Human beings are cultural animals; they ascribe meanings of their own creation to objects, persons, behaviours, emotions, and events and then proceed to act as if those meanings are real. All facets of their lives—death, birth, courtship, mating, food acquisition and consumption—are suffused with meaning.

Clifford Geertz suggests that human beings are compelled to impose meaning on their experiences because without those meanings to help them comprehend experience and impose an order on the universe, the world would seem a jumble, "a chaos of pointless acts and exploding emotions" (1973, 46). Geertz writes that human beings are "incomplete or unfinished animals who complete themselves through culture—not culture in general, but specific forms of it": Balinese, Italian, Ilongot, Chinese, Kwakiutl (known today as Kwakwaka'wakw), Canadian, and so on (1973, 49). When people share the meanings they give to experiences, they share and participate in the same culture.

Differences in culture arise, in part, from the fact that different groups of human beings, for various reasons, create, share, and participate in different realities; as a consequence, they assign different meanings to death, birth, marriage, and food. Objects, persons, behaviours, emotions, and events in a human world have meanings ascribed to them by those who share, use, or experience them. The clothes people wear, the foods they eat (or refuse to eat), even their gender, are defined through the meanings that people give them. Understanding culture, and the culturally situated meanings that flourish in various cultural contexts, is therefore the main object of anthropological study. In the next section, we will explore how anthropologists have approached the study of culture.

EXERCISE 1.1

Mere edibility is not enough to determine what counts as food. Food is a cultural creation; that is, human beings define what is and is not food. Consider, for example, the items listed below, all of which serve as food among one group of people or another. Which of these would you eat, and which would you not eat? If there are any you would not eat, explain why.

	Yes	No
eel		
kangaroo tail		
dog		
guinea pig		
raw squid		
sea urchin (sea slugs)		
ants		
monkey brains		
grubs		
opossum		
rattlesnake		
iguana		
horse		
dolphin		
pickled pig's feet		
haggis (stuffed intestines)		
cow brains		
blood sausage		
raw steak		
rotten meat		
armadillo		

QUESTION 1.2: IS IT POSSIBLE TO SEE THE WORLD THROUGH THE EYES OF OTHERS?

This question lies at the heart of the anthropological enterprise. The anthropologist must be able to look beyond everyday appearance to decipher the often hidden meanings of beliefs, objects, and behaviours, while setting aside her or his preconceptions about what is normal or proper. In addition to that, the anthropologist must also learn one culture and then relate what he or she has learned to members of another culture in order to translate the meanings of one world into the meanings of another. In the process, many anthropologists experience cultural traditions and values vastly different from their own. In this section, we explore the intricacies of two key concepts in anthropology: ethnocentrism and cultural relativism.

How Do People Explain the Beliefs and Behaviours of Others?

Richard Scaglion (1990) is fond of telling the story of his friend, a member of the Abelam tribe of Papua New Guinea, who was looking through an issue of *Sports Illustrated*. The friend, dressed in full ceremonial regalia with a feather through his nose, was laughing uncontrollably at a woman shown in a liquor advertisement. When he managed to stop laughing long enough to explain what he thought was so funny, he said, "This white woman has made holes in her ears and stuck things in them." When Scaglion pointed out that his friend had an ornament in his nose, the reply was "That's different. That's for beauty and has ceremonial significance. But I didn't know that white people mutilated themselves."

Scaglion's friend was confronting a problem that many do when the behaviour or beliefs of others seem to differ from their own, and his response was not unusual. He was both shocked and mystified at the strange behaviour. And this suggests a dilemma: Since there are so many versions of what the world is like, how do we go about trying to understand each of them without making positive or negative judgments? Which version of the world is correct? Are there any such versions we *can* reject or condemn? Can we say, as so many have, that one culture is superior to another?

In the catalogue of human behaviours and beliefs, it is not difficult to find practices or ideas that may seem bizarre or shocking even to trained anthropologists. Sociocultural anthropologists have described the beliefs of the Ilongots of the Philippines, who must kill an enemy to obtain a head that they can throw away in order to diminish the grief

Abelam villager in ceremonial costume.

© Rita Willaert/http://www.flickr.com/photos/rietje

and rage they feel at the death of a kinsman or kinswoman. They have studied the historical records of the Aztecs in Mexico, who believed that the universe underwent periodic destruction and that the only way to ward off disaster was to pluck the hearts from live sacrificial victims to offer to the gods. They have also studied modern states that routinely engage in or sanction torture, terror, and genocide. How, then, should we react to practices and beliefs such as these?

The Ethnocentric Fallacy and the Relativist Fallacy

If we do condemn or reject the beliefs or behaviours of others, we may be embracing the **ethnocentric fallacy**, or the idea that our beliefs and behaviours are right and true, while those of other peoples are wrong or misguided. Sociocultural anthropologists have long fought against **ethnocentrism**, that is, the tendency to judge the beliefs and behaviours of other cultures from the perspective of one's own. They try to show that what often appears on the surface to be an odd belief or a bizarre behaviour is functional and logical in the context of a particular culture. They find the ethnocentric fallacy *intellectually* and *methodologically* intolerable; if everyone everywhere thinks that they are right and that others must be wrong, an intellectual and social dead end is inevitable. Furthermore, if we, as anthropologists, assume that we have all the right answers, our study of other cultures becomes simply the study of other people's mistakes.

Because of the intellectual and methodological implications of ethnocentrism, sociocultural anthropologists emphatically reject this position. But the opposite pole to ethnocentrism, **cultural relativism**, raises issues of its own. Cultural relativism, simply stated, holds that no behaviour or belief can be judged to be odd or wrong simply because it is different from our own; instead, we must try to understand a culture on its own terms and to understand behaviours or beliefs for the purpose, function, or meaning they have to people in the societies in which we find them. In other words, cultural relativism holds that a specific belief or behaviour can be understood only in relation to the culture—the system of meanings—in which it is embedded.

For example, according to Renato Rosaldo (1989), the ceremonies and rituals accompanying a successful headhunting expedition help the Ilongot psychologically manage their grief over the death of a kinsperson. However, relativism poses a *moral* predicament. Once we concede, say, that it is permissible to rip out the hearts of living human beings, provided that you believe it necessary to save the world, or that it is permissible to subject young girls to genital modification to protect family reputations, we find ourselves falling quickly into the **relativistic fallacy**, or the idea that it is impossible to make moral judgments about the beliefs and behaviours of others. This standpoint, of course, seems morally intolerable because it implies that no beliefs or behaviours can be condemned. So, we are left with two untenable positions: the ethnocentric alternative, which is intellectually and methodologically unsatisfactory, and the relativistic alternative, which is morally unsatisfactory. How do we solve this problem?

ethnocentric fallacy
The mistaken notion that the beliefs and behaviours of other cultures can be judged from the perspective of one's own culture.

ethnocentrism
The tendency to judge the beliefs and behaviours of other cultures from the perspective of one's own culture.

cultural relativism
The effort to understand the beliefs and behaviours of other cultures in terms of the culture in which they are found.

relativistic fallacy
The idea that it is impossible to make moral judgments about the beliefs and behaviours of members of other cultures.

Virginity Testing in Turkey and Cannibalism Among the Wari'

To illustrate further the dilemma of relativism and the difficulty of appreciating the cultures of others without making moral judgments, consider this incident. Some time ago a human rights group based in the United States issued a report condemning the practice of virginity testing in Turkey. Traditionally, young women in Turkey, as in some other cultures, are expected to avoid sexual relations prior to marriage, although the same rule does not apply to men. In this tradition, the bride's virginity is revealed by displaying, the morning after the wedding, the sheet that was spread on the couple's wedding bed with the telltale hymeneal blood stain. The human rights report condemns the traditional testing as well as the reported practice of forcing tests on hospital patients, students, and applicants for government jobs. As anthropologists, we must ask: Is the human rights group being ethnocentric in judging Turkish customs by North American cultural norms, or is it correctly identifying abuses of women that must be corrected? Might it help if we better understood the logic behind the belief?

In her book on Turkish village society, *The Seed and the Soil*, anthropologist Carol Delaney (1991) describes how virginity testing relates to the way in which Turkish villagers conceptualize and explain the reproductive process. They see producing children as analogous to the planting and growing of crops; the man provides the "seed" with his semen, and the woman serves as the "soil" in which the seed germinates and grows. As a metaphor for reproduction, the idea of the seed and the soil provides villagers with a way of thinking about and understanding reproduction. However, the metaphor of seed and soil has at least one important implication; since seeds do not have a limited life span, as we know semen to have, villagers believe that once planted, the seed (semen) may grow at any time. Consequently, if a woman has had sexual relations with a man other than her husband at any time prior to her marriage, the paternity of the child will be in doubt. Since descent in traditional Turkish villages is closely tied to many things, including property rights, uncertainty about the identity of the true father can have major implications. Thus, in the context of Turkish beliefs about procreation, virginity testing may be said to make sense.

Furthermore, Turkish beliefs about conception are not that far removed from our own, since our language draws from the same agricultural metaphors as those of Turkish villagers to explain reproduction. We talk about women being "fertile" or "barren" and semen "fertilizing" "eggs." "Sowing one's oats," as an expression of sexual activity, is still heard in parts of the United States and Canada. Furthermore, these views are reinforced by religious proscription, legitimized in the Koran and the Hebrew Scriptures. Thus, before we either condemn or accept the Turkish villagers for their treatment of women, we need to examine what their beliefs tell us about our own. Ours may be equally problematical.

But what of cannibalism, such as the Wari' practice of roasting and eating the dead? Surely, there is no way to justify that! Cannibalism, as Beth Conklin (2001) points out in her study of Wari' cannibalism, *Consuming Grief*, pushes the limits of cultural relativism, guaranteeing reactions of revulsion and fascination. But in addition to that, it has political implications: for centuries, cannibalism was the ultimate smear tactic. To accuse one's enemies or people one wanted to degrade or dominate of cannibalism was the ultimate justification for conquest, domination, and exploitation. In 1503, Queen Isabella of Spain decreed that Spaniards could legally enslave specifically those American Indians who were cannibals. Pope Innocent IV, in 1510, ruled that Christians could punish, by force of arms, the sin of cannibalism. By claiming moral superiority in this way, Christians were claiming the right to decide ultimately what is right and what is wrong. Armed with that power, they felt justified in imposing their own views and way of life.

What Queen Isabella and Pope Innocent IV conveniently overlooked, however, was that Europeans at the time practised cannibalism. As Conklin notes, medicinal cannibalism—the consumption of human body parts for curative purposes—had a long tradition in Europe. Up until two centuries ago, European physicians prescribed the consumption of human flesh, heart, bones, and other body parts as cures for such afflictions as arthritis, reproductive disorders, sciatica, warts, and skin blemishes. Human blood was thought to be a cure for epilepsy, and physicians recommended that it be drunk immediately after the supplier died. Physicians also thought that the blood of someone who died violently was particularly effective. Thus, in Denmark, epileptics would stand around the scaffolds, cups in hand, waiting to catch the blood of executed criminals. And almost every apothecary kept dried and powdered human body parts on hand for anxious customers.

The people of medieval Europe accepted in their own lives the same types of practices they condemned in others; furthermore, they failed to understand the practices from the point of view of the others. The Wari' ate their dead, for example, because they believed it was the compassionate thing to do. As Conklin puts it, "More painful than having the corpse eaten would have been to have it *not* eaten" (2001, 81). For the Wari', a corpse left intact was a painful reminder of the deceased. People unrelated to the deceased ate the corpse, even when the smell or taste repulsed them, in the belief that it would help family members come to terms with their loss.

The Western practice of burying the dead (which missionaries and government officials forced the Wari' to do after contact) was almost as horrific to the Wari' as their cannibalism might have been for non-Wari'. "It's cold in the earth," a father who had recently lost a two-year-old son explained to Beth Conklin. "We keep remembering our child, lying there, cold. We remember and we are sad. It was better in the old days, when the others ate the body. Then we did not think about our child's body much. We did not remember our child as much, and we were not so sad" (xv). Burying the body also

violated many fundamental Wari' values. For them, the ground was "dirty" and "polluting." They never sat directly on the dirt, and discarding things on the ground was considered disrespectful. Special ritual objects were never supposed to touch the ground.

Without a deeper understanding of Wari' culture, we cannot know how consuming the dead aligns with the meaning they impose on their world, including how they deal with their emotions. By consuming the dead, Wari' are trying to obliterate the painful memories of their loss. The memory of the body is painful, but equally painful are the material objects associated with the deceased and the very mention of the deceased's name. Thus, the Wari' not only consume the body but also burn the house and personal possessions of the deceased. For months, too, they walk into the forest to find places associated with the deceased—where a hunter made a kill or a woman felled a fruit tree, or where there was something such as a favourite log on which the person liked to sit—cut the vegetation around it, and after it has dried, burn

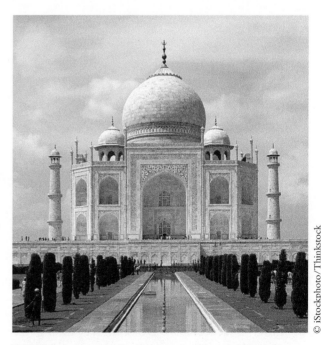

The Taj Mahal, a monument built to honour a 17th-century Mughal emperor's wife, who died in childbirth.

CULTURE AND MEANING

the spot, changing the appearance of the last earthly places to which memories of the deceased might cling. As they "sweep" (the Wari' term for it), they cry over the memories, but once done, "it is different," "there is not much sadness there." For most North Americans, a dead body is only a shell, its soul or spiritual essence gone. Thus, some societies can prepare the dead to look as they did in life and think of them buried in that way. The Wari', by contrast, want to separate the dead from the living, so obliterating their memories is perfectly logical. And they are not the only group to do so.

There are other aspects of Wari' beliefs about consuming the dead. For example, the Wari' believe that the spirits of the dead ultimately enter the bodies of animals they depend on for food, thus creating a cycle of eating and being eaten. The point, then, is that when we impose our own meanings on practices such as cannibalism and fail to see those practices the way others do, we miss a great deal.

EXERCISE 1.2A

In their funeral practices, Wari' attempt to obliterate the memory of the dead, as do many other societies. Other societies, however, memorialize the dead—forgetting them would be an act of disrespect. Think about your own cultural background and whether or not you are encouraged to preserve the memory of the dead. List the ways you try to keep the memory of deceased persons alive, and speculate as to why you do that instead of trying to forget them. If you are encouraged to forget the dead, how is that accomplished? Why? Compare your beliefs and practices with those of your classmates.

But does this mean that *any* practice or belief, once we understand it from "the native's point of view," is acceptable? Does understanding the cultures of others require that we accept and justify all beliefs and practices?

Objectivity and Morality

For anthropologists, the conflict between ethnocentrism and relativism is not just theoretical. When choosing their research subjects, anthropologists may face this dilemma: Should they maintain a "moral distance" from those they are studying and remain "objective," or should they engage in criticizing behaviour or beliefs they encounter (e.g., virginity testing)?

The contradiction between "objective" anthropology and a politically committed anthropology became apparent to Nancy Scheper-Hughes when she returned as an anthropologist to a shantytown in Brazil where, previously, she had worked as a community organizer. The women with whom she had worked in the past became angry. Why, they asked, was she now, as an anthropologist, so passive, so indifferent to the destruction around her when as a community organizer, she had helped them fight for clean water, decent wages, and protection from police brutality? She tried to explain that as an anthropologist, she was there now to observe, document, and write about their lives as truthfully as she could. The women refused to accept this view of her work and insisted that, if they were to work with her, she would have to work with them to fight for better lives. "What," they said, "is anthropology to us?"

On the basis of that experience, Scheper-Hughes (1995, 416) now argues for a politically committed, morally engaged, and ethically grounded anthropology. "Those of us who make our living observing and recording the misery of the world," she writes, "have a particular obligation to reflect critically on the impact of the harsh images of human suffering that we foist upon the public."

Scheper-Hughes proposes what she calls a more "womanly-hearted" anthropology, one that is concerned with how people treat one another. Moral relativism, she says, is no longer appropriate to the world in which we live, and anthropology, if it is to be worth anything, must be "critically grounded." Anthropologists cannot ignore the massacres and disappearances of vulnerable people that often occur in the communities in which anthropologists work. They must, she insists, serve as witnesses and reporters of human rights abuses and of the suffering of the poor and the oppressed. Witnessing, rather than just observing, therefore, requires not simply that we approach our subjects from a relativist perspective, but rather that we employ **critical cultural relativism**, through which anthropologists engage directly with questions of inequality, ethics, and power.

But serving as a witness for the poor and oppressed can itself lead to moral dilemmas for the anthropologist when the people with whom the anthropologist works engage in behaviour that may appear morally questionable. Scheper-Hughes confronted this question when she discovered and reported that impoverished women in the Brazilian shantytowns sometimes allowed their starving infants to die in the belief that they were doomed anyway. When Philippe Bourgois (2003) studied the world of crack dealers on the Upper East Side of New York City, he worried about the negative images he would be conveying if he reported the personal violence, sexual abuse, addiction, and alienation he witnessed. He recalled the advice of anthropologist Laura Nader, who advised others not to study the poor and powerless because whatever you say will be used against them.

Human rights activists, in particular, are skeptical about cultural relativism. If, they say, we must tolerate the beliefs and practices of other cultures because to do otherwise would be ethnocentric, how can we ever criticize what seem to be violations of basic human rights, such the right to bodily integrity, or the right to be free from torture, arbitrary imprisonment, slavery, and genocide?

critical cultural relativism
An alternative perspective on cultural relativism that poses questions about cultural beliefs and practices in terms of who accepts them and why, who they might be disproportionately harming and benefiting, and the cultural power dynamics that enable them.

Cultural relativism, they say, makes arguments about human rights meaningless by legitimizing almost any behaviour. Critical cultural relativism, on the other hand, might allow us to understand cultural beliefs and practices on their own terms without ignoring the cultural power dynamics that allow them to "make sense" within a given culture.

Take the case of the practice in some areas of India of *sati*, the burning of a widow on her husband's funeral pyre. In 1987, Roon Kanwar, an 18-year-old, was burned alive on her husband's pyre. Women's rights groups protested, but relatives claimed that *sati* is an ancient Indian custom and accused the protesters of being Western imperialists imposing their own cultural standards on them. Although India has outlawed the practice, prosecutors rarely enforce the law because of the difficulty of obtaining evidence. Would it matter if Roon Kanwar committed *sati* voluntarily? What would happen if she objected? Does it matter that only women are burned? Is the purpose of *sati* to deny a widow the inheritance of her husband's family's land?

Elizabeth Zechenter, who makes the argument for universal principles of human rights, says that cultural relativists are right to contend that endorsing or rejecting some foreign customs risks imposing one's cultural prejudices on others. She adds, however, that the idea we can make no judgments without being ethnocentric is illusory: "One simply cannot avoid making judgments when faced with oppression and brutality masquerading under the guise of cultural tradition. Such a nonjudgmental tolerance of brutality is actually an ultimate form of ethnocentrism, if not an outright ethical surrender" (1997, 336).

There is obviously no easy answer to the question of when, if ever, it is proper to judge the beliefs and practices of others to be right or wrong, or when, if ever, it is proper to work to change behaviours or beliefs judged to be wrong. Ideally, our attempts to understand what, at first, seemed puzzling in some cultures, and our arrival at some solution to that

CULTURE AND MEANING

puzzle, should lead us to ask ourselves what made the behaviour or belief puzzling in the first place. We also need to bear in mind that when cultures order the world in certain ways for their members, they are, in effect, masking other ways of viewing things. We need to appreciate that there are perspectives different from our own and that our ethnocentric biases may blind us to those alternatives. In other words, while culture provides us with certain meanings to give to objects, persons, behaviours, emotions, and events, it also shields us from alternative meanings. What our culture hides from us may be more important than what it reveals.

EXERCISE 1.2B

Think of a recent story reported in the mass media that challenges your sense of cultural relativism. What aspect of this story is problematic for you, and why? What aspects of your cultural background (e.g., religion, class, and gender) inform the judgments that you are inclined to make in this case? Do you think it is possible for us (as anthropologists and anthropology students) to overcome our ethnocentric biases? Support your opinion.

QUESTION 1.3: HOW CAN THE MEANINGS THAT OTHERS FIND IN EXPERIENCE BE INTERPRETED AND DESCRIBED?

In one Sherlock Holmes detective story, Dr. Watson, Holmes's assistant, decides to teach the great detective a lesson in humility. He hands Holmes a pocket watch owned by Watson's late brother and challenges Holmes to infer from the watch the character of its owner. Holmes's interpretation: "[Your brother] was a man of untidy habits—very untidy and careless. He was left with good prospects, but he threw away his chances and finally, taking to drink, he died."

Watson, astounded at the accuracy of Holmes's description of his late brother, asks if it was guesswork. "I never guess," replies Holmes.

"I began by stating that your brother was careless. When you observe the lower part of the watch case, you notice that it is not only dented in two places, but it is cut and marked all over from the habit of keeping other hard objects, such as coins or keys, in the same pocket. Surely it is no great feat to assume that a man who treats [an expensive] watch so cavalierly must be a careless man. Neither is it a very far-fetched inference that a man who inherits one article of such value is pretty well provided for in other respects."

"But what about his drinking habits?" asks Watson.

Holmes responds: "Look at the innerplate which contains the keyhole [where the watch is wound]. Look at the thousands of scratches all around the hole-marks where the key has slipped. What sober man's key could have scored those grooves? But you will never see a drunkard's watch without them. He winds it at night, and he leaves these traces of his unsteady hand. Where is the mystery in all this?"

Had Holmes been an anthropologist, he might have been tempted also to draw some inferences about the society in which the watch was manufactured, particularly about its conceptions of time. For example, in some societies, time is task oriented, not clock oriented; time might be measured by how long it takes to cook rice, as in Madagascar. In other societies, time patterns depend on natural events such as the rising of the sun or the ebb and flow of tides. British anthropologist E. E. Evans-Pritchard, in his classic account of the Nuer of the Sudan, noted:

the Nuer have no expression equivalent to "time" in our language, and they cannot, therefore, as we can, speak of time as though it were something actual, which passes, can be wasted, can be saved, and so forth. I don't think they ever experience the same feeling of fighting against time because their points of reference are mainly the activities themselves, which are generally of a leisurely character. Events follow a logical order, but they are not controlled by an abstract system, there being no autonomous points of reference to which activities have to conform with precision. Nuer are fortunate.

An anthropologist might also infer that clocks are instruments of discipline; they tell us when to get up, when to go to bed, when to eat, when to start work, and when to stop work. Our work patterns are defined by clocks, and our wages may depend on the constant repetition over time of a particular task. Historian E. P. Thompson (1967) notes that until the institution of modern notions of time and the need to measure it with clocks, work patterns were characterized by alternating bouts of intense labour and idleness, at least whenever people were in control of their own working lives. He even suggests that this pattern persists today, but only among a few self-employed professionals such as artists, writers, small farmers, and, he suggests, university students.

Watson's brother's watch was a product of Western society, part of its culture. Holmes "read" the watch as if it were a collection of symbols or words, a **cultural text** that revealed the character of its owner. He could just as easily have viewed it as a text inscribed with the symbols that revealed the ideas about time and work that characterized the civilization that produced it.

One way to think about culture is as a text of significant symbols: words, gestures, drawings, natural objects—anything, in fact, that carries meaning. To understand another culture we must be able, as

cultural text
A way of thinking about culture as a text of significant symbols, such as words, gestures, drawings, and natural objects, all of which carry meaning.

Modern notions of clock-based time tell us a great deal about the culture we live in. What measures of time are most important in your life as a student?

Holmes was with a pocket watch, to decipher the meanings of the symbols that comprise a cultural text. We must be able to interpret the meanings embedded in the language, objects, gestures, and activities that are shared by members of a society. Fortunately, the ability to decipher a cultural text is part of being human; in our everyday lives we both read and maintain the text that makes up our own culture. We have learned the meanings behind the symbols that frame our lives, and we share those meanings with others. Our task in understanding another culture is to take the abilities that have enabled us to dwell in our own culture and use them to understand the cultures of others.

Deciphering the Balinese Cockfight

To illustrate how an anthropologist might decipher a cultural text, imagine yourself coming upon a cockfight on the island of Bali. You see a ring in which two roosters with sharpened metal spurs attached to their legs are set at each other until one kills the other. Surrounding the fighting cocks are men shouting encouragement to their favourites, each having placed a wager that his favourite will kill its opponent.

CULTURE AND MEANING

What do you make of this? Your first reaction might be shock or disgust at the spectacle of the crowd urging the cocks to bloody combat. After a while you might begin to find similarities to events that are meaningful to you, such as some North American sports. But what if, like Sherlock Holmes—or like Clifford Geertz (1972), from whom this example is taken—you want to understand the meaning of what is happening and what that meaning tells you about how Balinese view their world? If you assume that the cockfight is a feature of Balinese culture, a Balinese text filled with symbols that carry meaning about what it is to be Balinese, how might you proceed to read this text?

You might begin by finding out the language the Balinese use to talk about the cockfight. You would no doubt discover that the double-entendre of cock both as a synonym for rooster and as a euphemism for penis is the same for the Balinese as it is for North Americans. The double-entendre even produces, says Geertz, the same jokes, puns, and obscenities in Bali as it does in North America. You would discover that *sabung*, the Balinese word for cock, has numerous other meanings and is used metaphorically to mean hero, warrior, champion, political candidate, bachelor, dandy, lady-killer, or tough guy. Court trials, wars, political contests, inheritance disputes, and street arguments are compared with cockfights. Even the island of Bali is

thought of as being cock shaped (in this case, meaning the fowl). You would also find that men give their fowls inordinate attention, spending most of their time grooming them and even feeding them a special diet. As one of Geertz's Balinese informants put it, "We're all cock crazy."

Having discovered the importance of cockfights to the Balinese and the connections they make between cocks and men, you next examine the cockfight itself. You learn that cockfights are public events held in arenas of about 4.7 square metres from late afternoon until after sundown. Handlers, expert in the task, attach sharp spurs to the cocks' legs; for a cock thought to be superior to an opponent, the spurs are adjusted in a slightly disadvantageous position.

In Balinese society, cockfighting is a major sporting event that is closely tied to cultural interpretations of manhood, competition, and status.

The cocks are released in the centre of the ring and fly at each other, fighting until one kills the other. The owner of the winning cock takes the carcass of the loser home to eat; the losing owner is sometimes driven in despair to wreck family shrines. You discover that the Balinese contrast heaven and hell by comparing them to the mood of a man whose cock has just won and the mood of a man whose cock has just lost.

You find out that while the Balinese place odds on cockfights, there are strict social conventions that dictate the wagering. For example, a man will never bet against a cock that is owned by someone of his family group or village or a friend's family group or village, but he will place large bets against a cock owned by an enemy or the friend of an enemy. Rarely is a cockfight without social significance (e.g., between two outsiders), and rarely do cocks owned by members of the same family or village fight each other. Moreover, the owners of the cocks, especially in important matches, are usually among the leaders of their communities. You might learn that cockfights come close to encouraging open expressions of aggression between village and kingroup rivals, but not quite, because the cockfight is, as the Balinese put it, "only a cockfight."

Given the social rules for betting and the ways in which odds are set, you might reason, as Geertz did, that the Balinese rarely make a profit betting on cockfights. Geertz says, in fact, that most bettors just want to break even. Consequently, the meaning of the cockfight for a Balinese has little to do with economics. The question is what meaning the cockfight *does* have for the Balinese. What is the cockfight really about, if it is not about money?

Geertz concludes that the Balinese cockfight is, above all, about status, about the ranking of people vis-à-vis one another. The Balinese cockfight is a text filled with meaning about status as the Balinese see it. Cocks represent men—more specifically, their owners; the fate of the cock in the ring is linked, if only temporarily, to the social fate of its owner. Each cock has a following consisting of the owner, the owner's family, and members of the owner's village, and these followers "risk" their status by betting on the cockfight. Furthermore, Geertz maintains that the more a match is between near equals, personal enemies, or high-status individuals, the more the match is about status. And the more the match is about status, the closer the identification of cock and man, the finer the cocks, and the more exactly they will be matched. The match will inspire greater emotion and absorption, and the gambling will be more about status and less about economic gain.

For Geertz, the cockfight is like any art form; it takes a highly abstract and difficult concept—status—and depicts it in a way that makes it comprehensible to the participants. The cockfight is meaningful to the Balinese because it tells them something real about their own lives, but in a way that does not directly affect their lives. They see the struggle for status that is part of everyday life vividly portrayed, even though, in the cockfight itself, no one really gains or loses status in any permanent sense.

A few words of caution are necessary concerning what we might learn about the Balinese from this particular cultural text. First, it would probably be a mistake to assume that the people gain status by being on the winning side or lose it by being on the losing side. The status outcomes of the cockfight do not translate into real life any more than the victory of your favourite sports team increases your status. Instead, says Geertz, the cockfight illustrates what status is about for the Balinese. The cockfight is a story the Balinese tell themselves about themselves. It would also be a mistake to assume that the character of the Balinese can be read directly from the cockfight; any conclusion that the cockfight is indicative of an aggressive, competitive, violent national character would quickly be dispelled. The Balinese are shy about competition and avoid open conflict. The slaughter in the cockfight is not how things are literally, but as they could be. Finally, the cockfight reveals only a segment of the Balinese character, as Watson's brother's watch revealed only a segment of its owner's character. The culture of a people, like the possessions of a person, is an ensemble of texts—collections of symbols and meanings—that must be viewed together to achieve a full understanding.

QUESTION 1.4: WHAT CAN LEARNING ABOUT OTHER PEOPLES TELL ANTHROPOLOGISTS ABOUT THEIR OWN SOCIETIES?

Anthropologists do not limit themselves to the study of cultures that are different from their own. They often apply concepts and techniques that are useful in understanding and interpreting other cultures as a means to understand and interpret their own. One objective of studying other cultures is to help us recognize the meanings we impose on our experiences. When Renato Rosaldo (1989) asked the Ilongots why they cut off human heads, they replied that rage, born of grief, drives them to kill others; by severing the heads of their victims, they are able to throw away the anger born of bereavement. Rosaldo found it difficult to accept the idea that the death of a kinsperson could cause anger or rage and that such rage in itself could drive a person to kill another. He questioned the Ilongots further but could obtain no other reason for their headhunting; he devised other theories to explain it, but none were satisfactory. Only his own experience of grief and anger at the accidental death of his wife, Michelle, while both were doing fieldwork among the Ilongots, helped him realize how grief can generate rage and how grief drove the Ilongots to hunt the heads of their enemies. At the same time that he began to understand the Ilongots, he began to understand his own grief and reaction to death.

A Balinese Anthropologist Studies Canadian Hockey

Whether we approach other cultures as anthropologists, as travellers, or as professionals who need to communicate with people of other cultures, the confrontation with other ways of believing and behaving should cause us to reflect on our way of viewing the world. To illustrate, try to step outside yourself and objectify an experience whose meaning you take for granted. Pretend you are a Balinese anthropologist who suddenly comes upon a spectacle as important in its way to Canadians as the cockfight is to Balinese: a hockey game.

As a Balinese, you might first react to this Canadian text with horror and revulsion at seeing men and women speeding from one end of an ice pad to the other with long wooden sticks in their hands, rudely pushing one another out of the way while thousands cheer them on. As you settled in, however, you would soon find some obvious similarities between the hockey game and the cockfight you are familiar with at home. Both are spectator sports in which the spectators sort themselves into supporters of one side or the other. In fact, in hockey, the sorting is even more carefully arranged, since fans of one team are often seated on one side of the arena and fans of the other on the opposite side.

Your next step (as in interpreting the cockfight) would be to examine the language Canadians use to refer to the hockey game. You discover that they use similar expressions in talking about hockey and fighting, for example, *roughing* and *slashing*. Coaches talk about getting "revenge" for defeats, as generals might talk about getting revenge on battlefields. You conclude that Canadians seem to feel the same way about hockey as they do about fighting. If you attend several hockey games, you will most likely witness players of opposing teams taking off their protective gloves and beginning to punch each other.

You soon discover that winning and losing hockey games is as important to Canadians as winning and losing cockfights is to Balinese. Winners engage in frenzied celebrations called "victory parties," and losers are often despondent in defeat. As anthropologists know, this behaviour is not always the case in other societies. For example, when the Gahuku-Gama of the Highlands of New Guinea started playing soccer, they always played until a committee of elders decided that the score was tied; the match was then considered completed. So you speculate that hockey is also about the meanings that Canadians give to the idea of success. You learn that success in Canada (like status in Bali) is a highly abstract idea; because it is abstract, its meaning is embedded in activities understood by members of the society. You need to find answers to certain questions about the meaning of success in Canadian society: How is success defined? How is it obtained? Why doesn't everyone who follows all the rules for gaining success attain it?

Through your fieldwork, you find that most North Americans believe that "all men are created equal" and that every person has (or at least should have) an equal opportunity to succeed. People compete for success, and they ought to compete on an equal footing, on a "level playing field," as some put it. Success, North Americans believe, comes from hard work, sacrifice, and self-denial. But you wonder why North Americans believe that hard work, sacrifice, and self-denial bring success. Aren't there instances where they do not? How do North Americans explain why women and minorities succeed less often than white males do? Why do some people achieve more success than others? You conclude that it is impossible to prove directly in real life the correctness of this North American success model. Faith in the value of work and self-denial must be generated in other ways. As a Balinese anthropologist studying the Canadian custom of hockey, you conclude, then, that the meaning of Canadian hockey lies in its demonstration of the North American success model as it is supposed to work. But the Canadian game of hockey is more than simply a mirror of society: Canadian hockey is also a ritual that creates meaning.

Rituals do not just reflect society. As Yngve Lithman (2004) suggests, they also draw attention to something and provide an explanation for something. One of the reasons why Canadian hockey has become a national symbol is that it brings Canadians from different parts of the country together with a common focus. During the hockey season, a team from Calgary competes against a team from Montreal, a team from Vancouver plays in the same ice rink as a team from Toronto, and so on.

An anthropologist might suggest that the meaning of hockey, for North Americans, is tied to our cultural understandings of success.

© AP Photo/Julio Cortez

Anthropologist Noel Dyck points out that Canadian hockey "is not only one of Canada's proudest contributions to the world of sport but also a national passion" (2000, 10). Hockey becomes important to children very early in life, and it involves the whole family. Tiny players, called "Tim Bits," sponsored by the Tim Hortons coffee shops throughout Canada, begin their training so young that their mothers or fathers, or even their grandfathers or grandmothers, help them put on their protective clothing in the dressing rooms. Young teams of children are grouped according to age into categories such as novice, atom, peewee, bantam, and midget, all progressing to secondary school and university teams. Those working toward professional play are called "Junior" and progress from Junior D to Junior A. At the other end of the life cycle, older players play on teams for "old timers," which are also grouped according to age.

Canadian hockey is also a ritual that, anthropologists Peter Collings and Richard Condon suggest, helps people adjust to sudden change by providing a way for players to gain status, achievement, and self-esteem. In the Kitikmeot region of the Northwest Territories, society is no longer based on hunting as a way of life, but communities are not yet fully integrated into the North American capitalist economy. In the Canadian Arctic, hockey has become a recreational activity that helps bridge this gap, and for most communities, it is a passion.

At first, when radio and television were introduced to the Arctic, and to the community of Holman, where Collings and Condon did their fieldwork in the 1980s, children played hockey on the snow-covered streets. Later, when a sporting organization in Yellowknife sent skates to Inuit communities, children began playing hockey on ice ponds. The initial hockey games were played Inuit style, with little emphasis on winning or losing, and were governed by flexible rules. Eventually, however, a league was established, and teams from different communities began to compete with each other.

With the formalization of hockey as a competition, violence became a standard feature of the game. Collings and Condon found that significantly more injuries were sustained playing hockey than during any other activity, including hunting, trapping, or fishing. Furthermore, being injured during a hockey game was a sure way to gain prestige, especially if an injured player returned to the ice before his injury was healed. Collings and Condon argue that the game of hockey, as it is played in Holman, models the values of achievement and self-reliance: "If achievement and self-reliance cannot be expressed in the conduct of everyday life, then it can be expressed on the ice while competing with one's peers. Status and control, so elusive to these young people in real life, become attainable goals when modeled in the context of play" (1996, 258).

Collings and Condon acknowledge the positive aspects of sports. Games such as hockey affirm the value of success, as well as a dramatic set of instructions on how it attain it. The games help build character and teach young people about cooperation. But Collings and Condon (1996) also suggest that there is a "darker side" to hockey. For some people, "games can teach violence, verbal aggression, subterfuge, cheating, poor sportsmanship, and other undesirable traits" (261). At the same time, hockey demonstrates the limits of acceptable violence. When players break the rules of how the game is supposed to be played, they incur penalties, just as citizens are penalized for breaking the laws in Canada. When players score a high number of points, they are rewarded with both prestige and, in the case of professional hockey, wealth. Violence and competition are part of Canadian life, and the game of hockey shows how both are important to Canadians, but both must be controlled.

Anthropologists, therefore, can conclude (as did Collings and Condon) that hockey provides for Canadians, as the cockfight does for the Balinese, a small-scale rendering of concepts too complex to be directly comprehended (status and success for Canadians, status only in the case of the Balinese). The audience for a hockey game is led to believe that if the rules that govern the world of hockey are equated with the rules that govern success outside the rink, then the principles that govern success on the hockey rink must also apply in the outside world. If hard work, dedication, submission to authority, and teamwork lead to success in a game, then surely they will lead to success in real life. The rules by which success is achieved in hockey can also be applied to life to succeed in the real world.

Of course, hockey is also a game that people enjoy. Analyzing it should not reduce our enjoyment of it but rather, should heighten our fascination with it. By looking at hockey from the same perspective that Geertz viewed the cockfight, we should gain an understanding of why the meaning carried by the game is important. Understanding the cockfight heightens our appreciation of the hockey game, but it also helps us see similarities between Canadians and Balinese. If you were shocked by the cockfight, seeing the similarities to hockey should lessen that shock, at the same time making hockey seem just a bit more exotic.

An Anthropologist Looks at a "Happy Meal"

Nothing is too mundane to provide some insights into the culture of which it is a part. Take the "Happy Meal" advertised by one of the many fast-food establishments in North America. It consists of a hamburger, French fries, a cola drink, and a plastic toy, which is often gendered—one chooses a "girl" toy or a "boy" toy. What can we learn about the culture of North America by looking beyond the taken-for-granted quality of this meal? Among other things, we can gain some idea of North American demographic and ecological patterns, agricultural and industrial history, and gender roles.

Why, for example, is meat the centre of the meal? Most cultures have diets centred on some complex carbohydrate—rice, wheat, manioc, yams, taro—or something made from these—bread, pasta, tortillas, and so on. It is the spice, vegetables, meat, or fish that when added to these foods gives cuisine its distinctive taste. Meat and fish are, however, generally at the edge, not the centre, of the meal. And why is beef the main ingredient in the Happy Meal, rather than some other meat, such as pork?

Anthropologists Marvin Harris and Eric Ross note that one advantage of beef is its suitability for the outdoor grill, which became more popular as people moved from cities into suburbs. Suburban cooks soon discovered that pork patties crumbled and fell through the grill, whereas beef patties held together better. In addition, to reduce the risk of trichinosis, pork had to be cooked until it was grey, which makes it tough.

In the United States, beef farmers, as well as the farmers who grew the corn fed to cattle to achieve a desirable fat content, benefited from the definition of a hamburger set by the United States Department of Agriculture: "'Hamburger'" shall consist of chopped fresh and/or frozen beef with or without the addition of beef fat as such and/or seasonings, shall not contain more than 30 percent fat, and shall not contain added water, phosphates, binders, or extenders. Beef cheek (trimmed Beef cheeks) may be used in the preparation of hamburgers only in accordance with the conditions prescribed in paragraph (a) of this section" (Harris 1998, 124).

As Marvin Harris noted, we can eat ground pork and ground beef, but we can't combine them into a patty and call it a hamburger. Hamburgers also cannot be made exclusively of lean beef,

as such patties would fall apart during cooking. Fat must be added as a binder, and the fat must come from beef scraps, not from vegetables or a different animal. This definition of the hamburger protects both the beef industry and the corn farmer, whose income is linked to cattle production. Moreover, it helps the fast-food industry because the definition of hamburger permits the use of inexpensive scraps of fat from slaughtered beef to make up to 30 percent of its hamburger. Thus, an international beef patty that has overcome the "pig's natural superiority as a converter of grain to flesh," as Harris (1998, 126) puts it, has been created.

The cola drink that accompanies the hamburger is the second part of the fat and sugar-centred diet that has come to characterize our culture. People in Canada consume, on average, about 38.6 kilograms of sugar a year. Why so much? Sugar, as anthropologist Sidney Mintz (1985) suggests, has no nutritional properties, but it provides a quick and inexpensive energy boost for hard-working labourers with little time for a more nutritious meal. Sugar also serves as an excellent complement to the fat in hamburgers: it has what nutritionists call "go-away" qualities that remove the fat coating and the beef aftertaste from the mouth.

From the Happy Meal, we can also learn that the fat-and-sugar diet is highly environmentally destructive. Beef raising is among the most environmentally inefficient and destructive forms of food raising. For example, the amount of water used to produce 4.5 kilograms (10 pounds) of steak equals the household consumption of a family for an entire year. Thirty-three times more water is needed to produce a kilogram of beef protein than an equivalent amount of plant protein.

Cattle raising is playing a major role in the destruction of tropical forests in Brazil, Guatemala, Costa Rica, and Honduras, where forests have been levelled to create pasture for cattle. Since most of the forest is cleared by burning, the creation of cattle pasture also creates carbon dioxide and, according to some environmentalists, contributes significantly to global warming.

Sugar is no less destructive a crop. Sugar production alters the environment in a number of ways. Forests must be cleared to plant sugar, wood or fossil fuel must be burned in the evaporation process, waste water is produced when sucrose is extracted from the sugar cane, and more fuel is burned in the refining process. Contemporary sugar production in Hawai'i has destroyed forests, and waste products from processing have severely damaged marine environments. "Big Sugar," as the sugar industry is called in Florida, is largely responsible for the pollution, degradation, and virtual destruction of the Everglades.

Thus, one of the "texts" that anthropologists can read from a Happy Meal relates to the extent to which consumption patterns associated with our culture create waste and environmental damage. Because of these consumption patterns, the average child born in Canada or the United States will, in the course of his or her lifetime, do twice the environmental damage of a Swedish child, 3 times that of an Italian child, 13 times that of a Brazilian child, 35 times that of an Indian child, and 280 times that of a Chadian or Haitian child.

And what of gendered toys—dolls for girls and toy cars for boys? Clearly, there is a message about the definition of gender roles, as dolls are expected to be chosen by girls and cars by boys. But, if you look closely enough, you can deduce even more about our culture from this meal.

EXERCISE 1.3

We have examined some of the lessons we can learn about our culture from the Happy Meal. There are obviously others. See what you can deduce about the following dimensions of life in North America from the Happy Meal.

1. What can you say about gender roles in North America?
2. What can you deduce about race relations?
3. What can you say about the physical attributes of people favoured in North America?

QUESTION 1.5: HOW CAN AN ANTHROPOLOGICAL PERSPECTIVE BE USED OUTSIDE ACADEMIA?

What Can You Do with a B.A. in Anthropology?

Students taking anthropology classes often say, "I like anthropology, but what can I do with it?" A more or less typical response is "Anything that you can do with any liberal arts major." That doesn't get us very far, though. Being a professional anthropologist—teacher, researcher, consultant—generally requires an advanced degree. However, an anthropological perspective and methodology can be invaluable in all sorts of career areas. In 2011, for instance, national newspaper *The Globe and Mail* identified ethnography as "the new buzzword in marketing." This buzz about ethnography does not necessarily mean that you will see scores of job postings looking specifically for candidates with an anthropology degree. However, the demand for candidates with ethnographic skills is on the rise. In 2015, a LinkedIn search using "ethnography" as a keyword yielded many hits that included jobs at Netflix, Skype, Microsoft, VISA, and Google. These examples are all from the corporate world, but many anthropologists are employed in the public sector or by nongovernmental organizations (NGOs), as well. Why are these companies looking for ethnographers? Anthropology, like any discipline, deals with problems and questions. In the contemporary lingo of human resources departments, ethnographers "add value" to the companies they work for by bringing a unique perspective to bear on the problems and questions they address. They often have distinctive insights and are able to suggest innovative solutions that accountants, marketers, doctors, or lawyers cannot. In particular, students of anthropology should graduate equipped with at least three problem-solving "tools" unique to the discipline:

- anthropological methods, especially close observation and detailed description and documentation of behaviour, as discussed in Chapter 2
- anthropological concepts, which help in understanding and comparing what observed behaviours, such as rites of passage (Chapter 6), kinship (Chapter 5), and reciprocity (Chapter 7), mean to the people studied
- anthropological theories, which aim to explain why human beings organize their experiences into meaningful categories in the ways that we do

Culture, our core disciplinary concept, is a tool that enables anthropologists to go beyond describing what people do and what it means to them to explain the deeper significance of *why* people do what they do. What kinds of problems can anthropologists help solve with their anthropological "toolkit"? People in management must address the problem of how to structure relationships among staff; people in government must address problems involved in designing public policy initiatives, such as reducing juvenile crime. Someone in a medical field may face the problem of how to educate the young regarding sexually transmitted disease, while someone employed in the tourist industry must address the problem of how to minimize the negative consequences of tourism for local populations. The solutions to all of these and other problems can benefit from an anthropological perspective because all involve ways that people give meaning to their experiences. Throughout the remaining chapters of this book, we will examine various examples of how anthropological perspectives are applied to real-world problems by anthropologists working both within and outside academia.

The best way to understand what anthropology is and how ethnographic insights have problem-solving potential is to look at what anthropologists and ethnographers do and at how they approach various kinds of social problems. The examples of applied anthropology discussed below demonstrate the important ways in which anthropological knowledge and ethnographic expertise matter in the real world. They also begin to suggest some (but certainly not all) of the ways that anthropology can be put to use outside the academy.

Applied Anthropology

Applied anthropology is the subdiscipline of anthropology that specializes in putting anthropological knowledge into practice outside academia. Sociocultural anthropology is, in part, about social and cultural differences, whether they occur from one country to another or within a single classroom. The fact that different peoples assign different meanings to events, objects, individuals, and emotions is a source of considerable conflict, miscommunication, and misunderstanding. Anthropologists seek to explain this diversity, to help people understand one another better, and, in the process, to apply their experience and knowledge to solving social, economic, educational, business, and political problems encountered in our diverse and increasingly interconnected world.

Applied anthropologists therefore work in a variety of topics and settings, and almost anything of interest to academic anthropologists might also be the focus of applied anthropologists. In practice, some branches of anthropology or areas of study lend themselves particularly well to applied anthropology: these include indigenous issues, political anthropology, environmental anthropology, medical anthropology, and corporate ethnography. The majority of applied anthropologists practise their trade with these.

Indigenous Issues

Julia Harrison and Regna Darnell (2006), scholars of the history of Canadian anthropology, have argued that, although the growth of anthropology in Canada has been influenced by the French, British, and American scholarly traditions, one thing that marks the Canadian disciplinary tradition as distinct is the strong focus on Indigenous peoples. They also suggest that an emphasis on applying research findings in order to serve the needs of the Indigenous communities that have been studied—that is, applied anthropology—has been a defining feature of the discipline in Canada.

Edward Hedican writes that more and more First Nations band administrations are employing anthropologists to conduct research in areas that the bands themselves find useful, such as research that helps to document the validity of First Nations land claims. Such collaborations makes anthropological research easier because, as Hedican suggests, "people will certainly be more willing to cooperate with researchers if they are able to see that the work has some direct relevance to their lives" (2008 [1995], 253).

Dawn Martin-Hill is a Canadian anthropologist and filmmaker of Mohawk ancestry whose work with the Lubicon Cree is discussed in detail in Chapter 8. Much of her research has focused upon exploring the lingering effects of colonialism upon First Nations groups. She also has a particular interest in understanding the historical and cultural basis of First Nations land claims. In her 2008 film, *Sewatokwa'tshera't: The Dish with One Spoon*, she documents and lends her support to the Haudenosaunee, who are involved in disputes with the federal and Ontario governments over land claims.

In February 2006, in what would come to be known as the Grand River Land Dispute, Haudenosaunee from the Six Nations of Grand River began public protests and road blockades. Their goal was to bring greater public awareness to a 40 hectare plot of land near Caledonia that was granted to them in 1754. The protests were sparked by the impending threat of the development of the land into a residential suburban area by Henco Industries Ltd., which claimed to have purchased the land in 1841 from what was then called "Canada West." The dispute is ongoing, and

it is relevant to note that throughout the ordeal, the Haudenosaunee have been portrayed in the mainstream media as violent, irrational, aggressive, and potentially dangerous. Such depictions function to garner public support and sympathy for the developers, and to delegitimize the validity of Haudenosaunee land claims.

In response to overwhelmingly negative mainstream media representations, Martin-Hill has organized numerous peaceful protests. Many of these have included not only Haudenosaunee protesters but also supportive members of the academic community. Such initiatives draw attention to the ways in which the agency and legal rights of Haudenosaunee community members have been threatened, if not delegitimized by both government and corporate interests.

Another way that anthropologists working with Indigenous peoples often apply their knowledge and insights is through efforts to influence and improve relevant public policy. One prominent example is the government-commissioned Hawthorne-Tremblay Report, published in two volumes in 1966 and 1967, which was the largest applied research project in Canadian anthropology. Titled *A Survey of the Contemporary Indians of Canada: Economic, Political, and Educational Needs and Policies*, the report was the result of a collaborative project that involved 35 researchers, both faculty and graduate students, who conducted interviews and surveys in Indigenous communities. The study differed from more traditional scholarly projects in several ways: it was written in readable language rather than academic jargon; it was expressly intended to address the concerns of bureaucrats and government officials rather than scholars; and it provided 151 recommendations with the potential to be implemented by the federal government (Dyck 2006, 82–83). As Dyck states:

> Although the discussion of the report was pre-emptied by the abortive White Paper proposals of 1969, it did popularize the concept of "citizen plus," a formulation firmly endorsed by

provincial and territorial Indian organizations in their opposition to the Trudeau government's new Indian policy (83).

Today, making contributions to land claims and to public policy pertaining to Indigenous peoples is a high-demand field for applied anthropologists. The Firelight Group, based in British Columbia, is a research cooperative that provides community-based research and technical support, most often to First Nations clients, on projects that are designed to support reconciliation between indigenous and non-indigenous interests, or to facilitate the inclusion of indigenous perspectives in decision making and public policy. The anthropologists employed by the Firelight Group work on a range of projects that include social, economic, and cultural impact assessments and traditional knowledge and land use studies.

Legal Anthropology

Another important branch of sociocultural anthropology involves the area of law and society, sometimes called "legal anthropology." Sally Falk Moore describes this approach as one that "inquires into the context of enforceable norms: social, political, economic, and intellectual. This includes, but goes farther than, what Western governments and courts define as law. In anthropology, while the 'socio-legal' includes formal juridical institutions and their social surroundings, it also encompasses law-like activities and processes of establishing order in many other social domains, formal and informal, official and unofficial, in our own society and in others" (2005, 1).

Anthropologists who study legal issues in a particular place ask questions about power, such as "who makes the rules, who can undo them, how are they normalized and enforced, and how are they morally justified" (Moore 2005, 2). These questions were first asked in egalitarian societies where legal institutions, such as courts and police, were absent; anthropologists tried to understand what prevented

total chaos. Other questions are now being asked in relation to the possible lasting effects of colonialism on "native laws," as the colonial powers enforced their own sense of what was right and just.

In his book *Culture and Power*, Stanley Barrett argues that globalization has increased conflict throughout the world and that anthropology's interest in the political is likely to grow. He suggests that "power, authority, influence, manipulation, and coercion (or force) constitute the basic terms in this field of inquiry" (2002, 19). With these concepts in mind, anthropologists have extended their interest in legal issues to include, for example, intellectual property issues and global human rights. They also look at global issues that involve international labour, immigration patterns and obstacles, and development schemes, continually asking: "Who is in control? Whose interests are being served?" We will touch on many of these issues in the chapters that follow.

Rosemary Coombe possesses both anthropology and law degrees, and much of her career has focused upon questions pertaining to the relationship between law, ethics, and culture. How do we come to believe that our systems of rules, regulations, and laws are "right," or natural? Moreover, how is our legal system changing in response to globalization and other phenomena?

Anthropologists such as Coombe are beginning to explore the volatile world of intellectual property law. In an increasingly globalized, digitized, and mediated world, where the flow of images of celebrities and commodities is unimpeded by geographical borders, Coombe's work (see Coombe 2013) asks how changing notions of ownership and authorship are understood in different societies. How, for instance, are representations of athletes or movie stars appropriated for different political causes or by advertisers? In the process, how do meanings of their bodies change, and who owns the appropriated images? In these contexts, differing cultural understandings of "ownership" have legal implications. In order to affect change and to educate current policymakers about the cultural implications of changing notions of intellectual property rights, Coombe conducts workshops with lawyers, law societies, government officials, and law schools. Through these efforts, she seeks to bridge the gap between theory and practice. For instance, if practising lawyers do not possess an understanding of the theoretical underpinnings of cultural notions of appropriation and ownership, then it becomes difficult, if not impossible, to represent the diverse needs of clients or to create culturally sensitive and appropriate legislation.

Political Ecology

A relatively new branch of sociocultural anthropology that is gaining popularity is *political ecology*, defined by Blaikie and Brookfield (1987, 17) as a field of study that "combines the concerns of ecology and a broadly defined political economy." One of the directions this approach has taken has involved challenging dominant explanations for environmental degradation and contesting some of the popular solutions to environmental problems (Paulson, Gezon, and Watts 2003, 205). Analyzing the politics of environment may uncover the interests of powerful elites that profit from directing public inquiry away from their activities and toward those of less powerful peoples, such as indigenous groups, who are forced into parts of the rainforest, where they clear plots of land to grow subsistence products.

Although political ecology usually focuses on land scarcity and access to material resources, two anthropologists at McMaster University have included community identity in their study of peri-urban political ecology. Tina Moffat and Beth Finnis combine a focus on access to land with access to education in a "squatter" community of 300 people called Nayabasti, in Kathmandu, Nepal. As in many such communities, most of Nayabasti's people lack both sewers and indoor plumbing and build houses out of rudimentary materials. The people of Nayabasti were given the land informally by the municipal government more than

30 years ago, but they have no legal documentation, and the only improvement that has been made is the partial installation of indoor toilets (unconnected to sewers) by a Danish nongovernmental organization (NGO). When the community was first formed, there were few others close by. However, the area now includes monasteries that were built by Tibetan refugees, as well as the homes of wealthy urbanites who have moved from the core of Kathmandu to the outskirts because the land is cheaper and the air is cleaner. The arrival of these newcomers, who have clear title to their land, has placed the community of Nayabasti at even more risk.

Moffat and Finnis discuss the difficulties the community has faced in its efforts to provide education for local children. In 1998, the residents pooled their resources and set about searching for a place to build their own school. After a period of negotiation with the municipal government, a plot of land was found. The community provided almost all the labour to build the school, with Lumanti, a local NGO, providing financial support. Moffat and Finnis caution that it is still uncertain whether the school will be sustainable in the long term, but the project did reinforce community identity, and the community's "ability to get this far is evidence of the incredible capacity of slum and squatter dwellers" (2005, 465).

Medical Anthropology

Medical anthropology is another branch of anthropology in which anthropologists are able to put their ethnographic skills and perspectives to good use. According to the Society for Medical Anthropology, it is "a subfield of anthropology that draws upon social, cultural, biological, and linguistic anthropology to better understand those factors which influence health and well being (broadly defined), the experience and distribution of illness, the prevention and treatment of sickness, healing processes, the social relations of therapy management, and the cultural importance and utilization of pluralistic medical systems" (http://www.medanthro.net/blog/about-the-blog/).

This area of anthropology has moved in many directions. Medical anthropologists may analyze the politics of healthcare access, local interpretations and experience of health and illness, the cultural and historical context of contemporary medical practice and policies, or perceptions and experiences of risk and stigma related to various illnesses.

Naomi Adelson is a medical anthropologist who has done fieldwork with the James Bay Cree of northern Quebec. In her ethnography, *Being Alive Well*, she notes that the Cree do not have a word that readily translates into what we call "health" in English. Rather, they talk about *miyupimaatisiiun*, or "being alive well." For the Cree, being alive well has less to do with individuals and physiology than with social and political relations. Adelson's informants asked, rhetorically, "If the land is not healthy, then how can we be?" (2000, 1). The Cree understanding and experience of health is grounded in what it means to "be Cree," which is itself grounded in connections to the land and to the past (25). Once, the James Bay Cree travelled and hunted across a vast swath of land in northwestern Quebec, but today many live in the village of Whapmagoostui at the mouth of the Great Whale River, hunting in the bush only on weekends. Since the 1970s, the Cree have been fighting with the provincial government of Québec over the appropriate uses of the land and its resources, most famously in the building of the James Bay I hydroelectric dam and the failed James Bay II project. While the Québec government saw the land as underused and underpopulated and as an untapped source of wealth and power, the Cree knew that the projects would drastically alter the ecosystem surrounding Whapmagoostui, changing the migration and survival patterns of land and sea mammals, fish, and birds. What would it mean to be Cree in the face of such changes? How could they manage to "be alive well"? Adelson (2000, 1) argues that "all definitions of health … are laden with ideological nuances and can never be separated from cultural norms and values."

Since Adelson conducted her initial fieldwork, there has been a fusing, at the local level, of health and politics. Adelson distributed copies of her research to local political and health authorities, and her use of "being alive well" to explain Cree understandings of health has been incorporated, via *The James Bay Experience: A Guide for Health Professionals Working Among the Cree in Northern Quebec*, into the vocabulary of doctors, dentists, and other healthcare workers in the area (115).

In her work on the social determinants of health among migrant farm workers in Ontario who come to Canada under the Seasonal Agricultural Workers Program (SAWP), anthropologist Janet McLaughlin (2009) bridges the gap between scholarly and applied anthropology. Her work exemplifies the potential overlap between several of the branches of anthropology we have described here, addressing concerns of medical anthropology, political ecology, and legal anthropology. McLaughlin notes that although health, or at least access to the highest attainable standard of health, is a human right, transnational migrant workers are in a paradoxical position when it comes to exercising this right. Although human rights are meant to be universally applicable, "they are also primarily premised on the relationship between individuals and the obligations of the state to respect, protect and fulfill the rights of citizens. What then are the implications for people who live and work in nations in which they are not citizens?" (McLaughlin 2009, 1). The health of migrant workers is shaped by a number of factors related to the nature of their employment, including the work they do, their working conditions, their access to healthcare, language barriers, and the type of housing in which they stay while in Canada. Yet they are also more vulnerable and neglected in terms of their healthcare needs because of the temporary nature and precarity of their employment, their transnational mobility, and their status as non-citizens. In addition to writing about these migrant workers for audiences that include other anthropologists and scholars of development, McLaughlin applies and disseminates her knowledge and findings beyond academia by writing policy papers and newspaper articles and working with several community groups that address the needs of migrant workers. Beyond that, she is the co-founder of the Migrant Worker Health Project (www. migrantworkerhealth.ca), a website that houses a collection of resources and information for healthcare workers to assist them in providing care to migrant workers.

Corporate Ethnography

Increasingly, corporations recognize that anthropologists possess many unique and beneficial skills that can assist with the marketing and advertising of key products. Specifically, anthropologists possess excellent qualitative research skills (discussed in Chapter 2), a commitment to cultural relativism, problem-solving skills and approaches unique to the discipline, and a focus on cross-cultural and multicultural understandings of the world. As such, corporations realize that anthropologists can often assist them in marketing particular products to people of specific demographics. If McDonald's, for example, is experiencing low revenue on the sale of a particular product in Norway, they may hire an anthropologist to go to Norway and interview potential consumers to understand why the product is not meeting target sales goals. The anthropologist may learn that the product does not appeal to Norwegian food preferences, that the product is perceived as too expensive, or that the advertising campaign is, perhaps for cultural reasons, unsuccessful at appealing to its target demographic.

The relationship between consumerism, culture, and "taste" (in terms of cultural preferences for certain foods, clothing styles, or particular aesthetic trends) is explored by Canadian anthropologist, corporate ethnographer, and blogger Grant McCracken (see McCracken 2005). McCracken has conducted fieldwork for a wide variety of corporations, including Nike, Ikea, and the Ford Foundation. McCracken's goal is to harness the unique perspectives and fieldwork methods of sociocultural anthropology for analyses of consumer trends. He is hired by large corporations to ask and answer questions such as these: How and why do consumers make the purchases that they do? Why is a particular product not meeting sales expectations? How can a product be re-designed to make it more appealing to the consumer? By interviewing consumers about their shopping and consumption habits, and synthesizing this information with analyses of broader cultural trends with respect to consumption, McCracken is hired to increase the net sales and revenue of large companies.

The alignment of anthropology with corporate interests, however, raises a number of ethical problems. As we will learn in Chapter 2, anthropologists have a primary ethical responsibility to ensure that their work does not harm their informants. But many people, including many anthropologists, would argue that the ultimate purpose of marketing and advertising is to manipulate people into mindless consumerism. From this perspective, the use of ethnography to increase corporate profits is harmful to those consumers who are being studied. Moreover, as we will discuss in Chapter 8, the rampant consumption that characterizes contemporary capitalism has global consequences that are often unseen, or at least not considered, by consumers, including environmental degradation, increased global inequality, and poor working conditions for those people who produce the goods we are encouraged to consume. Is it ethical to use our ethnographic problem-solving skills for corporate ethnography, when consumer culture might itself be considered a problem?

On the other hand, it is worth considering that not all anthropologists who work as corporate ethnographers try to increase sales of soft drinks or cars or sneakers. Some corporate ethnographers work in fields of design, urban development, education, or healthcare.

One example that confounds easy adjudications of the ethics of corporate ethnography is the work conducted by Lisa Reichenbach and Amy Maish (2006) on how pharmaceutical companies might best meet the needs of Type 2 diabetics, while simultaneously maximizing their benefits as a business. They argue that ethnography, with its focus on lived experience, is the best way to improve and encourage patient-focused healthcare and pharmaceutical interventions. In their ethnographic work on Type 2 diabetes patients as healthcare clients, they discovered that the key to understanding the illness experience was to realize that coping with diabetes entails a series of life transitions—from healthy to ill, and from dependent patient to self-care practitioner (through the self-administration of insulin).

The theorization of life transitions, as they are facilitated by what anthropologists call "rites of passage" (which we discuss in Chapter 6), is an example of the way in which these corporate ethnographers are able to bring the unique tools of anthropology to bear on interrelated problems that are of interest to patients and healthcare practitioners: how to improve the experience of taking insulin, and how to increase patient compliance. Of course, this work also addresses a problem for pharmaceutical companies: how to sell more insulin. Reichenbach and Maish suggest that the insights gleaned during their research might ultimately benefit both patients and pharmaceutical companies, though perhaps not necessarily to the same degree. The key question, they say, when addressing the issue of business opportunities is not just "What is your overall opportunity as a brand?" but also, "How do I realize that opportunity in the real and often painful world of the diabetic?"

CONCLUSIONS

This chapter has considered five questions, some having to do with the problem of how to understand ways of life that are different from our own and others with the problem of how to better understand our own lives. Why do human beings differ in what they believe and how they behave? One answer is that human beings, unlike other animals (or, at least, to a greater extent than other animals), create their own worlds and ascribe meanings to objects, persons, behaviours, emotions, and events: meanings that together constitute a culture. As Geertz (1973) suggests, human beings are compelled to create meanings if only to instill some sense of order in their lives.

The judgments we make about the beliefs and behaviours of other people create a dilemma. If, on the one hand, we assume that the meanings that others give to their experiences are wrong, silly, or absurd simply because they are different from ours, we are committing the ethnocentric fallacy. Ethnocentrism is intellectually awkward because it allows everyone to believe that their views are correct and that the views of others are wrong. This notion would make any kind of intercultural understanding virtually impossible. If, on the other hand, we conclude that the beliefs and behaviours of others can be judged only in the context of their cultures, we are confronted with the relativistic fallacy, which implies that any belief or behaviour is acceptable, provided it makes sense to the people of the society in which it occurs. This viewpoint places us in a moral dilemma because we must then accept virtually any belief or behaviour.

One way we describe and interpret the meanings other people find in their experiences is to consider a culture as a text inscribed with symbols whose meanings can be deciphered. We can examine virtually any cultural activity in this way and find in it a portion of the overall view of the world of a people. If we approach our own culture in the same way we approach other cultures, we should gain a better understanding of the meanings we give objects, persons, and events. If we objectify our own beliefs and behaviour in the same way that we objectify the beliefs and behaviours of others, our own culture should become more exotic, while the cultures of others become less strange, shocking, or bizarre. It is this ability to make the familiar exotic and the exotic familiar that makes the anthropological perspective so interesting and able to serve you well whether you go into a career as a professional anthropologist or simply apply your new-found insights to the world around you.

Regardless of your career path, the anthropological approach developed within this text should provide you with critical thinking skills. You will perhaps question your own beliefs and understandings of the world as you study, and recognize that much of what we are taught to accept as "natural" is really the byproduct of enculturation. In other words, our identities and worldviews are culturally constructed. This understanding encourages us to recognize the dangers of thinking about our beliefs as "natural' or "biological." Ultimately, by recognizing how culture shapes our experiences, we are in a better position to understand both ourselves and others around us.

CRITICAL THINKING QUESTIONS

1. In the introduction, we discussed the way that an anthropologist might find cultural meaning in a classroom chair. Think about the kinds of classroom spaces you are taking classes in—lecture halls, labs, seminar rooms. What other aspects of the classroom setup can you rethink from an anthropological perspective? How might an anthropologist explain your findings?

2. Sociocultural anthropologists are expected to engage ethically with their informants. Among other things, they must never harm (physically, emotionally, or otherwise) those that they work with. Over the years, this expectation has been particularly important because anthropologists have a long history of working with marginalized or oppressed groups. With this in mind, is corporate anthropology ethical? Is it ethical, for instance, to conduct field research on behalf of large multinational companies such as McDonald's and Starbucks?

3. Anthropologists explore the ways in which human beings make their experiences meaningful through culture. Is it possible to imagine life without systems of meaning to help us make sense of it? What would a life without culture be like?

KEY TERMS:

archaeology   (p. 7)
biological anthropology   (p. 6)
critical cultural relativism   (p. 17)
cultural relativism   (p. 13)
cultural text   (p. 19)
culture   (p. 9)
ethnocentric fallacy   (p. 13)
ethnocentrism   (p. 13)
linguistic anthropology   (p. 7)
relativistic fallacy   (p. 13)
sociocultural anthropology   (p. 3)

DOING FIELDWORK IN SOCIOCULTURAL ANTHROPOLOGY

© Rebekka Seigel, www.quiltartz.com

As noted below in the quotation by famous American anthropologist Margaret Mead, the process of doing sociocultural anthropology, called "ethnographic fieldwork," requires that anthropologists put cultural relativism into practice. When anthropologists study and learn about other cultures through their fieldwork, they often encounter seemingly unusual practices and beliefs. Mead's work was very popular with non-anthropologists and inspired many laypeople to learn about cultures other than their own. Rebekka Speigel's quilt pays tribute to Mead's influence. In this chapter, we learn how anthropologists do fieldwork, how fieldwork has developed and changed over time, how anthropologists navigate the ethical demands of the work, and how anthropologists depict, or represent, people when they write about their field experiences.

*Anthropology demands the open-mindedness with which one must look and listen,
record in astonishment and wonder that which one would not have been able to guess.* *

Margaret Mead

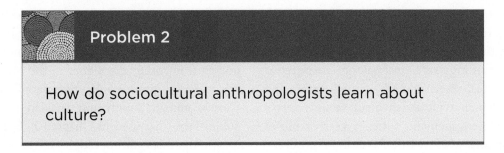

Problem 2

How do sociocultural anthropologists learn about culture?

INTRODUCTION

Think about what sometimes happens when your cellphone rings and you forget to check call display. It's a telemarketer, and you're faced with a request to complete a survey. While the immediate reaction for many people is to hang up the phone, sometimes you may "give in" and answer the telemarketer's questions. If you are busy or indifferent to the topic being discussed, you will probably not give much thought to your responses. Perhaps you are trying to relax, doing schoolwork, making dinner, or otherwise occupied. Because you do not know the individual who is asking you questions, you may have no feeling of interest or responsibility to engage with that person, or to be involved in the study.

This lack of connection with the surveyor is one of the potential methodological shortcomings of **quantitative research**. Moreover, because the telemarketer knows little or nothing about you, and cannot see you and judge your body language as you respond to the survey questions, it is entirely possible that you might simply lie, that your responses will be taken out of context, or that there might be contradictions between what you say and do that the telemarketer is unaware of. When a telemarketer asks you, for instance, to rank your responses to questions on a scale from 1 to 5, there is seldom any room to elaborate upon *why* you feel the way you do about a particular issue. Oftentimes, our answers to surveys are brief and given under time pressure. Telemarketing surveys may work well for answering questions about the *what* of certain behaviours and preferences; however, on their own, they are a much less appropriate tool for answering the kinds of *how* and *why* questions that anthropologists ask about cultural meanings, values, and beliefs.

> **quantitative research**
> Research methods that involve the generation of statistical data. Examples include surveys and censuses.

---

* Mead (1950, p. xxvi) cited in: Tom Boellstorff (2010) *Coming of Age in Second Life: An Anthropologist Explores the Virtually Human.* p. 71.

Although anthropologists do make careful use of quantitative tools, such as surveys and census data, in their own research, these tools are usually a supplement to the **qualitative research** of **ethnographic fieldwork**. Fieldwork is one of the defining features of sociocultural anthropology and something that has historically distinguished it as a unique field of inquiry. *Ethnographic fieldwork* refers to the principal research method used within the discipline, which typically involves various forms of long-term engagements (often a year or more) and interactions with a particular cultural group or community. This work many include participating in daily activities such as gardening and household tasks, attending religious ceremonies, or conducting interviews with community members. It also involves learning the local language in order to be able to communicate directly and effectively with people without the use of translators. As we will discuss in Chapter 3, understanding the local language also provides unique insights into the cultural transmission of beliefs and values.

Over time, anthropologists often develop a sense of **rapport** with the groups that they work with. In other words, they feel a sense of affinity with them and have a general concern for their well-being; friendships often develop. It is precisely this sense of rapport that allows anthropologists to obtain an in-depth understanding of various facets of culture. For example, while many people may feel uncomfortable or indifferent about responding to questions provided by an anonymous telemarketer, they are more likely to engage in open debates or frank discussion over coffee with someone who, they feel, cares about them, and vice versa. For this reason, most anthropological research necessitates the use of long-term fieldwork. Long-term engagements with people allow anthropologists to understand aspects of culture from an insider's perspective, or what is termed an **emic perspective**. Coming to understand a culture from an emic perspective requires that an anthropologist make use of the principle of cultural relativism. Once the anthropologist has conducted fieldwork and

grasped the insider's understanding of a culture, the task is then to situate this understanding within an **etic perspective**, that is, from the perspective of an outside observer. Ideally, anthropologists shift back and forth between these two perspectives when they write, analyze, and present their findings.

In the past, one feature that distinguished anthropology from other disciplines in the social sciences was its focus upon non-Western peoples and places. Closely affiliated with and enabled by European colonialism (discussed in Chapter 3), European and North American anthropologists often went to live, as guests of colonial administrators, among Indigenous peoples in the South Pacific, Africa, or the Americas. At the turn of the 20th century, anthropology was thus defined as the study of non-Western peoples and places. This focus would gradually shift throughout the 20th century, and today you are just as likely

qualitative research
Research methods that aim to explore, rather than measure, various phenomena, often through forms of observation such as interviews, focus groups, and direct participant observation.

ethnographic fieldwork
A research method in which sociocultural anthropologists have intensive, long-term engagements with a group of people. It may involve the use of both qualitative and quantitative methods, including interviews, participant observation, and survey-based research.

rapport
A feeling of affinity, friendship, and responsibility between an anthropologist and an informant. It is often developed through the use of long-term ethnographic fieldwork.

emic perspective
Traditionally refers to an "insider's perspective." The goal of most fieldwork is to employ cultural relativism to understand an issue or perspective from the point of view of one's informants.

etic perspective
Refers to the analysis of an aspect of culture using comparative categories, explanations, and interpretation from the perspective of an outside observer.

to see anthropologists studying their own cultures as the cultures of others. Some North American anthropologists, for instance, use ethnographic fieldwork to tackle important social issues or problems at home, such as racism, homelessness, poverty, and the gentrification of cities. Others study aspects of pop culture, such as the globalization of music industries, dance, or fashion.

Once an anthropologist has spent a sufficient time in the field and has generated enough data, whether it be in the form of field notes, photographs, video recordings, or a combination thereof, the next step is to disseminate an analysis of the fieldwork experiences for the benefit of a broader audience. Dissemination often takes written forms, for example, in journal articles, books, or in popular culture forms of writing such as magazine or newspaper articles. Some anthropologists also produce films about their fieldwork experiences, or they publish photographs, or other forms of visual media.

The production of anthropological knowledge based on ethnographic fieldwork is not without its potential pitfalls. What, for instance, are the ethical implications and responsibilities that result from the unique situation of ethnographic fieldwork? Another issue in the production of anthropological knowledge is that of **representation**, which refers to the ways in which anthropologists depict a particular group of people. Whenever we write about a cultural group, we are crafting particular representations for public consumption, and it is important to recognize that this privilege is connected to power. In other words, our representations will have an impact upon how people perceive others, and negative representations may have long-term, deleterious consequences for various peoples. In this chapter, we explore the history of anthropological fieldwork and the way that it has changed over the last century. We also discuss the various practical, ethical, intellectual, and representational challenges that arise during the process of doing and writing about ethnographic fieldwork.

QUESTIONS

2.1 How did ethnographic fieldwork develop during the formative years of anthropology?

2.2 How has fieldwork changed over the past century?

2.3 What are some of the challenges of conducting fieldwork?

2.4 What are the responsibilities of anthropologists toward the people they work with? What does it mean to "act ethically" as an anthropologist?

2.5 How do anthropologists represent the people they study and work with? Why is representation an important issue within anthropology?

QUESTION 2.1: HOW DID ETHNOGRAPHIC FIELDWORK DEVELOP DURING THE FORMATIVE YEARS OF ANTHROPOLOGY?

Anthropology from an Armchair

Anthropology began at a particular time in history: "the Age of Exploration," which was launched by Christopher Columbus when he arrived in the Americas in 1492 and which lasted until the early 17th century. It was during these centuries that Europeans first encountered people who looked and behaved very differently than themselves (Barrett 1996, 3).

representation
The way in which a group of people is depicted in writing or through images. Anthropologists are increasingly conscious of the fact that when they write about a group of people, they are constructing particular representations that may have positive or negative long-term effects for a group of people.

DOING FIELDWORK IN SOCIOCULTURAL ANTHROPOLOGY

Travellers and explorers returned home with stories about the seemingly "strange" people they had met in faraway places, sometimes bringing back live native "specimens," as well. Those at home debated at length whether these beings were fully human.

European countries established colonies throughout the world, often sending missionaries along to "civilize" the strange people; those missionaries then documented their encounters. One of the most famous of these accounts is the *Jesuit Relations*, first published in 1632, which describes the interactions between the Jesuit missionaries and the Indigenous peoples in southern Ontario. These missionaries' writings were a type of proto-anthropology, though it must be added that missionaries and anthropologists today have very different motivations for the work they do. For most missionaries, cultural understanding is a necessary means toward an end goal of changing or even eradicating certain beliefs; for most anthropologists, such understanding is an end in and of itself.

Notwithstanding these early cross-cultural interactions, anthropology did not emerge as a formal discipline until 1883, when Edward Tylor was appointed to the first academic position of anthropology in Britain, at Oxford. Decades later, in 1925, Thomas F. McIlwraith became the first anthropology appointment at the University of Toronto. Canada's first department of anthropology was founded at the same university in 1936.

In the late 1800s, as anthropology grew in popularity throughout Europe and North America, many early anthropologists, such as Tylor, were engaged in **armchair anthropology**. That is, instead of visiting various peoples and conducting their own first-hand research, they stayed at home and amassed diaries, reports, and various documents written by Europeans or Euro-Americans who had come in contact with non-Western peoples. Sitting in their "armchairs," or perhaps at their university office desks, these anthropologists applied a comparative method to explore differences and similarities in social institutions and belief systems in a variety of societies. This approach often included a comparison of family structures, forms of political and economic organizations, and religious or spiritual beliefs, among other things. Based on their comparisons,

armchair anthropology
Refers to an approach to the study of various societies that dominated anthropology in the late 1800s. It involved the collection, study, and analysis of the writings of missionaries, explorers, and colonists who had sustained contact with non-Western peoples. Armchair anthropologists used these documents to make comparisons and generalizations about the ways of life of various groups.

© Courtesy of the McIlwraith Family

Canadian anthropologist Thomas McIlwraith was the first anthropologist to be appointed to an academic position at the University of Toronto.

armchair anthropologists would try to make cross-cultural generalizations about such things as warfare, marriage patterns, religion, and other phenomena. These comparisons and generalizations were based entirely on etic interpretations and analysis.

Tylor relied on the accounts provided by travellers and missionaries as sources of information for *Primitive Culture* (1871). But he did so uncritically—that is, he did not acknowledge the inherent biases in their writings—taking their work at face value (as did many other armchair anthropologists of his day). Indeed, without any first-hand experience or emic understanding of the cultures he was reading about, it would have been difficult for him to detect or refute these biases.

It is worth noting the ways in which Tylor's own definition of culture reflected the methodological approach that he shared with his fellow armchair anthropologists. According to Tylor, "culture or civilization, taken in its wide [comparative] ethnographic sense, is that complex whole which includes knowledge, belief, art, morals, law, custom, and any other capabilities and habits acquired by man as a member of his society" (1871, 1). As in our working definition of culture outlined in Chapter 1, Tylor's definition emphasized the shared and learned aspects of culture; however, he and other Victorian anthropologists wrote about culture in the singular, believing that some peoples or cultural groups might have more or less culture or civilization than others. In this sense, both their methodology and their understanding of culture were not merely comparative, but hierarchical, as well. Ranking and ordering different cultural groups, many of whom were the subjects of colonialism, was an integral part of the intellectual justification and logic of colonial endeavours at the time. (This link between colonialism, ethnocentrism, and early anthropology is discussed more fully in Chapter 3.) Of relevance here is that contemporary anthropologists remain interested in the differences and similarities between cultures, but they no longer employ hierarchies when comparing human beliefs and behaviours.

Ethnographic Fieldwork

Anthropologists such as Bronislaw Malinowski and Franz Boas (often regarded as the "fathers" of social and cultural anthropology, respectively) would soon move beyond the armchair anthropology of Tylor and his contemporaries. Boas sought firsthand knowledge among the Inuit and the Kwakwaka'wakw of Canada, while Malinowski conducted much of his early fieldwork in the South Pacific. After Malinowski went to live in the Trobriand Islands during the First World War, extended periods of fieldwork became the required methodology of sociocultural anthropology.

Anthropologists, like other social scientists, use surveys, written documents, historical accounts, and questionnaires as part of their research toolbox. But the unique feature of sociocultural anthropology is the ethnographic method: investigators immerse themselves in the lives of the people they are trying to understand, systematically observe their day-to-day lives, and thereby attain some level of understanding of the meanings those people ascribe to their existence. This immersion process entails **participant observation**, defined as the active participation of observers in the lives of their subjects.

The ethnographic method is only the beginning of the anthropological enterprise. The anthropologist also seeks to explain why people view the world as they do and to contribute to the understanding of human behaviour in general by sharing findings with other anthropologists or the broader public. But this enterprise begins with fieldwork, which involves the meeting of at least two cultures: that of the researcher, and that of the people the researcher is trying to understand. Anthropological researchers must set aside their own views of

participant observation
An element of fieldwork that can involve participating in daily tasks, and observing daily interactions among a particular group.

DOING FIELDWORK IN SOCIOCULTURAL ANTHROPOLOGY

things and endeavour to see the world in a new way. In many respects, they must assume the demeanour and status of children, students, or novices who must be taught by their elders the proper view of the world.

Bronislaw Malinowski (1884–1942), Polish born and British trained, was one of the first anthropologists to abandon the armchair approach. He revolutionized anthropology by stressing the primacy of fieldwork. Malinowski's discovery of the efficacy of fieldwork for understanding culture could be described as something of an accident. In 1914, he travelled to New Guinea as part of a team of researchers, but when the First World War broke out, he found himself unable to travel back to Britain, as he was a citizen of the Austro-Hungarian empire and, therefore, an enemy of the state. He decided to stay and conduct long-term research, alone, in the Trobriand Islands as the guest of British colonial officials.

Soon after his arrival, Malinowski concluded that it would be necessary to spend each day with the Trobrianders if he hoped to obtain a comprehensive understanding of their daily lives. So he left the comfort of his colonial household, acquired a tent, and set up camp in a nearby Trobriand village. By living with Trobrianders, observing and participating in their daily tasks, and learning their language, he established the importance of participant observation as a fieldwork strategy.

© London School of Economics, Malinowski/3/18/2

Bronislaw Malinowski in the midst of Trobriand Islanders. Malinowski was one of the first anthropologists to conduct long-term fieldwork.

Participant observation requires long-term engagement with a group of people and their daily lives. It may involve living with group members as well as observing and participating in daily tasks, no matter how mundane. This fieldwork technique has become a defining feature of contemporary anthropological fieldwork. Even today, anthropologists regularly observe and participate in such things as gardening, harvesting, cooking, recreation, and various rituals and ceremonies.

Conducting participant observation is a balancing act that requires the anthropologist to shift back and forth between, or even attempt to simultaneously inhabit, two different roles: that of the participant, and that of the observer. Becoming too closely involved in participation may mean losing one's ability to see things from an etic, or outsider's, perspective; focusing too much energy on observation and note taking may mean missing out on the details and nuances that are such an important part of gaining a firsthand experience of the emic point of view.

As one of the first people to conduct this kind of fieldwork, Malinowski set the template for managing this balancing act, one that most anthropologists continue to follow today. He took detailed field notes by hand during his participatory interactions with Trobriand Islanders. In the evenings, he typed up his notes and spent more time thinking about his observations. Later, he would transform these into an **ethnography**, defined as a written description and analysis of an anthropologist's experiences and interactions with a group of people. In essence, the ethnography is the end product of a fieldwork experience. For Malinowski (1961, 3), the measure of a good ethnography was the extent to which the reader was able to follow

ethnography
A written description and analysis of a particular group of people, usually based upon anthropological fieldwork.

the anthropologist's analytic shifts between the emic and etic perspectives:

> I consider that only such ethnographic sources are of unquestionable scientific value, in which we can clearly draw a line between, on the one hand, the results of direct observation and of native statements and interpretations, and on the other, the inferences of the author, based on his common sense and psychological insight. *

Malinowski felt that by carefully documenting their experiences and observations with field notes, and combining this with participant observation and other qualitative fieldwork techniques, anthropologists would be able to obtain "the native's point of view" (Malinowski 1961, 25), his evocative term for the emic perspective. The differences between Edward Tylor's definition of *culture* and Malinowski's reflect the differences between armchair anthropology and ethnographic fieldwork. Malinowski was less interested in hierarchical comparisons than in understanding each culture on its own terms. His view was that cultures arise in order to meet the particular needs of specific peoples. Culture, in this sense, can be understood as plural. For Malinowski *(1944, 36)*, culture was

> the integral whole consisting of implements and consumers' goods, of constitutional charters for the various social groupings, of human ideas and crafts, beliefs, and customs. Whether we consider a very simple or primitive culture or an extremely complex and developed one, we are confronted by a vast apparatus, partly material, partly human, and partly spiritual, by which man is able to cope with the concrete, specific problems that face him.

When Malinowski returned to Britain, he took up a position teaching anthropology at the London School of Economics. The ethnography he wrote based on his Trobriand Islands fieldwork, *Argonauts*

---

* Malinowski, B. (1922). Argonauts of the Western Pacific: An account of native enterprise and adventure in the Archipelagoes of Melanesian New Guinea. London: Routledge and Kegan Paul.

of the Western Pacific (1922), was considered groundbreaking at the time, and remains a classic today. Malinowski is credited with being one of the first anthropologists to both utilize and formalize participant observation and long-term fieldwork, and he went on to train a wide range of influential anthropologists in these methods in the first half of the 20th century.

EXERCISE 2.1

Fieldwork involves a great deal of preparation and study before arriving in "the field." If you were asked to travel to the Trobriand Islands to study family relationships in a small village for a year, what steps would you take to prepare yourself for your fieldwork?

QUESTION 2.2: HOW HAS FIELDWORK CHANGED OVER THE PAST CENTURY?

Changing Notions of Fieldwork

Malinowski's insistence on long-term fieldwork and participant observation would have lasting effects on the discipline. These days, Ph.D. students in anthropology are still required to spend at least a year in the field, and they often incorporate participant observation as a fieldwork technique. However, fieldwork has also changed over the last century, and many of Malinowski's original ideas about fieldwork have been challenged. Nonetheless, his systematic approach to the collection and analysis of data, together with his evocative and eloquent presentation of Trobriand Islands culture, remain key to the ethnographic endeavour today.

In the late 19th century, anthropology was about the study of non–Western peoples and places. Most

DOING FIELDWORK IN SOCIOCULTURAL ANTHROPOLOGY

anthropologists were upper-class, educated, white men from Europe, Australia, Canada, and the United States. From their perspective, Indigenous peoples were the most appropriate subjects of study. In a somewhat paternalistic way, these early anthropologists viewed Indigenous peoples as groups in need of "rescue." Thus, a great deal of early-20th-century anthropology in North America was an outgrowth of **salvage anthropology**, an idea espoused by Franz Boas, among others, who felt that Indigenous peoples throughout the world were undergoing rapid assimilation and would eventually disappear (Darnell 1998a, 23). He felt that anthropologists had an obligation to document and collect the various traditions and cultures of these groups. Boas and his students began documenting Inuit and Northwest Coast indigenous cultures so to "preserve" them before they disappeared (which they never did).

Museums at the time took on the same task. Indeed, museums became integral to this culture of collecting and would play a prominent role in the development of Canadian anthropology. In 1911, the Anthropology Division of the Geological Survey of Canada was established, with Edward Sapir, Marius Barbeau, and Diamond Jenness on its staff. In the 1920s, this unit became part of the National Museum of Canada, since renamed the Museum of Civilization (Ervin 2001, 15).

Regna Darnell, an anthropologist at the University of Western Ontario who has conducted extensive research on the history of Canadian anthropology, contends that, although there are no features of Canadian anthropology that set it apart as utterly unique, "the national discipline combines

Diamond Jenness (1826–1969) is recognized as an early pioneer of Canadian anthropology. Chief of Anthropology at the National Museum of Canada between 1926 and 1948, he sought to expand the museum's collections and its international reputation. He also lobbied the federal government to fight against racism toward Indigenous peoples and to advocate for better living conditions for people living on reserves.

© "Diamond Jenness, Canadian Arctic Expedition, Northwest Territories" by G.H. Wilkins, Canadian Museum of History, 51236

features of disciplinary organization and historical context in patterns that *are* unique" (1998b, 155). It is difficult to define exactly what is "Canadian" about Canadian anthropology, but Darnell has an interesting suggestion: "In Canada, a critical mass of First Nations languages and cultures maintains them [traditional cultures] with a saliency in the national forum unparalleled in the United States" (2000, 170). Many Canadian anthropologists continue to focus on First Nations peoples, but they also conduct research in Latin America, the Caribbean, Asia, Africa, Europe (Eastern and Western), New Zealand, Australia, Melanesia, Polynesia, and the Middle East. Throughout this book, we will be looking at the work of many Canadian anthropologists as well as that of anthropologists in other places in the world.

The flow of anthropologists is still predominantly *from* former colonial powers *to* former colonies, despite the fact that most of the world's former colonies have achieved independence in the last

salvage anthropology
An approach to anthropology that arose in the late 1800s when anthropologists witnessed the extinction or assimilation of Indigenous peoples throughout the world. In response, some anthropologists, such as Franz Boas, suggested that anthropologists rapidly document the oral stories, songs, histories, and other traditions of Indigenous peoples before they disappeared.

century. However, ideas about appropriate "field sites" and subjects of study have changed since the days of Malinowski and Boas. Anthropologists no longer exclusively restrict themselves to the study of non-Western peoples and places; more anthropologists also study "up" rather than "down" in terms of power relationships. Today, Canadian anthropologists are just as likely to study aspects of their own communities.

This shift in thinking has had consequences for how anthropologists conduct their fieldwork. The field "site" is not necessarily a faraway place. Anthropologists might study office culture in Vancouver, homelessness in Toronto, or separatist ideologies in Quebec. As such, they do not necessarily travel long distances for fieldwork, and many no longer live among their informants for extended periods of time.

Perhaps the greatest transformations to the kinds of research anthropologists do, the research sites we choose, and the questions we ask have been made to address concurrent transformations in social and cultural life as a result of processes of globalization (discussed in further depth in Chapter 8). For instance, a key difference between the anthropology of today and in Malinowski's time has to do with how we think of the "native" in the "native's point of view." Anthropologists today are more likely to interrogate the difference between an insider's point of view and an outsider's point of view, not least because the people we study may negotiate more than one cultural point of view in their daily lives. Kirin Narayan (1993), for example, famously asked "How native is a 'native' anthropologist?" She was inspired to ask the question by her own position, as the daughter of German-American mother and an Indian father, who, when she conducted fieldwork in India, was considered a "native" anthropologist, despite the fact that she did not necessarily see herself as native. Not only did she question the oversimplified dichotomy between native and non-native, she also argued that, due to globalization, and the interpenetrating communities and power relations that come with

it, identities might better be thought of, studied, and written about as hybrid and in flux. Furthermore, regardless of the extent to which either an anthropologist or a "native" identifies as an insider or outsider, there are many other factors, such as gender, sexuality, education, race, and class, that mean that the category of "native" may be better thought of as plural, rather than singular (671–72).

Another key shift in the discipline and its methodologies in the last century has to do with the focus on a single research site. Malinowski advocated in-depth research in one specific location, but anthropologists today often conduct multi-locale fieldwork, or fieldwork in multiple locations. Other anthropologists advocate the use of multi-sited fieldwork, a term coined by George Marcus in 1995. **Multi-sited fieldwork** involves connecting the localized events and experiences of a community with broader regional, national, or global processes. This approach often goes hand in hand with multi-locale approaches. For instance, Canadian anthropologist Andrew Walsh (2010) has studied the commodification of sapphires and the growing preference for "natural" gems (sapphires that have not been subject to heat treatment to enhance their colour) from multiple perspectives. He has interviewed Malagasy miners and local sapphire traders in Madagascar as well as gemologists and jewellers in North America. His work has taken him not only to Madagascar but also to international gemological trade shows. In essence, Walsh is endeavouring to track the multiple meanings and relationships that form around the international sapphire trade, and he explores how international demand for "natural" sapphires is affecting the lives of miners in local communities in Madagascar. Sapphires "mean" different things to different

> **multi-sited fieldwork**
> This term, coined by George Marcus in 1995, refers to the process of connecting localized experiences of fieldwork with broader, global processes. It necessitates understanding various issues from multiple "sites," or perspectives.

groups of people, and the mining industries have different economic, political, social, and health consequences for different groups depending upon one's position within this complex international web of sapphire procurement, distribution, and consumption.

Finally, television, the Internet, and other media technologies have changed the ways we form and maintain social relationships, and some anthropologists have adjusted their methods accordingly. Today we are creating a sense of community not only through face-to-face interactions but also through Internet sites, chat rooms, online games, Skype, and Facebook, among others. Given that our contemporary interactions are mediated by technology, we increasingly see anthropologists conducting fieldwork online as well as face to face.

Tom Boellstorff's ethnography, *Coming of Age in Second Life* (2008), for example, documents his research on, and in, the three-dimensional, online gaming world of "Second Life." Boellstorff conducted all of his fieldwork online. He justified this by stating that this virtual space is a productive one for studying the unique "cultural logic" of gaming and gamers. In other words, the online communities created by gamers are just as valid an object of study as traditional face-to-face communities have been. Interestingly, Boellstorff cites Tylor's understanding of culture as a "complex whole," asking, "What is a virtual world if not a complex whole, however networked?" (2008, 66). He goes on to explain that he is not studying "virtual culture," but rather "culture in virtual worlds" (66). He also emphasizes the similarity between his research "site" and more traditional field sites by paying homage to Malinowski's famous "arrival" scene in his own ethnography, where he says:

> Imagine yourself suddenly set down surrounded by all your gear, alone on a tropical beach close to a native village while the launch of dinghy which has brought you sails away out of sight … You have nothing to do, but to start at once your

ethnographic work. Imagine further that you are a beginner, without previous experience, with nothing to guide you and no one to help you.

Thus far, his arrival is a verbatim re-creation of Malinowski's, which Boellstorff says, "exactly describes my first initiation into field work in Second Life" (2008, 3).

Thus, fieldwork has undergone changes since Malinowski's time, but the *content* of fieldwork, or data collection, has undergone relatively few changes. What counts as a site, or what counts as the emic, or insider's, point of view may have changed, but as Raymond Madden (2010, 32) has aptly put it, "being ethnographic" remains in many ways the same: "Being with people … in their time and space, in all their strangeness and in their mundane and quotidian flow, is still one of most valued ways to build a qualitative understanding of the particulars and generalities of the human condition."

Another key aspect of doing anthropology that remains relatively unchanged is that, as anthropologists, through our ethnographies we create bodies of knowledge about the people we are studying. Issues of how to accurately and ethically represent human beliefs and behaviours therefore remain central to the discipline.

Tom Boellstorff conducted his fieldwork for *Coming of Age in Second Life* entirely online.

QUESTION 2.3: WHAT ARE SOME OF THE CHALLENGES OF CONDUCTING FIELDWORK?

Ethnographic fieldwork can often be frustrating and lonely, and it can involve elements of **culture shock** and miscommunication. *Culture shock* refers to a feeling of disorientation in the initial stages of fieldwork when an anthropologist is often adjusting to a new language, beliefs, foods, or even climate. In the early stages of fieldwork, an anthropologist may also misinterpret the intent of his or her informants, which can lead to awkward or embarrassing situations. The following ethnographic vignettes by Richard Scaglion (1990) and Michael Kearney (1991) highlight the importance of long-term ethnography when it comes to interpreting the belief systems of another culture. In many ways, the anthropologist becomes a student during fieldwork, and through our mistakes and breaches of etiquette

> **culture shock**
> Refers to a feeling of disorientation in the initial stages of fieldwork when an anthropologist is adjusting to a new language, beliefs, food, or even climate.

we learn socially appropriate behaviours and ways of being and acting within a cultural group. Fieldwork is also a time when we can begin to challenge our own taken-for-granted assumptions about the world.

The Embarrassed Anthropologist

Awkwardness and embarrassment are a part of fieldwork, as well as a part of the process through which the fieldworker learns about another culture. Richard Scaglion (1990) spent over a year with the Abelam of Papua New Guinea. Shortly after he arrived in the field, he observed and photographed an Abelam pig hunt in which the men set out nets and waited while the women and children made lots of noise to drive the pigs into the nets. Soon after, he was invited by the Abelam to participate in a pig hunt, and he took this as a sign of acceptance, that the people "liked him." He started to go with the men, but they told him they wanted him to go with the women and children to beat the bush, explaining, "We've never seen anyone who makes as much noise in the jungle as you." Later, wanting to redeem himself, Scaglion offered to help an Abelam who was planting crops with a digging stick. A crowd gathered to watch as he used a shovel to try to dig a demonstration hole. After he had struggled for several minutes to get the shovel into the hard-packed soil, someone handed him a digging stick, and he was amazed at how easy it was to use. Later, he found out that several Abelam had shovels but rarely used them because they didn't work.

After months of answering Scaglion's questions about their view of the natural world, such as the moon, sun, and stars, some Abelam asked him about *his* views of the universe. Feeling on safe ground, he gave the usual grade-school lecture about the shape of Earth, its daily rotation, and its travels around the sun. Using a coconut, he showed them the relative positions on Earth of New Guinea, Australia, Europe, and the United States. Everyone listened intently, and Scaglion thought it had gone well—until a week later, when he overheard some elders wondering how it was that North Americans walked upside down!

Beginning again, Scaglion used the coconut to explain how, as Earth rotates, sometimes the United States is up right and New Guinea is on the bottom. The Abelam rejected this because they could see that they were *not* upside down, and no one, not even some of the old people in the community, remembered ever having walked upside down. Scaglion began to draw on the physics he had learned at university. As he tried to explain Newton's law of gravity (or "grabity," as his friends pronounced it), he suddenly realized that he didn't understand "grabity" either. The concept, something he had accepted since grade 3, was one that even physicists take for granted.

EXERCISE 2.3

Think of some awkward or embarrassing situation created by something you did or didn't do, said or didn't say. What was inappropriate about your behaviour, and why did it lead to misunderstanding or embarrassment? What did you learn from the experience about the meaning of your behaviour or that of others?

Confronting Witchcraft in Mexico

Awkward or embarrassing moments in the field may help anthropologists understand a culture and even question their own view of the world. But the question of whether one can ever see the world through others' eyes remains contentious among anthropologists. Obviously, to communicate with anyone—even members of their own society—people must share some of the meanings they ascribe to objects, persons, behaviours, emotions, and events. What happens, then, when views of the world are completely different?

Michael Kearney (1991) travelled to the town of Santa Catarina Ixtepeji in the valley of Oaxaca, Mexico, with the intention of studying the relationship between the people's view of the world

and their social arrangements and environment. He began his work secure in his knowledge of the scientific and materialist view of the world in which he was reared, but he was often fascinated by the differences between his view and that of the people of Santa Catarina Ixtepeji. Their world was controlled by mystic notions of "fate," the will of God, and malevolent witches and other harmful and sometimes lethal spiritual forces. He became familiar with the Ixtepejanos' worldview, never doubting that it was "unscientific"—albeit justified, perhaps, by a life in which suffering, disease, and death were common.

Kearney's faith in his own worldview was momentarily shattered by an incident that began innocently enough. While walking to an appointment, he came upon an obviously distressed woman, Doña Delfina. She was known as a witch, and Kearney had been trying unsuccessfully to interview her. When they met she explained that her sister-in-law had a "very bad disease in her arms" and that she wanted him to help. Kearney accompanied Doña Delfina to her house, where he found that the sister-in-law's arms were ulcerated with deep, oozing lesions that looked to him

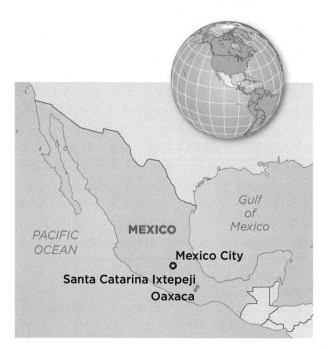

like infected burns. They rejected his offer to take the sick woman to a doctor for medical treatment, so Kearney said he had some ointment that might help, and they eagerly agreed that he should use it. He got the ointment, which contained an anaesthetic, and daubed it on the woman's sores. Much to the amazement of Doña Delfina, her sister-in-law immediately felt better. By the afternoon, her arms had greatly improved; by the following morning, scabs had formed; the day after, she had completely recovered.

Kearney was credited with a "miraculous cure," but encountered an unexpected reaction. The same day, an Ixtepejano friend asked Kearney what he had done, and the anthropologist proudly explained. The friend replied: "Why did you do that? It was not a good thing to do." The sick woman, he said, had been the victim of black magic; another woman, Gregoria, was trying to take Delfina's brother away from his wife and was using black magic to make Delfina's sister-in-law sick. Delfina was using *her* magic to keep her brother in the household, but Gregoria was winning. Now, the friend explained to Kearney, he had intervened, tipping the balance of power back to Delfina but creating a powerful enemy in Gregoria. "Maybe you should leave town for a while until Gregoria calms down," Kearney's friend suggested.

Kearney did not take the danger seriously, and he might never have done so were it not for two incidents that occurred soon afterward. A young doctor in town asked Kearney, who had medical training, to assist in an autopsy of a man who had died in a fall off a truck. It was a particularly long and gory autopsy accomplished only with rusty carpenter's tools in a dimly lit room. Images of the scene and the cadaver disturbed Kearney's sleep over the next few days. One night, about a week later, as the wind beat cornstalks against his house, Kearney felt an itching on his arm. Rolling up his sleeve, he discovered several angry welts that seemed to be growing as he watched them. Immediately, he thought of the chancrous arms of Delfina's sister-in-law, realizing at the same time that Gregoria's house was only 50 metres from his and

that she could be trying to kill him. "She got me!" he thought. The image of the cadaver on the table jumped into his mind, followed by a wish that he had got out of town while there was still time. As Kearney put it, he was witnessing the disintegration of his scientific, materialist view of the world and grappling with forces with which he was unprepared to deal.

Kearney is not sure how long his initial terror lasted—seconds, perhaps minutes. As he struggled against it, he realized that he was suspended between two worlds: his own and that of the Ixtepejanos. He was questioning a world of meanings that he had until then taken for granted. Kearney is not sure how long he was able to truly believe that the world was as the Ixtepejanos saw it, but as he retrieved his own view of the world, the Ixtepejanos' world-view, filled with witchcraft and magic, ceased to be only intellectually interesting. It acquired a reality and a sense of legitimacy for him that it had not had before he experienced the real fear that he had been bewitched. He came to realize through his experience that any system of belief is eminently reasonable when viewed from within that system.

The experiences of these anthropologists, Kearney and Scaglion, highlight certain features of the ethnographic method. They especially illustrate anthropologists' efforts to appreciate the views of others while at the same time questioning their own views of the world. They also illustrate what makes the ethnographic method unique: by participating in the lives of others and in their cultural practices, anthropologists can take *themselves* as subjects of investigation. Those who succeed in seeing the world as others do, if even for a brief moment, find it far easier to understand and describe that world. It also helps the anthropologist understand how others can believe what they do. Claude Levi-Strauss, one of the greatest anthropologists of the 20th century, once said that fieldwork, and anthropologists' efforts to immerse themselves in the worlds of others, makes anthropologists "marginal" men or women. They are never completely native because they cannot totally shed their own cultural perceptions, but they are never the same again after having glimpsed

DOING FIELDWORK IN SOCIOCULTURAL ANTHROPOLOGY

alternative visions of the world. Anthropologists are, as Roger Keesing put it, outsiders who know something of what it is to be insiders.

Scaglion and Kearney both succeeded because they were able to see things, at least temporarily, from the native's point of view or an insider's perspective. Doing this is by no means easy, especially when we are faced with practices and beliefs that we find incredible or troublesome. We may be able to overcome our initial shock or bewilderment on confronting different cultures if we understand something about why cultural differences exist. But how should we react if the meanings that others ascribe to experiences differ from our own? It is difficult enough to look beyond everyday appearances at our own beliefs and behaviours; it is far more difficult when we confront beliefs and behaviours of others that we initially consider wrong, horrible, or bizarre.

QUESTION 2.4: WHAT ARE THE RESPONSIBILITIES OF ANTHROPOLOGISTS TOWARD THE PEOPLE THEY WORK WITH? WHAT DOES IT MEAN TO "ACT ETHICALLY" AS AN ANTHROPOLOGIST?

As the previous sections demonstrate, fieldwork is challenging—to an anthropologist's worldview, sense of well-being, and even ego. In this section, we discuss another set of challenges: the ethical challenges of living with others and gathering data during fieldwork, and the related challenges of accurately and fairly representing informants in one's written (or visual) ethnography.

The ethical challenges posed by fieldwork, and especially by participant observation, arise from the fact that, rather than simply conducting naturalistic observations of behaviour, fieldwork is inherently interventionist. This characteristic is especially evident in applied anthropology, where anthropologists conduct their research with the goal of solving a particular problem. But it is just as true of "regular" anthropology: our presence in the field will inevitably have an effect on those we study. We get involved in the day-to-day lives of our research subjects, we develop a rapport, and we negotiate relationships with our informants. Human relationships can be complicated and unpredictable (not to mention rewarding and fulfilling) at the best of times. Relationships during ethnographic fieldwork are unique because ethnography, by definition, gives the ethnographer the power to create knowledge about the people he or she studies. The power dynamic involved in ethnographic fieldwork, therefore, adds an additional layer of responsibility to relationships in the field.

One way that anthropologists working in various institutions (e.g., universities, hospitals, and community groups) address the potential ethical dilemmas of fieldwork is by participating in an institutional ethics review process, which involves writing a proposal, reviewed by one's peers, that explains how the ethnographer will ensure that the ethical standards of the discipline (and the institution) are upheld.[1] Although these proposals consist of a series of elements that must be addressed, it might be better to think of fieldwork not as having an ethical element that must be present, but rather, as "an ethical commitment from the very outset, and through all phases of ethnographic research and writing" (Madden 2010, 34). Here, we discuss not so much the various ethical elements that might appear in one's ethics review at a particular institution, but rather, the various considerations that must be taken into account in fieldwork as an ethical commitment.

---

[1] For instance, all Canadian researchers who conduct research with human subjects, regardless of the discipline, must act in accordance with the *Tri-Council Policy Statement: Ethical Conduct for Research Involving Humans*. Interested readers can access the statement here: http://www.pre.ethics.gc.ca/pdf/eng/tcps2/TCPS_2_FINAL_Web.pdf

First and foremost, anthropologists are expected to "do no harm" to their informants. In other words, anthropological fieldwork must not result in any physical, psychological, or emotional harm to those that we work with. To protect the rights of informants, anthropologists are thus required to obtain **informed consent** before conducting research. Doing this requires anthropologists to disclose their identity, the goals of the project, and any potential risks involved. Satisfying this requirement is one of the key differences between anthropologists and spies or investigative journalists: our informants must always know about and understand our presence in the field; with rare exceptions, we need to do this even when it means that knowledge of our presence and our goals may change the way that people interact with us.

Ahead of our own goals and even ahead of our disciplinary pursuit of knowledge is our responsibility to our informants. This emphasis upon ensuring the well-being of one's informants is why building a rapport is so important to fieldwork. Anthropologists must also obtain permission to conduct any form of fieldwork, and while the use of written permission forms or letters is common, it can occasionally take the form of verbal consent. Individuals must also be told that they may withdraw from the project at any time, and to protect informants' confidentiality, people (and often places) are usually given pseudonyms. Furthermore, research participants have a right to know how an anthropologist will store and protect their data.

Our ethical commitments to our participants can lead to difficult situations and hard choices. For example, Philippe Bourgois (2003) has conducted fieldwork in El Barrio, New York, among gangs of Puerto Rican crack dealers and their families and communities. It took Bourgois over two years to obtain the

informed consent
The ongoing process of ensuring that research participants understand the goals, methods, and potential outcomes of the research process, and give permission for the researcher to conduct said research.

trust and loyalty of various crack dealers, and the goal of his project was to examine how poverty and urban economic restructuring (among other things) contributed to their choice to be crack dealers. Given the sensitive nature of his project, and the fact that the information he collected during his fieldwork (which details the names and addresses of dealers as well as the locations of crack houses) would be an invaluable resource to police, he found it necessary to change the names of informants and the specific locations where he conducted fieldwork. Indeed, because anthropologists, unlike journalists, do not have the legal right to protect their "confidential sources" in court, many anthropologists who find themselves in situations where they may witness illegal behaviour choose to remove themselves from the situation altogether. Although this decision may result in a "loss" of potentially rich data, it may be the only way to protect the rights of their participants and live up to their ethical responsibilities to those people with whom they have long-term relationships and commitments.

QUESTION 2.5: HOW DO ANTHROPOLOGISTS REPRESENT THE PEOPLE THEY STUDY AND WORK WITH? WHY IS REPRESENTATION AN IMPORTANT ISSUE WITHIN ANTHROPOLOGY?

Representation and Culture

Because they create knowledge about culture and relay other people's stories about themselves to a wider audience, anthropologists are concerned about issues of *representation*. All ethnographic depictions are based on interpretation, rather than a mere presentation of raw data, and as such are shaped, to

DOING FIELDWORK IN SOCIOCULTURAL ANTHROPOLOGY

varying degrees, by the perspectives and assumptions of the author. That is why anthropologists try to think critically about how they depict the people they are studying, be it in writing, photographs, art, films, and other media, or on the Internet. Representations can be created by anthropologists, by the media, or by the informants themselves. Increasingly, anthropologists are speaking out against racist, sexist, or homophobic representations produced by the mass media, or even by other anthropologists. In the wake of both 9/11 and the 2014–15 armed conflicts/air strikes against ISIS, for example, many mainstream American media outlets depicted Islamic people (especially men) as violent terrorists or as "uncivilized," "backward," and "primitive." The mass media have tended to resort to **essentialism** when representing particular groups. In essentialist representations, groups of people are depicted in ways that tend to homogenize and stereotype them (Mattingly, Lawlor, and Jacobs-Huey 2002). When essentialist representations are consumed by a public that is too often uncritical, racism is perpetuated, and domestic and foreign policy are often affected for the worse. Anthropologists are well positioned, because of their expertise and firsthand experience, to challenge the accuracy and analyze the repercussions of such representations.

Mass tourism is one social realm that tends to rely heavily on essentialist images and depictions of non-Western peoples. Such images are frequently circulated in brochures, on websites, and in other forms of advertising by airlines, hotels, and tour operators. Tourist brochures and websites often lure middle-class, Canadian travellers to warm, tropical islands by representing the island and its people as "primitive," "timeless," and "exotic." In fact, the tourist industry is built around producing marketable images or representations of particular peoples and places to attract foreign tourists (and their dollars) to various locations. In many developing

essentialism
The act of creating generalizations or stereotypes about the behaviour or culture of a group of people.

nations, non-white peoples (and especially Indigenous peoples) are frequently depicted as "primitive." We are often so accustomed to hearing this term used in uncritical ways and in association with Indigenous peoples, for instance, that we fail to understand how representations of particular groups as exotic or primitive are ethnocentric representations.

Let's analyze what the term "primitive" means. The term harkens back to a colonial period when non-Western peoples were erroneously positioned as "backward" and inferior in a biological, technological, and social sense to white Westerners. It is thus used to denote a group of people who are considered inferior, stuck in "another time," and, comparatively speaking, "uncivilized." The problem, of course, is that there are no primitive peoples, because the concept itself is simply a representation, or a depiction of another group of people based upon a subjective and oftentimes biased comparison with one's own society. Moreover, as we discuss in Chapter 3, markers of what is viewed as progress in our society (e.g., access to technology) are not necessarily viewed as desirable or necessary in other types of societies. So, the very criteria that are often used to label a group as "primitive" are themselves problematic.

Nevertheless, we still see the term "primitive" employed frequently in travel brochures. Since Western tourists tend to consider themselves as civilized, they may feel it is exciting and adventurous, not to mention a break from the stresses of modern life, to travel across the world to view seemingly simple, "primitive" peoples. If, however, you perceive another group of people as primitive, then mistreating and exploiting them become justified. Throughout her fieldwork in Sosua in the Dominican Republic, Denise Brennan (2004) explored the relationships that developed among heterosexual Afro-Dominican and Latina women and white, foreign male sex tourists. Sosua has become a magnet for sex tourism. Heterosexual men, in particular, travel to Sosua to engage in sexual relations with local women who often come from marginalized backgrounds and are reliant upon sex tourism for a source of stable income. When the men are asked why they come so far to engage in sex, they argue that the Dominican women are highly sexualized and are "exotic," "hot," and "primitive" (Brennan 2004, 45) compared to white women back home. The bodies of Dominican women thus become objectified, and their supposedly "exotic" and "primitive" nature is highlighted as a central component of their being. Representations of sex workers as "primitive" have led to their sexual exploitation and mistreatment, ranging from physical abuse at the hands of male sex tourists, to the pervasive view among Westerners that the lives of such women are somehow expendable, given their seemingly inferior, socially marginalized status.

With respect to representation, anthropologists also turn a critical lens upon themselves. An anthropologist who takes a photograph or writes an ethnographic account is crafting a particular representation of a group of people. Anthropologists must therefore ask themselves: Who has the right to produce representations of another group of people, and is there such a thing as a misrepresentation?

The people whom anthropologists study are becoming increasingly vocal in their concerns about how they are depicted. American anthropologist Margaret Mead travelled to American Samoa in 1925 to study adolescent girls' sexual habits; this research led to the publication of her now famous ethnography, *Coming of Age in Samoa* (1928). Throughout her book, Mead painted a picture of Samoan society as peaceful; she also noted that the girls were free to experiment with premarital sex. This acceptance contrasted sharply with American attitudes at the time regarding sexuality, where premarital sex was viewed as taboo. Her ethnography, which was widely read by anthropologists, students, and the mainstream public, cultivated (perhaps unintentionally) a romanticized and "exotic" representation of Samoans for a largely Western audience. Later generations of Samoans critiqued her work, often denying that teenagers engaged in gratuitous sex (Marshall 1993). Some anthropologists are quick

to point out that the "missionization" of Samoans has contributed to the development of stricter moral ideals of sexuality: ideals that, in turn, have affected their perceptions of Mead's text. Even so, their objections raise some interesting questions for anthropology students. What if the anthropologist's interpretations of culture differ from those of his or her informants? And what are the consequences of the representations cultivated by anthropologists?

There are no clear-cut answers for those questions, but it is worth noting that the representations crafted by anthropologists can have long-term ill consequences for the groups being depicted. For example, Napoleon Chagnon studied the Yanomamö, an Amazonian indigenous group in Brazil and Venezuela. He often labelled them as "fierce"

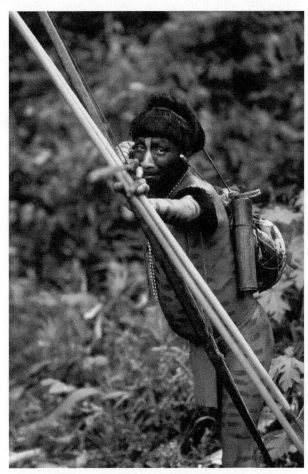

Images, like this one, depict the Yanomamö as fierce and warlike and have resulted in essentialist representations of the tribe.

and warlike. In fact, the title of his ethnography about them is *The Yanomamö: The Fierce People* (1968). Other anthropologists who have studied the Yanomamö (e.g., Ferguson 1995; Turner 2005) have challenged his interpretation of the Yanomamö as fierce. Terence Turner (2005) has argued that representations of the Yanomamö as "fierce" have done them harm. For instance, in the early 1990s, the British government wanted to provide financial assistance for various Amazonian groups for education and medical clinics. But after reading Chagnon's work, they decided that the money would be better spent on reducing levels of "violence" in the community.

Clearly, representations put forward by anthropologists, the mass media, and others have social, economic, and political consequences for various groups. So, it is important for anthropologists to consider the long-term impact of their work in various communities. Increasingly, the writings, films, and other visual and print media produced by anthropologists are read or viewed not only by academics, but also by their informants and their communities, by journalists, by government and nongovernmental organizations, and by others. As such, anthropologists have a responsibility to the people that they work with to ensure that the work they produce does not cause them any harm.

EXERCISE 2.4

Find a Canadian newspaper or magazine article that discusses a particular event involving a "minority" group. Outline how the author of the article represents this group. What words does the author use? What sorts of pictures (if any) are displayed? What is the tone of the article? Who was it written by, and for what audience?

CONCLUSIONS

Over the past century, ethnographic fieldwork has emerged as a defining feature of sociocultural anthropology. To understand cultural phenomena from the perspectives of those we work with and study, we must go into the field (whether or not this is a singular, physical locale or site) to learn about them firsthand. Through long-term fieldwork and the use of various qualitative methods such as interviews and participant observation, anthropologists develop a nuanced understanding of the different beliefs and cultural practices that they encounter in various societies. In addition, fieldwork helps us to comprehend how various societies are influenced by broader social processes, such as the effects of globalization or colonialism.

As discussed throughout this chapter, Bronislaw Malinowski is often credited with being one of the first anthropologists to break away from the "armchair" anthropology that dominated the discipline in the late 19th century. He immersed himself in Trobriand communities, living with his informants, learning the local language, participating in various cultural traditions, and observing aspects of daily life. Malinowski's emphasis upon participant observation stressed the importance of obtaining firsthand knowledge of and developing a sense of rapport with people. Under Malinowski, anthropology developed as a discipline that placed emphasis upon the use of qualitative research methods such as participant observation, stressed the importance of long-term fieldwork in a single locale, and focused largely on the study of Indigenous and non-Western peoples.

Given that anthropology at the turn of the 20th century was heavily influenced by colonialism and that Malinowski himself went to the Trobriand Islands as a guest of colonial administrators, it is not surprising that most early anthropologists "studied down." By this, we mean that there was a tendency to conduct fieldwork among peoples who were less powerful economically, socially, and politically than the anthropologist. Over the last century, however, we have seen gradual changes in anthropological methods and goals.

Anthropology has, indeed, grown and changed over the past century. Although there still exists a tendency for anthropologists from first world or developed nations to study those in developing nations, anthropologists are certainly no longer restricted to the study of "non-Western" peoples and places. Anthropologists are also increasingly cognizant of relationships of power, and more anthropologists "study up," including the study of corporate elites, celebrities, politicians, and others in positions of power and authority. Increasingly, anthropologists conduct fieldwork that is multi-locale and/or multi-sited, which allows them to better address questions about globalization and its implications for cultural beliefs, values, and practices. Despite these changes, the central tenets of ethnography remain the same: anthropologists still strive to systematically collect data that reflect and illuminate an emic point of view, while presenting and analyzing these data from an etic point of view for an audience of (mostly) outsiders. Ethnographic fieldwork, and especially participant observation, involves negotiating complex relationships and requires an ethical commitment on the part of the anthropologist to fairly and accurately treat and depict research subjects at all stages of the research process.

CRITICAL THINKING QUESTIONS

1. In section 2.1, we discuss participant observation, in which the anthropologist both observes and takes part in everyday life in order to understand an emic, or "native's" point of view. Is this objective knowledge or subjective knowledge or something in between? List the reasons for your answer.
2. Discuss some of the changes to fieldwork that have taken place over the past century. What factors do you think are responsible for some of these changes?

KEY TERMS:

armchair anthropology   (p. 40)
culture shock   (p. 47)
emic perspective   (p. 38)
essentialism   (p. 52)
ethnographic fieldwork   (p. 38)
ethnography etic perspective   (p. 38)
informed consent   (p. 51)
multi-sited fieldwork   (p. 45)
participant observation   (p. 41)
qualitative research   (p. 38)
quantitative research   (p. 37)
rapport   (p. 38)
representation   (p. 39)
salvage anthropology   (p. 44)

CHAPTER 3

THE MEANING OF PROGRESS AND DEVELOPMENT

© AFP Photo/Simon Maina/Getty Images

This photo of a fruit seller in the Kibera slum of Nairobi, Kenya, depicts some of the uneven effects of "progress" in the developing world. Below, in the epigraph to this chapter, John Isbister points out that modern technology has penetrated the Third World, but the results have not always been positive, as suggested by the background graffiti: "We want jobs not guns."

One of the myths prevalent about third-world people is that they are unchanging, that their societies are static. One often hears the word traditional used to describe the network of relationships in which they seem trapped. The opposite is true, however. The third world is undergoing rapid and sometimes chaotic social change: populations are growing and becoming more urbanized. Public health measures are lowering death rates ... Modern technology has penetrated the third world and transformed production. Education at all levels is spreading.

The lives of people in the third world are changing. They are not improving, however, at least for the majority. One can find privileged groups, or even entire countries and regions, in which economic conditions have progressed and human and political rights are respected ... These are exceptions, though; most people in the third world are desperately poor.

John Isbister, Promises Not Kept (2003)

Problem 3

How do we explain the transformation of human societies over the past 10,000 years from small-scale, nomadic bands of foragers to large-scale, urban-industrial states?

INTRODUCTION

What Do We Mean When We Talk About Progress?

For thousands of years, all human beings lived as **bands** in small, nomadic groups of 30 to 100 people, gathering wild vegetable foods and hunting large and small game. Ten thousand years ago, however, most human societies began to move away from this mode of livelihood and form of social organization. Today, no human beings anywhere in the world live exclusively by hunting and gathering, although every society in existence is descended from such people.

Today's world is radically divided into wealthy nations and poor nations. Some enjoy a standard of living that gives them abundant food, comfortable shelter, and a plethora of consumer goods, but more than a billion people worldwide suffer from hunger and poverty, live in urban and rural slums, and lack even the basics of healthcare.

bands
A term used by anthropologists to refer to egalitarian units of social organization, found mostly among foragers; these units usually consist of fewer than 100 people.

The gradual shift from a type of society that flourished for thousands of years, and the accompanying creation of a world divided into the wealthy and the poor, poses both a riddle and a moral predicament. The riddle is this: Why, after thousands of years of living as foragers, did some societies begin to change their way of life? Why did they begin to domesticate plants and animals and exchange their nomadic existence for a **sedentary** life in villages and towns? And how, over the next 10,000 years, did these villages and towns come to be divided into rich and poor states? The moral predicament involves our perceptions of the few remaining small-scale societies that exist today and of the millions of people who go hungry each day. Should we assume—as many have and still do—that human beings *chose* to abandon a nomadic, foraging life because they discovered better ways of living? Should we assume that the few remaining small-scale tribal societies are remnants of an inferior way of life and that, given the opportunity, their members would adopt modern farming, wage labour, or urban life? Should we assume that we can explain the world's division of wealth by saying that some nations have progressed while others have not? Or, is the concept of **progress**—namely, that human history has been a steady advance from a life dependent on nature's whims to a life of control and domination over natural forces—a fabrication of contemporary societies based on ethnocentric notions of technological superiority?

Throughout this chapter, we will seek to understand the monumental shift that has occurred in modes of livelihood and social organization over the past 10,000 years without relying on an uncritical use of the concept of progress. As we will see in section 3.5, many anthropological ideas about modes of livelihood can be put to good use outside the academy in the area of development; however, we will also see that "development" only works when we question the assumptions often inherent in the idea of progress. What, exactly, does progress mean, and for whom? And who determines what counts as progress and what does not?

QUESTIONS

3.1 How and why did foraging societies switch to sedentary agriculture?

3.2 How can we explain the vast inequality between the rich and the poor?

3.3 How do economic development, inequality, and cultural diversity relate to one another?

3.4 Have progress and development improved human health?

3.5 How can we apply a critical anthropological understanding of progress and development outside the academy?

QUESTION 3.1: HOW AND WHY DID FORAGING SOCIETIES SWITCH TO SEDENTARY AGRICULTURE?

A thumbnail sketch of what we know about the course of cultural history, modes of livelihood, and social organization will provide a useful starting point for understanding the meaning of progress and development. We will combine what we have learned about human history from the work of archaeologists and historians with information

sedentary
A mode of livelihood characterized by permanent or semi-permanent settlements.

progress
The idea that human history is the story of a steady advance from a life dependent on the whims of nature to a life of control and domination over natural forces.

provided by cultural anthropologists who have worked among contemporary foraging and tribal societies to create a relatively clear picture of **culture change**. Until around 10,000 years ago, humans were scattered in nomadic bands of 30 to 100 people, who lived by gathering wild plants and hunting small and large game. Because the search for food required mobility, it was probably not unusual for them to move every few days. Generally, people had few personal possessions or other forms of material culture. Such items would be a liability and hinder the ability to travel. With groups that were small and mobile, simple economic, social, and political arrangements sufficed: formal leaders were not needed, and there was little occupational specialization. If there was a specialist, it was likely to be a person who was believed to have special spiritual powers that could be used to cure illness or (if used malevolently) to cause illness or death. Kinship served as the main organizing principle of these societies, and social differences among people were based largely on age and gender. Because there was little occupational specialization and little difference in individual wealth or possessions, relations among people likely were egalitarian.

At some point in history, some foragers began to plant crops and domesticate wild animals. These groups became sedentary, living in permanent or semi-permanent settlements of 200 to 2,000 people. They practised **slash-and-burn, or swidden, agriculture**; they cleared forests by burning the trees and brush and then planted crops among the ashes. This land would be cultivated for one to three years; then, another plot of land would be burned and planted.

Larger, more sedentary groups required more formal leadership. Certain members assumed the roles of chief or elder, with the authority to make decisions and resolve disputes. Simple occupational roles developed. Villages consisted of extended family groups, and people organized themselves into **clans**, or groups of 200 to 500 people who claimed descent from a common ancestor. Now

that leadership roles had developed, members of some groups were ranked in importance.

Later in history, perhaps because of a need to defend themselves against other groups, settlements combined themselves under common leaders to form **states** consisting of many thousands of persons. The development of agriculture intensified, and slash-and-burn techniques were replaced by plough or **irrigation agriculture**. Leaders organized labour for the purpose of constructing public works such as roads (the Inca Highway), fortifications (the Great Wall of China), and religious structures (pyramids in Mexico, cathedrals in medieval Europe). Hereditary leaders emerged, settlements grew into cities, and competition between groups over available resources spurred the development of standing armies.

As technological complexity increased, people began to develop specific skills and to specialize in occupational tasks (e.g., herder, baker, butcher, warrior, potter); that occupational specialization led to increased trade and to the evolution of a merchant class. Some 300 years ago, some of these hierarchical societies began to develop into large-scale, industrialized states, which are now found all over the world. Table 3.1 summarizes this sketch of human social and cultural history.

---

culture change
The changes in meanings that a people ascribe to experience and changes in their way of life.

slash-and-burn, or swidden, agriculture
A mode of livelihood in which forests are cleared by burning trees and brush, and crops are planted among the ashes of the cleared ground.

clans
Unilineal descent groups whose members claim descent from a common ancestor.

states
Forms of society characterized by a hierarchical ranking of people and centralized political control.

irrigation agriculture
A form of cultivation in which water is used to deliver nutrients to growing plants.

TABLE 3.1 SUMMARY OF THE DEVELOPMENT OF SOCIETIES FROM GATHERERS AND HUNTERS TO AGRICULTURAL STATES

	HUNTERS AND GATHERERS	HORTICULTURALISTS	STATE SOCIETIES
Population density	Approximately 1 person per 2.6 square kilometres.	Approximately 10 to 15 people per 2.6 square kilometres.	Approximately 300 people per 2.6 square kilometres.
Subsistence	Hunting, gathering, and fishing.	Slash-and-burn agriculture with mixed livestock herding.	Plough or irrigation agriculture.
Work, labour, and production	Very high yield relative to labour expended.	High yield relative to labour expended.	High labour needs relative to yield. High degree of occupational specialization.
Political organization	Informal political organization. Few, if any, formal leaders. Conflict controlled by limiting group size, mobility, and flexibility of group membership. Little intergroup conflict.	More formalized political organization, often with well-established leaders or chiefs. Increased population density and wealth result in increased potential for conflict. Intergroup warfare, motivated by desire for wealth, prestige, or women, is common.	Highly developed state organization with a clear hierarchy of authority. Often a two-class society with rulers (landowners) and peasants. Authority of the elite backed by organized use of force (police or army). Warfare for purpose of conquest is common. Well-established mechanisms for resolving conflict (e.g., courts) exist side by side with informal mechanisms.
Social organization	Small family groups, whose major purpose is economic cooperation. Few status distinctions other than those of sex and age. Marriage for economic partnership and interfamily alliance.	Emphasis on extended family groups. Descent important for the distribution of wealth and property. Status distinctions based on wealth are common, but status mobility is usually possible.	Emphasis on nuclear family. Family is strongly patriarchal, with women holding low status. Strong bonds of intergenerational dependence are built on inheritance needs. Social distinctions between people are emphasized, sometimes based on occupations. Little or no status mobility.

Does the Idea of Progress Help Us Understand the Shift from Foraging to Sedentary Agriculture?

As we have seen, the shifts in modes of livelihood from foraging to horticulture to agriculture were accompanied by major social and cultural shifts. From the earliest days of their discipline, anthropologists have sought to explain these shifts. One possible explanation for why societies transformed themselves in this way is that human inventions resulted in better ways of doing things; in other words, human culture progressed. In the past 30 years, however, anthropologists have begun to question the idea that the life of foragers was harsh and difficult. In this section, we discuss the work of two early and influential anthropologists, Lewis Henry Morgan and Leslie White, who developed explanations of culture change based on the idea of progress.

We then explore case studies of foraging, slash-and-burn, and industrial agriculture; finally, we discuss the work of anthropologists who argue that agriculture is *not* the easiest mode of livelihood, nor is it the most efficient. If the notion of the steady march of progress through time does not adequately explain the shift in modes of livelihood, what does?

Evolutionary Explanations for Culture Change: Lewis Henry Morgan and Leslie White

One possible reason why foragers chose at some point to settle down and domesticate plants and animals is that sedentary agriculture was an easier, less dangerous, and more productive way to get food. People who discovered that they could plant and harvest crops and domesticate animals instead of searching for their food began to do so. According to this explanation, they had *progressed*.

The idea that change occurs because of a desire to progress is entrenched in Western societies, and beginning in the 19th century, anthropologists contributed significantly to this view. Many early anthropologists in the mid- to late-19th century were inspired by the work of British naturalists Charles Darwin and Herbert Spencer and their ideas of evolution.

In the 1830s, Darwin embarked upon a scientific voyage around the world on the HMS *Beagle*. Among other things, he documented physical variations in different species of non-human animals and plants, arguing that such processes as **natural selection** contributed to the formation of new species. Darwin published his theories of evolution in 1859 in his book, *On the Origin of Species*. Within the developing academic discipline of anthropology, many scholars misappropriated many of Darwin's ideas and applied them to the study of human societies. While Darwin's original publication dealt with notions of *biological* evolution, or physical, bodily changes over time, some scholars felt that his ideas could be applied to the study of social change, or how *societies* changed over time.

Meanwhile, the British philosopher and naturalist Herbert Spencer was working on his own theories of evolution; he suggested that change can be understood as progress over time and, moreover, that an end point, or final goal, exists for human societies. Spencer felt that, like biological organisms, societies grow, expand, and increase in complexity over time, and that the more complex and "advanced" a society was, the more "evolved" it was. While this link between social change and progress is considered ethnocentric by today's anthropological standards, notions of social progress would influence many early anthropologists via the theory of **unilineal evolution**.

Lewis Henry Morgan, for instance, was influenced by, and became a proponent of, unilineal evolutionary ideas, which posit that all societies go through a series of uniform, standardized stages of social evolution. Such theories typically (and ethnocentrically) positioned Western societies at the apex of a "ladder of civilization" and were informed by Morgan's own culturally informed notions of progress. Morgan, a lawyer in Rochester, New York, took a great interest in the historical evolution of culture, and he offered his own variant of unilineal evolution to explain how humankind had progressed. Morgan sent out questionnaires to travellers and missionaries all over the world asking them about the family organization and kinship terminology of the cultures they visited.

In *Ancient Society* (1877), Morgan postulated a unilineal theory of human development in which

natural selection
Refers to Darwin's idea that the survival of different species of organisms is partly contingent upon how well adapted they are to their physical environments. Those with favourable physical traits are more likely to survive to reproduce.

unilineal evolution
A late-19th-century theory of social evolution which posited that all societies go through a series of standardized stages of change. It ethnocentrically positioned Western societies at the apex of a "ladder of civilization."

human societies evolved through three stages that he labelled savagery, barbarism, and civilization. He further divided savagery and barbarism into early, middle, and late stages. Some societies—notably the United States, according to Morgan's theory—had evolved completely to civilization; others had yet to complete their transformation and remained in the stage of savagery or barbarism. The passage of societies from one stage to the next, Morgan reasoned, required some major technological invention. Thus, the advance from early to middle savagery was marked by the control of fire; from middle to late savagery, by the invention of the bow and arrow; from late savagery through late barbarism, by the invention of pottery, agriculture, and animal domestication; and so on. Eventually, some societies had progressed to civilization.

Particularly problematic with this model is the erroneous notion that "progress" can be universally defined by, and reduced to, technology. We must remember that Morgan, like all anthropologists, was a product of his times; he was influenced by developments that were occurring within Western nations like his own at the time of his writing. For example, the **Industrial Revolution** and the growth and dissemination of capitalism as the world's dominant economic model would undoubtedly have had an impact upon how he interpreted various societies. One consequence of the Industrial Revolution was the proliferation and dissemination of cheap, mass-produced goods—the result of standardization and mechanization within the context of factory labour—and the development of a middle class of mass consumers. Within this context, the accumulation of material things would become a measure and marker of one's "success" or social progress.

Industrial Revolution
A period of European history, generally identified as occurring in the late 18th century, marked by a shift in production from agriculture to industrial goods, urbanization, and the factory system.

Think about how many people in our society today, for instance, measure their success through the purchase and/or consumption of material culture: obtaining the "right" car or house, or having a particular brand of clothing or mobile phone. Although technology and material culture (for better or worse) are distinctive markers of success and progress within Western nations such as Canada, can we apply such notions of progress universally? What about nomadic hunting and gathering societies, for whom material culture and the accumulation of possessions may be a liability? The use of technology as a defining feature and marker of progress may be ethnocentric, but nonetheless, ideas about unilineal evolution have had a lasting impact upon how we think about different societies and culture change. Indeed, other writers —including many anthropologists—elaborated on Morgan's scheme, assuming, as he did, that humankind was progressing and would continue to do so.

For example, in the mid-20th century, Leslie White formulated what would be one of the more influential evolutionary schemes to explain the historical development of culture. Like Morgan, White saw technology as the driving force of cultural evolution. From his perspective, human beings sought to harness energy through technology and to transform that energy into things they required for survival, such as food, clothing, and shelter. By means of technology, energy was put to work, and the amount of food, clothing, or other goods produced by the expenditure of energy was proportional to the efficiency of the technology available. Because foragers had only their own muscle power to work with, the amount of energy produced by their work was limited. Once technological advances, such as the plough, the water wheel, and the windmill, enabled people to grow more crops and to domesticate animals, they were able to harness more and more energy for their own use. Still later, new forms of energy as in coal, oil, and gas were harnessed by means of steam engines and internal combustion engines, and the amount of energy human beings could control again leaped forward.

From White's perspective, cultural development varied directly with the efficiency of the tools employed. Technology that was more efficient allowed human societies to transform more energy to fulfill their needs; these societies could then produce more food and support larger populations. At some point, increased efficiency in food production allowed a few people to produce enough food for everyone, freeing others to develop different skills and thereby promoting occupational specialization. Specialization led to widespread trade and the development of commerce. Population growth and increased contacts among groups led to the development of states capable of coordinating group activities and organizing armies to defend group wealth.

EXERCISE 3.1

It is easy to look back at 19th-century anthropological theories, such as Morgan's theory of unilineal evolution, and critique them as being unduly influenced by norms and concerns of the time. It is more difficult to think about how more historically recent theories for thinking about human difference and social change are also culturally and historically situated. What kinds of contemporary issues might shape our theories for understanding humanity, progress, and development today? What kinds of scientific theories from other disciplines might we see imported into sociocultural anthropology?

What Are the Shortcomings of These Theories of Progress?

White's view of technology as the driving force in cultural evolution was highly influential in 20th-century anthropological theory. As with Morgan, White's theories encapsulated a point of view that many people hold to this day: that

technology is the true measure of progress, and that the more energy human societies can harness through the development of new power sources, the more social, economic, and political problems they will solve.

Technological progress remains a popular explanation for why societies transformed themselves, and many people continue to view technology as the solution to ongoing world problems. Yet even during the 20th century, some anthropologists were questioning the progress theory. Spurring these new doubts were studies of foraging societies that suggested the life of a nomadic forager was not nearly as harsh and dangerous as had been supposed. In fact, some anthropologists, such as Marshall Sahlins (1968), were beginning to suggest that foraging represented "the original affluent society," with minimal work and plenty of leisure time.

One of the first suppositions about life in foraging societies to be challenged had to do with the roles of males and females. Studies found that contrary to common belief, the gathering activities of women produced by far the greater share of food in these societies; men hunted, but except in areas such as the Arctic and Subarctic, meat and fish constituted only about one quarter of the diet. A second supposition—that foragers often went hungry—proved to be unfounded. Apparently, they had plenty of food. Moreover, contrary to opinion, they did not have to work very hard to get it. These findings raise two questions: Why did most foragers shift away from their mode of livelihood? And why do we often explain this shift in terms of progress?

Life Among Foragers: The Hadza and Ju/'hoansi

When James Woodburn studied the Hadza in the 1960s, they were a small group of nomadic foragers in Tanzania. Woodburn (1968) described their territory as dry, rocky savanna, characterized by one traveller as "barren land" and "desert." Foragers are often depicted as living on the verge of starvation, yet Woodburn found the Hadza area rich in food and resources. Wild game, such as elephant, giraffe, zebra, and gazelle, was plentiful. Plant foods—roots, berries, and fruits—were also abundant for those who knew where to look; they constituted about 80 percent of the Hadza diet. The Hadza spent about two hours a day obtaining food.

Hadza women were responsible for almost all the plant food gathered; hunting was exclusively a male activity. The men hunted with bow and poisoned arrows; at the time Woodburn lived among them, they used no guns, spears, or traps. The Hadza considered only meat as proper food and would say they were hungry when there was none; but there was, in fact, plenty of food available. For a Hadza to go hungry, Woodburn noted, was almost inconceivable. Plant food was so plentiful that the Hadza made no attempt to preserve it. Physicians who examined Hadza children in the 1960s found them in good health by tropical standards. Woodburn found that, from a nutritional point of view, the Hadza were better off than their agricultural neighbours.

The Ju/'hoansi[1] peoples of Namibia's Kalahari Desert are another foraging society that has contributed extensively to what anthropologists have learned about small-scale societies. Lorna Marshall, assisted by her children Elizabeth and John, began research among the Ju/'hoansi in the 1950s. Their work, along with intensive studies by Richard Lee and others, has provided us with a good description of Ju/'hoansi foraging activities. There is some controversy in anthropology over whether the Ju/'hoansi have always been foragers, but that was the way they lived when they were visited by the Marshalls and Lee during the 1960s.

Ju/'hoansi groups lived around water holes, from which they would wander as far as 10 kilometres in search of plant and animal foods. Their groups numbered from 30 to 40 people during the rainy season, when water holes were full and plentiful, but increased to 100 to 200 during the dry season, when only the larger holes retained water. Lee (1969) found that the food quest was constant among the Ju/'hoansi, as it was among the Hadza. They did little food processing, so they had to get food supplies every third or fourth day. Vegetable foods constituted 60 to 80 percent of the diet, and women gathered most of it, producing two to three times as much food as men.

Lee reports that the Ju/'hoansi never exhausted their food supplies. The major food source was the mongongo nut, which is far more nourishing than our own breakfast cereals and contains five times the calories and ten times the protein of cooked cereals (see Table 3.2). Mongongo nuts provided more than 50 percent of the Ju/'hoansi caloric intake; there are 1,260 calories and 56 grams of protein in 300 nuts. Ju/'hoansi territory contained more than 80 other species of edible plants, most of which they did not even use; they did, however, eat about 20 species of roots, melons, gums, bulbs, and dried fruits. In addition, meat was provided by an occasional giraffe, antelope, or other large game animal, as well as by the more usual porcupine, hare, or other small animal. Their meat intake was between 80 and 90 kilograms per person per year—an amount comparable to the meat consumption in developed countries.

In other words, Lee (1969) found that the environment of the Ju/'hoansi provided ample readily

Readily available plant foods were the mainstay of the Ju/'hoansi diet. Here, Ju/'hoansi women gather plant resources.

© David Cayless/Getty Images

[1] The terms that societies use to refer to themselves are often different from those assigned by others. Unfortunately, the latter sometimes become more widely accepted than the former. The Ju/'hoansi, for example, were referred to as "Bushmen" by Europeans and later as "!Kung" by anthropologists.

TABLE 3.2 THE MONGONGO NUT*—NUTRITION FACTS

SERVING SIZE 100 G			
Total fat	57 g		
Saturated fat	10 g		
Polyunsaturated	14 g		
Monounsaturated	10 g		
Protein	24 g		
Calcium	193 mg	Magnesium	527 mg
Iron	3.7 mg	Copper	2.8 mg
Zinc	4 mg	Vitamin B1 (Thiamine)	0.3 mg
Vitamin B2 (Riboflavin)	0.2 mg	Vitamin B3 (Nicotinic Acid)	0.3 mg
Vitamin E	565 mg		

* Mongongo nuts, the main staple of the Ju/'hoansi diet, are rich in nutrients and provide the core of a balanced diet.

Source: Adapted from Richard Borshay Lee (1973) Mongongo: The ethnography of a major wild food resource, Ecology of Food and Nutrition, 2:4, 307–321, Routledge.

accessible food. Their diet consisted of some 2,300 calories a day, with a proper balance of protein, vitamins, and minerals. If the Ju/'hoansi diet was deficient, it was in carbohydrates, since there was no equivalent to our white bread, pasta, rice, or sugar.

The Ju/'hoansi did not spend much time getting food. Lee conducted a careful study of Ju/'hoansi work habits. During the first week in which he recorded the time spent getting food, he found that individuals averaged 2.3 days at this work, with a typical working day of six hours. Overall, the average time spent getting food was 2.4 days, or less than 20 hours of work per week. The most active person Lee observed worked at obtaining food an average of 32 hours a week. Other time was spent doing housework or mending tools.

Lee concluded that, contrary to the stereotype that foragers struggle with limited technology to obtain the food they need for survival, they do not have to work hard to make a living. He added that the idea that foraging societies struggle for existence is an ethnocentric notion that assumes that our own technologically oriented society represents the pinnacle of development. If Lee, and others, are correct about foragers' ease of survival, and if their life is not harsh and dangerous, why did those foragers of 10,000 years ago abandon their old practices, begin to domesticate crops and animals, and settle in permanent villages and towns?

EXERCISE 3.2

Make a list of what you think are the advantages and disadvantages of life 10,000 years ago. Compare it to a list of what you think are the advantages and disadvantages of contemporary life in an industrialized society. Which way of life do you consider more affluent, and why?

THE MEANING OF PROGRESS AND DEVELOPMENT

The Transition to Agriculture

There is a perspective on cultural change that views the gradual shift from foraging to modern, industrial society less as development or progress and more as a necessary evil. This perspective emphasizes the influences of population growth and **population density**—defined here as the number of people living in a given area. To understand this point of view, we need to examine the transition from foraging to agriculture while also exploring the reasons for the eventual change from relatively simple slash-and-burn agriculture to more complex, labour-intensive irrigation agriculture. Comparing modern agricultural techniques with less complex methods used in the production of potatoes will also illustrate the point.

Anthropologist Mark Cohen set out to explain why individuals or groups abandoned foraging for agriculture and why so many did so in a relatively short time. First, he examined the reported food-gathering strategies of foraging societies. Foragers settle in a given area to collect food; then, as food resources decline in one spot, they enlarge the area within which they travel in search of them. Imagine this area as a series of concentric circles; as the outer circles are approached from the centre, the group may decide to move to another area where food is more plentiful in order to reduce the distance that members must travel. Cohen suggests that when population density in a given geographical area reached a point where different groups began to bump into one another, or found they had to travel farther and farther to get enough food to feed a growing population, they began to cultivate their own crops. He notes that anthropological and archaeological evidence suggests that they knew how to do this all along, but chose instead to gather crops until the labour involved in travelling to new food sources surpassed the labour involved in growing crops. In other words, the historical transition

population density
The number of people in a given geographic area.

from foraging to simple agriculture was a necessary consequence of population growth rather than a consequence of a discovery or invention that was adopted because it made life better. In a limited way, of course, this transition from gathering to cultivating did make life easier; when people began to harvest crops in a limited area and remained in villages, groups no longer needed to travel as much. However, Cohen and others argue that agriculture did not improve life at all; in fact, it made life worse (a claim we explore later in this chapter).

In most parts of the world, when societies abandoned foraging, they likely began to adopt slash-and-burn agricultural techniques. Slash-and-burn, or swidden, agriculture can be practised by relatively small, kinship-based groups. As a form of growing crops, it is highly efficient and productive. The Kuikuru, who inhabit the central Brazilian rainforest, annually produce about 5 million calories per hectare of land farmed—enough to feed five people more than 2700 calories per day for a year. Moreover, the Kuikuru work only about two hours a day.

Swidden agriculture, however, requires large tracts of available land because after a plot is farmed for a couple of years, it must lie fallow for 20 to 30 years to allow the brush and trees to grow back so that it can be used again. If the population and thus the amount of land needed to feed it both increase, plots must be used more frequently, perhaps every five or ten years. When land is cultivated more frequently, though, the yield per acre declines. Thus, swidden agriculture is efficient only as long as the population and the amount of land available remain constant.

Farmland may become scarce not only because of increasing population but also because of environmental changes or the encroachment of other groups. Then new agricultural techniques must be developed to increase the yield on the available land. The digging stick may be replaced with the plough, or irrigation systems may be devised, and developments like these require a great deal of labour. In other words, the more food the group needs to produce, the more complex the technology needed to produce it; the more complex the technology, the greater the amount of work involved. Note that this contradicts the idea that the shift from simple to complex technologies always makes life easier.

Tables 3.3 and 3.4 demonstrate the relationships among land, labour, population, and methods of agriculture. Table 3.3 indicates that the amount of labour required to produce a harvest increases with the complexity of agricultural techniques. For example, it requires up to ten times more labour to produce a harvest with irrigation agriculture than it does to produce one with swidden agriculture.

Why, then, abandon swidden agriculture? The answer: There is not enough land to support the population. Table 3.4 lists the amount of land needed to feed 100 families using various agricultural methods. For example, as little as 36.5 hectares of land are required to feed 100 families if irrigation agriculture is used, while around 1,200 hectares are needed if swidden agriculture is used. If a group has enough land, it might as well keep its farming methods simple, changing them only if population increases or the supply of land decreases.

But the history of humankind has been marked by an increase in population and an increase in the ratio of people to land. Robert L. Carneiro (1978) outlines the consequences of population density for cultural change.

TABLE 3.3 DAYS OF LABOUR PER ACRE PER HARVEST BY TYPE OF AGRICULTURE

TYPE OF AGRICULTURE	DAYS OF LABOUR PER ACRE
Advanced swidden	18–25
Plough cultivation	20
Hoe cultivation	58
Irrigation agriculture	90–178

Source: Data from Eric R. Wolf, Peasants (Englewood Cliffs, J.J.: Prentice Hall, 1966).

TABLE 3.4 LAND NEEDED TO FEED 100 FAMILIES USING DIFFERENT AGRICULTURAL METHODS

AGRICULTURAL METHOD	NUMBER OF HECTARES NEEDED TO FEED 100 FAMILIES
Swidden agriculture	1,200*
Swidden with garden plots	650*

*Includes unworked land that must be allowed to lie fallow to regain fertility.

Source: Data from Eric R. Wolf, Peasants (Englewood Cliffs, J.J.: Prentice Hall, 1966).

The increase in the number of people relative to the available land creates two problems. First, if there are more people than there is available land to feed them, conflict may arise between people vying for the available resources. Second, if a growing population decides to intensify methods of growing crops, there is a need for greater societal organization. Irrigation agriculture, for example, requires the digging of ditches, the building of pumps to bring water to the fields and to drain water from them, and the coordination of one and sometimes two harvests a year. Thus, whether a society deals with an increasing ratio between land and people by intensifying efforts to produce more food, or addresses the problem by denying some people access to the necessary resources, the groundwork is laid for a stratified society to emerge, with the concomitant need for a state organization.

Anthropologists such as Cohen and Carneiro are suggesting, then, that the change from foraging to gradually more labour-intensive methods of agriculture was not a matter of choice. Slash-and-burn agriculture wasn't easier than foraging, and plough and irrigation agriculture was not more efficient than slash-and-burn agriculture. Rather, changes in food production techniques were necessary responses to increases in population or population density, and these, in turn, created the need for more formal, more elaborate political and social institutions, both to organize labour and to maintain order among more and more people.

We might conclude from this—which not all anthropologists do—that the transition from foraging to complex agriculture, and the associated social, political, and economic transformations, do not represent progress. But is it not safe to say that at the very least, Western societies, particularly in North America, use agricultural techniques that are vastly superior to those of small, tribal societies? Those who claim that modern food production techniques are far more efficient than any others point out that in Canada and the United States, only 1 calorie of human energy is needed to produce 210 calories for human consumption; by contrast, foragers produce fewer than 10 calories of food for every calorie they use collecting the food. Others, however, argue that these figures are deceptive. At the same time that we have vastly decreased the amount of human labour required to produce food, they say, we have vastly *increased* the amount of nonhuman energy required. From that perspective, we expend 1 calorie of nonhuman energy in the form of non-renewable fossil fuels (e.g., oil and coal) for every 8 calories we produce.

Industrial Agriculture: Producing Potato Calories

To make this point about energy, John H. Bodley (1985) compared the production of sweet potatoes in New Guinea with potato production in the United States.

In New Guinea, people cultivate sweet potatoes by slash-and-burn agriculture; plots of land are burned, cleared, and planted using digging sticks. When the crops are ready, sweet potatoes are cooked in pits and eaten. In one New Guinea community, sweet potatoes accounted for 21 percent of the diet of 204 people. Some of the sweet potatoes were fed to pigs, thus producing protein and accounting for an even larger proportion of the diet. The people used only 10 percent of the arable land, and there was no danger of resource depletion. With their agricultural techniques, the New Guinea farmers could produce about 12.4 million calories per hectare.

Potato farms in Canada and the United States produce more than twice as many calories per acre as New Guinea farmers—about 29.6 million calories per hectare. However, as Bodley points out, in addition to the human energy that goes into North American farming, vast amounts of nonhuman energy are expended. Chemicals must be applied to maintain soil conditions and to control insects and fungus. For example, in the Washington State in the 1960s, 60 percent of the potato acreage was airplane-sprayed five to nine times per season to control insects; another 40 percent was treated for weeds. American potato farmers need specialized machines to cut, seed, harvest, dig, and plant.

In 1969, 36,000 tons of fertilizer was applied to 25,300 hectares—more than 1120 kilograms per hectare. Thus, while the American system produced more potatoes, the actual energy costs per calorie were lower in New Guinea. Moreover, all kinds of hidden costs from consequences such as soil erosion and pollution were incurred in the United States.

North Americans must also deal with distribution costs, which are minimal in traditional cultures, where most households consume what they themselves produce. In modern industrial societies, where 95 percent of the population is urban, the energy expended in distributing the food now exceeds the energy expended in producing it. If we take the food-producing process as a whole—the manufacture and distribution of farm machinery, trucks, and fertilizer; irrigation projects; food processing; packaging; transportation; truck manufacturing; industrial and domestic food preparation; and refrigeration—we'd discover that the American food industry expends 8 to 12 calories of energy to produce a single calorie of food!

Thus, the human and nonhuman energy required to convert a potato into potato chips is far greater than the energy expended in New Guinea to produce a more nutritious sweet potato! Moreover, North Americans do not fully appreciate the health risks of adding some 2,500 substances to our foods to colour, flavour, or preserve them.

QUESTION 3.2: HOW CAN WE EXPLAIN THE VAST INEQUALITY BETWEEN THE RICH AND THE POOR?

Even if we agree that hunters and gatherers don't struggle for food and that simpler forms of agriculture are more efficient than modern techniques, we still have not explained the vast divisions in the modern world between rich and poor. The pyramid in Figure 3.1 illustrates the economic disparities in the world economy.

FIGURE 3.1   THE GLOBAL ECONOMIC PYRAMID

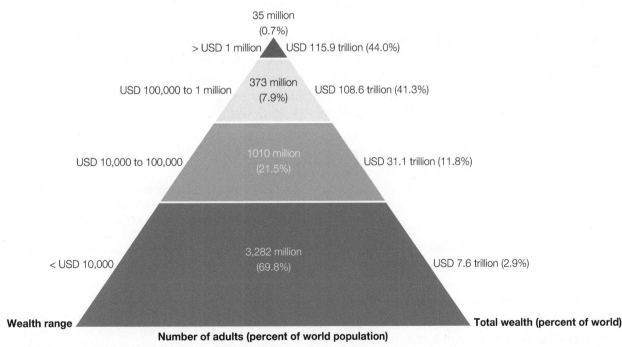

35 million (0.7%)
> USD 1 million   USD 115.9 trillion (44.0%)

USD 100,000 to 1 million   373 million (7.9%)   USD 108.6 trillion (41.3%)

USD 10,000 to 100,000   1010 million (21.5%)   USD 31.1 trillion (11.8%)

< USD 10,000   3,282 million (69.8%)   USD 7.6 trillion (2.9%)

Wealth range   **Total wealth (percent of world)**

Number of adults (percent of world population)

Source: The Global Wealth Pyramid (Figure 3-1) from Davies, James, Luberas, Rodrigo and Shorrocks, Anthony. Credit Suisse Global Wealth Report, 2014. p 24.

The bottom tier consists of the roughly 69.8 percent of the world's population (most from developing nations) who make less than $10,000 per year.

If progress is not the reason, why do most people in the industrial world enjoy a standard of living superior to those who live in underdeveloped countries? That question requires a complex discussion of 300 years of world history. Rather than try to pack three centuries into the next few pages, let's see what we can learn from the story of the expansion of one industry, in one country, during one phase of its development: the textile industry in England in the last half of the 18th century and the first half of the 19th. This period coincides with the advent of colonialism and the Industrial Revolution, which was marked by urbanization, by the factory system, and by a shift in production from agriculture to industrial goods.

The arrival of Christopher Columbus in the Americas and the subsequent "Age of Discovery" marked the advent of a period of European colonialism which has had a lasting legacy on world economics, politics, and ideologies. When Europeans encountered various Indigenous cultures, they often did not know how to interpret the vast differences in customs, religion, kinship, and political organization (among other things) that they experienced. Many even questioned whether Indigenous groups were human. Some felt that they were a sub-species of humans, or even animals.

While such attitudes are clearly ethnocentric by today's standards, such perceptions fuelled the implementation and dissemination of colonial rule. If you position yourself as morally superior or even as more "human" than other peoples, then it becomes easy to justify colonial atrocities such as slavery. As we will see below, European **colonialism** was a system predicated upon exploitative relationships between colonizer and colonized. Without the natural resources and raw materials supplied through slavery or the imposition of exploitative forms of labour upon local populations, European colonies would not have been able to expand their wealth. Indeed, the root of many contemporary global inequalities can be attributed to European colonialism and the advent of the Industrial Revolution.

Before the Industrial Revolution in Europe, the world was significantly different in its distribution of wealth. China was arguably the richest country in the world during the 16th and 17th centuries as gold and silver taken from the mines of South America by the Spanish and Portuguese were funnelled to China to pay for Chinese silks, spices, teas, and luxury goods; India was developing a thriving cotton textile industry as Indian calicoes flooded into Europe. Wealthy states developed in western Africa, and Islamic traders thrived from Africa to Southeast Asia. Seventeenth-century England was a largely rural and agricultural country; even by 1700, only 13 percent of the population lived in towns of 5,000 or more. England, however, had long enjoyed a thriving trade in raw wool and inexpensive wool textiles.

In its early days, textile production was largely a handicraft industry, and most steps in the production of wool cloth, from cutting and degreasing the wool, to dying and spinning the thread, to weaving the cloth, were in the hands of rural families or small cooperatives. The finished cloth or wool product might be sold at a local market or fair; more often, though, it was sold to urban-based merchants or traders for resale at fairs or for shipment overseas.

The trade in home-produced textiles was profitable for all; however, traders and merchants discovered that they needed to better control the type, quantity, and quality of cloth produced by spinners and weavers. The merchants' first solution to this problem was the **"putting out" system**, whereby merchants supplied weavers with materials and

colonialism
Refers to the acquisition of new territories throughout the world by European powers from 1492 until approximately 1945. Colonizers often imposed new forms of politics, economics, and religion upon colonized Indigenous or other cultures, and frequently exploited local populations for their labour.

"putting out" system
A means of production, common in the 16th and 17th centuries and surviving today, in which a manufacturer or merchant supplies the materials and sometimes the tools to workers, who produce the goods in their own homes.

required them to produce cloth of the desired type. Some merchants supplied only the wool, cotton, or linen, while others supplied everything, including the looms. The merchants delivered the supplies and tools and picked up the finished products, generally paying the producers for each piece produced. Putting out had many advantages for textile merchants: it gave them more control over production; it ensured cheap labour, for it brought women and children into the production process; and if demand for textiles slackened, the merchants could easily control how much was produced by limiting the materials they put out.

Increasingly, however, beginning in the 18th century, English merchants found it expedient to transform the "putting out" system into a **factory system** by bringing the spinners, weavers, and others together in one location to produce the cloth. Factories were neither new nor unique to England—factories employing more than 15,000 workers existed in France as early as 1685. Furthermore, merchants were not particularly anxious to invest in factories. Profits from manufacture were not nearly as great as profits from trade, especially long-distance exchange. Moreover, removing people from home-based families to urban-based factories required new mechanisms of discipline and control—a fact that explains why early factories were modelled on penal workhouses and prisons. Finally, the entrepreneur, who in the past could have halted putting out when demand slackened, now had to keep his factories busy to pay for his investment in buildings and technology. Consequently, he had to create demands for his products.

The only things that made a manufacturing investment attractive were the various government subsidies or laws (e.g., vagrancy laws requiring people to have jobs) that ensured a flow of cheap labour. Textile manufacturers were able to draw

on workers who had been forced from their land by the enclosure laws, which were pushing peasant farmers off their common lands at the behest of landowners, who wished to grow crops for sale to England's growing population. Since there were no minimum wage laws or laws restricting child labour, factory owners could exploit the cheap labour of women and children; thus, by 1834, children under 13 represented 13 percent of the British cotton industry, and by 1838, only 23 percent of textile factory workers in England were adult men. In addition, government played a major role in creating and defending overseas markets as well as sources of raw materials such as cotton.

The expansion of the textile industry had multiple effects. For one thing, it fuelled the growth of cities: by 1800, one-quarter of the English population lived in towns of 5,000 or more; and Manchester, a textile-manufacturing centre, grew from 24,000 inhabitants in 1773 to more than 250,000 by 1851. Moreover, factories spurred technological development. Mechanization of the textile industry began in earnest with Kay's flying shuttle in 1733, which doubled the weavers' output.

Spinners could not keep up with the need for thread for the new looms, however, so bottlenecks developed. To meet this need, James Hargreaves introduced, in 1765, the spinning jenny. In 1769, Richard Arkwright invented the water frame; then, in 1779, Samuel Crompton developed a spinning mule that combined features of the water frame and the jenny. Finally, in 1790, steam power was added to the production process. These inventions generated a staggering increase in textile production. A hand spinner in 18th-century India took more than 50,000 hours to process 100 pounds of cotton into thread; in England, Crompton's mule reduced that to 2,000 hours; the power-assisted mules of around 1795 reduced this time still further, to 300 hours. By 1825, it was taking only 135 hours to process 100 pounds of cotton.

The growth of the textile industry produced great wealth and employed millions of workers but led to two problems. In economic terms, the growth

factory system
A system of production characterized by the concentration of labour and machines in specific places. It is associated with the Industrial Revolution.

THE MEANING OF PROGRESS AND DEVELOPMENT

Three inventions that revolutionized the textile industry (clockwise): the flying shuttle, the water frame, and the spinning mule. These inventions were intended to increase product output and human efficiency. Both adults and children served as labourers within the textile industry.

transformed England into the wealthiest country in the world. And textiles were not, of course, the only industry that expanded—trade, the manufacture of iron, and food production further increased the wealth of the growing British empire. However, where was the market for all these textile products to be found? And where were the raw materials—notably the cotton—to come from?

Some historians point to the large domestic market available to English textile producers in the wake of the growth of the English population from 6 million in 1700 to 9 million in 1800. Moreover, English textile manufacturers were able to sell much of their product to markets in Europe and the growing markets of the Americas. But there

was still competition for these markets. England was not the only textile producer; Holland, France, and Spain were busy competing (and often fighting among one another) for overseas markets as well as for sources of raw materials. This competition, and the growing military superiority of Western Europe, often had dire consequences for once-prosperous industries in other parts of the world. The story of textiles in India is instructive.

The British in India

Mughal India of the 17th century was an empire created by Turks from Turkestan, who made their chief, Babur, the first Mughal emperor in 1527.

India was a major trading country, and centuries-old trade networks linked India to Europe, the Islamic world, and China. In 1690 the British East India Company was granted a monopoly in East Asian trade by the British government. A relative latecomer to the Indian trade, it established a trading centre in Bengal, in the city of Calcutta. "John Company," as it came to be known, soon had some 150 posts in India, which traded for fine silks, cotton, sugar, rice, saltpetre, indigo, and opium.

In the 1750s the British provoked the rulers of Bengal into war, defeating them conclusively in 1757. In the aftermath of their victory in Bengal, they plundered the state treasury of some £5 million and gained control of 10,000 Bengali weavers. By 1765, John Company was the civil administration of Bengal. It promptly increased the tax burden on peasants and artisans, which led to serious famines in 1770 and 1783. From its base in Bengal, moreover, the company began to extend its control over much of the Indian subcontinent.

Before the British military takeover, India had been producing cloth that was cheaper and better than English textiles; in fact, Indian cottons and calicoes —named after the city of Calicut—were the craze of Europe. To meet this challenge, the British government prohibited the British East India Company from importing calicoes into England. To take advantage of the import restriction, English factories began producing copies of popular Indian textiles for sale both in England and abroad. In addition, India was required to admit English manufacturers free of tariffs. These actions effectively destroyed what had been a thriving Indian textile industry. Although India was still a major producer of raw cotton, Indian cotton was not preferred or favoured by English or American manufacturers; however, China was willing to import plenty of it.

The British, and Western European nations in general, had a problem with trade into China. Chinese products, notably tea, were in high demand, but the Europeans were producing little that the Chinese wanted or needed. There was a market in China for opium, however, and by 1773, the British East India Company had a monopoly over opium sales. Opium was illegal in China, but the Chinese state seemed incapable of cutting off supplies. Smuggling opium into China was hugely profitable for British merchants, as well as for the Americans and the French. When the Chinese government tried to halt the trade in 1839 by seizing opium held by British merchants in warehouses in Canton, the British government intervened militarily and forced the Chinese government to stop enforcing its own opium laws. An analogy today might be the government of Colombia sending troops to the United States or Canada to force acceptance of Colombian cocaine shipments. Moreover, the British demanded and received additional trading rights into China, further opening a market, not only for opium but for textiles as well.

The British-led opium trade from India to China had three results. First, it reversed the flow of money between China and the rest of the world: during the first decade of the 19th century, China was still enjoying a yearly trade surplus of 26 million silver dollars; by the third decade, 34 million dollars per year were leaving China to pay for opium. Second, estimates are that by the end of the 19th century, one out of every ten Chinese was addicted to opium. Finally, textile exports from England to India and China increased from 6 percent of total British exports in 1815, to 22 percent in 1840, 31 percent in 1850, and more than 50 percent after 1873.

Cotton, Slavery, and the Trail of Tears

Cotton and the British textile industry also figure into the story of slavery and the removal of thousands of Native Americans from their homeland in the United States. The British were able to sell raw Indian cotton to China, but Indian cotton was not acceptable to European and North American markets. Indian cotton produced a shorter fibre, whereas cotton produced elsewhere, notably in Egypt and the southern United States, produced a longer, more desirable fibre. Cotton production in

THE MEANING OF PROGRESS AND DEVELOPMENT

the Americas was labour intensive, however, and to be profitable, it required slave labour.

Slavery was not created by the need for cotton—as an institution, it was far more ancient than that. It was never uncommon for groups at war to turn captured enemies into slaves. However, the slave trade grew rapidly between the 15th and 19th centuries in response to Europe's economic expansion and the demands of trade. The Spanish required workers for their silver mines; the Spanish, Portuguese, British, and French required cane cutters and millers for their sugar plantations in Brazil and the Caribbean; and Georgia, Alabama, Louisiana, Texas, and Mississippi required labourers for their cotton plantations. Between 1451 and 1600, some 275,000 slaves were taken from Africa to what is now the United States and to Europe. During the 17th century, 1.3 million slaves were forcibly exported from Africa; between 1701 and 1810, the figure was around 6 million. Another 2 million were taken from Africa between 1810 and 1870, many destined for Cuba.

Reliance on slave labour in the United States was closely tied to the rise of the British textile industry. Here, a slave family picks cotton on a plantation near Savannah, Georgia, during the early 1860s.

© Bettman/CORBIS

The production of cotton using slave labour fuelled the Industrial Revolution in the United States. England had long imported raw cotton from its possessions in the West Indies and from Turkey; by 1807, however, half its supply was from the United States. In fact, between 1815 and 1860, raw cotton constituted half the value of domestic exports from the United States.

The American cotton industry grew so rapidly, in part, because of Eli Whitney's cotton gin, an invention that efficiently separated the seeds from the raw cotton fibre. The gin allowed a person to clean cotton 50 times more quickly than in the past. American cotton production increased enormously as a result: from 3,000 bales in 1790 to 178,000 in 1810, 732,000 in 1830, and 4.5 million in 1860. But to be competitive, cotton production required cheap labour, and slave labour was half the price of wage labour. Each plantation required between 50 and 200 slaves, depending on the quality of the soil.

The British demand for American cotton was obviously not the cause of slavery, but it ensured its continuance in the United States into the second half of the 19th century. Between 1790 and 1860, 835,000 slaves were moved from Maryland, Virginia, and the Carolinas to Alabama, Louisiana, Mississippi, and Texas in one of the greatest forced migrations of all time. But this migration was not the only forced one spurred by the world demand for cotton. Another was the forced removal in the 1830s of 125,000 Native Americans from their homes in Georgia, Alabama, and Mississippi to the Oklahoma Territory, along the route known as the "Trail of Tears" (see Figure 3.2).

The story of the forced removal of the Cherokee (and other Native American nations) in the United States does much to explain why some of the world's people enjoy greater wealth than others. The Cherokee had always been viewed as among the more "advanced" Native American groups—the early European settlers had counted them as one of the "civilized tribes" of North America. They were horticulturists, living in large, autonomous villages

FIGURE 3.2   MAP OF THE TRAIL OF TEARS, SHOWING THE CHEROKEE REMOVAL

and, after the American Revolution, occupying large tracts of fertile land from North Carolina into Georgia. In 1802, to persuade the southeastern states to give up claims to territory in the west, President Thomas Jefferson instituted what became known as the "Georgia Compact of 1802." The Compact called for Georgia and the Carolinas to give up claims to western territories in exchange for land held by southeastern indigenous groups, including the Cherokee. The indigenous people fought the removal, embarking on a modernization plan; within a decade the Cherokee had built plantations, were holding slaves, and had their own newspaper, schools, and alphabet. They were also among the soldiers who served under Andrew Jackson in the War of 1812.

The Cherokee lobbied the U.S. Congress extensively to repeal the Georgia Compact, but to no avail. Andrew Jackson, who had made the removal of Native Americans a cornerstone of his presidential campaign in 1828, signed the final order. The army was sent in to forcibly move the population as land speculators flooded onto what had been prosperous Cherokee farms and plantations. Thousands of additional acres of what had been Cherokee land were taken over or converted to cotton production by white farmers using black slaves. In this way, white farmers using Native American land and African labour to produce cotton for the British and American textile industries created much of the future wealth of the young country. The political economy of cotton production, slavery, and land alienation during this period of history laid the groundwork for ongoing systemic racism in North America, as we discuss in Chapter 7.

Progress for Whom?

To summarize, the growth of the British textile industry produced great wealth for some people, but in the process, it destroyed textile manufacturing in India, led to the colonization of India, escalated imports of opium into China, and extended slavery in the United States while draining Africa of productive labour; it also enhanced the wealth of U.S. settlers while driving Native Americans from their lands. In addition, the mass production of textiles in Britain and elsewhere in Europe destroyed textile manufacture by artisans in areas of the world where British textiles were sold. Further, since women were the main textile producers in many societies, we might also speculate that the textile trade led to a decline in the status of women in these societies.

In assessing progress, we must also open up our critical review. Britain was not the only producer of textiles, nor was it the only country seeking to open and control overseas markets. France, Germany, the Netherlands, and (later) the United States also had thriving textile industries. It is important to remember, too, that the textile industry was only one industry among many in Western Europe that required raw materials and new markets. As a result of the growing European demand for sugar, cocoa, palm oil, tobacco, and coffee, millions of hectares around the world were converted from subsistence farming to cash crop farming; in turn, self-sufficient peasant farmers became dependent wage-labourers or unemployed poor. Finally, remember that we have examined only a brief period of time. The high point of European colonial expansion came later than the events described here, in the last quarter of the 19th century and the first decades of the 20th. By looking at the bigger picture, we can begin to understand why the problems of the non-industrial nations are due less to their own shortcomings than to the exploitative activities of others, and why a peasant farmer in India in 1400

was significantly better off economically than his Indian counterpart of 1960. In the next section, we explore the manifestations of this kind of economic "progress" on a global scale.

QUESTION 3.3: HOW DO INEQUALITY, ECONOMIC DEVELOPMENT, AND CULTURAL DIVERSITY RELATE TO ONE ANOTHER?

The Industrial Revolution radically transformed the lives of people in Western Europe and North America as the vast majority of the population went from being farmers to labourers. Usually, the change of job was not a matter of choice: people began selling their labour not because wage labour offered a better life, but because they no longer possessed land on which to secure a livelihood. Moreover, the availability of jobs was subject to the whims of the market and the rise and fall in the demand for products. As long as there was a demand for products, jobs were secure; when demand slackened, people were thrown out of work. The development of industry in the 19th century was marked by periodic downturns in economic growth and by economic depressions such as those of 1840 and 1873.

Overall, however, the rate of economic growth and technological advancement was astounding and resulted in a dramatic improvement in the standard of living of most people in Western countries. Nevertheless, many in the industrialized world did not enjoy increased wealth, and people in the Third World often saw their living standards decline as their countries fell under the influence of European powers.

As countries began to achieve independence from their colonial masters, new national leaders promised to improve the lives of their people, and the leaders in the rich countries promised to help; hence, the push for what became known as "**economic development**" ensued. Yet as John Isbister, whom we cite in this chapter's epigraph, argues in *Promises Not Kept: Poverty and the Betrayal of Third World Development*, these promises were empty.

The ideology of economic development included the assumption that the world's nonindustrial countries were backward and needed to progress or develop—*develop* being largely a code word for "Westernize." Tania Li, an anthropologist at the University of Toronto, documented how a development project in Indonesia typically began: "First, it is necessary to identify a target group with a deficiency to be rectified ... Second, there needs to be an agency tasked with planning and executing the appropriate development fix" (1999b, 298).

There flourished in the West an unprecedented resolve to know everything about the Third World, which experienced a massive invasion of experts, all of whom were tasked with investigating, measuring, and theorizing about every aspect of Third World societies. In *Encountering Development: The Making and Unmaking of the Third World*, Arturo Escobar suggests:

> development fostered a way of conceiving of
> social life as a technical problem, as a matter
> of rational decision and management to
> be entrusted to that group of people—the
> development professionals—whose specialized
> knowledge allegedly qualified them for the task.
> Instead of seeing change as a process rooted in
> the interpretation of each society's history and
> cultural tradition ... these professionals sought
> to devise mechanisms and procedures to make
> societies fit a preexisting model that embodied
> the structures and functions of modernity.
> Like sorcerers' apprentices, the development
> professionals awakened once again the dream of
> reason that, in their hands, as in earlier instances,
> produced a troubling reality. (1995, 52)

Three key assumptions shaped the idea of economic development that emerged: (1) economic growth and development is the solution to national as well as global problems; (2) global economic integration will contribute to solving global ecological and social problems; and (3) foreign assistance to undeveloped countries will make things better. Thus, countries that wished to develop sought foreign loans and investments to create an industrial infrastructure—dams, power stations, ports, roads, and railways, and so on—as well as schools for training local people to operate these. The loans, then, would allow undeveloped countries to produce export goods such as cotton, sugar, palm oil, tobacco, coffee, and cocoa (as well as other cash crops) and oil, metal ores, lumber (and other natural resources). This theory of economic development was nothing new; what *was* different was the degree of apparent support that the wealthier nations were offering the poorer. One major Western institution that promoted economic development was the **World Bank**.

The World Bank was founded in 1944 in Bretton Woods, New Hampshire, at a meeting of the representatives of major industrial nations. At the time of this conference, the Allied powers were still at war with Germany and Japan (which, of course, were not invited). The task of those attending was to develop plans for the economic reconstruction of those countries that were being devastated by the war and to develop a postwar plan for worldwide economic and monetary stability. It was decided at Bretton Woods

economic development
The term used to identify an increase in level of technology, and by some, standard of living of a population. Others view it as an ideology based on three key assumptions: (1) that economic growth and development is the solution to national as well as global problems; (2) that global economic integration will contribute to solving global ecological and social problems; and (3) that foreign assistance to undeveloped countries will make things better.

World Bank
One of the institutions created at the 1944 Bretton Woods, New Hampshire, meeting of Allied nations. The World Bank (or the Bank for Reconstruction and Development) functions as a lending institution to nations largely for projects related to economic development.

to establish the **International Monetary Fund** (IMF) and the International Bank for Reconstruction and Development (the World Bank). Funds for the bank were to be provided by member nations, largely in the form of loan guarantees. The bank would lend money to governments for specific projects: highways, dams, power plants, factories, and the like; those governments would agree to pay back the loans over a set time. The charter also specified that the loans must be made without regard for political or non-economic factors and that the bank must not interfere in the political affairs of any member or debtor nation.

The World Bank began operating in 1946, with the initial loans going to European countries. But soon the World Bank was making huge loans to countries such as Brazil, India, and Indonesia—loans that were supposed to transform their economies, generate wealth, and alleviate poverty. Many people have argued since that however benign their intentions, these loans only *increased* poverty in the Third World, besides leading to environmental devastation. How could this have happened?

The Case of Brazil

Brazil has been a major recipient of World Bank loans. In the 1960s the Brazilian government made a conscious decision to industrialize. Using loans from the World Bank and other Western lenders, along with money from private investors, Brazil built dams, roads, factories, and industries. It also modernized its agriculture, becoming a world leader in the export of crops such as soybeans. The economy surged, and Brazil became a model of modern industrialization: factories created jobs, and people flocked to the cities for employment as Brazil's cities began to rival any in the West.

> **International Monetary Fund**
> Created as an outcome of the 1944 Bretton Woods Conference to regulate currency transactions among countries. The IMF now makes loans and regulates the economies of lending countries.

But there was a downside: To repay its debts, Brazil needed to earn foreign income. Consequently, landowners were encouraged to expand their production of cash crops, especially those that could be sold in North America and Europe. Since the West already produced more than enough food (American farmers were being paid by the government not to grow food crops), Brazilian farmers turned to crops with other uses, such as soybeans, sisal, sugar, cocoa, and coffee. To grow more of these products required modern farming techniques and lots of land. Small farmers, forced off their land, had to find farm employment growing cash crops or migrate to the cities in search of jobs that, for the most part, did not exist. Moreover, those who found jobs on the large farms were not paid enough to purchase the food they had once grown themselves on their small plots. Brazil did increase production of some food crops, notably beef, but because poor Brazilians could not pay as much for beef as relatively wealthy North Americans and Europeans could, most Brazilian beef was exported.

To make matters worse, in the mid-1980s, Brazil and other debtor countries discovered that they could not keep up their payments to the World Bank and other Western financial institutions. To help these countries avoid default, the World

Between 2000 and 2009, more than 150,000 square kilometres of Amazon rainforest was burned down to make room for cattle farms, soybean farms, and roads. That area is larger than New Brunswick, Nova Scotia, and Prince Edward Island combined.

© luoman/Getty Images

Bank allowed them to renegotiate their loans. First, though, they had to agree to reduce their government spending—and typically, the targets for spending cuts were public education, welfare, housing, and health. These cutbacks resulted in still greater hardships for the poorest citizens.

In the wake of its program for economic development, Brazil has increased its total wealth. Some people have become very rich, but it is estimated that more than 40 percent of Brazilians are still living in poverty. And Brazil is not unique; most of Central and South America, Africa, and Southeast Asia followed the same formula for development, and most of these countries also experienced increased poverty and hunger for the majority of their people.

Economic development brought environmental destruction, as well. Between 1981 and 1983, the World Bank began delivering payments on a loan for Brazil to construct a road through the Amazon rainforest and to build new settlements. The economic goal of the Polonoroeste project was to open vast tracts of Amazon rainforest for settlement by displaced peasants, thereby transforming the forest into a cash producer. Nearly half a million settlers flooded into the area between 1981 and 1986. The government, however, was not prepared for that level of migration, and the new migrants were forced to burn forests to grow food to survive. The poor soil of the rainforests would not support agriculture for more than a couple of years, however, and people ultimately were left with worthless land. The only activity that proved worthwhile was cattle ranching, and that required the burning of still more rainforest. The area of Rondônia went from 1.7 percent deforestation in 1978 to 16.1 percent in 1991. Furthermore, life-threatening diseases developed, rates of malaria approached 100 percent, and infant mortality rates of 25 to 50 percent were not uncommon. Indian land was pillaged, and epidemics ravaged the population. The pesticide DDT (banned in North America) was used in an attempt to eradicate the mosquitoes that spread malaria, and rural violence broke out between ranchers and rubber tappers.

Do Progress and Development Inevitably Lead to Inequality?

Whether the price of progress through industrialization must be increased poverty, hunger, and environmental devastation is, for many, an open question. Many argue that economic and industrial development take time and that countries such as Brazil and India are now beginning to see a marked improvement in their economic situation. Some point to the countries deemed to be newly industrialized, Korea and Taiwan among them, as examples of what can be done. Yet the non-Western countries that have succeeded in emulating the West (and Japan is foremost among these) were never colonized by the West as were the poor countries of Africa and South America.

EXERCISE 3.3

It is 1967. You are members of a task force that the Botswana government has convened to evaluate the living conditions of the Ju/'hoansi. Another group of government officials, distressed over the foraging ways of the Ju/'hoansi, had recommended that they begin to enjoy the benefits of modern technology. Specifically, the group recommended that the government settle the Ju/'hoansi in permanent villages, dig wells to ensure a steady water supply, distribute domesticated animals to ensure a ready food supply, and introduce modern health services. The group had also recommended that jobs be found for the Ju/'hoansi.

You have toured the area and spoken to some of the Ju/'hoansi. Your specific task is to evaluate the recommendations of the previous government task force and make your own recommendations to the government on how the lives of the Ju/'hoansi could be improved. You may agree or disagree with the previous panel, but you must give reasons for your recommendations.

So, are the world's people better off now than they were before the Industrial Revolution?

Obviously, the answer depends on who you are. If you are fortunate enough to be a labourer, business person, or professional in a wealthy country, you are likely to be materially better off than your counterpart of five centuries ago, provided that the price you pay in health risks because of a damaged environment does not offset your material gains. If you are a labourer or small farmer in one of the world's poor countries, it is hard to see how you could be better off than your peasant counterpart of centuries past. If you are among the world's landless, unemployed, or underemployed, or one of the billion without enough food, it is difficult to see how your life could be an improvement over that of your counterpart two centuries before.

QUESTION 3.4: HAVE PROGRESS AND DEVELOPMENT IMPROVED HUMAN HEALTH?

Illness and Inequality

Even if the economic changes of the past two centuries have not improved many people's lives, can't we at least assume that *some* technologies—notably medical technologies—have done so? To answer this question, we need to consider two things: first, whether we have progressed in our ability to treat disease (using the **biomedical model**); and second, whether we fully understand the traditional medical techniques that modern medicine has sought to replace.

One of the supposed triumphs of modern society has been the treatment and cure of disease. Life expectancy more than doubled in the 20th century. In 1900, world life expectancy was around 30 years; by 2000, it was 63 years. Antibiotics save millions of people from death each year, and modern diagnostic methods and equipment allow medical

practitioners to identify the onset of disease more easily. Yet the progress we often take for granted is not available to all. In fact, the single most important determinant of a country's ability to protect its citizens from disease is the degree of economic equality.

In developing countries, infectious disease is responsible for 42 percent of all deaths, compared to just 1.2 percent in industrial countries. Around the world, 40 percent of all deaths are caused by environmental factors, including organic and chemical pollutants. These pollutants are far more deadly in poorer countries, where, for example, 1.2 billion people lack clean, safe water. However, the same contaminants can affect people in wealthy countries such as Canada. On Walpole Island in the St. Clair River, toxins from 52 industrial sources have been found in fish, ducks, and various animals that share the island with the 3,100 people of the Walpole First Nation. This contamination is in addition to a "toxic blob" that was discovered in 1985 (VanWynsberghe 2002). Thus, your income and dwelling place determine your chances of coming into contact with a deadly pollutant. The industrialized countries already ship 20 million tons of waste annually to the world's poorer countries.

We can, perhaps, better judge the extent to which we have "progressed" by examining what it takes for us to die of an infectious disease. At least four things have to happen. First, we have to come into contact with some **pathogen** or **vector** that

biomedical model
Also known as *Western medicine*, *scientific medicine*, or *modern medicine*, the model combines biology with the diagnosis and treatment of illness and views the body as a machine, independent of social context, that must be repaired periodically.

pathogen
An infectious agent such as a bacteria or a virus that can cause disease.

vector
An organism, such as a mosquito, tick, flea, or snail, that can transmit disease to another animal.

carries a disease. Second, the pathogen must be virulent—that is, it must be able to kill us. Third, if we come into contact with a deadly pathogen, it must evade our body's immune system. Finally, the pathogen must be able to circumvent whatever measures our society has developed to prevent it from doing harm. As we will see, our chances of dying are affected at every step by social and cultural patterns, particularly by the degree of economic and social inequality.

Cultural complexity has increased our exposure to infectious agents. Large, permanent settlements attract and sustain vermin such as rats and fleas, which serve as hosts for microorganisms and ensure their survival and spread. Permanent settlements also result in the buildup of human wastes. Sedentary agriculture requires altering the landscape in ways that can increase the incidence of disease. Schistosomiasis, for example, is a disease caused by worms and snails, which thrive in irrigation ditches. The domestication of animals such as dogs, cats, cattle, and pigs increases contact between people and disease-causing microorganisms. Large populations must store and process their food, which also increases the likelihood that disease-causing agents will survive and spread.

Coming into contact with an infectious pathogen is not in itself enough for death to ensue: the pathogen must be deadly. But this, too, depends on your social and cultural situation, including your income. Generally, it is not to the advantage of pathogens—viruses, bacteria, parasites—to kill their hosts; pathogens find it advantageous to allow their hosts to live and supply nutrients. However, if the pathogen does not need its host in order to survive, it can evolve into a more deadly form. Such is the case with waterborne infections. Pathogens that spread by contaminated water can survive regardless of how sick their host becomes, and by reproducing extensively in their host, they make it more likely that they can contaminate water supplies—for example, through bodily wastes. All of this means that you are far more likely to contract a deadly disease if you lack access to clean and treated water.

Even if you come into contact with a deadly pathogen, your immune system is designed to prevent it from killing you. The strength of your immune system, however, is clearly a function of diet, and diet is determined largely by income level. In this respect, we have not progressed. In 1950, 20 percent of the world's people (500 million) were malnourished. Today some 50 percent (3 billion) are malnourished. Insufficient food is one of the principal causes of immune system failure.

Finally, societies have developed methods to cure illnesses that our immune systems have failed to ward off. There is little doubt that the discovery of cures for infectious diseases is one of the great success stories of modern culture. Unfortunately, access to these cures is determined largely by individual wealth. This reality suggests why the United States, the wealthiest country in the world overall, ranks 38th in the world in life expectancy. It is no coincidence that the United States has the largest income gap between rich and poor of any industrialized country. Japan, which has the lowest gap between rich and poor, also has the highest life expectancy, even though Japanese are three times heavier smokers than Americans.

In sum, although we have indeed made dramatic progress in understanding and curing infectious disease, we have made no progress—and, indeed, have gone backward—in terms of our ability to provide access to these cures. At the same time, we have increased global exposure to environmental pollutants and infectious pathogens.

The Meaning of Illness

Even if we conclude that modern societies are more susceptible to contagious diseases, have they not at least improved their technologies for curing illness? In answering this question, it is important to grasp that the meanings members of different societies give to illness vary as much as the meanings they give to other aspects of their lives. In mainstream

North American society, illness is viewed as an intrusion by bacteria or viruses. Our curing techniques emphasize eliminating those agents. Death can occur, we believe, when we have failed to do so.

In many other societies, interpretations of illness are completely different. Illness may be attributed to witchcraft—that is, a witch or sorcerer has used magic to inflict illness on another person. Or it may be attributed to soul loss, or the soul having left the body. Or it may be understood as being about one's connection to the land, as is the case with the Whapmagoostui Cree (discussed in Chapter 1). Or it may be attributed to spirit possession, the idea that a foreign spirit has entered the patient. These explanations are not mutually exclusive; for example, the soul may flee the body as the result of witchcraft or sorcery.

Those who believe that illness has spiritual or magical causes do not believe that a witch or sorcerer strikes at random, that the soul leaves the body without cause, or that a spirit will possess just anyone. Rather, they believe there must be a social reason for these things to occur. Witchcraft involves relationships between people: the witch voluntarily or involuntarily afflicts someone who has caused offence or who has breached a rule of conduct. Likewise, the soul leaves the body of a person who is having difficulty with others, or a spirit possesses a person who has not honoured social obligations.

The Chewa of Malawi in southeastern Africa contend that illness and death are induced by witchcraft when someone fails to observe some social norm. Whereas Americans react to illness or death by seeking the disease or accident responsible, the Chewa ask what wrong the victim has committed, with whom the victim has quarrelled, or who is jealous of the victim. The Chewa explicitly recognize the connection between sorcery and social tension.

A Chewa who becomes ill consults a diviner to discover the cause of the illness. During the consultation, the patient and the diviner discuss the social roots of the illness. The diviner needs to

In a healing ceremony designed to restore the patient to his proper place in the world, a traditional Navajo doctor paints an image of the universe with coloured sand on an earthen floor.

know about the patient's relationships with kin and, if ancestral spirits may be responsible, the genealogy of the patient. Thus, Chewa medical theory, although couched in the idiom of sorcery, is a social theory of illness, not simply a supernatural one.

In Latin America there is a condition called "susto" (also known as *pasmo*, *espanto*, or *perdida de la somba*) that is believed to occur when the soul has detached itself from the body. Symptoms of *susto* include restlessness, listlessness, loss of appetite, lack of interest in dress or bodily appearance, loss of strength, and introversion. The onset of the illness is said to follow a fright brought on by a sudden encounter or accident, and the cure begins with a diagnostic session between the patient and a healer. After deciding what brought on the disorder, the healer coaxes the soul back into the body. The patient is then sweated, massaged, and rubbed with some object to remove the illness.

Anthropologist Arthur Rubel (1964) analyzed specific cases of *susto* and found that all cases share two characteristics. *Susto* occurs only when the patient perceives some situation as stressful and when the stress has been the result of difficulties in social relations with specific people. In one case, a father was afflicted when he discovered he could no longer provide for his family. In another, a mother was stricken when she was not able to take proper care of her child. In every case, according to Rubel, *susto* resulted when a person did not or could not fulfill an expected social obligation.

These theories of illness—soul loss, spirit possession, sorcery, and witchcraft—have one thing in common: all are expressions of the **interpersonal theory of disease**. Simply stated, in the interpersonal theory of disease it is assumed that illness is caused not by microorganisms but rather by tensions or conflicts in social relations. In this view, witches, spirits, and souls are mediating agents that link a social cause—tension and conflict—to a physical result—illness or death.

If an illness has social causes, then the cure, too, must be at least partly social. Therefore, a curer attempts not only to remove a spell, return the soul to the body, or remove a spiritual object that is causing illness, but also to repair the social problem. To illustrate, Victor Turner (1967) provides a look at one society, the Ndembu, an agricultural society in northwestern Zambia.

The Ndembu believe that a persistent or severe illness is caused either by the punitive action of some ancestral ghost or by the secret malevolence of a sorcerer or witch. The ghosts punish people when they forget to make a ritual offering to their ancestors or when, as the Ndembu put it, "kin are not living well together."

To effect a cure, the Ndembu patient consults a native doctor. The doctor first inquires about the patient's social relations: Has he or she quarrelled with anyone? What is the state of the patient's marital relations? Is anyone jealous of the patient? The doctor asks those with whom the patient has quarrelled to participate in the ceremony, which is a dramatic affair with chanting and drumming, sometimes lasting for hours. People who have complaints about the patient's social behaviour may come forward, and the patient may report grudges against neighbours. At the climax, the doctor may dramatically extract from the patient's body some object that could have been causing the illness.

The Ndembu recognize, at least implicitly, that social strain and stress may produce physical illness and that one way to treat illness is to treat the sources of social strain. Western medicine also recognizes the negative health effects that stress can have. Events such as the death of a spouse, the loss of a job, relocation to a new home, or even holidays such as Christmas can increase the chances of illness. These are the same kinds of events that can trigger the need for ceremonial cures in some societies. Thus, rather than viewing the healing practices of traditional societies as inferior, it makes far more sense to recognize that they focus on social stress as a cause of illness.

Cost is another consideration. Ethnomedical cures not only can be beneficial but also are affordable. One consequence of biomedical advances is increasing dependence on expensive technology. Consequently, while significant advances have been made in medicine, the cost to patients of many such advances has made them unavailable to all but a small percentage of the world's population. In societies where healing is everyone's responsibility instead of a commodity to be purchased, it follows the moral values of a social obligation rather than those of business.

interpersonal theory of disease
A view of disease in which it is assumed that illness is caused by tensions or conflicts in social relations.

EXERCISE 3.4

Can you think of any illnesses that we are familiar with in North America that are currently diagnosed and treated according to the biomedical model, but that might also be explained using the interpersonal theory of disease? How might we treat these illnesses from this perspective?

QUESTION 3.5: HOW CAN WE APPLY A CRITICAL ANTHROPOLOGICAL UNDERSTANDING OF PROGRESS AND DEVELOPMENT OUTSIDE THE ACADEMY?

As we have seen, efforts by countries to "progress" and modernize have often undermined the lives of indigenous peoples as well as the lives of craftspeople and small farmers. The idea of progress clearly contains some ethnocentric assumptions about what constitutes the "good life." Very often, the idea of development simply means the export of Western culture to sometimes willing, but often unwilling recipients.

That concern does not mean, however, that efforts should not be made to address economic, social, and human rights problems. In some parts of Brazil, for example, the mortality rate for children under five years is 116 per 1,000; among the wealthiest portion of the population it is 11 per 1,000. Around the world, 24,000 people die every day from hunger or hunger-related causes. Many women around the world have little or no access to education or job opportunities, yet they are responsible for the health and livelihood of their children. In Canada, the 2006 Census found that First Nations people who had been forced onto reserves faced unemployment rates of 18 percent, almost triple the national rate. That same year, only 8 percent of First Nations people had a university degree, compared to 23 percent of other Canadians, and 40 percent of First Nations people over 15 did not have a high school diploma. According to the Indian Affairs ministry, life expectancy among First Nations men is seven years less than for the general male population; for women, the difference is five years. Further, suicide rates are eight times higher for First Nations women and five times higher for First Nations men. The infant mortality rate is 11 per 1,000 live births among First Nations people, compared to 6 per 1,000 for all Canadians. These and other problems need to be addressed by those with the power and money to do so; in the case of First Nations peoples, addressing these problems is a matter of ensuring full and equal citizenship for all Canadians.

Governments, as in Canada's Department of Foreign Affairs, Trade, and Development, and international organizations, such as the World Bank, the United Nations, and U.S. AID (the official U.S. aid agency), along with nongovernmental organizations (NGOs), such as Oxfam, Amnesty International, and Doctors Without Borders/Médecins sans Frontières (MSF), recognize that anthropological perspectives are vital to addressing these problems. As a result, career opportunities have been created for professional anthropologists as well as for people with a background in anthropology. Anthropologists bring cultural expertise to the table, and their critical and ethnographically grounded understanding of what constitutes "progress" (and what does not) can be crucial to ensuring that development initiatives are culturally appropriate.

Anthropologists in Development

The failure of development professionals to understand the cultures and values of the people they are trying to help has had disastrous consequences in the past. The Mackenzie Delta in the western Canadian Arctic has been the home of Inuit, Métis, and Dene peoples for centuries. After the Second World War, the Canadian government wanted to develop the area in order to extract oil, gas, and mineral reserves. The government also wanted to prepare Aboriginal peoples for "modern" life through schooling and wage labour. Planning, however, was top-down, with little or no participation from the people themselves.

The centrepiece of the modernization plan was the construction of a large-scale "science town"

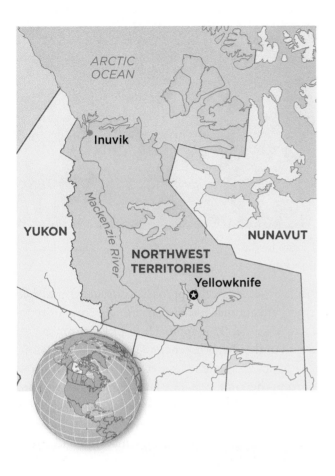

called Inuvik, which was to house a school, a commercial and service centre, and a hospital. The government planners encouraged the establishment of various businesses in the town, including oil companies, hotels, and restaurants.

As Alexander M. Ervin (2001) describes it, the town had a profoundly negative impact on the people of the Mackenzie Delta. Of 5,000 inhabitants, only 150 lived off the land. Half the population were "southerners"—transient workers from southern Canada who were paid generous salaries and allowances to encourage them to resettle, if only for a short time, in the Arctic. Few of the Aboriginal people were employed after the initial building phase, and they were overwhelmed by the social and economic advantages of the southerners. Southerners rarely interacted with the local people, and relations became hostile. School curricula, instead of being designed for northern youth, were modelled after programs in southern urban schools. This problem led to high dropout rates, and the alienation of young people was marked by a dramatic increase in petty crimes and assaults. Aboriginal women who had children with transient whites were stigmatized, and conflicts arose

A failure of development professionals to understand the cultures and values of people has had disastrous consequences in the past. A good example is the construction of the town of Inuvik in the Canadian Arctic.

THE MEANING OF PROGRESS AND DEVELOPMENT

between families with steady incomes and those who depended on government subsidies. All of this stress was evident in high rates of alcohol consumption and of crimes such as assault, theft, and wife battering, all associated with alcohol. Clearly, the government's optimism that the new town would better the lives of the local people was misplaced.

So, what went wrong? There was no consultation with the local Aboriginal people regarding the changes. The entire project had been planned and implemented by outsiders who had pre-existing notions about what would be good for Aboriginal people. Nobody considered the complex interactions among family structure, cultural values, economics, education, and new residents. No one attempted to integrate local knowledge into the planning process. Furthermore, no one considered the unintended consequences of the changes.

Contrast this with an agricultural project designed by anthropologist Ronald Nigh in Mexico. Like other Central American nations, Mexico has lost vast amounts of its rainforest—more than 100,000 square kilometres since the beginning of the 20th century. Much of the deforested land has been taken over by animal pastures, yet more than half of Mexico's population never consumes animal products. According to Nigh (1995), the destruction of the rainforest was the result of the **factory model** of agriculture, which involves producing a single product in as short a time as possible. This form of agriculture is technologically intensive and environmentally damaging. In Central America, the factory model of cattle raising has required that large tracts of land be cleared with fire and herbicides and then reseeded with grasses that are not well suited to the environment. The result has been degradation of the land by uncontrolled grazing and its eventual abandonment and return to secondary vegetation.

In his work, Nigh uses an **agroecological approach** that incorporates indigenous farming techniques, which are far more productive and less damaging to the environment than factory farming.

An agroecological approach produced multiple crops, enhancing the regeneration of land, flora, and fauna.

An agroecological approach produces multiple crops and animals, rather than a single crop, as in the factory model. This approach to production creates a system that helps regenerate land, flora, and fauna.

As an example, consider how the Maya grow corn in the rainforest. The farmers practise swidden agriculture, clearing a site, growing corn there for five to eight years, and then moving on to another site. At first glance, these sites may look identical to land that has been devastated and abandoned by cattle ranchers, but Mayan farmers do not abandon those sites. They continue to work the land so that native plant and animal life will return, eventually creating a highly productive space. The agroecological model, drawing as it does from indigenous systems developed over centuries, creates an ecologically sustainable system of production modelled after natural systems.

Nigh says that a similar model, emphasizing diversity, should be used to rehabilitate lands damaged by cattle grazing. One area of the land would be used

factory model
An energy-intensive, ecologically damaging form of agriculture intended to grow or raise as many crops or livestock as possible in the shortest time.

agroecological approach
An agricultural method that incorporates indigenous practices of food production along with contemporary agricultural research yet preserves the environment.

for annual crops, such as corn or squash. Another can be used for fruit trees and forage. Yet another can be devoted to intensive grazing using selected animal breeds and grasses. Intensive grazing, according to Nigh, frees up rainforest land that should never have been converted to pasture to begin with. He also maintains that by using organic fertilizers and controlled grazing, it is possible to recover aquatic areas and take advantage of water resources such as fish, mollusks, turtles, and birds.

Development projects might begin with good intentions, but they can quickly devolve into ethnocentric, socially damaging institutions. How, then, can development projects provide benefits to everyone involved? As the examples show, an anthropological perspective that carefully considers the cultures and values of indigenous people will go a long way to ease the potential pains of development.

EXERCISE 3.5

As an anthropologist, you have been asked to evaluate the mistakes that were made in the modernization of Inuvik. What are some key questions you would want to ask residents of the town? Which residents would you talk with? What specific questions might you ask women in the town? What recommendations would you make to remedy the problems created by the development project?

CONCLUSIONS

We began this chapter by noting that over the past 10,000 years, human societies have shifted away from a way of life that had survived for some 100,000 years. Why did so many societies begin to change from nomadic foraging to sedentary agriculture? Some anthropologists, such as Lewis Henry Morgan and Leslie White, have suggested that the need to progress and develop better ways of living might explain the change. Studies of forager societies, however, reveal that they live quite comfortably and with minimum effort. Indeed, Marshall Sahlins referred to the foraging way of life as "the original affluent society," characterized by minimal work coupled with ample leisure time.

If we reject the straightforward narrative of progress, how are we to explain the transformation of human societies over the past 10,000 years? It is possible that an increase in population or population density fuelled the transition of societies from foraging to swidden agriculture and then to plough or irrigation agriculture. But although the transition to more labour-intensive forms of agriculture may have been the result of population pressure, other anthropologists have argued that newer forms of agricultural technology may be simply better or more efficient. John Bodley's analysis of the energy expenditures of modern agriculture suggests, however, that it is difficult to conclude it is, in fact, simply better.

Explanations that equate culture change with progress have influenced the trajectory of global economic development. These explanations, though, fall short when we try to understand the gap between the wealthy and poor nations of the world. We find that we must consider the history of the economic expansion of Europe, as well as the military, political, and social exploitation of the countries of Asia, Africa, and the Americas. We find that hunger is not so much due to a lack of modern agriculture; rather, it is a consequence of poverty and attempts to industrialize. The need to repay bank loans secured for industrialization has led countries such as Brazil to encourage the development of large farms that grow mainly cash crops for export. As a result, people are dispossessed of their land and left without enough money to buy food.

For many small-scale societies, global economic development has led to cultural devastation at the hands of "civilized" countries. Unfortunately, notions of progress may simply be a convenient rationale for one society to impose its economic and political will on others. Perhaps when we talk about culture change in terms of progress, we should remember to ask: Progress for whom?

In the last two sections of the chapter, we explored the implications of an anthropological understanding of progress for thinking critically and cross-culturally about health, illness, and development. It may seem self-evident that Western standards of healthcare are higher than those of less developed societies. Researchers have concluded, however, that infectious diseases are more common in industrialized societies and that human behaviours associated with industrialization, modernization, and the unequal distribution of wealth often promote the incidence and spread of contagious disease. Moreover, traditional theories of illness and curing ceremonies can be effective in the diagnosis and treatment of illness or disease. Finally, we examined how an anthropological perspective can aid in planning development projects, and how knowledge of local concerns, the use of local knowledge, and the involvement of segments of the population who are sometimes ignored can mean the difference between helping people and disrupting their lives.

CRITICAL THINKING QUESTIONS

1. In Chapter 1, we discussed the concept of cultural relativism. How might you apply the idea of cultural relativism to the twin concepts of progress and development?
2. Western environmental activists often point to indigenous cultures and modes of livelihood as examples of a more environmentally friendly way to live. What are the possible advantages and disadvantages of this approach, both from the perspective of the environmentalists and from that of the indigenous groups to whom they refer?
3. Given what you have learned about how population, urbanization, agriculture, and technology relate to one another, what predictions might you make about future modes of livelihood and food production?

KEY TERMS:

agroecological approach   (p. 88)
bands   (p. 59)
biomedical model   (p. 82)
clans   (p. 61)
colonialism   (p. 72)
culture change   (p. 61)
economic development   (p. 79)
factory model   (p. 88)
factory system   (p. 73)
Industrial Revolution   (p. 64)
International Monetary Fund   (p. 80)
interpersonal theory of disease   (p. 85)
irrigation agriculture   (p. 61)
natural selection   (p. 63)
pathogen   (p. 82)
population density   (p. 68)
progress   (p. 60)
"putting out" system   (p. 72)
sedentary   (p. 60)
slash-and-burn, or swidden, agriculture   (p. 61)
states   (p. 61)
unilineal evolution   (p. 63)
vector   (p. 82)
World Bank   (p. 79)

CHAPTER 4

CONSTRUCTING REALITIES

© "Morning Star'' by Alex Janvier, Canadian Museum of Civilization, VI-D-276, photo Marie-Louise Deruaz, IMG2009-0085-0001-Dm

Dene artist Alex Janvier's painting, *Morning Star*, as described on the website of the Canadian Museum of Civilization, reflects many common Aboriginal beliefs and values. "Human life, for example, is believed to make a complete circle; a person dies and then life starts again." The Jesuit priest cited in the epigraph below would have been incredulous about the spiritual beliefs to which Janvier refers. The difficulties inherent in understanding and respecting others' belief systems is one of the issues we explore in this chapter.

It is amusing to hear them speak of their souls.... They think of the soul as divisible, and you would have all the difficulty in the world to make them believe that our soul is entire in all parts of the body.... God of truth, what ignorance and stupidity!

Jesuit reaction to Amerindian beliefs about life after death

Problem 4

Why do people believe different things, and why are they so certain that their view of the world is correct and that other views are wrong?

INTRODUCTION

The Central Question

How is it that people can believe in a God whose existence cannot be proven? How can they believe in the existence of ancestor spirits, or witches, or devils, or believe in the power of magic to call forth spirits of the dead? Although there is no material proof, people do believe these things, and even take these beliefs for granted. Many North Americans, for example, believe in the existence of God, and some firmly believe in the existence of Satan and the possibility of demonic possession. Such beliefs need not be tied to religion. For example, many North Americans daily consult their horoscope, believing that the position of the stars at their birth somehow affects their destiny.

When people try to make sense of their experiences, they do so by drawing from shared cultural assumptions about how the world works. These shared, learned cultural assumptions create an encompassing picture of reality (which can be religious or secular). This picture is called a "**worldview**."

Worldviews differ significantly between cultures. For example, E. E. Evans-Pritchard, a famous British anthropologist, is known for his 1920s fieldwork among the Azande of southern Sudan. Evans-Pritchard (1937) argued that witchcraft was "ubiquitous" among the Azande, and they tended to explain many acts of misfortune, such as death, illness, or even a bad hunt, as due to witchcraft. In other words, they claimed that someone was bewitching them, causing them misfortune. In contrast, in our society, many people may also

> **worldview**
> An encompassing picture of reality based on shared cultural assumptions about how the world works.

experience misfortune, perhaps falling down and getting a bad cut that causes infection. Although the Azande might use witchcraft to explain the infection, we might argue that the individual was clumsy for falling, or that he or she had "bad luck" to fall and get hurt. So, while all people have shared universal experiences—sickness, death, the birth of an infant, or other life events—we all interpret these experiences based upon our worldview. Unfortunately, many people tend to think that their worldview is the only correct way to interpret their reality, which often leads to ethnocentric assumptions about other cultures and their beliefs. These assumptions can range from believing that your religion is correct and that the spiritual beliefs of others are irrational or incorrect, to accepting that your model of politics or economics is "right" or better than that of others.

How to deal with the question of differing worldviews and beliefs has long been a concern of anthropologists. For example, early anthropological studies of religion sought to explain how people could believe in things that seemed illogical, such as witchcraft. Edward Tylor, considered by some to be the founder of modern anthropology, wrote in *Primitive Culture* (1870) that religion and a belief in the supernatural developed through people's efforts to explain basic phenomena, such as death and dreaming. Tylor imagined early human beings thinking, "What is the difference between a live person and a dead one, between a sleeping person and someone who is awake?" They must have reasoned that there was something, some kind of essence, that left the body at the moment of death or that travelled to distant places in the dreams of sleep. According to Tylor, from this reasoning came a belief in the idea of a soul that animated the body but that fled the body in death and sleep. In his view, this understanding was why the word for breath and the word for soul are the same or similar in so many languages. And it was not unreasonable, said Tylor, for these early philosophers to imagine that other animals and things were animated by souls as well.

Once people arrived at a belief in souls, it was a small step to reason that there were places where departed souls resided and an even smaller step to believe that souls became gods. It was logical, then, for human beings to appeal to these departed spirits for help in controlling life's uncertainties. For Tylor, then, beliefs in gods and spirits developed through the efforts of human beings to explain certain events, to understand why things happened as they did.

In his classic work *The Elementary Forms of the Religious Life* (1961 [1912]), French sociologist Emile Durkheim asked what led to the concept of God. Durkheim, like Tylor, speculated that the secret must lie in the beliefs of early human beings. Durkheim thought that the lives of these people could best be studied by looking at societies that were considered simple or underdeveloped. He decided to read about the religious beliefs of the Indigenous peoples of Australia, particularly their beliefs about **totemism**. The totem, said Durkheim, was some element of nature—an animal, an insect, a plant, or some celestial phenomenon—that served as a symbol for a group or clan. The totem was worshipped and was considered sacred and holy by the members of the group. It also served as a concrete representation of the group. If members of the group worshipped the totem and if the totem was a symbol of the group, was it unreasonable to suppose, asked Durkheim, that the group—the clan itself—was the object of worship?

What, however, would suggest to people that the totem had sacred power? The answer, said Durkheim, lay in the constraints that people feel are imposed on them by the group and by society and in the special power that people feel when groups come together in celebration and **ritual**. And if in small-scale societies people worship the group through their symbolic

totemism
The use of a symbol, generally an animal or a plant, as a physical representation for a group, generally a clan.

ritual
A dramatic rendering or social portrayal of meanings shared by a specific body of people in a way that makes them seem correct and proper. (*See also* symbolic actions.)

representations, as clans worship themselves through their totems, is it not reasonable to suppose that in large-scale societies people worship society through their god or gods? That God is society?

Early anthropologists approached the questions of God, in particular, and religion, in general, with the assumption that such beliefs were essentially in error. Nevertheless, they believed that religious beliefs served some purpose: the beliefs and rituals may have increased group cohesion or provided supernatural sanctions for the violation of group norms.

Recent anthropological efforts to understand differing beliefs and worldviews have built on these early efforts, but as Michael Lambek (2002, 5) argues:

> *If many of the nineteenth-century thinkers saw members of smaller-scale societies mired in superstition, ignorance, bliss, or folly, the personal connections forged in decent ethnographic fieldwork immediately deprived westerners of any illusions of intellectual or moral superiority … Theorists began to realize that rather than compare nonwestern systems of thought directly to western science, it was much more sensible to compare religion, common sense, and specialized knowledge about the world within any given society … and to compare western religious practices with nonwestern ones.*

Today, anthropologists' efforts to understand belief rarely start from the premise that other peoples' beliefs are irrational or incorrect. Rather, anthropologists try to understand the nature of belief or religious practice and how it is that people come to believe that their view of the world is correct.

In order to explain and contextualize people's beliefs, we need to examine a number of concepts. Metaphor is one of the tools we apply to make our knowledge meaningful to ourselves and to others; in that regard, it plays a major role in giving us a sense of the universe and ourselves. As we will see, **symbolic actions**—all the rituals, myths, arts, stories, and music that we enjoy or participate in—play a role in organizing and making concrete a particular worldview. We also need to explore how people learn to view the

world as they do and how they defend their beliefs against skeptics who challenge a particular view of the world. What we believe must also be, in some way, a product of our social, economic, and political lives. In addition, we need to ask and explain why people sometimes radically change what they believe.

QUESTIONS

In examining this problem, we will consider the following questions:

4.1 How does the use of metaphor affect the meanings people assign to experience?

4.2 How does symbolic action reinforce a particular view of the world?

4.3 How does the way we live affect our beliefs and rituals?

4.4 What happened to local worldviews when they were confronted by the religions of the European colonizers?

4.5 How can people reorder their view of the world if it becomes unsatisfactory?

QUESTION 4.1: HOW DOES THE USE OF METAPHOR AFFECT THE MEANINGS PEOPLE ASSIGN TO EXPERIENCE?

Borrowing Meaning with Metaphors

One major characteristic of language is its economy; the same words we use to describe one

> **symbolic actions**
> The activities—including ritual, myth, art, dance, and music—that dramatically depict the meanings shared by a specific body of people.

area of experience can also be used to describe another. This capability occurs primarily through metaphor. **Metaphors** take language from one **domain of experience**, such as the domain of the body or the domain of animals, and apply it to another domain, such as landscape features or persons. For example, "the shoulder of the road" is a metaphoric extension of a body part used to refer to landscape, while "Jeff is a dog" represents an extension from the animal world to the human world.

Metaphors are valuable tools for constructing worldviews. By directing attention to certain aspects of experience, while downplaying or ignoring others, metaphors can reinforce people's beliefs, as well as their understandings of reality, which ultimately come to be taken for granted as correct and true. To put it another way: "Through metaphors we understand the abstract in terms of the concrete" (Lakoff and Johnson 1980, 112).

Harvey Feit (2001) shows how the Cree in northern Quebec used the metaphor "hunting is like gardening" and "hunting lands are like a garden" as part of their strategy to defend their lands against a hydroelectric project that threatened to flood their land and destroy the habitat of their animals (this project is discussed in further detail in Chapter 8). The garden metaphor countered the view of the Quebec government that the northern areas were uninhabited and unproductive wilderness. The view of Cree hunting lands as a garden produced the image of the Cree as gardeners, who cared for Earth and all that Earth produced and who expected their lands to be treated as other special lands were in the rest of Canada.

metaphors
Figures of speech in which linguistic expressions are taken from one area of experience and applied to another.

domain of experience
An area of human experience (e.g., business, war, science, family life) from which people borrow meaning to apply to other areas.

In the words of a secondary student from Nemaska: "What do you think would happen if you were in Ottawa and saw a garden with a lot of roses and other flowers, and you started picking them? Or if you walked on someone's garden? You'd get a fine, of course, maybe we should give Hydro Quebec a fine too" (quoted in Feit 2001, 443–44). The "garden of the Cree" metaphor calls forth a perspective of Earth that, if protected and nurtured, will sustain Cree life. It also implies that if the Cree "garden" is destroyed, Cree people will be destroyed too.

When language is extended from one domain to another, meaning is also extended. In other words, metaphor involves not only speaking of one experience in terms of another but also *understanding* one experience in terms of another. For example, when those of us who speak English in North America describe an argument, we might say, "His point was right on target," or "Your claims are indefensible," or "She attacked my argument, and I had to defend my position." We might say, "She shot down my argument," or "I think I won the argument." We speak of argument in terms of conflict, taking the language from the domain of war and applying it to the domain of conversation. But we have not only transferred words; we have also transferred meaning. We don't simply talk about arguments in terms of war: we win and lose arguments.

Alternatively, think about the way the conception of illness is embedded in the language used to describe it. North Americans who speak English take language from the domain of war and use it to talk about health. We build our defences against illness; we get ill because our resistance was low. We fight a cold, destroy germs, wage war on cancer, and have heart attacks. The language that AIDS researchers use is full of metaphors drawn from war. Recent research reports that the AIDS virus weakens the "immune system attack force," and that "killer cells" are meant to "destroy virus-stricken cells." As one HIV researcher put it: "If you want to think of it with a war analogy, it's as though the soldiers are still on maneuvers, but they no longer have their weapons: When they encounter the enemy, they lose their weapons" (cited in Kolata 1995). It is worth thinking about the implications of the metaphors we use to discuss disease: How does our North American anglophone way of speaking of illness in terms of war and battle affect the kinds of treatment for illness that we devise and seek? Does this metaphor imply the need for cures that destroy the agent of disease rather than restore the patient to health?

The human body and war, of course, are not the only domains from which North American anglophones borrow to assign meaning to other areas of experience. North Americans who speak English borrow also from the domain of economic exchange. In English, time is spoken of not only as if it were a distinct thing, but also as if it were a specific type of thing: "Time is money," "You're wasting my time," "This gadget will save you hours," "I don't have the time to give you," "That flat tire cost me an hour," "You need to budget your time," "He's living on borrowed time," "Is that worth your while?" Time in North American cultures is a valuable commodity, a scarce resource that is quantified, invested, and spent.

© Domenic Gareri/Shutterstock

When North Americans use the term "slam dunk" to refer to ensured success, they are borrowing meaning from the domain of sports to make sense of another domain of experience.

CONSTRUCTING REALITIES

EXERCISE 4.1A

North American anglophones often borrow heavily from the domain of sports in their use of metaphor. Create a list of the sports-related metaphors with which you are familiar. How do such metaphors shape your understanding of experiences of romance, success, and failure? Can you think of alternative metaphors that might also describe those experiences? How might a shift in metaphor change your understanding of those experiences?

The fact that English speakers in North America borrow so heavily from the domains of war and economic exchange for metaphors suggests another way to understand how language operates to influence people's views of the world. Most societies seem to have one or more domains from which they borrow extensively for metaphor. These domains become **key metaphors** that give to each culture a style or cast that makes the culture distinctive. When a culture's members think and speak of many domains of experience in terms of a particular domain, that culture's meanings achieve a certain coherence, and a coherence of belief is thereby achieved as well.

Kwakwaka'wakw Metaphors of Hunger

Perhaps one of the most spectacular expressions of the elaboration of both a key metaphor and the human imagination is found among the Kwakwaka'wakw (once called the "Kwakiutl") of British Columbia. We owe much of our knowledge of the traditional life of the Kwakwaka'wakw to Franz Boas, one of the founders of American anthropology; his Kwakwaka'wakw assistant, George Hunt; and filmmaker and photographer Edward Curtis.

Stanley Walens (1981) suggests that the act of eating is a key metaphor for the Kwakwaka'wakw. A fundamental meaning the Kwakwaka'wakw find

in their experience is that the universe is a place in which some beings must die so that other beings may eat them and live. Eating gives life in at least two ways: it provides nutrition and it frees souls. The Kwakwaka'wakw believe that when a person dies, the soul leaves the body and enters the body of a salmon. But the soul cannot be freed until the physical body is destroyed. For this reason the Kwakwaka'wakw place their dead on scaffolds where the body can be devoured by ravens and other birds. Once the soul enters the body of a salmon, it remains there, living in a salmon world that socially resembles the human world. When the salmon is caught and eaten by human beings, however, the soul is once again freed and enters the body of a newborn child. Thus, for the Kwakwaka'wakw, the act of eating becomes a metaphor through which much of their life is understood and described.

key metaphors
A term to identify metaphors that dominate the meanings that people in a specific culture attribute to their experience.

The importance of eating as a metaphor that orders experience is evident in the dominance of mouths in Kwakwaka'wakw art, ritual, and **myth**. Their world, says Walens, is replete with the mouths of animals killing to satisfy their hunger. Their art is filled with gaping jaws of killer whales, fangs of wolves and bears, and tearing beaks of hawks, eagles, and ravens. Dancers wear masks of cannibal birds with three-metre-long beaks that shatter human skulls to suck out the brains. In their myths, wild women with protruding lips inhabit the woods, waiting to rip apart travellers and misbehaving children. It is a world where suckling infants turn into monsters and devour their mothers.

The Kwakwaka'wakw use the eating metaphor to give meaning to a wide range of their experiences. Hunger is associated with greed, for, like unrestrained hunger, greed causes people to accumulate wealth far beyond what they need. Hunger is also associated with immorality, as the Kwakwaka'wakw believe that human desires create conflict and destruction that can quickly get out of hand—people must work together to prevent and control conflict before it threatens to destroy the group. People who hoard food are, in effect, hoarding souls, preventing the return of a soul from the spirit world. Consequently, the Kwakwaka'wakw place great emphasis on gift giving and generosity. Hunger is also associated with children, who constantly demand to be fed and who will, if allowed, devour all the family's food.

The full impact of a metaphor lies in the fact that people are trying to impose order on their lives by describing the world according to a particular domain of experience. The Kwakwaka'wakw believe that greed, conflict, and child rearing can be solved by controlling hunger. Eating is thus highly ritualized and controlled. Food must be carefully handled and generously given to others to avoid accusations of greed. In fact, wealthy persons are said to vomit forth goods, vomit being for the Kwakwaka'wakw a life-giving substance. Animals that regurgitate their food, such as wolves and owls, occupy a special place in the Kwakwaka'wakw world. The socialization techniques of the Kwakwaka'wakw are geared to teaching children to control their hunger. In sum, a single domain of experience—eating—has been elaborated by the Kwakwaka'wakw to give to their world meaning.

myth
A story or narrative that portrays the meanings people give to their experience.

EXERCISE 4.1B

Some interesting parallels exist between the metaphors of eating and hunger among the Kwakwaka'wakw and the metaphors of sexual intercourse and sexual desire found in mainstream North American popular/expressive culture. Are there other ways in which North American popular culture uses sexual symbolism and metaphors of desire that are similar to the ways in which the Kwakwaka'wakw use hunger and food? Kwakwaka'wakw art, myth, and stories are filled with mouths and images of eating and hunger. What are some of the images that fill North American expressive culture (advertising, for example)? Similarly, vomit is a life-giving substance for the Kwakwaka'wakw; what symbolizes life giving in North America generally?

Metaphors of eating and being eaten abound in Kwakwaka'wakw life. In this religious ceremony, dancers portray cannibal birds with long beaks, and a totem pole includes faces with gaping mouths.

© Edward S. Curtis Collection/Library of Congress

The Metaphors of Contemporary Witchcraft and Magic

A metaphor is a theory, a system of interpretation that, once understood in the context of one domain of experience, can then be transferred to others. The metaphors may also be embedded in myth and history as well as everyday experience. Mutually sustaining metaphors work to reinforce belief systems and worldviews. A good example of that is witchcraft and magic.

Witchcraft refers to the belief that an individual (the witch) has the ability to cause harm to others through the manipulation of powerful substances or words. Indeed, witches are believed to use **magic** to harm or threaten their victims. In North American society, most people have come to associate the term "witch" with particular stereotypes: the witch is assumed to be elderly, female, dressed in black, riding on a broomstick, and able to cast nefarious spells on seemingly innocent people. Such stereotypes are rooted in European witch hunts during the Inquisition and the Reformation, when many women accused of witchcraft were tortured or killed. It is important to note, however, that witchcraft beliefs are widespread and found on all continents and in a variety of types of societies. In fact, when anthropologists compare witchcraft beliefs cross-culturally, they find that people of all ages and genders can be accused of witchcraft. In almost all societies, however, witchcraft beliefs function as metaphors that reinforce people's understandings about their world.

Modern Western forms of witchcraft persist in many areas of Europe and North America. Although in most contexts, witches are perceived as inherently evil, modern European forms of witchcraft draw upon aspects of New Age spirituality, and practitioners use witchcraft as a form of personal healing and as a means to achieve a sense of well-being. Anthropologist Tanya M. Luhrmann details the link between modern, urban witchcraft and worldview in *Persuasions of the Witch's Craft: Ritual Magic in Contemporary England* (1989). Luhrmann joined various covens and groups in England whose membership consisted of middle-class urbanites who situate their magic in "New Age" ideology, the "Age of Aquarius." They are people who place an emphasis on natural foods, good health, and personal stability and whose magical practices consist largely of conjuring spirits, reading the tarot, and magical healing.

Modern magic is based on the assumption that mind and thought can affect matter without the intervention of the thinker's actions. It assumes that thought and matter are one. Magicians believe, says Luhrmann, that it is a distortion to treat objects as isolated and unique. One manual describes magic as

> *the world view that sees things not as fixed objects, but as swirls of energy. The physical world is formed by that energy as stalagtites [sic] are formed by dripping water. If we can cause a change in the energy patterns, they in turn will cause a change in the physical world—just as, if we change the course of an underground river, new series of stalagtites will be formed in new veins of rock. (quoted in Luhrmann 1989, 118)*

A key metaphor embedded in modern witchcraft and magic is that of stratification, of "planes" and "levels." For the follower of good witchcraft, or magic, or the tarot, the universe is divided into a complex collection of entities and beings, each of which exists on different "planes," "astral planes," or "levels," of which the everyday plane of material life is but the lowest. After death, for example, the soul does not die, but goes to exist on another plane, with some souls remaining in contact with the material world. Other magical forces exist on

---

witchcraft
Refers to the belief that an individual (the witch) has the ability to cause harm to others through the manipulation of powerful substances.

magic
Refers to the manipulation of words or substances to influence spiritual beings for good or evil purposes.

other levels, but they, too, can be harnessed by human beings to influence events on the everyday plane of existence. Moreover, the properly trained human mind can, simply by imagining it, create forms on the "astral plane" that may, in turn, affect things in the material world.

Becoming a magician, Luhrmann says, requires the acquisition of specialized and esoteric knowledge; consequently, magicians read books, arrange and attend rituals, go to meetings, and learn the tarot, astrology, mythology, and 17th-century Gaelic cures.

The tarot deck consists of 78 cards that comprise an elaborate and complex system of metaphoric associations linking various domains of experience that range from an understanding of the planets and other celestial objects (e.g., sun, moon), to colours, material elements (e.g., mercury, iron, gold), emotions, personal qualities, and mythological beings. Each of the tarot cards is said to have some meaning that is determined by its association with a specific planet, an element, an emotion or human quality, and so forth. Aleister Crowley, one of the founders of modern magic and witchcraft and a designer of the modern tarot deck, says that each card is, in a sense, a living being.

The magician uses the tarot cards to divine the future, but the cards also provide ways for people to interpret their own lives. The cards, says Luhrmann, provide people with a symbolic map with which to interpret and understand themselves as they transfer the meanings of the cards to their own lives and experiences. Thus, some may associate themselves with the Empress, calm and fecund, or they may say that someone has the temperament of the Magician, mercurial and unpredictable. In associating themselves with a particular card, people also associate themselves with a specific planet (e.g., Mars—dominant and aggressive) or colour (e.g., red—emotional and passionate). In a sense, one may begin to define oneself in terms of the tarot and become the person that the cards delineate. The transfer of meaning creates meaning.

In examining the power of metaphor to define our realities and reinforce our beliefs, we must remember that there is no necessary connection between the domains from which people draw metaphors and the domains to which they apply them. There is no natural connection between commodities and time, war and health, eating and immortality, the tarot's Empress and someone's personality. These borrowings are the products of the human imagination. Many different metaphors can be applied to a specific experience, and one domain can never be the exact replica of the other. No man is really a tiger, no woman really a fox. On some level, then, metaphoric borrowings are intrinsically absurd. Yet we constantly seem to confuse one domain with another: we really do fight disease; we really win arguments. And so, as anthropologists, we need to explore by what cultural means people are convinced that by controlling one domain of experience (e.g., eating), they can really control another (e.g., greed). In the next section, we explore the way that symbolic action acts to reinforce worldview.

QUESTION 4.2: HOW DOES SYMBOLIC ACTION REINFORCE A PARTICULAR VIEW OF THE WORLD?

Metaphors are not the only way that we mediate between our senses and the meanings we assign to experience. We also participate in activities that express a particular view of the world and that reinforce particular beliefs about the way the world works. Especially important are symbolic actions such as ritual, myth, literature, art, games, and music. Symbolic actions carry bundles of meanings that represent public displays of a culture. They are dramatic renderings and social portrayals of the meanings shared by a specific body of people. More important, symbolic actions render particular beliefs and views of the world in a way that makes them seem correct and proper. The Kwakwaka'wakw and the Western witches and magicians described by

Tanya Luhrmann provide good examples of how ritual portrays, reinforces, and provides evidence for a particular view of the world. In addition to rituals, popular stories and myths—such as those about zombies and vampires in contemporary North America—are embedded with meanings that are closely intertwined with a particular world-view. Stories about zombies alone are not likely to convince anyone that the world works in the way it is portrayed in the stories. Instead, the meanings that characterize a culture are repeated again and again in other symbolic actions, particularly ritual.

The Kwakwaka'wakw Hamatsa Dance

The Kwakwaka'wakw view of the world, as we noted previously, rests on the metaphor of hunger and is graphically displayed in their language, myth, art, and ritual. One of the most important Kwakwaka'wakw rituals is the Cannibal Dance.

The Cannibal Dance is a four-day spectacle that serves as the highlight of the Kwakwaka'wakw Winter Ceremonial, a period of celebration and ritual observance in which all worldly activities cease. It is a time when the spiritual world of the Kwakwaka'wakw, filled with powerful beings and animal spirits, intersects with the real world. The dance varies in some detail from group to group, but in all, it is the focal point of a youth's initiation into the Cannibal Society, a group responsible for performing certain rituals. In the ceremony, the initiate plays the role of the cannibal dancer, or *hamatsa*. Members of the Cannibal Society and others gather in a ceremonial house to call back the cannibal to the human world from his sojourn in the realm of Man Eater, one of the most important of the supernatural beings in the Kwakwaka'wakw pantheon of spirits.

At the beginning of the ceremony, the *hamatsa* is believed to be in the woods frantically searching for human flesh to devour. Some early ethnographic accounts of the dance report that he would actually eat human mummified remains. Meanwhile, members of the Cannibal Society gather around a fire in the ceremonial house to sing and recite prayers to entice the *hamatsa* into the house, periodically sending out men to see if he is approaching the village. Finally, the prayers and calls of the Cannibal Society attract the *hamatsa*, who arrives, dressed in branches of the hemlock tree, pushing aside roof boards and jumping down among the celebrants. Jumping through the roof is supposed to symbolize descent from the spirit world above to the world of the living below. In a seeming frenzy, the *hamatsa* runs around the fire and then into an adjacent room, leaving behind only the sacred hemlock branches he had worn. During the four days of the ceremony, the celebrants try by various means to entice him back into the house and, in effect, tame and socialize him, convincing him to forsake his craving for human flesh and accept normal food. In one part of the ceremony, the *hamatsa* flees the house and a member of the Cannibal Society is sent as the bait to attract him. The *hamatsa* rushes upon him, seizes his arm, and bites it. Each time he bites someone, he dashes into a secret room and vomits, an act that is repeated various times during the ceremony.

During pauses, members of the audience exchange gifts. Later, the *hamatsa* appears naked and is given clothes, but he flees again. At another point a woman who serves as a co-initiate appears naked, carrying mummified remains. She dances backward, trying to entice the *hamatsa* to enter the house, but she fails. Finally, the group succeeds in subduing the *hamatsa* by bathing him in the smoke of cedar bark that has been soaked in menstrual blood. After the conclusion of the public part of the Cannibal Dance, the initiate and a few members of the Cannibal Society go to another house and eat a normal meal, the final symbol that the *hamatsa* has been tamed.

Ritual can be viewed as a symbolic representation of reality. In another sense, ritual presents participants with solutions to real problems, in the same way as symbolic representations suggest real solutions. For the Kwakwaka'wakw, the *hamatsa* is the ultimate projection of the power of hunger, and his desire for human flesh is a manifestation of the forces that can destroy society. The participants in the ritual, by symbolically taming the hunger of the *hamatsa*, are asserting their moral responsibility to control greed and conflict. The ritual is the acting out of the group's successful efforts to overcome forces that threaten their society. Here is how Walens (1981, 162) puts it:

> The hamatsa's hunger is fearsome; but it is the same hunger felt by every human, and thus every human has the power to control it. Ultimately the hamatsa and the bestial ferocity he embodies can be conquered … The winter ceremonials prove that no matter how terrible the power of hunger, no matter how many fearsome guises it assumes, no matter how many masks it wears, and no matter how many voices it speaks with, morality will be the ultimate victor. So long as humans have the knowledge to use food correctly, they need never fear hunger nor its awful accompaniment, death.

The Cannibal Dance also contains a powerful message about socialization. Children, like the *hamatsa*, come from the spirit world and enter the physical world naked. Like the *hamatsa*, children have a female assistant, their mother, who must feed and socialize them. Children come into the world hungry, threatening to devour their parents' wealth. Thus, in the Kwakwaka'wakw view of things, all humans are cannibals who must be socialized and tamed. Through swaddling, ritual fasting, denial of food, and other actions, parents transform their children from cannibals into moral human beings. Through ritual enactment, the Kwakwaka'wakw have made their symbols real.

A Ritual of Contemporary Witchcraft and Magic

> In a witches' coven in northeast London, members have gathered from as far away as Bath, Leicester, and Scotland to attend the meeting at the full moon … The sitting room has been transformed. The furniture has been removed, and a twelve-foot circle drawn on the carpet … Four candlesticks stake out the corners of the room, casting shadows from stag antlers on the wall. The antlers sit next to a sheaf of wheat, subtle sexual symbolism. In spring and summer there are flowers everywhere. The altar in the centre of the circle is a chest which seems ancient. On top an equally ancient box holds incense in different drawers. On it, flowers and herbs surround a carved wooden Pan; a Minoan goddess figure sits on the latter itself amid a litter of ritual knives and tools. (Luhrmann 1989, 42)

The scene just described is the setting for a ritual that Tanya Luhrmann attended in the course of her fieldwork on contemporary witchcraft and magic. These rituals, she says, were particularly important because they were one of the ways that people became convinced of the validity of their beliefs. Going on to describe the ritual in the above setting, Luhrmann (1989, 42) writes:

> The high priestess begins by drawing the magic circle in the air above the chalk, which she does with piety, saying "let this be the boundary between the worlds of gods and that of men" … On this evening a coven member wanted us to "do" something for a friend's sick baby. Someone made a model of the baby and put it on the altar, at the Minoan goddess's feet. We held hands in a circle around the altar and then began to run, chanting a set phrase. When the circle was running at its peak the high priestess suddenly stopped. Everyone shut their eyes, raised their hands, and visualized the prearranged image: in this case it was Mary, the woman who wanted the spell, the "link" between us and the unknown child … By springtime, Mary

reported, the child had recovered, and she thanked us for the help.[1]

Rituals, like this one, like the Hamatsa Dance of the Kwakwaka'wakw, or like those enacted in thousands of mosques, churches, temples, and synagogues across North America, are special occasions that not only involve the enactment of key metaphors but also serve as special events set aside from everyday existence: events that draw participants into an emotional involvement with the metaphors. Rituals really do produce special feelings; people are carried away with the symbolism, the music, and the social communion with others, and it is easy in this situation to come to believe that it is not the ritual that produces these feelings, but the forces or powers that the ritual is believed to summon or embrace.

EXERCISE 4.2A

The Hamatsa Dance and the rituals of contemporary witchcraft presented by Luhrmann may seem "exotic," but rituals are a key part of more familiar world religions as well (prayer is one example). Rituals can also be secular. What kinds of rituals are you familiar with from your own belief system? How do you feel when you practise your rituals? How would you describe the significance and meaning of these rituals to someone not familiar with them? What kinds of meanings are produced through the symbolic actions that comprise the rituals you are familiar with? How?

In contemporary witchcraft and magic, there is great emphasis placed on visualization and meditation as part of the ritual. The high priest or priestess may relate a story and ask the participants to imagine themselves in the story, perhaps a walk through a moonlit wood or a voyage with Sir Francis Drake around the Horn of Africa. After the ritual, people report experiencing the salt spray on their face or the pitching of the sea, and they experience fellow participants as shipmates aboard Drake's ship, *Golden Hind*. In other words, the ritual not only dramatically depicts a metaphor but also teaches the participants how to experience the world as if the forces, gods, and spirits were truly real. Consequently, it is not unusual, in any belief system, for people participating in ritual to claim to have had a "mystical experience" or to feel "one with the universe" or overwhelmed with love or light. Thus, ritual not only teaches us about the world depicted in our metaphors but also teaches us how to feel within the universe we create.

Zombies Are "Good to Think With"

Contemporary witchcraft and magic draw heavily from myth and literature for their language, symbols, and metaphors. When anthropologists speak of myth, they are not referring to stories that are untrue. Myths, like histories, are accounts that explain the past from a particular point of view. Luhrmann reports that many of the magicians she came to know were first attracted to their beliefs when they read J. R. R. Tolkien's *Lord of the Rings*, or Ursula LeGuin's Earthsea Trilogy, or Marion Zimmer Bradley's *Mists of Avalon*. The themes of many of these books, and of contemporary witchcraft and magic in general, are contained in North American popular culture. These books and movies contain **key scenarios**, stories, or myths that, like ritual, portray certain values and beliefs. In the same sense that people act out and communicate their view of the world in ritual and come to learn how

[1] Source: Reprinted by permission of the publisher, from *Persuasions of the Witches' Craft: Ritual Magic in Contemporary England*, by T. M. Luhrmann, p. 42, Cambridge, Mass.: Harvard University Press. Copyright © 1989 by T. M. Luhrmann.

key scenarios
Dominant stories or myths that portray the values and beliefs of a specific society.

to feel in that world, they can be said to act out the scenarios contained in their myths and histories.

Claude Levi-Strauss (1964), a key scholar of myth and meaning, coined the phrase "good to think with" to refer to the way that humans use aspects of the material world as a reservoir of metaphorical and symbolic meanings. Zombies may not be part of the material world as we know it, but zombie stories and myths are certainly good to think with. The proliferation of zombie movies, books, television shows, and video games in the 2010s in North America suggests that the "zombie apocalypse" genre contains key scenarios that embody how we think about our world today.

What is it about zombies that we find so compelling, and why now? Zombies, unlike their popular undead cousins, vampires, are barely recognizably human. Zombies are mindless wanderers; zombies are tireless; and zombies are almost uncontrollably contagious—turning loved ones against one another in an instant, creating a pandemic, producing hordes of relentless consumers with insatiable, never-ending appetites.

Anthropologists Jean and John Comaroff suggest that contemporary zombie stories have much to do with "the implosion of neoliberal capitalism at the end of the twentieth century" (2009, 451). The Comaroffs were interested in the proliferation of zombie stories in late 20th-century South Africa, but their insights are applicable to the North American case as well. Stories of a zombie apocalypse tap into our fears about what they call "millennial capitalism": zombies, like North Americans, consume relentlessly (think of shopping malls during the holidays), and zombies "work" without ceasing and for little reward (like "ideal" offshore workers under global capitalism). Furthermore, with rare exceptions, zombies do not possess a sense of consciousness and thus lack critical thinking abilities. This characteristic mirrors the oftentimes voracious and uncontrolled consumption habits of contemporary shoppers, with their seemingly "senseless" desire to possess particular brands of clothing or other commodities.

How might we explain the contemporary popularity of zombie and vampire myths and stories?

The increasing pop-culture interest in zombie pandemics, modelled after fears of the spread of diseases such as the avian flu, ebola, and H1N1, makes both intimate contact with and global flows of people and goods dangerous, even deadly. Zombie stories are thus linked with contemporary fears of the mobile "other" and function as a commentary on such phenomena as immigration, which is frequently blamed for the spread of disease and other social ills. Zombie stories are a metaphorical exploration of our fears and desires in our global, capitalist economy.

EXERCISE 4.2B

1. What skills are most valuable in the wake of an imagined zombie apocalypse? In zombie myths, who becomes the hero, and who is zombie fodder? What does this suggest about our anxieties related to our contemporary ways of making a living in North America?

2. The vampire genre is as popular, if not more so, than myths and stories about zombies. Why do you think this is the case? What do contemporary vampires tell us about ourselves?

CONSTRUCTING REALITIES

QUESTION 4.3: HOW DOES THE WAY WE LIVE AFFECT OUR BELIEFS AND RITUALS?

In answering this question, anthropologist Marshall Sahlins wrote:

> When we were pastoral nomads, the Lord was our Shepherd. We were his flock, and he made us lie down in green pastures … When we were serfs and nobles, the Lord was our king. Sat regnant on the throne of heaven, His shepherd's crook now a jeweled sceptre … Finally we are businessmen—and the Lord is our accountant. He keeps a ledger on us all, enters our good deeds in black and debits our sins in red. (1968, 96)

It is too easy to say, Sahlins points out, that people create gods in their own image or, as Emile Durkheim suggested, that "God is another name for society." Nevertheless, clearly the way we live, the organization of our social, economic, and political lives, must influence what we believe, how we represent those beliefs, and how we act them out. We need to understand, also, how our beliefs and the manner in which we act them out serve to maintain certain patterns of social, political, and economic relations, and how these beliefs and acts serve to reproduce these relations.

We also have a tendency to think that our own ways of living and worldviews are "natural," and, by extension, normal. In North American society, for instance, we have been enculturated to see capitalism and its attending effects as normal. Think, for instance, about how the notion of time is affected by capitalism. Capitalism and the Industrial Revolution, as discussed in Chapter 3, stress effective time management—a productive worker is a timely and efficient worker. Time thus becomes commodified, and to maximize productivity and profit, workers in office jobs or factories are encouraged to manage their time effectively. We value disciplined workers, and we use phrases such as "time is money." Time is also something that can be "wasted" or "saved." This commodification and valuation of time affects all areas of our lives. Think, for instance of how most of us set our daily tasks to calendrical and clock-based time, and how, with the advent of smartphones and calendar apps, we increasingly micro-manage our time to achieve greater productivity.

This commodification of time affects worldviews surrounding such seemingly "natural" processes as labour and birth, and is reflected in contemporary birthing rituals. Robbie Davis-Floyd (2004), for instance, has explored how Western, capitalist notions of time inform American hospital births. Davis-Floyd argues that most American women's experiences of birth are informed by a "technocratic" model that stresses the need for biomedical interventions such as ultrasound, Cesarean sections, epidurals, and intravenous infusions of pitocin (a synthetic form of oxytocin used to induce or speed up the labour process). Davis-Floyd suggests that while many of these procedures are often medically necessary, such as the use of Cesarean sections in emergency situations, most are not. Pitocin, for instance, is given to the vast majority of women who experience hospital births, and its purpose is to speed up the labour process and to allow for an "efficient" and timely labour that fits neatly within the schedules of obstetricians. In addition, when women labour for long periods of time, they become tired and are more prone to be "difficult" or demanding patients. According to Davis-Floyd, these procedures, through their predictability and repetition, turn hospital birth into a ritual, one that serves to reinforce fundamental beliefs about the superiority of technology over nature. Birth as a ritual is particularly effective because it is a part of a category of rituals called **rites of passage**, special

rites of passage
This term, coined in 1908 by Arnold Van Gennep, refers to the category of rituals that accompany changes in status, such as the transition from boyhood to manhood, living to dead, or student to graduate.

kinds of rituals (discussed in further detail in Chapter 6) that marks one's transition from one social state or status to another. In this case, birth as a rite of passage marks a woman's transition to motherhood. Ultimately, such interventions are naturalized and perceived as necessary for mother and baby, but, in fact, they reflect dominant Western capitalist worldviews about time and efficiency. So how we live (in this case, in a capitalist economic system) affects our beliefs about how we manage our bodies. To try to understand how what we believe is related to how we live, let's examine some other ways of knowing that challenge Euro-Canadians' beliefs about the world and their place in it.

In *Ways of Knowing: Experience, Knowledge, and Power Among the Dene Tha* (1998), Jean-Guy Goulet writes of his own experience learning about a worldview very different from the one he acquired as a child. For the Dene Tha living in three communities in northwest Alberta—Bushe River, Meander River, and Chateh—learning comes only through direct experience. In Chateh, the community where Goulet lived while he was a student of the Dene Tha, an adult cannot teach a child how to hunt or cook or perform a ritual by simply giving verbal instructions: to replace personal experience with objectified instruction is to turn knowledge into a commodity. All Dene Tha must learn by observing and by doing or imitating what they see when watching others. In the Dene Tha view, the only true knowledge is personal knowledge. This emphasis on firsthand knowledge is common among First Nations peoples; for instance, Richard Preston found that the Cree in Quebec "define certain truth value on the basis of what a man can see with his own eyes" (1975, 144). While Dene Tha stories can also contain knowledge, the narrator is careful to avoid making claims about the truthfulness of the story if it is not part of his or her own personal experience.

Along with the importance of personal knowledge comes the right of every Dene Tha to personal autonomy and the responsibility to respect the autonomy of others, including non-Dene Tha.

If someone interferes with another's direct experience, that person is seen to be infringing on the right of the other to gain knowledge properly. This understanding extends to small children as well as adults. Dene Tha children are allowed to explore their world in ways that Euro-Canadian children are not. For instance, setting and enforcing a particular bedtime for a child is considered by Euro-Canadians to be a sign of good parenting, but for a Dene Tha parent, this practice is a sign of an irresponsible parent who is blocking the child's access to knowledge and personal autonomy.

Dene Tha notions of power also differ from those of Euro-Canadians. In the Dene Tha worldview, "when Dene speak of a power, they think of a powerfulness inherent in plants, animals, or other substances, which can affect human beings knowingly or unknowingly" (Goulet 1998, 60). Dene Tha distinguish between two different "lands": *ndahdigeh*, "our land," and *echuhdigeh*, "the other land." Plants and animals in the bush are manifestations of the other land in our land; therefore, Dene Tha must be very respectful of all forms of life, human and nonhuman. This part of the Dene Tha worldview is another that is shared by many other First Nations peoples. Harvey Feit explains that the Waswanipi Cree in northern Quebec do not believe that animals are radically different from humans. Hunting is a very important part of Cree life, and the Cree in Waswanipi have a special word that encompasses their beliefs about humans, animals, and hunting. The Cree word *nitao* means "to see or to look at something; to go to get or to fetch something; to need something; to want something; and to grow or continue to grow" (Feit 2004b, 102). The Cree believe that animals are shy and difficult to see at times. To "get" an animal, in the Cree view, is to receive it. The animal must agree to give itself to the Cree hunter, and the hunter must agree to reciprocate with gifts to other Cree and to the spirits. One way to give a gift of appreciation to the spirits is to burn a small piece of meat in a fire so that the smoke goes up to where the spirits will receive it. Cree hunters reciprocate by providing the conditions for animals to survive and grow. Hunters must never waste the animals they are given and must kill the animals cleanly.

Sometimes, "our land" interacts directly with "the other land." An example given by Goulet is that of a young man's violent death producing an angry storm that was said to be the result of the man's feelings. In another example, when the animal helpers of a Dene Tha healer felt let down because a patient did not bring proper gifts, the village was covered with low clouds and drizzle for three days.

Dene Tha communicate with the other world through dreams and gain important knowledge about healing using plants and animal parts. However, like the Waswanipi Cree, they must always show respect by giving gifts or healing will not take place. If a piece of bark is taken from a tree or a plant is taken from the ground for its roots, a small portion of tobacco is placed at the bottom of the tree or in the ground at the spot the plant once grew.

In addition to providing meat for humans, animals are important because of their ability to share power with humans. This relationship of sharing goes back to a time when animals and humans were not as separated as they are now and when they married, spoke the same language, and lived together. Although this is no longer the case, the Dene Tha still view animals as superior to humans and believe that animals give to humans only the powers they no longer need.

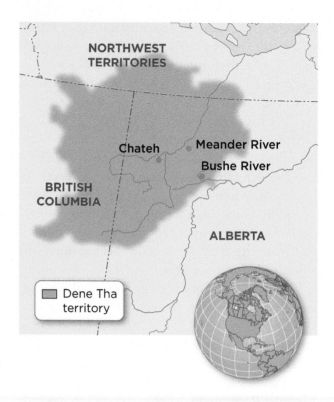

Like the Dene Tha, the Waswanipi Cree do not see humans as completely separate from other phenomena of the world, such as wind and water. For instance, animals do not act alone when they give themselves to hunters; they are also given by "wind persons" and the Christian God or Jesus. The Cree world is filled with all kinds of spirits that interact with people, and the whole Cree environment is thought of as a "society of persons," all of whom are dependent on one another. God and spirits may communicate with humans in dreams, and humans may communicate with spirits through their rituals.

Dreaming is the way that the Dene Tha gain powerful knowledge. When elders travel to the other land, they sometimes return with songs that are used in healing ceremonies. Dreams are also the process by which one can see the future and even take steps to avoid misfortune. Dreams may have a very pragmatic use, as when a Dene Tha hunter learns where to find animals that are willing to give themselves to humans. For the Dene Tha, the mind, or soul, is where one's will, memory, and intellect

© Arctic Photo/All Canada Photos

A Cree hunter.

reside. One's mind receives a power to heal or to cause harm from an animal helper. Although one's body may die, one's mind can choose to return to "this land" and become born again in a new body. In other words, human bodies are only temporary, but human minds are permanent.

Dreaming is understood by the Dene Tha as a journey in which the soul leaves the body and travels to other places in this land or spends time with relatives in the other land. If, however, the soul stays away too long, the body may become ill and a healer may be required to bring the soul back. If the soul doesn't return, the body will eventually die. For the Dene Tha in Chateh, some people (but not all) choose to come back to Earth once they die. Reincarnation in Chateh is a process whereby the spirit of a relative enters a woman's body to be born again. If the spirit was a female in her previous life and is born again as a male, family members may call the boy by female kinship terms such as "my sister" or "my daughter," once the former identity of the child is decided upon by the community. The same happens when a male is reborn as a female.

By exploring the examples of the Dene Tha and the Waswanipi Cree, we can see the mutual reinforcement of their beliefs about the relationships among humans, animals, and the land, and the social, economic, and political relations that are unique to their respective cultures. Many First Nations peoples view themselves as part of their environment, in contrast to the worldview of most Euro-Canadians, who see "culture" as separate from "nature." For instance, the most important being in the world of the Mi'kmaq in eastern and coastal Canada is the Sun. The Mi'kmaq believe that the Sun created Earth and everything on it, and both the Sun and the Moon are considered to be manifestations of the Great Spirit. When a person dies, that person's soul climbs the Milky Way to the land of the dead. Another prominent being of the Mi'kmaq spirit world is Glooscap, who was once on Earth and who created the natural features of the Mi'kmaq land. Glooscap also taught the Mi'kmaq how to make tools and weapons, and before he left

Earth to become the assistant of the Great Spirit, he predicted the arrival of the Europeans.

In *Do Glaciers Listen?* (2005), Julie Cruikshank explains how First Nations women who lived inland from the Saint Elias Mountains of Yukon told her stories in which glaciers had human-like qualities and interacted with humans: "The women I know portrayed glaciers as conscious and responsive to humans. Glaciers, they insisted, are wilful, sometimes capricious, easily excited by human intemperance but equally placated by quick-witted human responses" (2005, 8). In this worldview, the behaviour of humans could have grave consequences for the behaviour of the "natural" world. Cruikshank was told by local women that glaciers had a keen sense of smell and disliked the odour of cooking fat. These women warned against cooking bacon for breakfast when near a glacier because the glacier might react by causing a surge that produced ear-splitting sounds.

Indigenous peoples in other parts of the world have strikingly similar beliefs about their physical environments. For instance, the worldview of the Maori of New Zealand contains an origin story in which Sky Father and Mother Earth were joined together and produced many children. These children became the spirit beings of the sea, the winds, forests, plants, animals, and humans. Thus, Maori do not see themselves as separate from the physical world. As Manuka Henare (2001, 202) explains: "the resources of the earth do not belong to humankind; rather humans belong to the earth. While humans as well as animals, birds, fish, and trees can harvest the bounty of Mother Earth's resources, they do not own them."

These "ways of knowing" about the world and one's place in it differ greatly from the worldviews of Euro-North Americans, who believe that humans are superior to all other entities in the world and that everything in the world belongs to humans. The Euro-North American notion of human ownership of Earth's resources creates a very different way of interacting with the physical environment and justifies the ways of those who take resources from Earth—minerals, trees, animals, plants—without acknowledging any reciprocal responsibility.

EXERCISE 4.3

1. Take a few minutes to think about your own beliefs about the relationship between the cultural life of humans and the natural world. Are they connected to a particular religious or secular worldview (or both)? How do these beliefs reinforce the life you live (and vice versa)?
2. If you believed that all the entities of the world are somehow connected and have the same rights as humans, how would this belief change the way you think about resources, such as the foods you eat, the gas you put in your car, and the electricity and water you use in your house, as well as the disposal of your garbage?

However, not all humans in the world are able to "know," through direct observation, what is happening to Earth's resources. Multinational corporations, national companies, and even local businesses may behave in ways that local people are not able to investigate directly because they do not have access to the information they would need. In the next section, we look at two examples of how people cope with not knowing. The first example explores how people in northern Madagascar speculate on what happens to sapphires that are mined locally and then exported to other places. The second example shows how people in Cameroon use witchcraft to explain the conflicts of modernity.

Sapphire Mining in Northern Madagascar

Worldviews contain a people's understanding of how the world works, based on beliefs that are handed down through generations and tested against experience and knowledge. In the case of those who live on the periphery of the world

capitalist system, people often attempt to figure out how the world works without having direct experience or direct knowledge. Andrew Walsh describes this process in Ambondromifehy, a mining and trading town in northern Madagascar. Walsh describes the worldview of sapphire miners in Ambondromifehy as a complex process of speculation, deception, and knowledge. Sapphires, when uncut, seem to the Malagasy to be useless stones; prior to 1996, they were sometimes used as slingshot pellets. Based on this direct knowledge and experience, the Malagasy have trouble imagining why these stones are suddenly so valuable to outsiders. In an effort to understand, local miners and traders constantly asked Andrew Walsh, "What are sapphires used for?" (2004, 225). Because Walsh was an outsider, his answer to this persistent question—that they were used to make jewellery—was suspect, and many Malagasy speculated that the sapphires must have some other, far more important use. These speculations included the production of electronic parts for CD players or for military vehicles and weapons. The most common speculation was that "sapphires

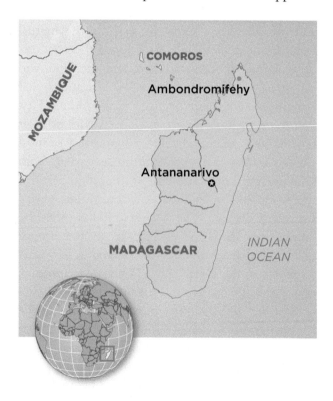

are used, largely by foreigners from the United States, in the production of bombs. Sapphires, this speculation goes, find their way from northern Madagascar to Bangkok to the United States, where they are transformed into arms of the sort that were being used in the U.S.-led coalition bombing of Iraq" (Walsh 2004, 233).

The act of speculation about what they are being told is a vital part of the Malagasy experience of the sapphire trade. Individual miners sell their stones to stationary traders who have booths along a strip on the outskirts of Ambondromifehy. The stationary traders, in turn, sell the stones to *demarchers*, who are mobile traders that run from booth to booth buying stones to sell to foreign traders, who, in turn, take the sapphires to the Malagasy capital, Antananarivo, and then leave the country. During the four or five trades, deception is often the rule. Because the sapphires are collected by groups of individuals in areas that are protected by the Malagasy state against large-scale mining, there is always the possibility that a miner may hide a stone in his mouth rather than share with the others. Each trader at the stationary booths tries to buy sapphires at a price low enough to make a profit, as does each of the *demarchers* and the foreign traders. But only the foreign traders know what is happening in the global market, so the local traders are always aware that they do not have full knowledge about the worth of the stones and must continually decide what to believe and what to reject. What the Malagasy do know for sure is that foreigners know something about the value of sapphires that the Malagasy do not know and cannot know.

To complicate matters further, every day several truckloads of tourists pass through Ambondromifehy on their way to the Ankarana Special Reserve, where they claim that the only things they take out of the area are pictures. The Malagasy don't know for sure if this is true, but they speculate that it is a cover for the extraction of something far more important because it is no coincidence that the only places the conservationists and ecotourists are interested in are those that have something valuable in "the belly of the land."

Because sapphires are traded locally and then globally for increasingly higher prices, and foreigners come and go without ever revealing their true purpose, the Malagasy belief that sapphires cannot be used simply for jewellery seems quite logical, given the world events that reach Ambondromifehy through the news media and the reports of foreigners. The Malagasy also know that knowledge is being actively withheld from them and that only foreigners have true knowledge about how the global market works; as a result, they speculate, both *in* and *about* the true value of sapphires, based on their own experience of the intimate connection between world trade and deception.

Using a worldview based on lived experience to decipher events that are unfamiliar may produce understandings that appear strange to outsiders. North Americans also do this—for example, when listening to political campaign speeches in which many promises are made but there is no way to verify the "truth" of the messages. North Americans know that they cannot know whether these promises are sincere, and the only choice they have is to speculate on the basis of what seems to be reasonable, given the uncertainty of outside forces such as the global market. In the case of Malagasy sapphire miners, as in the case of North American voters, the lives people live and the forces that shape them come to make sense through people's worldviews

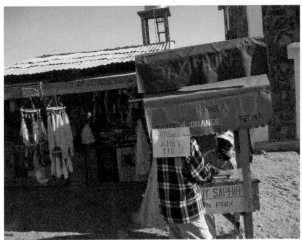

Selling sapphires in Illakaka, Madagascar.

CONSTRUCTING REALITIES

and beliefs (and those worldviews are shaped by the lives they live). In Cameroon, the process of evaluating the unknowable by using what is knowable (witchcraft, in this case) produces explanations that make sense to those who are living the experience but may seem totally illogical to outsiders who do not share their beliefs. The power of an anthropological perspective is that it gives us methodological and theoretical tools with which to contextualize and understand worldviews other than our own.

Modern Witchcraft in Cameroon

Peter Geschiere, who has been doing fieldwork among the Maka people in southeastern Cameroon since 1971, found that witchcraft had not decreased with modernization, as had been forecast by development experts. Quite the opposite: Cameroon newspaper reports about the "nightly escapades" of witches had multiplied since Cameroon became an independent state in 1960. In *The Modernity of Witchcraft: Politics and the Occult in Postcolonial Africa* (1997), Geschiere asked himself why. One of his Maka companions repeated a saying that he had heard from a Dutch missionary: "Where there is electric light, witchcraft will disappear" (1997, 2). Yet this man had been threatened by the occult in towns that were well lit by electricity.

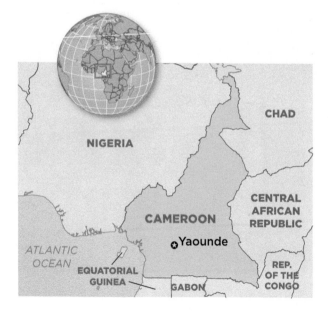

It is perhaps the ambiguity of witchcraft in Cameroon that enhances its connection to politics. In the Maka worldview, all events are the result of human action. Nothing happens simply by chance. If someone becomes ill, meets with misfortune, becomes wealthy, or gains a prominent position in politics, the cause is witchcraft. Witchcraft is the process by which inequalities are both created and overcome, because the new elites are believed to have gained their wealth through witchcraft. To gain access to wealth and power, a politician must have connections to the occult.

This ambiguity extends into the realm of kinship. Witchcraft is said to be "the dark side of kinship." The Maka believe that one's kin are the only people one can really trust, yet it is kin who trade the hearts of their kin for the favours of witches.

The Maka use the term *djambe* to refer to witches. A *djambe* is a small being that lives in the belly of humans. Some say it is like a small grey mouse; others describe it as a crab. Geschiere learned from the villagers that *djambe* used to live in the forest, where they helped hunters find animals to kill. As long as they stayed in the forest and hunters gave them part of the meat from their hunt, *djambe* did not harm humans. But one day a Maka woman became suspicious of her husband's success every time he went hunting. Unable to contain her curiosity, she followed him and saw him feed meat to a tiny being at the base of the tree. When her husband left, the woman went to the tree and asked the creature if it would help her the same way it was helping her husband. The *djambe* agreed, and the woman took it home. Once in the village, the *djambe* demanded that the woman feed it meat; when no more animal meat was to be found, it demanded that she feed it her children. Now that the *djambe* was in the village, it became the source of both fortune and misfortune.

In principle, all humans have a *djambe* in their belly, and as long as it is not activated, it does neither good nor harm. But the Maka say that no one can function without some connection with the occult. The way to activate one's *djambe* is to make it "go out" of one's body—to fly around and meet other *djambe*. To become a witch and be part of the nocturnal feasts held in the forest, one must sacrifice the hearts of one's parents because witches have an insatiable appetite for human flesh. A highly developed *djambe* also has a second pair of eyes and can see things not visible to those who are not witches.

In an effort to control witchcraft, the state justice system now involves itself in accusations of witchcraft. Unlike during colonial times, the state is anxious to prosecute witches to show its citizens that it is legitimate. However, because many of those who are employed by the state owe their good fortune to witchcraft, such prosecutions are paradoxical. As an example of how deep beliefs in witchcraft run in Cameroon, Geschiere tells of a civil servant, himself suspected of having connections to the occult because of his position, who accused villagers of using witchcraft to sabotage government projects.

Witchcraft in Cameroon exemplifies some of the tensions that have accompanied the end of colonialism and the incorporation of newly independent countries into the global capitalist market as individual entities. Beliefs about witchcraft help the Maka explain, in terms they understand, the changes that have taken place now that their own people are filling state positions and capitalism is creating previously inconceivable wealth. The existing worldview explains the sudden affluence of the elite that coexists with the poverty of the majority.

QUESTION 4.4: WHAT HAPPENED TO LOCAL WORLDVIEWS WHEN THEY WERE CONFRONTED BY THE RELIGIONS OF THE EUROPEAN COLONIZERS?

In most colonial encounters, some form of Christianity challenged the local worldviews of the colonized or Indigenous peoples. Christianity, with its close links to capitalism, was part of the bedrock of colonial rule. Many early anthropologists assumed that Christianity was such a powerful force that it destroyed all forms of indigenous worldviews. Recent research has shown that this is not always the outcome, which, in turn, raises a question: How do Indigenous or colonized peoples fit religions such as Christianity into their existing worldviews?

The Dene Tha and Christianity

Jean-Guy Goulet tells us that the Dene Tha live in a social context that presents many challenges to their worldview. Western institutions, such as "the school, the police station, the nursing station, and the church" (1998, 193), expect the Dene Tha to absorb the worldview of Euro-Canadians. The Dene Tha do accept some Euro-Canadian ways and incorporate them in a complementary fashion within Dene Tha ways of knowing.

Many indigenous cultures of the Americas practised variants of **shamanism** before the arrival of Europeans, and shamanism continues to be an important aspect of traditional spirituality. Shamanism is the oldest spiritual belief system in the world, and while it has many variants, it is a belief system in which spiritual practitioners, or "shamans," enter into an altered state of consciousness to seek guidance from spiritual beings. They work on behalf of an individual or on behalf of an entire community. In shamanic societies, spirituality and healing are closely intertwined, and the shaman is considered to have specialized knowledge of medicine, health, and healing. He or she can thus diagnose illness and help to cure a patient.

With the advent of European colonialism in Canada, however, many Indigenous peoples

shamanism
Refers to a spiritual belief system whereby spiritual practitioners, called "shamans," enter into an altered state of consciousness to seek guidance from spiritual forces.

were converted to Christianity. But they did not completely abandon their traditional shamanic beliefs. Indeed, many contemporary indigenous societies are a syncretism, or blend, of shamanic and Christian elements.

For instance, most Dene Tha say they are Christians, usually Roman Catholic or Anglican, but they still abide by their original worldview as well. It is not so much that missionaries and priests convinced them to reject their own view of the world as their determining that some aspects of Christianity make sense when evaluated by a Dene Tha worldview. For instance, the Christian figure of Jesus Christ is often incorporated into the category of those who now live in *echuhdigeh*, or "the other land," and who communicate with the living through dreams. The crucifix (or cross) has been accepted, and some shamans use it as a personal symbol, in conjunction with the drum.

An especially powerful role is given by the Dene Tha to the Roman Catholic rosary. A young Dene Tha told Goulet that "they were encouraged by the Elders to carry a rosary on their person as a protection against other Dene who might attack them with their power" (1998, 204). The rosary has a different meaning when used by the Dene Tha and is interpreted according to their own worldview, as a prophet explained to Patrick Moore and Angela Wheelock (1990, 62): "Each large bead represents a place where the Son of God came to earth. He walked along the earth and then went back to heaven. He did this many times, and each of the small beads represents his tracks on earth."

When the rosary is used in the Prophet Dance in conjunction with the dominant symbols of the circle and the path, it takes on the meaning of ritual. In the Prophet Dance the circle represents social and cosmic order; it takes its shape from important concepts and objects in Dene Tha life: the Sun, Earth, and the drum. Participants dance together in a circle around a fire in three or four rows. The path represents the journey between "our land" and "the other land," and the dancing performed during the Prophet Dance is believed to influence the quality of the journey the dancers will take when they die. The Dene Tha believe that when they dance, *Ndawota* (God) watches their feet and measures their steps; the more steps a dancer takes during the Prophet Dance, the fewer he or she will have to take on the journey to heaven. The same belief applies to the rosary: each bead of the rosary represents one prayer and one step on the way to heaven.

At the same time, the Dene Tha refuse to accept some of the most fundamental Christian beliefs. One of the most foreign to the Dene Tha is the belief in original sin and in the Christian "hell," with its implication that one is never forgiven for some sins and that punishment continues into eternity. The introduction of Christianity into the cultural world of the Dene Tha did not result in the wholesale abandonment of their existing beliefs and worldview; rather, they successfully incorporated certain aspects (but not others) of a Christian worldview into their own belief system.

Christianity was also introduced to the Kwara'ae of the Solomon Islands, but with different results. The difference between existing Dene Tha and Kwara'ae worldviews helps account for these different practices and beliefs of introduced Christianity.

Christianity in the Solomon Islands

Anglican missionaries first visited the Kwara'ae people in the Solomon Islands of Melanesia in the 1860s. The leaders of local communities met these missionaries with opposition. Ben Burt, an education officer at the British Museum of Mankind in London, has been researching Kwara'ae culture and history since 1979. He argues that when the Kwara'ae finally accepted Christianity (albeit with lingering reservations), it was for reasons that had less to do with belief in the Christian message than with the hope that once the Kwara'ae presented the appearance of acceptance, they could learn more about the power of the British colonizers and regain control of their lives under the rule of colonialism.

Before colonization in the 1920s and the arrival of Christianity in the 1860s, the rules for social order in Kwara'ae society were passed down from generation to generation and upheld by ghosts of the ancestors. The Kwara'ae believe that they are all descended from one man who came to the island 20 or 30 generations ago. As his sons and their sons grew, they cleared areas of the virgin forest to plant their gardens and build their villages. In places in these original clearings, Kwara'ae built shrines of stone, where their ancestors stayed in close contact with the land and their descendants.

Ghosts were located at the top of the Kwara'ae social hierarchy. Below them were "Tabu speakers," or priests, who interacted directly with ghosts, followed by men, and finally by women. Burt describes how vital ghosts were to Kwara'ae life: "It was the strength of ghosts which ensured people's health and prosperity, the growth of their gardens and pigs, kept the peace and ensured victory when the peace was broken, guided people's plans and endeavours and made some of them wealthy and successful. Ultimately the ghosts held power of life and death over their people" (1994, 54). The Kwara'ae had to treat ghosts with respect and follow their rules, or the ghosts would cause harm to the living. Making restitution to an angry ghost required sacrifices that ranged from roasting taro to killing the person who had committed an offence.

After colonization and the arrival of Christianity, people were encouraged to give up their ghosts. Some did this quite willingly, because the demands of ghosts were a definite burden. For others, however, life without ghosts didn't make sense. After the Second World War, there arose a resistance movement that called itself Maasina Rul (Rule of Brotherhood), which reaffirmed that all are descended from one common ancestor. The name was later changed to Masing Rul (literally, Marching Rule) (Burt 1994, 177). Its purpose was to challenge the British colonial authorities. Part of this challenge included a return to some of the pre-Christian values that nonetheless could be supported by the Christian Bible as interpreted

locally (1994, 184). The new indigenous Christian theology contained the origin story of common ancestry as well as the laws of correct social behaviour that had been passed on through generations from the original ancestor.

For some, the exchange of ghosts for God has been mainly a change in names. The connection of the pre-Christian worldview with the Christian one through reinterpretation of the Bible meant that many of the old ideas simply took on a different validation. As Burt explains, "a person's behaviour affects his relationship with God in much the same way as it affects relationships with ghosts, for God's support and protection is only given to those whose lives are kept clean and pure by following his rules" (1994, 258).

The way the Kwara'ae incorporated Christianity into their existing worldview was shaped by that worldview but also by the circumstances of their lives under British colonial rule. All reinterpretations of Christianity depend on local histories and local experiences. As discussed in the next example, Jamaicans living in poverty saw the European version of Christianity as intimately linked to colonialism and to the oppressiveness of the capitalist world system. This perspective was then reflected in the reinterpretation of the Christian Messiah in a new religion, Rastafarianism.

Rastafari in Jamaica

In 1834, slavery officially ended in the British West Indies, although there would be four more years of a bondage system known as apprenticeship before ex-slaves were able to leave the plantations. In places such as Jamaica, many of the newly freed people moved away from the sugar estates and began a new life on small plots of land where they could grow their own food and sell the surplus at community markets. In the early 1900s, however, United Fruit Company moved into Jamaica to start new plantations, employing the small-scale farmers as wage labourers. Within a few years, United Fruit was undercutting the prices of the surplus foods the small-scale farmers had been selling. By the mid-1930s, so many of the rural farmers had lost their lands that a vast pool of landless, unemployed people, numbering in the hundreds of thousands, had left the countryside and moved to the city of Kingston in search of jobs. When they arrived and found that the jobs were not there, they settled on the fringes of the city and tried to survive.

In 1930, Ras Tafari was crowned emperor Haile Selassie I of Ethiopia. The Jamaicans living in extreme poverty on the fringes of Kingston followed the crowning of a black king with great enthusiasm, for this event provided a clear sign that black men were not always destined to be at the bottom of society. During the coronation ceremonies, Ras Tafari was proclaimed King of Kings and Lion of Judah. To the poor living in Kingston, Haile Selassie was either the Messiah or the living God and a symbol of hope and salvation for all black people. His coronation fulfilled the biblical prophecies that a saviour would come for them and lead them back to Africa.

As Rastafari became organized, Rasta leaders founded communities in and around Kingston that emphasized what they understood to be traditional African values: cooperative work efforts, respect for life, and the unity of all peoples of African descent. Through their belief in their messiah, Rasta returned to what they saw as their African beliefs and rejected the values of capitalist society and the capitalist market. By the time Selassie was overthrown in 1974, the Rasta belief system was so widespread that the loss of the messiah had little effect. Rasta continued to reject the capitalist world, which they called Babylon, and to create their own understanding of the Christian Bible, in which they were heroes. Their present oppression (*downpression* in Rasta terms) comes from the United States, which has taken over the role as the centre of Babylon from Britain. The Rasta, however, believe that eventually Jah (God) will truly set them free (Henry 1997).

The Rastafari response to colonial and post-colonial forms of domination resonated with oppressed peoples around the globe. The continued global popularity of the reggae music of Bob Marley is evidence of this resonance. As discussed in section 4.2 (above), key scenarios, such as rituals, share and perpetuate values and beliefs; popular music often embodies these key scenarios. Bob Marley's extensive discography has been aptly named "Songs of Freedom," and his music remains both relevant and incredibly popular more than three decades after his death (in 1981). According to Jason Toynbee (2007), Marley can be considered the "herald of a postcolonial world." Toynbee points out that Marley is #12 on *Forbes* magazine's "Top-Earning Dead Celebrities List" (Kafka 2005), with tens of millions of albums sold, and that his music is most popular in the global South, where "most people listen to him on cassettes, generally copied and distributed outside of official music industry channels. No statistics are available for this activity. Nor is there any way to quantify the circulation of images of Marley in the form of posters and drawings, or the spread of stories about him" (2007, 8).

How can we explain Marley's ongoing global superstar status? Toynbee (2007, 27–28) elaborates:

Marley was among a handful of musicians who challenged the unwritten rules (the "mental slavery") that kept the great masses of the world in bondage to the rich and powerful. As he sang it:

> *Today they say that we are free*
> *Only to be chained in poverty*
> *Good god, I think it's all illiteracy*
> *It's only a machine that makes money*
>
> > Bob Marley, "Slave Driver"[2]

That these lines sound compelling and poignant is a testament to Marley's extraordinary creative powers … Marley combined an appreciation of the embeddedness of oppressive social relations with affirmation of the autonomy of human beings, and of their facility to "act back" upon the world in order to change it.

---

[2] Lyrics to "Slave Driver": Words and music by Bob Marley. Copyright © 1973 Fifty-Six Hope Road Music Ltd & Blackwell Fuller Music Publishing LLC. All Rights Reserved. Used By Permission. All rights administered by Blue Mountain Music Ltd.

Bob Marley.

The case of Bob Marley's reggae, and of Rastafarianism more generally, provides a powerful example of the often unexpected ways in which people incorporate introduced beliefs into existing belief systems, and of the ways in which one's living conditions shape and are shaped by one's worldview. Rather than ask, as some early anthropologists did, how European religions have destroyed the cultures of local people who have lived through colonization, anthropologists are now asking how colonized people have interpreted the colonial religion with regard to their own worldview. Although the arrival of colonial religions may change local people's worldviews, it is rarely the case that the beliefs and values that have worked to explain the ways of the world for a long time will be easily or completely discarded.

QUESTION 4.5: HOW CAN PEOPLE REORDER THEIR VIEW OF THE WORLD IF IT BECOMES UNSATISFACTORY?

The meanings that people assign to their experiences do not change easily. We very much take for granted that the view of the world created by the interaction of our own experiences of the world with the mediums of language, symbolic actions, humour, and collective judgments is the right view. But beliefs do change. Changes in the meanings that people assign to their experiences are often triggered by social upheavals, during which old ways of looking at the world, for whatever reason, are no longer satisfactory. Such social upheavals, and the resulting unease, are often the direct result of colonial encounters and subsequent inequalities. If sufficient numbers of people share this unease, they may together try to change both their view of the world and the organization of society.

Anthropologist Anthony F. C. Wallace (1966) suggests the term "**revitalization movements**" for these efforts by people to construct a more satisfying culture. The escalating political, economic, and cultural colonization of Indigenous peoples over the past few centuries has inspired a multitude of revitalization movements. These movements promise liberation from oppression by foreign powers and tend to incorporate and rework elements of pre-colonial culture. Wallace developed his theory in the context of North American indigenous peoples, but his framework has since been applied to colonial contexts around the world. It enriches our understanding of the effects of colonial contact on existing belief systems.

Generally, a period of social or economic upheaval or oppression leads to the development of a new or revised belief system that promises to return the society to a real or mythical previous state or that offers a new vision of the world that promises to relieve oppression or frustration. During such social upheavals, the usual explanations for events are unsatisfactory, traditional solutions to problems no longer work, and rituals may be abandoned. Doubts generated by social upheaval are replaced with new certainties born of religious fervour or conversion. Another way that people reorder their view of the

revitalization movements
The term suggested by Anthony F. C. Wallace for attempts by a people to construct a more satisfying culture.

CONSTRUCTING REALITIES **117**

world is **syncretization**, in which elements of two or more worldviews are combined to produce a new way of understanding lived experience. Examples of these two ways that people can change their worldviews are the Ghost Dance among Native Americans and Vodou among Haitians.

Wovoka and the Ghost Dance

As settlers moved west in the 19th century, they came into contact with hundreds of Native American groups. As more and more people migrated west, conflicts over land resulted in wars between these groups and U.S. military forces. The Indian Wars covered the period from about 1850 to 1880. During this time, the U.S. government negotiated and signed treaties with Native American groups, guaranteeing their rights over areas of land, financial compensation, and food and other provisions.

However, as more white settlers moved to Native American territories, the U.S. government insisted on renegotiating treaties when land that had been given to Native American groups was desired by settlers. For example, the Sioux were given rights to the Black Hills of South Dakota, but after gold was discovered there, the government unilaterally renegotiated the treaties and reduced the land of the Sioux by more than half in 1889. (In this case, however, the courts later ruled that the government's act was illegal and that the Sioux never ceded their rights.) In addition, the buffalo were virtually exterminated, sometimes in a conscious effort by the U.S. military to destroy the economic basis of Native American society.

As a result of the Indian Wars, treaty negotiations, government deceit, and the influx of new settlers, Native American groups were restricted to reservations, made dependent on government rations, and denied traditional pursuits such as

syncretization
The term given to the combination of old beliefs or religions and new ones that are often introduced during colonization.

National Anthropological Archives, Smithsonian Institution, Item 659–A–1

Wovoka, the major prophet of the Ghost Dance, is shown here in a photograph taken by anthropologist James Mooney in 1891.

hunting and horse raiding. Government deliveries of food and provisions were often late or did not arrive at all, and diseases brought to the New World by European settlers, to which the indigenous population had little resistance, decimated the population. Children were taken to boarding schools away from the reservations and prohibited from speaking their first languages. Government agents, often at the insistence of Christian missionaries, banned traditional ceremonies and rituals. In brief, the social fabric of indigenous society was virtually destroyed. Those traditional things that help filter experience—language, ritual, and the ability of groups to collectively sustain particular views of the world—virtually vanished.

Revitalization movements usually receive their impetus from a prophet who claims to have received a vision or dream about a new way of viewing the world or a set of moral injunctions governing people's lives. The major prophet for the Ghost Dance was a Paiute named Wovoka. In 1889,

Wovoka had a vision in which he was taken up to heaven, where he saw God and all the people who had died performing their traditional games and activities. God told him he must go back and tell people to live in peace with whites and with one another. Wovoka was also given instructions for a ritual dance. He was told that if this dance were performed for five days and nights, people would be reunited with their friends and relatives in the other world.

Converts to Wovoka's message spread the word from Nevada to Native American groups throughout the United States and Canada. Wovoka's message was sometimes reinterpreted as it spread from one Aboriginal group to another. In some versions, the world would be destroyed and only the Native Americans brought back to life; in others, Euro-Americans and Native Americans would live together in harmony. In some versions, the buffalo would return. In some cases, a specific date was set for the millennium (4 July was one date; another was the time of a major traditional ceremony). In some versions, Wovoka was even said to be the son of God. Whatever the interpretation, the Ghost Dance, as it came to be called, was adopted by many groups that were seeking a revival of a way of life disrupted by Euro-American expansion.

Among the groups that enthusiastically adopted the Ghost Dance were the Sioux. They had sent emissaries in 1889 to visit Wovoka; those emissaries had returned with descriptions of his vision and power. One account of the delegate's report is contained in James Mooney's *The Ghost Dance Religion and the Sioux Outbreak of 1890* (1897). An anthropologist working for the Bureau of American Ethnology, Mooney travelled around the country interviewing key figures, including Wovoka, and collecting firsthand accounts of the dance from Euro-Americans and Native Americans. Here is his description of the report of the Sioux delegates:

> They were gone all winter, and their return in the spring of 1890 aroused an intense excitement among the Sioux, who had been anxiously awaiting their report. All the delegates agreed that there was a man near the base of the Sierras who said that he was the son of God, who had once been killed by the whites, and who bore on his body the scars of the crucifixion. He had now returned to punish the whites for their wickedness, especially for their injustice toward the Indians. With the coming of the next spring (1891) he would wipe the whites from the face of the earth, and would then resurrect all the dead Indians, bring back the buffalo and other game, and restore the supremacy of the aboriginal race. (Mooney 2011 [1897], 64)

Based on these messages, the Sioux began to dance in October 1890, but for them, the Ghost Dance turned into a tragic reminder of Euro-American oppression. Frightened that the dance might turn into open rebellion, the Indian agent on one of the Sioux reservations called in the military. Some of the Sioux fled the reservation, chased by the Seventh Cavalry, General George Custer's group, which had been decimated by a combined Native American army at Little Bighorn in 1876. After a promise of a safe return to the reservation, the fleeing Sioux surrendered their arms at a place called Wounded Knee, where they were surrounded by the Seventh Cavalry equipped with Gatling guns. As soldiers rummaged through the Sioux shelters searching for guns, someone fired a shot and the army opened fire, killing hundreds of men, women, and children.

The Ghost Dance virtually ceased among the Sioux after the massacre at Wounded Knee, but it continued among other groups, each of which hoped for the return of their traditional culture. Today it represents one attempt of a people to build a new culture, a new system of meaning after the destruction of an earlier one.

Haitian Vodou

Another way people cope with drastic changes in their lives is by developing a different worldview. Doing so entails combining elements of a new view with those of an older one—the process called "syncretization," described earlier. In Haiti, Africans from many different parts of the continent were forcibly brought together by the slave trade. Having been captured inland, the Africans were taken to the coast, where they were sold to slave traders, loaded onto ships, and taken across the "Middle Passage" to a foreign land, where they were again sold to plantation owners. These Africans could not bring any of their belongings with them across the Middle Passage, but they could bring their beliefs and worldviews, stored in their memories. After they reached Haiti and were divided among individual plantations, they were unlikely to meet anyone from their own community; as a consequence, much of the initial adjustment they had to make involved learning to communicate with other slaves from other parts in Africa. Once new systems of communication had been established, Africans could create a distinctive Caribbean culture based on their former beliefs and those of the French planters. In this totally new world it must have been immediately obvious to all African slaves that their old worldviews would not work to explain their new experiences in Haiti.

The new worldview that Africans created in Haiti, then, was a **creole** view based on their lived experiences in their new world. That world was filled with work and suffering, first as slaves and then later as peasants living in a country that today is still the poorest in the Western hemisphere. Karen McCarthy Brown explains that Haitians created Vodou to find a way to live in conditions that are among the worst in the world: "Vodou is the system they have devised to deal with the suffering that is life, a system whose purpose is to minimize pain, avoid disaster, cushion loss, and strengthen survivors and survival instincts" (1991, 10).

> **creole**
> A term used commonly to refer to the formation of slave societies in the Caribbean in which elements of African and European cultures were merged, blended, or combined into something uniquely Caribbean.

Although the French introduced Roman Catholicism during the colonial period, the slaves they owned worshipped their Vodou deities in secret. After the Haitian Revolution ended in 1804, free Haitians combined the two religions to produce a third that looks like Catholicism on the outside but is something quite different. Haitians believe in the Christian God, whom they call "Bondye." They believe that this god created all things and that he is supreme. But they also believe that he is a European god who has many Europeans to attend to and is therefore much too busy to bother with poor Haitians. So, instead of trying to interact with Bondye directly, Haitians use African spirits, or *lwa*, to intercede for them. These *lwa* have names that connect them to Catholic saints: the Virgin Mary is Ezili, Saint Patrick is Danbala, Saint James is Ogou, Saint Gerard is Gede, and Isidore is Azaka. But this is where the similarities end, for Haitian *lwa* are anything but saintly.

Vodou *lwa* present models for Haitian life and address issues that real Haitians face. For example, Azaka, the poor peasant farmer, teaches Haitians to remember their roots: their land and their ancestors. In the worldview of rural Haitians, land, ancestors, and spirits are all the same thing. Azake also reminds people of the importance of their family, and part of what urban Vodou congregations do is provide families for those who have migrated to the cities.

As another model, Ezili represents women, and because women play various roles in Haiti, she has various manifestations. Three important Ezili manifestations are Ezili Danto, Ezili Freda, and Lasyrenn. Ezili Danto is the hard-working black single mother. She presents and works through the problems that single Haitian mothers face. Ezili Freda is the rich white woman who represents white privilege in Haiti. Freda is usually posed reclining on a sofa, dressed in beautiful clothes, covered with jewellery, and eating chocolates. This image reaffirms for Haitians the uselessness of white sensuality, because Freda does nothing except pose. Lasyrenn, often associated with the African "mammy water," is both black and white and lives just below the surface of the water, which Haitians say is "the back of the mirror." If one were to lean over a calm pool, one might catch a glimpse of Lasyrenn, but doing this is dangerous because sometimes she pulls people into the water and they disappear; some say she takes them back to Ginen (Africa). Sometimes, Lasyrenn will pull women under the water and keep them for several days, or as long as one year. When the women return, they are changed by the sacred knowledge they have learned and may become priestesses. Lasyrenn resembles the carved figure-heads that slave trading ships had on their bows. This image may mean that she reminds Haitians of the traumatic Middle Passage and slavery.

Danbala, Ogue, and Gede are male *lwa* who represent oppositions in Haitian life.

Danbala is the oldest and most respected of the *lwa* and, like Saint Patrick, is associated with snakes. The difference between Saint Patrick and Danbala is that snakes are creatures that have important survival skills. Snakes can curve their bodies to go over obstacles, and if a snake puts its tail in its mouth it becomes a circle with no beginning and no end. Thus, Danbala represents life, death, and rebirth in a continuous cycle. He also mediates opposites: as the symbol of the rainbow, Danbala is said to have one foot in the ocean and one in the Haitian mountains. Haitians say that Danbala is becoming angry with politics in Haiti and that he has taken his foot out of the water. People say that Haiti will now wither and die.

Ogue is a warrior who has subdivided into at least seven figures. In one of his manifestations, he is the handsome soldier riding a beautiful white horse who faces battle fearlessly. In another he is a liar and a beggar. In others he is a drunk or a coward. Ogue presents the lesson that while power may liberate, it also corrupts, as has happened to many of Haiti's leaders.

Gede is the master of the cemetery and is said to have one foot in life and one foot in death. Gede is a trickster, always making jokes, and he teaches that one way to overcome misfortune is to make fun of it. It should come as no surprise, then, that Gede is an important healer.

Haitian Vodou, then, is not just a set of exotic rituals, as it is often portrayed in the media. It is a worldview that helps Haitians cope with a life of poverty and hardship. Furthermore, as Brown argues, Haitian Vodou is a system of healing that applies to a variety of areas in the lives of its followers, including

© Photo courtesy and property of Anna E. Parmelee of Erzulie's, Inc. and www.erzulies.com

Mama Lola, the subject of Karen McCarthy Brown's (2001) ethnography, *Mama Lola: A Vodou Priestess in Brooklyn*

CONSTRUCTING REALITIES

troubled social relationships, physical illness, and the pain of the past in which families were torn apart by slavery.

Western Secularism

Increasingly, many Western industrialized nations, including Canada, are reporting higher rates of **atheism** and a preference for **secularism**, or the separation of spirituality/religion from government, economics, and politics. Atheists do not identify as "religious," and most do not believe in the existence of deities or spiritual forces. In 2011, the Canadian census reported that 23.9 percent of Canadians declared that they did not have any religious affiliation. This statistic raises interesting questions about the future of religion in a multicultural society like Canada. Increasingly, many influential scientists and thinkers, like best-selling author and evolutionary biologist Richard Dawkins (2006), label religion as a "delusion" and as a source of unnecessary violence and cultural conflict. Atheism and secularism, like religious beliefs, constitute worldviews.

What will be the future of religion in an increasingly globalized, multicultural, and secular world? It may be that the rise of atheism and the trend toward the abandonment or dismissal of organized forms of religion as "irrational" or "primitive" beliefs in favour of strictly scientific understandings of the world will lead to increasing intolerance of and ethnocentrism toward adherents of religion.

Such attitudes, for instance, were apparent in responses to the 2015 *Charlie Hebdo* shootings in Paris. On 7 January 2015, two gunmen (later identified as adherents of Al-Qaeda in Yemen) entered the headquarters of the satirical news magazine,

atheism
Refers to a lack of belief in supernatural forces or beings.

secularism
Refers to the separation of political and economic realms of society from religion or spirituality.

with the goal of assassinating cartoonists, artists, and key production team members. Eleven people were killed, and 11 more were injured. Five more people were killed and 11 wounded in additional attacks in other areas of Paris. *Charlie Hebdo*, renowned for its secular, irreligious, and irreverent political stance, had published satirical caricatures that mocked the Islamic prophet Muhammad. In the aftermath of this tragedy, interpretation and response became divided along religious/secular lines. For the secular mainstream French and Western public, the deceased *Charlie Hebdo* employees were commemorated and honoured for their secularism, bravery, and defence of freedom of speech. For many adherents of Islam, however, the organization, with its publications, had committed hate crimes, as it is considered sacrilegious to depict Muhammad in pictorial representations, and because the tone of the paper sought to depict Islam and its adherents as primitive, backward, and uncivilized. (Note that *Charlie Hebdo*'s religious satire was not limited to Islam; Catholicism, for example, has also been a target.)

This example draws our attention to the contested role of religion (or lack thereof) in an increasingly globalized world. In Western contexts, where religiosity is increasingly undermined by the rise and proliferation of scientific narratives, and where atheist worldviews are on the rise, how can anthropological principles of cultural relativism be used to avoid the proliferation of ethnocentric assumptions about different religions and worldviews? Moreover, how can such anthropological principles be used to help avoid, or at least better understand and address, secular/religious violence and conflict?

The work of anthropologist Mayanthi Fernando (2014) exemplifies one possibility. Fernando's ethnography of the paradoxes of being a Muslim French citizen in contemporary secular France reminds us that there is no single way of practising either Islam or secularity, and that seemingly universal ideas about freedom of speech are differently inflected in different cultural, social, and historical contexts. In a blog post written as an anthropologically informed response to the *Charlie Hebdo* incident, Fernando (2015) suggests:

> *We should not deny the horror of January 6. But, in its aftermath, rather than uncritically reaffirm French national identity and wring our hands about Muslims' refusal to integrate, we should use this moment of reflection to understand the various ways in which Muslims are consistently excluded from the [French] nation.*

Clearly, anthropologists and anthropology students have much to offer with respect to debates about the rise and proliferation of secularism in the coming years.

CONCLUSIONS

Human beings, as we have noted, live in a world of their own creation. In other words, by imposing meaning on experience through the metaphors we select, we construct our own realities and validate them collectively through rituals and myths. Our Haitian Vodou example demonstrates how an anthropological perspective on worldviews and belief systems can help us understand our own taken-for-granted desire to view our lives as meaningful, especially when faced with seemingly meaningless adversity.

Being aware of the ways that people assign meaning to their world relates also to fields such as counselling. Virtually any kind of counselling involves a manipulation of perspective to help people change or cope with the meanings they assign experience.

For example, in *Disrupted Lives: How People Create Meaning in a Chaotic World* (1997), anthropologist Gay Becker studies the ways in which people try to create continuity in their lives after some unexpected disruption, such as an illness, the death of someone close, or even the onset of aging. For Becker, an ongoing interpretation of experiences and events enables people to make sense of their personal world. People create continuity in their lives through ordinary routines or daily repetitive rituals such as drinking a cup of coffee with the morning newspaper. But, says Becker, when expectations about the course of one's life are not met, people experience inner chaos and disruption. Such disruptions represent the loss of the future. As Becker puts it, "restoring order to life necessitates reworking understandings of the self and the world, redefining the disruption and life itself" (1997, 4). Becker suggests that every culture has its own "cultural life course." This life course can be viewed as a collectively shared image that, through metaphor, provides persons with images to guide their lives. In North American societies, we hear people speak of life as a "journey" or a "life wheel."

Common in the United States, Becker says, is the view that life is predictable and continuous (the same view is shared by most people in Canada). People develop stories, or narratives, of how their lives should proceed, what they should accomplish, and what sort of person they will be. But when some unexpected event occurs—illness, death, infertility—they are forced to redo their narratives. Metaphors not only help people make sense of the disruptions, says Becker, but also enable people to alter their views of reality and restore a sense of coherence.

For many people, having a child is part of their narrative, part of the life course as they expect it to unfold, for example. A diagnosis of infertility would disrupt that narrative and require a reordering of experience and a way of coping with the disruption. In her infertility study, Becker found that people confronting this disruption felt trapped in the present and could not foresee the future. One metaphor that helped them get through this time was seeing it as a period of limbo, a temporary state that preceded a return to normalcy.

In her research on how people cope with illness, Becker interviewed a man of 40 who had been diagnosed with severe asthma but whose identity and life narrative had focused on being active and athletic. In reformulating his narrative, he drew on a military metaphor explaining how "people in midlife are wounded soldiers. And weary soldiers. We've been to the front and back." He thus identified himself with a social condition, extending it to his "war on illness" and redoing his biography to focus on his "fight with asthma."

Becker's point is that by recognizing life's disruptions as breaks in a cultural narrative of how life is supposed to proceed, we can better cope with the disruptions. In many ways, of course, Becker is addressing at the individual level the same revitalization processes engaged in by groups when they endeavour to construct a more satisfying culture.

We began the chapter by asking how it is that people can believe in things that cannot be proven—why, for example, people are convinced of the presence of God, the existence of unseen spirits, or of the powers of witchcraft. As we have seen, to answer this question requires us to examine the role of such areas of social life as metaphor, ritual, and myth, along with other features of social life that persuade people of the correctness of their beliefs or that convince them to change what they believe.

EXERCISE 4 (Conclusions)

Every culture has its version of how life is supposed to proceed; that is, there are cultural narratives about each person's life course. For this exercise, choose and interview a partner about how he or she expects life to unfold. For example, how would that person like to be remembered after death? Ask, too, whether your partner has experienced any disruptions that might alter attainment of the desired life course.

How does metaphor affect the meanings we assign to our experience? The selection of metaphors has an impact on the meanings we assign to experience. By taking the language from one domain of experience and applying it to another, we carry the meaning of one domain to another domain. Any effort to understand another culture (or to turn our anthropological analysis on our own culture) requires that we pay close attention to key metaphors.

The social and cultural construction of reality does not happen through metaphor alone. Symbolic actions also reinforce a particular view of the world. Ritual, for example, symbolically depicts a certain view of reality in such a way that it convinces us of the truth of that reality. Recall, for example, the Hamatsa Dance of the Kwakwaka'wakw, which portrays the values of Kwakwaka'wakw society and provides members with a way to control their lives. Recall, as well, the rituals of contemporary English magic and witchcraft, which convince participants that mental forces can influence the material world.

Relevant metaphors and rituals do not come from nowhere, and not just *any* metaphor or ritual will be meaningful or effective in a particular cultural context. The way we live (including social, political, and economic forces) influences what we believe and how we act out those beliefs. "Ways of knowing" among First Nations peoples differ from the kinds of knowledge that Euro-North Americans take for granted as correct because of the different ways these groups make their livelihood. People tend to act based on what they know about the world around them, which is shaped by their worldview. Sometimes, as we have seen in the examples from Madagascar and Cameroon, people are forced to speculate about what they cannot know—for example, what happens to sapphires when foreigners take them out of the country, or why some people are rich while others remain poor. People speculate using the tools provided to them by their existing worldview. These explanations may not make sense to an outsider, but knowing what we as anthropologists know about how belief systems work helps us begin to take such explanations seriously instead of dismissing them out of hand.

We also looked at three examples (Dene Tha, Kwara'ae, and Rastafari in Jamaica and beyond) of how people reinterpret new European religions using the worldviews that helped them explain their experiences before colonization or slavery. In most cases, people actively select parts of the new religion to incorporate within their own worldview. As the global popularity of Bob Marley shows, forces of globalization (see Chapter 8), and local responses to these forces, mean that many people around the world have had to reorient their belief systems in similar ways, despite differences in local histories and local experiences.

Under certain conditions, people might also be led to radically change what they believe. The experience of social upheaval may lead, as it did among the Plains Indians, to a new system of belief that promises to reorder society—and, in the case of the Ghost Dance, to resurrect the past. In the case of

CONSTRUCTING REALITIES **125**

Haitian Vodou, a new worldview has been constructed to help people cope with the new conditions of a life they don't believe they can change.

Finally, we explored the effects of the rise of Western secularism and atheism. We saw how secularism often contributes to the development of new struggles over competing worldviews (occasionally in the form of violence, as in the *Charlie Hebdo* case), as well as the development of problematic binaries between notions of a spiritual and a secular world. Overall, the key significance of understanding how and why people come to believe what they do is that doing so gives us insight into one of the things that makes us human: our desire—and, indeed, our need—to make our lives meaningful.

KEY TERMS:

atheism   (p. 122)
creole   (p. 120)
domain of experience   (p. 96)
key metaphors   (p. 98)
key scenarios   (p. 104)
magic   (p. 100)
metaphors   (p. 96)
myth   (p. 99)
revitalization movements   (p. 117)
rites of passage   (p. 106)
ritual   (p. 94)
secularism   (p. 122)
shamanism   (p. 113)
symbolic actions   (p. 95)
syncretization   (p. 118)
totemism   (p. 94)
witchcraft   (p. 100)
worldview   (p. 93)

CRITICAL THINKING QUESTIONS

1. If worldview is culturally and socially constructed, can there be such a thing as objective truth? What are the implications of taking a social constructionist approach to reality for the pursuit of knowledge? Is objectivity possible? What obstacles might this present for the anthropological study of culture?
2. Do we need to believe in rituals in order for them to be effective? Explain why or why not.
3. How have the forces and circumstances of globalization shaped belief systems around the world?

CHAPTER 5

CONSTRUCTING FAMILIES AND SOCIAL RELATIONSHIPS

This soapstone sculpture by Inuit artist Jonasie Quarqortoq Faber, simply titled "Family," depicts a family unit–mother, father, and child–that many North Americans would identify as the "typical" nuclear family. However, the dynamics of the Inuit nuclear family are not necessarily the same as the nuclear family dynamics described in the epigraph below by Whately. Indeed, as we will see throughout this chapter, family dynamics and configurations vary widely from culture to culture.

If ever thou purpose to be a good wife, and to live comfortably, set down this with thyself: mine husband is my superior, my better, he hath authority and rule over me; nature hath given it to him … God hath given it to him.

W. Whately, A Bride-Bush, or, A Wedding Sermon: London, 1617

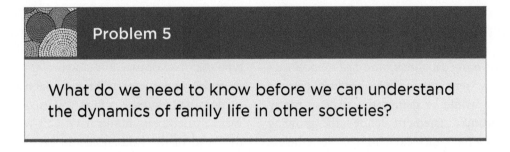

Problem 5

What do we need to know before we can understand the dynamics of family life in other societies?

INTRODUCTION

Family Relations in North American Popular Culture

In 1973, renowned anthropologist Margaret Mead reviewed a new, genre-defying television show, which aired on PBS, titled *An American Family*. The 12-episode documentary chronicled seven months in the lives of the Loud family of Santa Barbara, California, a "typical" nuclear family comprised of a husband, a wife, and their five children. Why would an eminent anthropologist be interested in a television program? For Mead, the controversial program—an early prototype for today's ubiquitous reality television shows—was "as important for our time as were the invention of drama and the novel for earlier generations: a new way to help people understand themselves" (cited in Ruoff 1996, 270). Ten million people tuned in weekly to "understand themselves." Much of the interest the show generated had to do with the unexpected, soap opera–like plot twists and character developments: Pat Loud, the mother, asked her husband William for a divorce; William's successful business fell on hard times; and Lance, the eldest son, was arguably the world's first openly gay TV "character."

An anthropologist might have learned a great deal about North American family relations in the 1970s by watching *An American Family*, noting the reasons for domestic strife, the choices characters made, and the impact those choices had on family members. Furthermore, an anthropologist would learn much by paying close attention to viewers' reactions to the show: What did they find plausible, scandalous, or relatable? What exactly was it about this family that made its members both typical and compelling?

Although North American viewers no longer find reality television especially groundbreaking, and many would be unfazed by the inclusion of divorced or gay characters, an anthropologist might still want to pay attention to the family structure and dynamics portrayed on popular television shows and the discussions they evoke. For instance, in May 2012, U.S. President Barack Obama publicly declared his support for same-sex marriage (which has been legal in Canada since 2005). In an interview with ABC News, he explained that he had taken his cue from his two young daughters, who had schoolmates whose parents were gay and who could not imagine why they would be denied the right to marry. President Obama's statement echoed the growing public support for same-sex marriage; nonetheless, it generated much controversy. For instance, Bristol Palin, daughter of 2008 Republican vice-presidential candidate Sarah Palin, criticized the president in her blog post titled "Hail to the Chiefs: Malia and Sasha Obama." She suggested that Obama's daughters had watched too many episodes of *Glee*—a popular television show with several prominent gay characters—and that President Obama should be a "proper" father and leader, teaching his daughters what to do and think rather than allowing them to teach him. Palin's critics, in turn, suggested that having become a single mother at the age of 18, she was in no position to judge others regarding issues pertaining to the family. Whose version of the North American family is the "correct" one?

The study of **kinship**, including family composition, descent, and marriage, has long been central to sociocultural anthropology. Franklin and McKinnon (2001, 1) argue that, in fact, "the study of kinship is itself symbolic of the anthropological tradition." Kinship has long intrigued anthropologists because it relates so closely to social organization. Many early anthropologists assumed that kinship was more important in small-scale societies, where it provided the entire basis of social organization, than in large-scale societies. But as we will find later in this chapter, contemporary kinship studies have demonstrated that kinship remains a meaningful element of social life in large-scale societies. When we study kinship, we are interested both in classifications—who is considered a relative and who is not—and in the ways people

make particular relationships meaningful. Anthropologists who study family relations often begin by exploring the composition of a typical family and how it is formed and maintained. They examine how the themes of sexuality, love, and wealth are dealt with and what kinds of situations or conflicts can disrupt family life. However, as we can see from the example above, the typical family is just that: an ideal type that may or may not closely align with people's everyday experiences. Questions about what does or does not count as a family, what kinds of rights various members should have, and who should be the head of the household can be contentious. By exploring both the typical family *and* the debates about its composition, however, we can learn much about a given society.

To make the task of understanding patterns of family relations cross-culturally more manageable, we will focus first on family life in three societies: the Ju/'hoansi of Namibia and Botswana, the Trobriand Islanders of the South Pacific, and a rural Chinese farm family in Taiwan. These have been selected for three reasons. First, they represent very different levels of social, cultural, and technological complexity. The Ju/'hoansi are gatherers and hunters living in small, mobile groups; the Trobriand Islanders are horticulturists living in villages of up to 400 people; and the rural Chinese in Taiwan represent a large agricultural society. Second, family structure and roles vary significantly among the three, as do notions about the bases of kinship relations and how kinship terms, such as mother, father, sister, and brother, are used. Finally, the three societies have been well studied in the anthropological literature. We will discuss these societies in what anthropologists refer to as the **ethnographic present**; that is, although the actual descriptions may

kinship
Refers to the anthropological, cross-cultural study of family composition, marriage, and descent patterns.

ethnographic present
Use of the present tense to describe a culture, although the description may refer to situations that existed in the past.

refer to situations that existed in the past, they will be described as if they still exist. In reality, the Ju/'hoansi, the Trobriand Islanders, and the rural Chinese are, to varying degrees, very different today than they were when they were studied by the anthropologists whose work we will mention. After this review, we will look at more recent kinship studies by anthropologists to show some of the problems they have encountered and the new directions they have taken.

QUESTION 5.1: WHAT IS THE COMPOSITION OF THE TYPICAL FAMILY GROUP?

To understand family composition in different societies, we need certain concepts and tools. One place to begin is by examining how unmarried North Americans would typically respond if asked about the composition of their families. They would likely list their mother, father, brothers, and sisters. If asked, "Who else?" they would likely add grandparents, aunts, uncles, and cousins. If married, they would add their spouse and children. Figure 5.1 shows how this family structure would be diagrammed using genealogical notations.

David Schneider was one of the first anthropologists to study American kinship systematically, and his 1968 study led him to conclude that kinship, in North America and elsewhere, is a cultural system, not a set of biological facts. For instance, although Americans talk about kinship in terms of biological relatedness (often using the metaphor of shared blood), in practice, kinship is not dictated by any biogenetic reality. Often, we call people kin who are not related to us biogenetically. Many of us, for instance, grow up referring to close friends of our parents as "aunt" or "uncle" despite the fact that we are not biologically related to them. Such relationships can even extend to companion animals. Many people think about their dogs or cats in terms of kinship. Dogs, for instance, are often perceived as family members, with owners taking on the role of "parents" and dogs as "kids." Conversely, we often deny kinship status to biogenetic relatives (Feinberg 2001, 8). Family members can become "estranged" due to familial disagreements or a family member's participation in illegal or seemingly unethical activities. Ultimately, we employ the language of blood, of love, and of solidarity strategically to determine whom we consider kin and whom we do not.

Certain features of some North American families stand out for the anthropological observer. Many North Americans consider themselves equally tied by kinship to both their mother and their father, and

FIGURE 5.1 COMPOSITION AND DEVELOPMENT OF THE CANADIAN NUCLEAR FAMILY

1. The traditional Canadian household generally begins with a husband and wife pair moving from the households of their parents.

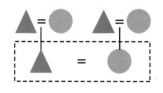

2. The arrangement is formalized with the birth of children, which produces a new nuclear family.

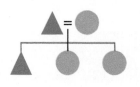

3. At some point the household might be composed of three generations, as married children join the household with their children.

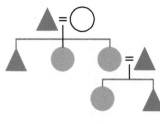

KEY

Female	●
Male	▲
Marriage	=
Blood Tie	⊓
Descent	I

4. At a later stage, the household might consist of the original couple or a single person.

▲ = ●

to both their maternal and their paternal kin. In other words, North Americans generally recognize **bilateral kinship**, or kinship through both parents. As we will see, however, not all societies do. Second, many North Americans make no linguistic distinction between the mother's siblings and the father's siblings; both are referred to as aunt or uncle, as are the spouses of their parents' siblings. Nor do they distinguish linguistically the children of aunts and uncles; all are referred to as cousins. For many North Americans, the most important family grouping is the **nuclear family**—the group that traditionally consists of father and mother and their biological or adopted children.

Notions of what constitutes a nuclear family, however, change over time. Increasingly within Canadian society, for instance, the concept of the nuclear family has shifted to also encompass same-sex partners who live with their biological or adopted children. With the increasing social acceptance of same-sex partnerships, and the advent of the *Civil Marriage Act* in 2005 that legalized them, the nuclear family does not necessarily imply the existence of heterosexual unions.

Families in other societies may be composed very differently. For example, other societies may place greater emphasis on ties to one parent or the other. In some cases, only people related through *either* the mother *or* the father are considered family. Societies that emphasize persons' ties to their mother are said to

bilateral kinship
A system in which individuals trace their descent through both parents.

nuclear family
The family group consisting of parents and their biological or adopted children.

have **matrilineal kinship** systems; those that emphasize persons' ties to their father are said to have **patrilineal kinship** systems. Few societies ignore an individual's relationship to one side of the family or the other; rather, in most societies, relationships with mothers' families and fathers' families are viewed differently. For example, North Americans traditionally inherit their surnames from their fathers, thus embracing the patrilineal principle; in cases of divorce, however, North American legal systems usually give priority to the matrilineal principle by awarding custody of the child to the mother.

Each of the three societies discussed in this chapter—the Ju/'hoansi, the Trobrianders, and the rural Chinese—defines the composition of the family and relations among members differently.

The Family Composition of Ju/'hoansi

For most of the year, the Ju/'hoansi live in groups numbering 10 to 30 or 40 people, bilaterally related (through both parents), who hunt and gather in a territory associated with a particular water hole. Camp groups are often organized around a brother-and-sister pair who claim ownership of the water hole. They bring their spouses and children into the group; in turn, the spouses may bring in their brothers, sisters, and even mothers and fathers.

A typical camp might look like the one described by Elizabeth Thomas in her classic work *The Harmless People* (see Figure 5.2). Membership in a camp is fluid. People move freely from camp to camp based on hunting alliances or because conflict develops in the group. Within the camp, however, the basic family group is the nuclear family of husband, wife, and children. Children spend most of their time with their mothers. The Ju/'hoansi acknowledge that pregnancy results from sexual intercourse (not the case in all societies). They also believe that conception

takes place at the end of the woman's menses, when the man's semen joins with the last of the menstrual blood.

A feature of Ju/'hoansi society that figures prominently in the dynamics of family life is the custom of **brideservice** at marriage, which requires that a groom work for the bride's parents for a specified time. Among the Ju/'hoansi, when a couple marries, the groom is expected to come and live in the bride's parents' camp and work for her parents for as long as ten years. Tales of Ju/'hoansi family life are often built around the effects of this arrangement on family dynamics.

---

matrilineal kinship
A system of descent in which persons are related to their kin through the mother only.

patrilineal kinship
A system of descent in which persons are related to their kin through the father only.

brideservice
The requirement that when a couple marries, the groom must work for the bride's parents for some specified time.

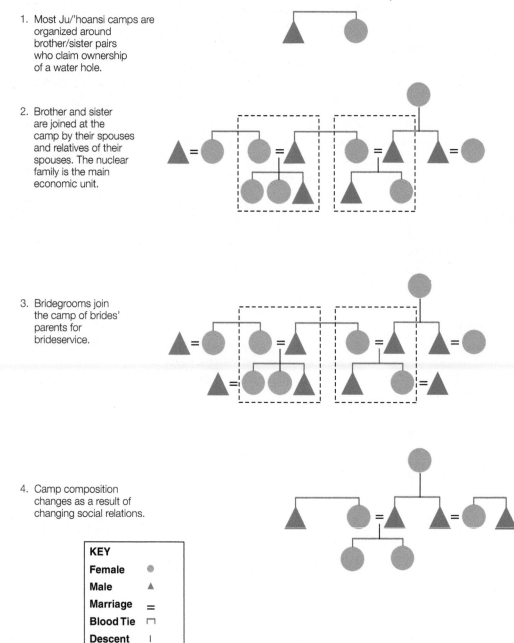

FIGURE 5.2 COMPOSITION AND DEVELOPMENT OF A JU/'HOANSI CAMP

1. Most Ju/'hoansi camps are organized around brother/sister pairs who claim ownership of a water hole.

2. Brother and sister are joined at the camp by their spouses and relatives of their spouses. The nuclear family is the main economic unit.

3. Bridegrooms join the camp of brides' parents for brideservice.

4. Camp composition changes as a result of changing social relations.

KEY

Female	●
Male	▲
Marriage	=
Blood Tie	⌐
Descent		

The Family Composition of Trobriand Islanders

The people of the Trobriand Islands live in some 80 villages, whose populations range from 40 to 400. Each village is surrounded by water holes, fruit trees, palm groves, and cultivated fields of yams, taro, and other crops. Each is further divided into hamlets, and each hamlet ideally consists of a **matrilineage**, or *dala*, as Trobrianders call it—that is, a group of

matrilineage
A lineage that is formed by tracing descent in the female line.

134 CHAPTER 5

NEL

men related to one another through the female line, along with their wives and unmarried children.

The matrilineages are ranked relative to one another, and each village has a chief who is the eldest male of the highest-ranking matrilineage. Since each person is a member of the lineage of his or her mother, neither a man's wife nor his children can be members of his own *dala* (see Figure 5.3).

Trobrianders' mythology and beliefs about procreation dramatically depict the matrilineal element in their lives. Their mythology contains stories of how,

a long time ago, pairs of brothers and sisters emerged from the ground to begin each *dala*. *Dala* members trace their descent back to their mythological ancestors, and they base their claims to specific plots of land on the fact that it was from there that their ancestors emerged. There is obviously an element of incest in Trobriand myth, since the originators of each lineage were brothers and sisters; however, Trobriand theories of procreation ostensibly deny a role to men in conception. They reinforce the matrilineal principle as well as the tie between brothers and sisters.

FIGURE 5.3   COMPOSITION OF A TROBRIAND ISLAND *DALA* AND HOUSHOLD

1. Each *dala* or matrilineage had its origin in a brother/sister pair who claim a plot of land.

2. *Dala* marriage is traced in the female line, and individuals must marry someone from outside their own *dala*.

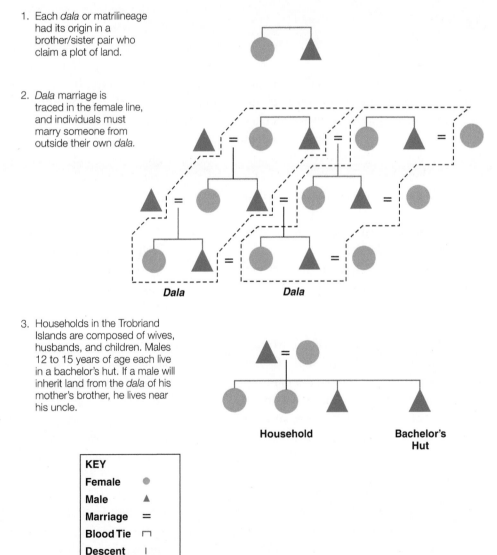

3. Households in the Trobriand Islands are composed of wives, husbands, and children. Males 12 to 15 years of age each live in a bachelor's hut. If a male will inherit land from the *dala* of his mother's brother, he lives near his uncle.

Household   **Bachelor's Hut**

KEY
Female   ●
Male   ▲
Marriage   =
Blood Tie   ⌐
Descent |

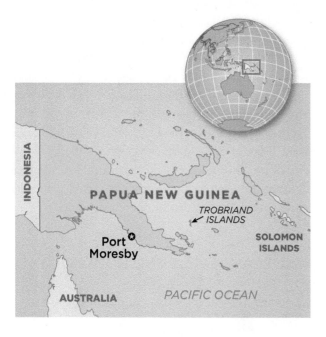

While Trobriand procreation beliefs may, at first glance, seem strange, in the context of their ideas about descent they make perfect sense. When a person is believed to be descended exclusively from the mother, possible relations and ties to the father are excluded not only socially but physically, as well. In fact, we find in strongly patrilineal societies corresponding beliefs about conception. Earlier in this book, we examined how Carol Delaney (1991, 26) explained how Turkish villagers had a "monogenetic" theory of procreation. "It is the males," she wrote, "who give life; women merely give birth." Turkish villagers use an agricultural metaphor to describe procreation: men provide the seed, and women are the soil. It is the seed that contains life; the soil simply nurtures it. The man is believed to plant the seed, and the woman is said to be the field in which the seed is planted. In this way, the male role in the patrilineal family system of the Turkish village is emphasized and the female role is diminished.

Trobrianders say that when a person dies, the soul or spirit becomes young and goes to live on an island called Tuma. There the soul ages, but it regenerates itself by bathing in the sea. As the skin is sloughed off, a spirit child, or *baloma*, is created, which returns to the world of the living and enters the womb of a woman of the same matrilineage as itself. In effect, a Trobriand matrilineage exists in perpetuity, as souls and spirits travel back and forth between the land of the living and the island of the dead.

The *baloma* may enter the woman through her head, or it may be carried by water into her womb. In some areas of the Trobriand Islands, if a woman wishes to become pregnant, a pail of water is brought to her dwelling by her brother. In fact, a woman cannot conceive without the "permission" of her brother. Consequently, the act of conception among Trobrianders is a matter of three agencies: a woman, the spirit or *baloma* of a deceased ancestor, and the woman's brother. Sexual intercourse is said to play no role in conception, but it does play a role in the development and growth of the fetus. Trobrianders believe that the man's semen provides food and nourishment for the fetus, and that is why children physically resemble their fathers. Sexual intercourse is also said to open the womb for the child to emerge.

Trobrianders can rationalize and "prove" their beliefs about procreation easily. Bronislaw Malinowski, who spent four years studying the Trobrianders, tells of their response when he suggested to them that sexual intercourse plays a role in procreation:

> *I sometimes made myself definitely and aggressively an advocate of the truer physiological doctrine of procreation. In such arguments the natives would quote, not only positive instances of women who have children without having intercourse; but would also refer to the many cases in which an unmarried woman has plenty of intercourse and no children. This argument would be repeated over and over again, with specially telling concrete examples of childless persons renowned for profligacy, or of women who lived with one white trader after another without having any baby. (Malinowski 1929, 185–86)*

To what extent Trobrianders really deny a role to men in procreation is a matter of some debate. Annette Weiner, who worked with them in the early 1970s, some 50 years after Malinowski's pioneering work, reported that they no longer denied the direct role of men in conception. However, she also reported a case where a grandmother claimed she had used magic to make her granddaughter pregnant when the woman conceived during her husband's absence.

Regardless of the extent to which Trobrianders recognize the role of coitus, their ideas about descent and procreation reflect important features of the composition of their families. First, the key family relationship for them is not, as it is among the Ju/'hoansi, between husband and wife; it is between brother and sister. Second, the father of the family is an outsider to his children, a member of another family group. His interest, ideally, is in his sister's children, since it is they who are members of his matrilineage. Third, since the matrilineal **extended family** group, the *dala*, is more important than the nuclear family, Trobrianders merge certain people under the same kin term the same way many North Americans refer to different kinds of kin as aunt, uncle, or cousin. In the Trobrianders' case, a person refers to all women of his or her matrilineage of the same generation by the same term; for example, a man refers to his mother, as well as his mother's sisters, by the term *ina*. A woman refers to her brother and to all other men of her matrilineage and generation as *luta*. Thus, a man has many "sisters," and a woman has many "brothers."

EXERCISE 5.2

The procreation beliefs of the Trobriand Islanders prompted debate among anthropologists about whether the Trobrianders really did believe that men played little or no role in reproduction or whether, to emphasize the matrilineal principle, they pretended not to acknowledge the male role. In either case, we would expect to find in societies that emphasize the patrilineal principle that a woman's role in reproduction is de-emphasized. What kind of belief about reproduction might deny the importance of the female? How does this compare with the biological roles of men and women in North American societies?

The Family Composition of Rural Chinese

Family life in rural China revolves around the patrilineal extended family household of a married couple, their married sons and daughters-in-law, and their grandchildren and unmarried daughters (see Figure 5.4). To understand a rural Chinese family, you have to understand the idea of *temporal depth*, for in China, the **patrilineage** exists as much in time as it does in space, and the family includes a long line of patrilineal ancestors. A patrilineage is a lineage that is formed by tracing descent in the male line. Anthropologist Francis L. K. Hsu notes that the identity of each male is defined by his relations to the dead as much as it is by his relations to the living. His social worth and destiny are but reflections of the actions of his ancestors. He thus exists, as Hsu (1967) says, "under the shadow of his ancestors." Likewise, the spirits of the dead are dependent on the contributions of the living. These contributions are ceremonially made at altars, prominently positioned in each home, from which people send gifts to their ancestors by burning paper money, paper clothes, or other paper articles.

Given the interdependence between the living and the dead men of the patrilineage, it is apparent why Chinese males deem it essential to have male descendants to look after their well-being and to provide for them in the afterworld. Male children and grandchildren are living proof to a man that his line will continue. For this reason, unlike the Ju/'hoansi or the Trobrianders, the Chinese express a marked preference for male children. Males are needed to maintain the patrilineal descent group, for if the only children born are daughters whose children will, in turn, belong to the patrilineage

extended family
A family group based on blood relations of three or more generations.

patrilineage
A lineage that is formed by tracing descent in the male line.

FIGURE 5.4 COMPOSITION AND DEVELOPMENT OF A RURAL CHINESE FAMILY

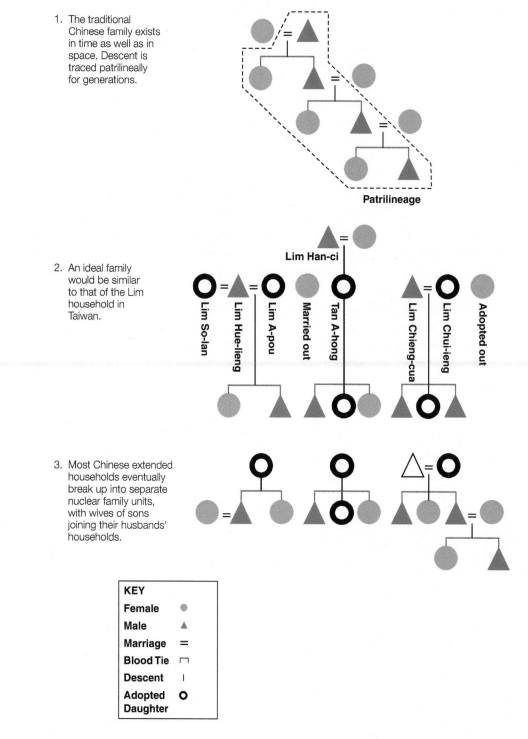

1. The traditional Chinese family exists in time as well as in space. Descent is traced patrilineally for generations.

Patrilineage

2. An ideal family would be similar to that of the Lim household in Taiwan.

Lim Han-ci

Lim So-lan — Lim Hue-lieng — Lim A-pou — Married out — Tan A-hong — Lim Chieng-cua — Lim Chui-ieng — Adopted out

3. Most Chinese extended households eventually break up into separate nuclear family units, with wives of sons joining their husbands' households.

KEY
Female	●
Male	▲
Marriage	=
Blood Tie	⌐
Descent	|
Adopted Daughter	O

of their husbands, a family line will die out. A son, as some Chinese put it, is a major happiness; a daughter is but a small happiness.

In addition to a long line of male ancestors, an ideal rural Chinese household should include several generations of fathers and sons sharing a common hearth or cooking stove and an ancestral altar: the symbols of the household. In the architecture of Peihotien, the village where Margery Wolf (1968) did her fieldwork, houses are constructed in such a way that they can easily be extended to accommodate additional sons and grandsons, who bring their wives to live in the family home. In reality it is very difficult to maintain this ideal; most households in villages such as Peihotien are small, consisting of a married couple and several dependent patrilineal relatives.

RESOURCE 5.1

The study of kinship organization and terminology can be highly complex, yet it is essential for understanding the patterns of social organization of many societies. You can find out more about this and engage in some entertaining exercises in an interactive tutorial, Brian Schwimmer's Kinship and Social Organization, at http://www.umanitoba.ca/faculties/arts/anthropology/kintitle.html

QUESTION 5.2: HOW ARE FAMILIES FORMED, AND HOW IS THE IDEAL FAMILY TYPE MAINTAINED?

Regardless of the size of family units or descent systems, most societies require the socially recognized union of a male and a female (we will discuss the exceptions later in this chapter). Generally, this union takes the form of marriage, a publicly recognized joining of two people or two families. However, while marriage makes or sustains families, the manner in which such an arrangement comes about varies significantly in different societies. In North American societies, for example, many children begin learning about courtship and marriage at an early age: five- and six-year-olds are teased about their "boyfriends" or "girlfriends," and playing house together is a popular preschool pastime. Most North Americans begin serious courting in their early teens and usually have a series of relationships before choosing a partner for their first marriage, most often when they are between the ages of 18 and 30. Although the choice of a marriage partner is supposedly based on feelings of love and sexual attraction, other factors also influence it. North Americans, like people in all societies, are prohibited by the **incest taboo** from marrying or having sexual relations with kin of certain categories, such as brothers or sisters, children or parents, or, in some cases, cousins. Preferences (sometimes tacit, sometimes explicit) also exist about choosing one's spouse from an appropriate income, ethnic, religious, gender, and/or racial group.

incest taboo
A rule that prohibits sexual relations among kin of certain categories, such as brothers or sisters, parents and children, or, in some cases, cousins.

The marriage ceremony in many North American societies is often arranged and financed by the bride's family. After the honeymoon, the couple ideally establishes an independent residence. Their relationship based on love expressed through regular sexual intercourse is later transformed by the arrival of one or more children, when a wife becomes a mother and a husband, a father. However, the cycles of events that create or sustain the family among the Ju/'hoansi, the Trobrianders, and the rural Chinese illustrate the diversity of such arrangements.

The Family Cycle of Ju/'hoansi

Ju/'hoansi men and women, like most North Americans, begin to learn about courtship, sex, and marriage early in life. Because there is little privacy in a Ju/'hoansi camp and children sleep with their parents, they soon are playing at marriage and imitating the bodily movements of parents making love. Most young men and women have had sexual experiences by the time they are 15.

Ju/'hoansi men usually marry for the first time between the ages of 18 and 25, when they are able to hunt and work for their wives' parents. Marriage is important for a man for a number of reasons. It marks him as an adult worthy of taking part in Ju/'hoansi public life, he gains a sex partner, and he gains a mate to provide his food. While men are obligated to share and formally distribute the meat they obtain in the hunt with everyone in the camp, women are not obligated to share what they gather outside their nuclear family group, and women gather from 60 to 80 percent of the food in a camp.

Women often marry as early as 12 to 14 years of age, generally before their first menstruation, which occurs at about 17. Girls have fewer reasons to marry than men. Single or married men are always available as sex partners, and since the product of male labour, meat, is widely shared, a woman need not have a husband to ensure her share of the hunt. A girl's parents, however, have good reasons for getting her married as soon as possible. The earlier she is married, the longer she and her husband will

In Ju/'hoansi culture, most marriages are arranged by the couple's parents, and the bride-to-be frequently objects to the chosen spouse or to the prospect of marriage itself.

remain with her parents until she is of age, and the longer her husband will work for her parents. Moreover, the bride's family gains an alliance with another family and is less likely to get involved in open conflict between men over their daughter.

Marriages are almost always arranged by the couple's parents. Typically, the mother or father of the male approaches the family of the girl with a proposal for marriage. If the girl's parents approve of the match, the families exchange gifts to indicate their agreement. An appropriate husband for a daughter is a man who is not too much older, is not yet married, is a good hunter, and is willing to accept responsibility. The prospective groom should also be cooperative, generous, and unaggressive.

The Ju/'hoansi not only avoid choosing a spouse who is a close kinsperson, but also are restricted in the choice of a marriage partner by their naming system. There are only about 30 to 40 names that can be chosen for newborns, and people with the same first name consider themselves connected, regardless of their actual kinship relation to one another. For example, if two people are named Toma, then everyone related by kinship to one Toma will be considered related in the same way to the other Toma. Consequently, if a man's name is Toma, all the brothers and sisters of everyone else named Toma would be considered his brothers and sisters, all the sons and daughters of any other Toma would be considered his sons and daughters, and so on. Therefore, a marriage partner should occupy neither an actual prohibited kinship category nor one created by the naming system. A woman, for example, could not marry a man with the same name as her father or a man whose father had the same name as her father, since she and the man would refer to themselves as brother and sister. When Richard Lee (1984) was working with the Ju/'hoansi kinship system, he found that interpretations of the naming system varied, and disagreements about the kin connection between people would always be resolved by the interpretation of the older person in the relationship.

Once a suitable match is made, one more obstacle to the marriage remains. Perhaps because they have little to gain or much to lose, young women often object strenuously to the marriage or to their parents' choice of a husband. If they protest long and hard enough, the marriage will be called off; if the protest is not sufficient to call off the arrangements, a marriage ceremony takes place. A hut set apart from the bride's family village is built for the couple by members of both families. Friends bring the couple to the hut, and the girl, head covered, is placed in the hut. Coals from the fires of both families are brought to start the fire in the couple's hut. Friends stay, joking, singing, and dancing, while bride and groom stay apart. Often, especially if the girl is young, a relative stays with them in the hut until she begins to adjust to her new status. These "honeymoons" are often the source of continuing conflict.

Working among the Ju/'hoansi, Marjorie Shostak (1983) forged a close relationship with a Ju/'hoansi woman, Nisa, who described her wedding night. Nisa said she cried so much and objected so strongly to spending the night with her new husband, Bo, that her parents asked a female relative, Nukha, to sleep between Nisa and Bo. She soon discovered that Nukha was having sex with Bo, and after a few nights, she told her parents. They took her and moved to another water hole, leaving Nukha and Bo behind.

Typically, half of all first marriages fail among the Ju/'hoansi, who may enter several marriages over the course of their lives. Nisa's second marriage, to Tashay, followed the same lines as her first; on her wedding night she cried and cried and eventually ran away into the bush. Relatives tried to explain the benefits of marriage and to convince her to accept Tashay. When she finally agreed, Tashay took Nisa to his parents' home to live, and Nisa's parents followed. But not until Nisa and Tashay had been living together for a long time did they have sex. Nisa remembers the aftermath of their first love-making as being painful, and it was a long time before she allowed it again and began to enjoy it.

The Family Cycle of Trobriand Islanders

Courtship and sexual play begin early in the Trobriand Islands. Children play erotic games at the ages of seven and eight and begin seeking sex partners at ages 11 to 13. Trobriand adolescents are permitted to openly display their affection for each other; girls scratch, beat, thrash, or even wound their lovers, and boys accept this treatment as a sign of love and display their wounds as proof of manliness and success in courtship. They sing about love, both successful and unrequited, and take great pains with their physical appearance. Here is what Malinowski says about adolescent courtship: "An adolescent gets definitely attached to a given person, wishes to possess her, works purposefully toward his goal, plans to reach fulfillment of his desires by magical and other means, and finally rejoices in achievement. I have seen young people of this age grow positively miserable through ill-success in love" (Malinowski 1929, 63).

Because sexual activity before marriage is common and expected among Trobrianders, the couple often has already been living together, and the marriage simply formalizes an existing relationship. Although the couple may take the initiative in arranging a marriage, parents approve or disapprove of the choice of a spouse and sometimes arrange matches. There are people of certain categories a Trobriander may not marry. All Trobrianders belong to one of four **clans**, groups whose members consider themselves descended from a common ancestor. They must observe **exogamy**, which requires one to marry outside one's own group—in this case, out of their own clan and into another (other societies practice **endogamy**, which requires marriage inside one's own group). In addition, the incest taboo applies to all close relatives, particularly brothers and sisters, who include all members of a matrilineage of the same generation. Trobriand myths tell of disastrous consequences of brother–sister incest that resulted in both parties committing suicide. Sexual relations between a father and daughter are prohibited, although Trobrianders tell stories about it and joke about the idea of a father being overwhelmed by the beauty of his daughter. From a Trobriand point of view, fathers are not related by kinship to their daughters. The best marriage for a man is to a woman from his father's clan, for then his children, who will trace their descent from their mother, will be members of his father's clan. Consequently, the close relationship a man has with members of his father's clan will continue into the next generation.

There is no formal marriage ceremony; the girl simply stays overnight in her boyfriend's house. The next morning the bride's mother brings the couple cooked yams to indicate the bride's family's approval of the marriage. If the girl's parents don't approve, they demand that their daughter return home with them. Sharing food is considered by Trobrianders to be more intimate than having sex. Later, the wife's mother and maternal uncle bring raw yams for the couple, while the groom's father and maternal uncle begin collecting **bridewealth**—valuables, such as stone axe blades, shells, and money—to give to the wife's kin and her father. The requirement of bridewealth makes young men dependent on members of their matrilineage. This relationship is unlike that of the brideservice required of a Ju/'hoansi man in that brideservice does not obligate a man to members of his family (see Question 5.1).

During the first year of marriage, the couple lives in the hut that served as the groom's adolescent retreat, and during that year the groom's mother brings meals for them to share. At the end of the year, the groom's mother builds a stone hearth for the couple. At that point the wife becomes responsible for the cooking.

The end of the first year of marriage marks a dramatic change in the husband–wife relationship. They no longer eat together, and the sexuality that bound them together as adolescents must be publicly submerged. After the first year of marriage it is shameful for anyone to refer to the couple's sex life together. In public, a husband and wife never hold hands or display affection. Their lives become segmented into a private domain in which affection and emotion can be displayed, and a public domain in which the meaning of their relationship is dictated by their obligation to help ensure the continuity and honour of their respective matrilineages.

The matrilineal principle in the life of a Trobriand husband and wife requires each to have a continued involvement with others outside the nuclear family. In addition to his ties to and concerns for his wife and children, the husband is also involved in the family life of his matrilineage: his sisters and their children. The wife is continually involved with her and her children's matrilineage—particularly her brothers. This involvement is

---

clans
Unilineal descent groups whose members claim descent from a common ancestor.

exogamy
A rule that requires a person to marry someone outside his or her own group.

endogamy
A rule that requires a person to marry someone inside his or her own group (e.g., a lineage, an ethnic group, a religious group).

bridewealth
The valuables that a groom or his family are expected or obligated to present to the bride's family.

economic and revolves around wealth, particularly yams, banana leaf bundles, and skirts, all of which are controlled ultimately by women.

One reason men marry is to obtain yams. Yams are more than food in the Trobriand Islands; they are valuable symbols or objects of wealth and are used as gifts to create and sustain relationships among people. They are particularly important in marriage transactions and in the continued tie of a woman to her matrilineage. Trobriand family yam gardens belong to the wife, but they are tended first by her father and later by a "brother." Each year at harvest time the yams grown in her garden by her father or brother are ceremoniously taken to her. The amount and quality of the yams grown by a woman's brother are usually proportional to the bridewealth given to the wife's family by the groom's family when the couple was married. Early in the marriage these yams are stored in the rafters of the couple's hut, and the husband uses them as valuables to be redistributed to those of his kin who contributed the bridewealth. Later—often 10 to 15 years later—if a man is recognized as important by his wife's kin, they construct a yam house for him to store the yams they bring each year. The amount and quality of the yams stored and displayed by a man are indications of the regard in which he is held by his wife's kin and of his status in the community. The yam house is, according to Weiner (1988), like a public bank account.

As a man seeks a wife to obtain the yams grown for him by his wife's brother, brothers seek husbands for their sisters, not only for the children nurtured by the husbands for their wives' matrilineage but also for the help of the brothers-in-law in obtaining banana leaf bundles. Sisters are obligated, with the help of their husbands, to prepare bundles of banana leaves to be used to finance the funerals of members of their matrilineage. Some are made by the woman, but her husband may have to purchase additional bundles. They are given away at funerals by members of the deceased's matrilineage to people who were important in the life of the deceased. The more important the person was to the deceased, the greater the number of banana leaf bundles he or she receives. In this way, members of a matrilineage uphold their honour and status; to fail to fulfill these obligations would bring dishonour to the matrilineage.

The development of Trobriand family life, then, must be understood in the context of the movement of such goods as yams and banana leaf bundles between husband and wife and members of the wife's matrilineage. It is the successful completion of the cycle of exchanges of yams and banana leaf bundles that ensures the stability of a marriage and a matrilineage.

The Trobriand nuclear family promotes stable bonds between husband and wife, although divorce is both frequent and easy to obtain. The initiative is usually taken by the wife. Most divorces occur in the first year of marriage; they are rare after the couple has been together for a few years.

Although fathers are not technically members of their children's family, they are important in the lives of the children. Once children are weaned they sleep with their fathers, and later the father is responsible for enhancing their beauty with presents of shells, necklaces, and tiny tortoise-shell earrings. These objects are evidence of a father's presence

Among the Trobriand Islanders, lineage is traced through the mother, and individuals must marry outside their own clan. Here, a Trobriand chief on Kiriwina Island is shown with family members at the home of one of his two wives.

in the life of his child; in fact, Weiner (1988) says the term for a child with unpierced ears is translated as "fatherless." So important is the tie that develops between a man and his son that when the son marries, the father may try to convince him to remain in his village rather than moving to the village of his maternal kin, as is expected.

The Family Cycle of Rural Chinese

The key relationship in Ju/'hoansi families is between husband and wife, and among Trobriand Islanders it is between brother and sister. In China, the family centres on the relationship between father and son. Marriage in traditional China is less a matter of a man getting a wife than of bringing a child bearer into the household. As Hsu (1967, 57) describes it, "a marriage is made in the name of the parents taking a daughter-in-law, not in the name of the son taking a wife."

Since marriage has far less to do with relations between husband and wife than with those between the husband's family and a daughter-in-law, marriages in rural China are almost always arranged, often far in advance, and there is little, if any courtship. When a boy is six or seven years old, his parents might hire a matchmaker to find a girl who will eventually be an appropriate bride for their son. Since they believe that the time of a person's birth influences his or her personality and fate, the parents may also enlist the services of a diviner to make the appropriate match. The matchmaker takes a red paper with the time and date of a girl's birth to a prospective groom's family. The boy's mother brings this paper (or papers, if there is a choice of brides) to a fortuneteller, who predicts the compatibility of the boy and girl. If a girl is deemed appropriate by the fortuneteller, the matchmaker tries to convince the girl's parents to accept the match. If she is successful, the bridewealth—that is, the marriage gifts of the husband's family to the wife's parents—is then negotiated.

Another way parents can obtain a wife for their son in rural China is to adopt an infant girl who will be reared in the household and later will marry the son. Although this kind of arrangement is not as prestigious as bridewealth marriage, it has two advantages: since the prospective bride was raised in the household of her future mother-in-law, she is more likely to be obedient, and paying a bridewealth for an adopted daughter-in-law is unnecessary. The major disadvantage is that the prospective bride and groom are raised as brother and sister and often find it difficult to make the transition to husband and wife.

The adoption of a boy to serve as a husband for a daughter is a third way that marriages are arranged in rural China. A family does this only when it has no sons. The adopted boy then assumes the family name, so that his sons continue the line of his adopted father. Such marriages are not as respected as others, and a man who is adopted into his wife's family bears the stigma of having abandoned his parents and ancestors. For poor or orphaned boys,

© Bettmann/CORBIS

In a rural Chinese wedding, the bride's mother places a rose in the bride's hair and then transfers it to the groom. The couple then proceed to the household of the groom's parents, where they will make their home.

however, the prospect of heading a thriving household may outweigh such a stigma.

Compared to Ju/'hoansi or Trobriand marriage ceremonies, the rural Chinese wedding is very formal and, for the groom's family, very expensive. The date and hour of the wedding are determined by a diviner, who even decides the exact time the bride will arrive in her sedan chair. The day before the wedding, the girl's **dowry**—goods and valuables that the bride's family supplies to the groom's family or the couple—is sent to the groom's home in a procession accompanied by a band, drummers, and ushers. The dowry consists of such goods as leather chests, tables, stools, cosmetics, housewares, clothing and cloth, but never land or a house. On the day of the wedding, the groom is carried in a sedan chair to the house of the bride; when he arrives, she shows token resistance, and she and her mother weep. She is then carried to the groom's house in a red sedan chair decorated to suggest the early birth of sons. Offerings are made at the ancestors' altar to ensure the success of the marriage. Then the couple is taken to pay respect to the boy's parents—the formal introduction of the bride to the groom's household. Feasting and dancing accompany the wedding and sometimes last for three or four days.

After the wedding, there is little time or place for romantic relations between husband and wife. Hsu (1967) reports that after the marriage, husband and wife sleep in the same bed for only seven days, and there is no public expression of affection between them. Once the wife enters into her husband's family, she finds herself among strangers, virtually cut off from her parents and siblings. She must treat her mother-in-law with respect and acquiesce to the demands of sisters-in-law or other members of her husband's family. She occupies the lowest place at the table, and she does not acquire full status in her husband's family until she produces a male child. Until then, the husband must show indifference to his wife, addressing her through a third party; after the birth of a son, he can refer to her as the mother of his child. For the groom, marriage is a continued expression of his duty to his father and his ancestors. Whereas divorce is fairly common among Trobrianders and among Ju/'hoansi, it is virtually unheard of in rural China. A husband can take mistresses with impunity, and in theory, he can murder an adulterous wife. Wives have no rights of divorce. A wife may flee her husband's household, commit suicide, or become a prostitute, but a woman who wishes to leave her husband and in-laws has few other alternatives.

QUESTION 5.3: WHAT ARE THE ROLES OF SEXUALITY, LOVE, AND WEALTH?

Sex, Love, and Wealth Among Ju/'hoansi

Wealth plays no part in the lives of the Ju/'hoansi, but especially for women, according to Nisa, sex, love, and beauty are very important. A Ju/'hoansi woman's sexuality is her major means of negotiating the conditions of her relationships with others. Sexuality is important first for her own well-being. Nisa told Marjorie Shostak (1983) that if a girl grows up not learning to enjoy sex, her mind doesn't develop normally; if a grown woman doesn't have sex, her thoughts are ruined and she is always angry. Moreover, a woman's sexuality maximizes her independence. Sex attracts lovers, and a love relationship, being voluntary, recognizes the equality of the participants. By taking lovers, a Ju/'hoansi woman proclaims her control over her social life, because she can offer her sexuality to men as a means of vitalizing them. Nisa talked candidly about sex,

> **dowry**
> The goods and valuables a bride's family supplies to the groom's family or to the couple.

CONSTRUCTING FAMILIES AND SOCIAL RELATIONSHIPS

male impotence, and the contributions women make to men:

> *A woman can bring a man life, even if he is almost dead. She can give him sex and make him alive again. If she were to refuse, he would die! If there were no women around, their semen would kill men. Did you know that? Women make it possible for them to live. Women have something so good that if a man takes it and moves about inside it, he climaxes and is sustained.* * (in Shostak 1983, 288)

There is one trade-off for Ju/'hoansi women who use their sexuality. Men see them as sources of male conflict and consequently as potentially dangerous.

Motherhood, unlike sexuality, is not easily bartered by Ju/'hoansi women. In other societies, parents may stress how much they have sacrificed or suffered for their children, thus using motherhood or fatherhood as a way of creating obligations and ties. It makes little sense for a Ju/'hoansi woman (or man, for that matter) to make such a claim. Children owe their parents little; there is no need for bridewealth or dowries for marriage, and food and kin to care for them are plentiful. The dynamics of Ju/'hoansi families are built on the need of individuals to avoid permanent ties and obligations and to maintain their independence.

Sex, Love, and Wealth Among Trobriand Islanders

The maintenance of sexuality is important throughout life among Ju/'hoansi; among Trobriand Islanders, it is important for women only prior to their marriage. Armed with the magic and bodily adornments contributed by her father, but without the wealth (yams, banana leaf bundles, other valuables) she will later acquire, an unmarried woman uses her sexuality to negotiate her relationships with others. Once married, she ceases to emphasize her beauty and sexual

attraction and, instead, emphasizes her fertility and motherhood. A woman's worth, once measured by her father's concern for her and by her own sexuality and beauty, is determined after marriage by her ability to collect yams for her husband, produce children, and provide banana leaf bundles for her matrilineage.

Men's sexuality is viewed very differently. Since Trobrianders claim that men play no role in reproduction, their sexuality is never very important anyway. Their physical attractiveness, however, is important, for this is what attracts lovers and later a wife to collect the yams by which a man measures his status. Beauty is especially important for chiefs. They must maintain an aura of sexual attractiveness in order to attract more wives, whose fathers and brothers will supply the wealth they need to maintain their influence.

Wealth also forms different kinds of links for Trobrianders. Because Ju/'hoansi have little wealth to contend for and what there is (e.g., meat) is widely shared, the links that men create with their wives' families are based not on wealth but on their labour. Among Trobrianders, however, men who want to marry must use the wealth of members of their matrilineage as bridewealth payments to their wives' families. They are required to return this wealth to members of their family by redistributing the yams they later receive from their wives' brothers. Moreover, the yams they receive from their brothers-in-law are in some ways payment for the children their wives produce—these children are members of the matrilineage of the wife and brothers-in-law.

Sex, Love, and Wealth Among Rural Chinese

The themes of sexuality, love, and wealth are played out very differently in Chinese rural families. Whereas Ju/'hoansi and Trobriand adolescents have considerable freedom to utilize their sexuality to attract and influence others, quite the opposite is true in China. If a girl comes from a family that is wealthy and influential enough to make an attractive match for her, she will have little to do with boys. Virginity is both valued and necessary for a Chinese

*NISA: The Life and Words of a !Kung Woman by Marjorie Shostak, Cambridge, Mass: Harvard University Press, Copyright (c) 1981 by Marjorie Shostak.

bride; for a Ju/'hoansi or Trobriander woman, it is almost no consideration. In China, if a girl is known to have been mixed up in an affair, her only chance of marriage is to someone in a distant village.

According to Margery Wolf (1968), romantic love and sexuality are irrelevant also in the relations between traditional Chinese husbands and wives. A wife's function is to produce children. A man who can afford it takes concubines. A man who can't afford it, but does so anyway, is criticized not for his infidelity to his wife but for squandering the wealth of his ancestors and descendants.

Sexuality figures little in the life of a rural Chinese woman either before or after her marriage. Her sexuality is simply not negotiable; instead, it is as a mother that most Chinese women establish significant relations. A woman's value consists in her potential to become the mother of a boy. Becoming a mother cements her relations with her husband, her father-in-law, and her mother-in-law, and it is her motherhood that secures her later life. While a son is obligated to care for his aged mother, the obligation is not so great as it is to care for a father. To compensate, Wolf argues, a woman must establish bonds of emotion and affection with her sons. She may do this with the assistance of her husband. After a boy is six or seven, fathers become aloof and withdrawn in order to assert and reinforce their authority and control over a son. A mother can use her husband's aloofness from his son to strengthen the son's ties to her. Even if she enjoys good relations with her husband, she will try to reserve the son's affections for herself, while preserving the son's respect for his father.

QUESTION 5.4: WHAT THREATENS TO DISRUPT THE FAMILY UNIT?

In the introduction, we briefly discussed contemporary debates about same-sex marriage and teenage and single motherhood in North America. Much of the debate focuses on whether or not these social phenomena pose a "threat" to the typical North American family. There are also threats to the stability and maintenance of traditional Chinese, Trobriand, and Ju/'hoansi families, but these differ from the ones that are perceived to threaten the North American family.

Threats to a Ju/'hoansi Family

The major threat to family stability among the Ju/'hoansi is conflict between husband and wife over infidelity or the efforts of a husband to secure a second wife. Like many societies around the world, the Ju/'hoansi allow **polygamy**, a form of marriage in which a person is permitted to have more than one spouse. Men are allowed to have more than one wife (**polygyny**), and apparently women are permitted to have more than one husband (**polyandry**), though this is rare. In fact,

polygamy
A form of marriage in which a person is permitted to have more than one spouse.

polygyny
A form of marriage in which a man is permitted to have more than one wife.

polyandry
A form of marriage in which a woman is permitted to have more than one husband.

EXERCISE 5.3

In North America, we tend to take romantic love and sexual attraction for granted as central to the development and maintenance of relationships. However, the cases explored above demonstrate that romantic love and sexuality are clearly not universal. Yet there seem to be features of love and sexuality in all three that are similar to life in North American families. Your problem is simply to list those features of conjugal relationships among Ju/'hoansi, Trobriand Islanders, and rural Chinese that resemble those of North American families. Put another way, what features of North American conjugal relationships would be familiar to a Ju/'hoansi, a Trobriand Islander, or someone from rural China?

CONSTRUCTING FAMILIES AND SOCIAL RELATIONSHIPS

polygamy is the exception rather than the rule. A survey conducted by Lee in 1968 of 131 married Ju/'hoansi men found that 93 percent were living monogamously, 5 percent were living in polygynous unions, and 2 percent were living in polyandrous relationships.

One reason that polygamy is rare, even though having more than one wife is a sign of prestige, is the family difficulties it creates. According to Marjorie Shostak (1983, 172), a popular saying is "There is never any peace in a household with two women in it." Stories of the complications resulting from polygamous unions are an endless source of humour for those who are single or monogamous. Here is how Nisa described polygyny in her society to Shostak:

> When a man married one woman, then marries another and sets her down beside the first so there are three of them together at night, the husband changes from one wife to another. First he has sex with the older wife, then with the younger. But when he goes to the younger wife, the older one is jealous and grabs and bites him. The two women start to fight and bite each other. The older woman goes to the fire and throws burning wood at them yelling "What told you that when I, your first wife, am lying here that you should go and sleep with another woman? Don't I have a vagina? So why do you just leave it and go without having sex with me? Instead you go and have sex with that young girl!" Sometimes they fight like that all night, until dawn breaks. A co-wife is truly a terrible thing.* (in Shostak 1983, 172)

While polygamy is rare, marital infidelity is not. At one water hole with 50 married couples, Lee (1984) recorded 16 couples in which one or another of the partners was having an affair. The Ju/'hoansi recognize certain benefits in taking lovers. For a woman, extramarital affairs add variety as well as economic insurance. Here is Nisa again:

> When you are a woman, you just don't sit still and do nothing—you have lovers. You don't just sit with the man of your hut, with just one man. One man can give you very little. One man gives you only one kind of food to eat. But when you have lovers, one brings you something and another brings you something else. One comes at night with meat, another with money, another with beads. (in Shostak 1983, 271)

Men say that the emotion and passion of extramarital affairs are wonderful—"hearts are on fire and passions great," as Ju/'hoansi say. When Shostak asked a young married man about his lover, he said they fantasized about running away. She asked what it would be like, and he smiled and replied, "The first few months would be wonderful!" Extramarital affairs are likely to be threatening to a husband, however, and they are the most common cause of conflict and violence among the Ju/'hoansi. Wives are important to Ju/'hoansi men because as long as they have wives they are dependent on no one. Male adulthood requires acquiring and demonstrating a willingness to fight for a secure marital status.

Threats to a Trobriand Island Family

Among Trobriand Islanders it is not threats to the husband–wife relationship that are critical but threats to the matrilineage. Because the matrilineage is the principal social unit, the honour of that family group relative to other groups is a central concern to all members. Lineages among Trobriand Islanders are ranked according to the closeness of their genealogical connection to the founders of the lineage. Each lineage must be able to maintain its position vis-à-vis others through the ceremonial presentation of valuables, particularly yams and banana leaf bundles. So important are yams in the relative

---

*NISA: The Life and Words of a !Kung Woman by Marjorie Shostak, Cambridge, Mass: Harvard University Press, Copyright (c) 1981 by Marjorie Shostak.

ranking of matrilineages that groups try to demonstrate their wealth by giving more yams to others than they receive. Since giving may be taken as a claim of superiority, however, it can be dangerous; as Trobrianders put it, "When you give too much, people worry."

Although it may seem implausible, yams could become the focus of a Trobriand soap opera or reality television show. For example, a man's political power, measured in yams, is a direct result of the support he receives from his wife's kin—her yams, grown for her by her father and brother, create status for him as her husband. However, the annual yam gifts received by a husband can also be a source of conflict. If the amount or size of yams harvested does not live up to a husband's expectations, he may be insulted. On the other hand, if a woman's brother is unhappy over the bridewealth he received from the husband's family or the support given by the husband to his sister in collecting banana leaf bundles, he may purposely communicate his unhappiness by not working hard in his sister's yam gardens. Other plots could be devised about unrequited love, about attempts by fathers to convince their sons to remain in their father's village, and even about incest. But a theme that would be sure to attract a Trobriand audience would be about sorcery.

Trobrianders claim to know of spells and magic forms that are capable of killing. Generally, only chiefs have this power, but others can seek out a chief and, for a price, convince him to use his power against their enemies. Someone who is believed to have this power is both feared and respected; Trobrianders tell of instances when they were challenged and retaliated with sorcery. Vanoi, an important Trobriand chief, told Weiner (1988) about being challenged by a Christian convert who openly mocked Vanoi's knowledge of sorcery. Vanoi offered the man a cigarette, saying that he should smoke it if he doubted the chief's knowledge of sorcery. The man did; he became ill later that night and died a week later.

A person who uses sorcery against another is dominating that person, and since each person's fate is tied to that of the matrilineage, a threat to one is considered a threat to all. That is why any death among Trobrianders is a serious matter. Since all deaths are attributed to sorcery, every death is a sign that the power of a matrilineage is being challenged by someone from another lineage. Each funeral marks an attempt by the members of a matrilineage to reassert its power; at the same time, the mourners assert their innocence of sorcery. The matrilineal kin of the deceased do this by distributing banana leaf bundles and other valuables to those who have come to publicly mourn the passing of the deceased and to assist with the funeral arrangements by decorating and carrying the corpse. In recognition of their contribution to the life of the deceased, they receive gifts. The deceased's matrilineage empties its treasury to announce its strength in the face of the threat to its integrity that is signalled by a death.

Maintaining one's identity and that of the matrilineage is a never-ending process among Trobrianders because death threatens the network by removing someone from it. Here is how Weiner sums up the meaning of death for them:

> *Because of the expanding possibilities in a person's life, each Trobriander represents her or his matrilineal identity—originally conceived through a woman and an ancestral baloma spirit—as well as the accumulation of all the other relationships that parenthood and marriage made possible. Therefore, a death demands attention to this full totality, as the members of a matrilineage seek both to repay all "others" for their past care and to hold on to them now that this death has occurred. (Weiner 1988, 161)*

Threats to a Rural Chinese Family

The biggest threat to the traditional rural Chinese family is, of course, the absence of a son. The lack of a male heir endangers not only the continuance of a household but also the entire patrilineage through time. A man without sons, a spirit without descendants, has no one to offer incense for him and no altar on which his spirit can find refuge and honour.

The existence of a son is no guarantee of smooth family relations, however. Fathers have enormous authority and power over sons, and sons are obligated to worship, respect, obey, and care for their fathers. But often fathers become overbearing or use force to assert their authority. Margery Wolf (1968) says that Lim Han-ci in the village of Peihotien (see Question 5.3) was unusual in the frequency with which he administered physical punishment to his sons; once he beat them with a hoe handle and left bruises that lasted for weeks.

Regardless of how harshly a person may be treated, however, breaking away from one's father is considered a violent act. Wolf reports a conflict between Lim Han-ci and his eldest son, Lim Hue-lieng, which illustrates both the dilemma of a father–son split and the difficulties that can arise in adopted marriages. When Lim Hue-lieng was a child, Lim Han-ci adopted Lim A-pou, then nine months old, to be reared as the eventual wife of his son. Growing up in the Lim household, Lim A-pou was a model daughter-in-law. She accepted reprimands and punishment without becoming sullen, she did not complain, and she worked hard. However, her relationship with her prospective husband was not a happy one. When Lim Hue-lieng was 19, he committed what in rural China is an act of moral violence: he left home and severed his relations with his father. If a son dies before his father and so is unable to care for the father in his old age, the father ritually beats the son's coffin to punish him. Lim Hue-lieng was able to leave home only because he had become a leader in the *lo mue*, a secret society that is involved in crime and extortion but that also protects the downtrodden and contributes heavily to religious festivals.

Dramatic splits between fathers and sons are rare in traditional China. More frequent is conflict between brothers over the division and sharing of the family wealth at the death of a male head of the household. In most other rural, peasant societies around the world, the male head of the household designates his heirs before his death. He may in some fashion divide his property among his offspring—**partible inheritance**—or he may leave all his property to one or another descendant—**impartible inheritance**. In rural China the ideal is for brothers to continue to live together and share the inheritance, usually under the direction of the eldest son, thus avoiding the division of property. In fact, however, brothers rarely continue to share, and ultimately conflict between them leads to a division of household property.

Wolf (1968) documents the ultimate disintegration of the Lim household after the death of Lim Han-ci and the resulting arguments over property by the sons and their wives. When Wolf went to live in the Lim household, Lim Han-ci and his oldest son, Lim Hue-lieng, had already died. The two remaining family units consisted of the family of the second oldest son, Lim Chieng-cua, and the family of Lim Hue-lieng's widow, Lim A-Pou. While Lim Han-ci was alive, his power and influence and his control over the family's wealth were enough to maintain the extended family. Once he died, conflict between Lim A-pou and her son on the one hand and Lim Chieng-cua on the other led to the division of family property. The wealth that had held the extended family together served, finally, to drive it apart. After dividing the property, brothers or their families often continue to live in the same house, but they partition it into separate family units with separate stoves, as did the son and grandson of Lim Han-ci. The once extended household becomes, in effect, a family compound.

partible inheritance
A form of inheritance in which the goods or property of a family is divided among the heirs.

impartible inheritance
A form of inheritance in which family property is passed undivided to one heir.

An international television production company has hired your company, Creativity Enterprises, to write a pilot episode of a soap opera to be marketed in rural China. The plot of the program you will create will revolve around the Wang family. The Wangs are a relatively well-off farming family in rural China. The characters in the show are to include the following family members: Wang Zhou, the 55-year-old male head of the family; Wang Lim, the wife of Wang Zhou; Wang Xiao, the eldest son of Wang Zhou; Wang Lao, the wife of Wang Xiao; Wang Jiang, the second son of Wang Zhou; Wang Jane, the wife of Wang Jiang; Wang Sally, the 20-year-old unmarried daughter of Wang Zhou; and Wang Nai-Nai, the mother of Wang Zhou. Xiao and Lao have four children, two boys and two girls. Jiang and Jane have two children, both girls. You may, if you wish, add other characters to the story. The story line should be simple but clear, and you are free to embellish the characters in any way you want. Keep in mind, though, the soap must appeal to a rural Chinese audience.

QUESTION 5.5: HOW HAS THE ANTHROPOLOGICAL STUDY OF FAMILIES CHANGED?

As we stated in our introduction, a lot has changed within Ju/'hoansi, Trobriand, and rural Chinese societies since the anthropologists noted in the previous sections of this chapter did their fieldwork. Culture is never static, and even small changes in both local societies and global politics may affect how different people in different places construct their beliefs about family relations and kinship. For instance, between the 1930s and the 1970s, China experienced almost constant turmoil: the war with Japan (1937 to 1945), a civil war (1945 to 1949), the Great Leap Forward (1959 to 1961), and the Cultural Revolution (1966 to 1976). Laurel Bossen suggests that throughout this time, women in Lu Village, in the southern province of Yunnan, have gained some benefits, such as "the end of footbinding, greater recognition of women's economic contributions, improved female health and education, lower infant mortality, a wider variety of employment options and family choices, more labor-saving technology and modes of communication, and a greater public voice" (2002, 19). Although patrilineal descent and patrilocality are still the rule, Bossen (2002, 229) found families in Lu Village that followed uxorilocal marriage, where the husband leaves his village and moves to the village of his wife. Lu villagers use the term "*zhao guye*" or "seek a son-in-law" to refer to uxorilocal marriage.

After the Cultural Revolution in China, women gained more control over their lives than they had in the 1960s when Wolf did her fieldwork. Ellen Judd (1994) has suggested that legal changes, such as the Inheritance Law of 1985, which allows daughters to inherit their parents' property, as well as the increase in women's access to employment in rural North China, have allowed some women to gain some freedom from previous constraints.

Challenges to Theory in Anthropology

Anthropologists experienced changes in the ways they think about and study family relations when they began to question the origins of some of their main assumptions. The idea that these assumptions might be rooted in Euro-American culture and then used to describe and analyze other cultures gained momentum in the 1970s and 1980s. In Canada, Martin Silverman (1979) questioned the relationship between political economy and anthropology as it applies to the ways that European and anglophone North American anthropologists view their own family relationships and those of other peoples in other cultures. Silverman argued that the view of marriage as an exchange of women, for instance, with men directing the exchanges, resembles the model of commodity exchange "in which something is bought and sold … a thing which has no rights of its own, and in which the direct producer has no rights" (1979, 71).

Linda Stone (2001) has reviewed two important factors questioned by David Schneider in the early 1980s: factors that led anthropologists to re-evaluate some of their underlying assumptions about how different societies establish connections among family members. The first was Schneider's critique of his own work among Yap families in the West Caroline Islands. The more Schneider thought about what he had written, the more he began to wonder how much of what he had described as Yap notions of relatedness were projections of his own Eurocentric beliefs about the role of biology in kinship. When he re-evaluated his account of Yap kinship, he found that two of the fundamental kinship terms in Western biological explanations of conception and birth—mother and father—did not apply to Yap notions of producing children. The biological term "father" as anthropologists were using it was only roughly equivalent to the mother's husband at the time she became pregnant in Yap society. Likewise, the term "mother" applied to the woman who gave birth to a child, but this child was placed in her womb by ghosts, not by the fertilization of her egg by the father's sperm.

The second factor was Schneider's critique of the ethnocentric evolutionism in studies that assume kinship is important in small-scale societies only where it provides the basis for social organization. In this argument, kinship loses importance as societies become more complex and disappears as a major institution in modern industrial states. Families likewise change from the large extended size in small-scale societies to the efficient nuclear size found in North America. This, according to Schneider, might actually be an anthropological myth, and if the myth itself is investigated, "kinship might … become a special custom distinctive of European culture" (Schneider 1984, 201).

When Schneider asked, "Is blood really thicker than water?", several anthropologists began to take a closer look at whether groups that used kinship terms for their association were related on the basis of biology or on the basis of some other factors. Co-residence on the basis of friendships, for instance, may look like kinship from the outside, especially when family terms are used as identifiers. The notion of whether "blood" or some other substance is the basis of how family members are related has also been debated. For example, whereas in the Western science model children are related to their parents through "blood," people in a neighbourhood of Gaborne, Botswana, told Frederick Klaits (2005) that husbands and wives become "of one blood" when they have sexual intercourse and produce children.

Food is another substance that may be more important than blood in creating kinship. David and Dorothy Counts (1998) tell a very instructive story about their own experience of being defined in kinship terms by the Kaliai people, whom they visited in New Guinea to do their research. They believed that their adoption into a Kandokan family had been basically only fiction and then learned to their surprise that it was very real: "We learned that when members of our Kandokan family brought us bananas, pineapples, and watermelons, and we gave them rice, fresh bread, and tinned beef, we were not just exchanging groceries. We and they were becoming family … When they fed us and our children and received food from us in return, we were exchanging the stuff of which substance is made: we were *becoming* Kaliai" (1998, 152).

Another major influence on how anthropologists study family relations is the feminist insight that we must question the ways in which the structure of families and their connections to biology reinforce gender inequalities. For instance, the fact that women give birth is consistently translated into a closer attachment of women to nature and to home, whereas men are more able to take part in the wider social sphere of politics and economics. But to what extent is this association between femininity and nature culturally constructed?

Several anthropologists have conducted studies of the ways in which the increased use of biomedical imaging technologies during pregnancy foster the development of an emotional attachment between mother and child. Rayna Rapp (2007) and Lisa Mitchell (2001), for instance, have examined the use of ultrasound in the United States and Canada respectively. We tend to think of ultrasounds as apolitical and "routine" elements of most pregnancies. Ultrasounds can be used to monitor the health and size of a developing fetus, to check its position within the uterus, and to determine sex, among other things. However, they were not routinely used within North America until the 1980s, when women's bodies became subject to increasing surveillance and monitoring with changes and improvements in biomedical imaging.

These days, for women who are intending to keep their babies after birth, ultrasound appointments are ritualized events. The woman typically brings her partner, a friend, or a family member to the appointment. Assuming that the pregnancy looks "healthy," the language employed by the sonographer functions to personify the fetus and to foster a bond between the mother and her otherwise invisible fetus. Rapp (2007, 615), for instance, writes that when sonographers are speaking with pregnant women, they "attribute motives to fetal activity and presence: a fetus that is hard to visualize is 'hiding' or 'shy'; an active fetus is described as 'swimming,' 'playing,' or even 'partying.'" "Showing the baby" drives its personification, and the mother-to-be is given a picture of the fetus to take home.

This process of visualization, according to Rapp (2007), becomes a key means through which mothers form a social bond with their fetus. Ultrasound pictures are often circulated on social media—on Facebook, Instagram, or Twitter; they are placed in albums, framed to hang on walls, posted on refrigerator doors, or even circulated to family and friends via e-mail. In this way, the fetus is perceived as a viable "baby" (even if, at this point, the fetus could not live on its own outside the womb), and the mother-to-be becomes engaged in social conversations about motherhood and pregnancy. Ultimately, ultrasound pictures, or what Mitchell (2001) calls "baby's first picture," are one of a multitude of ways in which the problematic association between femininity and "nature" can be shown to be informed by cultural processes.

These sorts of feminist critiques of our dominant perceptions of motherhood and family relations have encouraged studies in which a variety of other factors, such as history and power, are taken into account when anthropologists ask how family relationships have formed. A prime example of the influence of the heteronormative concept can be found in the history of colonization and the ways in which European colonizers viewed local family relationships as "primitive" when they differed from the European patriarchal model. In the Caribbean, for instance, family relations were defined as "abnormal" because many households appeared to lack a male figure who acted as the head of the family. Lisa Anderson-Levy, a Jamaican anthropologist, argues that colour, class, and gender work together to structure Caribbean families. Lower-class women tend to be the unmarried heads of their households or to live in extended households headed by their unmarried mothers. Upper- and middle-class women, whose skin colour is lighter, tend to be married and to live in nuclear families. Thus, "marriage was, and to a certain extent still is, something that rich people do" (2000, 195). Even female sexuality is race and class specific in Jamaica. Lower-class, dark-skinned women are thought to be unable to control their sexuality, whereas light-skinned, middle-class women are supposed to be fully in control.

Internal colonization, referring to the treatment of Indigenous peoples by the state, often follows the same pattern. Anthropologist Max Hedley (1998) has written about how families in the Walpole Island First Nation changed after the Department of Indian Affairs insisted that they reorganize their agriculture. No longer was growing food a community project, as in the past; instead, it was a matter of individual household production, with men as heads of the families. Around the same time, band government was imposed on the community, with women excluded from formal participation, unable to either hold office or vote. With the introduction of wage labour and formal education, the status of women within the family decreased as they left to work outside the home. Professional educators then took over important aspects of socializing children. All of this changed the meaning of motherhood.

The study of family relations has expanded to include gay and lesbian families and families produced by in vitro fertilization and by surrogate mothers. Gay and lesbian marriages became legal in Canada in July 2005, making Canada the fourth country in the world to recognize same-sex marriage (the other three were the Netherlands, Belgium, and Spain; since then, sixteen other countries have joined the list). As Meg Luxton (1997) points out, when families are formed by gay and lesbian couples, the definition of marriage is changed: both sexuality and child bearing are separated from legal marriage. This separation of marriage and child bearing has been one point of contention in the debate about gay marriage in Canada. Those who oppose gay marriage cite the family as the institution in which

children are produced and argue that the purpose of sexual intercourse—that is, between a male and a female—is to accomplish this.

Yet this does not mean that gay and lesbian couples cannot include children in their families. Children may be brought into the marriage from a former heterosexual relationship; other options for producing children are adoption, in vitro fertilization, and surrogate mothers. Indeed, all three methods are being used by heterosexual couples as well as by gay and lesbian couples.

QUESTION 5.6: HOW CAN UNDERSTANDING PATTERNS OF FAMILY RELATIONS BE RELEVANT OUTSIDE ACADEMIA?

As we have seen, knowledge of family relations helps us understand a whole range of things, from parent–child relations, to marriage and courtship patterns, to ideas about love, sexuality, and wealth. Understanding these relations can help societies address a multitude of issues involving families—for example, spousal abuse, divorce, and parent–child conflicts. The same knowledge can be valuable for those who work in a variety of fields that require an understanding of intimate human relations. Anthropologists, for example, can apply their understanding to prevent sexually transmitted diseases, especially HIV/AIDS.

The major problem in AIDS prevention (and in the prevention of sexually transmitted diseases, or STDs, more generally) is how to persuade people who are sexually active to protect themselves and their sex partners. Condom use is one of the simplest and most common measures. Yet even when people are aware of the risk of contracting an STD, they often fail to take this easy precaution. What do medical practitioners and those working in AIDS

Gay men celebrate the legalization of same-sex marriage in Canada.

© PETER JONES/Reuters/Landov

prevention need to know in order to design effective prevention programs? And what can anthropologists do to help?

AIDS Prevention in Namibia

As noted earlier, we have been using the "ethnographic present" when describing patterns of Ju/'hoansi family relations, though in reality, many aspects of daily Ju/'hoansi life have changed since anthropologists first studied them. Ju/'hoansi territory spans the border of the contemporary nation-states of Botswana and Namibia, and the Ju/'hoansi are being buffeted by the same local, national, and global forces as their fellow citizens. Richard Lee has been doing fieldwork with the Ju/'hoansi since the 1960s and has witnessed the effects of these forces firsthand. One unavoidable force that has shaped, and been shaped by, Ju/'hoansi kinship patterns and practices is the AIDS pandemic.

In the mid-1990s, when Lee and medical anthropologist Ida Susser began conducting research on the epidemic in southern Africa, one in every four adults aged 19 to 44 in South Africa, Namibia, and Botswana was HIV positive, and rates were rising (Lee 1996, 27). On the one hand, governments were making a concerted effort to mount publicity and education campaigns, even in remote areas where the Ju/'hoansi have traditionally lived. On the other, Lee and Susser were surprised by the relative "calm" surrounding the AIDS epidemic in the public sphere. Lee argues that silence and stigma about both sexual practices and AIDS in these southern African countries contributed to this deceptive sense of calm (28). Silence surrounded AIDS-related illness and deaths, and AIDS-related deaths were characterized simply as the result of "a long illness" or "unknown causes." In fact, physicians in Namibia were encouraged to omit any mention of AIDS from medical documentation (28). Such silences were a result of the strong stigma of having AIDS. Often, those who were infected hid their illness out of shame, and many transmitted the disease to their unknowing partners while they

kept their secret. At the time, Lee argued that "only when the magnitude of the problem is clear and the terrible stigma overcome will it be possible to make the critical behavioral changes that will prevent the further spread of AIDS" (30).

At first glance, the Ju/'hoansi would seem to be especially vulnerable to the AIDs epidemic. Anthropologists such as Paul Farmer (whose work we discuss in Chapter 7) have shown that poverty, inequality, and marginalization exacerbate the spread of AIDS throughout the world. Susser (2006) points out that contemporary Ju/'hoansi are in an unusual position in terms of poverty and inequality. Poverty is relative, and while the Ju/'hoansi may not have much in terms of material wealth, their relatively egalitarian society has helped them avoid the gap between the rich and the poor that often contributes to ill health. Although the Ju/'hoansi have not lived exclusively as hunter–gatherers for many years, many still gather some berries and nuts and snare small animals, and these unique patterns of subsistence have provided a slight cultural "buffer" against the encroachment of surrounding groups and the incursion of capitalism (206). Ju/'hoansi kinship practices—especially sharing and women's sexual autonomy—are central to this cultural buffer; moreover, Susser suggests that these practices have protected the Ju/'hoansi against the spread of HIV/AIDS.

These protective effects are most evident when we compare those Ju/'hoansi who continue to live in relatively remote areas to those who live in Tsumkwe, Namibia. Once a small Ju/'hoansi village, Tsumkwe has become an administrative centre, populated and visited by Ju/'hoansi, civil servants, tourists, cattle farmers, construction workers, and border guards. Ju/'hoansi living in more remote villages engage with capitalism by selling goods or services through community cooperative organizations, which mediate collectively between the villages and the market economy (Susser 2006, 215). However, the Ju'hoansi in Tsumkwe are not protected by the social organization and kinship relations of the (partial) subsistence economy;

instead, they enter into the lowest, most exploitative levels of the economy, which revolves around tourism and services. Besides living in poverty in Tsumkwe, many Ju/'hoansi spend a lot of time (and money) at local *shebeens* (makeshift bars that sell home brew), where Ju/'hoansi women often engage in "survival sex" (Susser 2009, 182), often with non-Ju/'hoansi itinerant workers.

Two important differences between life in remote villages and life in Tsumkwe stand out as relevant to understanding the spread of HIV/AIDS. The first is that, according to Susser, villagers "are somewhat protected from the individual risk and insecurity involved in marginal work and the lowest rung of the tourist economy, [and] appear to be less vulnerable to the ravages of HIV/AIDS" (2006, 215). The second is that, as we saw in section 5.3 above, Ju/'hoansi women living in small villages continue to exercise a great deal of sexual autonomy and authority, which has limited the spread of HIV infections in those villages. By contrast, rates of infection among Ju/'hoansi women in Tsumkwe are much higher. When Susser asked a group of young married women in a small "traditional" village if they would be able to use a box of male condoms, they replied, "Give us some, and we will teach our husbands how to use them" (2009, 171). This self-assuredness is markedly different from that of Ju'hoansi women living in Tsumkwe, and from that of women from other ethnic groups in Namibia, whose experiences of economic and gender inequality, coupled with silence and stigma around sexual practices, make it nearly impossible for them to ask their partners to wear condoms. Anthropologists and others note that the introduction of the female condom appears to be giving women some measure of autonomy and self-protection. Although exact figures are lacking, it is clear that the Ju/'hoansi—especially those *not* living in Tsumkwe—have a much lower incidence of HIV/AIDS infection than their neighbours (between 3 and 6 percent as opposed to the national average of 25 to 30 percent) (Lee and Susser 2002).

Women discuss the female condom. Dobe, 2001.

© Ida Susser

Clearly, prevention efforts aimed at the Ju/'hoansi will build on the insights of Lee and Susser's fieldwork. Maintaining aspects of a foraging way of life, which allows families to maintain their households and women to maintain aspects of their historic autonomy, will make all the difference in limiting or even preventing the spread of HIV infections among the Ju/'hoansi.

Elsewhere in Namibia we see an altogether different links among kinship patterns, sexuality, stigma, and HIV/AIDS. Robert Lorway conducted fieldwork in Windhoek, Namibia's capital, with a gay and lesbian community group, the Rainbow Project. He found that the greatest barrier to successful prevention initiatives in this community was the perception, perpetuated through public health initiatives, that "AIDS in Africa" is exclusively a Pattern II, or heterosexual, epidemic (Lorway 2007, 276). There are virtually no public health campaigns in Namibia that address homosexual behaviour in their prevention education, and as a result, men who have sex with men are more vulnerable to HIV infection (Lorway 2006, 435). For example, there was a common (mis)understanding among men who had wives or girlfriends, and who also enjoyed sex with men, that they were practising safer sex when sleeping with men. One of Lorway's informants explained: "Most of the men I know who have girlfriends are saying that they prefer to have sex with us *moffies* [effeminate males] because they don't want to catch STDs cheating on them, or HIV, or get someone pregnant. Most of them think they can even have sex with men without a condom because they think it is less risky than sex with a woman" (Jason, 21-year-old male from Katutura) (2007, 276).

Lorway's work shows that, although heterosexual intercourse *is* the main source of transmission of HIV in Namibia, the exclusion of any information about same-sex transmission was limiting possibilities for education and prevention. These transmission myths were compounded by intense anti-homosexual sentiment (and laws prohibiting homosexuality) in Namibia, which resulted in equally intense stigma, shame, and secrecy. Lorway's fieldwork demonstrated the urgent need for short-term interventions that would work even in a climate of intolerance and fear. During his fieldwork, he was actively involved in precisely this kind of prevention: through the Rainbow Project, he helped coordinate community-level education strategies that could "move safer sex information through secretive social networks without risking public exposure" (2007, 292). Maintaining secrecy may run counter to mainstream HIV-prevention goals, such as raising public awareness about homosexual transmission and encouraging acceptance of homosexuality in the public sphere, but Lorway's ethnographic evidence suggests that doing so is the most culturally appropriate and immediately effective way of promoting prevention. His work, like that of Lee and Susser, demonstrates just how important it is that "intensive ethnography is centrally incorporated within the methodologies of health science projects" (2006, 448).

EXERCISE 5.5

Developing a Program for Prevention of STDs

For this exercise, you play the role of an HIV/AIDS prevention specialist and help design a program for your culture to promote condom use. You need to answer the following questions:

1. What are some of the cultural barriers that might inhibit condom use? Are any similar to those in Namibia?

2. What are some measures that you would suggest to help people who are sexually active overcome these barriers?

CONCLUSIONS

In this chapter we have examined the structure and dynamics of family life among three peoples—the Ju/'hoansi, the Trobriand Islanders, and rural Chinese. Throughout the chapter, you have been asked to think about those aspects of the North American family that we tend to take for granted as natural but that are culturally situated and often unique. As we have seen, each society has different rules about whom a person regards as a family member, and family membership can vary based on variations in descent systems. In each case, we have also thought about how the family is formed and how the ideal family type is maintained in these societies. But it is important to keep in mind that these ideal types are not static and timeless; sometimes, the idea of an ideal family type can be contentious. Sexuality, love, and wealth each play a key role in family life, although as we have seen, the significance of each varies from culture to culture. Often, the forces that threaten the family unit are those that threaten sexuality, love, or wealth as they are understood in each cultural context.

Although kinship questions have always been central to anthropology, the ways that anthropologists think about and study family relations have changed a great deal in recent decades. Critiques such as those by David Schneider and various feminist anthropologists have inspired some researchers to be more aware of the effects of colonialism and of their own underlying Eurocentric assumptions about what families should look like. Nonetheless, knowledge of family and intimate relations in a society remains an important focus of anthropological research, and, it is important to note, can be applied to the development of culturally appropriate and effective programs to promote sexual health.

CRITICAL THINKING QUESTIONS

1. What are some common ways in which we use the idea of family as a metaphor for other kinds of social relationships (e.g., in the workplace or in teams)? What do we accomplish when we make these kinds of metaphorical comparisons?
2. Debates about same-sex marriage in North America often pit "traditional family values" against "universal human rights." What have you learned in this chapter (and the rest of the text) that might undermine this straightforward dualism?

KEY TERMS:

bilateral kinship (p. 132)
brideservice (p. 133)
bridewealth (p. 142)
clans (p. 142)
dowry (p. 145)
endogamy (p. 142)
ethnographic present (p. 130)
exogamy (p. 142)
extended family (p. 137)
impartible inheritance (p. 150)
incest taboo (p. 139)
kinship (p. 130)
matrilineage (p. 134)
matrilineal kinship (p. 133)
nuclear family (p. 132)
partible inheritance (p. 150)
patrilineage (p. 137)
patrilineal kinship (p. 133)
polyandry (p. 147)
polygamy (p. 147)
polygyny (p. 147)

CHAPTER 6

CONSTRUCTING IDENTITIES

From the moment we are born, interactions with others are shaped by their perceptions of us. Such interactions, as shown in the painting above by Mark Anthony Jacobson, are part of the "Celebration of a New Life." According to Goffman, quoted in the epigraph on the next page, we use our bodies in unconscious and conscious ways to communicate information about ourselves to others. Through our speech, clothing, gestures, postures, and other phenomena, people make assumptions and often judgments about our character and our place in the world. Similarly, we often consciously manipulate our bodies to show others who we think we are. These aspects of what we call "identity"—both individual and collective—form the subject of this chapter.

When an individual enters the presence of others, they commonly seek to acquire information about him or to bring into play information about him already possessed. They will be interested in his general socioeconomic status, his conception of self, his attitude toward them, his competence, his trustworthiness, etc. Although some of this information seems to be sought almost as an end in itself, there are usually quite practical reasons for acquiring it. Information about the individual helps to define the situation, enabling others to know in advance what he will expect of them and what they may expect of him. Informed in these ways, the others will know how best to act in order to call forth a desired response from him.

Erving Goffman

Problem 6

How do people determine who they are, and how do they communicate who they *think* they are to others?

INTRODUCTION

As human beings, we are not born knowing who we are or what our place is in the social landscape; we must learn our **social identity**: who we are and how we stand in relation to others. To appreciate the importance of the self as a social identity, try to imagine a society in which every person is physically indistinguishable from every other person. How would people in such a society know how to behave toward one another? Whenever we interact with another person, the interaction must be based on some idea of who the other is: Friend? Stranger? Family member? Teacher? At the same time, the other must have some idea of who *we* are, a conception of the relationship that exists between us. The need to know the social identity of others is apparent whenever two strangers meet and, directly or indirectly, seek to elicit information about each other. Each tries to place the other in some identity at some spot on the social landscape.

Imagine next a society in which every person is utterly unique. In this case, every interaction would be different, and there would be no way to learn from one situation how to behave in another similar situation.

social identity
The view that people have of their own and others' positions in society. These learned personal and social affiliations may include gender, sexuality, race, class, nationality, and ethnicity. Individuals seek confirmation from others that they occupy the positions on the social landscape that they claim to occupy.

Each person would need to have an infinite variety of behaviours with which to interact with people of an infinite number of types. We avoid this situation by categorizing people, placing them in groups so that not everyone in our social universe is unique. We group them into categories based on criteria such as gender (female, male, or some other gender), ethnicity (Irish, Italian, Chinese), personal characteristics (short, tall, husky, thin), and so on.

Try to imagine, also, a social landscape in which no person acknowledges any other person or communicates in any way who she or he thinks the other is. This scenario, too, would represent an impossible situation. People would have no way of acquiring from others confirmation that they occupy the social identities they think they occupy. In reality, our social identities are constructed in large part by others, who, by their behaviour toward us, confirm that we occupy the spot on the social landscape we claim to occupy. Put another way, nobody is anybody except in relation to somebody.

Finally, try to imagine a social landscape in which everyone communicates to everyone else that they occupy the wrong spot on the landscape. Every person actively disagrees with every other person about who they are. This situation would be, if not impossible, chaotic.

QUESTIONS

6.1 How is identity, and one's sense of self, learned?

6.2 How does the concept of personhood vary from society to society?

6.3 How do societies distinguish individuals from one another?

6.4 How do societies mark changes in identity?

6.5 How do individuals communicate their identities to one another?

6.6 How do people form identities through collective struggles?

To examine how people in a society determine who they are and communicate who they think they are to others, in this chapter we will explore the ways different societies define the person, the ways individuals are differentiated from others, the ways they find out who they are and convey to others who they are, the ways they mark transitions from one social identity to another, and the ways they form collective identities.

QUESTION 6.1: HOW IS IDENTITY, AND ONE'S SENSE OF SELF, LEARNED?

Learning Identities

Hugh Brody begins his book *The Other Side of Eden: Hunters, Farmers, and the Shaping of the World* (2000) with a description of a baby Inuit girl:

> *Imagine the darkness of the far north. Not as something in which the adventurous traveller moves in awe. But as a beginning, for those for whom the Arctic is home. Imagine the inside of a skin tent, or a snowhouse, or a government-regulation low-rental prefab. In this home, an Inuit baby girl wakes in the night. She is held, fed, cuddled—and talked to …*
>
> *In these words, the child is given the sounds of love, and can know that she is safe. Not safe just to feed, to sleep, but safe to do these things as and when she wants. For she is a baby who carries atiq, the spirit and name of her late grandmother. She is the adored baby; she is also her mother's mother, her grandfather's wife. Her grandmother is alive again in the baby. This means the baby is doubly and trebly loved. And she must be treated with respect. (2000, 11–12)*

Is this Inuit baby born with an identity? Or is her identity something she must learn? It is certainly clear to others in her Inuit community that she is the reincarnation of her grandmother, but how long will it take the baby to understand what that means?

Learning to Belong

Hugh Brody suggests that the Inuit baby begins to know that she is an important member of her family almost the moment she is born and that this knowledge expands daily as she interacts with others. As people tell her stories about her land and its creation, she builds up an image of her world and of her place in it. She learns that she is connected to her land and to all the other creatures that share the land with her.

Stories present people of all ages with ways of knowing about who they are and where they came from. Storytelling is also a way of communicating information from one generation to another (Ridington 1990, 14). No one censors Inuit stories, and children's understanding grows as they grow. Brody describes the Inuit child's experiences with stories told by her grandfather and other adults: "The small child listens for as long as she wishes—she is, after all, also her own grandmother. And she discovers that stories are always a mystery, for they have much that cannot be understood, and much that comes from knowledge and experience beyond understanding" (2000, 13).

As this child grows, she recognizes stories that are told over and over, with the same main characters and events. She also learns that no one understands everything in the stories, and she keeps her sense of wonderment about the world.

Brody's example highlights a key point about identity: we are not born knowing who we are or what our places are on the social landscape; we *learn* to be Canadian or Japanese, husbands or wives, Andrea, Gavin, Homa, Natasha, or Sebastian. We learn how we relate to others as sons, daughters, students, friends, or lovers. Both consciously and unconsciously, individuals form various identities so that they can relate to others and cultivate

a space for themselves within their social landscape. At the same time, identities are political and collective, formed around struggles against such threats as colonialism or the state. As we become who we are, we learn how we stand in relation to others.

Identities such as gender, sexuality, race, ethnicity, and national identity, to name a few, are not natural or biological. We are not born knowing instinctively what it means to "be Canadian," for instance. Our sense of Canadianness, like any other identity, is cultivated and learned through various agents of **enculturation**. These are sociocultural forces and institutions that teach us, consciously or unconsciously, about what it means to be a Canadian citizen. Agents of enculturation may include the mass media, parents, peers, school, and the government.

Think about the ways in which children are enculturated into the norms of "Canadian identity," for example, in many public school systems across Canada. In elementary school, most children learn how to sing the national anthem, and because provincial governments control the content of the school curriculum, students learn a government-sanctioned version of Canadian history. Students must demonstrate their successful acquisition and knowledge of this history on tests and papers in order to advance to the next grade. Even as they graduate and get older, Canadians continue to learn about Canada through participation in Canada Day parades and other public spectacles, or by watching the national news on Canadian television stations such as the CBC (Canadian Broadcasting Corporation). In Canada, the mass media play an important role in shaping ideals of Canadianness through their depictions of sport, for instance. Hockey, in particular, has long been promoted as a component of a distinctive

enculturation
The process through which individuals learn an identity. It can encompass parental socialization, the influence of peers, the mass media, government, and other forces.

CONSTRUCTING IDENTITIES **163**

Canadian identity; however, hockey's participants and spectators are mostly white, middle-class, and male (Gruneau and Whitson 1993; Hartman 2009). As such, it is a sport that (perhaps unintentionally) promotes a dominant, or normative, ideal of Canadian identity as white, middle-class, and male. Given that Canada is officially a diverse, multicultural nation in which no particular gender, sexuality, or ethnic or racial identity should be privileged as "more Canadian" than any other, this image is a problem. In this context, hockey's iconic status as a national symbol is ironic, for it excludes a large portion of the nation's multicultural population and promotes hierarchies of Canadianness. To be "truly" Canadian, we learn, is to consume and participate in hockey. In recent years, the sport has been trying to connect with the nation's increasingly multicultural and multilingual population base. Beginning in 2007, for instance, the CBC began broadcasting hockey games in Punjabi; even after hockey moved from the national public broadcaster to Rogers Media in 2014, Punjabi broadcasts were maintained on the private broadcaster's multicultural OMNI television stations.

Despite the problematical nature of hockey as a "Canadian" identity marker, it is important to note that shared experiences, such as sports and other mediated events, are often used to cultivate a sense of **imagined community**. This term, coined by political scientist Benedict Anderson in 1983, suggests that identities, including national ones, are culturally constructed through shared experiences, even in the absence of face-to-face contacts. So, even though a Canadian living in Halifax may never have visited Toronto, Regina, or Whitehorse, a shared sense of "Canadianness" is created through mediated experiences: watching and listening to stories about Canadian successes at the Olympics; attending Canada Day spectacles and ceremonies; following the national news on television, radio, and the Internet or in newspapers; and so on. Because this process of enculturation often begins when we are young, we often fail to see how various cultural forces shape our identities. Thus, we often view our identities as natural, primordial, or biologically

Canadians playing hockey.

based. Think of the many people who are willing to "sacrifice" themselves or die for their country, for instance. Often, individuals are willing to go to such lengths only if they feel that their identification with their nation is somehow instinctual and, by extension, natural.

Over the past century, anthropologists have engaged actively with precisely these sorts of debates. We live in a pop culture that privileges natural explanations for human behaviours. This has been the case since the late 1800s, with the rise of the **nature versus nurture** debate in academia. In 1874, British naturalist Sir Francis Galton, inspired by the principles of Darwinian evolution, coined

imagined community
A term coined by Benedict Anderson in 1983. It refers to the fact that even in the absence of face-to-face interactions, a sense of community (e.g., nationalism) is culturally constructed by forces such as the mass media.

nature versus nurture
A phrase, coined by Sir Francis Galton in 1874, that references a long-standing scholarly debate concerning whether or not human behaviours and identities are the result of nature (biological and genetic factors) or nurture (learned and cultural factors).

the term "nature versus nurture." Galton (whose work on race we discuss in Chapter 7) was a eugenicist who felt that some people, by virtue of their class, race, or other factors, were better suited to reproduce as they were more "fit" to survive in society. Galton believed that many human differences, including intelligence, were rooted in biology, or "nature." His ideas spawned wildly inaccurate assumptions and research on the part of academics throughout the late 19th and 20th centuries. At the time, many scholars felt that many of our identities, such as race and class, are genetic and thus "natural"—that we are born the way we are.

One of the first anthropologists to engage ethnographically with the nature versus nurture debate was Margaret Mead. In 1926, Mead set out for American Samoa to conduct research that would challenge widespread ideas among scientists that acts of teenage rebellion and experimentation were the result of hormonal or other physical changes brought on by puberty (or "nature"). Such behaviour was commonplace among American teenagers; Mead wondered whether similar behavioural patterns existed in other cultures. Under the direction of her doctoral supervisor, Franz Boas, she travelled to the island of Ta'u to study the behaviour of teenage girls. She observed that their experiences of adolescence were completely different from the experiences of American girls. In Samoa, girls were given a lot of freedom to experiment with their sexuality and did not go through periods of torment with parents. Samoan culture, she argued, did not possess the same Judeo-Christian ideals of sexual morality; this, in turn, contributed to different behaviours and attitudes toward sexuality. Mead thus argued that the experiences of adolescents varied depending on the culture in which they were raised. She therefore emphasized the role of culture or "nurture" in human behaviour.

Mead's methods and research findings would subsequently be disputed, but her continued ethnographic work on the "nature/nurture" debate in 1935 should be noted. Mead visited three tribes along the Sepik River in Papua New Guinea to

American anthropologist Margaret Mead in the Admiralty Islands.

explore differences in gender roles. She found that, in each tribe, men and women took on different responsibilities based on their gender. She was thus able to suggest, once again, that human behavioural differences (in this case, gendered divisions of labour) were the result of culture, not biology.

Research that seeks to link biology with human behaviours and identities is potentially dangerous, for it can provide powerful justifications for social inequalities in society. Back in 1968, for instance, Washburn and Lancaster sought to argue that women, for biological and evolutionary reasons, were better "nurturers" of children—an argument that has since been disputed by feminist scholars. But think of the consequences of this type of research. If women can be "proven" to be naturally better "nurturers," then it becomes easy to argue that a woman's place is in the domestic sphere. This information could then inform government policies relating to daycare funding, affirmative action, and other social issues.

Most anthropologists, on the other hand, would be quick to point out the significance of nurture when it comes to the explanation of gender identity, which, in all cultures, is one of the key aspects of personhood and identity. All societies use gender to divide their members into meaningful categories, yet the way in which this is accomplished varies widely

CONSTRUCTING IDENTITIES

from culture to culture and throughout history. In North America, gender assignment begins at birth with the announcement "It's a girl" or "It's a boy," conveniently ignoring the 4 percent of births in which the infant has various combinations of male and female characteristics (e.g., an infant with one testis and one ovary, an infant with one testis and aspects of the female genitalia, or an infant with ovaries and some aspect of male genitalia). Once the announcement of gender is made (or after a surgical procedure in which the infant is "corrected" to fit into either the male or female category), the infant is given a gender-appropriate name, dressed in properly designed or coloured clothing, and spoken to in gender-appropriate language. Parents and other caregivers then teach male children that it is manly to endure pain, to be strong and tough. Male children are discouraged from expressing discomfort and encouraged when they can withstand it. Female children, on the other hand, are comforted when they hurt themselves. Although gender stereotypes are changing, many North American boys are still encouraged to be aggressive and competitive; they learn to compete in games and play with toys that require aggressive behaviour. Girls are still taught to be caring and helpful; they are given toys such as dolls that encourage "feminine" behaviour. As we discuss in greater detail in Chapter 7, gender differences, regardless of whether they are understood as biological or cultural, often serve as a key form of social inequality.

Anthropological fieldwork in various societies has shed light on the problems associated with viewing all human identities in terms of "nature." Yet the development of genetic behavioural research and the ways in which such research is often discussed by laypeople continue to link identities with nature. Think of the ways in which some scientists are actively searching for specific genes that they believe are the cause of particular behaviours. We live in a society that valorizes the "gene" and that is fascinated by ongoing research on the so-called "gay gene" or the "selfish gene." Often, this fascination is more a reflection of popular cultural concerns than it is an accurate reflection of the science. As anthropologist Roger Lancaster (2003) has shown, science journalists misinterpret complex scientific findings in ways that imply that the diversity of human behaviours can be reduced to biology, that ignore the role of culture in shaping identities such as race, gender, and sexuality, and that serve to obscure the fact that many individual behaviours, such as selfishness, may be the result of complex interplays of culture and biology.

Recent developments in genetics suggest, however, that today, there is much more middle ground in the nature versus nurture debate. The consensus that is building among geneticists is that genes are not immutable, nor are genetics destiny. Rather, one's environment (including culture) has a profound effect on one's genes. Any effort to understand the relationship between genes and behaviour must take the cultural environment into account; similarly, geneticists argue that some, if not all, cultural behaviours (propensity to smoke cigarettes or drink alcohol, for example) may very well have important genetic underpinnings.

EXERCISE 6.1

Find a recent newspaper or magazine article that deals with the "nature/nurture" debate. For example, the mass media are always reporting on the latest "scientific" discoveries, which often seek to confirm a biological basis for certain identities—the "gay gene," for example. Outline some of the problems associated with this article from an anthropological perspective. How and why do scientists often overlook the "nurture," or cultural and learned, aspects of our identities?

Now that we have explored how anthropologists tend to emphasize the learned, culturally constructed nature of our personal and collective identities, in the next section we examine in greater detail how a sense of self or personhood is shaped by various cultural forces.

QUESTION 6.2: HOW DOES THE CONCEPT OF PERSONHOOD VARY FROM SOCIETY TO SOCIETY?

The Importance of Self

Of all the products of our culture, the one we most take for granted is our self.

In all societies a personal name is an intimate marker of a person, differentiating one individual from another. Names also can reveal how people conceive of themselves and their relations to others. For many North Americans, names are perhaps the most enduring aspect of the self. Assigned at birth, our names remain with us throughout our lives and represent the self. How much of the self is revealed by a name varies by culture and situation. University students meeting for the first time exchange personal names, rarely bothering with family names. Their sense of self is independent of any group or past. When North American businesspeople meet, they exchange first names, last names, and business titles. Businesspeople are linked to their organizations more than geographical location. In contrast, when Moroccans from different towns meet, the names they offer to others include not only the names of their families but the names of the towns they are from. The Moroccan self is embedded in family and place of origin. Among the Tsimshian of British Columbia, the names people use depend on their social position; when they enter adulthood, get married, or assume a higher rank in Tsimshian society, they change their names. The Tsimshian self is inseparable from one's position in society.

Jorge Chimbinda (2006) has explored the process of "naming" children among the Umbundu of Angola, where there are two ways of naming a child. The most common way is to name a child after a relative who is either alive or dead (an ancestor). The second way is to give

Some contemporary Tsimshian children continue to follow tradition by wearing traditional shawls and will change their names upon entering adulthood.

a child a new name that refers to some unusual circumstance that was present during the child's birth. For example, a child born during a severe drought will be given a name that refers to the drought and keeps the memory of the suffering alive. The child of a mother who dies in childbirth will be given a name that keeps the memory of the mother's suffering and death. The result of this way of naming is that each child has a last name of his or her own. At the same time, the Umbundu naming system is a historical version of cultural values, such as identity, kinship, geography, folktales, stories, and proverbs. From the Umbundu perspective, names are tools with which people reward the life they have received from their relatives and their world. Names serve to perpetuate the wide kinship web and stress the concept of extended family. Each child represents one of his or her living relatives or ancestors. All relatives and ancestors on both the father's side and that of the mother have equal value because each of them has contributed to the existence of the child. These names also inscribe the imprint of lived experiences on children, so that children named after unusual circumstances embody the meaning of the experiences.

Jorge Chimbinda also explores the effects of colonialism on his people. When Angola became a Portuguese colony, the colonial administrators found it too difficult to keep track of Umbundu people because the naming system did not group people in ways that the administrators understood. For the Portuguese, as for most Europeans, last names were shared among members of families and made family identification orderly. Thus, one of the first ways that the Portuguese colonizers tried to destroy Umbundu identity was to force people to discard their Umbundu names and to use Portuguese names instead.

The differences in naming practices among different societies reveal the different ways societies conceptualize what a person is and how that person relates to the group. Many North Americans believe that individuals are stable, autonomous entities who exist more or less independently of whatever situations or statuses they occupy. Even as they move from status to status or place to place—from student to husband or wife, to employee, to father or mother—they believe themselves to be the same persons. Otherwise, each time they changed situations or statuses they would in effect become different people and would have to change their names. In this regard North Americans are highly individualistic. In other societies, however, individuals are not seen as entities distinct from their social position or group. In societies such as the Umbundu, the relationship between the person and the group, or the person and his or her social position, is holistic; the person cannot be conceived as existing separately from society or apart from his or her cultural beliefs and values.

EXERCISE 6.2

If you were an Umbundu and lived in Angola, which of your ancestors would you choose for the name of your first child? Why would you make this particular choice? In other words, what are the qualities in your ancestors that you would want to transfer to your child? What about your second child and your third?

The Egocentric Self and the Sociocentric Self

Differences between the individualistic and holistic conceptions of the self led Richard A. Shweder and Edmund J. Bourne (1984) to delineate two distinct ways in which the person is conceived in different societies: the **egocentric** and the **sociocentric** views of self. Note that these terms are ideal types, or generalizations about the nature of self in different societies. There will, of course, be exceptions to these patterns, especially given the increasing influence of globalization in constructing our identities. So it is important to recognize that there exist multiple, often overlapping interpretations of self, even within the generalized contexts of the societies described below.

In the *egocentric* view, typified in many ways by the Western view adopted by North American societies, each person is perceived to be capable of acting independently from others, and the locus of motivations and drives is thus internal. For Westerners, the individual is the centre of awareness, a distinct whole set against other wholes. Social relations are regarded as contracts between autonomous, free-acting beings. Individuals are free to negotiate their places in society, and the dominant idea is that each individual is responsible for *what* and *who* he or she is. Moreover, individuals possess intrinsic qualities such as generosity, integrity, and beauty. The egocentric view of the person places a high value on individualism, self-reliance, and freedom of choice, such as the ability to select one's own marriage partner.

egocentric
A view of the self that defines each person as a replica of all humanity, as the location of motivations and drives, and as capable of acting independently from others.

sociocentric
A context-dependent view of self. The self exists as an entity only within the concrete situations or roles occupied by the person.

Keeping in mind that factors such as poverty and ethnicity may make individualism and self-reliance difficult to achieve, it is worthwhile to explore the beliefs associated with this view of the individual. Robert Bellah and his co-authors of *Habits of the Heart* (1984) examined ideas of the individual in the United States that seem to apply equally to Canada. The self in the United States, they say, seeks to work out its own life plot by individually pursuing happiness and satisfying its wants. Unlike individuals in some other societies, many Americans seek to cut themselves off from the past, especially from their parents. They each seek to become their own person, to find their own self. Young men and women need to demonstrate that they can stand on their own two feet and support themselves. This emphasis on self-reliance and independence underpins the belief Americans hold that success is the outcome of free and fair competition among individuals in an open market. Most successful Americans, say Bellah and his associates, claim that they achieved success through their own hard work, seldom acknowledging the contributions made by their families, their schooling, or their positions as members of the upwardly mobile middle class. The only way they can say they deserve what they have achieved is by succeeding through their own efforts.

Because of this dominant perspective of self, many people who were raised within Western, industrialized societies are inclined to view those afflicted with, for instance, eating disorders such as anorexia nervosa or bulimia, as suffering from an individual pathology. It is as if eating disorders were the result of an individual's "problem." Helen Gremillion (2003) conducted 14 months of ethnographic research at a small inpatient eating disorder clinic in the United States. She discovered there that the various cultural forces that have contributed to increases in diagnoses of eating disorders are being ignored in favour of "individualistic" explanations. For example, Gremillion and others often point out that mass media advertising plays a role in constructing normative expectations of an impossibly ideal femininity. Increasingly, the feminine ideal is being defined by physical appearance—in particular, by representations of predominantly white, youthful, slender, "beautiful" women. In this way, advertising on television and the Internet, in magazines, and on billboards is playing a powerful role in shaping Westerners' sense of self. Yet its images of ideal femininity have themselves been constructed and manipulated by computer technologies, which remove wrinkles or fine lines, minimize fat, and reshape facial features. Gremillion argues that many eating disorder treatment plans fail to recognize the role of culture in shaping the self. Such treatment plans replicate Western notions of individualism through the inclusion of careful daily monitoring of weight and patient "progress." These principles of egocentrism, of the individual monitoring of the body—and, by extension, the self—have led to a proliferation of eating disorders.

In contrast to the egocentric view, the *sociocentric* view of the self is context dependent. The self exists as an entity only within the concrete situations or roles occupied by the person. From a sociocentric perspective, there is no intrinsic self that can possess enduring qualities such as generosity, integrity, and beauty. These qualities can apply only to concrete social situations. Instead of saying that a man is generous, a sociocentric perspective would be that "he gives money to his friends." Instead of saying that a woman is principled, the perspective would be that "she does not give away secrets."

It may be the case, as some anthropologists have argued, that, in reality, most societies understand selfhood as both egocentric *and* sociocentric, and that the differences between the societal views of selfhood might lie less in which view they subscribe to than in how they see and practise the interrelationship between the two. For example, Anne E. Becker (1995) characterizes the relationship between body, self, and society in Fiji as one in which the relation of one's body to one's self is mediated through the relation of one's self to one's community (37). The cultivation of one's body (its shape and health, for instance) is understood mainly as a community, rather than a personal, enterprise; this view of the self and body may be more sociocentric than we are familiar with in North America, but it does not mean that Fijians do not also possess an egocentric view. Indeed, during subsequent fieldwork in Fiji, Becker (2004) discovered that the introduction of broadcast television, and specifically Western programming (along with other socioeconomic changes related to globalization), seemed to cause a dramatic shift away from the centrality of the sociocentric self and towards seeing the body as a personal project. As a result, the incidence of eating disorders among school-aged girls, previously almost unheard of, skyrocketed. However, as Gremillion's work above demonstrates, even in North America, the underlying logic of eating disorders must also be understood as sociocentric, even if our common-sense reaction to, and treatment of, these disorders privileges egocentric selfhood.

Personhood in Japan

Some anthropologists attribute a sociocentric view of the self to people in Japan. Anthropologist Christie Kiefer (1976) explained that the Japanese are more likely to include within the boundaries of the self the social groups of which the person is a member. Japanese children are not trained to rely solely on the self, as many North American children are. They are taught that interdependence between the person and the family or group is more important than independence.

Robert Smith (1983) noted that the Japanese view of the self is expressed in their language. For example, Japanese language does not include anything resembling English personal pronouns. In English, children quickly learn to use the two personal referents, *I* and *you*; Japanese boys, on the other hand, must learn six, and girls must learn five. The personal referent used in Japan depends on the speaker's relationship to the listener. It expresses how the self is defined relative to a specific social interaction.

In addition, wrote Smith, the Japanese language contains vocabulary that is very conscious of status. It is characterized by what the Japanese call *keigo*, or

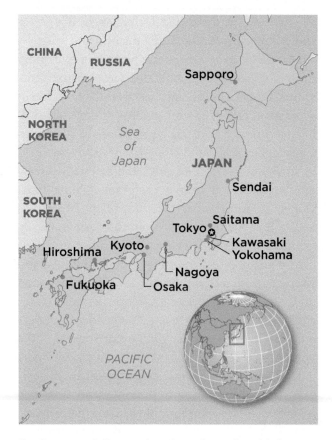

"polite speech." *Keigo* has the effect of establishing at the outset of a conversation the relative social standing and degree of intimacy of speaker and listener. Japanese speakers use different forms of address depending on their social position relative to the person to whom they are speaking. Since the Japanese language is status based, people must be careful of the linguistic forms they use in conversations. When conversing with someone in a superior social position, a speaker must linguistically acknowledge the social difference between speaker and listener. Japanese advertisers have a problem with *keigo* because actors should not give imperative commands (e.g., "Drink Coke") for fear of offending people. They solve the problem by using low-status people who are nonthreatening (e.g., clowns, coquettish women, or children) to issue the commands.

The sociocentric Japanese differ also in their approach to social interactions. Most North Americans believe it is desirable to assert themselves to stand out, and to take charge. The Japanese believe that social interactions should be characterized by restraint or reserve, traits they identify as *enryo*. With *enryo*, the giving of opinions is avoided; this attitude is summarized by the Japanese proverb "the nail that sticks up shall be hammered down."

EXERCISE 6.3

1. The contemporary popularity of social media and attendant forms of virtual selfhood poses some interesting challenges to a strictly dichotomous view of egocentric versus sociocentric selfhood. Many users of sites such as Facebook and Twitter use social media to present idealized versions of their "egocentric" selves. However, these sites also rely upon a more sociocentric sense of self, created through one's social network. Is a person really "on" Facebook if he or she has have no friend connections? Think about the way you construct yourself on social media (or in other virtual forms). Is your social media self described best as egocentric or sociocentric? Why?

2. In your opinion, how accurately does your virtual self reflect your physical self? Is one more real or true than the other?

3. Does your online self ever affect your virtual self? If so, in what ways?

4. How might social media use differ between North America and societies that are considered to have a more sociocentric view of the self?

Yet the Japanese *do* conceive of themselves as separate entities. They are as attached to their personal names as North Americans are, if not more so. Moreover, they believe in self-development. But for them, the autonomy of the individual is established, not in social situations where they actively distinguish themselves from others, but *away from* society, where self-reflection and introspection are legitimate. Through introspection the Japanese find their true heart (*kokoro*) and are put in touch with their true nature—their *hara* ("belly") and *jibub* ("self").

In *Crafting Selves*, an ethnography of Japanese factory workers, Dorinne Kondo (1990) approaches the sociocentric versus egocentric question from a slightly different perspective. She questions whether it is accurate to refer to selfhood, in Japan or elsewhere, as singular. Perhaps, she suggests, it would be better to think about how people craft *selves* through the practices of everyday life. From this perspective, personhood is not static or fixed, but processual and ongoing. According to Kondo, the way that Japanese factory workers craft selves is the result of how they envision and practise their belonging (or lack thereof) to entities such as company and family; selves are therefore crafted in relation to power and hierarchies. Rather than possessing a singular, decisively sociocentric "Japanese self," Kondo suggests that her informants adopt "multiple, infinitely graded, layers of selfhood," often described as oscillating between two ends of a continuum: *omote*, the front, formal side; and *ura*, the back, intimate side. This is not a straightforward dualism: what counts as *omote* or *ura* is always shifting, and the tension between the two is never fully resolved (Kondo 1990, 31).

In the remainder of this chapter, we will look at the self less from an egocentric perspective and more from a sociocentric perspective, as something contingent and relative to the situation. Our focus will be on that part of the self that is defined by social relations and social processes and that is subject to change and redefinition.

QUESTION 6.3: HOW DO SOCIETIES DISTINGUISH INDIVIDUALS FROM ONE ANOTHER?

Differences and similarities among persons are the materials from which we construct our social landscapes. Those materials allow us to distinguish individuals from one another or assign them to one group or another. From these similarities and differences we construct our social identities. However, all societies do not use the same similarities and differences to construct a social code, nor do they use these similarities and differences in the same way. Some characteristics of persons—some tools in the "identity toolbox," so to speak—are used almost universally to differentiate people or to group them together. For example, most societies use family membership, gender, and age as categories within a social code. But other characteristics figure prominently only in some societies—ethnic group membership, skin colour, and wealth, for example.

In many societies, the most important characteristics for defining the self are related to kinship and family membership. In these societies, kinship is the central organizing principle—the main determinant of a person's social identity. Anthropologists working with these societies are often "adopted" by a family. This act is a signal of acceptance, but it also serves the practical purpose of assigning an outsider a social identity through which she or he can be approached by others. To have no kinship label or designation in such a society is to have no meaningful place on the social landscape.

Language is another important identity marker, one sometimes viewed as essential for the maintenance of group identity. Language is often tied strongly to a national identity, and many countries have established institutions to oversee the "purity" of the national language. The Académie française has, for centuries, been charged with keeping the French language free of foreign borrowings, such as "le hot dog" or "le weekend." Sometimes, language becomes a flashpoint in political conflicts over collective identity. In Quebec, for example, efforts of one group to preserve French as the official language of the province, and thus protect what it sees as essential to group identity, have led to a movement for independence from the English-speaking remainder of Canada.

The Québécois, however, argue that Québec identity is not based solely on language. As they see

Continuing his support of Québec's Quiet Revolution, French president Charles de Gaulle declared, "Vive le Québec libre!" in his historic 1967 speech at Montreal's town hall.

it, their history in Canada is one of "slights, assaults, yet survival" (Eller 1999, 297). The conflict between British and French settlers in Canada has been ongoing since both arrived on North American shores. In 1759, the English drove the French Acadians out of eastern Canada; and after the Battle of the Plains of Abraham, outside the walls of Québec City, the Treaty of Paris gave Canada to the English. In 1791, two separate societies were formed: Lower Canada was French and Upper Canada was English, and each had its own culture, religion, stories, political views, and language. Then, in 1841, the Act of Union joined the two societies together, but this union was uneasy: Canada East was still French and Canada West, still English. Canadian Confederation, set out in the *British North America Act* of 1867, created two provinces out of the former Province of Canada: Québec for the French and Ontario for the English. Even so, the two were part of a single entity, Canada, and that entity was ruled by the English.

In the 1960s, during what is often referred to as the "Quiet Revolution," Québec began building its own sense of nationalism, which saw Québec as a "homeland" in which the French were "masters in their own house" (Eller 1999, 327). That "house" was no longer inhabited by French Canadians, or francophones; rather, it was the house of the Québécois—people who were ready to take control of their own lives and separate from the rest of Canada, if necessary.

QUESTION 6.4: HOW DO SOCIETIES MARK CHANGES IN IDENTITY?

Identities are not static, and people are constantly changing their identities as they move through the life cycle. These changes in identity are announced in myriad ways. Many societies have particular ceremonies or rituals that mark a change in a person's status or role in society. Most societies hold religious events, such as baptisms, confirmations, bat/bar mitzvahs, and secular events, including birthdays and graduations, to mark significant changes in an individual's status in society. In this section we explore cross-cultural examples of these phenomena.

The Transition to Adulthood

In a 1908 book now considered a classic of anthropology, Arnold van Gennep introduced the concept of **rites of passage**. The term refers to a category of rituals that mark a person's passage from one identity to another, in the same way that a person's progress through a house might be marked by entering one room after another. Van Gennep identified three phases in a rite of passage: separation, liminality, and reincorporation. First, the ritual separates the person from an existing identity; next, the person enters a transition phase; finally, the changes are incorporated into a new identity. These phases of rites of passage are not equally elaborated in all ceremonies. The separation phase, for example, is a major part of funeral ceremonies designed to help the living let go of the deceased; transition is a major part of initiation ceremonies marking the passage of a person from, say, childhood to adulthood; and incorporation

is emphasized in marriage ceremonies, which, in most societies, mark the transfer of a person from one social group to another.

Rites of passage are visible in Canadian society. For instance, a young man or woman who joins the military is required to undergo "boot camp." Geographically and spatially sequestered from mainstream society, the new recruit lives with other recruits in a dormitory. He or she marks this sense of separation by undergoing physical changes, such as cutting one's hair and wearing a uniform. These acts standardize physical appearances and visually mark an individual as a newcomer or initiate. Recruits then undergo a period of transition, or liminality, where they are expected to perform physically and emotionally draining tasks, such as running long distances when sleep deprived, or enduring verbal insults. Finally, a recruit who is able to endure the stresses of boot camp re-enters mainstream society with a new status: soldier. This period of reincorporation is marked by a new uniform and by a ceremony where the initiate is reintroduced to family and friends with the new status.

Prominent in most societies around the world are ceremonies that mark the transition of a male from boyhood to manhood. Most such ceremonies involve a test of courage. According to anthropologist David Gilmore (1990), one reason why so many societies incorporate tests of masculinity and tortuous initiation rituals for males is that the male identity is more problematical than the female identity. For every individual, there is at the beginning of life a subliminal identification with the mother, and men must make greater efforts to differentiate themselves from their mothers. Consequently, societies incorporate rituals that symbolically separate the boy from his mother, while at the same time incorporating him into manhood.

> **rites of passage**
> The term coined in 1908 by Arnold van Gennep to refer to the category of rituals that accompany changes in status, such as the transition from boyhood to manhood, living to dead, or student to graduate.

Victor Turner (1967) used van Gennep's model of rites of passage to describe the move from boyhood to manhood among the Ndembu of Zambia. When Ndembu boys reach puberty, they are taken, as a group of age mates, away from their mothers and out of the village (separation), to live in the forest (transition). There, the boys shave their heads and remove anything from their bodies that might identify them as individuals. While in the forest, the young Ndembu are circumcised and taught all of the special knowledge that Ndembu men know. But in the forest, they have no identity: they are no longer boys, but they are not yet men. In Turner's words, they are "betwixt and between." Once their circumcisions heal and the lessons are completed, the young men return to the village (reintegration) as new persons with new identities. These men, who made the transition to manhood together, will remain in close association throughout their lives as age mates, a category that cuts across kinship groups and that has special tasks in many societies, such as herding animals among pastoralists.

QUESTION 6.5: HOW DO INDIVIDUALS COMMUNICATE THEIR IDENTITIES TO ONE ANOTHER?

Both consciously and unconsciously, we make statements about our identity—who we think we are, or who we want to be—with objects and material things. The clothes we wear and the things we possess are used to display an identity that we desire or that we think we have. In North America, think about how designer clothing, shoes, and bags are coveted as markers of class and status.

Similarly, clothing can also express gender, sexuality, ethnicity, or religious affiliation. In some cases, clothing marks some individuals as "Other" even within their own society. Women who wear the Muslim veil in North America, for instance, have often been identified as "the enemy within," especially since 9/11. Some Muslims in Canada have dealt with this by removing visible signs of their Muslimness, particularly with regard to their dress. Still others have tried to show Canadians that the stereotype that all Muslims are terrorists is not only wrong but completely illogical.

In a study conducted by Homa Hoodfar (2003), young Muslim women in Canada reported that wearing the veil was not something their parents forced them to do. This finding contradicts the claims made by some North American feminists that banning the veil will free women from Islamic patriarchal oppression (2003, 15). In fact, most of the women Hoodfar talked to said they had had to fight with their parents in order to wear it. When Hoodfar and her research assistants asked young women why they wear the veil, one woman said that doing so "allowed her to be a 'person' rather than an object of male scrutiny" (2003, 17–18). Other women explained that they took up the veil when they began university because wearing it communicated certain values. In Hoodfar's words, "By taking up the veil, they symbolically but clearly announce to their parents and their community that, despite their unconventional activities and involvement with non-Muslims, they retain their Islamic mores and values. They are modern Muslim women who want to be educated and publicly active, but not at the cost of their moral principles" (2003, 21). In the same sense that "a picture is worth a thousand words," they believed that wearing the veil communicated identity in a way that saved them from having to explain why they behaved in certain ways. It is also worth noting that there are different interpretations as to what constitutes proper "Islamic dress." For example, some women wear a head scarf and a long dress over their clothes to cover the body completely and sometimes conceal part of the face; others believe that a head scarf suffices to fulfill the requirements of their faith. Still others do not believe that they need to wear a veil in order to maintain their Muslim identity.

While some Muslim women in Canada choose to wear veils or other garments to emphasize their modesty and to divert attention from the contours of their bodies and their sexual appeal, people in some societies may want to *highlight* their sexuality so that it is immediately visible to others. Men in some groups in New Guinea, for example, wear penis gourds. And in 17th-century Europe, men wore codpieces to emphasize their male anatomy.

Sexual identification is an important identity marker, but there are other signals that people use to display their identity. In some parts of Africa, people from different villages have different hairstyles; in North America, teenagers encode their schools or teams by the jackets they wear. People signal their connectedness to others by holding hands, by wearing rings, or by feasting and drinking together.

Rituals of Gift Giving and Hospitality

One of the most influential works in the history of anthropology is *The Gift* (1925), by Marcel Mauss. In it, Mauss identifies what he calls the **principle of reciprocity**: the giving and receiving of gifts. His main point is that gifts, which in theory are voluntary, disinterested, and spontaneous, are, in fact, obligatory. The giving of the gift creates a tie with the person who receives it and who, on some future occasion, is obliged to reciprocate. To Mauss, what matters is not what is given but the relationship that is maintained or established by the gift. The types of things given and received signal the identities of the participants in the exchange and the kind of relationship that exists between them. If the gifts are roughly of equal value, the relationship is one of equality. But if the gifts are unequal in value, the person who gives the more valuable gift is generally of higher status than the receiver.

EXERCISE 6.4

Suppose you were to travel to an island where no one knows anything about you or the society you came from. Suppose, too, that you could communicate with people on the island using only objects you carried with you and that you could take only five things to tell people about yourself. What would you choose, and why?

A well-known example of gift giving in the anthropological literature is the *kula* **ring** of the Trobriand Islanders. The seagoing Trobrianders leave their homes on islands off the eastern coast of New Guinea and travel from island to island, visiting and trading. Noteworthy in their travels is their pattern of gift giving. Each man has trading partners on the islands he visits, and these partnerships are signalled with gifts of red shell necklaces or white shell armbands. As a man travels and trades objects, he gives and receives necklaces and armbands. A man who receives either an armband or a necklace does not keep it but passes it along to another trading partner. There is a set pattern to the exchange: necklaces travel from island to island in a clockwise direction, while armbands move counterclockwise. The time between exchanges and the distances between the islands are so great that it may take two to ten years before the necklaces and armbands make a complete circle.

principle of reciprocity
According to Marcel Mauss, gift giving involves reciprocity. The idea is that the exchange of gifts creates a feeling of obligation, in that the gift must be repaid.

kula **ring**
A system of inter-island gift exchange documented by anthropologist Bronislaw Malinowski in the Trobriand Islands. It involves the exchange of shell necklaces and armbands. According to Malinowski, the *kula* ring serves, among other things, to create alliances and social ties among individuals living on different islands.

© I. DeVore/Anthro Photo

Trobriand Islanders define and maintain their social identities by participating in the *kula* ring, a ritualized pattern of gift giving involving the exchange of necklaces and armbands.

The *kula* ring serves as a concrete representation of ties among individuals. Any change in the pattern of gift giving reflects a change in the nature of the social ties. Special gifts that are individually owned are also circulated, and the owner's status and renown grow as the goods he owns circulate along predetermined paths. A successful *kula* operator participates in many such exchanges and can profit from them by keeping items for as long as he can before passing them along. Of course, if he keeps them too long, others will be reluctant to exchange, so a good deal of social skill is required to take successful part in a *kula* ring.

Anthropologist Margaret Anderson has devoted many years to studying another famous example of gift giving: the **potlatch** ceremony of the Indigenous

peoples of the Northwest Coast of British Columbia. Among the Tsimshian, the potlatch is typically a feast that legitimates a change in social relations, such as a funeral. Someone who dies is vacating a spot on the social landscape—or, more specifically, leaving a name empty. The Tsimshian are organized into matrilineal clans or houses. Each house has associated with it a fixed number of personal names, and each name has associated with it specific spiritual powers, honours, and objects of wealth. The man with the highest ranking name is recognized as the owner of the house. The name a Tsimshian holds when he dies is vacated until it is claimed by or given to someone else. If the name vacated belongs to a chief, the feasting will begin with his death and end with the acceptance of a new chief, who is usually the eldest son of the deceased chief's eldest sister. A person who disgraces his name by doing something wrong (such as having an automobile accident or being put in jail) must give a feast to "clean the name."

The potlatch feast, however, does more than allow a Tsimshian to obtain a new name and identity. It also serves to symbolically reorder and validate the names and, hence, the social positions of everyone at the feast through the distribution of gifts. Members of the house of the deceased generally serve as hosts to members of the deceased's father's house. The guests are feasted for the services they have performed (preparing the corpse, carving a pole) and as repayment for the gifts they formerly gave the deceased to help him acquire his name. When the guests are seated, the hosts announce the gifts they are giving to the guests, along with the name of the person from the host group who has contributed the gift. Higher ranking guests receive more gifts at a potlatch than lower ranking guests. Consequently, the seating

potlatch
A celebration, usually involving elaborate feasting and the redistribution of gifts, found among many indigenous Northwest Coast groups, such as the Tsimshian. The potlatch is a means of creating a new identity or of reinforcing social status within a group.

arrangements and the value of the gifts given to guests at the feast serve to announce or publicly notarize the social position or identity of each guest.

Anderson (2004) argues that, although the potlatch has changed since Christianity was introduced in 1857 (when William Duncan of the Church Missionary Society came to Fort Simpson), its meaning and symbolic value have remained, in part, because as long as the feasts began with a prayer, Duncan considered them respectable.

Exchanges that convey recognition of identities need not be limited to material goods. The exchanges also may consist of emotion and sentiment. Hawai'ians, for example, define a desired identity in part by expressions of gregariousness and hospitality. The emotional qualities of a person's relationships are one criterion by which others judge, interact with, and respond to that person. For example, if you accept an offer of hospitality in Hawai'i, it is a signal that you recognize the generous nature of the offer and that you wish to maintain the social link. If you reject the offer of hospitality, it is seen as a hurtful sign that you do not recognize the generous nature of the person making the offer and do not wish to maintain the relationship. Hawai'ians try to keep social pathways open through altruistic exchanges of love (*aloha*), sincerity, feeling (with heart, *na'au*), and warmth (*pumehana*).

Gifts and Commodities

An important characteristic of traditional *kula* and potlatch goods is that they have histories. A Trobriander who receives a necklace or armband can probably recite the history of the object, sometimes from its creation through all the persons who possessed it at one time or another. These goods are similar to heirlooms in our own society, whether it is the family wedding ring that has been worn by brides for three generations, the watch that was owned by a great-grandfather, or the quilt that was made by a great-aunt. The histories of these objects, especially when the objects are given as gifts, are vital to the identity of the person who gives them. They say something

special about the relationship between the giver and the receiver of the gift. The same is true to a lesser extent of gifts that are *produced* by the giver: these carry a special meaning apart from the object itself. A lamp made and given as a gift is often far more meaningful than a lamp purchased at a department store. However, we often must choose the gifts that we give from among thousands of mass-produced, largely impersonal goods available in department and chain stores. Herein lies a dilemma.

James Carrier, in his book *Gifts and Commodities: Exchange and Western Capitalism Since 1700* (1995), argues that since the 16th and 17th centuries, the production and distribution of goods has become impersonal, and that the spread of industrial and commercial capitalism has meant the spread of alienated objects and relations. In earlier times, commodities were personalized in various ways. The relationship between the producer and the seller of goods was a personal one between relatives or friends; the buyer knew who made and sold the object purchased. Even when stores replaced home trade and markets, the buyer knew the store owner, who further personalized the goods by buying them in bulk and individually packaging and displaying them. The buyer–seller relationship was further personalized by the extension of credit from seller to buyer and by the customer loyalty expressed by the buyer to the seller. Today the buyer knows neither the producer nor the seller, and if the item is bought on credit, it is through a credit card issued by some distant bank based on the filing of an impersonal application, with the transaction accomplished completely by mail. Eyes never meet.

Carrier labels goods that carry no special meaning as **commodities**, to distinguish them from

commodities
Traditionally, commodities are items that involve a transfer of value and a counter-transfer: *A* sells something to *B*, and the transaction is finished. As is typical of capitalist market-exchange systems, a long-standing personal relationship between buyer and seller is not established.

what he calls "possessions." Gifts, says Carrier, must be possessions before they can carry meaning in an exchange. Commodities involve a transfer of value and a counter-transfer: *A* sells something to *B*, and the transaction is finished. But in a gift exchange, a more or less permanent link is established between giver and receiver. Gifts are inalienable, that is, they are bound to people after the presentation; commodities are independent of their sellers (or producers). It is easy to return, destroy, or give away a commodity; it is a dilemma to do any of those things with a gift.

As noted, for North Americans the contrast between commodities and gifts poses a special problem. Most of the items we give as gifts are store-bought commodities, often mass produced. Their history is brief and undistinguished: an item of clothing was probably assembled in some factory in Mexico or Indonesia by a young woman earning perhaps a dollar an hour; a sports item was probably assembled in some factory in South America, shipped to a warehouse in Toronto or Chicago, and sold through a mass-produced catalogue; a radio, iPod, or mobile phone, assembled in Korea and distributed by a Japanese company, was probably sold in a North American chain store. These are commodities, not gifts.

For Carrier, the problem is how, in a world filled with impersonal, alienated commodities—goods without history, so to speak—we can turn these things into personal items with meaning and history, into possessions that carry something of the buyer's identity. In gift giving, how do we turn commodities into items that say something about the relationship between the giver and receiver? How do we make commodities meaningful?

We convert commodities into possessions and gifts, says Carrier, through a process of appropriation. For example, when a person takes an impersonal space—a dorm room, say, or a rented apartment—and decorates and modifies it, he or she has appropriated it and given it meaning. When a person buys an automobile, one virtually identical to thousands of others of the same make, model, year, and colour, and comes to think of it as unique, as an expression of his or her identity, that person has appropriated an object and made it a possession. Shopping itself, says Carrier, is a way of appropriating commodities; "wise shoppers" choose what is "right" for them or what is "right" for the recipient of the gift.

Gift Giving and the Christian Celebration of Christmas in North America

The dilemma of converting commodities into gifts is especially acute during the Christian Christmas holiday season, when most gift giving takes place in North America. Christmas as Christians know it did not really emerge until the height of the Industrial Revolution. Its precursors included the traditional end-of-year festivities that took place in England, where gifts consisted of food or feasts given by superiors to their dependants. In the 1770s in New York City, people began celebrating 6 December, the day of St. Nicholas, instead of the New Year. This celebration was actually something anti-Christmas; St. Nicholas was Dutch, and the colonists were celebrating things Dutch to protest British rule over what had been New Amsterdam before British colonization. Not until 1809 did the holiday begin to spread and did St. Nicholas turn into Santa Claus giving gifts of candy to children. The appearance of Clement Moore's *A Visit from St. Nicholas* in 1823 (or *'Twas the Night Before Christmas*, as it later became known) marked the movement of the holiday to the end of the year. At this point children began to receive toys rather than food. Even then, Christmas was celebrated largely on New Year's Day and in the industrial northeast.

The next major step in the evolution of Christmas was the appearance of Charles Dickens's *A Christmas Carol* in 1843. The story was an immediate sensation, especially with its victory of Bob Cratchit and Tiny Tim and their world of the home over Scrooge and the cold, impersonal world of work. By 1865, Christmas had been declared a national holiday, and in 1862, the Thomas Nast image of Santa Claus began appearing in *Harper's Weekly*, completing his construction as a fat, jolly, old man dressed in fur-trimmed robes (inspired, Nast later admitted, by the fur-trimmed clothing of the wealthy Astor family). By the 1880s, writers were beginning to complain about the commercialization of Christmas.

Most social scientists who have written about the Christian celebration of Christmas agree that it is largely a celebration of the family, serving especially to distinguish the world of the family from the outside world of work. Christmas serves to affirm the identity of Christians all over the world as members of specific family groups, and the circle of kin with whom gifts are exchanged defines the boundaries of the family. In one study conducted in a midwestern American city, 90 percent of all gifts exchanged at Christmas were exchanged with family members. Christmas heightens a person's sense of family identity, expressing how warm the family is and how cold the world outside may be.

Thus, it is within the family that the Christmas gift is most important. The question is how to resolve the problem of using commodities as family gifts, how to transform commodities to make them suitable as statements of the special role that family and family relations play in defining our identity. This problem, apparently, is not new. The dilemma of giving gifts that are manufactured and sold in stores existed as early as the mid-19th century, when department stores tried to convince buyers to purchase their gifts in stores by advertising them as "special Christmas stock." Even today, through Christmas decorations, music, and special attractions, such as the ever-present Santa Claus, retailers try to inject the spirit of Christmas into their stock of goods.

But there are other ways that consumers try to appropriate commodities and turn them into Christmas gifts. First, we may simply say that

In North American societies, the yearly ritual of Christmas shopping provides a means of converting impersonal commodities into personalized gifts that show one's love for family members and close friends.

the nature of the gift is immaterial, that "it's the thought that counts." A second way is to purchase things that aren't very useful, giving frivolous or luxurious gifts, or items that are Christmas specific, such as Christmas tree decorations or clothing with Christmas decorations on it. Third, and very important, there is the wrapping rule: Christmas gifts must be wrapped. The wrapping itself converts the commodity into a gift. Difficult-to-wrap presents (e.g., a piano, a horse, a bicycle) must be decorated with a bow. The only categories of things that needn't be wrapped are items made by the giver, such as breads or jams. These items need only a bow and a card.

Finally, says Carrier, there is the shopping itself, the time we spend getting the "right" gift for the "right" person. Why, he asks, do we go through all of this? It is onerous, it is stressful, and it is expensive. Yet one-third of all retail sales are made in November and December, most of them accounted for by Christmas shopping. One-sixth of all retail sales are related to Christmas. People complain about the materialism of Christmas and Christmas shopping. Yet people shop intensely for Christmas.

In the face of this bother and complaint, why do North Americans, even devout Christians, spend so much effort in Christmas shopping? Why not give homemade gifts? Indeed, why give presents at all? Why not give a Christmas card instead? It is true that the giving of purchased gifts reflects a number of motives, ranging from displays of affluence to a desire to shower a loved one with lovely things. However, these more commonly recognized motives do "not explain the intensity of Christmas shopping and people's ambivalence towards it" (Carrier 1993, 62).

Carrier suggests that the answer to this riddle lies in the fact that shopping in itself is a method of appropriation, of converting a commodity into a gift: we exercise a choice from among the mass of commodities presented to us. As Carrier (1993, 63) puts it, "Christmas shopping is an annual ritual through which we convert commodities into gifts. Performing this ritual indicates that we can celebrate and recreate personal relations with the anonymous objects available to us, just as it strengthens and reassures us as we undertake the more mundane appropriations of everyday life during the rest of the year."

Christmas shopping also demonstrates to people, says Carrier, that they can create a world of family, a world of love, out of the impersonal commodities that flood the world "out there." The Christian celebration of Christmas is a time when North Americans make a world of money into a world of family, a time of contrast between the impersonal world of commodities and the personal world of possessions and gifts.

EXERCISE 6.5

These days, gift cards for stores, restaurants, spas, or other goods and services are popular holiday gift items. After reading about Carrier's work, discuss how gift cards might fit into his discussion of commodities and gifts. How can gift cards, as commodities, be turned into gifts? Is this even possible?

QUESTION 6.6: HOW DO PEOPLE FORM IDENTITIES THROUGH COLLECTIVE STRUGGLES?

As this chapter's epigraph suggests, the formation of identity is a cultural process that involves the lived experiences and everyday practices of people. This cultural construction of identity creates both the individual and the collectivity, which we think of as society. In this section, we focus on the collectivity and ask how identity is produced through collective struggles.

The Meaning of "Indigenous"

After examining **Indigenous peoples** of Asia, Africa, Meso- and South America, North America, Eurasia, and Europe, Bruce Miller strives to arrive at a definition of what "Indigenous" means. He concludes his book *Invisible Indigenes* (2003) by looking at the common elements in the various ways the term has been used in different parts of the world. One common factor in all the societies Miller encountered is the association of indigenousness with both the presence and the absence of certain traits. The most critical element in the various definitions is that indigenes are recognized because they live in some clearly identifiable way that maintains their own distinct culture, and that they have been living exactly the same way since they were encountered by the colonizers. Furthermore, people are defined as indigenous because "broadly, definitions have come to focus on difference—the

> **Indigenous peoples**
> Groups of people whose ancestors predate the arrival of European or other forms of colonialism, who share a culture and/or way of life that they often identify as distinct from "mainstream" society, and who often feel that they have a right to self-government.

idea that indigenes are distinct—and the related idea that distinctions show up in many ways. These include self-identification and the recognition of distinction by others" (2003, 213).

Furthermore, people are defined as indigenous because "ancestors of members did not practice one of the world religions and therefore needed to be converted. Or members of a group are indigenous because they or their ancestors were not organized around Western values and practices, in particular Enlightenment values of universalism, secularism, rationalism, and subsequent modernist traits of bureaucratization and the centralization of authority" (2003, 213–14). Finally, indigenes are defined by their relationship to the state, in which they are recognized as having different rights than other citizens.

When Indigenous peoples try to gain rights to land or to resources that may lie beneath the surface of the land they occupy, the state or some other entity interested in blocking indigenous claims may use the definition of essential difference as a weapon against indigenous claims. For instance, issues such as wearing the same kinds of clothing as other Canadians have been cited by those who are opposed to Aboriginal rights as evidence that First Nations peoples no longer have a separate culture.

Social Movements

Kim Clark (2005) has explored the ways in which class struggles and state legislation created the space in which indigenous social movements could form in Ecuador. The actors in Clark's historical account of the growth of CONAIE (Confederation of Indigenous Nations of Ecuador), and of the eventual amalgamation of small, grassroots social movements, include the state, Ecuador's elites, and Indians. In the early 1900s, the aim of the state, backed by the elite class, was to turn the Indian population into proper "civilized" consumers; however, the Indigenous peoples took advantage of this undertaking to promote their own goals. For instance, they started a literacy program in order to be able to check the

account books of the haciendas, and they began to form small local groups.

As more grassroots indigenous organizations formed, the state used part of its revenues generated from an oil boom to modernize the Ecuadorian countryside, expecting the indigenous groups to passively accept the state's authoritarian paternalism. But local indigenous leaders were learning to interact with the administrators of the state's development projects and with NGOs from both inside and outside the country, and they were gaining confidence in their ability to express the common identity that was growing among the various groups that belonged to CONAIE.

The debt crisis of the 1980s compelled Ecuador to reduce its spending on social programs. When that happened, the state's influence in the countryside diminished rapidly, and indigenous organizations became more autonomous. The result has been that indigenous identity has strengthened rapidly, especially in the countryside. Clark argues that the "rural population of the Ecuadorian highlands is becoming more rather than less indigenous" (2005, 60).

The indigenous leaders of this new social movement now participate directly in negotiations with the state and rural elites over such matters as agrarian reform and the privatization of water.

In 2004, representatives of the indigenous movement were appointed to positions in the Ecuadorian government.

Palestinian Refugees

The plight of the Palestinian refugees has not had a happy ending. Randa Farah, a Palestinian-Canadian anthropologist living in exile, states: "Palestinians constitute the largest refugee population in the world, and their exile is one of the longest in contemporary history, spanning over half a century" (2003, 1550). In a refugee camp in Jordan, where 120,000 Palestinians live in an area of 1.4 square kilometres, Farah listened to the stories of three generations of Palestinian refugees. Her study revealed that the refugees reinforced their collective memory by invoking memories of the land, of original villages, and of shared experiences of exile. This reconstruction of the past cannot be separated from the present political struggles, which counter the plans of host societies to integrate the refugees. At the same time, the refugees reaffirm their hopes for repatriation. The Palestinian refugees also express their collective identity by reproducing symbols of home while they are away from home or, as Farah puts it, "a sense of place while out of place" (2005, 210).

When camps were not overcrowded, as they are today, Palestinian women planted gardens in front of their shelters as they did in their original villages, and they passed on to their children and grandchildren stories and images of what it was like to live in their villages before they had to flee. Public streets and walls in the camp are inscribed with political graffiti featuring Palestinian political history. Within refugee homes and shelters, Palestinian culture is displayed in Palestinian embroidery—especially embroidered peasant dresses—in pictures of the Dome of the Rock in Jerusalem, and in children's diplomas, decorative Koranic verses, and maps of Palestine and its flag.

The notion of prolonged temporary residence, which establishes that exile is not their permanent home, is vital to Palestinian identity. This is evident in the structures of refugee shelters. In the words of a refugee in Jordan interviewed by Farah:

No one at the time used concrete for their shelters ... They used to say this is not our Homeland, we should not build here ... My father used to say we want to return to our Homeland, if not this year, next year ... My father, until he passed away in the eighties, believed we shall return. He didn't even want to build a roof using cement, he kept saying we shall return, but we didn't! (2004, 177)

Land and return are at the centre of Palestinian identity, and keeping the memory alive is a form of resistance. As Farah explains, without the "Dream of Return," the older generation would have to concede that the younger generation—those born in the refugee camps—"are stateless refugees, without a past or a future" (2004, 181) and without an identity.

Conflict Within Collective Identity: Telefolmin and Land in Papua New Guinea

Creating a collective identity does not mean that everyone who assumes that identity experiences it in the same way. In Papua New Guinea (PNG), rights to land characteristically overlap and, as anthropologist Dan Jorgensen documents, are causing all kinds of problems in light of a proposed mining project, the Nena, at the site of Nena Mountain. Mineral exploration has been going on in PNG for quite some time, and the 1980s and 1990s saw a mining boom with four new mines in operation. Although mining brings some benefits to local people, such as employment and royalties, it also causes environmental damage, so compensation is paid to landowners. The Telefolmin people live in an area that has experienced mining since the 1960s, and many men have been employed in the industry.

The Ok Tedi mine.

The Telefolmin identify themselves as "Min," along with many of their neighbours. This identity is based on common descent from an ancestress known as Afek, who travelled through the area in the mythological past. When she came to the present site of Telefolip, she built a spirit house, which became the centre of important rituals for Min people. All Telefolmin men must be initiated at Telefolip, and they return at death in order to reach the "Land of the Dead." After Afek built Telefolip, she killed her younger brother, Umoim, and sent him along an underground passage to Mount Fubilan to establish Bagelam, "The Land of the Dead," located west of Telefolip. This place associated with the dead is also a source of wealth, for it is here that Umoim produced stone adzes used to clear gardens, and it is here that *bonang* shells, an important item of exchange in marriage and mortuary rituals, originated. In 1980, copper was discovered at Mount Fubilan and a mine called Ok Tedi was built there. The Telefolmin were hired during the initial construction phase and as wage labourers once the actual mining began. But they had no control over the land and the resources that Afek had given them. With another mine approaching, the connection between place and identity was crucial.

One way the Telefolmin and other Min peoples approached this problem was to propose the creation of a new province that would contain all of Afek's descendants. This province would give geographic expression to the collective identity that had been established in the story of Afek; it would also give the Min peoples a legal tool with which to assert more control over what was being taken out of their land and how they were compensated for environmental damage. But this would not solve all the problems, for the Min peoples relate to the land in different ways.

The Telefolmin hold a few basic principles that determine who has first rights to which pieces of land. The principle of first clearance means that whoever clears a plot of land has rights to that land as long as it is in use, and the principle of bilateral inheritance means that land can be passed on through both maternal and paternal connections. A third way that Telefolmin can gain access to land is through being granted permission to use some part of the land of another.

While all of this seems fairly simple in theory, when the principles are combined, the actual practice becomes much more complex. For instance, rights in land and rights based on residence may not be the same. The principle of bilateral inheritance may mean that a Telefolmin has rights in lands located in different places and that he or she, or the entire family, may move away temporarily in order to use land in another hamlet, giving permission to a friend to use land in the place they left. When the mining company agrees to pay occupation fees, royalties, or compensation to a landowner for environmental damage, the question becomes "Who and what is a landowner?"

Adding to the complexity is a history of conflict and warfare that has left some villages empty in the area of the mines but that has not destroyed old rights in land. Furthermore, when one group defeated another, women and children were often adopted into the victorious group, and their rights in land were passed on to their children. Over the years, this overlapping in land rights has created a vast puzzle that defies solution.

The Min conflict over rights to land highlights the connection between place and identity for Telefolmin; it also shows how "a self-conscious Min identity has multiple roots" (Jorgensen 1996, 202). Added to the variety of ways that Min people relate to one another through their common descent are colonial and missionary definitions that reinforce the notions of fixed categories and boundaries.

All three examples of how people form identities through collective action (indigenous groups in Ecuador, Palestinian refugees in Jordan, and Telefolmin in PNG) challenge the notion of fixed categories and boundaries. Common ancestry, the sense that people as much as plants and trees are grown from the land, and a sense of self and other all come into play as different facets of identity are reworked in relation to current experiences and events.

CONCLUSIONS

The concept of the self, or personhood, varies from society to society. In the egocentric view, the person is viewed as an autonomous, discrete individual; in the sociocentric view, the self is viewed as contingent on a situation or social setting. The sociocentric view is often taken by social scientists who are interested in the social processes by which social identities are formed and maintained.

Societies distinguish individuals from one another by using criteria such as age, gender, kinship, ethnicity, and language. Differences and similarities in characteristics among individuals are used to construct social landscapes on which each person's place or identity is indicated. The characteristics that determine identity, such as gender, are treated differently in various societies.

People must also be able to communicate their identities to one another. One way to do this is through gift exchange and the principle of reciprocity. The *kula* ring of the Trobriand Islanders is an example. North Americans and other people in modern industrial societies have a special problem with gift giving: somehow they need to convert an impersonal, store-bought commodity into a personal and meaningful gift. We examined how during the Christian celebration of Christmas, this is a special problem, and we explored some of the ways in which North Americans solve it.

Another way people form their identity is through collective struggle. Examples of how this is done include the indigenous social movements in Ecuador, the experiences of Palestinian refugees, and efforts to resolve land disputes in Papua New Guinea.

CRITICAL THINKING QUESTIONS

1. Even though anthropologists and other scholars view our identities as learned phenomena, we live in a society that privileges biological or "natural" explanations for our behaviour. What are some of the consequences of thinking about our identities as natural?
2. Hoodfar discusses what veiling means for many Muslim women and how they seek to express and communicate aspects of their identity through veiling. But many people use not just clothing but other forms of body modification to communicate their identity. How are tattoos and piercings markers of identity for many people?

KEY TERMS:

commodities (p. 177)
egocentric (p. 168)
enculturation (p. 163)
imagined community (p. 164)
Indigenous peoples (p. 180)
kula **ring** (p. 175)
nature versus nurture (p. 164)
potlatch (p. 176)
principle of reciprocity (p. 175)
rites of passage (p. 173)
social identity (p. 161)
sociocentric (p. 168)

CHAPTER 7

SOCIAL HIERARCHIES

© Paulo Ito

This mural, by graffiti artist Paulo Ito, was painted as a form of protest to the 2014 FIFA World Cup, hosted by Brazil. Through his representation of a starving child eating a soccer ball, Ito draws attention to pervasive social hierarchies (like class and race) within nation-states like Brazil. While large-scale sporting events are normally represented as celebratory events and viewed as opportunities to showcase the host country's "strengths," this mural highlights how massive expenditures on sporting spectacles often obscure pervasive social problems like poverty and ignore and/or exacerbate social inequalities.

Although it may never be possible to quantify the degree of racism that exists in a given society, the evidence unmistakably reveals that racism widely distorts the attitudes of white Canadians toward Aboriginal peoples. Whether blatantly or covertly, many Canadians still believe that Aboriginal people are inferior; as a result, these people believe that there is a sound, rational basis for discriminating against Aboriginal persons at both the individual and institutional level.

James S. Frideres and René R. Gadacz

Problem 7

Why are modern societies characterized by social, political, and economic inequalities? How are certain gender, class, racial, and other identities privileged or marginalized in various social contexts?

INTRODUCTION

The Rationale for Social Inequality

The maldistribution of wealth, status, power, and privilege is a significant problem throughout the modern world. To North Americans it is visible in the starving faces that stare out from our television screens in documentaries and on the evening news, interspersed with advertisements for luxuries such as automobiles, cosmetics, and household appliances. Some people can purchase the finest amenities, while others lack the necessities of life, such as food, shelter, and healthcare. There are few, if any, modern nations in which one part of the population does not in some way enjoy privileges that other parts do not share.

Anthropologists use the term **social hierarchy**, or *social stratification*, to refer to the ordering and ranking of individuals within a society. This ranking is normally based on pervasive systems of inequality that privilege particular classes, castes, races, or genders over others.

Social hierarchy is not an inevitable feature of human societies. For example, although groups such as the Ju/'hoansi and

> **social hierarchy**
> The ordering and ranking of individuals within society, also known as *social stratification*. Those at the top of the hierarchy are generally afforded more power, wealth, prestige, or privileges in a society. Hierarchies can be based on race, gender, class, caste, ethnicity, national affiliation, or other factors.

the Inuit are not totally egalitarian, people go out of their way not to appear better than others. Moreover, there does not seem to be a universal inclination to rank people by one criterion or another; in some societies, skin colour makes a difference, while in others, it does not. In some societies, men are accorded far greater status than women; in others, there is little, if any difference in gender rank. Even the use of age as a criterion of rank varies from society to society. The only general rule seems be that as societies become more complex and more populous, their propensity for social stratification increases.

Some people contend that the hierarchical ordering of people and groups is unavoidable. In their view, scarce resources, occupational specialization, and the power of an elite group to control the behaviour of others inevitably result in some form of social stratification. Others maintain that stratification is not only avoidable but also counter to human nature. According to anthropologist Thomas Belmonte, "since the emergence of stratification, man's[1] history (his changing ways of relating to nature and other men) has stood opposed to his humanity. The emergence of power-wielding elites … laid the basis for a new kind of anti-collective society whose vastly accelerated growth was founded, not on the reconciliation of antagonisms between men, but on their origination and amplification in slavery, caste, and class" (1989, 137).

Those who support Belmonte's view note that in societies such as those of Ju/'hoansi and Inuit, there are no "poor," "rich," "inferior," or "superior" people; nonetheless, these societies are not totally egalitarian, or equal — even in small-scale societies, valued statuses are not available to some members. The question at hand, though, is why modern societies are characterized by extremes of poverty and wealth.

It is worth noting here that poverty is not random. Indigenous populations, minorities, and women are the social categories of people most at risk for poverty. For instance, according to data collected by Statistics Canada, in general, poverty rates (measured by low income) decreased by 2.6 percent between 1981 and 2010. However, recent immigrants, Aboriginal peoples, racialized communities, and people with disabilities have been the least likely to benefit from this decrease; they are also more likely than other groups to remain poor for the long term. The poverty rate for all Canadians in 2010 was 9 percent, but it stood at 17.5 percent for recent immigrants, 18.7 percent for Aboriginal families, 42.8 percent for unattached Aboriginal people, and 13.6 percent for people with disabilities (Citizens for Public Justice 2012). Although the low income rate for women ages 18 to 64 in Canada was only slightly higher than average at 10.3 percent, children in single-parent households headed by women experience poverty at the disproportionately high rate of 21.8 percent (Statistics Canada 2013).

How do we explain the distribution of poverty, power, prestige, status, and wealth based on race, indigenous status, and gender, among other factors?

In this chapter we examine how societies construct social hierarchies and why some groups erect social edifices based on social dominance and submission, high and low status, and oppressors and oppressed. We examine why most people in stratified societies—both those at the top and those at the bottom—consider social ranks to be "the nature of things." We go on to discuss how social hierarchies such as race, gender, and class are intertwined in Canada, particularly in the experiences of immigrants who are also members of visible minorities. We also explore whether a relatively non-stratified community can exist within a large-scale society. Finally, we explore how an anthropological perspective can be applied to alleviate the effects of inequality.

---

[1] Note that Belmonte's use of "man," "men," and "his" in reference to humankind, including both men and women, is no longer accepted practice, especially in scholarly writing, as this usage is considered to be an example of gendered bias in language (see section 7.3 for a longer discussion of the relationship between gender, language, and social hierarchy).

7.1 How do societies use class and caste to rank people in social hierarchies?

7.2 How do people come to accept social hierarchies as natural?

7.3 How is gender a form of social hierarchy?

7.4 How are different forms of social hierarchy interwoven with each other?

7.5 Can a non-stratified community exist within a large society?

7.6 How can anthropology be applied to alleviate the effects of inequality?

Remember that social hierarchies are based on people's perceptions of others. Below is a list of personal attributes. Your task is to rank them by number from most to least important to you in judging a person's social or personal worth. No ties are allowed. If there is an attribute not included in the list that you wish to add, do so. What are some of your reasons for your rankings? Why are some attributes more important to you than others? What do your rankings tell us about our society?

Rank

___ Personal appearance

___ Income

___ Gender

___ Age

___ Religion

___ Ethnic or community origin

___ Family background

___ Intelligence (as indicated by school performance)

___ Athletic ability

___ Personal possessions (e.g., clothes, car)

___ Personality [Fill in your description of type of personality.] _____

QUESTION 7.1: HOW DO SOCIETIES USE CLASS AND CASTE TO RANK PEOPLE IN SOCIAL HIERARCHIES?

Social hierarchies in different societies vary along several dimensions: the criteria used to differentiate people into one level of society or another; the number of levels that exist; the kinds of privileges and rights that attach to people at different levels; and the strength of the social boundaries that separate the different levels. In Canada and the United States, for example, people are stratified by income and personal possessions into a social **class** (e.g., lower class, middle class, and upper class). They are classified by cultural or family background into ethnic groups (e.g., Italian, Jewish, Hispanic, or white Anglo-Saxon Protestant), or by physical appearance or skin colour into racial categories or visible minorities (e.g., black or white). They are also classified by gender and age, as well as by standards such as education. People in Canada and the United States may move from class to class, and they may choose to emphasize or de-emphasize their ethnic group membership, but generally, their racial category and gender are perceived as fixed.

Class as a Form of Social Hierarchy

Social class refers to perceptions of an individual's standing or status in society, normally based on economic criteria, status, or other factors, which may vary from society to society. Max Weber argued that social class can be based on economic wealth or "status class": prestige, honour, educational or occupational achievements, or religious or spiritual affiliation. In North American societies, for instance, we tend to place particular value on some occupations

class

A form of identity informed by perceptions of an individual's economic worth or status. It is also a form of social hierarchy.

that require years of post-secondary schooling over more "hands-on" professions such as construction work and trades. Although many tradespeople earn sizable incomes, their professions lack the "status" associated with medicine or law. Beyond that, we live in a commodified, consumer-driven society in which material possessions, such as cars, houses, and clothing of certain brands, are often perceived as markers of an individual's class background and, by extension, his or her access to wealth, power, and prestige.

Unlike social identities, such as race, which is normally perceived as an ascribed status, or one that is fixed or unchanging, class in North American society has long been viewed as a more fluid social identity. In other words, it can be either an **ascribed status** or an **achieved status**. An individual may be born into a life of wealth, power, and high status as a Rockefeller or a Massey; or alternatively, he or she may, through hard work and determination, overcome the odds and achieve a higher class status. The growing wealth gap between the rich and the poor in North America, and the decreased likelihood of upward class mobility, suggests that the former occurs much more frequently than the latter, and class comes to look, in reality, much more like an ascribed status. This popular myth that class is an achieved category is enshrined in American fiction (F. Scott Fitzgerald's *The Great Gatsby*) and in real life (Barack Obama). By suggesting that class identity is the result of a **meritocracy**, however, these stories overshadow the ways in which class intersects with other identities, such as gender and race.

In many ways, stories of opportunity, available for all, privilege a white male, middle- or upper-class perspective. As discussed earlier, ethnic minorities and women, for instance, are often positioned at the bottom of many social hierarchies, making it difficult for them to have the same opportunities or access to tools, such as post-secondary education, training, or other resources, which are needed to "achieve" a higher class status. The idea of North America as a meritocracy discounts the fact that

there is no "level playing field" when it comes to class, race, and gender. Unfortunately, when we think of class solely as an achieved status, too often we tend to blame the poor for their own fate.

Caste as a Form of Social Stratification

In a **caste system**, individuals are assigned at birth to the ranked social and occupational groups of their parents. A person's place in the social order is fixed; there is no mobility from one caste to another. This lack of mobility is one feature that distinguishes the notion of caste from class. Castes are also separated by strict rules that forbid intermarriage and other forms of interaction, such as eating together, speaking to one another, or working together. In other words, caste systems are endogamous, or closed.

Caste systems exist in societies all over the world (for instance, the Balinese, discussed in depth in Chapter 1, have a caste system). However, India presents the most well-known and paradigmatic example of a caste system of social stratification.

In any stratified society, people's access to jobs, wealth, and privilege is determined largely by

ascribed status
An identity that is perceived as fixed and unchanging because a person is believed to be born with it. In Canadian society, race is often assumed to be ascribed at birth.

achieved status
An identity that is believed to be in flux and that is dependent upon the actions and achievements of an individual.

meritocracy
A social system in which individuals are rewarded and resources are distributed according to achievement, effort, and ability.

caste system
A form of social stratification and identity where individuals are assigned at birth to the ranked and endogamous social and occupational groups of their parents.

their position in the hierarchy. In India, where the population is stratified into hundreds of different castes, these groups are based on traditional occupational roles and Hindu ritual categories of purity and pollution, for example. According to this traditional classification system, the Brahmins, the priestly caste whose lives were devoted to worship and teaching, occupied the top of the hierarchy. Directly under them was the Kshattriya caste, whose members comprised the soldiers, politicians, and administrators. Next was the Vaisya caste, made up of farmers and merchants. At the bottom of the hierarchy was the Sudra caste, whose members were devoted to the service of other castes. Although, traditionally, castes are occupational, they do not so much determine one's occupation as they exclude one from a certain job. Not all Brahmins are priests, nor are all members of the Vaisya caste farmers and merchants, but *only* Brahmins can be priests and *only* Vaisya can be farmers.

Beneath the religious hierarchy were the Harijans, "untouchable" or "unclean" persons, whose occupations were believed to be ritually polluting to others. Members of the Harijans caste have recently changed their name to *dalit*, which means "oppressed" or "ground down." *Dalit* include washermen, tanners, shoemakers, and sweepers—people whose occupations require them to come into contact with animal or human wastes.

For many years, debates about the practice of caste in India centred on which was the more important aspect of the caste system: concrete concerns with occupation roles or more abstract, symbolic issues of purity and pollution. However, rapid social and economic changes in contemporary India have required anthropologists to rethink how and why caste continues to be a salient social category there, and to what extent it continues to work as a justification and method of social stratification. For instance, no traditional caste rankings apply to modern professions such as pilots, call-centre operators, factory workers, or medical doctors. Furthermore, as Isabelle Clark-Decès (2011, 8). argues, "Nowadays ideas of relative purity

do not matter as much as they did in the past, [and] equality and democratic values have undermined the practice of caste ranking."

Yet caste still plays an important role in social hierarchy in India, even if it now overlaps with a newer hierarchy of class; nonetheless, the way in which caste links occupation to hierarchy has changed. Many traditional occupations continue to be filled by members of certain castes to the exclusion of all others, but, as Robert Deliège (2011, 47) has pointed out, "[t]oday everyone aspires to a better life and as a result, the struggle for attractive occupations has become a major issue in contemporary caste struggles." Today, many Indians think of members of other castes as rivals and as different, but not necessarily as inherently inferior or superior to themselves. The contemporary case of the *dalit* and their caste "rivals" provides an interesting example.

The Indian government has in its constitution outlawed discrimination against the *dalit*, or anyone else, based on caste membership. Although these legal measures did not lead to a sudden end to untouchability, they did have important consequences. Untouchables could now go to temple, attend school, apply for jobs, take the same buses and trains as anyone else, and so on. Deliège's *dalit* informants told him they did not find concerns about pollution to be particularly relevant to their lives, and although most people refused to do scavenging work within the village, they would be happy to find jobs as *municipal* scavengers if these jobs were salaried with benefits (2011, 54).

The *dalit* have also been able to use their designation as a "scheduled caste" to their collective socioeconomic advantage. As members of the scheduled caste, the *dalit* have been the recipients not only of constitutional protection against discrimination, but affirmative action in job allotments and higher education, as well as resources and benefits to bridge the socioeconomic gap with other groups. According to Deliège, the consolidation of the category "scheduled caste" has solidified the formerly ill-defined and somewhat fluid line between untouchable and non-untouchable. If you are within the *dalit* category, you are entitled to protection from the state; if you are outside, you are not. This solidification of categories has had drastic consequences, especially at the lower end of the caste hierarchy.

What, for instance, is the difference between an agricultural worker from a scheduled caste and another from a non-scheduled caste? Both earn similar wages and live in similar conditions. It may well be that members of a scheduled caste are insulted from time to time, but members of the non-scheduled caste may also be despised, even if no derogatory caste names are thrown at them. Moreover, the government usually gives non-scheduled communities fewer opportunities to improve their lot. All things being equal, then, it is often (but not always) better to be a member of a scheduled caste (Deliège 2011, 56). Clearly, caste continues to play a significant role in contemporary India; however, as Deliège's work shows, castes, especially those in similar socioeconomic circumstances, often see each other as rivals in a country where socioeconomic class hierarchies are becoming increasingly prevalent.

QUESTION 7.2: HOW DO PEOPLE COME TO ACCEPT SOCIAL HIERARCHIES AS NATURAL?

Race as a Form of Social Stratification

Sociocultural anthropology is about seeing behind the façade of everyday appearances to what lies behind those appearances. Understanding how societies construct rationales to justify and legitimize social discrimination is one of the most important and, to some extent, the most difficult tasks in anthropology. Franz Boas, a founder of anthropology, was among the first social scientists to discredit racist and sexist theories and ideologies that sought to legitimize the marginalization of people based on race, religion, gender, and ethnicity: see Boas (1940). Part of the problem is that racist and sexist theories exist not only in popular culture but also in science. It will be useful, then, to examine how such theories are constructed and often taken for granted, and how they are used to justify the ranking of people within the social hierarchy.

Constructing the Ideology of Racism

As discussed earlier, in Canada and the United States the ideology of class is based on the assumption that a person's position in the class hierarchy is determined largely by achievement or individual effort; that is, individuals who work hard and dedicate themselves to their work will succeed. Yet there is also the attempt to justify social position by a person's innate, biological makeup—largely by race, innate mental ability (intelligence), and other factors. Thus, the hierarchical ordering of society is seen as an expression of a natural law that some people are born better able to lead and succeed than others.

The term **race** is used here to refer to the presumed genetic, natural, heritable characteristics of a group of people, normally based on physical attributes such as skin colour, eye colour, or hair type. We live in a society that views race as a natural, ascribed category; it is something we believe we are born with. Unlike class, then, race in many industrialized societies (such as Canada) is seen as a fixed, unchanging form of identity.

race
A culturally constructed form of identity and social hierarchy, *race* refers to the presumed hereditary, physical characteristics of a group of people. These physical, or phenotypic, differences are often erroneously correlated with behavioural attributes.

association of anthropologists in the world, sums up this argument:

> *Both scholars and the general public have been conditioned to viewing human races as natural and separate divisions within the human species based on visible physical differences. With the vast expansion of scientific knowledge in this century, however, it has become clear that human populations are not unambiguous, clearly demarcated, biologically distinct groups. Evidence from the analysis of genetics (e.g., DNA) indicates that most physical variation, about 94%, lies within so-called racial groups. Conventional geographic "racial" groupings differ from one another only in about 6% of their genes. This means that there is greater variation within "racial" groups than between them. In neighbouring populations there is much overlapping of genes and their phenotypic (physical) expressions. Throughout history whenever different groups have come into contact, they have interbred. The continued sharing of genetic materials has maintained all of humankind as a single species.*

These days, most academics view race as a culturally constructed form of identity. In other words, they view race as a byproduct of cultural beliefs, not biology. Race may not exist from a strictly scientific perspective, but it remains an important topic for anthropologists to explore. In Canada, we live in a society in which the myth that race is natural or biological, as opposed to a cultural category, prevails. Because of this, race has had a variety of social consequences. Over the years, for instance, race has been conflated with behavioural characteristics, resulting in **racism**, or systems of prejudice based on the stratification of physical differences, which are erroneously thought to correlate with behavioural, physical, or intellectual differences in certain

Franz Boas (1858–1942) was one of the founders of anthropology and one of the first anthropologists to challenge racism and sexism in popular culture.

Anthropologists and other scholars, however, maintain that there is no scientific basis for positioning different groups of people into discrete "races" on the basis of physical features—no population of individuals anywhere in the world is morphologically distinct. In other words, for a "race" to scientifically exist, a certain physical feature (e.g., skin colour) would have to be demonstrated as occurring consistently and uniformly within a particular population. But no group of people, anywhere in the world, fits this criterion. Simply put, there is too much physical diversity within specific populations. The Executive Board of the American Anthropological Association (1998), the largest professional

racism
Refers to the discrimination and mistreatment of particular "racial" groups.

SOCIAL HIERARCHIES

populations. We tend to think of racism today as a practice limited to ill-educated or ill-meaning individuals against other individuals, but looked at from an anthropological perspective, it can be seen, rather, as a societal or systemic problem.

For centuries, European and North American societies have been characterized by racial stratification. In these societies, membership in certain racial or ethnic groups has been enough to place people in particular positions in a hierarchy that defines their social, political, and economic worth. In the United States, for example, one's position in the racial hierarchy has often determined whether a person can vote, hold political office, pursue a particular occupation, live in a certain area, use certain public facilities, attend certain schools, or marry a particular person.

Although most Canadians consider themselves to be far less racist than their southern neighbours, racism has a long history in Canada, and groups have been formed on the basis of white supremacy in both countries. The Ku Klux Klan, for instance, was founded in Tennessee in 1865 to terrorize newly freed slaves who questioned white supremacy. By the 1920s, the Klan was well established in Canada. When it arrived from the United States, it added French Canadians and Catholics to its list of inferior peoples. In the 1960s, the Canadian Nazi Party and the Edmund Burke Society, the forerunner of the Western Guard, openly supported racism. Ten years later, the Nationalist Party and the Aryan Nations took their place among the radical right. The common belief shared by these groups was that the "white race" was superior and that it was on the verge of being "wiped out" by the "dark-skinned races." As Stanley Barrett (2002, 92) put it, "according to white supremacists, interracial mixing, or as they preferred, mongrelization, was more dangerous to humankind than the atomic bomb, because without the genetic purity of 'the master race' the world could not survive."

African Canadians are not the only ones to experience racism in Canada. Racist beliefs about Aboriginal peoples are deeply rooted in Canadian history. James Frideres and René Gadacz call this "structural racism" (as opposed to prejudice and discrimination by individuals) because it is embedded in Canadian social institutions. Frideres and Gadacz argue that the Indian reserve is "an internal colony" in which "Canadians are seen as the colonizing people, while Aboriginal persons are considered the colonized people" (2001, 4).

Stratification by race has existed for a number of reasons. It was economically profitable to people who could buy black slaves or obtain workers from among groups legally or socially barred from anything but low-paying jobs. It was advantageous, also, to those who did not have to compete for jobs with people who were socially or legally barred from them. However, stratified societies often claim that the ranking of people by race and ethnicity is natural and that social hierarchies are not socially constructed. In the case of racial stratification, some proponents claimed that it was the Christian God's will that some persons were inferior to others; others claimed that God created different races as He created different species of animals, and furthermore, that the Bible says the species are to be kept apart. Others claimed that members of one race or another were intellectually or morally superior to members of other races. Generally, of course, it was the race of the person making reference to the Christian God or the Bible that was somehow superior.

Canadians assisted fugitive slaves, as depicted in the Charles T. Webber painting *The Underground Railroad*.

Most people had little trouble constructing an ideology to justify racial stratification, especially since it was reinforced by state and religious authorities. Even the supposedly objective findings of scientists assisted in building a racist ideology. In the 19th century, reputable scientists devoted much time and energy to proving that the racial stratification of society was "in the nature of things." Indeed, many contemporary forms of racism emerged out of 19th-century scientific studies of race. Both misguided and ethnocentric by today's standards, they functioned to maintain what Peggy McIntosh refers to as **white privilege**—the positioning of "white" individuals at the top of racial hierarchies. Science thus became a tool for naturalizing the power, authority, and privileges afforded to individuals with white skin. Their research findings supposedly proved that members of one race (usually whites or Europeans) were intellectually superior to members of another race (usually blacks or Asians).

Samuel George Morton was a respected scientist and physician who began in the 1820s to collect and measure skulls from all over the world. When he died in 1851, he left a collection of some 6,000 skulls. Like many in the 19th century, Morton believed that a person's intelligence was related to the size of his or her brain; the larger the brain, the more intelligent the person. Since the size of the brain could be determined by the size of the skull, he believed that a ranking of the races could be objectively achieved by a ranking of skull size.

Morton first measured the size—more specifically, the cranial capacity—of skulls by filling them with mustard seed and then pouring the seed into a container to measure the skull's volume in cubic inches. Dissatisfied with the inconsistency of measurements obtained with mustard seed, he later used 1/8-inch-diameter lead shot. He concluded

white privilege
Refers to the fact that, in many societies, "white" people have access to greater power, authority, and privileges than non-white people.

from his measurements that "white" skulls had a mean value of 92 cubic inches, "American Indian" skulls 79 cubic inches, and "black" skulls from America, Africa, and Australia 83 cubic inches. Among "white" skulls, the largest were those of Germans and English people; in the middle were those of Jews; and at the bottom were those of Hindus. Thus, the social hierarchy of whites at the top, with the English and Germans at the top of the top, and blacks on the bottom, was said to be supported by the evidence of brain size and intelligence.

Morton concluded from all this that "whites" (specifically, northern European "whites") were not only socially superior but also biologically superior. He believed he had provided objective evidence that the distribution of status and power in 19th-century North America accurately reflected not merely social, but biological merit.

When Stephen Jay Gould, a Harvard paleontologist, re-examined Morton's published data, he concluded that Morton's summaries were a "patchwork of fudging and finagling" (1981, 54) to reach conclusions that supported the socially constructed hierarchy. Gould found no evidence of conscious fraud. He concluded that Morton had simply selected or rejected certain data to ensure that the results confirmed what he and most other Americans believed: that whites were naturally more intelligent than the people they called "Indian" or "black."

Working with the same skulls Morton had used more than 150 years earlier, Gould discovered that the sample of 144 Native American skulls included proportionally more small-brained Inca skulls from Peru and fewer large-brained Iroquois skulls. This choice naturally produced a lower mean cranial capacity for indigenous Americans than would have occurred had Morton correctly adjusted for this discrepancy. Moreover, Gould discovered that Morton's failure to include the small-brained Hindu skulls with his "white" skulls had produced a higher average cranial capacity for white skulls. When Gould corrected for Morton's sample biases, he discovered that there was no difference between

Apollo Belvidere

Greek

Negro

Creole Negro

Young chimpanzee

Young chimpanzee

Nineteenth-century scientists attempted to "prove" that whites were naturally superior to other races. In this illustration from an 1868 racist tract, the proportions of the skulls were distorted, giving the impression that blacks might even rank lower than the apes.

Euro-American and indigenous American cranial capacity. As for comparisons between "white" and "black" skulls, Gould discovered that Morton had ignored the facts that brain size is related to body size and that male skulls are larger than female skulls. Examination of Morton's black skulls indicated that the group included proportionally more female skulls and fewer male skulls. When Gould remeasured the "black" and "white" skulls, he discovered that the mean cranial capacity of black males was slightly higher than the mean for white males, while the mean for white females was slightly higher than that for black females.

Gould did not believe that Morton consciously manipulated his skull measurements to prove that whites were intellectually superior to Native Americans or blacks. Rather, he thought that Morton had simply assumed what his measurements would prove and set about achieving the results he expected.

For example, Gould observed that when Morton used mustard seed to measure cranial capacity, he obtained even greater differences between his "white" and "black" skulls than he had obtained using lead shot. Gould concluded that because mustard seeds are smaller and lighter than lead shot, Morton, probably unconsciously, packed more mustard seed into "white" skulls to obtain a greater difference in cranial capacity between "blacks" and "whites." Unfortunately, while Morton's measurements were obviously in error, as was his assumption that cranial capacity reveals intelligence, and though his conclusions were dictated by the socially constructed hierarchy of his day, they were used well into the 20th century to support the ideology that the racial ranking of persons in society could be justified on natural rather than social grounds.

Class, Race, and the Social Construction of "Intelligence"

Morton's experiments were just one example of the efforts in North America and Europe to show that people somehow deserve their ranking in society: that it is not the result of chance or family privilege but, rather, the result of innate attributes. To believe otherwise would threaten a key assertion of North American ideology: that everyone in Canada and the United States enjoys an equal opportunity for success. Moreover, there are serious political and economic consequences to believing otherwise. If poverty and a low ranking in society are not the fault of the poor, then they must be the result of some failure of society. Such an admission provides a strong reason for governments to enact social and economic policies such as affirmative action, programs of economic redistribution, and laws barring racial and other forms of discrimination. Such changes, however, might lead to a loss of privilege for those who benefit from present policies; therefore, there is strong motivation to find some concept that legitimizes inherited privilege while still placing the blame for poverty or lack of success on the poor.

The concept of intelligence neatly solves this problem: if people accept the idea that intelligence can explain how well people do, then the fiction that people's rank in society depends solely on their own innate ability can be maintained. Moreover, if it can be shown that intelligence is inherited, then we can explain why the children of successful people tend to be successful, and why certain groups, notably people of colour and immigrants of certain characteristics, are disproportionately poor.

The failure of the thesis that cranial capacity, and hence brain size, reveals intelligence did not end all attempts to link intelligence to success and to race and ethnic class membership. There has been, instead, a continuing effort on the part of some members of the scientific establishment to marshal evidence that intelligence is inherited and varies among racial groups. These efforts have included the work of Arthur Jensen in the 1960s and 1970s and, more recently, the publication in 1994 of *The Bell Curve* by Richard J. Herrnstein and Charles Murray. Missing from most of these accounts is any acknowledgment that intelligence itself is a social construct, an invented idea. We need, then, to look closely at our concept of intelligence. How did it evolve?

To begin, anthropologist Allan Hanson (1993) notes that the concept of intelligence contains several questionable assumptions. First, intelligence is assumed to be a single entity. Second, it is assumed to be measurable and unequally distributed in the population. Third, the amount people have is assumed to be relatively fixed throughout life. Fourth, the amount people have is assumed to largely explain their degree of success in life. Finally, it is assumed to be largely inherited.

Each of these assumptions is critical to the intelligence construct as most people think of it, and each has been the subject of enormous scientific attention and criticism. The first assumption requires that we accept the idea that if someone is intelligent in one way, they will be intelligent in other ways, rather than believing that some people can be intelligent in some ways but not in others. The second assumption implies that we can somehow measure innate intelligence, as opposed to achievement, and the third presumes we can show that whatever is measured does not vary throughout a person's life. The fourth is built on the idea that people who have more measurable intelligence are more likely to be successful, while the fifth assumption requires us to show that the children of people with high measurable intelligence also have high measurable intelligence.

In spite of the number of assumptions that lie behind the notion of intelligence, and in spite of the studies that illustrate how questionable each of these assumptions really is, most North Americans take the notion for granted. Yet it is an almost unique idea, one not shared by many other societies. Indigenous maritime navigators of the South Pacific, for example, learned to read wave patterns, wind direction, celestial constellations, and other signs and find their way thousands of miles from one island to another. Yet others in the same society who are unable to duplicate this feat did not view the navigators as somehow being smarter—they saw them as people who could navigate. The Japanese view what we call intelligence in much the same way as we view health: except in certain (and generally temporary) circumstances, we all have enough of it.

This book is not the place to summarize all those works that call the concept of intelligence into question. Nevertheless, we might learn something about the social construction of ideologies of class by looking briefly at the early history of the intelligence construct and by reviewing how reputable scientists proceeded to develop it. Three pioneers—Francis Galton, Karl Pearson, and Charles Spearman—supplied the basic ideas and experimental proofs for the classic concept of intelligence as a fixed "mental" entity that is differentially distributed in the population, is measurable, largely explains a person's educational and occupational success, and is inherited.

Francis Galton was one of the leading intellectual figures of the late 19th century. He was the founder of modern statistics as well as the founder of eugenics, or the attempt to identify the most desirable human traits, specify the individuals who possess them, and through selective reproduction, enhance the number of people possessing those desired characteristics. In his best-known work, *Hereditary Genius* (1869), he sought to demonstrate that the "genius" of selected eminent men was linked to the fact that they had eminent parents and, it followed, that their "genius" was largely inherited. In his sample of 997 eminent British men, he found that 31 percent had eminent fathers, 48 percent had eminent sons, and 41 percent had eminent brothers—far higher percentages than one would expect by chance. For Galton, this illustrated the power of heredity in the distribution of "genius." He was, of course, rightly criticized for ignoring the impact of environment. But he did something else that was more interesting, something that went largely unchallenged: he selected the eminent men from the British upper and upper-middle classes, ignoring the "captains of industry and finance," as well as any women. For Galton, eminence was eminence only within a select range of activities and occupations. A nephew of Charles Darwin and of upper-middle-class background, he was faithfully reproducing the judgments of his own status as to what constituted intelligence.

Much of Galton's later research was devoted to arguing that what he called "genius," "mediocrity," and "imbecility" were analogous in their statistical distribution within a society to certain physical characteristics. He developed a number of tests for cranial capacity and for sensory capacities—the ability to discriminate between colours or smells, for example. Around 1900, however, there was a move away from these kinds of measures because they weren't showing any correlations with one another and, more important, because they showed only a low correlation with teachers' estimates of the mental capability of their students. Regardless, by 1900 the classic

intelligence construct had been laid out, although its proof was somewhat wanting.

The next figure is Karl Pearson, one of the most fascinating figures of the late 19th and early 20th centuries. In 1901, Pearson published a study in the *Proceedings of the Royal Society of London* in which he concluded that "the mental characteristics in man are inherited in precisely the same manner as the physical. Our mental and moral nature is quite as much as our physical nature, the outcome of hereditary factors" (155).

It is instructive to look at how Pearson reached this conclusion. He took pairs of brothers and measured specific physical characteristics, such as stature, forearm length, hair colour, eye colour, and cephalic, or cranial, index. He found, not surprisingly, that there were high correlations among brothers for these traits, as well as a mean correlation of .5171. He then asked teachers, using a separate sample, to rank brother-pairs on seven "mental characteristics": intelligence, vivacity, conscientiousness, popularity, temper, self-consciousness, and shyness. Thus, under "conscientiousness" teachers were asked to rate each child as "keen" or "dull" and to choose among six subdivisions of intelligence. When the teachers' evaluations of brother-pairs were tabulated, Pearson found a strong correlation between brother ratings and a mean correlation of .5214, thereby proving the power of inheritance.

Much about this study is questionable, but of particular note is the role of teachers' judgments. Clearly, teachers were evaluating selected behaviour patterns and personal characteristics: patterns and characteristics that they judged to be evidence of various "mental characteristics." In other words, the teachers' judgments were highly subjective and, at best, questionable. But Pearson's work marked an important development in the construction of our concept of intelligence: he claimed to show that whatever intelligence was, it was obviously inherited at least as much as physical characteristics.

Let's now move forward a few years to the next important stage in the construction of the intelligence construct: Charles Spearman and "general intelligence."

Spearman's research, published in the *American Journal of Psychology* in 1904, was designed to prove that there were different degrees of correspondence between an individual's performance on different types of tests. Thus, one would expect a high correspondence between one's performance on geometrical tests and tests of spatial perception, and a low degree of correspondence between one's performance on, say, tests of musical ability and tests of weight discrimination.

If some degree of correlation existed between all the test results, it would point to some general factor, or *g*, that affected performance on all tests. Thus, tests that resulted in a high correlation (e.g., geometrical ability and spatial perception) would be heavily saturated with *g*, while tests with little correlation would not be. For example, to use an athletic analogy, if someone hits both a baseball and a golf ball a long way, we might assume that there exists some general factor for athletic ability accounting for both skills.

Spearman was suggesting that the *g* factor underlay all mental operations and that if it could be found, it would approximate true intelligence. His was a major claim, for if the existence of *g* could be proved, it would dismiss the idea—widely held at that time—that different people can be intelligent in different ways and that each person has a unique contribution to make. With *g*, people would be intellectually different in only one way, and people with lots of *g* would have more to contribute than people with only a little *g*.

To experimentally prove the existence of general intelligence, Spearman isolated four kinds of intelligence that, he claimed, when correlated would show a high degree of correspondence: "present efficiency," "native capacity," "general impression produced upon other people," and "common sense." "Present efficiency" referred to the "ordinary classification according to school order" in subjects such as Greek, Latin, and mathematics. "Native capacity" was arrived at by taking the difference between a child's rank in school and the child's age, while "general impression produced on other people" was obtained by asking the teacher of a class who

was the brightest pupil, the next brightest, and so on. "Common sense" was arrived at by asking the oldest child in a class to rank her school fellows on the basis of "sharpness and common sense out of school." As Spearman said, she seemed "to have no great difficulty in forming her judgments concerning the others, having indeed known them all her life." As a check on the reliability of judgments, he also asked the rector's wife to rank the children, although as Spearman notes regretfully, she did not know some of them. Spearman, not surprisingly, found that children who ranked high on one kind of intelligence tended to rank high on others, thereby validating the existence of *g*.

Obviously, the methodology of these classic studies was seriously flawed, relying as it did on subjective judgments as to who was intelligent and who was not—judgments that were bound to be biased by such factors as the social class of teachers and students. From Galton's first major work on hereditary genius through Spearman's work on general intelligence, members of the professional middle class were selecting as intelligent those people whose behaviour patterns and appearance most conformed to their own. Moreover, little effort was made to conceal the fact: subjective judgments of members of the professional class were the principal means for defining intelligence. Regardless, the intelligence construct as we know it was generally complete and was perceived by reputable scientists as having been validated experimentally: intelligence, represented by *g*, was a singular trait that was inherited and differentially distributed in the population.

Much more was to come, of course, in the social construction of intelligence. Most notable in this regard was the development of the Stanford-Binet IQ test and later the Scholastic Aptitude Test (SAT; recently renamed the Scholastic Assessment Test). Among the additional and more sophisticated experiments performed were some that claimed to support the conclusions of Galton, Pearson, Spearman, and other early researchers. But the most interesting feature was the continued part played by the social judgments of people—largely teachers, psychologists, and school administrators—in determining what did or did not constitute intelligence. As late as the 1960s, intelligence test results were still being cross-checked with teachers' judgments and students' ranks in class; if the test scores failed to correlate with the teachers' judgments, the tests were changed.

QUESTION 7.3: HOW IS GENDER A FORM OF SOCIAL HIERARCHY?

Constructing Male and Female

We often assume that gender, like race, is biological. But there is an academic distinction between the terms "**sex**" and "**gender**." *Sex* refers to biological, hormonal, and chromosomal differences between males and females; *gender*, by contrast, is cultural. In other words, gender is the cultural interpretation of sex. Cross-culturally, different standards apply to being male and female. As such, there is no cross-cultural, universal understanding of what is considered to be "appropriate" dress, demeanour, behaviours, occupations, or roles for men or women; rather, these understandings must be learned in their respective cultural contexts.

---

sex
Hormonal, chromosomal, or physical differences between males and females.

gender
Culturally constructed ideals of behaviour, dress, occupations, roles, and comportment for particular sexes.

third gender
A gender role given to someone who does not fit within strictly masculine or feminine gender roles in a society that recognizes the possibility of at least three genders.

Societies also vary in the number of gender categories they recognize. For example, many Native American societies recognize a **third gender**, such as that of the *two-spirit* among the Cheyenne and Lakota. The *two-spirit* is a biological male who does not fill a standard male role. Such individuals are not seen as men, nor are they defined as women. They occupy a third role, one that is culturally defined, accepted, and, in some cases, revered. Male children among the Lakota and Cheyenne thus can choose from two gender categories, rather than learning that gender roles are defined by physiology. Among the Lakota, male children learn that, if they desire, they can adopt the dress and work roles of women and have sex with men, although the *two-spirit* role does not necessarily involve sexual behaviour. The *two-spirits* do not play only women's roles, however; some are noted for their hunting skills and exploits in war. In North American societies, in contrast, individuals who do not assume the gender roles associated with their anatomy are most often defined as deviant, abnormal, or nonconformist, unless the reversal of gender roles is framed as play.

One way to learn about how a society constructs gender differences and relationships is to explore theatrical and ritual transvestism, as Michael Taft (1997) did on the Canadian Prairies when he studied mock weddings. The principal feature of a mock wedding is role reversal: men dress and act like women and sometimes women dress and behave like men. These mock figures are often as much caricatures as stereotypes, reflecting some feature of the identities of the actual wedding pair.

Taft's (1997) study focused on men who dressed as women in these rituals of reversal, which were filled with ludic, or playful, behaviour. He repeatedly asked men why they did this, and the most frequent answer he received was that they were just being "good sports." As good sports, men do not attempt to become women in their role in the mock wedding. In Taft's words, "they play clownish and distorted women. They exaggerate the female physique with over-large breasts and behinds. They mince and wiggle in mockery of femininity" (135).

Courtesy of Saskatchewan Archives Board

In this photograph of a mock wedding ritual on the Canadian prairies, transvestism represents a form of gendered social commentary on notions of power, equality, and the position of women in this community.

Thus, these men are expressing their views of women to one another. Taft suggests that one reason men do this may have something to do with the economic conditions of farming on the Prairies. Although farmers or ranchers may *seem* to be independent, in reality they are dangerously dependent on government bureaucrats, subsidies, and the world market. In contrast, women have considerable power on farms and often do the same work as men, besides working part-time off the farm in order to pay the bills. By making fun of women, men may be reasserting their own importance. Whatever the men's motives, Taft (1997, 137) argues that "wherever it is found, theatrical transvestism acts as a sounding board for commentaries on gender relations."

Constructing Stratification by Gender

As discussed earlier, the biases that falsely linked race to biology and intelligence to class also led to the belief in the "natural" (as opposed to socially constructed) superiority of men over women. Many people believed that women's bodies defined both their social position and their function, which

was to reproduce, in the same way that men's bodies dictated that they manage, control, and defend.

The view that the biology of females makes them lesser persons than males is embedded in North American cultures, sometimes in subtle ways. An example is the language used by professionals to describe women's bodily processes of menstruation and menopause. Anthropologist Emily Martin (1987) says that during the 19th century, Americans regarded the female body as if it were a factory whose job was to "labour" to produce children. Menopause was viewed negatively because it marked the end of productive usefulness, and menstruation was described as a sign of the failure of the implantation of a fertilized egg. Medical writers of the time, such as Walter Heape, a Cambridge zoologist and militant antisuffragist, described how in menstruation the entire epithelium (cellular tissue) is torn away, "leaving behind a ragged wreck of tissue, torn glands, ruptured vessels, jagged edges of stroma, and masses of blood corpuscles, which it would seem hardly possible to heal satisfactorily without the aid of surgical instruments" (Martin 1987, 35).

According to Martin, the same attitudes toward female reproductive functions that existed in the 19th century persist today, encoded in contemporary medical and biology textbooks. Menstruation is likewise described even today as a breakdown in the reproductive process. When an egg is not implanted, the process is described in negative terms as a disintegration or shedding. Here is one example Martin found:

> The fall in blood progesterone and estrogen "deprives" the "highly developed endometrial lining of its hormonal support," constriction of blood vessels leads to a "diminished" supply of oxygen and nutrients, and finally "disintegration starts, the entire lining begins to slough, and the menstrual flow begins." Blood vessels in the endometrium "hemorrhage" and "the menstrual flow consists of this blood mixed with endometrial debris." The "loss" of hormonal stimulation causes "necrosis" (death of tissue). (Martin 1987, 45)

Another otherwise objective text states that "when fertilization fails to occur, the endometrium is shed, and a new cycle starts. This is why it used to be taught that 'menstruation is the uterus crying for lack of a baby'" (quoted in Martin 1987, 45).

In yet another textbook, menstruation is depicted as a sign of an idle factory, a failed production system, a system producing "scrap" or "waste." However, Martin notes that very different language is used in the same textbooks to describe male reproductive functions. For example, the textbook from which the above description of menstruation is taken describes the production of sperm as follows: "The mechanisms which guide the remarkable cellular transformation from spermatid to mature sperm remain uncertain. Perhaps the most amazing characteristic of spermatogenesis is its sheer magnitude: the normal human male may manufacture several hundred million sperm per day" (Martin 1987, 48).

This text, which describes menstruation as "failed production," fails to mention that only about one of every 100 billion sperm ever makes it far enough to fertilize an egg. Moreover, other bodily processes that are similar to menstruation are not spoken of in terms of breakdown and deterioration. Seminal fluid picks up shredded cellular material as it passes through the male ducts, and the stomach lining is shed periodically. Why are these processes not described in the same negative terms as menstruation? According to Martin, the reason is that both men and women have stomachs, but only women have uteruses. The stomach falls on the positive side, the uterus on the negative.

Rather than describing menstruation as failed production, Martin suggests that it might be more accurate to describe it as the successful avoidance of an egg implant. If a couple has done anything to avoid the implantation of an egg, is it still appropriate to talk of the reproductive cycle in terms of production?

Emily Martin's analysis reveals that in contemporary North American societies, the ideology of gender stratification remains embedded in our language and in our ideas about the bodily functions of males and females. Describing the bodily processes of women in negative terms makes women seem to be lesser human beings. Moreover, describing menstruation and menopause in negative terms leads women themselves to believe that their bodily functions are less clean and less worthy than those of men.

Gender Stratification and the Privileging of Hegemonic Masculinities

All societies have particular images and stereotypes of masculinity and femininity that are privileged as normative—that is, as societal ideals. These ideals of masculinity, for instance, are referred to as **hegemonic masculinity**. Industrialized societies, for example, often view traits such as athleticism, courage, rationality, and heterosexuality as markers of an ideal "manliness."

Hegemonic masculinities are often used to construct gendered hierarchies in societies. For instance, those individuals who fall outside hegemonic gendered ideals are often labelled as "less masculine" than others, which can lead to the proliferation of homophobia and the objectification of women. Canadian anthropologist David Murray (2002), for instance, has studied how performances of a hegemonic masculinity on the Caribbean island of Martinique are dependent on "proving" one's heterosexuality through the aggressive pursuit of women, cat calling, and flirting with the opposite sex. Men who fail to pursue women aggressively are often labelled *macumé,* a derogatory word in Martinique that is equivalent to "sissy." In a society marked by intense homophobia, all men, whatever their sexual orientation, go to great lengths to uphold the norms of hegemonic masculinity

hegemonic masculinity
Refers to ideals and norms of masculinity in a society, which are often privileged over others.

in public settings. To be labelled *macumé* is a social liability, and a man risks physical and verbal abuse if he does not conform to societal ideals of gender.

Hegemonic masculinities are also constructed, performed, and maintained within societies through sports, competitions, and rituals. Fraternities, for instance, are a means of constructing hegemonic masculinities; they are also a way to promote often dangerous gendered hierarchies within university settings, which lead to the objectification, abuse, and marginalization of women.

Peggy Reeves Sanday (2007 [1990]), in her study of college fraternity gang rape, provides a vivid portrait of how male identity is defined and reinforced in American society. Gang rape, or "pulling train," as it is called in fraternities, begins with the coercion of a vulnerable young woman who is seeking acceptance. The ritual incorporates the man into a group whose activities reinforce a male identity, defined largely by the degradation of female identity through sexual conquest and physical abuse. "Pulling train" is both an expression of male sexuality and a display of the brotherhood's power to control and dominate women. In other words, gang rape is but one instance of the abuse and domination that begin during the initiation and that are continued later in relations with women and new pledges.

When a woman is too weak or intoxicated to protest, a "train" of men have sex with her. Gang rape is not limited to college campuses; it is also associated with sports teams, street gangs, and other groups of men for whom the act often serves, according to Sanday, as a male bonding ritual.

Sanday and her associates interviewed fraternity members, women who were associated with them, and victims of rape, seeking to explain what it was about male identity that encouraged these actions. Three things seemed to stand out in her account.

First, there is a heavy emphasis in fraternities on male bonding and male-bonding behaviour, to the extent that a college man's self-esteem and social identity depend on gaining entry to a fraternity and being accepted by the brothers. Fraternities

confer status; on most college campuses they are recognized as places "where the action is." They also provide reassurance, security, and a ready-made identity. Membership in a fraternity transforms outsiders into insiders.

Second, sex constitutes a major status and identity marker. Masculinity is defined and demonstrated by sexual conquest. In the fraternity in which the gang rape occurred, a major activity was persuading a woman to have sex. Men who had more success gained status, while those who often failed were in danger of being labelled "nerds" or, worse, "fags." Sex in this case is a public thing. Men in the fraternities that Sanday interviewed bragged publicly about their sexual conquests and arranged for brothers to witness them. Some fraternities posted weekly newsletters listing brothers' sexual conquests.

A third element in the identity of fraternity men concerns their attitudes toward women. Many of the fraternity members in Sanday's study implied that women were sex objects to be abused or debased. A woman's identity among fraternity men was determined largely by her sexual interactions with them. Women who were sexually unresponsive were "frigid," women who allowed advances only up to a point were "cockteasers," and women who had sex with many men were "sluts." Such labels indicate that the role of "girlfriend" is virtually the only role without negative connotations that a woman can play for fraternity men. The debasement of women is interwoven with the themes of male bonding and sexual conquest.

Part of the reason men bond in college, says Sanday, is to achieve the domination and power they think is owed to males. Sanday uses the term "phallocentrism," "the deployment of the penis as a concrete symbol of masculine social power and dominance" (2007 [1990], 40), to describe the use of sex and the debasement of women to demonstrate masculinity. Phallocentrism, as well as the themes of male bonding, sexual prowess, and the debasement of women, are all manifested in the act of pulling train. It is a form of bonding, it publicly legitimizes a male's heterosexuality, and it makes women an object of scorn and abuse.

Sanday is quick to emphasize that not all college men subscribe to the ideology of phallocentrism and that not all fraternity men measure their masculinity by sexual conquest. In the case that initiated her study, all the women who knew them described the six men charged with gang rape as "among the nicest guys in the fraternity." Individually, probably none of them would have committed the act they were charged with. In the context of the fraternity, however, gang rape was the credible outcome of a process of identity formation manifested in fraternity life in general and in the fraternity initiation ritual in particular.

Gender Stratification and the Feminization of Poverty

Throughout the world, gender and age are significantly related to whether a person lives in poverty. In *Women and Children Last* (1986), Ruth Sidel draws an analogy between the doomed ship *Titanic* and society in the United States at the end of the 1980s. Both, she says, were gleaming symbols of wealth that placed women and children at a disadvantage. When the *Titanic* went down, women and children were indeed saved first, but only those who were travelling in first- or second-class accommodations. Women and children in third class and steerage were not saved. Although only 8 percent of the women and 3 percent of the children in first and second class drowned on the night the *Titanic* sank, 45 percent of the women and 70 percent of the children in steerage died. As with the *Titanic*, Sidel says, certain women and children in the United States are not the first to be saved; instead, they are the first to fall into poverty.

Most of the world's poor are women and children. As Michael Todaro, an economist, explains: "[Women] are more likely to be poor and malnourished and less likely to receive medical services, clean water, sanitation, and other benefits" (2000, 172). Female-headed households make up the poorest segments of Third World populations. For instance, as of 2000, 40 percent of all households in Kenya and 20 percent in India had no male wage earners. The percentages have increased since then. Women's potential earnings are far below those of males. Women have less access to education and government employment programs, and are more likely to be employed in the informal sector, where neither wages nor working conditions are regulated. Even in households where there is a male wage earner, women may not have access to the household income. In countries where there is a strong male bias, such as India and China, household resources may be distributed unevenly. In India, it is estimated that "girls are four times more likely to suffer from acute malnutrition and boys are 40 times more likely to be taken to a hospital when ill" (Todaro 2000, 173–74). This imbalance not only results in more female infant deaths, but also contributes to an extremely high female child mortality rate.

When gender is combined with other factors that contribute to poverty, such as indigenous status, women face a combination of risks. Linda Gerber argues that in Canada, Métis, Inuit, and "Indian" women face "multiple jeopardy"—first as women, then as members of a "visible minority," and finally "as residents of uniquely dependent communities" (1990, 72). In the area of education, 7.7 percent of all Canadian females have not completed grade 9, but the percentages are much higher for Métis women (34.8 percent), Inuit women (62 percent), and "Indian" women (35.9 percent) (1990, 75). Moreover, Métis women have an average income 70 percent that of Métis men, Inuit women earn 76 percent of what Inuit men earn, and the average income of "Indian" women is 73 percent that of "Indian" men (1990, 79).

Body Image and Gender Hierarchies

One of the most important identity features for many North Americans is body shape. Although desired body shapes vary cross-culturally and across historical periods, in the West today a thin person is judged to be superior to a heavier person. When researchers asked children aged six to nine to examine three body silhouettes and to describe the kind of person represented by each body type, the children described the "thinner" figure as friendly, kind, happy, and polite, while they described the heavier figure as lazy, lying, and cheating. When ten- and eleven-year-olds were shown drawings of other children, they consistently ranked heavier figures lowest, even below drawings of children with missing limbs or a child in a wheelchair.

Weight is a handicap also in the education system, where teachers perceive heavy children as having more behavioural problems than others and as being less well liked by their classmates. Later in life, people who are overweight face hostile work environments and job discrimination. Workers judged unattractive by their peers—especially women—are consistently described in more negative terms.

The relationship between self-image and body shape is particularly relevant for female adolescents, as anthropologist Mimi Nichter (2000) discovered during a three-year study among high-school girls in Arizona. Adolescent girls are particularly vulnerable to body image issues because during adolescence girls will gain up to 11.5 kilograms of body fat and thus are likely to be more critical of their own bodies. Young girls, says Nichter, are embedded in a morality play in which thinness is good, fatness is bad, and dieting is the way to get in shape. Nichter found that most of the girls in her study were thinking about their bodies either "all of the time" (24 percent) or "a lot of the time" (31 percent) and that 90 percent of white girls in the study were dissatisfied with their weight.

The adolescent girls in Nichter's study formed their idea of the "perfect" body largely from television, films, magazines, and, of course, Barbie. The ideal woman was tall (170 centimetres) and had long hair (preferably blond), long legs, a flat stomach, a clear complexion, and "good" clothes.

Weight, however, was the key factor: being "thin" was believed to be the ticket to happiness and popularity. As with many adult women that Nichter knew, the girls seemed to see the world in terms of fat and thin.

The girls rarely talked about weight with classmates whom they judged to be "fat"; nevertheless, they made moral judgments about them, believing that if someone who was overweight really wanted to lose weight, she could. Not losing weight implied that the girl was unconcerned about her personal appearance or was lazy. The lack of respect for overweight girls, says Nichter, was a theme that emerged repeatedly in discussions with the students. One girl explained:

> *I have a friend that's overweight and I feel that she should—I mean, I don't have anything against her 'cause she's overweight—but I guess it makes me mad that she doesn't do anything about it. She could do something about it and she doesn't. It's like her responsibility … like last night I went over there and right when I walked in she had a bag of Doritos—she was just, I mean, it's just like she's constantly eating. She's addicted to food. She just can't stop. (Nichter 2000, 42)*

EXERCISE 7.2

Men and Body Image

Men rarely talk about dieting, or at least not as much as women do, but concerns about body image are not restricted to women. How, then, do men address the gap between their body image and the cultural ideal represented in advertisements and the media? Do men talk about this issue, and, if so, how is it articulated?

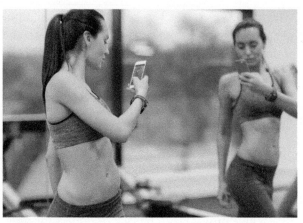

Anthropologist Mimi Nichter argues that in North America, women and girls are often subjected to, and subject themselves to, moral judgment based on their weight.

Language, Gender, and Racial Hierarchies

Societies provide a social landscape along with the symbols or codes through which a person's place on the landscape is conveyed to others. For individuals these symbols or codes serve as toolboxes from which to fashion an identity. Societies may vary in the extent to which people are allowed to negotiate their place on the landscape, but all allow people some leeway.

Language, as we mentioned, is one tool that people have to signal how they want to be placed in society. Voice pitch, for example, does tend to differ because men's vocal tracts are longer, thus giving men a deeper voice. But children, whose voice tracts do not yet differ in size, will unconsciously lower or raise their pitch to conform to gender expectations; that is why you can usually tell from the voice the gender of a child. As Penelope Eckert and Sally McConnell-Ginet point out in *Language and Gender* (2003), people use language to present themselves as a certain kind of person, to project an attitude or a style, along with gender. All parts of language can be used in this way. The phonology, that is, the sounds, of a language can convey gender. For example, the /s/ sound can be made by pressing the tip of the tongue against the teeth. When pressed against the teeth it is still recognized as /s/, but this creates a slight lisp associated among English speakers in the United States and Canada with femininity in women and gayness in men.

Grammar can signal gender. Thus in French, there are male and female forms of nouns; in English, the third-person singular *he* and *she* force us to differentiate gender. In Japanese there are sentence-final particles that add to or soften the force of an utterance, with so-called women's language characterized as more mild. Thus "I am going" can be said as a mild assertion (*iku wa*), as a neutral assertion (*iku*), or as an emphatic assertion (*iku ze / iku zo*), with the latter being characterized as more masculine.

Whether or not to speak can convey gender. Children, for example, are encouraged to speak or to remain silent. Among the Araucanians of Chile, men are encouraged to talk since it is a sign of masculine intelligence and leadership, while the ideal woman is submissive and silent in her husband's presence.

Conversational styles may also convey gender. Linguist Robin Lakoff (1975) was one of the first to draw attention to the way a woman's identity in society influences how she speaks. Women, said Lakoff, are constrained to minimize their expression of opinion with various linguistic devices such as tag questions ("This election mess is terrible, **isn't it**?"), rising intonations on declaratives ("When will dinner be ready? **Six o'clock**?"), the use of hedges ("That's **kinda** sad" or "It's **probably** dinnertime"), boosters or amplifications ("I'm **so** glad you're here"), indirection (e.g., saying "I've got a dentist's appointment then," to convey an inability or reluctance to meet at that time and asking the other to propose another time).

The general thrust of Lakoff's argument has to do with the relative powerlessness of women stemming from their relatively weak social position. Speaking "as a woman," suggests Lakoff, requires avoiding firm commitment or expressing strong opinions and, in general, being restricted to using a "powerless" language.

Language can also be used to construct others, or groups from which people want to separate themselves. Ward Churchill (1994) discusses the consequences of naming sports teams the "Braves," "Chiefs," "Redskins," "Seminoles," and "Savages," names that he suggests are deeply demeaning to Native Americans. Since apologists claim that this is just "fun," with no harm intended, Churchill suggests that we spread the fun around and use nicknames from other groups to name sports teams, such as the Kansas City "Kikes," the Hanover "Honkies," the Dayton "Dagos," the Wisconsin "Wetbacks," and so on. Churchill draws attention to the way we use language, often unknowingly, that stigmatizes the identities of others.

QUESTION 7.4: HOW ARE DIFFERENT FORMS OF SOCIAL HIERARCHY INTERWOVEN WITH EACH OTHER?

In the preceding section of this chapter, we unpacked a few of the most common forms of social stratification and discussed the ways in which they come to seem natural, inevitable, or commonsense ways of explaining and perpetuating inequality. We have discussed them as separate phenomena, but in practice, different forms of inequality are often experienced as overlapping or interwoven. For instance, as noted earlier, Canada's Aboriginal peoples experience disproportionately high levels of poverty, and Aboriginal women are faced with a "multiple jeopardy" because their gender makes them even more vulnerable to the structural forces of inequality. Furthermore, as we see in the examples below, race and class, or race and immigrant status, or race and gender, often overlap and sustain each other conceptually, as well.

Race, Class, and Social Hierarchies in Brazil

Despite the efforts of some scientists to find a biological basis for racial hierarchies, it should now be clear that race is culturally constructed, as is class. We can now turn our attention to an ethnographic example of how categories such as race and class are negotiated in Brazil. Anthropologist Alexander Edmonds (2010) has explored the ways in which race and class converge in Brazil to form social hierarchies. While conducting his doctoral dissertation fieldwork in Rio de Janeiro, Edmonds noticed that plastic surgery clinics proliferated in urban areas of Brazil. Furthermore, while access to plastic surgery had once been a marker of middle- or upper-class status (due to the high cost of such surgeries), the attainment of physical "beauty" was regarded as a necessary means of achieving social mobility. In Brazil, plastic surgery rates are among the highest in the world, and the government subsidizes plastic surgeries for the working classes. There are even plastic surgeons who practise "charity" surgeries on behalf of the urban poor. "Beauty" is thus a marker of class status and is increasingly viewed as a "right" that should be available for everyone.

Plastic surgery, however, is also a means by which non-white Brazilians can seek to "whiten" their appearance by correcting what some of Edmonds's informants viewed as undesirable—a "Negroid" nose, for instance. In Brazilian society, race exists along a continuum, and white skin and stereotypically "white" facial features are associated with power, privilege, and prestige. Indeed, many of Edmonds's informants, especially young women, did improve their employment prospects, and ultimately their class status, by undergoing plastic surgery. In this context, plastic surgery represents a means by which some Brazilians can "whiten" their bodies and, by extension, improve their social standing in Brazilian society. Interestingly, Brazil has been mythologized as a multicultural nation, and while its citizens are encouraged to celebrate diversity, there exists enormous social pressure to emulate the powerful—that is, the white upper class—in Brazilian society. Racial identity is also understood to be malleable and linked to one's social class: according to a popular Brazilian adage, "money whitens." Ultimately, this ethnographic example highlights the fluid and interconnected nature of social hierarchies such as class and race, as well as the ways in which the conscious manipulation of features like "attractiveness" are viewed as a means of achieving a sense of individual fulfillment, well-being, and status.

Constructing a New Racism

In 2006, a soup kitchen in Paris discovered by chance that poor Muslims and Jews would not eat soup made with pork. Their response? They began making soup only with pork. The soup kitchen leader, Odile Bonnivard, declared that "European civilization and Christian culture is our choice," proclaiming the right to racial preference and initiating a campaign across France labelled "Ours Before the Others" (Goldberg 2009, 179–80).

The "identity soup" campaign, as it came to be called, is an example of **new racism**—based not on biological characteristics but on cultural

differences that are assumed to be insurmountable. And counter to the claims by some that we have achieved a "raceless" society, it is just one bit of evidence that racism persists in one form or another. Quite simply, being "white," however "whiteness" is defined, still matters. As such, anthropologist Leith Mullings (2005, 684) says that racism is not a singular phenomenon, but rather, a "relational concept":

> a set of practices, structures, beliefs, and representations that transform certain forms of perceived differences, generally regarded as indelible and unchangeable, into inequality. It works through modes of dispossession, which have included subordination, stigmatization, exploitation, exclusion, various forms of physical violence, and sometimes genocide. Racism is maintained and perpetrated through coercion and consent and is rationalized through paradigms of both biology and culture. It is, to varying degrees at specific temporal and special points, interwoven with other forms of inequality, particularly class, gender, sexuality, and nationality.

The fieldwork of Alexander Edmonds, described above, thus demonstrates the way that racism, gender, and class are interwoven in Brazil, but this issue is equally salient in Canada, if in different ways. Despite our policy of multiculturalism, recent immigrants are one group whose collective experiences often exemplify the ways in which new racism is interwoven with other forms of equality. However, one's country of origin and ethnic background may result in very different experiences of these forms of inequality, as we discuss below in reference to recent experiences of Pakistani immigrants to Canada.

---

new racism
A form of "soft" racism that posits racial differences as cultural, rather than biological, but which still views such differences as immutable or insurmountable.

Pakistani Immigrant Women and the Construction of the "Sanitized Body"

Anthropologist Lalaie Ameeriar (2012) has conducted fieldwork in Karachi, Pakistan, and in Toronto with women who migrated to Canada for work. In Toronto, her work focused particularly on the kinds of spaces where multiculturalism is negotiated: government offices, settlement services agencies, mosques, cultural festivals, immigration consulting offices, and women's homes; she conducted interviews not only with recent Pakistani immigrants, but also with government workers, translators, mullahs (Islamic clerics or leaders), and non-profit workers. Her work was, at least in part, an effort to understand and contextualize the marginalization and poverty experienced within Toronto's Pakistani community. Despite the fact that many come to Canada as highly skilled professionals, many Pakistani immigrants experience their move to Canada in terms of decline: Pakistani women have an unemployment rate of over 20 percent; Statistics Canada puts the poverty rate for the Pakistani community at 40 percent; and many in the community "become deskilled, working in what are known as 'survival jobs,' such as cashiering, and living in pockets of poverty in marginal parts of the city" (Ameeriar 2012, 511).

Based on her fieldwork, Ameeriar found that there are two contradictory strains of multicultural practice in Canada, both of which she frames in terms of embodiment: there exist simultaneously a denial of the "difference" of immigrant bodies, and a recognition of that very difference. For Pakistani immigrants, this phenomenon was experienced through, on the one hand, the celebration of "multiness" in South Asian cultural festivals and public celebrations; on the other, Pakistani women experienced the "imposition of the dominant culture through government-funded settlement services that institute new ideals of bodily comportment ... by teaching them how to dress and act" (509–510).

Ameeriar proposes the concept of "the sanitized sensorium" to understand the forms of embodiment required for inclusion in the multicultural public sphere, including smell and appearance. Her research suggests that, when it comes to the integration of foreign labour in the workplace, multiculturalism is less about getting employers not to discriminate and much more about making oneself, as an immigrant, into someone who will not be discriminated against. For instance, women in a government-funded workshop about finding employment were told, "Don't show up smelling like foods that are foreign to us," "make sure your clothes are clean," "don't wear the shalwar cameeze," and "don't wear headscarves" (509). The painful irony is that while, foreign food smells, clothes, and practices are deemed repugnant or inappropriate when too closely associated with immigrant bodies, when disembodied—at cultural festivals, restaurants, and stores—the same smells are fragrant, the clothes deemed beautifully exotic, and the practices considered entertaining. Pakistani women, many of whom do most of the cooking for their families at home, and who are routinely exhorted by government agencies to "dress plainly," find themselves particularly vulnerable to these contradictions when seeking employment. Their often impressive education and qualifications are not enough to overcome this. In this way, the body of the Other is sanitized, and the "Canadian" body is rendered neutral (that is, non-immigrant and non-racialized). At the same time, the smell of food becomes both a private "problem" for Pakistani immigrant women (one with real, negative socioeconomic consequences) and a "public, commodified, accessible form of pleasure for white Canadian consumption" (510).

EXERCISE 7.3

In Canada, we tend to pride ourselves on being an accepting, multicultural nation. However, there are many examples of embedded or institutionalized racism in our society. Select a recent Canadian newspaper or magazine article that offers an example of embedded racism. By "recent," we mean published within the past two years. Provide a brief overview of the article, and outline how institutionalized racism is at work.

QUESTION 7.5: CAN A NON-STRATIFIED COMMUNITY EXIST WITHIN A LARGE SOCIETY?

Many people who are convinced of the harmful effects of social stratification believe nevertheless that in a modern, industrial society, the system is inevitable. It may be possible for the Inuit or the Ju/'hoansi to have a relatively egalitarian society, for example, but it is not possible in a modern, industrial state. Yet for thousands of years, there have been attempts by groups in stratified societies to create classless, egalitarian, utopian social settings. Christianity began as a utopian dream of universal equality, and the idea of a real-life utopia emerged with the idea that man, under God, has the power to create an earthly paradise. Among the earliest expressions of this idea was Christian communalism, which led to the founding of Catholic monastic orders: isolated, virtually self-sufficient communities in which the work was collective and egalitarian. In the 19th century, industrialists such as Robert Owen endeavoured to build utopian factory communities, and Karl Marx's goal was to build a national-utopian society. All of these efforts to construct utopian societies are evidence of the long history of the search for an egalitarian social order.

Anthropologist Charles Erasmus (1977) examined hundreds of utopian communities in an effort to discover why most failed, but some succeeded. He concluded that the main problem for these communities is trying to motivate community members to work and contribute to the common good without the promise of individual material rewards, status, or prestige. Of the successful utopian communities in North America, the most notable are those of the Hutterites, a Christian Protestant sect that originated in Moravia in the 16th century. Why did the Hutterites succeed while so many others failed? Is it possible to use communities such as theirs as models for modern egalitarian communities?

The Hutterites and the Colony of Heaven

"If there will ever be a perfect culture it may not be exactly like the Hutterites—but it will be similar." These words of a member of a Hutterite colony express the feeling that the group has succeeded in building utopian communities. The Hutterites originated during the Protestant Reformation. In 1528 they began to establish colonies throughout what are now Germany, Austria, and Russia. Their pacifism and refusal to perform military service brought them into conflict with European governments, and, in 1872, to avoid conscription, they immigrated to the United States and established colonies in South Dakota. During the First World War, a confrontation over military conscription with state and federal authorities in the United States resulted in the imprisonment of Hutterite men in Alcatraz, where some of them died from abusive treatment. As a consequence, many colonies moved to Canada and settled in Alberta and Saskatchewan. Although a significant number of Hutterites returned to the United States after 1920, many remained in western Canada. By the early 1970s there were more than 37,000 Hutterites in the United States and more than 21,000 in Canada. Peter Stephenson, a Canadian anthropologist, has conducted long-term fieldwork among Hutterite communities in western Canada.

Cooperation is valued in Hutterite society, where community members worship, work, and eat as a group. Here, women are shown preparing a meal for the entire community.

The goal of Hutterites is to create a "colony of heaven." Drawing their inspiration from the Old and New Testaments of the Christian Bible, the Hutterites believe in communal living and the proper observance of religious practice. They reject competition, violence, and war and believe that property is to be used, not possessed. They respect the need for government but do not believe they should involve themselves in it or hold public office. A Hutterite colony is governed by an elected board that includes the religious leaders and the community teacher, so authority is group centred. It is a family-based, agricultural community in which everyone is expected to contribute to the work and to share equally in the bounty. Unlike the Amish, whose beliefs they in essence share, the Hutterites accept and use modern technology; they are acknowledged to be among the most successful agriculturists in North America. Hutterite colonies in Canada are often million-dollar farm enterprises, and because no labour costs are involved in their farming expenses, the colonies are able to maintain a competitive edge on other farmers in Canada.

It is important to keep in mind that Hutterites are not totally egalitarian. Their society is ranked by age and gender; members do not participate in decision making until they are baptised and married. Baptism is a very important event in a Hutterite community because it marks a person's entry into adulthood. Until a member is baptised, that person is not thought to be "morally accountable for his or her actions and thoughts" (Stephenson 1991, 127). Although women are considered intellectually and physically inferior to men, Hutterites reject the unequal distribution of wealth as well as competition among members for status, prestige, or personal possessions. Hutterites minimize competition by renouncing private adornment and ostentatious displays of wealth and by practising collective consumption. There is little difference in dress, and adornment is usually frowned on. All the housing is plain and utilitarian. And, as in most Christian communes, the Hutterites are careful to indoctrinate their children against competition within the colony. Children are taught to avoid seeking honours or placing themselves above others. They are taught never to envy others.

One way Hutterites build commitment to the group is through frequent face-to-face interaction. Members eat together in a communal dining hall, work together, and meet frequently to discuss the affairs of the community. Almost every evening the entire community gathers for a church service. Although the Hutterites have no formal means of punishing those who violate group rules, they do practise a form of ostracism called *den Frieden nehmen*, "taking away the individual's peace of mind." An ostracized man, for example, is not allowed to talk to other members, including his own wife. He may also be assigned a special room in which to sleep apart and may be required to eat alone.

Stephenson points out that social movements have difficulty maintaining long-range goals, especially as wealth accumulates. The Hutterites address this problem by dividing the communities, or branching, every 15 years. During a 15-year period, each community saves a portion of its earnings to purchase additional land, build houses and barns, and accumulate necessary machines and livestock to start a new colony. When the new physical facilities are complete, members of the community draw lots to determine which families will relocate. Branching provides each Hutterite community with a tangible goal. Wealthier colonies that delay branching are often disrupted by internal quarrels and become examples of the danger of failing to branch on schedule. Branching also has a built-in renewal factor; new communities reproduce the founding enthusiasm and ideals. If there is competition, it is between colonies, rather than individuals.

In sum, the Hutterites, by a collective effort, have created within the larger societies of Canada and the United States communities without poverty, without economic classes, and with little or no crime, where each person, without the promise of material reward, contributes to the common good. There are, however, some negatives: the Hutterites are a Christian

SOCIAL HIERARCHIES

Bible-based religious community that teaches male supremacy and severely limits individual freedoms. Nonetheless, it is worth asking whether cooperative communities, such as Hutterites, can serve as a model for the poor in the larger society; that is, does the establishment of closed, collective communities offer a solution to the endemic poverty of those at the bottom level of modern society, and does the success of Hutterites suggest that it is within our means to build societies without poverty?

EXERCISE 7.4

Imagine for a moment that you have just been hired by NASA (National Aeronautics and Space Administration) to plan the development of the first human extraterrestrial settlement. NASA wants you to use your knowledge of other societies to build an ideal community, avoiding the problems of modern society. How would you go about the task? For example, what communities or societies that you know about might you choose as models for an extraterrestrial settlement? Which core values would you build into your community? How would people be rewarded for the work they performed? How would you maintain order and settle conflicts? What kind of education system would you propose? Finally, what are the most serious problems in modern society that you would want to avoid?

QUESTION 7.6: HOW CAN ANTHROPOLOGY BE APPLIED TO ALLEVIATE THE EFFECTS OF INEQUALITY?

It is all too easy, and perhaps even understandable, to resign oneself to hopelessness or helplessness when it comes to permanently alleviating poverty and oppression caused by social stratification. Inequality, as we discussed earlier, is striking and is growing worse both within wealthy countries and between the rich and the poor countries of the world. Worse yet, inequality produces differential access to life's necessities—food, water, shelter, healthcare, and protection from torture and cruel punishment and polluted environments. The question is, of course, what can be done to alleviate these problems, and what role might anthropology play in addressing them?

There are various ways that a background in anthropology is relevant for dealing with problems stemming from inequality. Anthropology prepares people for careers in, for example, delivering health services, administering treatment programs, counselling dysfunctional families, and finding the connections between old age and depression. We have already examined in previous sections anthropological work in the areas of economic development, HIV/AIDS prevention, and counselling for adolescent girls. But perhaps some of the most significant contributions that can be made by people with a background in anthropology are in the design and implementation of measures to protect people from human rights abuses.

Anthropology and Human Rights

The idea of individual rights comes to us from the 17th- and 18th-century Enlightenment, as codified most notably by Thomas Jefferson in the U.S. *Declaration of Independence*. That idea, however, is clearly biased by the notion of the egocentric view of society (discussed in Chapter 6). However, some of the rights outlined in the *Universal Declaration of Human Rights*,[2] adopted on 10 December 1948 by the General Assembly of the United Nations, could be extended across cultures. These might include the right to be free of the threat of torture or cruel, inhuman, or degrading treatment or punishment,

---

[2] You can access the *Universal Declaration of Human Rights* at http://www.un.org/Overview/rights.html.

and the right to freedom of opinion and expression. Besides these legal rights, the UN declaration also includes the right to a standard of living adequate for health and well-being, which encompasses the rights to food, clothing, housing, medical care, and necessary social services, along with the right to security in the event of unemployment, sickness, disability, widowhood, old age, or other lack of livelihood in circumstances beyond the person's control.

Similar rights have been incorporated into various other international treaties and conventions, but most of the rights outlined in these agreements are largely ignored or unenforceable. For example, the member countries of the UN that were signatories to the *Convention on the Prevention and Punishment of the Crime of Genocide* all stood by in 1994 while more than 800,000 Rwandans were slaughtered by their countrymen. These countries avoided taking action simply by refusing to define the killing as genocide until it was over. Amnesty International and Human Rights Watch, two of the major nongovernmental organizations (NGOs) addressing issues of human rights, have documented violations of individual rights in at least 150 countries. In those countries, nonviolent dissidents have been held without trial, imprisoned, tortured, killed, or raped, or have "disappeared" due to police, military, or paramilitary forces. When the UN instituted the post of High Commissioner for Human Rights, the position was allocated only $700,000, small even by NGO standards. In his first year on the job, the High Commissioner did not criticize a single government anywhere in the world.

Furthermore, as we have seen earlier in this chapter, the economic and social inequality that creates the conditions for human rights violations continues to grow. Billions of people are living in poverty and experiencing oppression while the top 358 global billionaires had a combined income equal to that of the 2.3 billion poorest people in the world.

Anthropologists Carol Nagengast and Carlos G. Vélez-Ibáñez (2004) suggest that, of all social scientists, anthropologists are the best prepared for human rights work. That is because they are the best prepared to deal with cultural variation and to understand complex community struggles. They are trained to understand the workings of official bureaucracies and global processes, and they have "a strong penchant for supporting the underdog." The issue, say Nagengast and Vélez-Ibáñez, is that while anthropologists often discover and reveal human rights abuses, they must also find a way to predict such abuses and do something about them, be it indirectly through participation in the design of public policy or directly in the delivery of services. As Canadian General Roméo Dallaire explained regarding conflict resolution in Rwanda: "What you need now are people who can not only fight—because they may need to protect and defend—but people who have a whole new set of skills … You need them to have more intellectually based skills like anthropology, sociology and philosophy" (*Toronto Star*, 13 February 2005, A14).

In *Human Rights: The Scholar as Activist* (2004), Nagengast and Vélez-Ibáñez suggest also that the human rights agenda, besides addressing individual and political abuses such as land grabs, torture, murder, rape, and disappearances, must include collective rights, including economic, social, and cultural ones. There are, they point out, no binding or enforceable laws or guidelines to constrain the power of corporations and their support agencies, such as the World Bank and International Monetary Fund, to set working conditions or wages or to impose development projects that displace persons or leave them worse off than before. Basically, all internationally written and customary law has left it to nation-states to enforce the recognition of rights. But nation-states, which claim the right to self-determination, are also the major violators of human rights either directly, through the operations of the military or the police, or indirectly, by allowing extra-state or paramilitary groups to violate human rights.

Nagengast and Vélez-Ibáñez then ask, "What can scholars do?" First, they say, anthropologists, who among all social scientists most often work with the poor, can publicize human rights abuses. Anthropologists can work with groups whose rights have been violated to help them develop the means to defend themselves.

Terence Turner (2005), for example, has been working with the Kayapo of central Brazil since 1962, to prevent development projects that threaten their land. Turner, a founding member of the American Anthropological Association's Committee on Human Rights, has also been directing the Kayapo Video Project, during which the Kayapo have been shooting and editing their own videos about their lives and culture and their relations with Brazilians.

The Kayapo Video Project.

Anthropologist Robert Hitchcock has worked with the San peoples of Botswana and Namibia. He has done much to map their homelands, institute land claims, and stave off settler takeovers of their land. Hitchcock has ensured that the San participate actively in these efforts. As a result, San communities have created their own human rights and development agencies.

People with anthropological training work on behalf of refugees, too, by helping service providers alleviate their plight, an enormous task. As of 2013, the UN High Commission on Refugees (www.unhcr.org) recognized that there are more than 17 million refugees, with "refugee" defined as a person who "owing to a well-founded fear of being persecuted for reasons of race, religion, nationality, membership of a particular social group, or political opinion, is outside the country of his nationality, and is unable to or, owing to such fear, is unwilling to avail himself of the protection of that country." In addition to these 17 million, over 33 million people are displaced internally—that is, within their own country.

These are just a few examples of how anthropological skills and perspectives can help protect and restore human rights, but a description of such efforts would be incomplete without the story of Paul Farmer and his efforts, according to one author, to "cure the world" (Kidder 2003).

Anthropology and Medical Rights: The Work of Paul Farmer

In his Pulitzer Prize–winning book, *Mountains Beyond Mountains* (2003), about the work of anthropologist and physician Paul Farmer, Tracy Kidder described how Farmer's background in anthropology and his experiences in Haiti moulded his view of the links among anthropology, medicine, and human rights. While at Duke University and studying anthropology as an undergraduate, Farmer met and began visiting with Haitians working on tobacco farms and became fascinated with Haitian history and culture. Consequently he visited Haiti in 1983, when the country was still controlled by

Anthropologist Paul Farmer has worked intensively with a variety of local and international agencies in Haiti, to help plan, implement, and deliver health and social services to local communities.

the U.S.-supported dictatorship of the Duvalier family. Haiti, a country of some 7.5 million people, is the poorest country in the Western hemisphere; 80 percent of Haitians live in poverty.

Farmer began to work with local and international agencies that were delivering health and social services to the local population and conducting a health census on infant and juvenile mortality, the results of which he characterized as "horrific." He watched a young pregnant woman with malaria die because even after he had helped to raise the $15 needed to purchase blood, he couldn't raise enough for the inexpensive equipment needed for the transfusion.

Among the lessons that Farmer drew from his initial experience in Haiti was that a knowledge of anthropology was critical for addressing the health problems of that country's poor. In one instance, a mother permitted a Vodou priest to treat her child for malaria, while at the same time agreeing to let Farmer treat the patient with chloroquine. It was critical, Farmer says, to appreciate the role of Vodou, a religion that combines traditional Catholicism with traditional African beliefs, in the life of most Haitians. A doctor who knew nothing about local beliefs might end up at war with Vodou priests, mistaking patient complaints for bizarre superstitions. However, a doctor with a background in anthropology could find a way to work with the priest. For example, a female patient might complain of something Haitians call *move san, lét gate*. The condition is brought on by *sezisman*, a surprise of some sort or a frightening action. The result is "bad blood," in which a nursing mother's milk stops flowing. While such a description might be dismissed by someone without knowledge of local culture, Farmer notes that, metaphorically, the explanation turns two vital fluids, blood and milk, into poison, thus serving as a symbolic warning about the abuse of pregnant women, particularly those who are nursing.

A second defining lesson that emerged from Haiti for Farmer touched on liberation theology. In the 1960s in Latin America, during heightened periods of human rights abuses by often dictatorial states, Roman Catholic churches became centres for the defence of human rights and attacks against government repression. Church leaders in Latin America attacked inequality and injustice and began to participate in forming organizations and social movements to give the poor a political and economic voice. As some put it, this effort was meant to apply the Gospel, or good news, to everyday life in the hope that these efforts would ultimately replace the old order of things. Farmer considered liberation theology to be, as he put it, "a powerful rebuke to the hiding away of poverty" (Kidder 2003, 78). Reacting to the poverty and repression he witnessed in Haiti, Farmer thought that

> *someone is witnessing this horror show? … I know it sounds shallow, the opiate thing, needing to believe, palliating pain, but it didn't feel shallow. It was more profound than other sentiments I'd known, and I was taken with the idea that in an ostensibly godless world that worshipped money and power or, more seductively, a sense of personal efficacy and advancement … there was still a place to look for God, and that was in the suffering of the poor. (Kidder 2003, 85)*

Farmer was attracted to liberation theology because it was driven by a need to accomplish something concrete in the lives of the poor and was characterized by what he called "pragmatic solidarity" with the communities that it sought to assist. Liberation theology argued for giving the poor, not equal treatment, but preferential treatment.

Farmer also gained an understanding of the context in which poverty and oppression occurred. He understood that, as he put, "a minor error in one setting of power and privilege could have an enormous impact on the poor in another" (Kidder 2003, 78). For example, in the 1950s, with money from the U.S. Export–Import Bank, the U.S. Army Corps of Engineers built the Péligre dam, which displaced thousands of Haitian farmers. The farmers were forced either to rebuild on the sides of mountains unsuited for growing crops or to move to cities such as Port-au-Prince to look for jobs as housekeepers or as low-paid labourers in American-built assembly plants. The most valuable asset for the remaining farmers was their Creole pigs, but an outbreak of swine fever in the Dominican Republic led the United States to destroy all the Haitian pigs in order to protect the American pork industry. The pigs were replaced with pigs purchased from Iowa farmers, but these were delicate and most of them died, leaving the peasants with little. These are examples of what Farmer refers to as **structural violence**, the systematic ways in which social structures or social institutions harm or otherwise disadvantage local individuals. Structural violence is often invisible, and often lacking one specific person who can (or will) be held responsible. In the examples discussed by Farmer, structural violence refers to the actions of remote governments or international agencies that result in denial to the poor of basic rights of food, shelter, and livelihood.

After his initial experiences in Haiti, Farmer enrolled at Harvard University in both medical school and the Ph.D. program in anthropology, completing both programs while spending much of his time travelling back and forth to Haiti, where he worked to build a public health program in the village of Cange. That effort included vaccination programs, protected water supplies, and sanitation. He also trained people to administer medicines, treat minor ailments, and recognize symptoms of serious illnesses such as tuberculosis, malaria, and typhoid. He received both his Ph.D. in anthropology and his M.D. in 1992, writing his Ph.D. thesis, *AIDS and Accusation*, on HIV/AIDS in Haiti. Since that time, Farmer has applied his expertise with infectious diseases to problems of drug-resistant tuberculosis in Russian prisons and in impoverished communities in Peru; and he has worked to help develop health services in Chiapas, Mexico. All the while he has continued to work in Haiti.

Health as a Human Right

Based on his experiences in Haiti, Farmer became convinced that health is a basic human right and that medical workers, along with social scientists, are uniquely situated, both in temperament and in profession, to address the problems of structural

> **structural violence**
> Refers to the systematic ways in which social structures or social institutions harm or otherwise disadvantage local individuals. Structural violence is often invisible and lacking one specific person who can (or will) be held responsible.

violence and to engage with the poor in the spirit of pragmatic solidarity. In *Pathologies of Power: Health, Human Rights, and the New War on the Poor* (2003), Farmer outlines a rationale and a strategy for addressing human rights abuses.

Farmer offers as an example the case of Russian prisons, where multi-drug-resistant tuberculosis (MDRTB) emerged. In Russia, prisoners are crowded together in cells where the air is thick with tubercle bacilli. As a consequence, tuberculosis is the leading cause of death among Russian prisoners. Clearly, says Farmer, the situation is rife with human rights abuses.

The first set of abuses begins with pre-trial detention and the violation of the human right to a speedy trial. The Russian court system is backlogged for months, and people who are being held for trial must live in deplorable conditions that are ripe for the contraction of TB, even before it is determined that they have committed a crime.

The second set of abuses occurs if they are convicted and are held in a prison in conditions that guarantee exposure to MDRTB.

Next, they are denied adequate food and medical care. As one of the Russian physicians put it, "I have spent my entire medical career caring for prisoners with tuberculosis. And although we complained about shortages in the eighties, we had no idea how good we had it then. Now it's a daily struggle for food, drugs, lab supplies, even heat and electricity" (Farmer 2003, 215).

Finally, of course, prisoners are dying because of ineffective treatment, a clear violation of article 25 of the *Universal Declaration of Human Rights*, which states that everyone has a right to "share in scientific advancement and its benefits."

Farmer points out that people are dying not because there are no effective treatments (in the vast majority of cases, there are combinations of drugs that can cure MDRTB), but because they or the agencies responsible for their care lack the money to pay for the medicine. "Untreatable" has become a euphemism for "too expensive." And the case of

MDRTB in Russia is mirrored in the cases of HIV/AIDS and malaria in Africa and HIV/AIDS and TB in Haiti, as well as in most of Latin America. Worldwide, 32 percent of all deaths are caused by infectious disease, but in the poor countries, infectious disease is responsible for 42 percent of all deaths, compared to 1.2 percent in industrial countries.

Once we have defined health as a human right and recognized the structural violence that either creates conditions for disease or that denies the afflicted access to medicine, what can anthropologists, other social scientists, and medical professionals accomplish?

First, says Farmer, they can place human rights violations in their proper contexts so as to identify their structural causes. Russian prison doctors, for example, lack the medicines to cure their patients because international financial agencies, such as the International Monetary Fund, require most countries, including Russia, to cut government services as a condition for receiving loans. As another example, pharmaceutical companies, which often receive sizable government subsidies and support for research, refuse to waive patent rights to supply generic forms of drugs that could help HIV/AIDS patients in poor countries. Anthropologists can do a great deal to place human rights abuses in these broader perspectives. As Farmer (2003, 219) puts it: "Social inequalities based on race or ethnicity, gender, religious creed, and—above all—social class are the motor force behind most human rights violations. In other words, violence against individuals is usually embedded in entrenched structural violence."

But, says Farmer, it is not enough to understand the context for violations of health rights. Russian penal codes already prohibit overcrowding in prisons, long pre-trial detentions, and the exposure of patients to malnutrition and disease. Prison officials already recognize the problem of MDRTB—that is why they sought Farmer's help.

Consequently, says Farmer, we need a strategy to confront structural violence. The problem, he says, is that traditional government agencies and NGOs are restricted when it comes to addressing rights issues. International institutions such as the UN and organizations such as Amnesty International and Physicians for Human Rights are constrained by the fact that they must work through governments. What's more, often, the major violators of rights are the governments themselves. For this reason, Farmer suggests that independent groups, such as First World universities, hospitals, churches, and healthcare professionals, can best serve local communities. If healing and healthcare can become the "symbolic core," as he puts it, of a new human rights agenda, we will be able to tap into an almost universal concern for the sick, while involving persons in medicine, public health, and the natural and social sciences.

Farmer's own efforts provide a model for the approach to addressing human rights abuses that he is suggesting. On one of his trips back to Boston from Haiti, he tried to raise money to build a bread oven in Cange, the village where he was working. He approached a local charity that gave him the money and that also put him in contact with one of its regular donors, Tom White, a local contractor. White became so interested in what Farmer was doing in Haiti that he founded a public charity called Partners in Health, as well as a corresponding organization in Haiti called Zamni Lasante on which Farmer could draw for his work in Cange. White began by donating $1 million. Soon, Farmer expanded the membership of Partners in Health, adding a fellow anthropology and medical student, Jim Yong Kim, along with Ophelia Dahl, then Farmer's fiancée. Partners in Health has since provided funds to develop various public health projects in Haiti, such as the HIV Equity Initiative to complement prevention efforts with antiretroviral drugs for those for whom treatment has failed. Health workers visit patients each day and administer the drugs. Although funds from standard health organizations such as the World Health Organization are limited for expensive drug treatments, Partners in Health can provide them from private donations. After the 2010 earthquake, Partners in Health and Zamni Lasante designed and implemented the Stand with Haiti Fund, and a 2.5 year, $125 million plan to help to rebuild the country. In 2013, Partners in Health, in collaboration with the Haitian government, opened the new Mirebalais hospital, funded by the donations that poured in from the international community after the earthquake. In addition to designing the hospital as a training hospital (as both the nursing and medical schools had been destroyed), they focused on strengthening the country's health infrastructure, particularly in specialties such as mental health and rehabilitative medicine, which had been weak even before the earthquake.

Summarizing his approach, Farmer (2003, 238) says that "we have a long way to go in the struggle for health and human rights. We cannot merely study this topic without proposing meaningful and pragmatic interventions; but to succeed, we must distinguish between our best analysis and our best strategies. The focus on health offers a critical new dimension to human rights work and is a largely untapped vein of resources, passion, and good will."

CONCLUSIONS

The problem underlying this chapter is why extremes of poverty and wealth exist in modern societies. The criteria customarily used to rank people in social hierarchies include wealth or income, occupation, ethnic group membership, personal appearance, race, gender, and age. The consequences of such rankings, especially in the creation of poverty and the gap between the rich and the poor, have raised some of the most challenging questions in modern societies.

People come to accept social hierarchies as natural because they believe that hierarchy is a biological principle. Some people are thought to be naturally more or less intelligent than others or otherwise more or less worthy. Female biological functions, for example, have been described in terms that make women seem less worthy than men. Even when social categories such as race or ethnic identity are understood as being defined by cultural rather than biological differences, the idea that such categories, and subsequent social hierarchies, are immutable often remains.

A few groups have demonstrated that it is possible to build egalitarian, relatively non-stratified communities within a larger industrial society. Perhaps the most successful in North America have been the Hutterites, a religious group that emphasizes communal ownership of property and equal distribution of production, while rejecting competition, violence, and war. Nonetheless, the Hutterites have not avoided social hierarchy completely, as they use gender and age as key forms of stratification within their society.

Finally, we have examined various areas in which persons with a background in anthropology can help address the poverty and oppression that often arise from inequality. We focused largely on human rights abuses, since most of these arise from differential access to wealth. The work of anthropologists such as Carole Nagengast and Paul Farmer show that anthropologists can apply their unique skills and knowledge to help mitigate against forms of structural violence and alleviate the pernicious effects of growing social inequality.

CRITICAL THINKING QUESTIONS

1. In this chapter, we have discussed how most people tend to perceive their identities as natural, or biological. What might be some strategies for getting people to think differently about their identities, and for recognizing the culturally constructed nature of identity? Furthermore, why is it important to understand the role that culture plays in shaping social hierarchies?
2. Think of some examples of both explicit and implicit "white privilege" in our own society.
3. In section 7.6, we discuss how anthropologists can help alleviate the effects of inequality. On reading the examples of Terence Turner and Paul Farmer, both of whom work in non-Western contexts, can you apply any of these ideas to our own Canadian society? As anthropologists and anthropology students, what can we do in Canada to make a difference in people's lives and confront the issue of social inequality?

KEY TERMS:

achieved status   (p. 190)
ascribed status   (p. 190)
caste system   (p. 190)
class   (p. 189)
gender   (p. 200)
hegemonic masculinity   (p. 202)
meritocracy   (p. 190)
new racism   (p. 208)
race   (p. 192)
racism   (p. 193)
sex   (p. 200)
social hierarchy   (p. 187)
structural violence   (p. 216)
third gender   (p. 200)
white privilege   (p. 195)

CHAPTER 8

GLOBALIZATION, NEOLIBERALISM, AND THE NATION-STATE

Frances Heinrich's *Globalized Nicaragua* evokes the flow and movement of both people and commodities in an increasingly globalized and neoliberal environment. Cross-cultural flows and contacts often result in the syncretism, or blending, of different cultural traditions. This phenomenon is represented visually here with images of Nicaraguan textile motifs on "Western" clothing like T-shirts.

The incredible concentration of wealth and power that now exists in the upper echelons of capitalism has not been seen since the 1920s. The flows of tribute into the world's major financial centres have been astonishing. What, however, is even more astonishing is the habit of treating all of this as a mere and in some instances even unfortunate byproduct of neoliberalization. The very idea that this might be—just might be—the fundamental core of what neoliberalism has been about all along appears unthinkable.

David Harvey, *The History of Neoliberalism* (2005)

Problem 8

What are the economic and cultural effects of globalization, and what is the relationship between globalization, the nation-state, and neoliberalism?

INTRODUCTION

On 26 June 2010, political leaders from around the world gathered in Toronto, Ontario, for the fourth meeting of the G-20 heads of government. Here, the leaders of 20 of the wealthiest nations in the world convened to discuss the future of global capitalist economies, international aid and development strategies, measures for promoting open markets, and means of stimulating economic growth in the wake of a worldwide recession. The two-day event was the most expensive security event in Canada's history, costing $868 million. A 10-metre-high fence was erected in the downtown core, and 10,000 uniformed officers were brought in to protect the delegates.

In many ways, however, the actual content of the conference was obscured within the mass media. Much of the national and international media attention afforded to this event focused on the various protests. During the event, more than 1,100 protesters were arrested. The mainstream media homogenized and sensationalized the protesters as young, selfish, violent criminals and emphasized their role in the destruction and vandalism of storefronts, cars, and other public spaces, inciting fear among the general public. Few media outlets stressed that most protests were peaceful, and even fewer focused on what, specifically, the protesters were protesting against. While there is no question that a handful of them used the G-20 as an opportunity for mayhem, the vast majority were peacefully voicing the underrepresented perspectives of marginalized populations around the world—populations directly affected by decisions made by

Protesters at the 2010 G20 meetings in Toronto.

the G-20 leaders. Indigenous groups, gay rights activists, environmentalists, and anti-poverty groups were among the protesters. In specific, these groups were questioning the ways in which globalization, as a social and economic force, had benefited the wealthiest and most powerful segments of society.

The term "globalization" has been bandied about by academics and the mass media and within our popular culture over the past three decades. Anthony Giddens (1990, 64) defines **globalization** as "the intensification of worldwide social relations which link distant localities in such a way that local happenings are shaped by events occurring many miles away and vice versa." Globalization can have both economic and cultural effects on various populations. The worldwide spread of large multinational companies such as Walmart and Starbucks has been documented as having deleterious economic

---

globalization

Defined by Anthony Giddens as the intensification of worldwide social relations that link distant localities in such a way that local happenings are shaped by events occurring many miles away, and vice versa.

---

consequences on local communities. Walmart, for instance, may seem like an attractive option for shopping because of its low price points, but because of its size and buying power, it can sell products more cheaply than most small, local businesses, effectively driving them out of business.

In many ways, globalization is not a new phenomenon. As we saw in Chapter 3, Europe's colonization of the world was a global phenomenon. But as Roxana Ng (2002, 74) points out, "what is new in this era of globalization is the ability of capital to move sites of production across national borders with relative ease." The production, circulation, and consumption of a common commodity, the T-shirt, provides an instructive example of the mechanisms and consequences of economic globalization and contemporary forms of capitalism. Many protesters at the G-20 sported T-shirts emblazoned with anti-globalization slogans, or with the logos of the protest groups with which they were affiliated. By examining what Igor Kopytoff (1986) calls the biography of a commodity (in this case, the T-shirt), we can understand much about the global processes that the protesters were criticizing.

For instance, economist Pietra Rivoli (2005) wanted to understand the impact, on workers and on the environment, of the policies of multilateral institutions such as the World Trade Organization (WTO), the International Monetary Fund (IMF), and the World Bank (first discussed in Chapter 3). Rivoli assumed that globalization was a good thing, that the increased production and sale of commodities such as T-shirts were helping to create jobs in poor countries as well as supplying inexpensive goods to consumers. To convince herself of the benefits of trade, she wanted to trace the chain of production and distribution of a T-shirt, from the growing of the cotton to the delivery of the final product to a chain store in Fort Lauderdale, Florida. She began by locating the company that printed and distributed the T-shirt, Sherry Manufacturing of Fort Lauderdale. Sherry Manufacturing had purchased the shirt from China, one of about 25 million cotton T-shirts shipped from China that year. Rivoli then travelled to China to visit the factory that had assembled the T-shirt, the place where the fabric had been knit, and finally, the factory where the yarn had been spun out of raw cotton. The cotton, she was surprised to discover, had been grown in Lubbock County, Texas. The unexpected (yet increasingly typical) biography and global itinerary of her T-shirt—purchased in Fort Lauderdale, printed and distributed by a Florida textile manufacturer, assembled, sewn, and spun in Chinese factories out of cotton grown in Texas—can tell us much about globalization and our role in it as T-shirt consumers in North America. The aspects of capitalism, neoliberalism, and economic globalization that underpin the biography of the T-shirt are the focus of the first half of this chapter.

In the second half of this chapter, we examine the often ambiguous cultural effects of globalization. For some societies, the process has been empowering: a means to strengthen cultural identity as a society's arts, material culture, and values and beliefs circulate around the world. To understand these effects, it is first necessary to understand the relationship between the nation-state and globalization, and between nation-states and national identity. Think, again, about T-shirts and how often they communicate not just political slogans or brand names, but sentiments of national pride and affiliations of national identity (as we saw when Canada hosted the 2010 Winter Olympics in Vancouver, or the 2015 Pan-Am Games in Toronto). When we wear T-shirts purchased in popular tourist destinations, we demonstrate our own global itineraries while simultaneously conveying carefully crafted messages about the locales in which we purchased the T-shirts. To understand both the forces of economic globalization that make it possible for us to buy cheap T-shirts produced elsewhere, and the forces of cultural globalization that compel us to wear our identity and our global itineraries, literally, on our sleeves, we need to explore the four questions that comprise this chapter.

QUESTIONS

8.1 What is neoliberalism, and what role does it play in capitalist economic globalization?

8.2 What role do nation-states play in market economies?

8.3 What is the relationship between the nation-state and identity under globalization?

8.4 How do engagements with global capitalism affect local cultural identities and livelihoods?

QUESTION 8.1: WHAT IS NEOLIBERALISM, AND WHAT ROLE DOES IT PLAY IN CAPITALIST ECONOMIC GLOBALIZATION?

"The Great Transformation"

To understand the various economic effects of globalization, we must explore what we mean by an "economic system." **Economic systems** are about the distribution of goods and services—that is, the rules, mechanisms, institutions, and systems of relations through which people get what they want. This process can be as simple as the borrowing of a cup of sugar or a pair of shoes, or as complex as the production, distribution, consumption, and disposal of automobiles, houses, or military weapons.

Markets go back thousands of years. Communities would set up areas where merchants, farmers, and artisans could bring their goods or services for sale or barter. But as new modes of transportation and manufacturing developed, markets were no longer only places to trade, but entire networks whereby silk manufactured in China, for example, could be sold in Paris. At some point 200 to 300 years ago, technological changes led to what economist Karl Polanyi termed "the great transformation," or the Industrial Revolution. As discussed in Chapter 3, the Industrial Revolution had enormous worldwide economic and social consequences, and it was intimately linked with colonialism. Indeed, the Industrial Revolution contributed to the development and perpetuation of many of our existing forms of social inequalities—classism and racism, for example—and it solidified the rise of capitalism as a dominant, worldwide economic system.

Capitalism has, of course, expanded, such that we engage in the sale or barter of goods and services on large, international scales that involve complex exchanges between different countries. States have always played a major role in the economy. Some 18th-century economists, however, argued that the state should play as small a role as possible. Ideally, they argued, people will supply only those goods and services for which there is demand; and generally, a balance will be established between what is demanded and what is supplied. In his classic treatise *The Wealth of Nations* (1776),

---

economic systems
The rules, mechanisms, institutions, and systems of relations through which goods and services are distributed and people get what they want.

Adam Smith saw the workings of the market as an "invisible hand" by which a benevolent God administered a universe in which human happiness was maximized; the market was an ideal system in which each person, seeking his or her own ends, contributed to the betterment of society as a whole. Thus, by seeking money and wealth, each person would work toward supplying what others needed or demanded. For Smith, the market represented a utopian vision in which wealth was perpetually created for the benefit of all.

The problem was that an unregulated market, in which the generation of wealth was the only goal, resulted in abysmal working conditions, environmental degradation, and wild economic fluctuations that saw people plunged into poverty. In *The Great Transformation* (1944), Polanyi addressed the tension between the need to allow the market—that is, the mechanisms for buying and selling—to operate freely without government interference and the need to somehow minimize the social and natural damages inflicted by the market. Polanyi suggested that the market, if allowed to operate unhindered, would soon destroy the very foundations of society. It would disrupt social relations though the operations of the labour market; it would destroy the environment; it would reduce freedom. Yet regulating the market by enacting laws on pollution, land use, and working conditions could destroy the market. Polanyi saw the working out of this dilemma as one of the driving forces of history since the early 19th century.

When it comes to the market's workings, governments have tried to maintain a balance between regulation and noninterference. At one extreme are the almost completely state-run economies of Cuba and North Korea; at the other are capitalist economies such as those of Canada and the United States. Economic systems are generally categorized as market-driven or state-run; in practice, though, almost all represent some mix of the two. North Korea is one of the last of the state-run economies, with the government controlling virtually every economic activity; yet the North Korean government also sponsors the Kaesong Industrial Region, a development zone that welcomes foreign investment and that encourages market principles. The United States, by contrast, is a hallmark example of a market economy. Nevertheless, during the recent global recession, there was significant government intervention in the form of corporate bailouts and promises of stricter financial controls. Rarely are even the most capitalist economies free of significant state involvement, and the tension between the state and the market that Polanyi wrote about results in ebbs and flows of regulation.

The British economist John Maynard Keynes called on governments to regulate their economies through spending, tax policies, interest rates, and so on. Government involvement in the economy, support of labour unions, and a progressive tax system in which marginal tax rates ranged as high as 90 percent resulted in rapid economic growth in the United States and Canada through the 1960s.

This rapid growth was followed, in the 1970s, by a period of slow economic growth, which generated pressure to change economic policies. Economists began to abandon Keynesian economics, arguing that the state should withdraw from any involvement in regulating the economy. This economic philosophy, known as **neoliberalism**, is often synonymous with contemporary capitalism under globalization. Since the application of neoliberal principles may determine your career path as well as what goods and services you can acquire for what price, not to mention the natural, political, and social environment in which you live, it is useful to understand where it came from and what it is trying to accomplish.

The Emergence of Neoliberalism

Neoliberalism emerged from a group of economists, historians, and philosophers who gathered around political philosopher Friedrich von Hayek to establish the Mont Pelerin Society in 1947. Their ideas were prompted by concerns about the spread of totalitarian societies and religious and racial intolerance in the aftermath of the Second World War. They argued that totalitarian philosophies both endanger freedom and threaten private property and the free market, without which, they believed, freedom cannot be preserved. They called themselves "liberals" because they adhered to ideals of freedom, and "neo" because they adhered to neoclassical economic theory, which was opposed to the Keynesian ideas about state involvement in the economy.

Well-being, neoliberals argued, is best served by liberating individual entrepreneurs to operate within a framework of strong property rights, free markets, and **free trade**. The state's role should be limited to safeguarding the integrity of money and maintaining military, police, and legal structures to secure property rights and protect markets. The state should also open markets in areas such as education, water, land, healthcare, and social security. Other than that, state intervention should be kept to a minimum, because states can never have enough information to second-guess markets on matters such as prices, and because their involvement allows special interest groups such as unions, environmentalists, and trade groups to distort market operations.

One of the first applications of neoliberalism was in New York City in the 1970s. By the start of the decade, industry was fleeing New York and people who could afford new housing were

neoliberalism
An economic philosophy that argues for minimal government involvement in the economy and greatly accelerated economic growth. Well-being, neoliberals argue, is best served by liberating individual entrepreneurs to operate in a framework of strong property rights, free markets, and free trade.

free trade
The removal of barriers to the free flow of goods and capital between nations by eliminating import and export taxes as well as subsidies paid to farmers and businesspeople. It may also mean reducing environmental or social laws when they restrict the flow of goods and capital.

moving to the suburbs. The city was left with a diminished tax base and an impoverished and socially restive inner city—what became known as the "urban crisis." The initial solution was typical Keynesian economics: expand public employment and public assistance. When President Richard Nixon declared the urban crisis over in the early 1970s, however, he also reduced federal aid to the city. The economic slowdown of the 1970s that hit New York, combined with a reduced tax base and reduced federal aid, drove New York City to the brink of bankruptcy. Financial institutions were unwilling to negotiate the city's debts unless it met strict conditions that included severe budget cuts. They also required unions to put their pension funds in city bonds, which meant that if the city went bankrupt, workers would lose their pensions. The overall result was a diminished standard of living for New Yorkers, particularly the poor. But ultimately, the city became financially solvent and represented to neoliberals what could be done through free market principles.

This pattern soon became the one applied to countries in trouble. The economic stagnation of the 1970s adversely affected developing countries that, encouraged by banks, had borrowed heavily but could no longer repay their debts. As a condition for restructuring their loans, multilateral institutions such as the World Bank and the International Monetary Fund (IMF) (discussed in Chapter 3) imposed neoliberal economic policies on these countries: these included privatizing state-run enterprises; reducing the value of their currency, thus making goods produced in the country cheaper for foreign buyers (and thereby encouraging exports); and making foreign goods more expensive for citizens (thereby discouraging imports). Other conditions included reducing state funding for education, welfare, and health and imposing user fees for school attendance.

These neoliberal policies had few positive results. Only a few countries were able to escape debt, and more than $4.6 trillion flowed from poorer to wealthier countries. According to economist Joseph E. Stiglitz (2002), the poor countries ended up subsidizing the richest. As David Harvey (2005) suggests in the epigraph to the chapter, this result may not be an unfortunate byproduct of neoliberalism, but rather, its fundamental purpose.

Removing government involvement in the economy is central to neoliberal economic philosophy. When such involvement ends, so the theory goes, business can be more profitable, create more jobs, and so on. One way that less government involvement can help economic growth is by allowing costs that are involved in the production, distribution, consumption, and disposal of goods and services to be externalized. All along the commodity chain, from the production of goods to their transport to their sale and disposal, there are market externalities, costs that are not included in the prices that people pay, such as environmental degradation, health risks, and waste disposal. In the next section, we discuss the relationship between the nation-state and market economies under neoliberalism, and look at the market externalities of chocolate bars and T-shirts.

QUESTION 8.2: WHAT ROLE DO NATION-STATES PLAY IN MARKET ECONOMIES?

Although neoliberal philosophy is the driving force behind what we call "globalization," there is a basic contradiction in how it is applied. The central idea behind neoliberalism is to keep governments from interfering in the functioning of the market, but the nation-state still plays a vital role in how the economy functions.

What do we mean by "nation-state"? The concept of the **nation-state** is relatively recent,

> **nation-state**
> A political community that has clearly defined territorial borders and centralized authority.

dating back in its present form to the 19th century. Furthermore, the terms **nation** and "state" do not mean the same thing. Most states have more than one nation, as in Canada, where there are many First Nations; moreover, one nation can be scattered across many states, either by choice or by force, as in the case of diasporic communities or refugees.

Nation-states typically keep public order, maintain armies, collect tribute or taxes, and so on. The main difference between earlier states and the modern nation-state concerns the extent to which the modern state influences and controls trade. In historical terms, the increasing importance of trade gave governing elites a greater interest in creating conditions to accumulate profits from trade. Of course, ruling elites have always been interested in the economic lives of their subjects. Early states protected the privileges of the elites by regulating the production of goods from resources, offering protection from other elites, and extracting surplus wealth in the form of tribute and taxes from a largely peasant population. The state also issued coins and paper money, established standards for weights and measures, protected the movement of merchants and goods, purchased goods, and created and maintained marketplaces where merchants could sell their products.

In 13th- and 14th-century China and, later, in 16th- and 17th-century Europe and Japan, states began to actively promote and regulate trade. By the 18th century, rulers were beginning to view trade as the ultimate source of well-being. Consequently, states regulated money. They also passed laws to protect their manufacturers and merchants by imposing taxes and tariffs on goods coming from other states. They used military force to open markets in other places and granted trading monopolies to their own groups. They granted charters to trading companies, such as the East India Company and the Hudson's Bay Company, giving them exclusive

---

nation

A collection of people who share a common language, worldview, and ancestry.

---

rights to trade in specific areas. These were the forerunners of today's transnational corporations.

States also created and maintained the infrastructure that made trade possible. They developed and maintained ports, built roads and canals, and later, subsidized railway construction. In Canada, for instance, the Canadian Pacific Railway was completed in 1885. Connecting a vast expanse of the nation from east to west, the railway facilitated trade and economic links between provinces that would otherwise have been impossible to maintain. States also became important customers.

In brief, nation-states began to develop into partnerships between ruling elites and the merchant classes. As Eric Wolf (1982, 109) put it:

> *The state bought arms and ships. Goods won by force of arms paid for the hiring of mercenaries, for the manufacture of guns and cannon, and for the construction of more ships. The armed merchants foraging overseas needed the state to shield them against competitors and to provide the officialdom capable of holding and consolidating the newly won areas. At the same time the state needed the merchants to lend money to the Crown or to the captains of expeditions; to collect, ship, and sell the goods obtained abroad; and—increasingly—to acquire and export the goods needed in the far-flung outposts of the realm.*

In these ways, states became the building blocks of an emerging global economic network. Each state was now the guardian of its own "national economy," functioning largely to advance the economic lives of its own citizens. In fact, the modern nation-state sought to create the conditions that made business profitable, while at the same time ensuring that its citizens could afford the things they wanted to buy. As we will see, though, this ideal is possible only if manufacturers do not have to pay the full production costs of what they make and sell, and only if consumers don't have to pay the real costs of things. One need only examine the real costs

GLOBALIZATION, NEOLIBERALISM, AND THE NATION-STATE

of even the most basic commodities to appreciate the role that nation-states played in making possible their production and purchase. Take, for example, the cost of a Snickers bar.

The Nation-State and the Cost of a Snickers Bar

Snickers bars are described by their producers, Mars, Incorporated (listed by *Forbes* in 2014 as the 6th largest privately held company in the United States) as chocolate treats that are "packed with roasted peanuts, nougat, caramel and milk chocolate." More precisely, Snickers bars have more than 20 ingredients, the main one being sugar or sugar derivatives. Snickers is the most popular chocolate bar in Canada and the United States, and one package of Snickers sells for about $1.50. But that is only the store price. To arrive at the real price, we need to examine the hidden costs, owing to **market externalities**, of each ingredient; in other words, we need to calculate the additional monetary and nonmonetary expenses that go to produce and distribute each ingredient in a Snickers bar: expenses that are not reflected in the store price. In fact, without the intervention of the nation-state, the real cost of a Snickers bar would probably be $10 or higher. It is only about $1.50 because of the various ways the nation-state functions to keep costs accessible and sales profitable.

To illustrate, let us examine just one ingredient that goes into a Snickers: cane sugar. Sugar cultivation requires a tropical climate and is not grown in Canada, but it is a popular and lucrative crop in parts of the United States (southern Florida and Hawaii) and throughout the Caribbean and South America, among other regions. Environmentally, sugar is not a benign crop. Its production is responsible for dying coral reefs in Hawai'i, water pollution in Buenos Aires, and damage to river estuaries in Brazil and waterways in the Philippines. Florida's sugar cane industry, centred just south of one of North America's largest freshwater lakes, Lake Okeechobee, dumps phosphorus-laden agricultural

One function of the nation-state is to ensure that businesses and corporations profit and that commodities are affordable to consumers. Thus, laws and regulations are written (or not written) to permit corporations to externalize costs. Rarely, if ever, do consumers pay the real prices for things. Even a Snickers chocolate bar, which might sell for $1.50, would likely cost far more if externalized costs were included in the purchase price.

runoff into the lake, which destroys native species and results in the growth of non-native species. In 2000, the *Comprehensive Everglades Restoration Plan* was enacted, which saw almost $8 billion spent to fix the Everglades. Although sugar producers paid some of that cost, most of it was passed on to American taxpayers.

Sugar production is heavily subsidized by some nation-states, including the United States, which, through import quotas, limits the amount of sugar that can be imported from other countries. This arrangement raises the cost of sugar for consumers, but it also makes sugar production more profitable and so has resulted in the conversion of more than 200,000 hectares of Everglades wetlands to sugar cane production.

The nation-state also manipulates the prices of things by regulating the price of labour. For example, paying sugar workers less than a living wage minimizes the price of sugar. Although countries

market externalities
Costs that are not included in the prices people pay, for example, health risks and environmental degradation.

such as the United States and Canada have a "minimum wage," it does not apply to agricultural workers, many of whom come from the English-speaking Caribbean or Mexico and are permitted to enter North America temporarily only for the purpose of work.

Indirect subsidies for sugar include government funding of the infrastructure for sugar production and processing. This infrastructure includes, among other things, roads, power systems, water and sanitation systems, and waste disposal. The entire water management infrastructure that supports the Florida sugar cane industry, for example, was built with U.S. federal tax dollars. Finally, the tax policies of the nation-state are constantly being adjusted to ensure the maintenance of corporate profits and low prices. Thus, in the 1950s, the tax bill of corporations in the United States accounted for 39 percent of all federal tax income; by the 1990s, the corporate tax bill had been cut to 19 percent. By 2014, approximately one-third of the most financially lucrative U.S. corporations were paying corporate taxes that equalled 10 percent or less of their net annual revenue (Pyke 2014).

These are only some of the hidden costs of one ingredient in a Snickers bar. To arrive at a real economic cost, we would need to examine each of the other ingredients and then add the hidden costs of processing, packaging, delivery, and waste disposal. The energy and pollution costs of distribution alone would be considerable. In Europe and North America, a typical food item travels 1,600 kilometres before it reaches consumers' meal plates. A head of lettuce in the local supermarket has travelled an average of 1,900 kilometres from where it was grown. The shipment of foods, while sometimes necessary, is further encouraged by energy subsidies that allow North Americans to enjoy some of the lowest fuel prices in the world. Economists estimate that if tax subsidies, government program subsidies, and environmental damage were calculated and if other externalities of vehicle use were discontinued, the price of gasoline would be as high as $16.40 a gallon in the United States and about $4.00 a litre in Canada.

It is also important to note that our insatiable desire for sugary treats such as Snickers is closely intertwined with a long history of exploitative labour that began during the colonial period. In his analysis of the link between sugar and colonialism, Sidney Mintz (1985), for instance, argues that sugar would never have become such a significant and seemingly "necessary" commodity within European and other Western countries without the use of slave labour. In Chapter 3, we discussed the significance of the production and trade of cotton to colonialism and the slave trade in the Americas, but sugar, too, was an integral part of this history. With the European colonization of the Caribbean, for instance, the Caribbean became the largest producer of sugar in the world. To cultivate and distill sugar cane at a high yield and profitable rate, European plantation owners brought over one million individuals from West Africa to work as slaves in the 1700s and 1800s.

Even after slavery was abolished, exploitative forms of labour would continue. For instance, about 20,000 poor and dispossessed Haitian workers are lured annually to the Dominican Republic with the promise of jobs, only to find themselves working in horrific conditions on sugar cane plantations. With little or no rights, and no passports, workers are underpaid and overworked; as many cross the border illegally and without official passports, they lack legal or official representation in the Dominican Republic. Ultimately, when we think about the different products that we "can't live without"—sugar often being one—we should also consider how colonial relationships among nation-states persist into the post-colonial present. Some of these issues pertaining to labour and the production of commodities in an increasingly neoliberal environment are elaborated upon below.

In brief, then, the nation-state develops such instruments as tax laws, financial policies, environmental regulations, and labour laws that help corporations and consumers avoid paying the real costs of production and consumption. The costs of these measures are then passed on to future

GLOBALIZATION, NEOLIBERALISM, AND THE NATION-STATE

generations or to people in other countries in the form of low wages, a polluted environment, health risks, and the like. Yet this, it seems, is what citizens want. Corporations look to nation-states to further their interests; to ensure this, they spend billions of dollars each year to help elect office-holders who are sympathetic to their interests. Consumers look to the nation-state to keep the prices of things (e.g., chocolate bars and gasoline) within their reach. And workers expect the nation-state to enact policies to enhance job and wage growth. None of this would be possible without nation-states to enact and enforce rules and regulations that allow their citizens to pass on the real costs of things, such as environmental damage, health risks, and poverty, to people in other countries, to marginalized people in their own countries, or to future generations.

EXERCISE 8.1

Calculating the Real Cost of Things

Each morning, most students begin the day by brushing their teeth, washing their face, and using the toilet facilities. Then, perhaps, they drink a glass of orange juice and maybe sip a cup of coffee. But what are the hidden costs of these activities? What sorts of indirect environmental, health, and economic costs are involved in the activities?

Activity or Product	Hidden Cost
Brushing teeth:	
Flushing the toilet:	
Drinking orange juice:	
Sipping coffee:	

What Is the Role of the Nation-State in an Increasingly Neoliberalized Global Economy?

Nation-states are currently the political building blocks of the modern world. All individuals derive whatever political rights and privileges they enjoy from their nation-state. Each person is educated, is given or denied permission to travel, and is bound by the laws of his or her state. Yet some people, such as David Korten (1995), claim that the nation-state is a thing of the past, that in an increasingly globalized world, national boundaries are no longer relevant. Millions of people migrate from their home countries in search of jobs, further blurring national boundaries. More than 230 million people currently live and work in countries of which they are not citizens, and this number will continue to grow (International Labor Organization 2015). Some say that new **transnational** institutions, such as transnational corporations and transnational treaty organizations, such as the World Trade Organization (WTO), are rapidly replacing nation-states. Is the nation-state a thing of the past?

The major candidate to replace the nation-state is the transnational corporation. Currently, half the richest institutional entities in the world are not nation-states, but transnational corporations. Walmart is the 28th-richest financial entity in the world, well ahead of Denmark (37), Venezuela (40th), and Hong Kong (47th). Five petroleum companies (including Exxon Mobile and British Petroleum) are included in the top 50 (http://dstevenwhite.com/2012/08/11/the-top-175-global-economic-entities-2011/). One of the reasons why nation-states emerged was to integrate national economies. The expansion of the modern global economy, however, requires global, not just state, integration, and transnational corporations have both a vested interest in expanding across national boundaries and the power and financial resources to accomplish that end. One consequence of this development has been that corporate interests, as opposed to human interests, now dominate the policy agendas of nation-states and the international agencies they create, support, and control.

transnational
Involving more than one nation-state; reaching beyond or transcending national boundaries.

A good example of how international agencies have begun to "escape" nation-states' strictures involves the role of the World Trade Organization. The WTO was established in 1995 by international treaty. Its stated goal was to reduce trade barriers among its 140 member nations. Its proponents argued that when these barriers were reduced so that goods and services could flow freely across national boundaries, citizens of all countries would benefit.

But despite its apparently high-minded goals, the WTO has been the focus of mass public protests. In Seattle in 1999 and in Québec City in 2001, thousands of protesters representing hundreds of labour, environmental, and human rights groups organized to demonstrate against the inequalities resulting from world trade. What were these protests against the WTO all about? Why does it matter that you know? And what *does* this have to do with anthropology?

Basically, anti-WTO protesters are demanding to know how an unelected body that makes decisions behind closed doors with no provisions for appeal can force sovereign countries to dismantle environmental, health, labour, and social laws that it deems to be "unfair restrictions on trade."

In brief, when a member country, generally acting for a domestic corporation, feels that the laws or regulations of another country constitute an unfair restriction on trade, it can ask the WTO to investigate. If a WTO panel, appointed by the member countries, agrees with the claim, the complaining country can then impose trade taxes and tariffs on goods imported from the offending country. Table 8.1, below, outlines the WTO's assessment of its value.

TABLE 8.1 PROPOSED BENEFITS OF THE WORLD TRADE ORGANIZATION

The system helps promote peace
Disputes between nations are handled constructively
Free trade rules make life easier for all
Freer trade cuts the costs of living
Free trade provides more choice of products and qualities
Free trade raises incomes
Free trade stimulates economic growth
The basic principles of free trade make life more efficient
Governments are shielded from lobbying
The system encourages good government

*See http://www.wto.org/english/thewto_e/10ben_e/10b00_e.htm. Reproduced courtesy of the World Trade Organization.

An example follows. Most European countries impose a tariff on bananas imported from Central America but not on those from some Caribbean countries, such as Jamaica, Dominica, St. Lucia, and St. Vincent. This policy favours Caribbean countries, since it makes Central American bananas more expensive for European consumers. The rationale for these tariffs dates back to when Caribbean countries were colonial outposts of Britain and France.

The United States appealed the European tariff on Central American bananas to the WTO, claiming it constituted an unfair trade barrier. The Americans acted largely because most Central American banana plantations are owned by U.S. corporations, some of which had contributed considerable amounts of money to the election campaigns of both Republican and Democratic politicians. The WTO ruled that the tariffs imposed by European countries on Central American bananas did, in fact, constitute an unfair restriction on trade.

The WTO does not have the power to force countries to change their trade rules, but it can permit offended countries (the United States, in this case) to impose tariffs on selected goods of offending countries. The WTO permitted the United States to impose import tariffs on such things as British cashmere and French cheeses, thus increasing their costs to American consumers and likely reducing the profits of British wool producers and French cheese makers.

Some of the WTO's rulings have deeply disturbed health, labour, and environmental advocates because the WTO can pressure countries to change their health, labour, and environmental laws if its dispute panel rules that these laws constitute an unfair restriction on trade. For example, when a country has banned a product from another country because of health risks, the country in which the product was manufactured or produced can accuse the banning country of creating an unfair barrier to trade. The country passing the law then has to prove to the WTO panel that the ban was "scientifically based." If it cannot, then trade sanctions and penalties can be applied to the banning country.

A prominent case here involves the European ban on hormone-treated beef produced in the United States and Canada. Injecting hormones into beef cattle is legal in the United States and Canada, but some research suggests that treated beef may be harmful. Europeans are especially sensitive to health threats in meat because of the emergence of mad cow disease (Creutzfeldt-Jakob disease) in Great Britain, which is spread by eating meat from animals that have eaten infected feed, the subsequent ban on British beef by European countries, and fears about cancer-causing dioxins in meat and egg products in Belgium.

The United States, at the request of its ranchers and beef processors, brought the case to the WTO, claiming that the ban on beef was an "unfair restraint of trade" and that there was no clear scientific evidence of health risks. The WTO ruled in favour of the U.S. corporations, thus forcing European consumers to accept American hormone-treated beef or accept restrictive tariffs on selected European products sold in the United States. So far, Europe has refused to overturn the ban, and the United States has been permitted to impose tariffs on selected European imports, including truffles from Italy.

Disputes such as these threaten the "precautionary principle" of risk management, which states that if a product or process poses risks to health or the environment, scientific certainty is not necessary in order for other countries to prohibit or control that product or process. The Europeans reason that, while there is no absolute scientific proof that hormone-treated beef is harmful to health, enough research has been done to raise real health concerns. Yet the WTO has rejected the precautionary principle in the case of North American beef, ruling that the Europeans must either let it in or allow Canada and the United States to impose penalties on European products.

As a result of such developments, some critics claim that "free trade" has less to do with trade and helping citizens of WTO countries than it does with allowing global corporations to force nation-states to change or erase environmental, health, and social regulations that interfere with their business. Critics claim that international agencies are being controlled and manipulated by corporate powers that determine not only what we buy but also the conditions under which our goods are produced and how they are distributed.

Globalization, Free Trade, and the Canadian Garment Industry

An ethnographic approach to studying the Canadian garment industry can yield insights into the local, everyday effects of economic globalization and international trade. First, recall the example at the beginning of this chapter, of Pietra Rivoli's (2005) T-shirt—purchased in Florida, made from cotton grown in Texas, but spun into cloth and assembled in China. One important chapter in the biography of this particular commodity concerns the garment workers. The young women working in the Chinese factories visited by Rivoli were happy to have the work. However terrible the conditions in the factories, they told her, "it sure beats work on the farm" (110).

Roxana Ng (2002) has done similar research on the Canadian garment industry. Her findings with respect to the effects of free trade have led her to ask, "Freedom for whom?" From the perspective of Canadian garment workers, longer hours, lower wages, and job loss have been the concrete, everyday results of the neoliberalization and restructuring of the garment industry under free trade. The industry has always relied on low wages to be competitive and has always used immigrants as a pool of inexpensive labour; 50 percent of workers in the garment industry are immigrants, and 76 percent are women (Ng 2002, 75). Since the mid-1990s, control within the garment industry has shifted away from manufacturers, first toward large retail chains such as the Hudson's Bay Company, but increasingly toward transnational retail chains such as Walmart. At the same time that control over the industry has been centralized, production has become fragmented. This fragmentation takes the form of subcontracting. According to Ng (2002, 77), manufacturers have responded to their loss of control by reducing plant sizes and sending work to subcontractors, or "jobbers," who increasingly are using home workers or sweatshop operations to maximize their profit margins and reduce their operating costs.

The implementation in 1993 of the North American Free Trade Agreement (NAFTA), which enabled the freer movement of production and goods between the United States, Canada, and Mexico, also played a major role in the restructuring of the garment industry. Canadian companies such as Gildan, the largest T-shirt manufacturer in Québec, have since opened plants in Mexico (and throughout the Caribbean). Wages are much lower than Canadian wages, and when labour costs go down, these companies' profits go up. Unfortunately, the direct results in Canada have been job losses, the depressing of wages, and deteriorating working conditions. One garment worker that Ng interviewed demonstrated the unpredictability of wages in this sector:

> The lowest salary I earned was about $3 per hour, with the same employers I'm now working. [I asked why she didn't complain about the low rate.] I didn't say anything at the beginning. I dared not. But now I start to talk to them about this. This kind of pocket-cover sewing I'm doing now also requires me to cut certain fabric before I can start sewing. But the employers don't count the cutting time. I told the employers about this. But they said that almost every homeworker asks them for a raise. But they get no raise from their contractor who gives them the fabric. I don't know other homeworkers who also work for them. It would be better if I know. Their factory is very small. They only have two workers in their factory, plus some part-timers, and the two owners.
>
> The highest salary I earned was around $8 per hour. That was at the beginning when I first worked for these employers, when they let

me know the piece rate before I sewed. But now they don't tell me the piece rate before I sew.
(Ng 2007, 197)

One effect of economic globalization has been the movement of capital, production, and goods around the globe. There has been a corresponding movement of people around the world, as well. People migrate in search of a better livelihood or because they have been displaced by the lack of economic and social opportunities in their home country. As mentioned earlier, the Canadian garment industry has always relied heavily on immigrant labour; to this, Ng adds that illegal migrants and undocumented workers now represent a larger and larger portion of Canada's garment-sector workforce (necessarily, the official data are scarce). Undocumented garment workers—indeed, all undocumented workers—are among the most vulnerable participants in the global economy.

EXERCISE 8.2

Biography of a Commodity

Take a look at the label on your shirt, T-shirt, sweatshirt, or whatever article of clothing you are wearing. What company made it? Where was it made? By whom? Try to find information online about clothing manufacturing practices (location of factories and labour policies) for your particular label.

The anti-sweatshop movement has increased awareness of the poor working conditions for garment workers in parts of the developing world. In 1999, students at the University of Toronto successfully lobbied for a Code of Conduct for Trademark Licensees. The Code now ensures that suppliers of school-trademarked merchandise (including T-shirts) have met minimum employment standards. Gildan, one of the university's suppliers, was forced to directly address allegations of unethical treatment

of its workers in the developing world (Ng 2002, 79). So, it is important to note that free trade regulations, in particular, and neoliberalism, in general, have not only sent manufacturing jobs to the developing world, but also led to sweatshop conditions for Canadian workers. "In other words, globalization has created Third World working conditions within the geographical boundaries of the so-called First, or developed, world" (Ng 2007, 204).

QUESTION 8.3: WHAT IS THE RELATIONSHIP BETWEEN THE NATION-STATE AND IDENTITY UNDER GLOBALIZATION?

The integration and maintenance of the national economy is, then, one of the most important tasks facing the modern nation-state. But there are others. The state must be recognized by its citizens as the legitimate source of authority. And it must establish and uphold its own citizenship rules.

To achieve these ends, the state must create a nation out of groups who share (or who believe they share) a common culture, language, and heritage and who willingly identify themselves as members of the nation (review the discussion of the "imagined community" in Chapter 6). Given that almost all of the world's nation-states are composed of peoples with different cultures, languages, and heritages, creating a nation is no easy task. Somehow, these diverse entities must come to see themselves as sharing a common culture, tradition, and heritage; only when they do can state leaders claim to represent "the people," whoever they might be. Furthermore, when people can be persuaded to identify themselves as members of a common political entity, they more easily accept integration into the national economy—the same wages, the same currency, and the same goods.

But how does one go about constructing a national identity? In addition to the creation of a sense of "imagined community," this challenge often involves creating *Others*—that is, persons or groups who, having been somehow excluded from or pushed to the margins of the nation-state, accent those persons or groups who are more legitimate. The Others may be citizens of rival countries who are thought to embody characteristics that are mocked or feared by members of the nation-state. Thus, for centuries the British could pride themselves on not being Irish or French, and Canadians could take pride in not being "American," that is, citizens of the United States. Colonial empires established by the Germans, French, Dutch, and British substantiated each of those countries' claims that God or Providence had chosen them to rule over "inferior" peoples. In Canada, as in many other nation-states, we maintain our sense of "nationhood," in part, by drawing boundaries and by making Others of migrants who enter the country, legally or illegally, to work.

Others may be constructed out of largely arbitrary criteria, including physical characteristics, religion, or language. In Canada, for example, the Meech Lake Accord, a constitutional amendment that was debated in 1990, attempted to make English and French the only "official languages" of the nation-state, thereby implying that anyone who did not speak one of those languages did not quite belong. The Accord was vigorously challenged and defeated by First Nations leaders, including Elijah Harper, a member of the provincial legislature in Manitoba, who argued that the denial of First Nations languages was a denial of Aboriginal existence. People who are immigrants, refugees, non-Christians, or members of visible minorities often experience negative reactions from those who claim to be "authentic Canadians." In this way, Canadians heighten their sense of exclusivity; by creating boundaries, they more clearly define for themselves their membership in the nation-state.

Political scientists, anthropologists, and political philosophers have generally assumed that membership in the state is voluntary and contractual. In exchange for protection against enemies and the enforcement of rules of behaviour, the idea goes, citizens agree to cede to the state the power to use force. Yet the idea that citizens make voluntary contracts with the state is not entirely true. Rather, people are born into nation-states much as they are born into their families; they assume the citizenship of one or both of their parents.

Another way to obtain citizenship in a nation-state is through immigration, which is a prime location for policies of racism. Canada has a long history of immigration policies based on race and ethnicity. Examples include the special head taxes imposed on Chinese immigrants between 1885 and 1923, the setting of quotas for different "racial" groups, and the refusal to allow Jewish refugees into Canada during the Second World War. During the decades when Canada was trying to populate its territory, British and American immigrants were actively recruited, northern Europeans were welcome, and other Europeans were accepted if they were the only ones available. "Peoples of colour," such as Chinese, East Indians, and blacks, were the least welcome. However, the Canadian state found ways to admit Chinese workers when labour was needed to build the Canadian Pacific Railway, and in the 1970s, a program was written into the Immigration Act to allow non-Canadians into Canada on a temporary basis as agricultural workers and domestics. For example, the Foreign Agricultural Resource Management Services (FARMS) was created to allow Ontario growers to import workers from Mexico and various Caribbean countries to work on Ontario farms during planting and harvest. In 1967, Canada introduced the "point system," based on a match between the country's labour needs and applicants' education and skills, to accommodate a growing need for skilled workers from outside its borders.

In the same way that the nation-state creates membership rules, it creates rules for categorizing people. In the case of "race," the nation-state again uses notions of birth tempered by geography.

According to Statistics Canada, there are three "races" in Canada: "visible minorities," Aboriginal peoples, and Whites. "Visible minorities" include the following: South Asian, Chinese, Black, Filipino, Latin American, Arab, Southeast Asian, West Asian, Korean, Japanese, or Other (http://www12.statcan.gc.ca/NHS-ENM/ref/Questionnaires/2011NHS-ENM-eng.cfm). These classifications group people in very strange ways: Chinese, Filipino, and Japanese are based on a specific nationality, whereas several categories, such as South Asian, are based on geographical region, and Black is based completely on skin colour, with no geographical specification. Besides being imprecise, these classifications create ready-made target groups for hatred, as people of "Arab" descent found after the 9/11 attacks on New York City in 2001. Police in Toronto reported an increase in hate -crimes from 1 in 2000 to 121 in 2001. Police in Ottawa, Montréal, and Calgary reported similar increases.

Nation-states carefully define the places occupied by the various groups within their borders. Through these definitions, they clearly privilege some groups over others and some individuals over others.

One way in which this is done is by creating official accounts of history. As Eva Mackey (1999, 23) argues, "nationalism often depends upon mythological narratives of a unified nation moving progressively through time—a continuum beginning with a glorious past leading to the present and then onward to an even better future. These mythical stories ensure that specific versions of history are highlighted, versions that reaffirm the particular characteristics ascribed to the nation." In Canada, that "glorious past" was filled with "nature," and First Nations peoples were part of the natural landscape. In settler narratives about the creation of the Canadian nation, Aboriginal peoples play the role of helpful "children" who join with the "adult" Euro-Canadians in bringing prosperity to the land. The history that children read in Canadian public schools describes Canada as much kinder to First Nations peoples than the United States was to the Native American population, but even in this gentle

version of history, "real Canadians are, by definition, not 'Native' or not from those 'other cultures'" (Mackey 1999, 89).

Canadians pride themselves on being tolerant of ethnic differences, but these differences are carefully managed through the policy of **multiculturalism**, defined by Fleras and Elliot as an official policy that "involves a process of engaging diversity as different yet equal" (2002, 16). Prime Minister Pierre Elliott Trudeau announced Canada's multicultural policy on 8 October 1971. However, multiculturalism has not been accepted by all Canadians. Himani Bannerji (2000, 44) argues that its ultimate purpose was to sidestep the real issues that were becoming more and more obvious among many new Canadians: poverty, unemployment, and racism. According to Eva Mackey, Canadian multicultural policy has not lived up to its promises. It has produced a core of "Canadian Canadians," with tiny segments of ethnic cultures that contribute to the value of the core. "Ordinary Canadians" are the *unmarked* category of the population, the ones who set the standards from which ethnic groups differ.

Furthermore, the meaning of "culture" changes within the policy of multiculturalism. Culture becomes merely a collection of fragments, such as "folklore, food, dancing, music, and customs," when it is used to refer to ethnic groups, whereas Canadian national culture is "conceived of as a whole, entire, way of life" (Mackey 1999, 90). The *Multiculturalism Act* was, in part, an effort to defuse Québec's threat to separate from Canada, yet Québec has rejected the implication that it is just another "ethnic" group. Although Canada claims to have two founding nations, French and British, many of the French in Québec believe that they will never

multiculturalism
A term that Eva Mackey defines as a Canadian policy in which all hyphenated cultures, such as African-Canadian and French-Canadian, are described and celebrated as part of a "cultural mosaic." Contrast with the "cultural melting pot" image that is used in the United States.

attain equality with the rest of Canada until they separate and form their own nation-state.

Education and the Nation-State

The creation and cultivation of inferior Others through such means as religion, racial classifications, empire building, and the marginalization of peoples based on their geographic origins is not in itself enough to build identity, loyalty, and devotion to the nation-state. A nation-state also requires institutions that integrate all of its members. For example, it needs to impose some sort of common language on its citizens; facilitate travel from one part of the state to another; establish national media to disseminate information from the state; and create a bureaucracy for collecting taxes and revenues, as well as a judicial system through which to maintain authority. It must establish a military and, perhaps most important, oversee an education system to train and socialize children to be "good citizens."

Ernest Gellner (1983) has suggested that today the control of education is even more important than the control of armed force. In order to regulate the national economy, a nation-state must build education systems that enable people to communicate with others in a common standardized language. People must be taught to deal with meanings rather than with things such as shovels or ploughs, and they must learn the complex processes through which buttons and other controls activate machines. In a complex industrial society, people cannot be taught in the family; they must be instructed by specialists operating within a national education system. Most important, students must be trained to identify themselves as members of a nation-state as well as to learn the identity of Others. They must be taught loyalty to their nation-state and be instructed in patriotism.

In Canada, the state sponsored residential schools in order to teach First Nations children how to become Canadians. In *Victims of Benevolence: Discipline and Death at the Williams Lake Indian Residential School, 1891–1920* (1992), Elizabeth Furniss tells the

stories of two young boys who died as a result of their experiences in a residential school in British Columbia. One ran away and was found dead at the side of a road; the other committed suicide. Residential schools, which were operated by churches, lasted in Canada for about a century. First Nations children were removed from their homes and sent to these schools, where they were taught Christian beliefs and morality and were trained in agriculture, trades, and domestic skills. They were also taught that the beliefs of their elders and their parents were wrong and immoral. The underlying assumption of the residential schools was that First Nations peoples were inferior to Euro-Canadians and that they needed the guidance of Euro-Canadians in order to survive. Through the residential school system, First Nations children became wards of the Canadian state, and corporal punishment was used on children who made the mistake of reverting to their own languages or religious beliefs. When students actively resisted, the resistance was typically interpreted as confirmation that Aboriginal people did not know what was best for them.

EXERCISE 8.3

Creating Citizens of the Nation-State

Students are experts on the role of education in the formation of the nation-state. They are expert because they are most directly involved in the process of creating state citizens, or "patriots." Turn yourself momentarily into an anthropological fieldworker examining the role of education in creating the nation-state. What are some of the activities and programs that contribute to your identifying with your nation-state?

The First Nations' Challenge to the Canadian State

Thus far, we have discussed the nation-state only from the perspective of its power over the people who live within its territory. Tania Li, whose work we also discussed in Chapter 3, argues that development projects carried out by the state are not simply neutral acts of concern by the state for the less fortunate; they are also a way for the state to manage its population. The state typically defines the people it wants to bring under its control as "primitive," "backward," and in need of "proper" housing and education. The critical focus of Li's study was "the ways in which meanings and outcomes are negotiated, albeit within an uneven field of power" (1999b, 297). Li wanted to learn more about "categories that manifestly do not fit, plans that fail, and compliance withheld or withdrawn [that] expose the fragile nature not only of government agencies promoting this or that development program but of the very idea of 'the state' as knower, arbiter, and provider for 'the people' " (1999b, 297).

Li's focus challenges those who would see the state as a source of unquestioned power and its citizens as mindless victims. People who become victims of the state's efforts to create a nation rarely accept their fate quietly. A good example of how marginalized peoples challenge the power of the state is happening right now in Canada.

Canada's history is laced with demonstrations of the power of the colonizers over the colonized. The first step was to define Aboriginal peoples as Other in a way that allowed Europeans to take possession of the land, which they declared "empty" in the sense that no Europeans were living on it. Dara Culhane (1998) points out that from the first moment of contact, the position of the British colonizers was based on an assumed hierarchy wherein the British Crown asserted its will by declaring its sovereignty over First Nations peoples and land and then supported that assertion through armed force whenever necessary.

At first, the French and the British *needed* the Aboriginal peoples; it was they who trapped fur-bearing animals and transported their skins to the trading posts, which brought great wealth to the European traders. Both the British and the French recruited the First Nations peoples to fight their

battles for them as they struggled to determine which European power would control what is now Canada. Because they depended on Aboriginal peoples in these matters (and in others), the Europeans had to show them some respect, at least initially. The first treaties were signed in order to ensure peace and friendship between Aboriginal nations and Europeans. These early friendship treaties were between the French and the Mi'kmaq, Maliseets, Montagnaix-Naskapi, Huron, and Abenake; those same treaties were then transferred to the British under the Treaty of Utrecht in 1713. When Canada became a British colony, the Colonial Office issued the Royal Proclamation of 1763, which declared that Aboriginal lands could be surrendered only through a legal treaty signed by a representative of the Crown and a representative of the appropriate First Nation.

After Confederation, "numbered treaties"— which focused on land far more than on friendship— were signed by the British and various First Nations. The meaning of these treaties is still being debated, which has led to confrontations between First Nations and the Canadian state. (Some First Nations, including the Lubicon Cree, discussed later in this chapter, never had treaties.) Because the treaties were modelled more on agreements that First Nations had negotiated among themselves than on European models of legal contracts, the Aboriginal leaders who signed them did not believe that they were surrendering their land or their rights; they also expected the agreements to be renewed periodically through the exchange of gifts. From the viewpoint of the Colonial Office, the treaties were intended to protect the "primitive" Aboriginal peoples while they were being "civilized." From the viewpoint of the European settlers, the point was to get rid of the "obstacles" that were hindering progress. As the population of European settlers grew and land became more important than people, the Canadian state began to deny the few promises it had made in the treaties.

Increasingly, First Nations have been refusing to surrender any more of their rights. When Clifford

White and David Bob, members of the Saalequn First Nation in Nanaimo, British Columbia, went deer hunting in the spring of 1963, they were arrested and charged under the Game Act (passed by British Columbia in 1960) for hunting out of season. White and Bob argued that they were exercising their Aboriginal right to hunt and fish on unoccupied Crown lands throughout the entire year, a right guaranteed in an 1853 treaty and protected by the Indian Act. The matter went to court and became the first modern Aboriginal rights case in British Columbia. A B.C. court found White and Bob guilty; however, the Supreme Court of Canada overturned that verdict and supported the Aboriginal right to hunt and fish on unoccupied Crown lands. Legal tests for Aboriginal rights continue to come before the courts. Some of the most important have involved the James Bay Cree.

FIGURE 8.1   MAP SHOWING APPROPRIATION OF CREE LAND FOR QUÉBEC GOVERNMENT HYDROELECTRIC PROJECTS

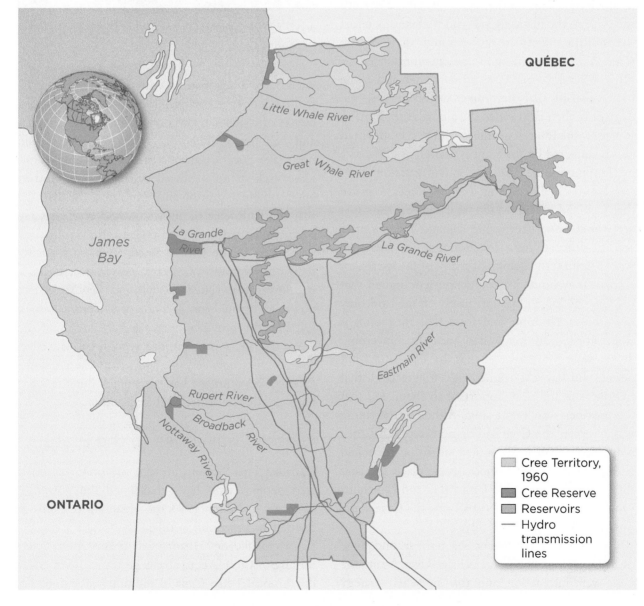

The James Bay Cree have fought for years against the Québec government and developers that want to build dams on Cree land. By the time Harvey Feit began his work among the Cree in the 1960s, railway and road networks had already expanded into Cree territory, and logging and mining had already been established. The position of the Québec government was that the Cree didn't need all their land because hunting was no longer a viable way of making a living and any "rational" person would much rather have a steady job. When the Québec government set out to build a series of hydroelectric dams in the region, it did not involve the Cree in the planning, nor did it make any effort to assess the effects the project might have on the Cree. As soon as the government announced its plans, several young Cree leaders met and came to a consensus that the project would cause severe damage to their land and to the animals they hunted. Joined by the Inuit of northern Québec, who would also be affected by the project, the Cree initiated a legal injunction in 1972 to stop construction.

The burden was now on the Cree to prove that they had a claim to the land and that the project would cause irreversible damage. They argued, among other things, that flooding the wetlands would destroy the habitat of many of the species of animals they hunted. The government argued that the Cree no longer lived primarily off the land; they had houses, clothing, and food that they bought from stores, and many had jobs. In November 1973, Judge Malouf ruled that the Cree and Inuit people did have Aboriginal title to the land, that hunting was still very important to them, and that the province was "trespassing." Although the ruling was appealed, the Cree had demonstrated that they would hold firm in their demand to be consulted before development projects took place on land they deemed theirs. The James Bay and Northern Québec Agreement (JBNQA) gave the Cree some power to back up their resolve.

In 1989, Hydro-Québec began the second phase of its project, on the Great Whale River. Again, the Cree went into action, only this time their strategy

Grand Chief Stan Beardy and Chief Glenn Nolan of Missanabie Cree First Nation with Treaty No. 9 Scroll.

went beyond negotiations with the Québec government. Cree representatives approached the potential buyers of Québec hydro power in the United States and convinced them that Hydro-Québec would not make good economic or environmental sense. Cree spokespeople showed videos of their land to environmental groups and explained the damage that the hydroelectric project would do. The Cree even conducted their own polls to show politicians that voters in the United States favoured reducing their consumption of electric power over importing power from Québec. When the New York State power company cancelled one of its contracts with Québec, the province's premier conceded that the Great Whale River project would be cancelled. The conflict between the James Bay Cree and the Québec government has not ended, but the Cree have greatly strengthened their position.

Global Challenges to the State

Canada's First Nations are not the only marginalized peoples who have challenged the power of the state. In March 1990, the Huaorani of Ecuador formed an organization called the Organizacion de las Nacionalidades Huaorani de la Amazonia Ecuatoriana, or ONHAE, to challenge Texaco, Petroecuador, Unocal, Petro-Canada, and other oil companies that were conducting large-scale exploration projects in the Amazon. When the oil companies built roads into the forest, settlers followed and began clearing the land in preparation for agriculture. Tourists then followed the settlers. One of the first steps taken by ONHAE was to secure title to Huaorani lands. The main problem in this was that the government retained all rights to subsurface minerals. The government immediately divided the Huaorani territory into numbered "blocks" and auctioned them off to the oil companies. Although ONHAE has signed contracts permitting oil exploration, it did secure a Huaorani voice in negotiations.

Then, in January 2000, the Huaorani joined with the powerful Confederation of Indigenous Nations of Ecuador (CONAIE) to block government cutbacks that had resulted in thousands of people losing their jobs and in an increase of 400 percent in the price of water. When the government tried to repress the resistance, CONAIE and other protesters blocked the roads to the capital city, Quito, and seized the Congress, proclaiming a new government. Without support from the urban labour movement, however, the protest came to an end. However, in early July of the same year, joined by labour unions and community organizations, the protesters closed the international airport, the banks, and government offices for two days. It is clear that when Indigenous peoples and urban workers join together, the state must pay attention.

In 1999, the government of Bolivia sold its water system in its second-largest city, Cochabamba, to Bechtel Enterprises, based in San Francisco. The price of water immediately rose by 100 percent, and the "water war" began. Indigenous groups joined with Bolivia's Federation of Workers and began to block the streets and hold public meetings to plan strategy. The protesters set 4 April as the date by which the government had to cancel the sale. The government held out until 10 April, but finally had to admit defeat.

Ronald Niezen (2003) examines the concept of "**Indigenism**," a term he uses to "document the international movement that aspires to promote and protect the rights of the world's first peoples."

The Cree and the Huaorani are part of a much larger phenomenon that includes Indigenous peoples everywhere who are pursuing the right of self-determination through human rights standards. For most Indigenous peoples, this effort includes a rejection of state legal systems but not necessarily a rejection of the law, as the Cree example shows.

QUESTION 8.4: HOW DO ENGAGEMENTS WITH GLOBAL CAPITALISM AFFECT LOCAL CULTURAL IDENTITIES AND LIVELIHOODS?

Globalization is having a variety of cultural impacts, both positive and negative. The transnational flow of ideas, commodities, and images can help groups cultivate a sense of collective identity. Some commentators worry that globalization will challenge and perhaps even destroy the autonomy of nation-states and that it will homogenize the world's cultures. There is a pervasive worry, for example, that companies such as McDonald's and Starbucks will destroy local food cultures. These fears are not completely unfounded; however, many globalization theorists point out that such fears are essentialist and that they fail to take into account the unique ways in which cultures adapt to and transform new ideas.

Nuxalk Identity in an Age of Globalization

The Nuxalk are a First Nations community in the Bella Coola Valley in central British Columbia.

Indigenism
Refers to an international, collaborative movement that aims to protect the rights and livelihoods of Indigenous peoples.

Nuxalk artists are renowned within their communities—and, indeed, internationally—for their intricately carved and painted spirit masks, and for other forms of art, such as totem poles, paintings, jewellery, and murals.

Canadian anthropologist Jennifer Kramer (2007) conducted participant observation and interviews with Nuxalk artists, elders, and art school representatives. She spent time in museums and galleries in Vancouver, talking to art dealers and curators about the display and sale of Nuxalk art to national and international audiences. She also talked to Nuxalk individuals with the goal of understanding how they felt about seeing their art displayed in national and international museums and art galleries, and how they interpreted the increasing commodification of their art.

More and more Nuxalk artists, in an effort to earn money for themselves and for their community, are putting images of spiritual figures on mugs, T-shirts, jewellery, and other tourist commodities. Others are selling their art to art dealers. Kramer set out to understand how the Nuxalk engage with the forces of globalization, which include tourism as well as increasing exposure for their art on the Internet and in the international art market.

When she entered the remote Bella Coola Valley by car for the first time to conduct fieldwork, Kramer was struck by the number of dangerous mountain switchbacks that face motorists. Often inaccessible in winter except via ferry or boat, the Nuxalk have historically been proud of their geographic isolation

Nuxalk mask.

© Seattle Art Museum, 91.1.35, Mask with Humanoid Face, Nuxalk, ca. 1880, alder, red cedar bark, cotton cloth, paint, 14 1/2 x 8 3/4 x 6 in; gift of John H. Hauberg; photographer: Paul Macapia.

from mainstream Canadian society. Throughout her research, Kramer adopted the metaphor of "switchbacks" to explain how her Nuxalk informants felt about the commodification and global flow of Nuxalk art. She argues that most Nuxalk oscillate between feelings of theft and feelings of pride. Many people felt that they were "selling out": that the commodification of their culture and heritage was devaluing local meanings and interpretations of art. Many were opposed to seeing important Nuxalk spiritual figures on mugs or T-shirts and were upset that most Westerners interpreted the images differently. Tourists, for instance, often buy T-shirts as souvenirs and as proof to friends and family that "I was there," or for their aesthetic value. Because tourists and art dealers map new meanings onto Nuxalk art and have different interpretations of its "value," many Nuxalk feel that the global flow of their art has resulted in a loss of cultural heritage.

Yet many of the same Nuxalk individuals that Kramer spoke with who were upset about the potential loss of Nuxalk traditions were also filled with pride at seeing their art displayed in national and international museums, and with the level of interest expressed by tourists. Many felt that the global flow of their art outside their small community was a form of external validation for their culture as a whole. A sense of Nuxalk national identity was being cultivated through the flow and positive international consumption of their art.

Figure Skating, Globalization, and Canadian Identity

The ambiguous cultural effects of globalization can also be explored in the context of elite, high-performance sport. Karen McGarry (2015) conducts fieldwork among national and Olympic-level Canadian figure skaters, coaches, choreographers, journalists, corporate sponsors, and others involved in the production of Canadian figure skating. In Canada, figure skating is the second-ranked sport behind hockey in terms of television sponsorship and spectatorship. One reason for its popularity is that

Canada has a long history of producing top world- and Olympic-level figure skaters. Olympic gold medallists, such as Jamie Salé and David Pelletier, or Tessa Virtue and Scott Moir, the 2010 medalists from Vancouver, have become celebrity figures who derive much of their power as "national symbols" not simply by winning medals, but by circulating their bodies in international arenas of influence.

Canada has historically had an ambivalent relationship with the United States. On the one hand, Canadians live in a world saturated with American popular culture, from television shows to American-based retail outlets, food chains, and other cultural phenomena. Canada's geographical and social proximity to America has resulted in a pervasive fear of American economic and cultural influences, or

Canadian Olympic gold and silver medallists, Tessa Virtue and Scott Moir.

what Kieran Keohane (1997 refers to as a "theft of national enjoyment." In other words, Canadians construct themselves as victims in relation to the United States. Economically, we see this in contemporary debates and concerns relating to American appropriation of natural resources such as oil, water, and lumber, and in concerns over the impact of NAFTA. Yet at the same time, Canadians yearn for the approval of Americans to evaluate their sense of self-worth as a nation on the international stage. So, for instance, Virtue and Moir, like other Canadian celebrities, become a symbol of "Canadianness" not simply because they won an Olympic gold medal, but also because their image has been heavily circulated in the United States: they appear on their own reality show, on talk shows and other television shows, in magazines, and in ice shows and other pop culture venues. The positive international (especially American) reception and consumption of their image has boosted Canadians' national pride. The global flow of commodities (such as Nuxalk art) and bodies (as in athletes) provides countries such as Canada with a means of constructing and promoting a sense of national identity.

Intersections of Nationalism and Economic and Cultural Globalization in Vanuatu

As the Nuxalk example suggests, tourism is an aspect of contemporary life in which the simultaneous impacts of economic and cultural globalization are most obvious. The recent growth of tourism has been staggering. By 2010, around 8 percent of the world's entire workforce was employed in the tourism sector, and this number continues to grow.

Tourism is a relatively new phenomenon. Lofgren (2002, 5) describes it as a mode of consumption "based on the idea of leaving home and work in search of new experiences, pleasures, and leisure." To some extent, our society is obsessed with the need for "experiences." We constantly ask one another, "How was it? How did it feel?" We are also entranced by the thought of being "on holiday," especially as its opposite, being "at work," becomes more burdensome. We often display our experiences as tourists and convey our ability to consume other cultures by buying a souvenir T-shirt. Given what we have discussed earlier in this chapter about

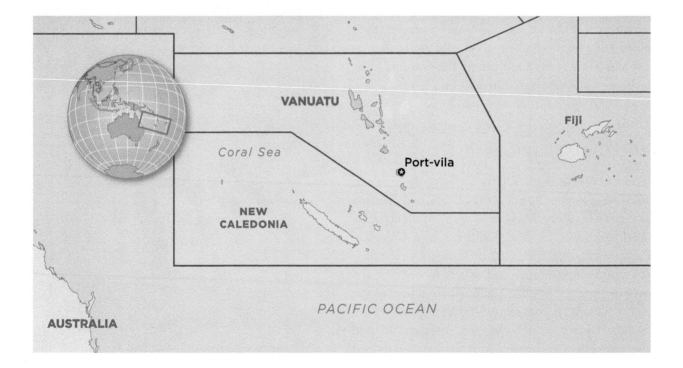

T-shirts as global commodities, the centrality of the T-shirt (and other inexpensive souvenirs) to the tourist experience begins to hint at the fact that tourism is more than simply a leisure practice: it is an important indicator that globalization is linking us all together economically and culturally. By examining the local impacts of the global tourist economy on Vanuatu, we can begin to understand some of the ambiguous, or simultaneously positive and detrimental, effects that global forces are having on local cultures.

Vanuatu, formerly known as the New Hebrides, is an archipelago nation in the southwest Pacific that was jointly ruled by France and Britain from 1906 to 1980. In terms of climate, geography, and culture, Vanuatu has all of the "assets" required of the ideal tropical tourist destination: dense rainforests, swaying palm trees, warm turquoise seas, accessible coral reefs, and so-called "primitive" cultures. The tourism industry in Vanuatu has its roots in the 1960s, which the United Nations declared the "Decade of Development." During that decade, Vanuatu's first international resort, the French-owned Hotel Le Lagon, was built on a former plantation. Between 1970 and 1990, tourism arrivals by air grew from 5,000 to 25,000 per year (Douglas 1996, 216); today, around 7,000 tourists arrive by air each month, and every month another 15,000 tourists arrive by cruise ship for day visits. Tourism is the key economic sector in Vanuatu, accounting for 40 percent of the gross domestic product (GDP).

In its efforts to entice foreigners to visit, the Vanuatu Tourism Office has employed various slogans that draw from its imagined status as a land of idyllic, simple pleasures and the easy life: "The Untouched Paradise," "The Friendly Face of the Pacific," "Vanuatu: Discover What Matters." At the same time, many of the attractions and activities geared toward tourists highlight the "darker" aspects of traditional culture, such as cannibalism, tribal warfare, and sorcery. Tourists flow into Vanuatu with particular expectations about the local people and their culture. At the same time, *ni-Vanuatu* (the local name for Indigenous citizens) have

their own expectations about what tourists are like, as well as their own sense of national identity, which has been forged at least, in part, by encounters with foreigners.

If, as a tourist in Vanuatu, you want to purchase an "Untouched Paradise" T-shirt as a souvenir, you will likely do so at one of the market stalls on the seafront in Port Vila, the national capital. You will find a vast array of cheap T-shirts (made in and imported from China), but few if any of the women working in the stalls will be wearing T-shirts. Rather, they will being wearing what they refer to as the "island dress," a long, loose, floral-patterned dress—similar to the Hawai'ian *mumu*—which they consider to be both their "national dress" and the most culturally appropriate and modest clothing for women. Maggie Cummings conducted fieldwork in Vanuatu on gender, dress, and national identity and found that women, especially single, childless young women living in the capital, embody a range of ambivalent and contradictory sentiments about national pride, the commodification of culture for tourist consumption, and the global flow of goods and fashions. The island dress was first introduced in Vanuatu during the colonial period by British missionaries, who were scandalized by the scantily clad natives they were trying to convert. Wearing an island dress became a visible sign of one's conversion to Christianity—and to British gender norms, according to which women wore dresses while men wore the pants, both literally and figuratively. Most ni-Vanuatu today are devout Christians, and on achieving independence in 1980, ni-Vanuatu women took up the island dress with pride as a symbol of their uniquely Melanesian Christianity and of their difference from white foreigners. In this context, it makes sense that the island dress, as a symbol of cultural authenticity, would be the appropriate choice for women selling souvenirs to tourists, for whom consuming cultural authenticity is one of the most significant parts of the trip.

The young women Cummings worked with acknowledged the symbolic significance of the island dress (and the importance of wearing it in

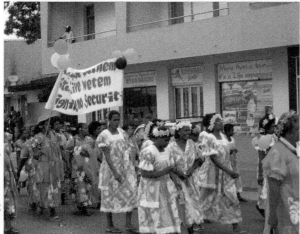

© Maggie Cummings

The island dress is considered the "traditional" dress for women in Vanuatu, but many younger women prefer to wear shorts and T-shirts.

tourist encounters), but they were also drawn to the kinds of clothing they saw tourist women wearing—T-shirts and shorts rather than skirts. Young women who chose to wear shorts, however, were often chastised and even fined by their elders, pastors, and chiefs for trying to look "like foreigners." Furthermore, chiefs often accused young women of turning their backs on tradition and destroying *kastom* (traditional culture) when they chose to wear even long, modest surf shorts. They were too young to remember the struggle for independence.

Cummings (2008) highlights the ironies of ni-Vanuatu national identity in the context of increasing globalization. As Vanuatu attempts to increase visits (and revenues) from tourism, more and more ni-Vanuatu are moving to the capital, leaving behind—at least temporarily—their traditional subsistence horticultural livelihoods in search of wage labour in the tourist economy. Yet within the tourist industry, they must perform "ni-Vanuatu-ness" that is perceived as culturally authentic, which includes wearing the island dress and sometimes grass skirts. However, as ni-Vanuatu women admire and appropriate tourist fashions for themselves (and the availability of cheap imports from China is what makes this possible), they are less and less inclined to wear the "authentic" island dress in their daily lives. One of Cummings's informants

neatly summarized the ironies of trying to dress authentically in contemporary Vanuatu: ironies that have their origin in the uneven intercultural encounters in the context of decades of global contact and movement:

> *When the missionaries came, they told us we were practically naked when we were wearing grass skirts, and that we had no shame. So we put on the island dress to show that we were good Christians, and now we wear it to show our respect for God and for our kastom. Now all these tourists, whose grandparents told our grandparents to cover up, they come and they flaunt themselves, half-naked on the beach in their bikinis and shorts. Meanwhile, we young women are told, now by our own elders, we have to cover up in the island dress to show our national pride!*

Cultural policy in Vanuatu (created, in part, by a former head of the Vanuatu Cultural Centre, Ralph Reganvanu, a ni-Vanuatu with a degree in anthropology) demands that all foreign anthropologists create a product or provide a service that will benefit the nation. Cummings therefore worked with local fieldworkers (who were trained in ethnographic research skills by the Vanuatu Cultural Centre) to produce a video for local audiences about the dress conundrum. One intention of the video was to bridge the gap between chiefs and young women: a gap that seemed to be widening in the face of increased tourism and globalization.

The Vanuatu Cultural Centre has created many important and innovative programs and policies based on ethnographic insights and collaborations with anthropologists (and historians and archaeologists). For instance, the Vanuatu National History Curriculum Project led to the publication of the three-volume *Histri Blong Yumi Long Vanuatu* (Lightner and Naupa, *Our History*, 2005), which aimed to provide a core high-school history curriculum. One effect of the curriculum project, and related projects and policies, has been to ensure that young ni-Vanuatu are able to participate meaningfully in and contribute to the ongoing vibrancy and viability of *kastom* in a global world.

Globalization and Cultural Diversity

With the increasing emphasis upon market-driven economies and neoliberalism, what is to be become of societies that seek to retain their traditional way of life? Modern societies, as we shall see, have not been kind to groups that have retained or tried to retain a way of life that is thousands of years old. Societies such as the Ju/'hoansi and the Inuit of the Canadian Arctic and Alaska have not always fared well when contacted by more complex civilizations. Living in small, scattered groups with little need for complex political structures, Western technologies, or market-driven economic systems, these societies have often been no match for the well-armed, organized, acquisitive people and governments that have coveted their land or labour.

The vulnerability of small-scale cultures has increased in recent years, largely because of globalization and the expansion into virtually all areas of the world of a culture that assumes that economic trade is the source of all well-being. For example,

in their efforts to pay off debts accumulated over the past three decades, countries have been forced to export goods and commodities to gain cash to repay these debts. Support for small-scale agriculturists or peasant farmers has been reduced as a result.

When Mexico signed the North American Free Trade Agreement (NAFTA) with the United States and Canada, it precipitated a revolt in the State of Chiapas by peasant farmers (the Zapatistas) whose livelihood would be destroyed by the agreement. NAFTA's terms compelled Mexico to allow large-scale corn farmers in the United States to sell their product in Mexico at a price lower than what the peasants could meet. Small Mexican farmers might still have been able to compete except that the Mexican government nullified a portion of the national constitution that gave peasant farmers access to land on which to grow their crops. Instead, Mexico's large-scale cattle ranchers got more land to produce beef to sell to American consumers. As anthropologist James D. Nations pointed out, peasant farmers in Chiapas were faced with a choice of moving to a city to sell Popsicles from a pushcart, working for a cattleman punching cows, or rebelling against a situation that seemed to have them trapped.

Often, the same economic forces that are undermining traditional cultures are promoting environmental destruction. A case in point is that of the Guaraní of Paraguay. There are about 15,000 Guaraní. For centuries their lives centred on the rainforest, where they gathered tree crops, grew food crops, raised animals, and hunted and fished. The first European governor of the area described them, in 1541, as "the richest people of all the land and province both for agriculture and stock raising." They quickly entered into trade with Europeans, mostly by gathering and selling a caffeine-bearing plant called "yerba mate." These trade arrangements did not greatly affect Guaraní life, since they would gather and sell yerba mate only when they needed some Western trade item, such as a metal pot. Consequently, Guaraní culture was able to sustain itself and thrive. Just as important, the Guaraní exploited the rainforest in sustainable ways by adapting to it rather than trying to change it. Then in the 1970s, due largely to international trade arrangements, both the Guaraní and the rainforest began to decline.

In the 1970s, Paraguay, like most developing countries, enjoyed an economic boom fuelled largely by loans from the World Bank and other international lenders. Increasing production of crops such as soy, wheat, and cotton also fuelled the boom. The "economic miracle" was accomplished by bringing more land under cultivation; this, however, involved cutting down forests, selling the timber, and converting the cleared land into farmland or pasture. The rate of rainforest destruction accelerated rapidly. Between 1970 and 1976, Paraguayan rainforests were reduced from 6.8 to 4.2 million hectares. The country had cleared half its rainforest by 1984, and an additional 5 percent a year is being cut. At this rate, the entire Paraguayan rainforest will be gone by 2020.

Guaraní culture has been one more casualty of global capitalism and "economic development." This group's livelihood has been destroyed, and new roads through the rainforest have brought with them thousands of new settlers eager to stake claims to some portion of the forest, clear it of trees, and grow cash crops. Unfortunately, rainforest soil quickly loses its nutrients once the forest canopy that protects it is destroyed. Furthermore, all the animals and plants that the Guaraní once depended on have been decimated. As a result, the Guaraní have been displaced to squatter settlements in towns and cities or along the roads that have been built through the rainforests. The wages they can make working for farmers or in other odd jobs are inadequate to support families; illness and disease have increased; and suicide rates between 2000 and 2013 have more than tripled over the previous ten years, making the suicide rate among the Guaraní 12 times the Brazilian national average (http://www.nytimes.com/2015/01/04/opinion/sunday/suicides-spread-through-a-brazilian-tribe.html?_r=0).

Finding Hope in the Face of Cultural Devastation

The experiences of peoples such as the Guaraní raise an important question: What does it mean to experience cultural devastation? This question is important, not only for what it tells us about the experiences of other people, but also for how we understand what culture is and what culture change can mean. Clearly, all cultures are vulnerable. People's views of the world, what they count as important, what they value, and what the good life means to them are all subject to sudden upheaval.

One of the best examples is what has happened to Indigenous peoples of the Americas. When Columbus arrived in the "New World," there were hundreds of thriving societies. These were quickly devastated by European diseases, which wiped out nearly 90 percent of the population. That devastation continued well into the 19th century as the remnants of these peoples struggled to adapt to the westward expansion of settlers.

Note that adaptation is not the only possibility, nor is what counts as "adaptation" particularly straightforward, especially if we recognize that it has generally been the colonizers who have defined the terms of engagement. Dawn Martin-Hill's work with the Lubicon Cree of Alberta provides an instructive example of what it means to go from being an independent hunting society to one struggling for recognition, self-determination, and cultural survival within the Canadian nation-state.

For centuries, the Lubicon Cree have lived, hunted, and trapped within a 110 kilometre radius of Lubicon Lake in northern Alberta. Because of their relative isolation, the Lubicon avoided much contact with white settlers until the end of the 19th century. Then, in 1899, Lubicon elders, wanting to secure their territory against the encroachment they saw happening elsewhere, approached the Canadian government about signing a treaty. The treaty, however, failed to materialize over the following years. In 1939, the Lubicon were finally recognized as a band under federal law, and the groundwork was laid for establishing a reserve of 65 square kilometres. But the Second World War created a shortage of surveyors, and the required survey never happened. The Lubicon population was decimated by illness in the first half of the 20th century, and in 1942, many remaining Lubicon were removed from the band registry by the Department of Indian Affairs. As a result of that, they were deemed too small a population to warrant a treaty or a reserve (Martin-Hill 2004, 315–16).

The Lubicon elders decided that their young people should learn English in order to pursue their land claims. One of these youth, Walter Whitehead, was elected chief in the early 1970s and began to lay the legal groundwork for the land claim. Unfortunately, he was doing so at the same time that oil exploration was beginning in northern Alberta. Since then, the Lubicon Cree have been embroiled in an unsettled land claim. Meanwhile, oil and gas corporations have been extracting resources from land that the Lubicon have never legally relinquished, all the while contaminating it. In their struggle for recognition, the Lubicon must walk a fine line between trying to work within the Canadian legal system on the one hand and maintaining their own indigenous knowledge on the other.

As Martin-Hill points out, "from the West's perspective, Indigenous peoples [like the Lubicon] are always standing in the way of progress, development, and civilization" (2008, 153). She also points to the Lubicon's determination to reach a fair deal with the Canadian government; their resolve "is rooted in their firm belief that good always overcomes bad" (158). They are using their own indigenous knowledge to their advantage (as best they can under the circumstances), "restructuring their damaged traditional system by recreating a modern anti-colonial community" (159). Martin-Hill recounts a conversation, excerpted here, with Albert Laboucon, a Lubicon elder, who explained the transformative possibilities of such a community:

> I met Albert Laboucon [a Cree-speaker in his 70s] during my second trip to Little Buffalo in December 1989 … I asked Albert to tell me about himself, and for his thoughts on the land claim. His answers were short and often direct.
>
> "I was raised in the bush, trapping, hunting, a hard life but a good one. There has been much change. No more animals, no wildlife, everything is disappearing, our ways are. They came in the road and destroyed everything in their path. They cut right through trap lines, right through

everything. Everything is dirty, water and animals are not so clean. I want the children, the grandchildren, to have something, that's why I stay with it. I think they are trying to wipe us out. I never thought that really before—to wipe us out … just to get us out of the way. They are greedy, greed like we don't know. There is nothing for me, just doing this for my grandchildren now … This has been going on a long time, since I was young. I thought it would all be okay; we would get our reserve, no big deal. They seem to want to wipe us out instead, don't know why. I think they have money, no word for the money they have. We don't want much … A lot they do doesn't make sense, destroying the land, water, air. No matter, they think they're above all this—they're not. They're needing air, water, food, and they can't see what will happen to us will happen to them too. They don't think about their children either. What will these young ones have to drink if all the water no good? Maybe if we keep hollering they will hear us, if we keep making enough noise. It's good that other Indians like you [Martin-Hill is Mohawk] come here and help. We need to help one another the way the Creator intended. I feel better when there are other Indians helping."

I asked Albert to tell me what he wanted me to take back to my people, what to tell them from him. He sat quietly for a long time and then said in Cree, "We should put our voices together, our drum, it will be heard across the country." (117–18)[1]

Albert Laboucon's drumming inspired the Drum Beat Conference, held by McMaster University and the Six Nations community in 1989, which hosted indigenous people from all over North America and was aimed at raising awareness of First Nations issues. The conference laid the groundwork for the creation of the Indigenous Studies program at McMaster.

The dilemma of peasant farmers, the Guaraní, and the Lubicon Cree is shared by thousands of other societies and groups around the world. Equally involved in the dilemma are the societies that are responsible for driving small-scale societies to the edge of cultural devastation or forcing them to experience development through its dark side of poverty, disease, and forced labour. By systematically destroying small-scale societies, we may be eliminating systems of meaning that hold solutions to compelling world problems, such as environmental destruction, intergroup and intragroup conflict, poverty, and sickness.

---

[1]Source: From *The Lubicon Lake Nation: Indigenous Knowledge and Power,* by Dawn Martin-Hill, © University of Toronto Press, 2008. pp. 117–118. Reprinted with permission of the publisher.

CONCLUSIONS

How might we use an anthropological perspective on neoliberalism, economic globalization, and the nation-state outside the academy? What might we gain by taking an anthropological perspective on neoliberalism, globalization, and the nation-state? How can this perspective be put to use in the development of public policy? As we saw in section 8.4, one important contribution that anthropologists have made to globalization studies has been to extend the ethnographic focus not just to the economic impacts of globalization but also to the cultural ones, both negative and positive. As a cultural force, globalization is far from uniformly negative and homogenizing; in fact, transnational flows of ideas, images, and commodities often *activate* and *animate* new local cultural meanings and practices, even as they often devastate traditional modes of livelihood. Indeed, people often actively engage with the forces of globalization in an effort to revitalize and reconstruct a sense of collective identity. As anthropologists, we learn and experience firsthand how culture is both dynamic and shifting in the process.

As we saw in section 8.2, nation-states exist, in part, to regulate and promote the growth of national economies. In fact, economic growth is clearly the primary directive of market-based industrial societies such as the United States, Canada, and Japan. We measure our economic progress by the growth of GDP, or the sum total of all goods and services transactions in a country in a given year. Failure to maintain GDP can have dire economic, social, and political consequences, including job losses, bank failures, and general political chaos.

So, governments devise economic policies to achieve economic growth. Often forgotten, however, is that market activities have effects that economic policy makers do not consider. We noted some of these effects in section 8.2, when we examined the real cost of a Snickers bar and the externalities relating to the cost of sugar, which include underpaid labour and environmental pollution. Yet policy planners rarely consider such externalities. As we saw with the effects of NAFTA on the Canadian garment industry, the local and everyday effects of international trade agreements are unlikely to be taken into account during the drafting of the agreements.

Sometimes, organized forms of resistance to neoliberalism and globalization emerge. As with the Toronto G-20 protests discussed in the chapter opening, many protests are portrayed negatively in the media. In the case of the G-20 summit, the protesters were homogenized and represented as young, rebellious, and violent. Images of smashed windows on storefronts and masked protesters became the norm within mainstream media outlets. In many ways, such representations overshadow the politics behind acts of resistance. One goal of the G-20 protesters, for example, was to draw attention to the gaps between economic policies, market externalities, and public policies.

A major contribution of anthropology in the area of public policy and planning is that it makes people aware of market externalities and of the need to craft policies to eliminate or at least minimize those externalities. As we saw in section 8.3, challenges to the state, both from within and outside, are always possible, and an anthropological perspective can strengthen those challenges.

CRITICAL THINKING QUESTIONS

1. In section 8.1, we noted how neoliberalism manifests itself in the context of various nation-states. Think of three ways in which neoliberalism affects Canadian politics, economics, or social life differently than in the United States.
2. From a student's perspective, can you think of examples of how principles of neoliberalism affect your education? How does it operate on your university or college campus?
3. Sections 8.3 and 8.4 include examples of the ways in which First Nations peoples have resisted state control. Think of two other cultural or ethnic groups in Canada that have resisted the state's homogenizing tendencies. How do they seek to define their sense of identity against that of "mainstream" Canadian society?

KEY TERMS:

economic systems   (p. 224)
free trade   (p. 225)
globalization   (p. 222)
Indigenism   (p. 241)
market externalities   (p. 228)
multiculturalism   (p. 236)
nation   (p. 227)
nation–state   (p. 226)
neoliberalism   (p. 225)
transnational   (p. 230)

CHAPTER 9

RESOLVING CONFLICT

© Bilderbuch/Design Pics/Thinkstock

Canadian memorials to fallen soldiers, such as the Canadian National War Memorial, often evoke the sentiment "Lest We Forget." In the second half of the 20th century, Canada saw itself as a peacekeeper nation, striving to prevent or diminish violent conflict. However, as Richler notes in the chapter epigraph on the next page, Canada more recently became a "warrior nation," especially since it assumed a combat role in Afghanistan. How do Canadians make sense of our ambivalent relationship with war?

Often it is illuminating to see how history puts on different disguises even as the underlying habits of a place are fundamentally unaltered. This is to say either that Canada today is a "warrior nation"—that the peacekeeping version of Canada was a fifty-year aberration and a public that believes otherwise genuinely has ignored Canada's long military history—or that the Canada with an innate disposition toward "soft power," "making a difference" and the sort of peacekeeping work that is now so disparaged is the underlying constant and the "warrior nation" is the fiction.

Noah Richler, What We Talk About When We Talk About War (2012)

Problem 9

How do societies give meaning to and justify various forms of conflict resolution, both peaceful and violent?

INTRODUCTION

Justifying Violence and Imagining Peace

We often tend to think of violence and peace as conditions of existence that are universally understood, transparent, and commonsense: that violence is an innate human tendency and that peace is simply the absence of violence. It may be more useful, as anthropologists, to focus on peace-making and violence as two sides of the coin of conflict resolution. As with all human behaviours and experience, violence and peace are processes to which we collectively assign meaning within particular contexts. For instance, as Noah Richler points out in the epigraph to this chapter, when Canada sends its soldiers into conflict zones, their role can be understood and has been understood as peacekeeping or as war-making, depending on the dominant narratives of national identity at the time.

Throughout this text, we have taken a problem-based approach to understanding humanity, and many of the problems we have explored may give rise to conflicts, perhaps over resources, over identity, over inequality or injustice, and these conflicts demand some sort of resolution. In some cases, conflict results in collective violence: think, for instance, of the Cherokee Removal discussed in Chapter 3 or Sanday's analysis of fraternity gang rape in Chapter 7. In other cases, more peaceful forms of conflict resolution are favoured, as among the

Ju/'hoansi or the Hutterites, or in Wovoka's Ghost Dance revitalization movement, discussed in Chapter 4. In order to understand why humans choose one form of conflict resolution or another, it is necessary to think about how humans make sense of and justify violence and peace.

Violence, "a category in between peaceful disputing, and major planned warfare and fighting" (Strathern and Stewart 2002, 1), may seem to be an intrinsic feature of human societies. It is, in fact, difficult to find societies that do not sanction violence for one reason or another. But why is collective violence nearly universally sanctioned? Some suggest that human beings have an innate instinct toward aggression and that the roots of war and collective violence lie somewhere in the biological mechanisms that animals and humans have in common. Violent conflict is regarded, in this view, as a part of human nature. Others reject this explanation as simplistic; collective violence, they say, is, above all, a cultural construction whose roots lie in the human mind, not in the genes.

Moreover, some anthropologists argue that there is compelling ethnographic and historical evidence that "humans have a solid capacity for getting along with each other peacefully, preventing physical aggression, limiting the scope and spread of violence, and restoring peace following aggression" (Fry 2007, 21). We tend to overlook and underappreciate this capacity precisely because violence is exceptional and aberrant. It commands our scrutiny, attention, and concern. Put another way, "the view that [violence and] warfare is inevitable because it is an immutable part of human nature is also a cultural convention masquerading as fact" (Sahlins 2008, quoted in Lohmann 2014, 255). The ethnographic realities of conflict resolution suggest that "neither fully peaceful nor fully violent outcomes are actually the norm" (Strathern and Stewart 2011, ix); as anthropologists, we must endeavour to understand the factors that lead to or favour one form of conflict resolution over the other in different circumstances.

The fact that human beings construct systems of meaning to justify violent conflict and to distance themselves from its consequences suggests that it has little to do with a natural aggressive impulse. Acts of collective violence are rationalized as purposeful, noble, or inevitable, not as evidence of wanton cruelty. The problem is to discover how societies construct meanings for violent conflict that mask its consequences and that convince people it is right and proper.

It is equally important to understand what peace is and how it is created and maintained. As anthropologist Brian Ferguson (2008, 46–47) has argued, "peace is more than the absence of war." Rather, peace is an active social process, one that must be first imagined and then acted upon. Lohmann (2014) defines peace, therefore, as

A group activity, carried on by members of one community toward members of another community, in which the primary purpose is to maintain mutual benefit by successfully deploying means for enhancing political relations and preventing violence, by either directing contacts with goodwill or avoiding one another with an attitude of peace. (259)

Just as violence must be justified, peace must be imagined and maintained; both are deeply social and political processes.

To make sense of these issues, the first question to be addressed is how societies create a bias in favour of collective violence. In other words, what kinds of meanings are constructed to encourage people to commit violence against others? Then, if there are societies without collective violence, how do they create a bias against it? How do they create peace? If violent conflict is not natural and inevitable but culturally constructed, it may be possible to learn from societies in which there is little if any violence. This focus raises the following question: are there significant social, economic, or political differences between violent and peaceful societies? Beyond that, what is the relationship between violence and the nation-state? Since collective violence is sanctioned in North American societies, it is instructive to ask how we have created a bias toward violent conflict and constructed meanings that allow us to contemplate, plan for, and pursue the destruction of millions of people in other nations. We will go on to explore the potential pitfalls and possible insights to be gained by conducting participant observation of, and during, violent conflicts. Finally, as a conclusion to the chapter and to the text as a whole, we will think about the roles that anthropologists can play in promoting peaceful forms of conflict resolution to the kinds of problems we have discussed throughout this book.

QUESTIONS

9.1 How do societies create a bias in favour of collective violence?

9.2 How do societies create a bias in favour of peaceful conflict resolution?

9.3 What are the economic, political, and social differences between peaceful and violent societies?

9.4 What is the relationship between violence and the nation-state?

9.5 How is it possible to justify the creation of weapons of mass destruction?

9.6 How do anthropologists do fieldwork in the midst of violent conflict?

QUESTION 9.1: HOW DO SOCIETIES CREATE A BIAS IN FAVOUR OF COLLECTIVE VIOLENCE?

Horses, Rank, and Warfare Among the Kiowa

One way societies create a bias toward collective violence is by rewarding it. Among the Native Americans of the western plains, for example, raiding other groups for horses was a means by which a man gained status. Horses symbolized wealth, and in many groups a man's importance was measured by the number of horses he owned and gave to others as gifts.

Horses are not indigenous to North America; they were brought to the continent by the Spaniards in the 1500s. Native American groups such as the Kiowa captured some horses and acquired others in trade with the Spaniards. The Kiowa also obtained horses by attacking other Native American groups with horse-raiding parties of as many as 30 men. The objective of these raids was to secure as many of the enemy's horses as possible and, as well, to demonstrate bravery. Among the Kiowa, rank was determined in two ways: by the number of horses a man possessed and by the honours accruing to him in warfare.

Kiowa society was divided into four ranks, or grades. In the top rank were *ongop*, men who were generous, who held considerable wealth, and, most important, who had distinguished themselves in war. In the second rank were *ondeigupa*, men who had property (especially horses), who were generous, but who had not yet distinguished themselves in war. The lower ranks of Kiowa society were occupied by *keen* or *dupom*, people who were poor, propertyless, or helpless.

To rise in status, a young Kiowa male needed to acquire a horse. Often, he began his climb through the ranks of Kiowa society by borrowing a horse from a kinsperson to go on a raid, hoping to repay the loan with another horse he had captured. With a horse of his own, he could participate in more raids, gradually obtaining enough horses to rise to the rank of *ondeigupa*, or, as the Kiowa put it, "rise out of the bush of *keen*." Several years of raiding might bring him 20 or 30 horses, at which point people would begin speaking of him with respect.

To rise to the top rank of *ongop*, however, also required the accumulation of honours won in war. The Kiowa had a very elaborate system of battle honours divided into three groups of brave deeds, with group I being the most honoured (see Table 9.1). Counting first coup, for example, involved

TABLE 9.1   KIOWA RANKING AND HONOURS

GROUP I	GROUP II	GROUP III
Counting first coup	Killing an enemy	Dismounting, turning horse loose, and fighting on foot
Charging an enemy while the party is in retreat, thus covering the retreat	Counting second coup	Counting third and fourth coup
Rescuing a comrade while the party is retreating before the enemy	Receiving a wound in hand-to-hand combat	Serving as raid leader
Charging the leading man of the enemy alone before the parties have met	Success in stealing horses	Efficiency in war camp life

Information from Bernard Mishkin, Rank and Warfare Among the Plains Indians (Seattle: University of Washington Press, 1940)

charging the enemy alone and striking one of them with a stick. The number of feathers a man wore in his headdress was a measure of his heroic exploits.

Anthropologist Bernard Mishkin (1940) estimates that about 10 percent of the men would rise to the top rank of Kiowa society by obtaining a significant number of horses and accumulating sufficient battle honours. In this way, the Kiowa rewarded aggressive behaviour and bravery in battle.

Good Hosts Among the Yanomamö

Another way societies create a bias in favour of collective violence is by making it a necessary means for protecting valuable resources. As we discussed in Chapter 2, a classic (but contentious) example is the Yanomamö of Venezuela. The Yanomamö live in villages of 40 to 250 people and practise slash-and-burn (swidden) agriculture, living primarily on the crops they grow in their gardens.

Warfare between villages is endemic among the Yanomamö. Anthropologist Napoleon Chagnon, who conducted fieldwork with them from the mid-1960s until the latter half of the 1990s, reports that one village of 200 people was attacked 25 times and that ten people were killed during a 15-month period, representing a loss of 5 percent of the village population. He estimates that 20 to 25 percent of all male deaths are the result of warfare.

For the Yanomamö, women and children are valuable resources. The men believe that to protect themselves and their resources, they must be fierce, and raiding another village is one way for them to demonstrate their ferocity. Raids may be conducted to avenge the death of a village member at the hands of an enemy village or as the result of an act of sorcery by an enemy. Raids may also be made to capture women or children. Violence can take the form of inviting members of another village to a feast and—usually with the aid of allies from another village—killing the guests and abducting their women. Raiding by other villages forces them to move fairly frequently, and sometimes they take refuge from their enemies in the villages of their allies. This practice is risky, however, because host villages generally expect sexual access to the wives of their guests or expect unmarried female guests to marry men of their village. These expectations often lead to open hostilities between hosts and guests.

people were created from the blood of the moon, which had been shot with an arrow by beings who believed that their children's souls were being devoured by the moon. The first Yanomamö born of the blood of the moon were exceptionally fierce and waged constant war on one another.

The Yanomamö also socialize male children to be aggressive and hostile. Boys are teased to strike tormentors and to bully girls. At one gathering of two villages attended by Chagnon, men were to satisfy their grievances against each other with a chest-pounding duel. Prior to the duel the men gathered all the boys between the ages of 8 and 15 and forced them to fight one another. At first, says Chagnon, the boys were reluctant and tried to run away, but their parents dragged them back and insisted that they hit each other. At the first blows the boys cried, but as the fight progressed, fear became rage, and they ended up pounding each other while they screamed and rolled in the dirt, to the cheers and admiration of their fathers.

Constructing Religious Justifications for Violence

Another way to justify violence is by framing it as a cosmic struggle between good and evil. Most modern religions contain sacred texts describing violent confrontations between the forces of good and the forces of evil. The Book of Revelation, with its description of the forces of Satan and the ultimate battle between good and evil, provides one of the most powerful (and most violent) metaphors of war and redemption in Western literature. As Elaine Pagels (1995) notes, the characterization of one's enemies as "Satanic" and of oneself as God's people has long been a formula for justifying hatred and mass slaughter.

So, it should not be surprising that people use religious rhetoric to justify violent acts, but more than that is often at work. When devout adherents to Christianity, Judaism, Sikhism, Buddhism, or Islam commit violent acts in the name of God or some spiritual mission, they are often responding

Expressions of ferocity may be directed among village members, as well. For example, men often vent anger and demonstrate their ferocity by beating their wives. A man who accuses another of cowardice or of making excessive demands for goods or women may challenge his opponent to a chest-pounding duel in which they take turns hitting each other in the chest as hard as they can. The duel generally ends when one of the contestants is too injured to continue. Fights with clubs are another form of settling disputes between men, although these generally result in free-for-alls, which can be deadly.

In this environment, where each man strives to acquire women from others, it is necessary to adopt an antagonistic stance toward others. This stance, in turn, encourages the development of what the Yanomamö call *waiteri* (ferocity). The *waiteri* complex, as Chagnon calls it, is evidenced in ways other than direct conflict. The Yanomamö express it in their origin myth, which tells how the original to social, political, or economic grievances, as well. Osama bin Laden sought the establishment of an Islamic caliphate, or form of government, but he was also protesting the Israeli occupation of Palestinian territories, the stationing of U.S. troops in Saudi Arabia, and the American support for oppressive governments in the Middle East. Of course, violence is not the only response to cosmic conflict and social grievances that the devout of any religion might be expected to make. Indeed, many adherents vehemently protest against such violence and advocate for peace in the name of their respective religions. For example, the Hutterites, as discussed in Chapter 7, reject violence and war as part of their interpretation and practice of Christianity.

Nonetheless, all religions have their violent militants. On 20 March 1995, five members of the Aum Shinrikyo movement, all of whom had scientific training, walked into the Tokyo subway and, with sharpened umbrellas, punctured plastic bags filled with deadly sarin gas, killing 12 people and poisoning more than 5,500. The group's members explained to Mark Juergensmeyer (2003) that Aum Shinrikyo represented for them a critique of Japanese religion and the "hierarchical" Japanese social system. The movement was founded by Shoko Asahara based on the idea that there would occur a world catastrophe—a Third World War or "Armageddon"—in which the forces of good and evil would confront each other and members of Aum Shinrikyo would survive.

Asahara justified his acts by reference to Tibetan Buddhism and the concept of *phoa*. Instead of focusing on the effect that killing has on the killer's moral purity, this doctrine focuses on the one who is killed and on the merit that comes after death. According to Asahara, if a person is a scoundrel or is part of an evil social system, he or she is accumulating negative karmic debt. Killing such people represents a mercy killing that allows their souls to move to a higher plane than if they continued to exist in sin.

Juergensmeyer (2003) asks under what conditions people are likely to use religious justifications

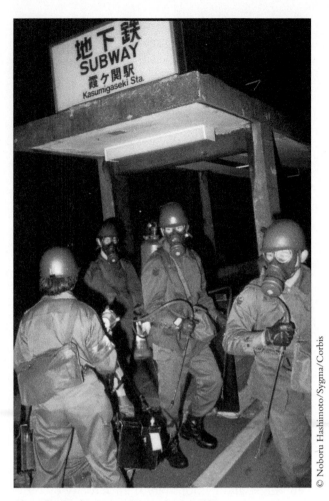

Aftermath of sarin attack on Tokyo subway in 1995.

for violence. He suggests that by locating a struggle on a cosmic scale, aggressors elevate its importance beyond local concerns and, instead, invoke legendary battles between good and evil. Osama bin Laden justified violence by projecting the struggle as one between the forces of Islam and those trying to destroy it. The rhetoric of wars of good versus evil is even part of the U.S. political mainstream, with terms such as "axis of evil."

There is real power, suggests Juergensmeyer, in elevating a political conflict to a cosmic war. To live in a state of war, he writes,

> is to live in a world in which individuals know who they are, why they have suffered, by whose hand they have been humiliated, and at what

expense they have persevered. The concept of war provides cosmology, history, and eschatology and offers the reins of political control. Perhaps most important, it holds out the hope of victory and the means to achieve it. In the images of cosmic war this victorious triumph is a grand moment of social and personal transformation, transcending all worldly limitations. One does not easily abandon such expectations. To be without such images of war is almost to be without hope itself. (2003, 158)

EXERCISE 9.1

Examples of group-sanctioned conflict are readily available in reports in newspapers and on the Internet. To examine the justifications for such conflict, follow a daily newspaper or news website for a couple of days and document the instances you find of group-sanctioned violence and the reasons attributed for it. What options, if any, are discussed or proposed for peaceful resolutions to such conflicts?

QUESTION 9.2: HOW DO SOCIETIES CREATE A BIAS IN FAVOUR OF PEACEFUL CONFLICT RESOLUTION?

Anthropologist Thomas Gregor (1990) suggests that since war is so widespread in human societies, the task of the social scientist is not so much to explain war as to explain peace. Peaceful societies, he says, are difficult to find. By peaceful, he means a society that is not involved in internal collective violence and in which there is little interpersonal violence. A peaceful society has no special roles for warriors and places a positive value on nonaggressive behaviour

and the peaceful resolution of conflict. Societies that have been characterized as relatively peaceful include the Ju/'hoansi, the Semai of Malaysia, and the Xinguano of the Amazon.

Characteristics of Peaceful Societies

Peaceful societies avoid conflicts over material resources through a strong emphasis on sharing and cooperation. It is understood that everyone in the group has a legitimate claim to what the group possesses. Among the Ju/'hoansi, the person whose arrow kills an animal is considered to be the owner of the game, but he is obligated to distribute it. The Ju/'hoansi will share arrows with the understanding that if they kill an animal with an arrow given to them by someone else, they will give the owner the game to distribute. This practice also works to spread out the responsibility for meat sharing and the glory (and perhaps the hostility) that accompanies meat distribution.

The Semai of Malaysia are known for their nonaggressiveness and avoidance of physical conflict. The approximately 15,000 Semai live in hamlets of fewer than 100 people each. Understanding Semai nonviolence, says anthropologist Clayton Robarchek (1990), requires understanding the Semai notion of *pehunan*, a state of being in which a person is unsatisfied in regard to some need or want, such as food or sex. The Semai believe that to refuse a request and deny a person a need intensifies the danger to both the individual and the group; for that reason, the group is obligated to help. The idea of *pehunan* encompasses a depiction of the community as nurturant caregivers. Instead of understanding that each person is obligated to meet his or her own needs, the Semai believe that all members of the community are obliged to help and give nurturance to others. Thus, Semai values stress affiliation, mutual aid, and the belief that violence is not a viable option for settling disputes.

Another way that people in peaceful societies create a bias against violence is by condemning those who boast or who make claims that can be interpreted as a challenge to others. Among the Ju/'hoansi, for example, no one is praised for gathering food or making a kill, and people go out of their way to minimize their accomplishments. Those who make boastful claims are ridiculed. Anthropologist Richard Lee (1969) painfully learned this lesson himself when, to show his appreciation to the Ju/'hoansi for the help they had given him, he brought a fine ox to be slaughtered and distributed at a Christmas feast. The Ju/'hoansi, much to Lee's chagrin, ridiculed the ox, claiming it was thin and unappetizing. Lee later realized that they were acting toward him as they would have to one of their own. They were letting him know that he wasn't as important as the gift and the killing of the ox made him think he was.

Thomas Gregor (1990) says that villagers in the Xingu basin of the Amazon maintain harmony by purposely sanctioning village monopolies in the production of certain goods such as shell belts, stone axes, salt, cotton, fish spears, and ceramic pots. In this way, each village has something that other villages need. The villages therefore maintain good relations, since to alienate another village might deprive one's own village members of a desired good. Moreover, trade is positively valued in itself. When villagers are asked why they don't make the goods they need themselves, they reply that doing so might anger those who do make them. Or they may claim that they do not have the knowledge to produce the items. (When temporarily cut off from a supply, though, they seem to learn how to make or acquire them very quickly.) Gregor says it is unlikely that any village could not produce the goods desired: marriage between groups is common so each village contains people with the skills of other villages.

The Xinguanos place a strong negative value on aggression and on things that symbolize aggression. Killing is wrong because it produces blood; even animal blood is considered defiling. Most game animals are considered inedible, and even fish must be well cooked so that there is no blood. The Xinguanos also hold strong negative stereotypes of aggressive groups. They consider non-Xingu Indians to be "wild Indians" who are violent, beating their children, raping their women, and shooting arrows at white men's planes. The wild Indian has almost the status of an animal and represents everything a Xinguano does not want to be. When Xingu villages have been the object of aggression by others, they have defended themselves, but successful warriors take no trophies and are given no special honour. In fact, they have to take special medicine to cleanse themselves of the defilement of the blood of those killed.

Peaceful societies also minimize violence and conflict through ceremony. The Ju/'hoansi believe that everyone has "medicine" or power. In the same way that nearby Bantu tribes have witchcraft and sorcery, and Europeans have pills and syringes, the Ju/'hoansi have *n/um*, a substance they say lies in the pit of the stomach. *N/um* has the capacity to keep people healthy and to help cure people who are sick. Most important, *n/um* can be transferred from someone who is acting as a healer to others through the medium of the trance dance, their most common ceremony. The idea of the dance is for a person to "heat up" his or her *n/um* by dancing; as the person dances, the *n/um* in the stomach is

© Ueslei Marcelino/Reuters

This Xinguano will ensure that his catch is well cooked, so that there will be no blood.

vaporized and travels up the spinal cord into the brain, which causes the dancer to go into a trance. The dancer then goes from person to person laying on hands and transferring power to those who are touched, thereby enabling them to ward off sickness and death. Anyone can be a healer among the Ju/'hoansi; in a lifetime, each person is likely to serve as a healer at least once.

The trance dance has meanings that go beyond the power to heal, however. Some Ju/'hoansi are thought to have special powers that allow them to see the ghosts of dead ancestors who hover around the fires, to see distant scenes, to see through things, and, in special cases, to change themselves into lions and stalk the veldt in search of human prey. Trance dances are most frequent when large numbers of people come together (from about once a month in small groups, up to four times a week in large camps) and during certain occasions such as the arrival of visitors to a camp, the presence of meat, or sickness. The congregation of large numbers of people, the presence of meat, and the arrival of new people are all occasions that, in one way or another, create the potential for interpersonal conflict. The fact that trance dances are more frequent during such times seems to indicate that they may serve to heal social conflict as well as individual maladies. By bringing people together in the ceremony, by the sharing of *n/um* and the ritual recognition of common threats, the trance dance unites people and symbolizes the relationship between group harmony and individual well-being.

In sum, peaceful societies create a bias against violence by sharing, by valuing nonaggressive behaviour, by building relations of dependence between individuals and groups, and by engaging in collective behaviours that promote harmony. They are not, of course, always successful, and even among some societies characterized as peaceful, there is violence. Lee (1984, 148) collected accounts of 22 homicides among Ju/'hoansi groups during a 35-year period from 1920 to 1955, for example, but found little, if any sanctioned group violence.

QUESTION 9.3: WHAT ARE THE ECONOMIC, POLITICAL, AND SOCIAL DIFFERENCES BETWEEN PEACEFUL AND VIOLENT SOCIETIES?

Thomas Hobbes, a 17th-century philosopher, proposed that human beings in their natural state, without government or laws, are driven by greed and the quest for gain. Without some common power to keep them in awe, Hobbes said, they live in a state of war, with every person against every other person. In his book *Leviathan*, Hobbes famously describes his vision of life before civilization as "solitary, poore, nasty, brutish, and short" (Hobbes 1881 [1651], 94–96).

Hobbes saw human beings as having a natural inclination to be violent, an inclination that can be controlled only by some form of centralized authority. However, as anthropologists have discovered, societies with little formal government, such as the Ju/'hoansi and the Semai, are among the most peaceful in the world. Furthermore, these peaceful societies are small in scale and people make their living primarily by hunting and gathering or by swidden agriculture. Most are relatively isolated and lack formal mechanisms for resolving conflict once it begins. There are no courts, no police, no jails, and no formally sanctioned threats of violence, even against wrongdoers. Since there is little that people in these societies can do once violence begins, they go to great lengths to avoid it.

Had Hobbes (1881) known the Yanomamö, however, he might have found that his vision of a stateless society, "where every man is enemy to every man," was verified. Their social and economic life closely resembles that of the Semai, and they live in virtually the same environment and are neighbours of the peaceful Xinguano. But Yanomamö society creates attitudes favouring collective violence in order to protect its women and children. In this case, the lack of any centralized control or formal mechanisms for putting an end to conflict results in unrestrained violence rather than the avoidance of conflict.

The Need to Protect Resources

In societies without any form of centralized control and a bias toward collective violence, such as that of the Yanomamö, individuals must protect their own resources through force. Because the Yanomamö, for example, do not effectively control intravillage conflict, men of their own as well as other villages are constantly seeking to seduce one another's wives. Consequently, the men, individually or in groups, must build a reputation for fierceness in order to protect themselves and their families. Failure to control conflict and the need for men to build a reputation for aggressiveness in order to protect their resources combine to produce a society that places a positive value on violent behaviour.

The conditions that give rise to violent conflict among the Yanomamö are not unlike those that promote violence in street gangs in the United States. When he worked in the 1960s with the Vice Lords, a Chicago street gang (or "club," as they preferred to call themselves), Lincoln Keiser (1968) concluded that boys joined gangs because alone they could not protect themselves from shakedowns or safeguard their interests in girls. Where the Yanomamö encouraged *waiteri*—fierceness—the Vice Lords valued heart—a willingness to follow any suggestion regardless of personal risk. Where a Yanomamö demonstrated fierceness through chest-pounding duels, axe fights, and raids against enemy villages, members of street gangs in Chicago confirmed their heart in gang fights. Street gangs even formed alliances against other gangs, as do Yanomamö villages with each other. The similarities in the dynamics and values of violent conflict among Yanomamö and among street gangs in Canada and the United States illustrate how under certain conditions, individuals form groups to protect themselves against other groups. To discourage attacks from others in the absence of protection from other agencies, these groups cultivate a reputation for violence.

The gang violence that Keiser observed in Chicago during the late 1960s has escalated since, and weapons more typical of armed soldiers in the military are now being used. Alex Kotlowitz, in *There Are No Children Here* (1991), reported how the Vice Lords, one of three gang factions in Chicago in the early 1990s, made use of an arsenal that included Uzis and grenades. The purpose was the same, although the stakes were higher. Drugs have become the major source of contention among Chicago gangs (the head of one Vice Lord faction grossed $50,000 to $100,000 a week). When drug wars erupt over territory, the violence reflects the increased stakes and more massive firepower. A couple of years ago, four members of the Vice Lords came upon a rival gang member in the lobby of a housing project and shot him five times with an Uzi, two sawed-off shotguns, and a .25-calibre automatic handgun to establish their dominance in the neighbourhood.

The social and political conditions that characterize the societies of the Vice Lords and the Yanomamö are such that in each of them, individuals must mobilize and use force to protect or acquire desired resources. In neither case is there

Innocent bystanders may be killed in the midst of gang warfare waged due to a lack of other ways to protect valued resources or to settle disputes. Here, spokespeople for Toronto youth groups plead for help from municipal politicians to combat unchecked gang violence.

any effective centralized authority to guarantee the safety of resources or to stop violence once it begins. Although there is a centralized force in Chicago—the police—they rarely intervene in gang violence because they are unwilling or lack the resources to do so, or because local residents are afraid or reluctant to report violence.

Creating the Conditions for Violence

Napoleon Chagnon characterized Yanomamö warfare as a "truly primitive cultural adaptation … before it was altered or destroyed by our culture." It was, he said, the normal state of affairs before it was suppressed by colonial governments. There is, however, considerable evidence that Yanomamö warfare and aggression were less a product of their existence or nature than they were consequences of Western contact.

Brian Ferguson (1995) maintains that the period of Chagnon's fieldwork (1964 to 1972), on which he based his best-selling ethnography, *The Fierce People* (1968), was one of the most turbulent in Yanomamö history. Violence and aggression, writes Ferguson, were a product of three major changes: (1) the presence of new outpost settlements of government agents, missionaries, and researchers; (2) competition for Western manufactured goods, particularly steel cutting tools, and (3) a breakdown of social relations brought about by epidemics and the depletion of game and other food resources.

The Yanomamö, Ferguson points out, had been in contact with outsiders for centuries. Europeans began raiding Yanomamö villages for slaves as early as the mid-17th century and continued to do so until around 1850. In the late 19th century, the rubber boom in the Amazon—a horrendous period for indigenous groups, who were forced to collect rubber under the threat of torture and death—brought the Yanomamö into increased contact and conflict with other indigenous groups. After the Amazon rubber boom collapsed in the 1920s as a result of competition with Asian rubber

plantations, the area in which the Yanomamö lived was relatively peaceful until the 1950s and 1960s; then, influenza and measles epidemics swept the area, leaving only one-quarter of the children with both parents. More disruptive yet was the presence of new Western outposts.

The new outposts made available to the Yanomamö desired manufactured items, such as steel knives, machetes, aluminum pots, and shotguns. Steel cutting tools, for example, were ten times more efficient than the stone cutting tools they had long been using. Shotguns were effective both for hunting and for raiding.

The Yanomamö could obtain these items in various ways. They could relocate their villages near the outposts, they could send trading parties on long voyages to get them, or they could raid other groups for them. But the greatest advantage went to what Ferguson called "anchor villages," those that relocated near outposts. The result was a hierarchy of settlements ranging from anchor villages whose members were able to monopolize the new desired goods to more isolated settlements whose members had fewer and lower quality goods.

Yanomamö in anchor settlements traded Western items to distant groups for local handicrafts such as cotton hammocks, spear points, or manioc flour. But trading parties were also targets of raids by groups desiring Western goods. To protect themselves and their monopoly on Western trade goods and to discourage raiding, Yanomamö groups found it advantageous to cultivate reputations for violence and aggression. A reputation for fierceness was also an advantage in negotiating for desired goods. Thus, one man told of the number of people he had killed on raids just before demanding a machete.

Proximity to Western outposts incited violence in other ways. For example, once people relocated their village near an outpost settlement, they were reluctant to move. One way that small-scale, mobile societies such as the Yanomamö avoid conflict is by moving villages away from enemies when conflict is threatened. But since moving would mean giving up access to and a monopoly on Western goods, members of anchor villages were reluctant to move and, hence, needed to protect themselves and the goods they obtained from Westerners. In addition, more permanent settlements quickly depleted game resources: resources that had been used in reciprocal exchanges with other people and groups. Thus, sharing patterns, which as we noted earlier are crucial for maintaining peaceful relations, began to break down, leading to more conflict.

In these ways, deaths from disease and war disrupted traditional social relations, the depletion of game weakened traditional patterns of sharing and cooperation, and access to Western technology provided new sources of conflict. Furthermore, the new technology introduced a new way of ordering society and enhanced the ability of people in anchor villages to make war.

Access to Western goods also explains the aggressive attitudes of Yanomamö men to women. Traditionally, Yanomamö practised brideservice; grooms were obligated to work for their bride's family for up to four years. But families of grooms in anchor villages were able to substitute Western goods for brideservice, one result being a movement of wives to villages with greater access to Western goods. This, combined with the Yanomamö practice of female infanticide and polygamy, resulted in a shortage of and greater competition for females and the more frequent raiding of other villages for women. In addition, Yanomamö wives go to live in their husbands' family villages, particularly where Western goods take the place of brideservice. The result is that women are removed from the protective influence of their families and are more likely to be victims of abuse.

In sum, many of the patterns of Yanomamö warfare, violence, and aggression cannot be understood without knowledge of their history of contact with Western society and the contact conditions that increased the likelihood of violence and war. Even the power of chiefs, whose feast giving played such an important role in Chagnon's descriptions of alliance formation and aggression, was largely a function of Western contact. Outsiders, following traditional customs, brought gifts to local leaders. But the gifts that outsiders brought were far more valuable. Thus, Chagnon gave one chief a gift of 25 machetes, providing him with items that he could use to enhance his power. And thus, as Ferguson (1992, 225) says, "if villages were not anchored to outposts but were able to move freely, if long-established marital alliances were not disturbed by massive mortality, if communal sharing of meat were still the norm, and, above all, if necessary technology were widely and equally available, my theoretical expectation is that there would be little collective violence among the Yanomami."

EXERCISE 9.2

Some anthropologists have explained the tendency toward violence of both Yanomamö and the Vice Lords of Chicago as being the result of competition over, and protection of, resources. Brian Ferguson, however, contends that violence among the Yanomamö must be understood within the broader context of colonialism and its attendant physical and structural violence. What kinds of broader societal forces, and forms of structural violence (as discussed in Chapter 7), might apply to the context in which the Vice Lords struggle to protect their resources?

Sexism and Violent Conflict

Another difference between peaceful and violent societies that has been suggested has to do with gender roles. Among the Ju/'hoansi, the Xinguano, and the Semai, men and women are relatively equal and there is little institutionalized violence against women. In contrast, the Yanomamö and the Vice Lords are characterized by male dominance, and both sanction violence against women.

Several reasons have been advanced to support the link between sexist values and violent conflict. First, it is men that make war, though women may fill certain positions in the armed forces.

While there have been societies in which women engage in armed combat, these instances are the exception rather than the rule. During the Sandinista rebellion in Nicaragua in the 1980s, women took an active role in combat, but they were banned from active combat once the Sandinistas gained power. Second, there is a strong cross-cultural link between patriarchy and violent conflict. After examining information on more than one thousand societies, William Tulio Divale and Marvin Harris (1976) concluded that the intensity of collective violence is significantly higher in societies characterized by a strong male bias—patrilocal residence, patrilineal descent, polygyny, postmarital sex restrictions on females, male secret societies, and men's houses. Finally, there is evidence that societies characterized by sexual violence against women tend to be more warlike and prone to collective violence. Peggy Sanday's 1981 study of 95 societies in which there was evidence of frequency of rape supports this conclusion. The question is, does a sexist ideology promote violent conflict, or does the incidence of violent conflict promote sexism?

Those who claim that sexism promotes violent conflict make that connection in various ways. Betty Reardon (1985) and Leslie Cagan (1983) suggest that societies that relegate women to an inferior position explicitly or implicitly sanction violence against women. Moreover, violence toward women serves as what they call a "primal" paradigm for violent warfare against other peoples; once violence is allowed as a means of domination of one group such as women, it can serve as a model for dominance and violence against other groups.

For Peggy Sanday, and for many others, sexism and violent conflict both have their roots in competition over scarce resources. During periods in which resources are not scarce, males and females are valued equally. When there is an imbalance between food supply or distribution and needs, or when groups are competing for resources, males become of greater value, females become objects to be controlled, and sexual violence becomes one way that men demonstrate dominance. Among cattle-herding people in East Africa, for example, raiding for cattle was common and sometimes led to violent conflict between groups. Violence was defined as a manly activity, leading East African societies to place great emphasis on masculinity and manliness. Manliness, however, was tested not only in battle but in male–female relations as well, for sex was a way of demonstrating strength.

In sum, factors such as a lack of centralized control, competition over scarce resources, private property, and sexism may lead societies to construct an ideological bias toward violence. Examining the effects of violent conflict to see if they produce changes in societies may provide insights into the factors that promote violent conflict.

EXERCISE 9.3

There is some suggestion of a link between militarism and competitive sports; that is, societies that are prone to collective violence are more likely to value games in which men aggressively compete against other men. How does this apply to North American societies? Which sports in North America most closely resemble or promote the values of militarism and war? Does the language of these sports reflect militaristic values? Do gender roles reflect these values? In what ways does Canada differ from the United States on these issues?

QUESTION 9.4: WHAT IS THE RELATIONSHIP BETWEEN VIOLENCE AND THE NATION-STATE?

Violence and the Nation-State

As we discussed in Chapter 8, the symbolic barriers of excluded Others, infrastructure, and education are essential for nation building. The use of violence or the threat of armed force is another key instrument in creating and maintaining the nation-state. Killing is the ultimate tool of nation-states. In fact, some anthropologists, among them Pierre van den Berghe, Leo Kuper, and Carol Nagengast, view the nation-state as a genocidal or ethnocidal institution, one that conspires to kill or remove those citizens who fail to (or refuse to) conform to the dictates of the imposed national culture. "Ethnic cleansing" is not only a phenomenon of the late 20th century. For example, the United States, through policies of either aggressive extermination or benign neglect, attempted to kill all Native American indigenous peoples and assimilate those who remained. Between 1975 and 1979, the government of Cambodia, the Khmer Rouge, systematically murdered 2 million of its 7 million citizens, and in 1994, the Rwandan state slaughtered 800,000 of its citizens. According to Carol Nagengast (1994),

> *the numbers of people worldwide subjected to the violence of their own states are staggering. More than a quarter of a million Kurds and Turks in Turkey have been beaten or tortured by the military, police, and prison guards since 1980; tens of thousands of indigenous people in Peru and Guatemala, street children in Brazil and Guatemala, Palestinians in Kuwait, Kurds in Iraq, and Muslim women and girls in Bosnia have been similarly treated. Mutilated bodies turn up somewhere everyday. Some 6000 people in dozens of countries were legally shot, hung, electrocuted, gassed, or stoned to death by their respective states between 1985 and 1992 for political misdeeds: criticism of the state, membership in banned political parties or groups, or for adherence to the "wrong" religion; for moral deeds: adultery, prostitution, homosexuality, sodomy, or alcohol or drug use; for economic offenses: burglary, embezzling, and corruption; and for violent crimes: rape, assault, and murder. (119–20)*

Pierre van den Berghe (1992) contends that what is euphemistically called "nation building" is nothing but a blueprint for at best **ethnocide** (an attempt to destroy the culture of a people) and at worst **genocide** (an attempt to exterminate a people). Social scientists, he writes, tend to ignore the genocidal character of the nation-state because of the widespread assumption that nation-states are necessary for maintaining peace and economic stability. Instead, he says, nation-states are, in effect, mafias or gangs that, through the use or threat of violence, extract booty for themselves or their elites from rival "gangs" and extract "protection money" from their own citizens.

Other anthropologists share van den Berghe's view of the nation-state as an instrument of force and violence. Nagengast (1994) examined not only state killing but also the use of torture, rape, and homosexual assault to draw the boundaries of the nation-state. State-sponsored violence, she says, serves not only to inflict pain but also to create "punishable categories of people"—that is, people whose existence creates and maintains an Other. These punishable individuals represent an ambiguous underclass believed capable of undermining the accepted order of society. Arrest and torture, she says, stigmatize people and mark them as people no one would want to be. Arrest and torture provide a way to symbolically mark, discipline, and stigmatize categories of people whose existence or demands threaten the idea, power, and legitimacy of the nation-state. Because torture and violence are committed against only "terrorists," "communists," or "separatists," these methods become legitimate. "We only beat bad people," said a Turkish prison official in 1984. "They are no good, they are worthless bums, they are subversives who think that communism will relieve them of the necessity of working."

ethnocide
The attempt to destroy the culture of a people.

genocide
The attempt to exterminate a people.

The official described with apparent pride the order that he had given that "all prisoners should be struck with a truncheon below the waist on the rude parts, and warned not to come to prison again." "My aim," he said, "is to ensure discipline. That's not torture, for it is only the lazy, the idle, the vagabonds, the communists, the murderers who come to prison" (Nagengast 1994, 121).

Nation-states, and national identity, can also be an integral, if complicated, part of the process of creating and maintaining peace. For instance, since the 1994 genocide in Rwanda, the Rwandan government has embarked on a "deethnicization campaign." Ethnic labels on national identity cards are outlawed, and to identify as Hutu or Tutsi is to "risk accusations of 'divisionism' or genocide ideology" (Eramian 2014, 96).

Violence, the Nation-State, and Peace in East Timor

One of the most recent instances of state violence against its own citizens occurred on the island of Timor on the southern edge of Indonesia. East Timor had been colonized by the Dutch and the Portuguese and was granted its independence by the Portuguese in 1975. Five days after a state visit by then U.S. Vice-President Gerald Ford and Secretary of State Henry Kissinger, Indonesia invaded East Timor. Over the following two decades, Indonesians, especially members and friends of the ruling family, invested millions of dollars in various enterprises there. And, as many other countries have done, Indonesia embarked on a campaign of violence and terror in its effort to integrate the East Timorese into the Indonesian nation-state.

Indonesian anthropologist George Aditjondro (2000), who faced an indefinite jail term for criticizing Indonesian leaders, described the campaign of terror, violence, and torture embarked on by the Indonesian state against its most recent citizens. It included, among other things, a "pacification war," which lasted from 1975 to 1979, and repression

that continued even after a 1999 UN-sponsored referendum in which 80 percent of the population voted for independence from Indonesia.

Torture, says Aditjondro, was a standard method of subjugation. Techniques included physical beatings, the use of cigarette butts to burn holes in the skin, electric shock, the crushing of hands and feet with chair or table legs, the poking of the mouth with bamboo sticks, the infliction of pain on the genitals, the rape of women, and immersion in a metal tank filled with water charged with electricity.

Torture was used for five reasons, according to Aditjondro. First, to obtain information from victims. Second, to crush the fighting spirit of freedom fighters. Third, to weaken the political power of the Catholic Church by obtaining "confessions" of church complicity in pro-independence politics or in sacrilegious or criminal acts. Fourth, to protect the business interests of Indonesians in East Timor. And finally, to minimize critical press reports from East Timorese newspapers.

But torture was not the only technique of state terror used by Indonesia. There was, for example, physical terror, including mass killings of guerrillas along with women and children that took place during the first decade of the Indonesian occupation.

Some 200,000 people—around one-third of the population—were killed or died of deprivations brought about by the terror. Prisoners were thrown to their death from helicopters; people were killed by napalm bombings that also destroyed crops, and thousands died from resulting famines. Many people died in overcrowded prison barracks, some of which were covered with black canvas to turn them into human ovens.

There was also a campaign to "depurify," as Aditjondro calls it, the bodies of East Timorese women through rape and forced fertility control. Rape was often committed against the wives or daughters of men suspected of being involved with the resistance. In other cases, rape was committed against women who failed to produce identity cards or who refused to accompany or submit to the sexual demands of soldiers. Other women were forced to spy on resistance forces while serving as sex slaves of Indonesian troops. In still other cases, East Timorese women were forced into brothels for use by Indonesian troops. Rape, says Aditjondro, was also a way to destroy the East Timorese resistance by biologically depurifying their ethnic constituency.

Another way to biologically depurify the population was through forced contraception. Family planning programs were used as means to discipline the population; they symbolically represented state control over human bodies. Thus, high-school girls were injected with Depo-Provera, a birth control drug, without being told of its function.

Other forms of symbolic violence included erecting pro-Indonesian monuments and forcing citizens to participate in Indonesian political rituals (flag raisings, parades, and parties), subjecting them to arrest, interrogation, and physical torture if they resisted. Language itself was modified, with new linguistic expressions for torture and execution becoming common. *Jalan-jalan ke Jakarta* ("taking a trip to Jakarta") and *Berangkat studi lanjut ke Jawa* ("going for further study in Java") were euphemisms for executions. *Mani laut* ("taking a sea bath") referred to the practice of weighting the

© Supri Supri/Reuters

The brutalization of East Timor by the Indonesian military and by Indonesian-supported militia from 1975 to 1999 is but one example of how nation-states use force to control their citizens. Here, East Timorese youth are staging a drama portraying the killings of some 271 unarmed protesters by Indonesian troops at the Santa Cruz cemetery on 12 November 1991.

bodies of people with rocks and dumping them from a helicopter into the sea. *De-Santa Cruz-kan* ("Santa Cruz-ified") was an expression used by mothers to threaten their children with the sinister connotations of a notorious 1991 massacre of East Timorese high-school students who were protesting Indonesian occupation. Finally, 200,000 people were taken from East Timor and relocated to other parts of Indonesia.

Many East Timorese became **refugees**—forced to flee their home country to seek protection in another. Refugees that comprise a **diaspora**, or dispersed population living outside their homeland, escape direct violence and harm; however, the effects of living through sustained, everyday violence are long-lasting. Amanda Wise

refugees
Groups of people who have left their homeland due to warfare, forced expulsion, acts of terrorism, or other factors.

diaspora
A population whose members are dispersed and living outside their homeland.

(2006) conducted fieldwork with the refugee diaspora in Sydney, Australia. She found that the experience of shared violence and trauma was a key element in the collective identity of the refugees, who came together to create what she called a "community of suffering." The embodied memories of pain and suffering drew the community together. The Indonesian military inflicted violence on the East Timorese, and "such practices symbolically and affectively bind the pain of the individual to the fate of the ethnic collectivity." The shared memory and common suffering became the foundation of solidarity among her informants (2006, 15).

East Timor finally regained its independence from Indonesia in 1999, but the break did not come easily. Eighty percent of the population voted for independence in a UN-sponsored referendum; however, before they withdrew from East Timor in September 1999, the Indonesian military and military-trained and -supported militias laid waste to virtually the entire country, killing thousands of people and driving 200,000 people out of East Timor and into Indonesia, where many remain under the control of fleeing militia members.

For Wise's informants, living in exile in Australia, independence opened up the possibility of a return to their homeland. But many of them, having spent so many years in Australia, had mixed feelings about where they belonged. They had developed a sense of identity based on collective suffering. An exiled journalist described these mixed feelings: "Perhaps the worst condemnation of all is to watch our country recede from our reach like a foreign, distant, indecipherable tide and to witness how indecisively our bodies begin to seek stability after many precarious years; our bodies, unconsenting and perhaps irremediably, grow accustomed to a country which they did not choose of their free will" (in Wise 2006, 163).

Canada's part in the tragedy of the East Timorese is documented in the video *Bitter Paradise: The Sellout of East Timor*, by Elaine Brière. Probably the last tourist to visit East Timor while it was still a peaceful, welcoming society in 1974, Brière dedicated her life to making the genocide public. The video followed Brière's journey into the business world, where she was told that Canadians who were commercially involved in Indonesia did not know about the genocide or believed that it was an exaggeration; to the world of the media, where she was told by the host of a talk show that Canadians didn't "connect" with the killing of East Timorese; and to Ottawa, where her questions were ignored by the External Affairs minister. Canada continued to give enormous amounts of economic aid to the Suharto regime in spite of the killings and in spite of cutbacks in social programs at home; and Canadian businesses, such as Inco and Bre-X, continued to see Indonesia as a haven for international investment.

The tactics used by Indonesia to subdue people who resisted integration into the Indonesian nation-state are not unique. In fact, virtually all these tactics have been used by most, if not all, nation-states at one time or another. You can get some idea of how nation-states today sponsor violence against their citizens by going to the Internet, where information is readily available from organizations such as Amnesty International and Human Rights Watch.

EXERCISE 9.4

Protesting the Genocide in East Timor

Many Canadian students protested Canada's continued financial support of Indonesia with international aid. What do you think would have happened to Canada's ability to do business in Indonesia if Canada had stopped the aid? Do you think Canadian businesses should have continued to operate in Indonesia in spite of the genocide? Do you think that if Canada had taken a stand against the genocide (stopped the aid, withdrawn all businesses), the rest of the world would have followed? Defend your opinions.

QUESTION 9.5: HOW IS IT POSSIBLE TO JUSTIFY THE CREATION OF WEAPONS OF MASS DESTRUCTION?

Anthropologist Hugh Gusterson, who had been an antinuclear activist, wanted to know how nuclear weapons scientists could justify conducting research on and testing of weapons of mass destruction. What could create a worldview that enabled people to justify performing that kind of work? To answer that question, he set out to study the culture of the Lawrence Livermore National Laboratory in Livermore, California.

Gusterson (1995) suggests that those who justify nuclear weapons and who question nuclear disarmament make four assumptions about the world. First, they claim that anarchy characterizes international relations. Second, they assume that states must rely on self-help since no one else is going to offer them protection. Third, they assume that nuclear weapons are the ultimate form of self-help, because they vastly increase the cost of aggression against them. And fourth, they assume that relatively little can be done in the short term to change the anarchistic nature of the international system.

Critics of nuclear weapons make very different assumptions. They argue that international relations are not as anarchistic as they are made out to be and that rules and norms that control aggression exist. Many critics see the nuclear arms race as "objective social madness." People who work in the area, they assume, must be in denial and must demonize the Other to justify their work.

Gusterson wanted to find out not so much who was "right," but rather how people came to hold such divergent opinions about ways of resolving conflict, especially when the stakes are so high. Nuclear weapons scientists did not, says Gusterson, avoid the ethical concerns of their research. Most, however, accepted the central axiom that nuclear research is necessary to make the world safe. To some, working on nuclear weapons was more ethical than working on conventional weapons, since conventional weapons were more likely to be used. Nuclear weapons, the scientists assumed, were simply symbolic chips in a game, the goal of which was to avoid using them. When asked if he could ever foresee a circumstance in which nuclear weapons would be used, one scientist said, "No, even if we were under attack." In other words, deterrence was the only reason to develop nuclear weapons; if you were attacked, the whole enterprise had failed. Others rationalized their work more baldly, saying they were not responsible for how what they designed would be used. "Are automobile designers," they ask, "responsible for deaths caused by drunk drivers?" (Gusterson 1995, 58)

When Gusterson asked people why they chose to work at Livermore, most cited the intellectual freedom they enjoyed working in a weapons laboratory. Almost all compared Livermore favourably to working in universities (which they characterized as "stodgy," "cutthroat," or "high-pressure") or in private organizations. Some also cited the challenges of weapons research and the opportunity to work with state-of-the-art equipment. Beyond those attractions, Livermore paid about twice as much as a university position.

Once a person was hired, secrecy played a major role in forging a person's identity. Livermore employees were investigated before being given security clearance to laboratory facilities. Personnel were divided into different security categories and given coloured badges indicating their level of clearance. "Q" clearance (a green badge) was necessary for classified research; "L" clearance (yellow badge) allowed access to classified areas but not to classified information. The labs themselves were divided into areas of lesser and greater security. As Gusterson (1995, 70) put it, the laboratory was "an enormous grid of tabooed spaces and tabooed topics."

Without a green badge, a weapons scientist was not considered a full adult in the lab. The process of getting "Q" clearance was elaborate and could take six months to two years. Virtually every aspect of a person's life was subject to investigation in search of clues that he or she was unfit to handle classified material. Most people passed, though, and because secrecy was not so well guarded in practice, the security clearance process functioned mostly as a rite of passage that added to the mystique of weapons research and that disciplined the initiate.

Secrecy was one of the principal ways that the lab's diverse population was brought together. Knowing secrets, regardless of how mundane they might be, marked a person as a member of a special group and lent an air of drama and importance to one's work. Secrecy also served to limit discussion that could change people's views of the work that they were doing. As Gusterson (1995, 68) put it, "the laboratory's culture of secrecy does tend to produce certain effects in its scientists: it segregates laboratory scientists as a privileged but somewhat isolated elite; it inculcates a sense of group loyalty; and it thrusts on laboratory scientists an amorphous surveillance, which can become internalized."

The process of testing nuclear weapons was, in many ways, the critical step in creating the nuclear scientist. Any Livermore scientist could propose a weapons test, but reviewers (senior scientists at the laboratory) selected only about one out of 20 ideas for testing. Nuclear tests had elements of myth and ritual. Approval of an idea for testing reaffirmed the scientist's membership in the group, not unlike a rite of passage. Testing produced not only weapons but also weapon designers. It was a way of creating the elite. The more tests one participated in, the greater the prestige and power that accrued. A successful test validated status and credentials and brought forth congratulatory support and reinforcement. Tests provided a symbolic simulation of the reliability of the entire system of deterrence: "Each time a nuclear test is successfully carried off, the scientists' faith in human control over nuclear technology is further reinforced. Seen in this light, the 'reliability' the tests demonstrate has an expandable meaning, extending out from the reliability of the particular device being tested to the entire regime of nuclear deterrence" (Gusterson 1995, 161).

The Language of Nuclear Destruction

Carol Cohn (1987, 1991) spent one year studying the culture of a strategic studies institute, or "think tank," for government defence analysts who plan nuclear strategy. She began her study with this question: How are people whose job it is to plan nuclear destruction able to do it? As we discussed in Chapter 4, language is one of the key ways in which members of a particular culture come to understand their shared worldview as true and natural. One of Cohn's conclusions was that the planners used language to distance themselves from the consequences of the actions they were planning. The language they used obfuscated and reassembled reality in such a way that what was really being talked about—the destruction of human lives—was hidden behind metaphors and euphemisms.

During her first weeks at the centre, as she listened to the participants talking matter-of-factly about nuclear destruction, she heard language that she labelled *technostrategic*. This language included terms such as *clean bombs* (fusion bombs, which release more energy than fission bombs), *penetration aids* (technologies that help missiles get through enemy defences), *collateral damage* (human deaths), and *surgical strikes* (bombing that takes out only military targets). Domestic metaphors were common in the technostrategic language: missiles were based in *silos*, piles of nuclear weapons in a submarine were *Christmas tree farms*, bombs and missiles were *re-entry vehicles* or *RVs*, and massive bombing was *carpet bombing*. According to Cohn, the domestic images were more than a way for people to distance themselves from the grisly reality they were discussing. Calling the pattern in which a bomb would fall a "footprint" removed the speakers from any position of accountability for the acts they were contemplating.

Cohn also discovered that the language and metaphors of those working at the institute seemed incapable of expressing certain realities. The aftermath of a nuclear attack was described in technostrategic language as "a situation bound to include EMP blackout, brute force damage to systems, a heavy jamming environment, and so on" (1987, 707). She contrasted this with eyewitness accounts of the bombing of Hiroshima. There was, Cohn wrote, no way of describing this experience in technostrategic language. It removed the speakers from having to think about themselves as victims of nuclear war.

Cohn also discovered that she could not use ordinary language to speak to the defence analysts. When she tried, they acted as if she were ignorant or simpleminded. To communicate, she had to use terms along the lines of *subholocaust engagement* and *pre-emptive strike*. The word *peace* was not a legitimate part of the vocabulary; to use it was to brand oneself as a softheaded activist. The closest she could come to *peace* in technostrategic language was *strategic stability*.

To an anthropologist, the fact that people are limited by their culture, their language, and their worldview is, of course, no surprise. All cultures give a characteristic meaning to violent conflict, and to peace, whether it is viewed as the act of an animal in possession of a human body, or as the will of God, or as a game. The more serious implication of Cohn's observations is that scientists, academics, and nuclear planners give weight to their claim that their perspective is "objective" and therefore has greater truth value than other perspectives. Moreover, says Cohn, if one can speak to defence analysts only in technostrategic language, and if the language is constructed in such a way as to be incapable of expressing different realities, then there is no way for these analysts to appreciate or understand the other realities involved in the use of nuclear weapons.

QUESTION 9.6: HOW DO ANTHROPOLOGISTS DO FIELDWORK IN THE MIDST OF VIOLENT CONFLICT?

As often as possible, anthropologists try to learn about and understand various social and cultural phenomena through fieldwork and participant observation. However, striving to understand violent conflict firsthand can be difficult at best and dangerous at worst. Often, it is contentious as well. Should anthropologists place themselves in danger in the name of fieldwork? What if, through our very presence, we put others at risk or promote the conditions for further violence? Can we use ethnography to understand war from a soldier's perspective? Below, we discuss three different examples of the possibilities and pitfalls of studying violence and conflict, either directly or indirectly.

The Endangered Anthropologist

The risk of injury, disease, or hostile reactions has always been a feature of anthropological fieldwork. As anthropologists increasingly work in areas where human rights violations are common, these risks are intensified. At least four anthropologists have been murdered because of their fieldwork. In 1982, South African anthropologist and anti-apartheid activist Ruth First was killed by a mail bomb in her office at Maputo University in Mozambique. In 1984, Melanesian anthropologist Arnold Ap was tortured and killed by the Indonesian army, his body dumped by helicopter into the sea. In 1989, South African anthropologist David Webster was shot and killed by members of a pro-apartheid death squad. And in 1990, Guatemalan anthropologist Myrna Mack was stabbed to death by a soldier, ostensibly for her work with Mayan refugees and their experiences in the government's counterinsurgency war of the early 1980s, through which hundreds of thousands of people died. In addition, at least two anthropologists,

Ricardo Falla and George Aditjondro, went into exile under threat of assassination because of their work. These real dangers that anthropologists face may provide insights into how the people with whom they are working experience the threat of violence.

In 1989 and 1990, Linda Green was doing fieldwork in the Guatemalan community of Xe'caj. Like many similar communities, Xe'caj was only beginning to recover from some 35 years of violence. Beginning with a military coup orchestrated largely by the Central Intelligence Agency (CIA) against a democratically elected government in 1954, Guatemala experienced regular violence as the militarized state tried to suppress attempts to overthrow the military regime. Hundreds of thousands of Guatemalans were killed, mostly by the government, in an attempt to suppress the revolt. The late 1970s and early 1980s were particularly brutal as the government embarked on a campaign to destroy peasant villages and relocate people to government-controlled towns. In addition, paramilitary groups, largely supplied and supported by the regular military, embarked on campaigns of terror and torture in an effort to control the peasant population.

The people of Xe'caj lived in a state of constant surveillance from the military encampment located above the town. Many of the residents had husbands, fathers, or sons taken away by the military. There were rumours of death lists. People had difficulty sleeping and reported nightmares of recurring death and violence. Soon, said Green, "I, too, started to experience nighttime hysteria, dreams of death, disappearances, and torture."

Green interviewed women who had been widowed by the conflict. Without prompting, the women recounted in vivid detail their stories of horror, the deaths and disappearances of husbands, fathers, sons, and brothers, as if they had happened last week or month rather than six to eight years earlier.

Then, one day when Green arrived to continue the interviews, the women were anxious and agitated. When she asked what had happened, they told her that the military commissioner was looking for her and that people were saying she was helping the widows and talking against other people in the community. When Green told the women she was going to see the commissioner, they pleaded with her not to do so, telling her that they knew of people who had gone to the military garrison and never returned. Green decided to visit the garrison alone, and that visit would provide a vivid experience of the fears confronted by the villagers. As she approached the garrison, she noted the following:

> I saw several soldiers sitting in a small guardhouse with a machine gun perched on a three-foot stanchion pointed downward and directly at me. The plight of Joseph K. in Kafka's Trial flashed through my mind, he accused of a crime for which he must defend himself but about which he could get no information. I didn't do anything wrong, I must not look guilty, I repeated to myself like a mantra. I must calm myself, as my stomach churned, my nerves frayed. I arrived breathless and terrified. Immediately I knew I was guilty because I was against the system of violence and terror that surrounded me. (1995, 116)

Fortunately, the *commandante* said he knew nothing about why she was being harassed. He assured her that she could continue with her work, and everything went smoothly from there. But Green had gained a fuller understanding of the experiences of people who must live under the constant threat of violence.

Is There a Place for Anthropology–Military Collaborations?

In 2005, Montgomery McFate, a military adviser with a background in anthropology, published an article in *Military Review* arguing that there was a "culture gap" in our understanding of the conflict in Iraq caused by "the almost total absence of anthropology within the national-security establishment." She argued that successful counterinsurgency requires a total understanding of local culture. To achieve victory, the United States needed to understand Iraq's traditional authority structure and the competing interests of different groups such as the Shia, Sunni, and Kurds. In a second article, co-written with Andrea Jackson, McFate outlined a proposal to establish an "Office for Operational Cultural Knowledge," which would train teams to provide battlefield commanders with knowledge of local culture, or as it was being called, the "human terrain."

The need for cultural knowledge was echoed by retired Major General Robert H. Scales, Jr., (2005, 43) who argued that these new conflicts required not technological superiority but "an exceptional ability to understand people, their culture, and their motivation."

One outcome of this interest in cultural knowledge was the development of the Human Terrain System (HTS), which ran from June 2006 to September 2014. The centrepiece of the program was Human Terrain Teams (HTTs), each of which had a staff of five: an army officer serving as team leader, a cultural analyst, a regional studies analyst, a Human Terrain (HT) research manager, and an HT analyst. Each team studied the local culture, interviewed local people, and provided valuable information to the battalion commander.

Anthropologists who joined the HTS project explained their service as an effort to do something meaningful. Marcus Griffin wrote: "I have an obligation to use my skills to learn about people and to share what I learn." Working as a member of an HTT in Iraq, Griffin saw his job as finding out what Iraqis needed and helping them meet those needs.

Not everyone, however, shared this positive assessment of the Human Terrain System. In 2007, the American Anthropological Association issued a formal statement condemning the project, arguing that it would lead anthropologists to violate ethical standards and that it posed a danger to both anthropologists and the people they were studying. Another notable critic, Roberto Gonzales (2009), pointed out a number of dangers of the Human

Terrain System. First, was it possible for informants to *consent* to their participation? Second, what type of information was being gathered by anthropologists, and how would it be used? Third, how well would informants be protected from retaliation by hostile groups or political rivals?

Despite such reservations, in 2008, the Canadian Forces began a program of "white situational awareness teams," or WSATs, which are similar to HTTs. In military terminology, "white" refers to the civilian population (as opposed to the "red" and "blue" of enemy and friendly forces, respectively). Each WSAT included two military intelligence officers and three civilian Department of Foreign Affairs employees, and aimed to provide a more nuanced understanding of the cultural terrain for military leaders and advisers (Fenton 2010).

Maximillian Forte, an anthropologist at Concordia University, expressed concerns about the Human Terrain System, WSATs, and the potential militarization of anthropology in general: "Their [WSATs'] job seems to be no different from that of HTS, except that for now the civilians they use are government employees, not academics. They have breached a barrier however: the idea that social and cultural knowledge can be useful for counterinsurgency, at least that door has now been opened in Canada" (in Fenton 2010).

What bothers many critics of the Human Terrain System, in particular, is that regardless of the efforts of the military and others to put a humanitarian face on the contributions of social scientists, the information gathered by HTTs was clearly going to be used for military purposes. HTS advocates wanted to make whatever information was gathered available to other agencies and to the governments of Iraq and Afghanistan, to "enable them to more fully exercise sovereignty over their country" (Gonzalez 2009, 74).

This idea reminds many anthropologists of the disastrous CORDS program, implemented during the Vietnam War. Like the Human Terrain System, CORDS was designed to gather cultural knowledge in order to win "hearts and minds." Using information from social scientists, military

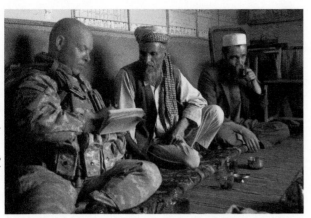

A U.S. soldier takes notes as he talks and drinks tea with local Andar District Special Needs School administrators during a cordon and search of Nani, Afghanistan, in June 2007. Can anthropological expertise be put to (good) use in a war zone?

personnel exploited Vietnamese superstitions and religious beliefs to frighten and terrorize civilians. When CORDS data were given to the South Vietnamese government, they were used to target political opponents and dissidents. This experience points to the need to take precautions to ensure that the Iraqi and Afghan governments do not use HTT information to target political rivals or to create blacklists for personal vendettas.

The use of social scientists for HTTs in Iraq and Afghanistan raises a larger issue: the responsibility of anthropologists and other social scientists to be aware of how their data may be used. The Pentagon, for example, is using information collected by social scientists to help identify dangerous neighbourhoods in Baghdad and Kabul. This knowledge allows the military to predict which neighbourhoods are at risk for riots, gun violence, or bombings; it also helps them develop lists of possible participants and their relatives, friends, and associates.

Perhaps more ominous, the military is awarding grants to social scientists to forecast human behaviour. The U.S. Department of Defense is developing a project called Human Social Culture Behavior (HSCB) Modeling. Much of this work will be contracted out to private corporations eager to secure lucrative government contracts. One corporation, Aptima, in conjunction with Carnegie Mellon University, has developed Social Network Analysis, or SNA, software. SNA has been used by the U.S. military "to predict a state's potential for instability or civil unrest in terms of nine key factors," which range from "lack of essential services" to "corruption level" to "tension."

One danger, of course, is that the philosophy of the Human Terrain System, as well as the development of elaborate surveillance technologies using vast quantities of information now available on citizens, will move from military applications in places such as Iraq and Afghanistan to domestic uses that seriously undermine democratic freedoms. Gonzalez (2009, 123–24) concludes his critique of the Human Terrain System as follows:

> *What comes across from the accounts of many social scientists supporting counterinsurgency initiatives in Iraq and Afghanistan is a fundamental acceptance of modern warfare in general and the U.S.-led occupations in particular. Furthermore, they generally accept the false notion that counterinsurgency—the "graduate level of war" to quote one military enthusiast—is more antiseptic, more humane, less damaging than conventional warfare. As technicians of power, some adhere to Machiavellian principles: do not question the prince or his war, but instead use the most efficient means to help him achieve victory. War's inevitability is taken for granted. Basic assumptions are left unquestioned. Missing from these accounts is the question of whether war is appropriate at all today.*

Making Sense of Combat: Canadian Soldiers in Kandahar

Throughout this chapter, we have explored the ways in which people in various societies and cultures make sense of violent conflict, or alternatively, create meaningful, peaceful solutions to conflict. As we have seen, language and ritual are both employed, quite successfully, to make nuclear proliferation and the subsequent possibility of mass destruction seem both feasible and meaningful. As noted at the outset of the chapter, until recently, pride in peacekeeping was a key part of Canadian national identity. For the first time since the Korean War, however, Canada had soldiers in active combat (in Afghanistan) between 2001 and 2014. In her work with Canadian Forces soldiers stationed in Kandahar, Anne Irwin analyzed the ways in which they use storytelling and ritual to make sense of their experiences in combat.

A former member of the Canadian Forces, Irwin spent many years studying Canadian soldiers, both while they trained for peacekeeping operations (Irwin 2002) and, more recently, with a unit that would undertake "full-spectrum operations," including combat (2012, 61). Irwin spent several months with the unit during its tour in 2006, living with them both at Kandahar's air force base and "outside the wire," on patrol and in combat. Irwin found that whereas time and routine on the base were quite structured, time outside the wire

was completely disrupted—"there was no day-to-day routine for sleeping and eating, not even predictable shifts" (64). Even when there was no engagement—"troops in contact," in military parlance—the soldiers experienced all time outside the wire as being in combat, not least because of the omnipresent danger of IEDs (improvised explosive devices). Soldiers who spent time outside the wire together seemed to go through a rite of passage and shared a liminal period together during combat (69). However, Irwin is reluctant to cast combat as a rite of passage that turns boys into men. Indeed, she argues that although combat has some of the elements of a rite of passage, soldiers who return to Canada seem to be both permanent adolescents (referring to themselves and their fellow soldiers as "the boys") and, at the same time, old men: prematurely aged, grief stricken, and often scarred or disabled (76).

Irwin has also collected and analyzed soldiers' narratives about the war in Afghanistan. Often, these address and link individual morality to social and political debates about Canada's combat role. One soldier, in telling the story of his experiences, said that "a lot of people in Canada think that we

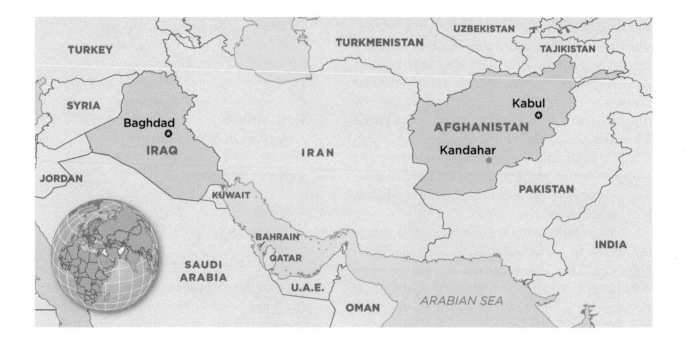

should not be here in Afghanistan, but those people don't see the remarkable changes happening here. One interpreter told me, 'Because Canada is here, our people are happy again.' So to all those Canadians who continue to harp about what they don't know—here's your straw, suck it up" (Cpl Sanders, in Pengelly and Irwin 2011, 52).

Here, the soldier has turned his combat experience into a morality tale, one that takes the qualities of a good solider—responsible, tough, and uncomplaining—and transposes them onto the Canadian public. Moreover, he is attempting to show the moral justness of the war by drawing on "the moral character of a helpful and caring Canada" (2011, 53). By examining these kinds of narratives, we can see how their circulation helps soldiers understand and justify their participation in this violent conflict. Moreover, when such combat narratives draw on a sense of national identity and pride, of Canada as "helpful and caring," we can begin to make sense of the rather rapid (though contested) shift, at the turn of the 21st century, of Canada's role from peacekeeper to warrior nation.

CONCLUSIONS

One of the unique disciplinary strengths of socio-cultural anthropology is our ability bring ethnographic and cross-cultural insights to bear on various contemporary social problems. Knowing what we know about the twin human capacities for violence and peace-making as forms of conflict resolution, how might anthropologists encourage the latter? Anthropologist Roger Lohmann (2014) makes the following suggestions:

> Anthropology is in a position to fulfil some of the prerequisites of world peace if we direct research and communication efforts accordingly. If we wish to stop war and establish peace locally or universally, temporarily or indefinitely, we need to answer several questions of the sort that anthropologists … are well positioned to address: What conditions motivate people to resort to organized violence between polities and how can these positions be manipulated to diffuse conflicts before they escalate? Is peace established and maintained only and ironically through the threat of violence, or can a foundation of non-violent ideology be laid and kept up, and if so, how? Under which conditions are people able to make peace an actively maintained and indefinitely sustainable condition, and not just the cessation of warfare? (255)

In other words, anthropologists interested in promoting peace need to apply their ethnographic and critical thinking skills to the task at hand. Moreover, anthropologists need to communicate the results of these efforts broadly, not just to other anthropologists, but to those in positions to influence relevant policy and conflict resolution efforts. For example, Kevin Avruch, anthropologist and dean of the School of Conflict Analysis and Resolution at George Mason University, makes a case for the importance of including anthropology in the core curricula of conflict resolution programs. Avruch (2009, 12–13) argues that anthropology can be applied to conflict resolution education in at least three ways: in terms of "subject matter expertise" in particular ethnographic topics (about a specific ethnic group or particular kinds of agricultural practices, for instance); in terms of methodology (including methods of ethnographic inquiry such as participant observation); and by encouraging reflexive sensitivity to practitioners' own cultural beliefs and biases. Of course, graduates of conflict management programs are not the only people with the capacity to imagine and create peace; as we have seen, different peoples have their own culturally meaningful ways of doing so. However, this awareness is precisely why an anthropological perspective is so important for those outside "experts" who are called upon to intervene or lend a hand in conflict resolution.

Finally, anthropologists, or students of anthropology, with an interest in promoting peace can remember, and remind others, that both violence and peace are culturally meaningful and situated processes. Neither form of conflict resolution, it seems, is innate in humans. As we have seen throughout the text, most of the problems we have explored have the potential to incite conflict. The first, and most illuminating, task that we as anthropologists face is to understand each problem on its own terms and situate it within a wider, cross-cultural perspective.

CRITICAL THINKING QUESTIONS

1. Is world peace possible? Given what you have learned in this chapter, what are the barriers to world peace in the contemporary world? Can they be overcome, and if so, how?
2. Depictions of graphic violence have become commonplace in contemporary popular culture. How might an anthropologist explain this phenomenon?

KEY TERMS:

diaspora   (p. 270)
ethnocide   (p. 268)
genocide   (p. 268)
refugees   (p. 270)

GLOSSARY

achieved status   An identity that is believed to be in flux and that is dependent upon the actions and achievements of an individual. (p. 190)

agroecological approach   An agricultural method that incorporates indigenous practices of food production along with contemporary agricultural research yet preserves the environment. (p. 88)

archaeology   The branch of anthropology that studies human history and its artifacts. Archaeologists typically look at the material remains of human groups in order to learn how people lived. (p. 7)

armchair anthropology   Refers to an approach to the study of various societies that dominated anthropology in the late 1800s. It involved the collection, study, and analysis of the writings of missionaries, explorers, and colonists who had sustained contact with non-Western peoples. Armchair anthropologists used these documents to make comparisons and generalizations about the ways of life of various groups (p. 40).

ascribed status   An identity that is perceived as fixed and unchanging because a person is believed to be born with it. In Canadian society, race is often assumed to be ascribed at birth. (p. 190)

atheism   Refers to a lack of belief in supernatural forces or beings. (p. 122)

bands   A term used by anthropologists to refer to egalitarian units of social organization, found mostly among foragers; these units usually consist of fewer than 100 people. (p. 59)

bilateral kinship   A system in which individuals trace their descent through both parents. (p. 132)

biological anthropology   A subdiscipline of anthropology that focuses upon the study of the evolution, function, and health of the human body and our closest primate ancestors across time and space. (p. 6)

biomedical model   Also known as *Western medicine*, *scientific medicine*, or *modern medicine*, the model combines biology with the diagnosis and treatment of illness and views the body as a machine, independent of social context, that must be repaired periodically. (p. 82)

brideservice   The requirement that when a couple marries, the groom must work for the bride's parents for some specified time. (p. 133)

bridewealth   The valuables that a groom or his family are expected or obligated to present to the bride's family. (p. 142)

caste system   A form of social stratification and identity where individuals are assigned at birth to the ranked social and occupational groups of their parents. (p. 190)

clans   Unilineal descent groups whose members claim descent from a common ancestor. (pp. 61, 142)

class   A form of identity informed by perceptions of an individual's economic worth or status. It is also a form of social hierarchy. (p. 189)

colonialism   Refers to the acquisition of new territories throughout the world by European powers from 1492 until approximately 1945. Colonizers often imposed new forms of politics, economics, and religion upon colonized Indigenous or other cultures, and frequently exploited local populations for their labour. (p. 72)

commodities   Traditionally, commodities are items that involve a transfer of value and a counter-transfer: *A* sells something to *B*, and the transaction is finished. As is typical of capitalist market-exchange systems, a long-standing personal relationship between buyer and seller is not established. (p. 177)

creole   A term used commonly to refer to the formation of slave societies in the Caribbean in which elements of African and European cultures were merged, blended, or combined into something uniquely Caribbean. (p. 120)

critical cultural relativism   An alternative perspective on cultural relativism that poses questions about cultural beliefs and practices in terms of who accepts them and why, who they might be disproportionately harming and benefiting, and the cultural power dynamics that enable them. (p. 17)

cultural relativism   The effort to understand the beliefs and behaviours of other cultures in terms of the culture in which they are found. (p. 13)

cultural text   A way of thinking about culture as a text of significant symbols, such as words, gestures, drawings, and natural objects, all of which carry meaning. (p. 19)

culture   The system of meanings about the nature of experience that are shared by a people and passed on from one generation to another, including the meanings that people give to things, events, activities, and people. (p. 9)

culture change   The changes in meanings that a people ascribe to experience and changes in their way of life. (p. 61)

culture shock   Refers to a feeling of disorientation in the initial stages of fieldwork when an anthropologist is adjusting to a new language, beliefs, food, or even climate. (p. 47)

diaspora   A population whose members are dispersed and living outside of their homeland. (p. 270)

domain of experience   An area of human experience (e.g., business, war, science, family life) from which people borrow meaning to apply to other areas. (p. 96)

dowry   The goods and valuables a bride's family supplies to the groom's family or to the couple. (p. 145)

economic development   The term used to identify an increase in level of technology, and by some, standard of living of a population. Others view it as an ideology based on three key assumptions: (1) that economic growth and development is the solution to national as well as global problems; (2) that global economic integration will contribute to solving global ecological and social problems; and (3) that foreign assistance to undeveloped countries will make things better. (p. 79)

economic systems   The rules, mechanisms, institutions, and systems of relations through which goods and services are distributed and people get what they want. (p. 224)

egocentric   A view of the self that defines each person as a replica of all humanity, as the location of motivations and drives, and as capable of acting independently from others. (p. 168)

emic perspective   Traditionally refers to an "insider's perspective." The goal of most fieldwork is to employ cultural relativism to understand an issue or perspective from the point of view of one's informants. (p. 38)

enculturation   The process through which individuals learn an identity. It can encompass parental socialization, the influence of peers, the mass media, government, and other forces. (p. 163)

endogamy   A rule that requires a person to marry someone inside his or her own group (e.g., a lineage, an ethnic group, a religious group). (p. 142)

essentialism   The act of creating generalizations or stereotypes about the behaviour or culture of a group of people. (p. 52)

ethnocentric fallacy   The mistaken notion that the beliefs and behaviours of other cultures can be judged from the perspective of one's own culture. (p. 13)

ethnocentrism   The tendency to judge the beliefs and behaviours of other cultures from the perspective of one's own culture. (p. 13)

ethnocide   The attempt to destroy the culture of a people. (p. 268)

ethnographic fieldwork   A research method in which sociocultural anthropologists have intensive, long-term engagements with a group of people. It may involve the use of both qualitative and quantitative methods, including interviews, participant observation, and survey-based research. (p. 38)

ethnographic present   Use of the present tense to describe a culture, although the description may refer to situations that existed in the past. (p. 130)

ethnography   A written description and analysis of a particular group of people, usually based upon anthropological fieldwork. (p. 42)

etic perspective   Refers to the analysis of an aspect of culture using comparative categories, explanations, and interpretation from the perspective of an outside observer. (p. 38)

exogamy   A rule that requires a person to marry someone outside his or her own group. (p. 142)

extended family   A family group based on blood relations of three or more generations. (p. 137)

factory model   An energy-intensive, ecologically damaging form of agriculture intended to grow or raise as many crops or livestock as possible in the shortest time. (p. 88)

factory system   A system of production characterized by the concentration of labour and machines in specific places. It is associated with the Industrial Revolution. (p. 73)

free trade   The removal of barriers to the free flow of goods and capital between nations by eliminating import and export taxes as well as subsidies paid to farmers and business people. It may also mean reducing environmental or social laws when they restrict the flow of goods and capital. (p. 225)

gender   Culturally constructed ideals of behaviour, dress, occupations, roles, and comportment for particular sexes. (p. 200)

genocide   The attempt to exterminate a people. (p. 268)

globalization   Defined by Anthony Giddens as the intensification of worldwide social relations that link distant localities in such a way that local happenings are shaped by events occurring many miles away, and vice versa. (p. 222)

hegemonic masculinity   Refers to ideals and norms of masculinity in a society, which are often privileged over others. (p. 202)

imagined community   A term coined by Benedict Anderson in 1983. It refers to the fact that even in the absence of face-to-face interactions, a sense of community (e.g., nationalism) is culturally constructed by forces such as the mass media. (p. 164)

impartible inheritance   A form of inheritance in which family property is passed undivided to one heir. (p. 150)

incest taboo   A rule that prohibits sexual relations among kin of certain categories, such as brothers or sisters, parents and children, or, in some cases, cousins. (p. 139)

Indigenism   Refers to an international, collaborative movement that aims to protect the rights and livelihoods of Indigenous peoples. (p. 241)

Indigenous peoples   Groups of people whose ancestors predate the arrival of European or other forms of colonialism, who share a culture and/or way of life that they often identify as distinct from "mainstream" society, and who often feel that they have a right to self-government. (p. 180)

Industrial Revolution   A period of European history, generally identified as occurring in the late 18th century, marked by a shift in production from agriculture to industrial goods, urbanization, and the factory system. (p. 64)

informed consent   The ongoing process of ensuring that research participants understand the goals, methods, and potential outcomes of the research process, and give permission for the researcher to conduct said research. (p. 51)

International Monetary Fund   Created as an outcome of the 1944 Bretton Woods Conference to regulate currency transactions among countries. The IMF now makes loans and regulates the economies of lending countries. (p. 80)

interpersonal theory of disease   A view of disease in which it is assumed that illness is caused by tensions or conflicts in social relations. (p. 85)

irrigation agriculture   A form of cultivation in which water is used to deliver nutrients to growing plants. (p. 61)

key metaphors   A term to identify metaphors that dominate the meanings that people in a specific culture attribute to their experience. (p. 98)

key scenarios   Dominant stories or myths that portray the values and beliefs of a specific society. (p. 104)

kinship   Refers to the anthropological, cross-cultural study of family composition, marriage, and descent patterns. (p. 130)

kula ring   A system of inter-island gift exchange documented by anthropologist Bronislaw Malinowski in the Trobriand Islands. It involves the exchange of shell necklaces and armbands. According to Malinowski, the *kula* ring serves, among other things, to create alliances and social ties among individuals living on different islands. (p. 175)

linguistic anthropology   *A study of* the relationship between language and culture. Linguistic anthropologists explore how people use language, both in a physical sense with regard to how communication is structured, and in a historical sense with regard to how different languages have developed and spread throughout history. (p. 7)

magic   Refers to the manipulation of words or substances to influence spiritual beings for good or evil purposes. (p. 100)

market externalities   Costs that are not included in the prices people pay, for example, health risks and environmental degradation. (p. 228)

matrilineage   A lineage that is formed by tracing descent in the female line. (p. 134)

matrilineal kinship   A system of descent in which persons are related to their kin through the mother only. (p. 133)

meritocracy   A social system in which individuals are rewarded and resources are distributed according to achievement, effort, and ability. (p. 190)

metaphors Figures of speech in which linguistic expressions are taken from one area of experience and applied to another. (p. 96)

multiculturalism A term that Eva Mackey defines as a Canadian policy in which all hyphenated cultures, such as African-Canadian and French-Canadian, are described and celebrated as part of a "cultural mosaic." Contrast with the "cultural melting pot" image that is used in the United States. (p. 236)

multi-sited fieldwork This term, coined by George Marcus in 1995, refers to the process of connecting localized experiences of fieldwork with broader, global processes. It necessitates understanding various issues from multiple "sites," or perspectives. (p. 45)

myth A story or narrative that portrays the meanings people give to their experience. (p. 99)

nation A collection of people who share a common language, worldview, and ancestry. (p. 227)

nation-state A political community that has clearly defined territorial borders and centralized authority. (p. 226)

natural selection Refers to Darwin's idea that the survival of different species of organisms is partly contingent upon how well adapted they are to their physical environments. Those with favourable physical traits are more likely to survive to reproduce. (p. 63)

nature versus nurture A phrase, coined by Sir Francis Galton in 1874, that references a long-standing scholarly debate concerning whether or not human behaviours and identities are the result of nature (biological and genetic factors) or nurture (learned and cultural factors). (p. 164)

neoliberalism An economic philosophy that argues for minimal government involvement in the economy and greatly accelerated economic growth. Well-being, neoliberals argue, is best served by liberating individual entrepreneurs to operate in a framework of strong property rights, free markets, and free trade. (p. 225)

new racism A form of "soft" racism that posits racial differences as cultural, rather than biological, but which still views such differences as immutable or insurmountable. (p. 208)

nuclear family The family group consisting of father, mother, and their biological or adopted children. (p. 132)

partible inheritance A form of inheritance in which the goods or property of a family is divided among the heirs. (p. 150)

participant observation An element of fieldwork that can involve participating in daily tasks, and observing daily interactions among a particular group. (p. 41)

pathogen An infectious agent such as a bacteria or a virus that can cause disease. (p. 82)

patrilineage A lineage that is formed by tracing descent in the male line. (p. 137)

patrilineal kinship A system of descent in which persons are related to their kin through the father only. (p. 133)

polyandry A form of marriage in which a woman is permitted to have more than one husband. (p. 147)

polygamy A form of marriage in which a person is permitted to have more than one spouse. (p. 147)

polygyny A form of marriage in which a man is permitted to have more than one wife. (p. 147)

population density The number of people in a given geographic area. (p. 68)

potlatch A celebration, usually involving elaborate feasting and the redistribution of gifts, found among many indigenous Northwest Coast groups, such as the Tsimshian. The potlatch is a means of creating a new identity or of reinforcing social status within a group. (p. 176)

principle of reciprocity According to Marcel Mauss, gift giving involves reciprocity. The idea is that the exchange of gifts creates a feeling of obligation, in that the gift must be repaid. (p. 175)

progress The idea that human history is the story of a steady advance from a life dependent on the whims of nature to a life of control and domination over natural forces. (p. 60)

"putting out" system A means of production, common in the 16th and 17th centuries and surviving today, in which a manufacturer or merchant supplies the materials and sometimes the tools to workers, who produce the goods in their own homes. (p. 72)

qualitative research Research methods that aim to explore, rather than measure, various phenomena, often through forms of observation such as interviews, focus groups, and direct participant observation. (p. 38)

quantitative research Research methods that involve the generation of statistical data. Examples include surveys and censuses. (p. 37)

race A culturally constructed form of identity and social hierarchy, *race* refers to the presumed hereditary, physical characteristics of a group of people. These physical, or phenotypic, differences are often erroneously correlated with behavioural attributes. (p. 192)

racism Refers to the discrimination and mistreatment of particular "racial" groups. (p. 193)

rapport A feeling of affinity, friendship, and responsibility between an anthropologist and an informant. It is often developed through the use of long-term ethnographic fieldwork. (p. 38)

refugees Groups of people who have left their homeland due to warfare, forced expulsion, acts of terrorism, or other factors. (p. 270)

relativistic fallacy The idea that it is impossible to make moral judgments about the beliefs and behaviours of members of other cultures. (p. 13)

representation The way in which a group of people is depicted in writing or through images. Anthropologists are increasingly conscious of the fact that when they write about a group of people, they are constructing particular representations that may have positive or negative long-term effects for a group of people. (p. 39)

revitalization movements The term suggested by Anthony F. C. Wallace for attempts by a people to construct a more satisfying culture. (p. 117)

rites of passage The term coined in 1908 by Arnold van Gennep to refer to the category of rituals that accompany changes in status, such as the transition from boyhood to manhood, living to dead, or student to graduate. (pp. 106, 173)

ritual A dramatic rendering or social portrayal of meanings shared by a specific body of people in a way that makes them seem correct and proper. (*See also* symbolic actions.) (p. 94)

salvage anthropology An approach to anthropology that arose in the late 1800s when anthropologists witnessed the extinction or assimilation of Indigenous peoples throughout the world. In response, some anthropologists, such as Franz Boas, suggested that anthropologists rapidly document the oral stories, songs, histories, and other traditions of Indigenous peoples before they disappeared. (p. 44)

secularism Refers to the separation of political and economic realms of society from religion or spirituality. (p. 122)

sedentary A mode of livelihood characterized by permanent or semi-permanent settlements. (p. 60)

sex Hormonal, chromosomal, or physical differences between men and women. (p. 200)

shamanism Refers to a spiritual belief system whereby spiritual practitioners, called "shamans," enter into an altered state of consciousness to seek guidance from spiritual forces. (p. 113)

slash-and-burn, or swidden, agriculture A mode of livelihood in which forests are cleared by burning trees and brush, and crops are planted among the ashes of the cleared ground. (p. 61)

social identity The view that people have of their own and others' positions in society. These learned personal and social affiliations may include gender, sexuality, race, class, nationalism, and ethnicity. Individuals seek confirmation from others that they occupy the positions on the social landscape that they claim to occupy. (p. 161)

social hierarchy The ordering and ranking of individuals within society, also known as *social stratification*. Those at the top of the hierarchy are generally afforded more power, wealth, prestige, or privileges in a society. Hierarchies can be based on race, gender, class, caste, ethnicity, national affiliation, or other factors. (p. 187)

sociocentric A context-dependent view of self. The self exists as an entity only within the concrete situations or roles occupied by the person. (p. 168)

sociocultural anthropology A comparative approach to the study of societies and cultures that focuses on differences and similarities in the ways that societies are structured and cultural meanings are created. (p. 3)

states Forms of society characterized by a hierarchical ranking of people and centralized political control. (p. 61)

structural violence Refers to the systematic ways in which social structures or social institutions harm or otherwise disadvantage local individuals. Structural violence is often invisible and lacking one specific person who can (or will) be held responsible. (p. 216)

symbolic actions The activities—including ritual, myth, art, dance, and music—that dramatically depict the meanings shared by a specific body of people. (p. 95)

syncretization The term given to the combination of old beliefs or religions and new ones that are often introduced during colonization. (p. 118)

third gender   A gender role given to someone who does not fit within strictly masculine or feminine gender roles in a given society. (p. 200)

totemism   The use of a symbol, generally an animal or a plant, as a physical representation for a group, generally a clan (p. 94)

transnational   Involving more than one nation-state; reaching beyond or transcending national boundaries. (p. 230)

unilineal evolution   A late-19th-century theory of social evolution which posited that all societies go through a series of standardized stages of change. It ethnocentrically positioned Western societies at the apex of a "ladder of civilization." (p. 63)

vector   An organism, such as a mosquito, tick, flea, or snail, that can transmit disease to another animal. (p. 82)

white privilege   Refers to the fact that, in many societies, "white" people have access to greater power, authority, and privileges than non-white people. (p. 195)

witchcraft   Refers to the belief that an individual (the witch) has the ability to cause harm to others through the manipulation of powerful substances. (p. 100)

World Bank   One of the institutions created at the 1944 Bretton Woods, New Hampshire, meeting of Allied nations. The World Bank (or the Bank for Reconstruction and Development) functions as a lending institution to nations largely for projects related to economic development. (p. 79)

worldview   An encompassing picture of reality based on shared cultural assumptions about how the world works. (p. 93)

BIBLIOGRAPHY

Abu-Lughod, Lila. 1995. "A Tale of Two Pregnancies." In *Women Writing Culture,* edited by Ruth Behar and Deborah A. Gordon. Berkeley: University of California Press.

Adelson, Naomi. 2000. *"Being Alive Well": Health and the Politics of Cree Well-Being.* Toronto: University of Toronto Press.

Aditjondro, George. 2000. "Ninjas, Nanggalas, Monuments, and Mossad Manuals." In *Death Squad: The Anthropology of State Terror,* edited by Jeffery A. Sluka. Philadelphia: University of Pennsylvania Press.

Alford, Richard D. 1988. *Naming and Identity: A Cross-Cultural Study of Personal Naming Practices.* New Haven: HRAF Press.

Ameeriar, Lalaie. 2012. "The Sanitized Sensorium." *American Anthropologist* 114(3): 509–20.

American Anthropological Association. 1998. *Statement on Race.* http://www.aaanet.org/stmts/racepp.htm

American Anthropological Association. 2005. *Anthropology News* 46:1.

Anderson, Benedict. 1991. *Imagined Communities: Reflections on the Origin and Spread of Nationalism.* New York: Verso.

Anderson, Margaret (Seguin). 1984. *Interpretive Contexts for Traditional and Current Coast Tsimshian Feasts, 98.* Ottawa: Canadian Ethnology Service Paper. National Museum of Canada.

—, ed. 1984. *The Tsimshian: Images of the Past, Views for the Present.* Vancouver: UBC Press.

—. 2004. "Understanding Tsimshian Potlatch." In *Native Peoples: The Canadian Experience,* edited by R. Bruce Morrison and C. Roderick Wilson. Toronto: Oxford University Press.

—, and Marjorie Halpin, eds. 2000. *Potlatch at Getsegukla.* Vancouver: UBC Press.

Anderson-Levy, Lisa. 2000. "Colliding/Colluding Identities: Race, Class, and Gender in Jamaican Family Systems." In *New Directions in Anthropological Kinship,* edited by Linda Stone. Lanham: Rowman and Littlefield.

Angeloni, Elvio. 1990. *Anthropology 90/91.* Guilford, CT: Dushkin.

Arat-Koc, Sedef. 1999a. "'Good Enough to Work but Not Good Enough to Stay': Foreign Domestic Workers and the Law." In *Locating Law: Race / Class / Gender Connections,* edited by Elizabeth Comack. Halifax: Fernwood.

—. 1999b. "Neoliberalism, State Restructuring, and Immigration: Changes in Canadian Policies in the 1990s." *Journal of Canadian Studies* 34(2): 31–57.

Asch, Michael, ed. 2002. *Aboriginal and Treaty Rights in Canada: Essays on Law, Equality, and Respect for Difference.* Vancouver: UBC Press.

Austin-Broos, Diane. 1997. *Jamaica Genesis: Religion and the Politics of Moral Orders.* Chicago: University of Chicago Press.

Avruch, Kevin. 2009. "Transforming Conflict Resolution Education: Applying Anthropology Alongside Your Students." *Learning and Teaching* 2(2): 8–22.

Bannerji, Himani. 2000. *The Dark Side of the Nation: Essays on Multiculturalism, Nationalism, and Gender.* Toronto: Canadian Scholars' Press.

Barker, John, ed. 1990. *Christianity in Oceania: Ethnographic Perspectives.* Lanham: University Press of America.

Barrett, Stanley R. 1987. *Is God a Racist? The Right Wing in Canada.* Toronto: University of Toronto Press.

—. 1996. *Anthropology: A Student's Guide to Theory and Method.* Toronto: University of Toronto Press.

—. 2002. *Culture Meets Power.* Westport, CT: Praeger.

Barsh, Russel Lawrence. 2002. "Netukulimk Past and Present: Mikmaw Ethics and the Atlantic Fisheries." *Journal of Canadian Studies* 37(1): 15–44.

Basok, Tanya. 2004. *Tortillas and Tomatoes: Transmigrant Mexican Harvesters in Canada.* Montreal and Kingston: McGill–Queen's University Press.

Beaud, Michel. 1983. *A History of Capitalism, 1500–1980.* New York: Monthly Review Press.

Becker, Anne E. 1995. *Body, Self, and Society: The View from Fiji.* Philadelphia: University of Pennsylvania Press.

—. 2004. "Television, Disordered Eating, and Young Women in Fiji: Negotiating Body Image and Identity During Rapid Social Change." *Culture, Medicine, and Psychiatry* 29: 533–59.

Becker, Gay. 1997. *Disrupted Lives: How People Create Meaning in a Chaotic World*. Berkeley: University of California Press.

Behar, Ruth, and Deborah Gordon, eds. 1995. *Women Writing Culture*. Berkeley: University of California Press.

Bellah, Robert, Richard Madsen, William M. Sullivan, Ann Swidler, and Steven M. Tipton. 1984. *Habits of the Heart*. Berkeley: University of California Press.

Belmonte, Thomas. 1989. *The Broken Fountain*. New York: Columbia University Press.

Benedict, Ruth. 1934. *Patterns of Culture*. New York: Houghton Mifflin.

Bielawski, Ellen. 2004. *Rogue Diamonds: Northern Riches on Dene Land*. Seattle: University of Washington Press.

Blackwood, Evelyn. 2005. "Wedding Bell Blues: Marriage, Missing Men, and Matrifocal Follies." *American Ethnologist* 32(1): 3–19.

Blaikie, Piers, and Harold Brookfield. 1987. *Land Degradation and Society*. London: Methuen.

Blaser, Mario, Harvey Feit, and Glenn McRae, eds. 2004. *In the Way of Development: Indigenous Peoples Life Projects and Globalization*. London and New York: Zed.

Blundell, Valda. 1989. "The Tourist and the Native." In *A Different Drummer: Readings in Anthropology with a Canadian Perspective,* edited by Bruce Alden Cox, Jacques Chevallier, and Valda Blundell. Ottawa: Carleton University Press.

Boas, Franz. 1940. *Race, Language and Culture*. New York: Macmillan.

Boas, Franz, and George Hunt. 1905. *Kwakiutl Texts*. Memoir of the American Museum of Natural History, vol. 5.

Bodley, John. 1985. *Anthropology and Contemporary Problems*, 2nd ed. Palo Alto, CA: Mayfield.

——. 1994. *Cultural Anthropology: Tribes, States, and the Global System*. Mountain View: Mayfield.

——. 1999. *The Victims of Progress*. Mountain View: Mayfield.

Boellstorff, Tom. 2008. *Coming of Age in Second Life: An Anthropologist Explores the Virtually Human*. Princeton: Princeton University Press.

Bohannan, Laura. 1966. "Shakespeare in the Bush." *Natural History Magazine*, August/September.

Bonanno, Alessandro, Lawrence Busch, William Friedland, Lourdes Gouveia, and Enzo Mingione, eds. 1994. *From Columbus to ConAgra: The Globalization of Agriculture and Food*. Lawrence: University Press of Kansas.

Bossen, Laurel. 2002. *Chinese Women and Rural Development: Sixty Years of Change in Lu Village, Yunnan*. Lanham: Rowman and Littlefield.

Bourgois, Philippe. 2003. *In Search of Respect: Selling Crack in El Barrio*, 2nd ed. Cambridge: Cambridge University Press.

Branford, Sue, and Jan Rocha. 2002. *Cutting the Wire: The Story of the Landless Movement in Brazil*. London: Latin American Bureau.

Braudel, Fernand. 1982. *The Wheels of Commerce. Volume 2 of Civilization and Capitalism, 15th–18th Century*. New York: Harper and Row.

Brennan, Denise. 2004. *What's Love Got to Do with It?: Transnational Desires and Sex Tourism in the Dominican Republic*. Durham, NC: Duke University Press.

Brettell, Caroline, and Carolyn Sargent, eds. 2005. *Gender in Cross-Cultural Perspective*. Upper Saddle River: Prentice Hall.

Briggs, Jean. 1970. *Never in Anger*. Cambridge, MA: Harvard University Press.

Brody, Hugh. 2000. *The Other Side of Eden: Hunters, Farmers, and the Shaping of the World*. Vancouver: Douglas and McIntyre.

Brown, Karen McCarthy. 1991. *Mama Lola: A Vodou Priestess in Brooklyn*. Berkeley: University of California Press.

Burt, Ben. 1994. *Tradition and Christianity: The Colonial Transformation of a Solomon Islands Society*. Philadelphia: Harwood.

Burt, Martha. 1992. *Over the Edge: The Growth of Homelessness in the 1980s*. New York: Russell Sage Foundation.

Cagan, Leslie. 1983. "Feminism and Militarism." In *Beyond Survival: New Directions for the Disarmament Movement,* edited by M. Albert and D. Dellinger. Boston: South End.

Canadian Council on Learning. 2009. *The State of Aboriginal Learning in Canada: A Holistic Approach to Measuring Success*. Ottawa: Canadian Council on Learning.

Carneiro, Robert. 1978. "Political Expansion as an Expression of the Principle of Competitive Exclusion."

In *Origins of the State: The Anthropology of Political Evolution,* edited by Ronald Cohn and Elman Service. Philadelphia: Institute for the Study of Human Issues.

——. 1979. "Slash-and-Burn Cultivation Among the Kuikuru and Its Implication for Cultural Development in the Amazon Basin." In *The Evolution of Horticultural Systems in Native South America: Causes and Consequences. Anthropologica Supplement 2,* edited by Johannes Wilbert. Caracas.

——. 1990. "Chiefdom-Level Warfare as Exemplified in Fiji and Cauca Valley." In *The Anthropology of War,* edited by Jonathan Hass. New York: Cambridge University Press.

Carrier, James G. 1993. "The Rituals of Christmas Giving." In *Unwrapping Christmas,* edited by Daniel Miller. Oxford: Clarendon.

——. 1995. *Gifts and Commodities: Exchange and Western Capitalism Since 1700.* London: Routledge.

Carter, Sarah. 1999. *Aboriginal People and Colonizers of Western Canada to 1900.* Toronto: University of Toronto Press.

Cesara, Manda. 1982. *Reflections of a Woman Anthropologist: No Hiding Place.* Toronto: Academic Press.

Chagnon, Napoleon. 1968. *Yanomamö: The Fierce People.* Toronto: Holt.

——. 1990. "Reproductive and Somatic Conflicts of Interest in the Genesis of Violence and Warfare Among Tribesmen." In *The Anthropology of War,* edited by Jonathan Hass. New York: Cambridge University Press.

Chambers, Erve. 2000. *Native Tours: The Anthropology of Travel and Tourism.* Prospect Heights: Waveland.

Chen, Zhongping. 2004. "Chinese Minority and Everyday Racism in Canadian Towns and Small Cities: An Ethnic Study of the Case of Peterborough, Ontario, 1892–1951." *Canadian Ethnic Studies* 36(1): 71–91.

Chimbinda, Jorge. 2006. "The Umbundu Naming System." M.A. thesis, Department of Anthropology, University of Western Ontario, London.

Chodkiewicz, Jean-Luc, and Raymond E. Wiest, eds. 2004. *Globalization and Community.* Winnipeg: University of Manitoba Press.

Chomsky, Noam. 1984. *Turning the Tide: U.S. Intervention in Central America and the Struggle for Peace.* Boston: South End.

Churchill, Ward. 1994. *Indians Are Us? Culture and Genocide in Native North America.* Monroe: Common Courage.

Citizens for Public Justice. 2012. *Poverty Trends Scorecard Canada 2012.* www.cpj.ca.

Clammer, John, Sylvie Poirier, and Eric Schwimmer, eds. 2004. *Figured Worlds: Ontological Obstacles in Intercultural Relations.* Toronto: University of Toronto Press.

Clark, Kim. 2005. "Ecuadorian Indians, the Nation, and Class in Historic Perspective: Rethinking a 'New Social Movement.'" *Anthropologica* 47(1): 53–65.

Clark-Decès, Isabelle. 2011. "Introduction." In *A Companion to the Anthropology of India,* edited by Isabelle Clark-Decès, 1–21. Malden, MA: Blackwell.

Cohen, Mark. 1977. *The Food Crisis in Prehistory.* New Haven: Yale University Press.

——. 1989. *Health and the Rise of Civilization.* New Haven: Yale University Press.

Cohn, Carol. 1987. "Sex and Death in the Rational World of Defense Intellectuals." *Signs* 12: 687–718.

——. 1991. "Decoding Military Newspeak." *Ms.* 5.

Cole, Sally. 2000. "Reflections on Anthropology in Canada: Introduction." *Anthropologica* 42(2): 123–26.

Collier, Jane E., and Michelle Rosaldo. 1981. "Politics and Gender in Simple Societies." In *Sexual Meanings: The Cultural Construction of Gender and Sexuality,* edited by Sherry B. Ortner and Harriet Whitehead. New York: Cambridge University Press.

Collings, Peter, and Richard G. Condon. 1996. "Blood on Ice: Status, Self-Esteem, and Ritual Injury Among Inuit Hockey Players." *Human Organization* 55(3): 253–62.

Comaroff, Jean, and John Comoraff. 2009. "Alien-Nation: Zombies, Immigrants, and Millennial Capitalism." In *Enchantments of Modernity: Empire, Nation, Globalization,* edited by Saurabh Dube, 451–81. New Delhi: Routledge India.

Conklin, Beth. 2001. *Consuming Grief: Compassionate Cannibalism in an Amazonian Society.* Austin: University of Texas Press.

Coombe, Rosemary. 2013. *Dynamic Fair Dealing: Creating Canadian Culture Online.* Toronto: University of Toronto Press.

Corten, Andre, and Ruth Marshall-Fratani. 2001. *Between Babel and Pentecost: Transnational Pentecostalism in Africa and Latin America.* Bloomington: Indiana University Press.

Counts, David, and Dorothy Counts. 1998. "Fictive Families in the Field." In *Fieldwork and Families: Constructing New Models for Ethnographic Research,* edited by Juliana Flinn, Leslie Marshall, and Jocelyn Armstrong. Honolulu: University of Hawai'i Press.

Cowan, Jane K., Marie-Benedicte Dembour, and Richard A. Wilson, eds. 2001. *Culture and Rights: Anthropological Perspectives.* Cambridge: Cambridge University Press.

Cowell, Daniel David. 1985/86. "Funerals, Family, and Forefathers: A View of Italian-American Funeral Practices." *Omega* 16: 69–85.

Cox, Bruce Alden, Jacques Chevalier, and Valda Blundell, eds. 1989. *A Different Drummer: Readings in Anthropology with a Canadian Perspective.* Ottawa: Carleton University Press.

Crick, Malcolm R. 1982. "Anthropology of Knowledge." *Annual Review of Anthropology* 11: 287–313. Palo Alto: Annual Reviews.

Crowley, Aleister. 1985. *The Book of Thoth.* Stamford: U.S. Games Systems.

Cruikshank, Julie. 1998. *The Social Life of Stories: Narrative and Knowledge in the Yukon Territory.* Lincoln: University of Nebraska Press.

——. 1990. *Life Lived Like a Story: Life Stories of Three Yukon Native Elders.* Lincoln: University of Nebraska Press.

——. 2005. *Do Glaciers Listen? Local Knowledge, Colonial Encounters, and Social Imagination.* Vancouver: UBC Press.

Culhane, Dara. 1998. *The Pleasures of the Crown: Anthropology, Law, and First Nations.* Burnaby: Talonbooks.

Culhane Speck, Dara. 1987. *An Error in Judgement: The Politics of Medical Care in an Indian/White Community.* Vancouver: Talonbooks.

Cummins, Bryan D. 2004. *"Only God Can Own the Land": The Attawapiskat Cree.* Toronto: Pearson Education.

Cummings, Maggie. 2008. "The Trouble with Trousers: Gossip, *Kastom,* and Sexual Culture in Vanuatu." In *Making Sense of AIDS: Culture, Sexuality, and Power in Melanesia,* edited by Leslie Butt and Richard Eves Honolulu, 133–49. University of Hawai'i Press.

Daniel, Valentine. 1996. *Charred Lullabies: Chapters in an Anthropology of Violence.* Princeton: Princeton University Press.

Darnell, Regna. 1990. *Edward Sapir: Linguist, Anthropologist, Humanist.* Berkeley: University of California Press.

——. 1998a. *And Along Came Boas: Continuity and Revolution in Americanist Anthropology.* Amsterdam and Philadelphia: John Benjamins.

——. 1998b. "Toward a History of Canadian Departments of Anthropology: Retrospect, Prospect, and Common Cause." *Anthropologica* 40(2): 153–68.

——. 2000. "Canadian Anthropologists, the First Nations, and Canada's Self-Image at the Millennium." *Anthropologica* 42(2): 165–74.

——, and Julia Harrison. 2006. "Introduction." In *Historicizing Canadian Anthropology,* edited by Julia Harrison and Regna Darnell, 3–18. Vancouver: University of British Columbia Press.

Darwin, Charles. 1859. On the Origin of Species by Means of Natural Selection, or the Preservation of Favoured Races in the Struggle for Life. London: John Murray.

Davis, D. L., and R. G. Whitten. 1987. "The Cross-Cultural Study of Human Sexuality." *Annual Review of Anthropology* 16: 69–98.

Davies, James, Rodrigo Luberas, and Anthony Shorrocks. 2014. *Credit Suisse Global Wealth Databook 2014.* Credit Suisse Research Institute. http://economics.uwo.ca/people/davies_docs/credit-suisse-global-wealth-report-2014.pdf

Davis-Floyd, Robbie E. 2004. *Birth as an American Rite of Passage.* Oakland, CA: University of California Press.

Dawkins, Richard. 2006. *The God Delusion.* Boston: Houghton Mifflin.

D'Andrade, Roy. 1995. "Moral Models in Anthropology." *Current Anthropology* 36: 399–408.

Day, Richard J. F. 2000. *Multiculturalism and the History of Canadian Diversity.* Toronto: University of Toronto Press.

Delaney, Carol. 1991. *The Seed and the Soil: Gender and Cosmology in a Turkish Village Society.* Berkeley: University of California Press.

Deliège, Robert. 2011. "Caste, Class, and Untouchability." In *A Companion to the Anthropology of India,* edited by Isabelle Clark-Decès, 45–61. Malden, MA: Blackwell.

Desai, Ashok V. 1972. "Population and Standards of Living in Akbar's Time." In *Indian Economic and Social History Review* 9: 42–62.

Devita, Philip, ed. 1990. *The Humbled Anthropologist: Tales from the Pacific.* Belmont: Wadsworth.

——. 1991. *The Naked Anthropologist: Tales from Around the World*. Belmont: Wadsworth.

Dickason, Olive Patricia. 2002. *Canada's First Nations: A History of Founding Peoples from Earliest Times*. 3rd ed. Toronto: Oxford University Press.

Divale, William Tulio, and Marvin Harris. 1976. "Population, Warfare, and the Male Supremacist Complex." *American Anthropologist* 78: 521–38.

Douglas, Mary. 1966. *Purity and Danger*. New York: Praeger.

Douglas, Mary, and Aaron Wildavsky. 1982. *Risk and Culture: An Essay on the Selection of Technical and Environmental Changes*. Berkeley: University of California Press.

Douglas, Ngaire. 1996. *They Came for Savages: 100 Years of Tourism in Melanesia*. Lismore: Southern Cross University Press.

Dréze, Jean, and Amartya Sen. 1991. *Hunger and Public Action*. New York: Cambridge University Press.

Dumont, Louis. 1970. *Homo Hierarchicus: An Essay on the Caste System*. Chicago: University of Chicago Press.

Durham, William H. 1990. "Advances in Evolutionary Culture Theory." *Annual Review of Anthropology* 19: 187–210.

Durkheim, Emile. 1961. *The Elementary Forms of the Religious Life*. New York: Collier.

Dyck, Noel. 2000. "Games, Bodies, Celebrations, and Boundaries: Anthropological Perspectives on Sports." In *Sports, Games and Cultures*, edited by Noel Dyke. Oxford: Berg.

Dyck, Noel. 2006. "Canadian Anthropology and the Ethnography of 'Indian Administration.'" In *Historicizing Canadian Anthropology*, edited by Julia Harrison and Regna Darnell, 78–92. Vancouver: University of British Columbia Press.

Dyck, Noel, and James B. Waldram, eds. 1993. *Anthropology, Public Policy, and Native Peoples in Canada*. Montreal and Kingston: McGill–Queen's University Press.

Eckert, Penelope, and Sally McConnell-Ginet. 2003. *Language and Gender*. Cambridge: Cambridge University Press.

Edmonds, Alexander. 2010. *Pretty Modern: Beauty, Sex, and Plastic Surgery in Brazil*. Durham: Duke University Press.

Eisler, Riane. 1987. *The Chalice and the Blade*. New York: Harper and Row.

Eller, Jack. 1999. "Quebec: Masters in Our Own House." In *From Culture to Ethnicity to Conflict: An Anthropological Perspective on International Ethnic Conflict*. Ann Arbor: University of Michigan Press.

Epp, Marlene, Francis Iacovetta, and Francis Swyripa, eds. 2004. *Sisters or Strangers? Immigrant, Ethnic, and Racialized Women in Canadian History*. Toronto: University of Toronto Press.

Eramian, Laura. 2014. "Ethnicity Without Labels: Ambiguity and Excess in 'Postethnic' Rwanda." *Focaal: Journal of Global and Historical Anthropology* 70: 96–109.

Erasmus, Charles. 1977. *In Search of the Common Good*. Glencoe: The Free Press.

Ervin, Alexander M. 2001. *Canadian Perspectives in Cultural Anthropology*. Toronto: Nelson Education.

——. 2005. *Applied Anthropology: Tools and Perspectives for Contemporary Practice*. Boston: Allyn and Bacon.

Escobar, Arturo. 1995. *Encountering Development: The Making and Unmaking of the Third World*. Princeton: Princeton University Press.

Evans-Pritchard, E. E. 1937. *Witchcraft, Oracles and Magic Among the Azande*. Oxford: Clarendon.

——. 1940. *The Nuer: A Description of the Modes of Livelihood and Political Institutions of a Nilotic People*. Oxford: Clarendon.

——. 1985. *Theories of Primitive Religion*. San Francisco: Greenwood.

Farah, Randa. 2003. "The Marginalization of Palestinian Refugees." In *Problems of Protection: The UNHCR, Refugees, and Human Rights*, edited by Niklaus Steiner, Mark Gibney, and Gil Loescher. New York and London: Routledge.

——. 2004. "But Where Shall I Return? Where To? 1948 Palestinian Refugees: Land and Return." *Mediterranean Journal of Human Rights* 8(2): 157–84.

——. 2005. "Out of the Shadows: Listening to Place-Based Narratives of Palestinian Women." In *Women and the Politics of Place*, edited by Wendy Harcourt and Arturo Escobar. Bloomfield: Kumarian.

Farmer, Paul. 1992. *AIDS and Accusation: Haiti and the Geography of Blame*. Berkeley: University of California Press.

——. 2003. *Pathologies of Power: Health, Human Rights, and the New War on the Poor*. Berkeley: University of California Press.

Fausto-Sterling, Anne. 1993. "The Five Sexes: Why Male and Female Are Not Enough." *The Sciences* 33: 20–24.

Fei, Hsiao-Tung. 1939. *Peasant Life in China: A Field Study of Country Life in the Yangtze Valley*. London: Routledge and Kegan Paul.

Feinberg, Richard. 2001. "Introduction: Schneider's Cultural Analysis of Kinship and Its Implications for Anthropological Relativism." In *The Cultural Analysis of Kinship: The Legacy of David M. Schneider*, edited by Richard Feinberg and Martin Ottenheimer. Urbana: University of Illinois Press.

Feit, Harvey A. 1973. "The Ethno-Ecology of the Waswanipi Cree; or How Hunters Manage Their Resources." In *Cultural Ecology*, edited by B. Cox. Toronto: McClelland & Stewart.

——. 1982. "The Income Security Program for Cree Hunters in Quebec: An Experiment in Increasing the Autonomy of Hunters in a Developed Nation State." *Canadian Journal of Anthropology* 3(1): 57–70.

——. 2001. "Hunting, Nature, and Metaphor: Political and Discursive Strategies in James Bay Cree Resistance and Autonomy." In *Indigenous Traditions and Ecology: The Interbeing of Cosmology and Community*, edited by John A. Grim. Cambridge, MA: Harvard Divinity School.

——. 2004a. "Hunting and the Quest for Power: The James Bay Cree and Whiteman Development." In *Native Peoples: The Canadian Experience*, edited by R. Bruce Morrison and C. Roderick Wilson. Don Mills, ON: Oxford University Press.

——. 2004b. "James Bay Crees' Life Projects and Politics: Histories of Place, Animal Partners and Enduring Relationships." In *In The Way of Development: Indigenous Peoples, Life Projects, and Globalization*, edited by Mario Blaser, Harvey A. Feit, and Glenn McRae, 92–110. London and New York: Zed Books in association with the International Development Research Centre, Ottawa.

Fenton, Cameron. 2010. "The Ethnography of an Airstrike: Canada's Military Academics in the Afghan War and at Home." http://www.dominionpaper.ca/articles/3295

Ferguson, R. Brian. 1992. "A Savage Encounter: Western Contact and the Yanomami War Complex." In *War in the Tribal Zone: Expanding States and Indigenous Warfare*, edited by R. Brian Ferguson and Neil L. Whitehead. Santa Fe: School of American Research Press.

——. 1995. *Yanomami Warfare: A Political History*. Santa Fe: School of the American Research Press.

——. 2008. "Ten Points on War." *Social Analysis* 52(2): 32–49.

Fernandez, James W. 1978. "African Religious Movements." *Annual Review of Anthropology* 7: 195–234.

Fernando, Mayanthi. 2014. The Republic Unsettled: Muslim French and the Contradictions of Secularism. Durham, NC: Duke University Press.

——. 2015. *The French Myth of Secularism*. http://theconversation.com/the-french-myth-of-secularism-36227

Fienup-Riordan, Ann. 1990. *Eskimo Essays: Yup'ik Lives and How We See Them*. New Brunswick: Rutgers University Press.

Fisher, William. 1997. "Doing Good? The Politics and Antipolitics of NGO Practices." *Annual Review of Anthropology* 26: 439–64.

Fleras, Augie, and Jean Leonard Elliot. 2002. *Engaging Diversity: Multiculturalism in Canada*. Toronto: Nelson Education.

Foucault, Michel. 1979. *Discipline and Punish: The Birth of the Prison*. New York: Vintage.

Francis, Daniel. 1992. *The Imaginary Indian: The Image of the Indian in Canadian Culture*. Vancouver: Arsenal Pulp.

Franklin, Sarah, and Susan McKinnon, eds. 2001. *Relative Values: Reconfiguring Kinship Studies*. Durham: Duke University Press.

French, Hilary. 2000. *Vanishing Borders: Protecting the Planet in the Age of Globalization*. New York: Norton.

Frideres, James. 2003. *Native Peoples in Canada: Contemporary Conflicts*. Toronto: Prentice Hall.

Frideres, James S., and René Gadacz. 2001. *Aboriginal Peoples in Canada: Contemporary Conflicts*. Toronto: Prentice Hall.

Fried, Morton, Marvin Harris, and Robert Murphy. 1967. *War: The Anthropology of Armed Conflict and Aggression*. Garden City: Natural History Press.

Fry, Douglas. 2007. *Beyond War: The Human Potential for Peace*. Oxford: Oxford University Press.

Furniss, Elizabeth. 1992. *Victims of Benevolence: Discipline and Death at the Williams Lake Indian Residential School, 1891–1920*. Williams Lake: Cariboo Tribal Council.

Gagne, Marie-Anik. 1994. *A Nation Within a Nation: Dependency and the Cree*. Montreal: Black Rose.

Galton, Francis. 1879. *Hereditary Genius: An Inquiry into Its Laws and Consequences.* New York: Appleton.

Gardner, Katy, and David Lewis. 1996. *Anthropology, Development, and the Post-Modern Challenge.* London: Pluto.

Geertz, Clifford. 1972. "Deep Play: Notes on the Balinese Cockfight." *Daedalus* 101: 1–37.

———. 1973. "The Impact of Culture on the Concept of Man." In *The Interpretation of Cultures: Selected Essays by Clifford Geertz.* New York: Basic Books.

Gellner, Ernest. 1983. *Nations and Nationalism.* Ithaca: Cornell University Press.

George, Susan, and Fabrizio Sabelli. 1994. *Faith and Credit: The World Bank's Secular Empire.* Boulder: Westview.

Gerber, Linda. 1990. "Multiple Jeopardy: A Socio-Economic Comparison of Men and Women Among the Indian, Metis, and Inuit Peoples of Canada." *Canadian Ethnic Studies* 22(3): 69–84.

Geschiere, Peter. 1997. *The Modernity of Witchcraft: Politics and the Occult in Postcolonial Africa.* Charlottesville: University Press of Virginia.

Gibson, Thomas. 1990. "Raiding, Trading, and Tribal Autonomy in Insular Southeast Asia." In *The Anthropology of War,* edited by Jonathan Hass. New York: Cambridge University Press.

Giddens, Anthony. 1990. *The Consequences of Modernity.* Cambridge: Polity.

Gilmore, David D. 1990. *Manhood in the Making: Cultural Concepts of Masculinity.* New Haven: Yale University Press.

Ginsburg, Faye, and Rayna Rapp. 1991. "The Politics of Reproduction." *Annual Review of Anthropology* 20: 311–43.

Gledhill, John. 1994. *Power and Its Disguises: Anthropological Perspectives on Politics.* London: Pluto.

Goffman, Erving. 1999. *The Presentation of Self in Everyday Life.* New York: Peter Smith.

Goldberg, David Theo. 2009. *The Threat of Race: Reflections on Racial Neoliberalism.* Hoboken, NJ: Wiley-Blackwell.

Gonzales, Roberto. 2009. *American Counterinsurgency: Human Science and the Human Terrain.* New York: Prickly Paradigm.

Gould, Stephen Jay. 1981. *The Mismeasure of Man.* New York: Norton.

Goulet, Jean-Guy A. 1998. *Ways of Knowing: Experience, Knowledge, and Power Among the Dene Tha.* Vancouver: UBC Press.

———. 2004 "The Dene Tha of Chateh: Continuities and Transformations." In *Native Peoples: The Canadian Experience,* edited by R. Bruce Morrison and C. Roderick Wilson. Toronto: Oxford University Press.

Green, Linda. 1995. "Living in a State of Fear." In *Fieldwork Under Fire: Contemporary Studies of Violence and Survival,* edited by Carolyn Nordstrom and Antonius C. G. Robben. Berkeley: University of California Press.

Greenhouse, Carol. 1987. "Cultural Perspectives on War." In *The Quest for Peace: Transcending Collective Violence and War Among Societies, Cultures, and States,* edited by Raimo Vayrynen. Beverly Hills: Sage.

Gremillion, Helen. 2003. *Feeding Anorexia: Gender and Power at a Treatment Center.* Durham: Duke University Press.

Gregor, Thomas. 1990. "Uneasy Peace: Intertribal Relations in Brazil's Upper Xingu." In *The Anthropology of War,* edited by Jonathan Hass. New York: Cambridge University Press.

Grim, John A., ed. 2001. *Indigenous Traditions and Ecology: The Interbeing of Cosmology and Community.* Cambridge, MA: Harvard University Press.

Gruneau, Richard, and David Whitson, eds. 1993. *Artificial Ice: Hockey, Commerce, and Culture.* Peterborough: Broadview.

Gusterson, Hugh. 1995. *Nuclear Rites: A Weapons Laboratory at the End of the Cold War.* Berkeley: University of California Press.

Gwynne, Margaret A. 2003. *Applied Anthropology: A Career-Oriented Approach.* Boston: Allyn and Bacon.

Hall, Edgar T. 1966. *The Hidden Dimension.* Garden City: Doubleday.

Handler, Richard. 1988. *Nationalism and the Politics of Culture in Quebec.* Madison: University of Wisconsin Press.

Hanson, Allan. 1993. *Testing Testing.* Berkeley: University of California Press.

Harris, Marvin. 1977. *Cannibals and Kings: The Origins of Culture.* New York: Vintage.

———. 1998 [1985]. *Good to Eat: Riddles of Food and Culture.* Long Grove, IL: Waveland Press.

Hartman, Anne. 2009. "'Here for a Little Pickup?' Notes on Women's Shinny Hockey in Toronto Public Parks."

In *Now Is the Winter: Thinking About Hockey,* edited by Jamie Dobb and Richard Harrison. Toronto: Wolsak and Wynn.

Harvey, David. 2005. *The History of Neoliberalism.* New York: Oxford University Press.

Hass, Jonathan, ed. 1990. *The Anthropology of War.* Cambridge: Cambridge University Press.

Hedican, Edward J. 1986. *The Ogoki River Guides: Emergent Leadership Among the Northern Ojibwa.* Waterloo: Wilfrid Laurier University Press.

——. 2001. *Up in Nipigon Country: Anthropology as a Personal Experience.* Halifax: Fernwood.

——. 2008 [1995]. *Applied Anthropology in Canada: Understanding Aboriginal Issues,* 2nd ed. Toronto: University of Toronto Press.

Hedley, Max. 1998. "Shadow of Domination: Colonialism, Household, and Community Relations." In *Transgressing Borders: Critical Perspectives on Gender, Household, and Culture,* edited by Suzan Ilcan and Lynne Phillips. Westport: Bergin and Garvey.

Helly, Denise. 2004. "Are Muslims Discriminated Against Since September 2001?" *Canadian Ethnic Studies* 36(1): 24–47.

Helm, June. 1965. "Bilaterality in the Social Organization of the Arctic Drainage Dene." *Ethnology* 4: 361–85.

Henare, Manuka. 2001. "Tapu, Mana, Mauri, Hau, Wairua: A Maori Philosophy of Vitalism and Cosmos." In *Indigenous Traditions and Ecology: The Interbeing of Cosmology and Community,* edited by John A. Grim. Cambridge, MA: Harvard University Press.

Henderson, Paul. 1976. "Class Structure and the Concept of Intelligence." In *Schooling and Capitalism: A Sociological Reader,* edited by Roger Dale, Geoff Esland, and Madeleine MacDonald. London: Routledge and Kegan Paul in association with Open University Press.

Henry, Paget. 1997. "Rastafarianism and the Reality of Dread." In *Existence in Black: An Anthology of Black Existential Philosophy,* edited by L. R. Gordon. New York: Routledge.

Herrnstein, Richard J., and Charles Murray. 1994. *The Bell Curve: Intelligence and Class Structure in American Life.* New York: The Free Press.

Hertz, Robert. 1960. *Death and the Right Hand.* Glencoe: The Free Press.

Herzfeld, Michael. 2001. *Anthropology: Theoretical Practice in Culture and Society.* Malden: Blackwell.

Hobbes, Thomas. 1881 [1651]. *Leviathan.* London: Oxford University Press.

Hoben, Allan. 1982. "Anthropologists and Development." *Annual Review of Anthropology* 11: 349–75.

Hobsbaum, Eric. 1959. *Primitive Rebels: Studies in Archaic Forms of Social Movement in the 19th and 20th Centuries.* New York: Praeger.

Hoerder, Dirk. 2002. *Cultures in Contact: World Migrations in the Second Millennium.* Durham: Duke University Press.

Holmes, Teresa. 1997. "Contested Kinship and the Dispute of Customary Law in Colonial Kenya." *Anthropologica* 39: 79–90.

Honigmann, John J. 1963. *Understanding Culture.* New York: Harper and Row.

——. 1976. *The Development of Anthropological Ideas.* Homewood: Dorsey.

Hoodfar, Homa. 2003. "More Than Clothing: Veiling as an Adaptive Strategy." In *The Muslim Veil in North America,* edited by Sajida Sultana Alvi, Homa Hoodfar, and Sheila McDonough. Toronto: Women's Press.

Hostetler, John. 1974. *Hutterite Society.* Baltimore: Johns Hopkins University Press.

House, James S., Karl R. Landis, and Debra Umberson. 1988. "Social Relationships and Health." *Science* 241: 540–45.

Howell, Signe, and Roy Willis, eds. *Societies at Peace: Anthropological Perspectives.* London and New York: Routledge.

Hsu, Francis L. K. 1967. *Under the Ancestors' Shadow.* New York: Anchor.

Hutchinson, John, and Anthony D. Smith, eds. 1994. *Nationalism.* Oxford: Oxford University Press.

Inhorn, Marcia C., and Peter J. Brown. 1990. "The Anthropology of Infectious Disease." *Annual Review of Anthropology* 19: 89–117.

International Labor Organization. 2015. *Mainstreaming of Migration in Development Policy and Integrating Migration in the Post-2015 UN Development Agenda.* http://www.ilo.org/wcmsp5/groups/public/---ed_protect/---protrav/---migrant/documents/genericdocument/wcms_220084.pdf

Irwin, Anne. 2002. "The Social Organization of Soldiering: A Canadian Infantry Company in the Field." Ph.D. diss., Manchester University.

———. 2012. "'There Will Be a Lot of Old Young Men Coming Home': Combat and Becoming a Man in Afghanistan." In *Young Men in Uncertain Times,* edited by Verid Amit and Noel Dyck. New York: Berghahn.

Isbister, John. 2003. *Promises Not Kept: Poverty and Betrayal of Third World Development.* Bloomfield: Kumarian.

Jensen, Arthur. 1972. *Genetics and Education.* New York: Harper and Row.

Johnson, Norris Brock. 1985. *Westhaven: Classroom Culture and Society in a Rural Elementary School.* Chapel Hill: University of North Carolina Press.

Jorgensen, Dan. 1990. "Placing the Past and Moving the Present: Myth and Contemporary History in Telefolmin." *Culture* 10(2): 47–56.

———. 1996. "Regional History and Ethnic Identity in the Hub of New Guinea: The Emergence of the Min." *Oceania* 66(3): 189–210.

———. 1997. "Who and What Is a Landowner? Mythology and Marking the Ground in a Papua New Guinea Mining Project." *Anthropological Forum* 7(4): 599–627.

Judd, Ellen R. 1994. *Gender and Power in Rural North China.* Stanford: Stanford University Press.

Juergensmeyer, Mark. 2003. *Terror in the Mind of God: The Global Rise of Religious Violence, 3rd ed.* Berkeley: University of California Press.

Kafka, Peter. 2005. "Top Earning Dead Celebrities." *Forbes.* http://www.forbes.com/2005/10/25/highest-earning-dead-celebrities_deadceleb05_land.html.

Karier, Clarence J. 1976. "Testing for Order and Control in the Corporate Liberal State." In *Schooling and Capitalism: A Sociological Reader,* edited by Roger Dale, Geoff Esland, and Madeleine MacDonald. London: Routledge and Kegan Paul in association with the Open University Press.

Kearney, Michael. 1991. "A Very Bad Disease of the Arms." In *The Naked Anthropologist: Tales from Around the World,* edited by Philip Devita. Belmont: Wadsworth.

Keesing, Roger. 1991. "Not a Real Fish: The Ethnographer as Inside Outsider." In *The Naked Anthropologist: Tales from Around the World,* edited by Philip Devita. Belmont: Wadsworth.

Kehoe, Alice. 1989. *The Ghost Dance: Ethnohistory and Revitalization.* New York: Holt, Rinehart, and Winston.

Keiser, Lincoln. 1969. *The Vice Lords: Warriors of the Streets.* New York: Holt, Rinehart, and Winston.

Kelly, John D., and Martha Kaplan. 1990. "History, Structure, and Ritual." In *Annual Review of Anthropology* 19: 119–50. Palo Alto: Annual Reviews.

Kennedy, Paul. 1993. *Preparing for the Twenty-First Century.* New York: Random House.

Keohane, Kieran. 1997. *Symptoms of Canada: An Essay on the Canadian Identity.* Toronto: University of Toronto Press.

Kets deVries, Manfred, and Danny Miller. 1987. "Interpreting Organizational Texts." *Journal of Management Studies* 24: 233–47.

Kidder, Tracy. 2003. *Mountains Beyond Mountains.* New York. Random House.

Kiefer, Christie. 1976. "The Danchi Zoku and the Evolution of the Metropolitan Mind." In *Japan: The Paradox of Progress,* edited by Lewis Austin, with the assistance of Adrienne Suddard and Nancy Remington. New Haven: Yale University Press.

Kinkade, Kathleen. 1973. *A Walden Two Experiment: The First Five Years of Twin Oaks Community.* New York: William Morrow.

Klaits, Frederick. 2005. "The Widow in Blue: Blood and the Morality of Remembering in Botswana's Time of AIDS." *Africa* 75(1): 46–62.

Kolata, Gina. 1995. "Researchers Offer Clue to How AIDS Virus Survives Prolonged Attack by Immune System." *New York Times,* November 24, 1995. http://www.nytimes.com/1995/11/24/us/researchers-offer-clue-aids-virus-survives-prolonged-attack-immune-system.html

Kondo, Dorinne K. 1990. Crafting Selves: Power, Gender, and Discourses of Identity in a Japanese Workplace. Chicago: University of Chicago Press.

Kopytoff, Igor. 1986. "The Cultural Biography of Things: Commoditization as Process." In *The Social Life of Things: Commodities in Cultural Perspective*, edited by Arjun Appadurai, 64–91. Cambridge: Cambridge University Press.

Korten, David C. 1995. *When Corporations Rule the World.* Hartford: Kumarian.

Kotlowitz, Alex. 1991. *There Are No Children Here.* New York: Anchor.

Kramer, Jennifer. 2007. *Switchbacks: Art, Ownership and Nuxalk National Identity.* Vancouver: UBC Press.

Kroeber, Alfred L. 1948. *Anthropology.* New York: Harcourt, Brace.

Kuper, Leo. 1981. *Genocide: Its Political Use in the Twentieth Century.* New Haven: Yale University Press.

Labov, William. 1966. *The Social Stratification of English in New York City.* Washington: Center for Applied Linguistics.

Lakoff, George, and Mark Johnson. 1980. *Metaphors We Live By.* Chicago: University of Chicago Press.

Lakoff, Robin. 1975. *Language and Women's Place.* New York: Harper and Row.

Lambek, Michael. 2002. "General Introduction." In *A Reader in the Anthropology of Religion,* edited by Michael Lambek. Malden: Blackwell.

Lancaster, Roger. 2003. *The Trouble with Nature: Sex in Science and Popular Culture.* Berkeley: University of California Press.

Lang, Sabine. 1998. *Men as Women, Women as Men: Changing Gender in Native American Cultures.* Austin: University of Texas Press.

Langlois, Kellie, and Didier Garriguet. 2011. *Sugar Consumption Among Canadians of All Ages.* http://www.statcan.gc.ca.myaccess.library.utoronto.ca/pub/82-003-x/2011003/article/11540-eng.htm

Lappé, Frances Moore, and Joseph Collins. 1977. *Food First: Beyond the Myth of Scarcity.* New York: Random House.

Lee, Richard. 1969. "Eating Christmas in the Kalihari." *Natural History Magazine.* December.

—— . 1984. *The Dobe !Kung.* New York: Holt, Rinehart, and Winston.

—— . 1996. "AIDS: The Conspiracy of Silence." *Southern Africa Report* 12(1): 8. https://tspace.library.utoronto.ca/bitstream/1807/18005/1/TSpace0114.PDF

—— , and Irven DeVore, eds. 1968. *Man the Hunter.* Chicago: Aldine.

—— , and Ida Susser. 2002. "Facing the Challenge of HIV/AIDS." *Cultural Survival Quarterly* 26(1). http://www.culturalsurvival.org/publications/cultural-survival-quarterly/botswana/facing-challenge-hivaids

Leslie, Heather Young. 1998. "The Anthropologist, the Mother, and the Cross-Cultured Child." In *Fieldwork and Families: Constructing Models for Ethnographic Research,* edited by Juliana Flinn, Leslie Marshall, and Jocelyn Armstrong. Honolulu: University of Hawai'i Press.

Levi-Strauss, Claude. 1964. *Totemism.* Translated by Rodney Needham. (London: Merlin Press).

—— . 1966. *The Savage Mind.* Chicago: University of Chicago Press.

—— . 1974. *Tristé Tropiques.* New York: Atheneum.

Lewellen, Ted. 2002. *The Anthropology of Globalization: Cultural Anthropology Enters the 21st Century.* Westport: Bergin and Garvey.

Lewin, Ellen, and William L. Leap, eds. 2002. *Out in Theory: The Emergence of Lesbian and Gay Anthropology.* Chicago: University of Chicago Press.

Li, Tania, ed. 1999a. *Transforming the Indonesian Uplands: Marginality, Power, and Production.* Amsterdam: Harwood.

—— . 1999b. "Compromising Power: Development, Culture, and Rule in Indonesia." *Cultural Anthropology* 14(3): 295–322.

—— . 2002. "Local Histories, Global Markets: Cocoa and Class in Upland Sulawesi." *Development and Change* 33(3): 415–37.

Lightner, Sara, and Anna Naupa. 2005. *Histri Blong Yumi Long Vanuatu.* Port Vila: Vanuatu Cultural Centre.

Lithman, Yngve G. 2004. "Anthropologists on Home Turf: How Green Is the Grass?" *Anthropologica* 46(1): 17–27.

Lofgren, Orvar. 1999. *On Holiday: A History of Vacationing.* Berkeley: University of California Press.

—— . 2002. *On Holiday: A History of Vacationing.* Oakland, CA: University of California Press.

Lohmann, Roger Ivar. 2014. "Investigating the Causes of Peace to End War: An Introduction." *Anthropologica* 56(2): 255–60.

Long, David, and Olive Patricia Dickason, eds. 2000. *Visions of the Heart: Canadian Aboriginal Issues.* Toronto: Harcourt Canada.

Longres, John F. 1990. *Human Behavior in the Social Environment.* Itasca: F.E. Peacock.

Lorber, Judith. 1994. *Paradoxes of Gender.* New Haven: Yale University Press.

Lorway, Robert. 2006. "Dispelling 'Heterosexual African AIDS' in Namibia: Same-Sex Sexuality in the

Township of Katutura." *Culture, Health, and Sexuality* 8(5): 435–49.

——. 2007. "Breaking a Public Health Silence: HIV Risk and Male–Male Sexual Practices in the Windhoek Urban Area." In *Unravelling Taboos: Gender and Sexuality in Namibia,* edited by Suzanne LaFont and Dianne Hubbard. Windhoek: Gender Research and Advocacy Project, Legal Assistance Centre.

Luhrmann, T. M. 1989. *Persuasions of the Witch's Craft: Ritual Magic in Contemporary England.* Cambridge, MA: Harvard University Press.

Luxton, Meg, ed. 1997. *Feminism and Families: Critical Policies and Changing Practices.* Halifax: Fernwood.

Lyons, Andrew P., and Harriet D. Lyons. 2004. *Irregular Connections: A History of Anthropology and Sexuality.* Lincoln: University of Nebraska Press.

Mackey, Eva. 1999. *The House of Difference: Cultural Politics and National Identity in Canada.* London and New York: Routledge.

Macnair, Peter. 2004. "From Kwakiutl to Kwakwaka'wakw." In *Native Peoples: The Canadian Experience,* edited by R. Bruce Morrison and C. Roderick Wilson. Toronto: Oxford University Press.

Madden, Raymond. 2010. Being Ethnographic: A Guide to the Theory and Practice of Ethnography. London: Sage Publications.

Malinowski, Bronislaw. 1929. *The Sexual Life of Savages in North-Western Melanesia.* New York: Halcyon House.

——. 1944. *A Scientific Theory of Culture, and Other Essays.* Chapel Hill: University of North Carolina Press.

——. 1948. *Magic, Science, and Religion, and Other Essays.* Boston: Beacon.

——. 1961 [1922]. *Argonauts of the Western Pacific.* New York: Dutton.

Marchak, Patricia M. 2003. *Reins of Terror.* Montreal and Kingston: McGill–Queen's University Press.

Marcus, George E. 1995. "Ethnography in/of the World System: The Emergence of Multi-Sited Ethnography." *Annual Review of Anthropology* 24(1): 95–117.

Marshall, Lorna. 1976. *The !Kung of Nyae Nyae.* Cambridge, MA: Harvard University Press.

Marshall, Mac. 1993. "The Wizard of Oz Meets the Wicked Witch of the East: Mead, Freeman, and Ethnographic Authority." *American Ethnologist* 20: 604–17.

Martin, Emily. 1987. *The Woman in the Body: A Cultural Analysis of Reproduction.* Boston: Beacon.

Martin-Hill, Dawn. 2004. "Resistance, Determination, and Perseverance of the Lubicon Cree Women." In *In the Way of Development: Indigenous Peoples, Life Projects, and Globalization,* edited by Mario Blaser, Harvey A. Feit, and Glenn McRae. New York: Palgrave Macmillan.

——. 2008. *Sewatokwa'tshera't: The Dish with One Spoon* [film]. http://www.lock3media.com/doc6.html

——. 2008. *The Lubicon Lake Nation: Indigenous Knowledge and Power.* Toronto: University of Toronto Press.

Marwick, Max. 1965. *Sorcery in Its Social Setting.* Manchester: University of Manchester Press.

Matsubara, Hisako. 1985. *Cranes at Dusk.* New York: Dial.

Mattingly, Cheryl, Mary Lawlor, and Lanita Jacobs-Huey. 2002. "Narrating September 11: Race, Gender, and the Play of Cultural Identities." *American Anthropologist* 104(3): 743–53.

Mauss, Marcel. 1967 [1925]. *The Gift: Forms and Functions of Exchange in Archaic Societies.* Translated by Ian Cunnison. New York: Norton.

Maybury-Lewis, David. 1997. *Indigenous Peoples, Ethnic Groups, and the State.* Boston: Allyn and Bacon.

McCauley, Clark. 1990. "Conference Overview." In *The Anthropology of War,* edited by Jonathan Hass. New York: Cambridge University Press.

McCracken, Grant. 2005. Culture and Consumption II: Markets, Meaning and Brand Management. Indianapolis: Indiana University Press.

McElroy, Ann, and Patricia Townsend. 1979. *Medical Anthropology.* North Scituate: Duxbury.

McFate, Montgomery. 2005. "Anthropology and Counterinsurgency: The Strange Story of Their Curious Relationship." *Military Review,* March–April.

McFate, Montgomery, and Andrea Jackson. "An Organizational Solution for DOD's Cultural Knowledge Needs." *Military Review,* May–June.

McGarry, Karen. 2011. "Mass Media and Gender Identity in High Performance Canadian Figure Skating." In *The Gendered Society Reader,* 2nd Canadian ed., edited by Amy Aronson, Amy Kaler and Michael S. Kimmel. Cambridge: Oxford University Press.

——. 2015. "Ethnographic Frictions and the Ice Scandal: Affect, Mass Media and Canadian Nationalism in High

Performance Canadian Figure Skating." In *Reclaiming Canadian Bodies*, edited by Lynda Mannik and Karen McGarry, 105–43. Waterloo, ON: Wilfrid Laurier University Press.

McGee, R. Jon, and Richard Warms. 2000. *Anthropological Theory: An Introductory History.* MountainView: Mayfield.

McIntosh, Peggy. 1988. "White Privilege and Male Privilege: A Personal Account of Coming to See Correspondences Through Work in Women's Studies." *Working Paper No. 189.* Wellesley, MA: Wellesley College Center for Research on Women.

McLaughlin, Janet. 2009. Migration and Health: Implications for Development—A Case Study of Mexican and Jamaican Migrants in Canada's Seasonal Agricultural Workers Program. Policy Paper. Ottawa: Canadian Foundation for the Americas (FOCAL), Labour Mobility and Development Project.

McNally, David. 2002. *Another World Is Possible: Globalization and Anti-capitalism.* Winnipeg: Arbeiter Ring.

Mead, Margaret. 1928. *Coming of Age in Samoa: A Psychological Study of Primitive Youth for Western Civilization.* New York: Morrow.

Miller, Bruce Granville. 2003. *Invisible Indigenes: The Politics of Nonrecognition.* Lincoln: University of Nebraska Press.

Mills, Antonia. 1988. "A Preliminary Investigation of Cases of Reincarnation Among the Beaver and Gitksan Indians." *Anthropologica* 30: 23–59.

Mills, Antonia, and Richard Slobodin, eds. 1994. *Amerindian Rebirth: Reincarnation Belief Among North American Indians and Inuit.* Toronto: University of Toronto Press.

Mintz, Sidney W. 1985. *Sweetness and Power: The Place of Sugar in World History.* New York: Viking.

Mishkin, Bernard. 1940. *Rank and Warfare Among the Plains Indians.* Monograph No. 3, American Ethnological Society. Seattle: University of Washington Press.

Mitchell, Lisa. 2001. Baby's First Picture: Ultrasound and the Politics of Fetal Subjects. Toronto: University of Toronto Press.

Moffat, Tina, and Elizabeth Finnis. 2005. "Considering Social and Material Resources: The Political Ecology of a Peri-Urban Squatter Community in Nepal." *Habitat International* 29: 453–68.

Monture-Angus, Patricia A. 2000. "Lessons in Decolonization: Aboriginal Over-Representation in Canadian Criminal Justice." In *Visions of the Heart:*

Canadian Aboriginal Issues, edited by David Long and Olive Patricia Dickason. Toronto: Harcourt Canada.

Mooney, James. 2011 [1897]. *The Ghost Dance Religion and the Sioux Outbreak of 1890.* Chicago: University of Chicago Press.

Moore, Henrietta. 1988. *Feminism and Anthropology.* Cambridge: Polity.

Moore, Henrietta, and Todd Sanders, eds. 2005. *Anthropology in Theory: Issues in Epistemology.* Malden: Blackwell.

Moore, Patrick, Angela Wheelock, and Dene Wodih Society. 1990. *Wolverine Myths and Visions: Dene Traditions from Northern Alberta.* Lincoln: University of Nebraska Press.

Moore, Robert B. 1976. *Racism in the English Language.* New York: Council on Interracial Books for Children.

Moore, Sally Falk. 2005. *Law and Anthropology: A Reader.* Oxford: Blackwell.

Moos, Robert, and Robert Brownstein. 1977. *Environment and Utopia.* New York: Plenum.

Morgan, Lewis Henry. 1964 [1877]. *Ancient Society.* Cambridge, MA: Belknap.

Morin, Eugene. 2008. "Evidence for Declines in Human Population Densities During the Early Upper Paleolithic in Western Europe." *Proceedings of the National Academy of Sciences of the United States of America.* 105(1): 48–53.

Morrison, David. 2000. "Canadian Aid: A Mixed Record and an Uncertain Future." In *Transforming Development, Foreign Aid for a Changing World,* edited by J. Freedman. Toronto: University of Toronto Press.

Morrison, R. Bruce, and C. Roderick Wilson, eds. 2004. *Native Peoples: The Canadian Experience.* Toronto: Oxford University Press.

Morton, Samuel G. 1844. *An Inquiry into the Distinctive Characteristics of the Aboriginal Race of America.* Philadelphia: Penington.

Mukhopadhyay, Carol C., and Patricia J. Higgins. 1988. "Anthropological Studies of Women's Status Revisited: 1977–1987." *Annual Review of Anthropology* 17: 461–495.

Mullings, Leith. 2005. "Interrogating Racism: Toward an Antiracist Anthropology." *Annual Review of Anthropology* 34: 667–93.

Murray, David A. B. 2002. *Opacity: Gender, Sexuality, Race, and the "Problem" of Identity in Martinique.* New York: Peter Lang.

Myer, Fred R. 1988. "Critical Trends in the Study of Hunters-Gatherers." *Annual Review of Anthropology* 17: 261–82.

Nader, Laura, ed. 1996. *Naked Science: Anthropological Inquiry into Boundaries, Power, and Knowledge*. New York: Routledge.

Nagengast Carole. 1994. "Violence, Terror, and the Crisis of the State." *Annual Review of Anthropology* 23: 109–36.

Nagengast, Carol, and Carlos G. Vélez-Ibáñez, eds. 2004. *Human Rights: The Scholar as Activist*. Oklahoma City: Society for Applied Anthropology.

Narayan, Kirin. 1993. "How Native Is a 'Native' Anthropologist?" *American Anthropologist* 95(3): 671–86.

Nations, James D. 1994. "The Ecology of the Zapatista Revolt." *Cultural Survival Quarterly* 18: 31–33.

Neider, Charles. 1966. *The Complete Travel Books of Mark Twain*. New York: Doubleday.

Ng, Roxana. 2002. "Freedom for Whom? Globalization and Trade from the Standpoint of Garment Workers." *Canadian Woman Studies* 21/22(4/1): 74–81.

——— . 2007. "Garment Production in Canada: Social and Political Implications. *Studies in Political Economy* 79 (Spring): 3–11.

Nichter, Mimi. 2000. *Fat Talk: What Girls and Their Parents Say About Dieting*. Cambridge, MA: Harvard University Press.

Niehaus, Isak. 2001. Witchcraft, Power and Politics: Exploring the Occult in the South African Lowveld. New York: Pluto Press.

Niezen, Ronald. 1993. "Power and Dignity: The Social Consequences of Hydro-Electric Development for the James Bay Cree." *Canadian Review of Sociology and Anthropology* 30(4): 510.

——— . 2003. *The Origins of Indigenism: Human Rights and the Politics of Identity*. Berkeley: University of California Press.

——— . 2004. "Indigenous Peoples in a Global Era." In *Globalization and Community: Canadian Perspectives,* edited by Jean-Luc Chodkiewicz and Raymond E. Wiest. Winnipeg: University of Manitoba Press.

Nigh, Ronald. 1995. "Animal Agriculture for the Reforestation of Degraded Tropical Rainforests." *Culture and Agriculture* 51/52: 2–5.

Nordstrom, Carolyn. 2004. *Shadows of War: Violence, Power, and International Profiteering in the Twenty-First Century*. Berkeley: University of California Press.

Omohundro, John T. 2001. *Careers in Anthropology.* Mountain View: Mayfield.

Ontario Ministry of Aboriginal Affairs. Aboriginal Labour Force. http://www.aboriginalaffairs.gov.on.ca/english/services/datasheets/labour.asp.

Ortner, Sherry B., and Harriet Whitehead, eds. 1981. *Sexual Meanings: The Cultural Construction of Gender and Sexuality*. Cambridge: Cambridge University Press.

Otterbein, Keith F. 2004. *How War Began*. College Station: Texas A&M University Press.

Pagels, Elaine H. 1995. *The Origin of Satan*. New York: Random House.

Paine, Robert, ed. 1985. *Advocacy and Anthropology: First Encounters*. St. John's: Institute of Social and Economic Research.

Palgi, Phyllis, and Henry Abramovitch. 1984. "Death: A Cross-Cultural Perspective." *Annual Review of Anthropology* 13: 385–417.

Parkin, Robert, and Linda Stone, eds. 2004. *Kinship and Family: An Anthropological Reader*. Malden: Blackwell.

Patrick, Donna. 2003. *Language, Politics, and Social Interaction in an Inuit Community*. Berlin: Mouton de Gruyter.

Paulson, Susan, Lisa L. Gezon, and Michael Watts. 2003. "Locating the Political in Political Ecology: An Introduction." *Human Organization* 62(3): 205–17.

Pearson, Karl. 1901. "On the Inheritance of Mental Characteristics in Man." In *Proceedings of the Royal Society of London* 69: 153–55.

Pengelly, Ryan. D., and Irwin, Anne. 2011. "Twenty-First Century Narratives from Afghanistan: Storytelling, Morality, and War." In *The Routledge Handbook of War and Society: Iraq and Afghanistan,* edited by Steven Carlton-Ford and Morten G. Ender. New York: Routledge.

Philips, Susan U. 1980. "Sex Differences and Language." In *Annual Review of Anthropology* 9: 523–44. Palo Alto: Annual Reviews.

Polanyi, Karl. 1957 [1944]. *The Great Transformation*. Boston: Beacon.

Pratt, Cranford. 2000. "Alleviating Global Poverty or Enhancing Security: Competing Rationales for

Canadian Development Assistance." In *Transforming Development: Foreign Aid for a Changing World,* edited by J. Freedman. Toronto: University of Toronto Press.

Preston, Richard J. 1975. *Cree Narrative: Expressing the Personal Meaning of Events.* Ottawa: National Museum of Canada.

——— . 2004. "Cumulative Cultural Change in the Moose and Rupert River Basins: Local Cultural Sites Affected by Global Influences." In *Globalization and Community,* edited by J. L. Chodkiewicz and Raymond E. Wiest. Winnipeg: University of Manitoba Press.

Pryce, Paula. 1999. *"Keeping the Lakes' Way": Reburial and the Re-creation of a Moral World Among an Invisible People.* Toronto: University of Toronto Press.

Pyke, Alan. 2014. "A Third of America's Most Successful Corporations Pay Less Than a 10 Percent Income Tax Rate." *ThinkProgress* (February 28).

Rapp, Rayna. 2007. "Real-Time Fetus: The Role of the Sonogram in the Age of Monitored Reproduction." In *Beyond the Body Proper: Reading the Anthropology of Material Life,* edited by Margaret Lock and Judith Farquhar, 608–23. Durham, NC: Duke University Press.

Read, Kenneth E. 1965. *The High Valley.* New York: Columbia University Press.

Reardon, Betty. 1985. *Sexism and the War System.* New York: Columbia University Teachers College Press.

Reed, Richard. 1997. *Forest Dwellers, Forest Protectors: Indigenous Models for International Development.* Boston: Allyn and Bacon.

Reichenbach, Lisa, and Amy Maish. 2006. "Larger Than Life: Personal and Social Transitions Within Type 2 Diabetes." *Ethnographic Praxis in Industry Conference Proceedings,* 4–18. Arlington, VA: American Anthropological Association.

Rich, Bruce. 1994. *Mortgaging the Earth: The World Bank, Environmental Impoverishment, and the Crisis of Development.* Boston: Beacon.

Richler, Noah. 2012. *What We Talk About When We Talk About War.* Fredericton, NB: Goose Lane Editions.

Ridington, Robin. 1990. *Little Bit Know Something: Stories in a Language of Anthropology.* Iowa City: University of Iowa Press.

Rindos, David. 1984. *The Origins of Agriculture.* New York: Academic Press.

Rivoli, Pietra. 2005. *The Travels of a T-Shirt in the Global Economy: An Economist Examines the Markets, Power, and the Politics of World Trade.* Hoboken: John Wiley.

Robarchek, Clayton. 1990. "Motivations and Material Causes: On the Explanation of Conflict and War." In *The Anthropology of War,* edited by Jonathan Hass. New York: Cambridge University Press.

Robbins, Richard H. 2005. *Global Problems and the Culture of Capitalism,* 3rd ed. Boston: Allyn and Bacon.

Rosaldo, Renato. 1989. *Culture and Truth: The Remaking of Social Analysis.* Boston: Beacon.

Rosaldo, Michele, and Jane Monnig Atkinson. 1975. "Man the Hunter and Woman: Metaphors for the Sexes in Ilongot Magical Spells." In *The Interpretation of Symbolism,* edited by Roy Willis. New York: John Wiley.

Ross, Rupert. 1992. *Dancing with a Ghost: Exploring Indian Reality.* Markham: Octopus.

Rothstein, Frances Abrahamer, and Michael L. Blim, eds. 1992. *Anthropology and the Global Factory: Studies of the New Industrialism in the Late Twentieth Century.* New York: Bergin and Garvey.

Rowe, Allen. 2004. "'The Mysterious Oriental Mind': Ethnic Surveillance and the Chinese in Canada During the Great War." *Canadian Ethnic Studies* 36(1): 48–70.

Roy, Ramashray. 1985. *Self and Society: A Study in Gandhian Thought.* Beverly Hills: Sage.

Rubel, Arthur. 1964. "The Epidemiology of a Folk Illness: Susto in Hispanic America." *Ethnology* 3: 268–83.

Ruoff, Jeffrey. 1996. "'Can a Documentary Be Made of Real Life?': The Reception of *An American Family.* In *The Construction of the Viewer: Media Ethnography and the Anthropology of Audiences,* edited by P. I. Crawford and S. B. Hafsteinnsson. Denmark: Intervention.

Russell, Wendy. 2004. "The People Had Discovered Their Own Approach to Life: Politicizing Development Discourse." In *In the Way of Development: Indigenous Peoples, Life Projects, and Globalization,* edited by Mario Blaser, Harvey A. Feit, and Glenn McRae. London and New York: Zed Books in association with International Development Research Centre, Ottawa.

Rutherford, Blair. 1999. "To Find a Witch: Anthropology, Witch-Finding in North-West Zimbabwe." *Critique of Anthropology* 19: 89–109.

Sahlins, Marshall. 1968. *Tribesmen.* New York: Prentice Hall.

Sanday, Peggy Reeves. 1981. "The Socio-Cultural Context of Rape: A Cross-Cultural Study." *Journal of Social Issues* 37: 5–27.

——. 2007 [1990]. *Gang Rape: Sex, Brotherhood and Privilege on Campus,* 2nd ed. New York: NYU Press.

Satzewich, Vic. 1991. *Racism and the Incorporation of Foreign Labour: Farm Labour Migration to Canada Since 1945.* London: Routledge.

——, ed. 1992. *Deconstructing a Nation: Immigration, Multiculturalism, and Racism in '90s Canada.* Halifax: Fernwood.

Scaglion, Richard. 1990. "Ethnocentrism and the Abelam." In *The Humbled Anthropologist: Tales from the Pacific,* edited by Philip Devita. Belmont: Wadsworth.

Scales, Robert H. 2005. "The Second Learning Revolution." In *Rethinking the Principles of War*, edited by Anthony D. McIvor, 41–57. Annapolis MD: Naval Institute Press.

Schieffelin, Bambi B., and Elinor Ochs. 1986. "Language Socialization." *Annual Review of Anthropology* 15: 163–91.

Scheper-Hughes, Nancy. 1992. *Death Without Weeping: The Violence of Everyday Life in Brazil.* Berkeley: University of California Press.

——. 1995. "The Primacy of the Ethical: Propositions for a Militant Anthropology." *Current Anthropology* 36: 409–20.

Scheper-Hughes, Nancy, and Philippe Bourgois, eds. 2004. *Violence in War and Peace.* Malden: Blackwell.

Schmidt, Bettina E., and Ingo W. Schroder, eds. 2001. *Anthropology of Violence and Conflict.* London and New York: Routledge.

Schneider, David M. 1984. *A Critique of the Study of Kinship.* Ann Arbor: University of Michigan Press.

Schrire, Carmel. 1984. "Wild Surmises on Savage Thoughts." In *Past and Present in Hunter Gatherer Studies,* edited by Carmel Schrire. Orlando, FL: Academic Press.

Sharma, Parnesh. 1998. *Aboriginal Fishing Rights: Laws, Courts, Politics.* Halifax: Fernwood.

——. 2001. "On Not Being Canadian: The Social Organization of 'Migrant Workers' in Canada." *Canadian Review of Sociology and Anthropology* 38(4): 415–39.

Shewell, Hugh. 2004. *"Enough to Keep Them Alive": Indian Welfare in Canada, 1873–1965.* Toronto: University of Toronto Press.

Shipton, Parker. 1990. "African Famines and Food Security." *Annual Review of Anthropology* 19: 353–94.

Shore, Chris, and Susan Wright. 1997. *Anthropology of Policy: Critical Perspectives on Governance and Power.* London: Routledge.

Shostak, Marjorie. 1983. *Nisa: The Life and Words of a !Kung Woman.* New York: Vintage.

Shweder, Richard A., and Edmund J. Bourne. 1984. "Does the Concept of the Person Vary Cross-Culturally?" In *Cultural Conceptions of Mental Health and Therapy,* edited by A. J. Marsella and G. M. White. Boston: Reidel.

Sidel, Ruth. 1986. *Women and Children Last: Social Stratification in America.* New York: Penguin.

Silverman, Martin G. 1979. "'Kinship': An Informal, Critical Guide to Some Problems." In *Challenging Anthropology,* edited by David H. Turner and Gavin A. Smith. Toronto: McGraw-Hill Ryerson.

Sipes, Richard G. 1973. "War, Sports, and Aggression: An Empirical Test of Two Rival Theories." *American Anthropologist* 74: 64–86.

Skinner, B. F. 1962. *Walden Two.* New York: Macmillan.

Slobodin, Richard. 1994. "Kutchin Concepts of Reincarnation." In *Amerindian Rebirth: Reincarnation Belief Among North American Indians and Inuit,* edited by Antonia Mills and Richard Slobodin. Toronto: University of Toronto Press.

Smith, Adam. 1994 [1776]. *The Wealth of Nations,* edited by Edwin Cannan. New York: Modern Library.

Smith, Gavin. 1999. *Confronting the Present: Towards a Politically Engaged Anthropology.* Oxford and New York: Berg.

Smith, Raymond T. 1984. "Anthropology and the Concept of Social Class." In *Annual Review of Anthropology* 13: 467–94.

Smith, Robert J. 1983. *Japanese Society: Tradition, Self, and the Social Order.* New York: Cambridge University Press.

Solway, Jacqueline, ed. 2003. "Politics and Practice in Critical Anthropology: The Work of Richard B. Lee." Special Edition of *Anthropologica* 45(1): 1–128.

Solway, Jacqueline S., and Richard B. Lee. 1990. "Foragers, Genuine or Spurious? Situating the Kalahari San in History." *Current Anthropology* 31(2): 109–46.

Spearman, Charles. 1904. "General Intelligence." *American Journal of Psychology* 115: 201–92.

Stafford, James. 1992. "The Impact of the New Immigration Policy on Racism in Canada." In *Deconstructing a Nation: Immigration, Multiculturalism, and Racism in '90s Canada,* edited by Vic Satzewich. Halifax: Fernwood.

Statistics Canada. 2011. *Religions in Canada—Census 2011.* Ottawa: Statistics Canada.

——. 2013. *Persons in Low Income After Tax (in Percent, 2007–2011).* http://www.statcan.gc.ca/tables-tableaux/sum-som/l01/cst01/famil19a-eng.htm?sdi=low%20income

Stephenson, Peter H. 1991. *The Hutterian People: Ritual and Rebirth in the Evolution of Communal Life.* Lanham: University Press of America.

Stern, Jessica. 2003. *Terror in the Name of God: Why Religious Militants Kill.* New York: HarperCollins.

Stevens, Jacqueline. 1999. *Reproducing the State.* Princeton: Princeton University Press.

Stewart, Pamela J., and Andrew Strathern. 2002. *Violence: Theory and Ethnography.* London and New York: Continuum.

Stiglitz, Joseph E. 2002. http://www.nybooks.com/articles/archives/2002/may/23/a-fair-deal-for-the-world

Stone, Linda, ed. 2001. *New Directions in Anthropological Kinship.* Lanham: Rowman and Littlefield.

Strathern, Andrew, and Pamela J. Stewart. 2011. *Peace-Making and the Imagination.* St. Lucia, AU: University of Queensland Press.

Strong, William. 1929. "Cross-Cousin Marriage and the Culture of the Northeast Algonkian." *American Anthropologist* 31: 277–88.

Susser, Ida. 2006. The Other Side of Development: HIV/AIDS Among Men and Women in Ju/'hoansi Villages." In *The Politics of Egalitarianism: Theory and Practice,* edited by J. S. Solway. New York: Berghahn.

——. 2009. "Ju/'hoansi Women in the Age of HIV: An Exceptional Case." In *AIDS, Sex, and Culture: Global Politics and Survival in Southern Africa,* edited by Ida Susser. Malden: Blackwell.

Taft, Michael. 1997. "Men in Women's Clothes: Theatrical Transvestites on the Canadian Prairie." In *Undisciplined Women: Tradition and Culture in Canada,* edited by Pauline Greenhill and Diane Tye. Kingston and Montreal: McGill–Queen's University Press.

Tator, Carol, and Francis Henry. 2000. "The Role and Practice of Racialized Discourse in Culture and Cultural Production." *Journal of Canadian Studies* 35(3): 120–41.

Thomas, Elizabeth. 1959. *The Harmless People.* New York: Knopf.

Thompson, E. P. 1967. "Time, Work-Discipline, and Industrial Capitalism." *Past and Present* 38: 56–97.

Thrasher, Frederic. 1963 [1927]. *The Gang.* Chicago: University of Chicago Press.

Todaro, Michael. 2000. *Economic Development.* Reading: Addison Wesley.

Toynbee, Jason. 2007. *Bob Marley: Herald of Postcolonial World?* Cambridge: Polity.

Trigger, Bruce. 1986. "Evolutionism, Relativism, and Putting Native People into Historical Context." *Culture* 6(2): 65–79.

Turner, Terence. 2005. "Ethical Issues Arising from Patrick Tierney's *Darkness in El Dorado* and the Ensuing Controversy." In *Yanomami: The Fierce Controversy and What We Can Learn from It,* edited by Rob Borofsky. Berkeley and Los Angeles: University of California Press.

Turner, Victor. 1967. *The Forest of Symbols: Aspects of Ndembu Ritual.* Ithaca: Cornell University Press.

——. 1995 [1969]. *The Ritual Process.* Hawthorne: Aldine de Gruyter.

Tylor, Edward. 1871. *Primitive Culture.* London: Murray.

Valentine, Charles A. 1968. *Culture and Poverty: Critique and Counter-Proposals.* Chicago: University of Chicago Press.

van den Berghe, Pierre L. 1965. *South Africa: A Study in Conflict.* Middletown: Wesleyan University Press.

——. 1970. *Race and Ethnicity.* New York: Basic.

——. 1992. "The Modern State: Nation-Builder or Nation-Killer?" *International Journal of Group Tensions* 22: 191–208.

——, and George P. Primov. 1977. *Inequality in the Peruvian Andes: Class and Ethnicity in Cuzco.* Columbia: University of Missouri Press.

van Gennep, Arnold. 1960 [1906]. *The Rites of Passage.* Translated by Monica B. Vizedom and Gabrielle L. Chaffe. Chicago: University of Chicago Press.

Van Wynsberghe, Robert M. 2002. *AlterNatives: Community, Identity, and Environmental Justice on Walpole Island.* Toronto: Allyn and Bacon.

Vergano, Dan. 2014. Amazon Warriors' Names Revealed Amid "Gibberish" on Ancient Greek Vases. *National Geographic.* http://news.nationalgeographic.com/news/2014/09/140923-amazon-greek-vase-translations-science

Vincent, Joan, ed. 2002. *The Anthropology of Politics.* Oxford: Blackwell.

Von Gernet, Alexander. 1994. "Saving the Souls: Reincarnation Beliefs of the Seventeenth-Century Huron." In *American Rebirth: Reincarnation Belief Among North American Indians and Inuit,* edited by Antonia Mills and Richard Slobodin. Toronto: University of Toronto Press.

Wagner, Roy. 1984. "Ritual as Communication: Order, Meaning, and Secrecy in Melanesian Initiation Rites." *Annual Review of Anthropology* 13: 143–55.

Waldram, James B. 1997. *The Way of the Pipe: Aboriginal Spirituality and Symbolic Healing in Canadian Prisons.* Peterborough: Broadview.

Waldram, James B., and J. O'Neil. 1989. "Native Health Research in Canada." Special Issue of *Native Studies Review* 5(1): 1–213.

Walens, Stanley. 1981. *Feasting with Cannibals: An Essay on Kwakiutl Cosmology.* Princeton: Princeton University Press.

Wall, Denis. 2000. "Aboriginal Self-Government in Canada: The Cases of Nunavut and the Alberta Métis Settlements." In *Visions of the Heart: Canadian Aboriginal Issues,* edited by David Long and Olive Patricia Dickason. Toronto: Harcourt Canada.

Wall, Ellen. 1992. "Personal Labour Relations and Ethnicity in Ontario Agriculture." In *Deconstructing a Nation: Immigration, Multiculturalism and Racism in '90s Canada,* edited by Vic Satzewich. Halifax: Fernwood.

Wallace, Anthony F. C. 1966. *Religion: An Anthropological View.* New York: Random House.

Wallerstein, Immanuel. 1989. *The Modern World-System III. The Second Era of Great Expansion of the Capitalist World-Economy, 1730–1840s.* New York: Academic.

Walsh, Andrew. 2002a. "Responsibility, Taboos, and 'The Freedom to Do Otherwise' in Ankarana, Northern Madagascar." *Journal of the Royal Anthropological Institute* 8(3): 451–68.

—— . 2002b. "Saving Souls, Preserving Bodies: Religious Incongruity in a Northern Malagasy Mining Town." *Journal of Religion in Africa* 32(3): 366–92.

—— . 2003. "'Hot Money' and Daring Consumption in a Northern Malagasy Town." *American Ethnologist* 30(2): 290–305.

—— . 2004. "In the Wake of Things: Speculating in and About Sapphires in Northern Madagascar." *American Anthropologist* 106(2): 225–37.

—— . 2010. "The Commodification of Fetishes: Telling the Difference Between Natural and Synthetic Sapphires." *American Ethnologist* 37(1): 98–114.

Washburn, Sherwood L., and C. S. Lancaster. 1968. "The Evolution of Hunting." In *Man the Hunter,* edited by R. B. Lee and Irvene Devore. New York: Aldine.

Watson-Ellam, Linda. 2001. "Living Against the Wind: Pathways Chosen by Chinese Immigrants." *Canadian Ethnic Studies* 33(1): 71–101.

Weiner, Annette B. 1976. *Women of Value, Men of Renown.* Austin: University of Texas Press.

—— . 1988. *The Trobrianders of Papua New Guinea.* New York: Holt, Rinehart, and Winston.

Weston, Kath. 1991. *Families We Choose: Lesbians, Gays, Kinship.* New York: Columbia University Press.

White, Leslie. 1949. *The Science of Culture.* New York: Farrar, Straus and Giroux.

—— . 1959. *The Evolution of Culture.* New York: McGraw-Hill.

Whitehead, Harriet. 1981. "The Bow and the Burden Strap: A New Look at Institutionalized Homosexuality in Native North America." In *Sexual Meanings: The Cultural Construction of Gender and Sexuality,* edited by Sherry B. Ortner and Harriet Whitehead. New York: Cambridge University Press.

Whitehead, Neil Lancelot. 1990. "The Snake Warriors— Sons of the Tiger's Teeth: A Descriptive Analysis of Carib Warfare, ca. 1500–1820." In *The Anthropology of War,* edited by Jonathan Hass. New York: Cambridge University Press.

Williams, Walter L. 1986. *The Spirit and the Flesh: Sexual Diversity in American Indian Culture.* Boston: Beacon.

Wilmsen, Edwin N., and James R. Denbow. 1990. "Paradigmatic History of San-Speaking Peoples and Current Attempts at Revision." *Current Anthropology* 31: 489–512.

Wilson, Richard A. 1997. *Human Rights, Culture, and Context: Anthropological Perspectives.* London: Pluto.

Wise, Amanda. 2006. *Exile and Return Among the East Timorese*. Philadelphia: University of Pennsylvania Press.

Wolf, Eric. 1964. *Anthropology*. Englewood Cliffs: Prentice-Hall.

——. 1966. *Peasants*. Englewood Cliffs: Prentice Hall.

——. 1969. *Peasant Wars of the Twentieth Century*. New York: Harper and Row.

——. 1982. *Europe and the People Without History*. Berkeley: University of California Press.

Wolf, Margery. 1968. *The House of Lim*. Englewood Cliffs: Prentice Hall.

Woodburn, James. 1968. "An Introduction to Hadza Ecology." In *Man the Hunter,* edited by Richard Lee and Irven DeVore, with the assistance of Jill Nash. Chicago: Aldine.

Worsley, Peter. 1982. "Non-Western Medical Systems." *Annual Review of Anthropology* 11: 315–48.

Yan, Yunxiang. 2002. "Practicing Kinship in Rural North China." In *Practicing Kinship: Lineage and Descent in Late Imperial China,* edited by Michael Szonyi. Stanford: Stanford University Press.

Yanagisako, Sylvia Junko. 1979. "Family and Household: The Analysis of Domestic Groups." *Annual Review of Anthropology* 8: 161–205.

Yanagisako, Sylvia, and Carol Delaney, eds. 1995. *Naturalizing Power: Essays on Feminist Cultural Analysis*. New York: Routledge.

Young, Allan. 1982. "The Anthropologies of Illness and Sickness." *Annual Review of Anthropology* 11: 257–85.

Young, K. 1988. *Health Care and Culture Change: The Indian Experience in the Central Subarctic*. Toronto: University of Toronto Press.

Zechenter, Elizabeth. 1997. "In the Name of Culture: Cultural Relativism and the Abuse of the Individual." *Journal of Anthropological Research—Universal Human Rights Versus Cultural Relativity* 53: 319–48.

Ziegler-Otero, Lawrence. 2004. *Resistance in an Amazonian Community: Huaorani Organizing Against the Global Economy*. New York and Oxford: Berghahn.

Ziemba, Christine. 2011. "The Beer Archaeologist: Tasting World History: …The "Indiana Jones of Alcohol." *Slate* magazine. www.slate.com: John Alderman.

INDEX

Abelam, 12, 47–48

Abenake, 238

Aboriginal peoples. *See* Indigenous peoples

Achieved status, 190

Act of Union, 172

Adelson, Naomi, 31

Aditjondro, George, 269, 270, 275

Adolescence, 165, 205

Adulthood, transition to, 173–174

Afek, 183

Afghanistan, 276, 277–279

Agriculture
    factory model, 88
    industrial, 70–71
    irrigation, 61, 62*t*
    labour days per acre by type of, 69*t*
    land need to feed 100 families, by type of, 69*t*
    slash-and-burn, 61, 62*t*, 88
    transition to, 68–70

Agroecological approach, 88–89

AIDS, 154–157, 217

AIDS and Accusation (Farmer), 216

Ambondromifehy, Madagascar, 110–112

Ameeriar, Lalaie, 209

American Anthropological Association, 193, 276

American Family, An (documentary), 129

American Journal of Psychology, 199

American Samoa, 53, 165

Amnesty International, 213, 271

Anchor villages, Yanomamö, 265–266

Ancient Society (Morgan), 63–64

Anderson, Benedict, 164

Anderson, Margaret, 176, 177

Anderson-Levy, Lisa, 153

Anthropology, 4–6
    alleviation of inequality and, 212–218

applied, 27–33

archaeology, 7

armchair, 40–41

biological, 6–7

challenges to theory in, 151–154

changes to study of family in, 151–154

development and, 86–89

formative years of, 39–43

globalization and, 45

human rights and, 212–214

legal, 29–30

linguistic, 7–8

medical, 30–32

medical rights and, 214–216

in midst of violent conflict, 274–279

military collaborations, 275–277

morality and, 16–18

objectivity and, 16–18

outside of academia, 26–33

representation, 51–54

salvage, 44

sociocultural, 3–6, 8–9, 27–33

Ap, Arnold, 274

Applied anthropology, 27
    corporate ethnography, 32–33
    indigenous issues, 27–29
    legal anthropology, 29–30
    medical anthropology, 30–32
    political ecology, 30

Appropriation, 178, 179, 180

Aptima, 277

Araucanians, 206

Archaeology, 5, 7

Arctic, 23–24

Argonauts of the Western Pacific (Malinowski), 43

Arguments, metaphors regarding, 96

Arkwright, Richard, 73

Armchair anthropology, 40–41

Aryan Nations, 194

Asahara, Shoko, 260

Ascribed status, 190

Atheism, 122

Aum Shinrikyo, 260

Australia, 271

Awkwardness, during fieldwork, 47–48

Azaka, 120

Azande, 93

Aztecs, 13

"Bad blood", 215

Balinese cockfight, 19–21

Baloma, 136

Banana leaf bundles, Trobriand Islands, 143

Bananas, tariffs on, 232

Bands, 59

Bannerji, Himani, 236

Baptism, in Hutterite community, 211

Barbarism, 64

Barbeau, Marius, 44

Barrett, Stanley, 29, 194

Beardy, Stan, 240

Bechtel Enterprises, 241

Becker, Anne E., 169–170

Beef industry, 25, 232

Behaviours
    differences in, 9–11
    judging others', 12–18

Being Alive Well (Adelson), 31

Beliefs
    differences in, 9–11
    judging others', 12–18
    relation to way of life, 106–110
    religious, 94–95
    worldviews and, 93–95

Bell Curve, The (Herrnstein and Murray), 197

Bella Coola Valley, 242

Bellah, Robert, 169

Belmonte, Thomas, 188

Bengal, 75
Berangkat studi lanjut ke Jawa, 270
Berghe, Pierre van den, 268
Bilateral inheritance principle, 183, 184
Bilateral kinship, 132
Bin Laden, Osama, 260
Biography of commodity, 222–223
Biological anthropology, 5, 6–7
Biomedical imaging, 153
Biomedical model, 82
Birth, as rite of passage, 106–107
Bitter Paradise (video), 271
Boas, Franz, 41, 44, 98, 165, 192, 193
Bob, David, 239
Bodley, John H., 70
Body image, 204–206
Body shape, 204–205
Boellstorff, Tom, 46
Bolivia, 241
Bonang shells, 183
Bondye, 120
Bonnivard, Odile, 208
Book of Revelation, 259
Boot camp, 173
Bossen, Laurel, 151
Botswana, 155
Bourgois, Philippe, 17, 51
Bourne, Edmund J., 168
Brahmins, 191
Branching, by Hutterites, 211
Brazil
    debts, 80–81
    economic development, 80–81
    mortality rate for children, 86
    race, class, and social hierarchies in, 207–208
Brennan, Denise, 52–53
Bretton Woods Agreement, 79–80
Bride-Bush, or, A Wedding Sermon, A (Whately), 129
Brideservice, 133, 142, 266
Bridewealth, 142, 144
Brière, Elaine, 271
British East India Company, 75
British North America Act of 1867, 172

British Petroleum, 230
British textile industry, 75–78
Brody, Hugh, 162–163
Brown, Karen McCarthy, 120, 121–122
Burt, Ben, 114–115

Cagan, Leslie, 267
Cambodia, 268
Cameroon, modern witchcraft in, 112–113
Canada
    East Timor tragedy and, 271
    family composition, 131–132, 132f
    First Nations' challenge to, 237–240
    garment industry, 233–234
    globalization and Canadian identity, 243–244
    hockey, 22–24, 163–164
    Hutterites, 210–212
    identity of, 163–164
    immigration, 235
    multiculturalism policy, 236
    national identity in, 235, 243–244
    Pakistani immigrant women in, 209
    potato industry, 70–71
    poverty in, 188
    races in, 236
    racism in, 194
    residential schools in, 237
    soldiers in Kandahar, 277–279
Canadian Forces, 278–279
Canadian National War Memorial, 254
Canadian Nazi Party, 194
Canadian Pacific Railway, 227, 235
Cannibal Dance, 102–103
Cannibal Society, 102
Cannibalism, 14–16
Capitalism, 224
Caribbean bananas, 232
Carnegie Mellon University, 277
Carneiro, Robert L., 69–70

Carpet bombing, 273
Carrier, James, 177–178, 179–180
Caste system, 190–192
Catholicism, Vodou and, 120
"Celebration of a New Life" (Jacobson), 160
Central American bananas, 232
Chagnon, Napoleon, 53–54, 258, 259, 265, 266
Charlie Hebdo shootings, 122, 123
Cherokee, 76–77
Chewa, 84
Cheyenne, 200
Chiapas, Mexico, 247
Chimbinda, Jorge, 167–168
China. *See also* Rural Chinese
    during 16th and 17th centuries, 72
    changes benefiting women in, 151
    death in, 10
    opium trade, 75
Christianity
    Christmas gift giving, 178–180
    communalism, 210–212
    Dene Tha and, 113–114
    effect on local worldview, 113–117
    Haitian Vodou and, 120
    Rastafarianism and, 115–117
    in Solomon Islands, 114–115
    utopian dreams related to, 210
Christmas, 178–180
Christmas Carol, A (Dickens), 178–179
Christmas tree farms, 273
Churchill, Ward, 206–207
Civil Marriage Act, 132
Civilization, 64
Clans, 61, 142
Clark, Kim, 181
Clark-Decès, Isabelle, 191
Class
    in Brazil, 207–208
    definition, 189
    as form of social hierarchy, 189–190
    intelligence and, 196–200

Classroom chairs, 3–4
Clean bombs, 273
Clocks, 19
Clothing, as identity marker, 174–175
Cochabamba, Bolivia, 241
Cockfight, Balinese, 19–21
Code of Conduct for Trademark Licensees, 234
Cohen, Mark, 68
Cohn, Carol, 273–274
Cola drink, 25
Colarusso, John, 8
Collateral damage, 273
Collective identity, 180–184
Collective violence
    bias in favour of, 257–261
    justifications for, 256–257
Collings, Peter, 23–24
Colonialism
    in Canada, 238
    definition, 72
    heteronormative concept, 153
    internal colonization, 153–154, 194
    naming systems and, 167–168
    revitalization movements, 117
    worldview of colonized peoples, 113–117
Colony of heaven, 210–212
Columbus, Christopher, 39, 72
Comaroff, Jean, 105
Comaroff, John, 105
Coming of Age in Samoa (Mead), 53
Coming of Age in Second Life (Boellstorff), 46
Commodification of time, 106
Commodities, 177–178, 179–180
Common sense, 199
Communalism, Christian, 210–212
Community, imagined, 164, 234–235
Community identity, 30
Comparative method, 40–41
Competition, in Hutterite community, 211
Comprehensive Everglades Restoration Plan, 228

Conception, theories of, 133, 135–137
Condon, Richard, 23–24
Confederation of Indigenous Nations of Ecuador (CONAIE), 181, 241
Conflict, fieldwork in midst of violent, 274–279
Conflict resolution, 255–257, 261–263
Conklin, Beth, 14, 15
Consent, informed, 51
Consumerism, 32
Consuming Grief (Conklin), 14, 15
Contraception, forced, 270
Convention on the Prevention and Punishment of the Crime of Genocide, 213
Conversational style, gender and, 206
Coombe, Rosemary, 29–30
Cooperative communities, 210–212
CORDS program, 276–277
Corporate ethnography, 32–33
Corporate taxes, 229
Cosmic war, framing violence as, 259–261
Cotton gin, 76
Cotton trade, 75–77
Counterinsurgency, 275–276
Counts, David, 152
Counts, Dorothy, 152
Courtship, 139, 141
Crafting Selves (Kondo), 171
Cree, 84, 238
    being alive well, 31
    challenge to Canadian state by, 239–240
    cultural devastation, 248–250
    metaphors used by, 96
    worldview of, 107–108
Creole, 120
Creutzfeldt-Jakob disease, 232
Critical cultural relativism, 17
Crompton, Samuel, 73
Crowley, Aleister, 101
Cruikshank, Julie, 109
Culhane, Dara, 238

Cultural devastation, 248–250
Cultural diversity, 247–248
Cultural globalization, 241–250
Cultural relativism, 13, 17
Cultural text, 19–21
Culture
    counterinsurgency and knowledge of, 275–276
    death and, 10
    deciphering others', 18–21
    definition, 9–10, 41, 43
    differences in, 11
    food and, 10–11
    globalization and, 241–250
    judging others', 12–18
    multiculturalism, 236
    representation and, 51–54
    study of one's own, 22–26
Culture and Power (Barrett), 29
Culture change, 60–62
    definition, 61
    evolutionary explanations for, 63–65
Culture shock, 47
Cummings, Maggie, 245–246
Curtis, Edward, 98
Custer, George, 119

Dahl, Ophelia, 218
Dala, 134–135, 137
Dalit, 191–192
Dallaire, Roméo, 213
Danbala, 121
Dancing with a Ghost (Ross), 3
Dani, 10
Darnell, Regna, 27–28, 44
Darwin, Charles, 63
Davis-Floyd, Robbie, 106
Dawkins, Richard, 122
Death, 10, 15–16, 22, 149
Deethnicization campaign, Rwanda, 269
Deforestation, 80, 81, 248
Delaney, Carol, 14, 136
Deliège, Robert, 191–192
Demarchers, 111

Den Frieden nehmen, 211
Dene Tha, 107–109, 113–114
De-Santa Cruz-kan, 270
Development, 60
    anthropology and, 86–89
    economic, 78–82
    health and, 82–85
    inequality and, 81–82
Diabetes, 32–33
Diaspora, 270–271
Dickens, Charles, 178–179
Disease, 85, 96–97
Divale, William Tulio, 267
Diversity, globalization and, 247–248
Divorce, 141, 143, 145
Djambe, 112–113
Do Glaciers Listen? (Cruikshank), 109
Domain of experience, 96
Dominican Republic, 52–53, 229
Dowry, 145
Dreams, in Dene Tha worldview,
    108–109
Drug wars, 264
Drum Beat Conference, 250
Duncan, William, 177
Dupom, 257
Durkheim, Emile, 94–95, 106
Dyck, Noel, 23, 28–29

East India Company, 227
East Timor, 269–271
Eating disorders, 169, 170
Eating metaphor, 98–99
Echuhdigeh, 107, 114
Eckert, Penelope, 206
Economic development, 78–82
Economic exchange metaphors, 97
Economic globalization, 223–226,
    233–234, 244–247
Economic pyramid, 71*f*
Economic systems, 224–228
Ecuador, 181, 240–241
Edmonds, Alexander, 207–208
Edmund Burke Society, 194
Education, 237
Egalitarian communities, 210–212

Egocentric self, 168–170
Elementary Forms of the Religious Life,
    The (Durkheim), 94
Embarrassment, during fieldwork,
    47–48
Embodiment, multiculturalism
    and, 209
Emic perspective, 38, 43
Encountering Development
    (Escobar), 79
Enculturation, 163–164
Endogamy, 142
Energy, 64–65, 70–71
English textile industry, 72–77
Enlightenment, 212
Enryo, 171
Environment, politics of, 30
Environmental destruction, 247–248
Erasmus, Charles, 210
Ervin, Alexander M., 87
Escobar, Arturo, 79
Espanto, 84–85
Essentialism, 52
Ethics, 32–33, 50–51
Ethnic cleansing, 268
Ethnocentric fallacy, 13
Ethnocentrism, 13
Ethnocide, 268
Ethnographic fieldwork, 38–39
    challenges of conducting, 47–50
    changing notions of, 43–47
    definition, 38
    development of, 41–43
    ethical challenges of, 50–51
    globalization and, 45
    in midst of violent conflict,
        274–279
    multi-locale, 45–46
    multi-sited, 45
    representation and, 51–54
Ethnographic method, 41–42
Ethnographic present, 130–131, 155
Ethnography, 26, 32–33, 42
Etic perspective, 38, 43, 50
Eugenics, 198
Europe, WTO cases involving, 232
European colonialism, 72

Evans-Pritchard, E. E., 18–19, 93
Evolutionary explanations for culture
    change, 63–65
Exogamy, 142
Extended family, 137
Extramarital affairs, among
    Ju/'hoansi, 148
Exxon Mobile, 230
Ezili, 120–121
Ezili Danto, 120
Ezili Freda, 120

Faber, Jonasie Quarqortoq, 128
Factory model, 88
Factory system, 73
Falla, Ricardo, 275
Families. *See also* Kinship
    anthropological study of, 151–154
    applying understanding of,
        154–157
    Christmas gift giving in, 179
    extended, 137
    feminist critiques, 152–153
    formation of, 139–145
    nuclear, 132
    threats to, 147–151
"Family" (Faber), 128
Family composition, 131–133
    Canadian, 131–132
    Ju/'hoansi, 133, 134*f*
    rural Chinese, 137–139
    Trobriand Islanders, 134–137
Family cycle
    Ju/'hoansi, 140–141
    rural Chinese, 144–145
    Trobriand Islanders, 141–144
Family planning programs, 270
Farah, Randa, 182
Farmer, Paul, 155, 214–218
Fat-and-sugar diet, 25
Federation of Workers, Bolivia, 241
Feit, Harvey, 96, 107, 240
Feminism, 152–153
Feminization of poverty, 204
Ferguson, Brian, 256, 265, 266
Fernando, Mayanthi, 122–123

Fieldwork. *See* Ethnographic fieldwork
Fierce People, The (Chagnon), 265
Figure skating, 243–244
Fiji, 169–170
Finnis, Beth, 30
Firelight Group, 29
First, Ruth, 274
First clearance principle, 183
First Nations. *See* Indigenous peoples; *specific First Nations*
Florida sugar cane industry, 228–229
Flying shuttle, 73, 74
Food
    culture and, 10–11
    kinship based on, 152
Footprint, bomb, 273–274
Foraging societies, 59–60
    culture change and, 60–62, 63–65
    Hadza, 65–66
    idea of progress and, 62–63, 65
    Ju/'hoansi, 66–67
    as original affluent society, 65
    transition to agriculture, 68–70
Foreign Agricultural Resource Management Services (FARMS), 235
Forensic anthropology, 6–7
Forte, Maximillian, 276
Foucault, Michel, 3–4
Fraternities, 203–204
Free trade, 225, 232–234
Frideres, James, 194
Frideres, James S., 187
Funeral customs, 10, 15–16
Furniss, Elizabeth, 237

G factor, 199
G-20, 221–222
Gadacz, René R., 187, 194
Gahuku-Gama, 22
Galton, Francis, 164–165, 197–198
Game Act, 239
Gang rape, 203–204
Gangs, 264–265
Garment industry, 233–234

Gay marriage, 130, 132, 154
Gede, 121
Geertz, Clifford, 11, 20, 21
Gellner, Ernest, 237
Gender
    constructing, 200–201
    definition, 200
    as form of social hierarchy, 200–207
    language and, 206
    third, 200
Gender identity, 165–166
Gender stratification
    body image and, 204–206
    constructing, 201–202
    feminization of poverty and, 204
    hegemonic masculinity and, 202–204
Gendered toys, 25, 26
General impression concept, 199
General intelligence, 198–199
Genetics, 166
Genocide, 268, 269–271
Geological Survey of Canada, 44
Georgia Compact of 1802, 77
Gerber, Linda, 204
Geschiere, Peter, 112, 113
Ghost Dance, 118–119
Ghost Dance Religion and the Sioux Outbreak of 1890, The (Mooney), 119
Ghosts, in Kwara'ae worldview, 115
Giddens, Anthony, 222
Gift, The (Mauss), 175
Gift giving, 175–180
Gifts and Commodities (Carrier), 177
Gildan, 233, 234
Gilmore, David, 173
Glaciers, 109
Glee (television show), 130
Global economic pyramid, 71*f*
Global economy, nation-states and, 230–233
Globalization, 29, 222–223
    anthropology and, 45
    Canadian garment industry and, 233–234

    Canadian identity and, 243–244
    cultural diversity and, 247–248
    cultural effects of, 241–250
    definition, 222
    economic, 223–226, 233–234, 244–247
    environmental destruction and, 247–248
    nationalism and, 244–247
    nation-state and, 234–241
    neoliberalism and, 223–226
    tourism and, 244–247
Globalized Nicaragua (Heinrich), 220
Glooscap, 109
God, belief in, 93, 94–95
Goffman, Erving, 161
Gonzales, Roberto, 276, 277
Goodall, Jane, 6
Gould, Stephen Jay, 195–196
Goulet, Jean-Guy, 107, 108, 113, 114
Government involvement in economy, 224–226
Grammar, as signaling gender, 206
Great Transformation, The (Polanyi), 224
Green, Linda, 275
Gregor, Thomas, 261, 262
Gremillion, Helen, 169
Griffin, Marcus, 276
Guaraní, 247–248
Guatemala, 275
Gusterson, Hugh, 272–273

Habits of the Heart (Bellah), 169
Hadza, 65–66
Haile Selassie I, 116
Haiti, 119–122, 214–216
Hamatsa dance, 102–103
Hamburger, 25
Hanson, Allan, 197
"Happy Meal", 24–26
Hargreaves, James, 73
Harijans caste, 191–192
Harmless People, The (Thomas), 133
Harper, Elijah, 235
Harper's Weekly, 179

Harris, Marvin, 25, 267
Harrison, Julia, 27–28
Harvey, David, 221, 226
Haudenosaunee, 28
Hawai'i, hospitality in, 177
Hawthorne-Tremblay Report, 28–29
Headhunting, 12–13, 22
Health, 31, 82–85, 216–218
Heape, Walter, 201
Hedican, Edward, 28
Hedley, Max, 153–154
Hegemonic masculinity, 202–204
Heinrich, Frances, 220
Henare, Manuka, 109
Hereditary Genius (Galton), 198
Herrnstein, Richard J., 197
Heteronormative concept, 153
Hierarchical methodology, 41
High Commissioner for Human
     Rights, 213
Hiroshima, 274
Historical linguists, 8
History, official accounts of, 236
History of Neoliberalism, The (Harvey),
     221
Histri Blong Yumi Long Vanuatu,
     246–247
Hitchcock, Robert, 214
HIV Equity Initiative, 218
HIV/AIDS, 154–157, 217
Hobbes, Thomas, 263
Hockey, 22–24, 163–164
Hoe cultivation, 69t
Holistic view of self, 168
Holmes, Sherlock (fictional
     character), 18
Hominids, 6
Homophobia, 202–203
Hoodfar, Homa, 174
Hormone-treated beef, 232
Horses, in Kiowa society, 257–258
Horticulturalists, 62t
Hospitality rituals, 175–177
Hsu, Francis L. K., 137, 144, 145
Huaorani, 240–241
Hudson's Bay Company, 227, 233
Human rights, 212–214

Human Rights (Nagengast and
     Vélez-Ibáñez), 213–214
Human Rights Watch, 213, 271
Human Social Culture Behavior
     (HSCB) Modeling, 277
Human Terrain System (HTS),
     276, 277
Human Terrain Teams (HTTs),
     276, 277
Hunger, metaphors of, 98–99
Hunt, George, 98
Hunters and gatherers, 62t. *See also*
     Foraging societies
Huron, 238
Hutterites, 210–212
Hydro-Québec, 240

Identity, 161–162
     Canadian, 243–244
     changes in, 173–174
     clothing and, 174–175
     collective struggles and, 180–184
     communication of, 174–180
     enculturation and, 163–164
     kinship and, 172
     language and, 172–173
     learning, 162–166
     national, and globalization,
          234–241
     nature versus nurture, 164–166
     social, 161
"Identity soup" campaign, 208
Illness
     inequality and, 82–83
     meaning of, 83–85
     metaphors regarding, 96–97
Ilongots, headhunting by, 12–13, 22
Imagined community, 164, 234–235
Immigration, 209, 235
Immune system, 83
Impartible inheritance, 150
Ina, 137
Incest taboo, 139, 142
India
     British in, 74–75
     caste system in, 190–192

death in, 10
feminization of poverty in, 204
opium trade, 75
sati custom, 10, 17
in 16th and 17th centuries, 72
Indian Act of Canada, 239
Indian Wars, 118
Indigenism, 241
Indigenous peoples. *See also specific*
     peoples
     agroecological approach, 88–89
     in applied anthropology, 27–29
     challenges to nation-states by,
          237–241
     collective identity, 180–181
     cultural devastation, 248–250
     definition, 180
     ethnic cleansing of, 268
     feminization of poverty among,
          204
     internal colonization, 153–154
     Meech Lake Accord, 235
     poverty among, 188, 204
     progress and development issues,
          86
     racism against, 194
     residential schools, 237
     revitalization movements, 117,
          118–119
     salvage anthropology, 44
     social movements, 181–182
     third gender, 200
     worldview of, 107–109, 113–117
Individualistic view of self, 168–169
Individuals, distinguishing between,
     171–173
Indonesia, 269–271
Industrial agriculture, 70–71
Industrial Revolution, 64, 72, 76, 78,
     224–225
Inequality
     alleviating effects of, 212–218
     economic development and,
          78–82
     explanations for, 71–78
     gender differences and, 165–166
     global economic pyramid, 71f

illness and, 82–83
   rationale for, 187–189
Infectious disease, 82–83, 217
Infidelity, among Ju/'hoansi, 148
Informed consent, 51
Inheritance, in rural China, 150, 151
Innocent IV (pope), 14
Insider perspective, 38, 43, 50
Intellectual property law, 29–30
Intelligence
   general, 198–199
   skull size and, 195–196
   social construction of, 196–200
Internal colonization, 153–154, 194
International Bank for
      Reconstruction and
      Development (World Bank),
      79–80, 81, 223, 226
International Monetary Fund (IMF),
      80, 223, 226
Internet research, 46
Interpersonal theory of disease, 85
Inuit, 2, 162–163, 187–188, 204, 240
Inuvik, 86–88
Invisible Indigenes (Miller), 180–181
Iraq, 275–276, 277
Irrigation agriculture, 61, 62*t*,
      68–70, 69*t*
Irwin, Anne, 278
Isabella, Queen, 14
Isbister, John, 58, 59, 79
Islam, 122–123
Island dress, 245–246
Italy, funeral customs in, 10
Ito, Paulo, 186

Jackson, Andrea, 276
Jackson, Andrew, 77
Jacobson, Mark Anthony, 160
Jalan-jalan ke Jakarta, 270
Jamaica, 115–117, 153
James Bay and Northern Québec
      Agreement (JBNQA), 240
James Bay Cree, 31, 239–240
James Bay Experience, The, 31
Janvier, Alex, 92

Japan, 83, 170–171, 197
Jefferson, Thomas, 77, 212
Jenness, Diamond, 44
Jensen, Arthur, 197
Jesuit Relations, 40
Jobbers, 233
John Company, 75
Jorgensen, Dan, 182
Judd, Ellen, 151
Juergensmeyer, Mark, 260–261
Ju/'hoansi, 130
   AIDS prevention among, 155–156
   family composition, 133, 134*f*
   family cycle, 140–141
   foraging by, 66–67
   gender roles, 266
   kinship, 140–141
   lack of social hierarchy among,
      187–188
   marriage, 140–141
   peacefulness of, 261, 262–263
   sex, love, and wealth among,
      145–146
   threats to family, 147–148
   trance dance, 262–263

Kaesong Industrial Region, 225
Kaliai, 152
Kandahar, Afghanistan, 277–279
Kanwar, Roon, 17
Kathmandu, Nepal, 30
Kayapo Video Project, 214
Kearney, Michael, 48–50
Keen, 257
Keesing, Roger, 50
Keigo, 170
Keiser, Lincoln, 264
Kenya, 204
Keohane, Kieran, 244
Key metaphors, 98
Key scenarios, 104, 116
Keynes, John Maynard, 225
Khmer Rouge, 268
Kidder, Tracy, 214
Kiefer, Christie, 170
Kim, Jim Yong, 218

Kinship. *See also* Families
   bases of, 152
   bilateral, 132
   definition, 130
   Ju/'hoansi, 140–141
   matrilineal, 133
   patrilineal, 133
   self and, 172
   study of, 130–131
Kiowa, 257–258, 258*t*
Kitikmeot, Northwest Territories,
      23–24
Klaits, Frederick, 152
Kondo, Dorinne, 171
Kopytoff, Igor, 222
Korten, David, 230
Kotlowitz, Alex, 264
Kramer, Jennifer, 242–243
Kshattriya caste, 191
Ku Klux Klan, 194
Kuikuru, 68
Kula ring, 175–176
Kuper, Leo, 268
Kwakwaka'wakw, 10, 98–99,
      102–103
Kwara'ae, 114–115

Laboucon, Albert, 249–250
Labour, 228–229
Labov, William, 8
Lake Okeechobee, 228
Lakoff, Robin, 206
Lakota, 200
Lambek, Michael, 95
Lancaster, Roger, 166
Land rights, 182–184
Language
   construction of Others based
      on, 235
   gender and racial hierarchies and,
      206–207
   as identity marker, 172–173
   Japanese, 170
   technostrategic, 273–274
Language and Gender (Eckert and
      McConnell-Ginet), 206

Lasyrenn, 120–121
Law, and society, 29
Lawrence Livermore National
        Laboratory, 272–273
Leakey, Mary, 6
Lee, Richard, 66–67, 141, 148, 155,
        262, 263
Legal anthropology, 29–30
Leviathan (Hobbes), 263
Levi-Strauss, Claude, 49–50, 105
Li, Tania, 79, 238
Liberation theology, 215–216
Life expectancy, 82, 83
Linguistic anthropology, 5, 7–8
Lithman, Yngve, 23
Lo mue, 150
Lorway, Robert, 156–157
Love, 145–147
Lu Village, China, 151
Lubicon Cree, 238, 248–250
Luhrmann, Tanya M., 100–101,
        103–104
Luta, 137
Luxton, Meg, 154
Lwa (African spirits), 120–121

Maasina Rul (Rule of Brotherhood),
        115
Mack, Myrna, 274
Mackenzie Delta, 86–88
Mackey, Eva, 236
Macumé, 202–203
Mad cow disease, 232
Madagascar, 45, 110–112
Madden, Raymond, 46
Magic, 100–101, 103–104
Maish, Amy, 32–33
Maka, 112–113
Malagasy, 110–112
Male bonding, 203
Malinowski, Bronislaw, 5, 41, 42–43,
        46, 136, 141
Maliseets, 238
Mama Lola, 121
Mani laut, 270
Maori, 109

Marcus, George, 45
Market economies, 224–228
Market externalities, 226, 228–230
Marley, Bob, 116–117
Marriage, 139–140
    heteronormative concept, 153
    Ju/'hoansi, 133, 140–141
    rural Chinese, 144–145
    same-sex, 130, 132, 154
    Trobriand Islanders, 141–144
    uxorilocal, 151
Mars, Incorporated, 228
Marshall, Lorna, 66
Martin, Emily, 201–202
Martin-Hill, Dawn, 28, 248, 249–250
Martinique, 202–203
Marx, Karl, 210
Masculinity, hegemonic, 202–204
Masing Rul (Marching Rule), 115
Matchmakers, 144
Material culture, 64
Matrilineage, 134–135, 136, 137,
        142–143, 148–149
Matrilineal kinship, 133
Mauss, Marcel, 175
Maya, 88
McConnell-Ginet, Sally, 206
McCracken, Grant, 32
McFate, Montgomery, 275–276
McGarry, Karen, 243
McGovern, Pat, 7
McIlwraith, Thomas F., 40
McIntosh, Peggy, 195
McLaughlin, Janet, 31–32
McMaster University, 250
Mead, Margaret, 36, 37, 53, 129, 165
Meat, 25
Medical anthropology, 30–32
Medical rights, 214–216
Medicinal cannibalism, 15
Meech Lake Accord, 235
Membership rules, nation-states, 235
Menopause, 201
Menstruation, 201–202
Meritocracy, 190
Metaphors, 95–101
Métis, 204

Mexico, 48–49, 88–89, 247
Migrant Worker Health Project, 32
Migrant workers, 31–32
Mi'kmaq, 109, 238
Military collaborations,
        anthropological, 275–277
Military Review, 275–276
Millennial capitalism, 105
Miller, Bruce, 180–181
Min peoples, 182–184
Mining, land rights and, 182–184
Mintz, Sidney, 25, 229
Mirebalais hospital, Haiti, 218
Mishkin, Bernard, 258
Missanabie Cree, 240
Mitchell, Lisa, 153
Miyupimaatisiiun, 31
Mock weddings, 200–201
Modern medicine, 82
Modernity of Witchcraft, The
        (Geschiere), 112
Moffat, Tina, 30
Moir, Scott, 243, 244
Mongongo nut, 66, 67*t*
Mont Pelerin Society, 225
Montagnaix-Naskapi, 238
Mooney, James, 119
Moore, Patrick, 114
Moore, Sally Falk, 29
Morality, in anthropology, 16–18
Morgan, Lewis Henry, 62, 63–64
Morin, Eugene, 6
Morning Star (Janvier), 92
Morton, Samuel George, 195–196
Motherhood, 146, 147, 152–153
Mountains Beyond Mountains
        (Kidder), 214
Mughal India, 74–75
Mullings, Leith, 208
Multiculturalism, 209, 236
Multiculturalism Act, 236
Multi-drug-resistant tuberculosis
        (MDRTB), 217
Multi-locale fieldwork, 45–46
Multi-sited fieldwork, 45–46
Murray, Charles, 197
Murray, David, 202

Muslims, 122–123, 174–175
Myth, 99, 102, 104–105

Nader, Laura, 17
Nagengast, Carol, 213–214, 268
Names, 167–168, 176
Namibia, AIDS prevention in,
        155–157
Nast, Thomas, 179
Nation, definition, 227
National Museum of Canada, 44
Nationalist Party, 194
Nations, James D., 247
Nation-states
    cost of Snickers bar and, 228–230
    definition, 226
    education and, 237
    global challenges to, 240–241
    in market economies, 226–228
    national identity and globalization,
        234–241
    in neoliberalized global economy,
        230–233
    violence and, 267–271
Native, category of, 45
Native Americans. *See* Indigenous
        peoples; *specific peoples*
Native capacity, 199
Natural selection, 63
Nature versus nurture, 164–166
Nayabasti, 30
Ndahdigeh, 107
Ndembu, 85, 174
Neoliberalism, 221, 225–226,
        230–233, 234
Nepal, Nayabasti community in, 30
New Age spirituality, 100
New Guinea, sweet potato
        production in, 70–71
New racism, 208
New York City, urban crisis in,
        225–226
Ng, Roxana, 222, 233–234
Nicholas, Saint, 178
Nichter, Mimi, 205, 206
Niezen, Ronald, 241

Nigh, Ronald, 88–89
Ni-Vanuatu, 245–247
Nixon, Richard, 226
Nolan, Glenn, 240
North American Free Trade
        Agreement (NAFTA), 233, 247
North Korea, 224–225
Northwest Territories, 23–24
Nuclear family, 132, 132f
Nuclear weapons, 272–274
Nuer, 18–19
N/um, 262–263
Numbered treaties, 238
Nuxalk, 241–243

Obama, Barack, 130
Objectivity, in anthropology, 16–18
Office for Operational Cultural
        Knowledge, 276
Ogue, 121
Ok Tedi mine, 183
Omote, 171
On the Origin of Species (Darwin), 63
Ondeigupa, 257
Ongop, 257
Online research, 46
Opium trade, 75
Organizacion de las Nacionalidades
        Huaorani de la Amazonia
        Ecuatoriana (ONHAE),
        240–241
Ostracism, in Hutterite community,
        211
Other Side of Eden, The (Brody),
        162–163
Others, 235–237, 268
"Ours Before the Others" campaign,
        208
Owen, Robert, 210

Pagels, Elaine, 259
Pakistani immigrant women, 209
Paleoanthropology, 6
Palestinian refugees, 182
Palin, Bristol, 130

Papua New Guinea, 165, 182–184
Paraguay, 247–248
Partible inheritance, 150
Participant observation, 41–42
Partners in Health, 218
Pasmo, 84–85
Pathogen, 82–83
Pathologies of Power (Farmer), 217
Patrilineage, 136, 137–138
Patrilineal kinship, 133
Peace, imagining, 255–257
Peaceful societies
    conflict resolution in, 261–263
    vs. violent societies, 263–267
Pearson, Karl, 197, 198
Pehunan, 261
Peihotien, Taiwan, 139
Péligre dam, Haiti, 216
Pelletier, David, 243
Penetration aids, 273
Perdida de la somba, 84–85
Permission to conduct fieldwork, 51
Persuasions of the Witch's Craft
        (Luhrmann), 100
Phallocentrism, 203
Pharmaceutical companies, 32–33
Phoa, 260
Phonology, 206
Plastic surgery, 207–208
Plough cultivation, 69t
Point system, 235
Polanyi, Karl, 224
Political anatomy, 3–4
Political ecology, 30
Political economy, 151–152
Political organization, 62t
Pollutants, 82
Polonoroeste project (Brazil), 81
Polyandry, 147–148
Polygamy, 147–148
Polygyny, 147, 148
Population density, 62t, 68–70
Possessions, gifts as, 178
Potato industry, 70–71
Potlatch, 176–177
Poverty, 188, 204
Precautionary principle, 232

Pregnancy, ultrasound during, 153
Present efficiency, 199
Preston, Richard, 107
Primatology, 6
"Primitive," analyzing use of term, 52–53
Primitive Culture (Tylor), 41, 94
Principle of bilateral inheritance, 183, 184
Principle of first clearance, 183
Principle of reciprocity, 175
Prisons, Russian, 217
Procreation, theories of, 133, 135–137
Progress, 59–60
    assessing in textile industry, 78
    definition, 60
    health and, 82–85
    inequality and, 81–82
    theories of, 62–65
Promises Not Kept (Isbister), 59, 79
Prophet Dance, 114
Provenience, in archaeology, 7
"Pulling train", 203–204
"Putting out" system, 72–73

Qualitative research, 38
Quantitative research, 37
Québec, 31, 172–173, 236–237, 239*f*, 240
Quiet Revolution, 172–173

Race
    in Brazil, 207–208
    definition, 192
    intelligence and, 196–200
    language and, 206–207
    national identity and, 235–236
    skull size and, 195–196
Racism, 187, 192–196, 208, 235
Rainbow Project, 156–157
Rainforest destruction, 80, 81, 248
Rank, in Kiowa society, 257–258, 258*t*
Rape, 203–204, 270

Rapp, Rayna, 153
Rapport, 38
Rastafarianism, 115–117
Reality television, 129
Reardon, Betty, 267
Reciprocity principle, 175
Re-entry vehicles, 273
Refugees, 182, 214, 270, 270–271
Reganvanu, Ralph, 246
Reggae music, 116–117
Reichenbach, Lisa, 32–33
Reincarnation, 109
Relationships, during fieldwork, 50
Relativistic fallacy, 13
Religion
    anthropological studies of, 94–95
    of Dene Tha, 113–114
    of European colonizers, 113–117
    Haitian Vodou, 119–122, 215
    justifications for violence, 259–261
    Rastafarianism in Jamaica, 115–117
    secularism and, 122–123
    in Solomon Islands, 114–115
Representation, 39, 51–54
Residential schools, 237
Resources, protecting through violence, 264–265
Revelation, Book of, 259
Revitalization movements, 117, 118–119
Richler, Noah, 255
Rights
    Aboriginal, 238–239
    health as, 216–218
    human, 212–214
    medical, 214–216
Rites of passage, 106–107, 173–174, 278
Ritual, 102
    of contemporary witchcraft and magic, 103–104
    definition, 94
    of gift giving and hospitality, 175–177
    hamatsa dance, 102–103

hockey as, 23
    relation to way of life, 106–110
Rivoli, Pietra, 223, 233
Robarchek, Clayton, 261
Rondônia, Brazil, 81
Rosaldo, Renato, 13, 22
Rosary, 114
Ross, Eric, 25
Ross, Rupert, 3
Royal Proclamation of 1763, 238
Rubel, Arthur, 84–85
Rural Chinese, 130
    death, concept of, 10
    family composition, 137–139, 138*f*
    family cycle, 144–145
    marriage, 144–145
    sex, love, and wealth among, 146–147
    threats to family, 149–151
Russian prisons, 217
Rwanda, 213, 268, 269

Saalequn First Nation, 239
Sabung, 20
Sahlins, Marshall, 65, 106
Salé, Jamie, 243
Salvage anthropology, 44
Same-sex marriage, 130, 132, 154
Samoa, 53, 165
San peoples, 214
Sanday, Peggy Reeves, 203–204, 267
Sandinistas, 267
"Sanitized sensorium", 209
Santa Catarina Ixtepeji, Mexico, 48–49
Sapir, Edward, 44
Sapphires, 45–46, 110–112
Sati, 10, 17
Savagery, 64
Scaglion, Richard, 12, 47–48, 50
Scales, Robert H., Jr., 276
Scheduled castes, in India, 191–192
Scheper-Hughes, Nancy, 16–17
Schistosomiasis, 83
Schneider, David, 131, 152

Scientific medicine, 82
Second Life online gaming world, 46
Secrecy, in nuclear weapons facilities, 272–273
Secularism, 122–123
Sedentary, 60
Seed and the Soil, The (Delaney), 14
Self
    crafting, 171
    egocentric, 168–170
    holistic view of, 168
    importance of, 167–168
    individualistic view of, 168–169
    Japanese view of, 170–171
    kinship and, 172
    North American view of, 168, 169
    sociocentric, 168, 169–170, 171
Self-image, 205
Semai, 261, 263, 266
Sewatokwa'tshera't (film), 28
Sex, definition, 200
Sex tourism, 52–53
Sexism, 266–267
Sexual identification, 175
Sexuality
    among Ju/'hoansi, 141, 145–146
    among rural Chinese, 146–147
    among Trobriand Islanders, 141, 146
    hegemonic masculinity and, 203
    nature versus nurture, 165
    Trobriand theories of, 136–137
Sexually transmitted diseases (STDs), 154–157
Sezisman, 215
Shamanism, 113–114
Shopping, Christmas, 179–180
Shostak, Marjorie, 141, 145–146, 148
Shweder, Richard A., 168
Sidel, Ruth, 204
Silverman, Martin, 151–152
Sioux, 118, 119
Skull size, 195–196
Slash-and-burn (swidden) agriculture, 61, 62t, 68–69, 69t, 88

Slavery, 75–77, 229
Smith, Adam, 224
Smith, Robert, 170
Snickers bars, 228–230
Social hierarchy/social stratification
    anthropology's role in alleviating, 212–218
    in Brazil, 207–208
    caste, 190–192
    class, 189–190
    definition, 187
    gender, 200–207
    interwoven forms of, 207–209
    language and, 206–207
    new racism, 208
    non-stratified communities, 210–212
    race, 192–200
    rationale for, 187–189
Social identity, 161. *See also* Identity
Social movements, 181–182
Social Network Analysis (SNA) software, 277
Social organization, 62t
Social theories of illness, 84–85
Societies
    development of, 61, 62t
    distinguishing between individuals in, 171–173
    effect of globalization on small-scale, 247–250
    evolution of, 63–64
    identity changes and, 173–174
    non-stratified communities within, 210–212
    peaceful, 261–263
    peaceful vs. violent, 263–267
Society, law and, 29
Society for Medical Anthropology, 30–31
Sociocentric self, 168, 169–170, 171
Sociocultural anthropology, 3–4
    applied, 27–33
    definition, 3
    uniqueness of, 5–6, 8–9
Sociolinguists, 8
Solomon Islands, Christianity in, 114–115

Sorcery, 84, 85, 149
Sosua, Dominican Republic, 52–53
Soul loss, 84–85
South Africa, AIDS epidemic in, 155
Spearman, Charles, 197, 198–199
Speigel, Rebekka, 36
Spencer, Herbert, 63
Spinning jenny, 73
Spinning mule, 73, 74
Spirit possession, 84
Sports metaphors, 97
Stand with Haiti Fund, 218
State-run economic systems, 224–225
States, 61, 62t
Statistics Canada, 188, 236
Status class, 189–190
Stephenson, Peter, 210, 211
Stiglitz, Joseph E., 226
Stone, Linda, 152
Storytelling, 163
Strategic stability, 274
Strategic studies institute, 273–274
Street gangs, 264–265
Structural racism, 194
Structural violence, 216–218
Subcontractors, 233
Sudra caste, 191
Sugar, 25, 26, 228–229
Surgical strikes, 273
Survey of the Contemporary Indians of Canada, A (report), 28–29
Susser, Ida, 155, 156
Susto, 84–85
Sweatshop operations, 233–234
Sweet potato production, 70–71
Swidden agriculture, 61, 62t, 68–69, 69t, 88
Symbolic actions, 95, 101–105
Syncretization, 114, 118, 119–122

Taft, Michael, 200–201
Taj Mahal, 15
Tariffs, WTO, 231–232
Tarot cards, 101
Taxes, 229

Technology, 64–65, 68–69
Technostrategic language, 273–274
Telefolip, 183
Telefolmin, 182–184
Telemarketing, 37
Temporal depth, 137
Testing, nuclear, 273
Textile industry, 72–78
Theatrical transvestism, 200–201
"Theft of national enjoyment", 244
There Are No Children Here
    (Kotlowitz), 264
Think tank, 273–274
Third gender, 200
Thomas, Elizabeth, 133
Thompson, E. P., 19
"Tim Bits", 23
Time, 18–19, 97, 106
Timor, 269–271
Titanic (ship), 204
Todaro, Michael, 204
Torture, 268–269
Totemism, 94–95
Tourism, 52, 244–247
Toynbee, Jason, 116
Trail of Tears, 76–77, 77*f*
Trance dance, 262–263
Transnational, definition, 230
Transnational corporations, 230
Transnational migrant workers,
    31–32
Transnational treaty organizations,
    230, 231
Transvestism, 200–201
Treaties, with First Nations, 238
Treaty of Paris, 172
Treaty of Utrecht, 238
Trobriand Islanders, 42, 130
    family composition, 134–137,
        135*f*
    family cycle, 141–144
    kula ring, 175–176
    marriage, 141–144
    sex, love, and wealth among, 146
    threats to family, 148–149
    view of death, 149
Trudeau, Pierre Elliott, 236

T-shirts, biography of, 222–223
Tsimshian, 167, 176–177
Tsumkwe, Namibia, 155–156
Tuberculosis, 217
Turkey, 14, 136
Turner, Terence, 54, 214
Turner, Victor, 85, 174
Two-spirit, 200
Tylor, Edward, 40, 41, 94
Type 2 diabetes, 32–33

Ultrasound, 153
Umbundu, 167–168
Umoim, 183
UN High Commission on Refugees,
    214
Underground Railroad, The (Webber),
    194
Unfair restrictions on trade, 231–232
Unilineal evolution, 63–64
United Fruit Company, 115–116
United States
    Canada's relationship with, 243–244
    cotton, slavery, and Trail of Tears,
        75–77
    egocentric self, 169
    ethnic cleansing in, 268
    feminization of poverty, 204
    Hutterites, 210
    life expectancy in, 83
    market-driven economic system,
        225
    potato industry, 70–71
    sugar cane industry, 228–229
    Trail of Tears, 76–77
    WTO cases involving, 232
Universal Declaration of Human Rights,
    212–213, 217
University of Toronto, 234
Untouchables, 191–192
Ura, 171
Urban crisis, 225–226
U.S. Army Corps of Engineers, 216
U.S. Department of Defense, 277
Utopian communities, 210–212
Uxorilocal marriage, 151

Vaisya caste, 191
Van Gennep, Arnold, 173
Vanuatu, 244–247
Vector, 82
Vélez-Ibáñez, Carlos G., 213–214
Vice Lords, 264–265, 266
Victims of Benevolence (Furniss), 237
Vietnam, 276–277
Violence
    bias of societies against, 261–263
    collective, 256–261
    creating conditions for, 265–266
    fieldwork in midst of, 274–279
    justifications for, 255–257
    nation-states and, 267–271
    peaceful vs. violent societies,
        263–267
    for protection of resources,
        264–265
    religious justifications for, 259–
        261
    sexism and, 266–267
    in stateless societies, 263–264
    structural, 216–218
Virginity testing, in Turkey, 14
Virtue, Tessa, 243, 244
Visible minorities, 236
Vodou, 119–122, 215
Voice pitch, and gender, 206
Von Hayek, Friedrich, 225

Waiteri, 259, 264
Walens, Stanley, 98–99, 103
Wallace, Anthony F. C., 117
Walmart, 222, 230, 233
Walpole Island, 82, 153–154
Walsh, Andrew, 45–46, 110–111
War, 96–97, 257–258
Wari', 10, 14–16
Waswanipi Cree, 107–108
Water frame, 73, 74
Water war, Bolivia, 241
Waterborne infections, 83
Watson, John H. (fictional
    character), 18
Ways of Knowing (Goulet), 107

Wealth, 143, 145–147
Wealth of Nations, The (Smith), 224
Weapons of mass destruction
    (WMD), 272–274
Webber, Charles T., 194
Weber, Max, 189
Webster, David, 274
Weddings. *See* Marriage
Weight, body image based on,
    205–206
Weiner, Annette, 136–137, 143,
    144, 149
West Caroline Islands, 152
Western Guard, 194
Western medicine, 82
Whapmagoostui Cree, 31, 84
*What We Talk About When We
    Talk About War* (Richler),
    255
Whately, W., 129
Wheelock, Angela, 114
White, Clifford, 238–239
White, Leslie, 62, 64–65
White, Tom, 218
White privilege, 195
White situational awareness teams
    (WSATs), 276
White supremacists, 194
Whitehead, Walter, 249
Whitney, Eli, 76
Windhoek, Namibia, 156–157
Wise, Amanda, 270–271

Witchcraft
    in Cameroon, 112–113
    definition, 100
    interpretations of illness, 84, 85
    metaphors of contemporary,
        100–101
    in Mexico, 48–49
    ritual of, 103–104
    worldviews and, 93, 94
Wolf, Eric, 9, 227
Wolf, Margery, 139, 147, 150
Women. *See also* Gender stratification
    body image issues, 204–206
    hegemonic masculinity and, 203
    language used by, 206
    Pakistani immigrant, 209
    poverty among, 188, 204
    violence against, 266–267
Women and Children Last (Sidel), 204
Woodburn, James, 65–66
World Bank, 79–80, 81, 223, 226
World Trade Organization (WTO),
    223, 230, 231–233, 231*t*
Worldview, 93–95
    Cree, 107–108
    definition, 93
    Dene Tha, 107–109, 113–114
    effect of religion of colonizers,
        113–117
    ethnographic fieldwork and,
        48–49
    Haitian Vodou, 119–122

Kwara'ae, 114–115
Maka, 112–113
Malagasy, 110–112
relation to way of life, 106–110
reordering of, 117–123
revitalization movements, 117,
    118–119
secularism, 122–123
Wounded Knee massacre, 119
Wovoka, 118–119

Xe'caj, Guatemala, 275
Xinguanos, 262, 266

Yams, in Trobriand Islands, 143, 146,
    148–149
Yanomamö
    bias toward violence, 258–259
    conditions for violence, 265–266
    essentialist representations of, 53–54
    statelessness and violence,
        263–264
Yanomamo (Chagnon), 54
Yap kinship, 152

Zamni Lasante, 218
Zapatistas, 247
Zechenter, Elizabeth, 17
Zhao guye, 151